R

Clucas

URBN 650F
503 725-3258

# POLITICS IN THE AMERICAN STATES

please

return

# Politics in the American States

## A COMPARATIVE ANALYSIS

### EIGHTH EDITION

*Editors*

VIRGINIA GRAY, *University of North Carolina at Chapel Hill*

RUSSELL L. HANSON, *Indiana University*

CQ PRESS

A Division of Congressional Quarterly Inc.
Washington, D.C.

CQ Press
1255 22nd Street, N.W., Suite 400
Washington, D.C. 20037

Phone, 202-729-1900
Toll-free, 1-866-4CQ-PRESS (1-866-427-7737)

www.cqpress.com

∞ The paper used in this publication exceeds the requirements of the American National Standard for Information Sciences—Permanence of Paper for Printed Library Materials, ANSI Z39.48-1992.

Cover design: Kathleen Sims

Printed and bound in the United States of America

07  06  05  04  03    5  4  3  2  1

**Library of Congress Cataloging-in-Publication Data**

Politics in the American states : a comparative analysis / editors,
    Virginia Gray, Russell L. Hanson. — 8th ed.
        p.    cm.
        Includes bibliographical references and index.
        ISBN 1-56802-773-7 (alk. paper)
        1. State governments—United States.    I. Gray, Virginia, 1945–
II. Hanson, Russell L., 1953–    III. Title.
JK2408.P64  2004
320.973—dc22                              2003015130

# Contents

# Tables, Figures, and Boxes

## FIGURES

## BOXES

# Preface

State government and politics changed dramatically after al Qaeda terrorists crashed fully fueled jets into both the World Trade Center and the Pentagon. The nation responded by declaring war against terrorism, and in this conflict the American states have important duties on the home front. Units of the National Guard protect power plants, water supplies, and airports. Law enforcement agencies monitor suspected terrorists, bolster the defense of state buildings, and prepare disaster plans in case of attack. Police and emergency medical technicians receive antiterrorist training and equipment, while public health facilities develop vaccines and antidotes for biological and chemical agents. Almost all of this activity proceeds under the direction of state and local officials, who in spite of budgetary problems must supply most of the resources for domestic countermeasures.

Homeland security is an addition to states' other commitments, which are extensive. States are reshaping their economies, reforming education, supplying social services, and regulating citizens' behavior. They are also constructing prisons, building roads, and acquiring land for parks and nature preserves. These activities, and others like them, are the traditional preserve of subnational units of government in the United States. States' responsibilities are growing, however, as a more conservative national government devolves authority in certain areas, including welfare, transportation, and environmental regulation. In other areas, most notably education, congressionally mandated changes are adding to states' burden by imposing new obligations on governors and legislatures.

The declining financial capacity of the national government will accelerate these trends. Defense expenditures are rising, and will continue to increase as long as terrorism is a serious threat. Moreover, outlays for Social Security are growing as "baby boomers" reach retirement age. Revenues are not keeping pace because of a stagnant economy, and even if economic recovery happens soon, Congress has enacted a series of substantial tax cuts that will likely be permanent—ensuring further revenue shortfalls. The resulting deficits will persist for years, limiting the ability of Congress and the president to undertake new domestic ventures, or to assist states in meeting current commitments or future needs.

Simply put, demands on state governments are increasing at a time when they can ill afford them. Right now, state economies are weak, revenues are down, and the cost of public services is rising as unemployment grows and more people seek social services. This confluence of events is generating a "perfect storm" that is battering state budgets across the nation. In fact, budget shortfalls in the states are the worst in fifty-five years, and the situation is unlikely to improve soon. According to current projections, states' fiscal problems will get worse before they get better.

Unlike their national counterpart, state governments cannot engage in deficit spending. To balance their budgets—which most must do by law—most states are reducing expenditures in nonessential areas, such as state park systems, and deferring road maintenance and highway construction. They have also slowed the growth of spending for core services, including education, Medicaid, and prisons. To generate more revenue, many states have increased "sin taxes" on cigarettes and alcohol; a few have increased sales and income taxes. Some are considering an expansion of gambling operations in order to increase revenue. More will do so in the next year or two as officials encounter political resistance to further spending reductions.

Raising taxes and cutting expenditures are unpopular, and it is never easy for elected politicians to solve fiscal problems that require one or both remedies. The difficulty is compounded when political parties are sharply divided over the best strategy for balancing budgets, as they are now. On economic grounds, Republicans generally oppose tax increases and favor reductions in social spending. Democrats typically want to maintain or expand social spending for needy people, even if that increases taxes on the wealthy. The clash of ideologies is intensifying, since parties are more evenly matched in many states. This increases the likelihood of divided government, which makes difficult choices ever more difficult. Political stalemates, protracted negotiations, and special sessions of the legislature are the result, which could undermine citizens' confidence in state governments.

The strain on governors and legislatures is showing, but the institutions of state government are resilient. Indeed, the capability of state governments has increased noticeably over the past three decades. Institutions have been streamlined, operations are more efficient, and more officeholders are professional politicians, administrators, or jurists. State capitals teem with interest groups, media coverage of state politics is improving, and campaigns for state elections resemble those for national offices. The modernization of state government and politics is continuing, and while the pace of change varies considerably across the states, the direction is the same.

Understanding these developments in today's context is the object of the eighth edition of *Politics in the American States*. The contributors to this volume seek to advance our knowledge about state politics, building on their own research and the work of professional scholars in the field. In that sense, this volume is a handbook for academicians, administrators, policy makers, consultants, and other experts in state politics. At the same time *Politics in the American States* provides teachers with instructional resources that students can grasp, appreciate, and use for their own purposes. Our contributors address both audiences, appealing to students' curiosity about their own states and professionals' interest in generalizations. Thus, each chapter provides nuanced treatments of individual states in the context of rigorous analyses of the fifty states as a whole. Readers can therefore make systematic comparisons between states while remaining sensitive to the diversity and subtlety of political life at the state level.

Nine chapters from the previous edition have been revised, updated, and streamlined for this edition. Two other policy chapters were rewritten completely by new authors, and two entirely new chapters were added to the volume. Thus Virginia Gray describes the current socioeconomic and political context of states, drawing on the latest information from the U.S. Bureau of the Census. Russell L. Hanson reviews the intergovernmental context of state governments, including relations between state and tribal governments. John Bibby and Thomas Holbrook analyze parties and elections in the states, incorporating results from the 2002 elections. Clive Thomas and Ronald Hrebenar assess the role of interest groups in state politics, and in a new chapter Shaun Bowler and Todd Donovan analyze the prevalence and impact of initiatives and referenda on state politics.

Each institution of state government is treated at length in a separate chapter. Keith Hamm and Gary Moncrief explore legislative politics in the states, and Thad Beyle discusses the governors. Both include results of 2002 campaigns and elections. Henry Glick reprises his coverage of state courts, adding a discussion of courts' role in legislative redistricting. Richard Elling again considers civil service, administrative agencies, and state bureaucracies.

Because state agendas are evolving, the chapters on state policy have been reconceived for the eighth edition. Martin Saiz and Susan Clarke trace the evolution of economic development policy, and Mark Rom evaluates reforms in health and welfare programs. Kenneth Wong, a new author, discusses education policy in view of states' increasing interest in making schools more effective and holding them accountable for their performance. Two other newcomers, Kenneth Meier and Matthew Eshbaugh-Soha, categorize state regulatory policies in a chapter that subsumes two narrower chapters from the seventh edition. James Garand and Kyle Baudoin also join the roster of contributors, offering a new perspective on examining fiscal policy in the American states and the politics of budgeting.

Such changes follow the example of the late Herbert Jacob, who was the lead editor for the first six editions of this volume. Although he worked on this book for more than thirty years, Herb always thought the anthology could be improved. To each edition he brought new ideas about how to organize the volume, who the authors should be, and what new pedagogical features should be added. We honor that tradition here, knowing that readers will spot the remaining gaps in our treatment of state politics, but hoping they will be inspired to fill those gaps in future editions of *Politics in the American States*.

For help in preparing this edition, we thank the staff at CQ Press: Charisse Kino, our sponsoring editor; Michael Kerns, our development editor; Tracy Villano, our copy editor; and Daphne Levitas, our production editor. Each of them made important contributions to this volume, and it was indeed a pleasure to work with such dedicated and skilled professionals.

*Virginia Gray*
*Russell L. Hanson*

# Contributors

KYLE BAUDOIN is a graduate student in political science at Louisiana State University. His research interests include state politics, legislative politics, and public policy.

THAD BEYLE is the Thomas C. Pearsall Professor of Political Science at the University of North Carolina at Chapel Hill and was board chairman of the North Carolina Center for Public Policy Research for ten years. He has worked with the North Carolina Governor's Office and with the National Governors Association. He is editor of *Governors and Hard Times* (1992), *North Carolina DataNet*, and edits annual editions of *State and Local Government*, formerly known as *State Government: CQ's Guide to Current Issues and Activities*.

JOHN F. BIBBY is professor emeritus of political science at the University of Wisconsin–Milwaukee. He is the past chair of the political parties section of the American Political Science Association and the 2001 recipient of the section's Samuel J. Elderveld Lifetime Achievement Award. In addition to having contributed to the four previous editions of *Politics in the American States*, Bibby is a coauthor of *Party Organizations in American States* (1984); *Two Parties or More? The American Party System* (1998); and the author of *Governing by Consent: An Introduction to American Politics* (1995).

SHAUN BOWLER is professor of political science, University of California–Riverside. Bowler's research interests include comparative electoral systems and voting behavior. His work examines the relationship between institutional arrangements and voter choice. Bowler is the author of *Demanding Choices: Opinion Voting and Direct Democracy* (1998), with Todd Donovan, and editor of *Elections in Australia, Ireland, and Malta Under the Single Transferable Vote* (2000), with Bernard Grofman. He and Todd Donovan recently coauthored two books examining America's electoral system. He has published in several journals, including the *American Political Science Review, American Journal of Political Science, Journal of Politics*, and *American Politics Quarterly*.

SUSAN E. CLARKE is professor of political science at the University of Colorado at Boulder and the director of the Center to Advance Research and Teaching in the Social Sciences (CARTSS). She is also editor of *Urban Affairs Review*, with Michael Pagano and Gary L. Gaile. Her research currently centers on economic development policies, workforce development issues, and cross-border regionalism in Europe and North America. She is coauthor, with Gary L. Gaile, of *The Work of Cities* (1998).

TODD DONOVAN is professor of political science at Western Washington University. His research examines electoral politics and representation in many settings, including the American states. His latest books include *Reforming the Republic: Democratic Institutions for the New America* (2004), with Shaun Bowler, and *Electoral Reform and Minority Representation* (2003), also with Shaun Bowler. He and Bowler have also coauthored two previous books on direct democracy in America. Donovan has published his research in *Electoral Studies, Journal of Politics, American Journal of Political Science, British Journal of Political Science*, and several other journals.

RICHARD C. ELLING is professor and chair of the Department of Political Science at Wayne State University in Detroit. Much of his research has examined issues of state management and administrative politics and includes his book *Public Management in the States* (1992). His current research includes a comparative study of state managers' perceptions of impediments to effective management and another on how the careers of state managers develop.

MATTHEW ESHBAUGH-SOHA received his Ph.D. in 2002 from Texas A&M University. Currently, he is visiting assistant professor in political science at Texas A&M University. He has published in the *American Journal of Political Science* and has authored or coauthored chapters in *The Encyclopedia of Public Opinion* and *Regulation and Consumer Protection*. His current research focuses on presidential signaling and its impact on the economy as well as on public policy in Congress and the bureaucracy.

JAMES C. GARAND is the Emogine Pliner Distinguished Professor in Political Science at Louisiana State University. He has teaching and research interests in the fields of legislative politics, electoral politics, public policy, state politics, domestic political economy, and methodology and statistics. His research on a wide range of topics in American politics has been published in numerous journals, including the *American Political Science Review, American Journal of Political Science, Journal of Politics*, and *British Journal of Political Science*, among other journals. He is the coauthor (with James Campbell) of *Before the Vote: Forecasting American National Elections* (2000). He is former editor of the *American Politics Quarterly* and is president-elect of the Southern Political Science Association.

HENRY R. GLICK recently retired from the department of political science and the Pepper Institute on Aging and Public Policy at Florida State University. Much of his scholarly work and teaching has been on state court systems and judicial policy. Recently, he has been concerned with the development and evolution of government policy concerning the right to die, and he is the author of *The Right to Die: Policy Innovation and Its Consequences* (1992). He has written numerous other books and journal articles on the judicial process and the impact and implementation of right to die policy.

VIRGINIA GRAY is the Robert Watson Winston Distinguished Professor of Political Science at the University of North Carolina at Chapel Hill. She teaches and does research on state politics and public policy and on interest groups. She has published a number of books and articles on these topics, including most recently *Minnesota Politics and Government* (1999), written with Daniel J. Elazar and Wyman Spano, and *The Population Ecology of Interest Representation* (1996), written with David Lowry.

KEITH E. HAMM is professor of political science at Rice University. He is the author or coauthor of several articles and book chapters on American state legislatures, interest groups, and political parties. He served as co-editor of *Legislative Studies Quarterly* from 1997 to 2002.

RUSSELL L. HANSON is professor of political science at Indiana University–Bloomington, where he has taught since 1980. He is interested in American federalism and has published articles on political culture, economic development, and social policy in the American states. Among his edited books are *Governing Partners: State-Local Relations in the United States* (1998) and *Reconsidering the Democratic Public* (1993). He also writes on American political thought.

THOMAS M. HOLBROOK is professor of political science at the University of Wisconsin–Milwaukee. He is the author of *Do Campaigns Matter* (1996), has published in the leading political science journals, and is also a former editor of *American Politics Research*.

RONALD J. HREBENAR is professor and chair of the Political Science Department at the University of Utah. His research and teaching focuses on interest groups, political parties, public policy and Japanese politics. He has published several books and articles including *Interest Group Politics in America* (3d ed., 1997). He was a Fulbright Scholar in Japan from 1982 to 1983.

KENNETH J. MEIER is the Charles Puryear Professor of Liberal Arts and Professor of Political Science at Texas A&M University. He also holds the Sara Lindsey Chair in Government in the George Bush School of Government and Public Service at Texas A&M University. He is pursuing two major research agendas. One is a national study of Latino and African American education policy in 1,800 school districts. The other is building and testing an empirical theory of public management.

GARY F. MONCRIEF is professor of political science at Boise State University. He has written many journal articles and book chapters on legislatures in the United States and Canada and is a frequent speaker at legislative conferences and workshops. He is co-editor of two books on state legislatures, and coauthor of *Who Runs for the Legislature?*, a book about candidate recruitment (2000).

MARK CARL ROM is associate professor of government and public policy at Georgetown University in Washington, D.C. He has written *Fatal Extraction: The Story Behind the Florida Dentist Accused of Infecting His Patients with HIV and Poisoning Public Health* (1997), *Public Spirit in the Thrift Tragedy* (1996), and *Welfare Magnets: A New Case for a National Welfare Standard* (1990, with Paul E. Peterson), among other book chapters and articles. Most recently, he has focused on interstate policy competition.

MARTIN SAIZ received his Ph.D. from the University of Colorado at Boulder in 1992 and is professor of political science and the director of the Center for Southern California Studies at California State University, Northridge. He has written extensively on issues of urban politics, local political parties, economic development, and the effects of voting turnout on public policy. He was a community activist in Denver, Colorado where he served two terms as a planning commissioner. His articles have been published in *Journal of Politics, Urban Affairs Review, Political Research Quarterly, Policy Studies Journal,* and *Economic Development Quarterly,* as well as other books and journals.

CLIVE S. THOMAS is professor of political science at the University of Alaska, Juneau. His publications include works on interest groups, political parties, legislative process, and state politics. He has been a volunteer lobbyist and teaches seminars on lobby organization and tactics. During 1997–1998 and spring 2000 he was a Fulbright Senior Research Scholar in Brussels studying American interest groups operating in the European Union.

KENNETH K. WONG is professor in the Department of Leadership, Policy, and Organizations and the Department of Political Science at Vanderbilt University. He also serves as the associate director of the Peabody Center for Education Policy. He has published widely in the areas of federalism, urban and state politics, policy implementation, and educational reform. His research on federal Title I programs contributed to the design of the No Child Left Behind legislation and his notion of "integrated governance" influenced central office functions in the Chicago district. He currently serves as president of the Politics of Education Association, whose national membership consists of professors in educational policy and politics.

# CHAPTER 1

# The Socioeconomic and Political Context of States

V I R G I N I A   G R A Y

American national government is often the focus of our attention; yet in November of 2000 all eyes turned to the operation of Florida government where the actions of state officials and volunteer precinct workers turned out to critically affect the outcome of the nation's presidential election. For thirty-six days the nation and the world watched as local officials counted hanging and dimpled chads, and lawyers argued over butter-fly ballots; Florida's Supreme Court ordered this manual recount in certain counties where voting machines malfunctioned, but later the recount was halted by the U.S. Supreme Court's 5-4 decision in the case of *Bush v. Gore*.

The 2000 election was a particularly dramatic example of our federal system at work. It demonstrated how the quality of one state's administration affects us all; in fact, nearly all states, realizing they could have easily been in Florida's shoes, tightened up their electoral procedures, redesigned their ballots, or bought new voting machines. The critical importance of the Electoral College, and of the states' role within it, was also illustrated: the president is not actually elected by a vote of the people at the polls (in this case Al Gore, Jr., won that vote). Rather, fifty separate state elections select slates of delegates pledged to presidential candidates. It is the votes of those delegates, constituting the Electoral College, that determine the winner (George W. Bush won that vote, according to the U.S. Supreme Court).

On September 11, 2001, the nation's and the world's attention was riveted by the collapse and destruction of the World Trade Center and many of the people within it. The president immediately mobilized the armed forces for a "war on terrorism" fought in Afghanistan; as in previous wartime situations he asked for and received expanded national powers: the Office of Homeland Security (now a cabinet-level department), federal takeover of airport security, additional money for the defense budget, and so forth. But "9-ll," as the event came to be known, also focused the spotlight on the critical importance of state and local government. Previously dull topics such as city services, infrastructure, and emergency management loomed large as the extent of devastation in Lower Manhattan became clear. Fortunately, New York City government was up to the challenge: from its mayor and the state's governor to its policemen and -women, Port Authority police officers, and firefighters, we saw effective governments responding to an unprecedented crisis.

Like the Florida electoral experience, the terrorist attack in NYC was a wake-up call for other states and cities: local and state police everywhere have taken on additional public safety duties, whether it be providing heightened security at airports or crowd control at sporting events. State health officials, who used to worry about naturally occurring threats, now have geared up to fight anthrax, smallpox, and various potential biochemical threats. Some states have enacted laws giving more leeway to law enforcement in surveillance of criminal activity; most have tightened up the requirements to get a driver's license, the most commonly used form of personal identification. All tightened security in their own capital buildings; a few inserted more patriotic content into the public school curriculum. Though not always headline news, the domestic "war on terrorism" has fully engaged state and local governments as well as the national government; Chapter 2 explores the intergovernmental aspects of the "war" in greater detail. States have passed new legislation aimed at terrorism and have already spent billions of dollars in their "war on terrorism."

The need to wage such a war came at an unfortunate time, as both the national and state governments were feeling the effects of the 2001 recession. In an economic downturn state tax revenues fall; expenditures already budgeted cannot be met; unemployment claims increase; state policy makers then can choose to raise taxes or cut current spending. By early 2002 nearly every state's revenues failed to meet budgeted expenditures; all states chose to cut their budgets, while adding on new security and public health initiatives, rather than raise taxes significantly. However, during 2002 the states' fiscal crises worsened significantly: the twenty-four new governors taking office in January 2003 faced the worst set of financial problems since World War II. Will state leaders have the will to deal with this challenge? Do state governments have the capacity to deal with the problems and issues that come before them?

The purpose of this book is to help the reader understand the governments that conduct elections and wage the domestic "war on terrorism," that is, the state governments. Not only do state governments deal with these pressing issues of the day; they also build and operate large public enterprises, such as highways, prisons, and universities. They are important regulators of private business and private behavior and important partners in the federal system. Many national politicians got their start in state capitols: George W. Bush and Bill Clinton are but two examples of governors who became president.

The authors of this volume share a common perspective on how to study state politics. We compare the fifty states in terms of their policy differences and explain these differences using the methods of political science. We find these political differences both fascinating and intriguing to analyze. The social and economic differences among states are also significant. This chapter will make you aware of some of the differences among states in population, natural resources, and wealth, differences that affect what policy makers can do, and the sort of problems they face.

Political and economic differences, in turn, relate to another way in which states differ. States offer different levels of services and benefits to their citizens and allocate costs for those benefits differently. In this book we explore these policy differences and some of the political reasons for them. Expect to learn how state government operates in general—that is, the similarities among the fifty states—and expect to learn how the politics of various states differ. As the authors develop these points, you will also see that state governments and their politics are different from the national government and its politics. States are subject to many competitive pressures from other states. These pressures constrain state actions on taxation and ratchet up spending on economic development, among other things.

## DIFFERENCES AMONG THE STATES

Differences among the states abound. If you pay close attention to the news, you will begin to notice that different states have different problems, and different solutions to them. California often leads the way on the environment; it is the first to attempt to regulate carbon dioxide emissions from motor vehicles, for example. The legislature aims to reduce greenhouse gas emissions from automobiles and light trucks to the "maximum feasible and cost-effective," starting with vehicles in model year 2009 and later. California is counting on its market size to provide leverage with automakers to change their designs.

Small states can blaze trails too. In 2002 North Dakota voters used the referendum mechanism to overturn a new state law that allowed banks to sell customers' financial data without getting their written permission. The state legislature had passed the measure at the urging of banks and credit unions; these institutions then mounted an expensive advertising campaign against the referendum. Their main argument was that repealing the law would drive away business that a small, cold state could ill afford to lose. The referendum's supporters spent relatively little money in their grassroots campaign but garnered 74 percent of the vote. Privacy advocates argued that North Dakotans' clear message at the ballot box would encourage lawmakers in other states to strengthen their privacy laws too.

A more systematic way to see the differences among states is to look at rankings of the states on various quantitative policy indicators. Political scientists often select issues on which liberals and conservatives differ; they score the states as to whether they have liberal or conservative policies on these issues; then they sum up and average the scores to produce an index of overall policy liberalism. Table 1-1 presents state rankings on a new index of policy liberalism on which

**Table 1-1** 2000 Policy Liberalism Index

| State | Policy liberalism | Gun law index | Abortion index | TANF index[a] | Tax progressivity |
|---|---|---|---|---|---|
| Alabama | 38 | 36 | 27 | 33 | 40 |
| Arizona | 32 | 31 | 17 | 31 | 32 |
| Arkansas | 42 | 41 | 32 | 44 | 26 |
| California | 1 | 2 | 5 | 7 | 5 |
| Colorado | 19 | 19 | 20 | 25 | 27 |
| Connecticut | 5 | 3 | 4 | 26 | 28 |
| Delaware | 10 | 22 | 26 | 12 | 1 |
| Florida | 47 | 18 | 23 | 45 | 46 |
| Georgia | 45 | 42 | 36 | 48 | 21 |
| Idaho | 37 | 35 | 28 | 46 | 7 |
| Illinois | 18 | 6 | 25 | 27 | 38 |
| Indiana | 28 | 30 | 35 | 41 | 35 |
| Iowa | 23 | 9 | 21 | 24 | 22 |
| Kansas | 30 | 32 | 30 | 23 | 20 |
| Kentucky | 33 | 46 | 46 | 37 | 15 |
| Louisiana | 44 | 47 | 48 | 10 | 41 |
| Maine | 15 | 48 | 13 | 21 | 9 |
| Maryland | 12 | 4 | 7 | 42 | 19 |
| Massachusetts | 4 | 1 | 19 | 22 | 16 |
| Michigan | 22 | 14 | 42 | 16 | 36 |
| Minnesota | 6 | 12 | 16 | 3 | 8 |
| Mississippi | 40 | 33 | 41 | 32 | 33 |
| Missouri | 21 | 13 | 44 | 15 | 25 |
| Montana | 8 | 44 | 12 | 6 | 2 |
| Nebraska | 26 | 16 | 40 | 13 | 14 |
| Nevada | 36 | 28 | 15 | 18 | 48 |
| New Hampshire | 16 | 27 | 8 | 9 | 39 |
| New Jersey | 14 | 5 | 10 | 40 | 29 |
| New Mexico | 11 | 25 | 11 | 2 | 34 |
| New York | 2 | 7 | 6 | 5 | 13 |
| North Carolina | 29 | 10 | 22 | 47 | 10 |
| North Dakota | 46 | 43 | 47 | 30 | 31 |
| Ohio | 24 | 20 | 38 | 36 | 12 |
| Oklahoma | 34 | 38 | 18 | 39 | 23 |
| Oregon | 7 | 24 | 2 | 20 | 6 |
| Pennsylvania | 25 | 23 | 45 | 8 | 37 |
| Rhode Island | 9 | 8 | 33 | 4 | 11 |
| South Carolina | 20 | 11 | 29 | 19 | 3 |
| South Dakota | 48 | 37 | 39 | 35 | 45 |
| Tennessee | 41 | 26 | 31 | 28 | 44 |
| Texas | 31 | 45 | 14 | 11 | 42 |
| Utah | 39 | 29 | 43 | 29 | 30 |
| Vermont | 3 | 40 | 3 | 1 | 4 |
| Virginia | 35 | 17 | 34 | 38 | 17 |
| Washington | 17 | 15 | 1 | 17 | 47 |
| West Virginia | 13 | 34 | 9 | 14 | 18 |
| Wisconsin | 27 | 21 | 37 | 43 | 24 |
| Wyoming | 43 | 39 | 24 | 34 | 43 |

SOURCE:  Gray et al., 2002.

NOTE:  Each index is ranked: 1 = Most Liberal, 48 = Most Conservative. Right-to-work laws were not included in table since this is a binary variable.

[a] Temporary Assistance to Needy Families.

California ranks first and South Dakota last (column one). The index makes intuitive sense: other liberal states joining California are New York, Vermont, Massachusetts, Connecticut, Minnesota, and Oregon. Clustering at the bottom are traditionally conservative southern states such as Mississippi, Arkansas, Louisiana, Georgia, Tennessee, and Florida, and smaller western or plains states such as Wyoming and the Dakotas.

Our policy liberalism index is based on five indicators measured between 1995 and 2001. The first is gun control policies; Massachusetts has the strictest gun control laws and Maine the loosest. The second component is a scale of abortion laws: Washington state has the most facilitative laws and Louisiana has the most restrictive laws. The next column contains a ranking on TANF welfare eligibility and work requirements: Vermont's rules seem designed to ease eligibility, whereas Georgia's rules appear to be the most restrictive. The last column reports rankings on tax progressivity (the extent to which the tax burden falls on the top 5 percent of earners as compared to the lowest 40 percent of earners): by this measure Delaware taxes the rich while Nevada burdens its poor. The fifth component of our index has to do with unionization: whether a state has laws that facilitate collective bargaining or whether it has a "right to work" law which impedes unionization. Since this is a simple binary variable (1 or 0) rather than a ranking, we do not present the data in the table. But it is included in the policy liberalism index.

The sharp-eyed reader will have noticed that a specific state is not necessarily liberal (or conservative) in every category. The best way to see this is to select a state and look at its overall policy liberalism ranking and then how it ranks on each component. For example, I live in North Carolina, which ranks twenty-ninth overall or slightly conservative; it is tenth on both the gun law index and the progressivity of its tax system (i.e., quite liberal), twenty-second on the abortion index (in the middle of the pack), but it is almost the tightest in the nation on welfare (forty-seventh) and has a right-to-work law, both of which are conservative positions. Thus my state averages out at twenty-ninth on policy liberalism.

So the question is: why do some states make liberal policy choices while others make conservative ones? What separates California and other liberal states from South Dakota and other conservative states? This is the type of question we ask in this book and in the field of state politics; we will answer the question later in the chapter.

## EXPLAINING POLICY DIFFERENCES

The second half of this book focuses on a state government's many activities. These outputs of a government's activities are called *public policies,* which are usually defined as means to governmental ends. The public policies reviewed in this book deal with taxation, health and welfare, education, social and economic regulation, economic development and infrastructure.

Scholars have spent years investigating the differences among states' public policies and the reasons for those differences. The intellectual task is to explain interstate patterns—that is, what conditions or characteristics of states lead to generous educational expenditure, low welfare expenditure, or innovation in health policy? In general these investigations focus on two broad sets of variables: political characteristics and socioeconomic factors. Among a state's political variables, researchers have found the following to be important: political party control and interparty competition, interest group strength, gubernatorial power, the political background of judges, professionalism of the legislature, public and elite opinion, and political culture. Subsequent chapters in this book examine the major governmental institutions, both in their own right and as policy makers. Other chapters focus on key political actors such as interest groups and political parties.

In this chapter I examine the set of socioeconomic factors that may affect patterns of state policy. Included in these factors are the following: population size and composition, migration and urbanization, physical characteristics and natural resources, types of economic activities stemming from a state's physical endowments, wealth, and regional economic forces. These factors structure a state government's problems and affect a state government's ability to deal with them. I also explore the broader political context that affects state governments, such as political culture, public opinion, other states' actions, and national political forces. An understanding of the broader context will aid in understanding the role of political players and each state's governmental institutions.

Understanding the magnitude of state differences also helps us to understand the existence of federalism. The states are so different it is hard to imagine they would get along within a single government. Only federalism could accommodate the cultural distance between, say, clean-living Utah and gambling-mecca Nevada. Federalism allows these differences to flourish.

### THE PEOPLE

The first state resource that I examine is the human resource. What kinds of people live where? How does the movement of people back and forth affect states? Why are trends in population growth and economic competition important for a state's future?

### Population Size

A fundamental fact influencing a state's policies is its population size. In Table 1-2, I list each state's population in 2002 and, for comparative purposes, the populations of selected nations. The largest state, California, has 35 million residents or one in eight Americans. California can be considered more the size of a major nation than of a state. In fact, California's population is a bit larger than Canada's, and California's provision for education, highways, hospitals, and housing is on the same scale as that of many large nations; its state legislative districts are the size of congressional districts in other states.

**Table 1-2** State Population Contrasted with Similar Country Population Rank, 2002

| State rank | State/Country | Population | State rank | State/Country | Population |
|---|---|---|---|---|---|
| 1 | California | 35,116,033 | 25 | South Carolina | 4,107,183 |
|  | *Canada* | *31,300,000* | 26 | Kentucky | 4,092,891 |
| 2 | Texas | 21,779,893 | 27 | Oregon | 3,521,515 |
|  | *Australia* | *19,700,000* | 28 | Oklahoma | 3,493,714 |
| 3 | New York | 19,157,532 | 29 | Connecticut | 3,460,503 |
| 4 | Florida | 16,713,149 |  | *Albania* | *3,100,000* |
|  | *Kazakhstan* | *14,800,000* | 30 | Iowa | 2,936,760 |
| 5 | Illinois | 12,600,620 | 31 | Mississippi | 2,871,782 |
| 6 | Pennsylvania | 12,335,091 | 32 | Kansas | 2,715,884 |
| 7 | Ohio | 11,421,267 | 33 | Arkansas | 2,710,079 |
| 8 | Michigan | 10,050,446 |  | *Jamaica* | *2,600,000* |
|  | *Sweden* | *8,900,000* | 34 | Utah | 2,316,256 |
| 9 | New Jersey | 8,590,300 | 35 | Nevada | 2,173,491 |
| 10 | Georgia | 8,560,310 | 36 | New Mexico | 1,855,059 |
| 11 | North Carolina | 8,320,146 | 37 | West Virginia | 1,801,873 |
| 12 | Virginia | 7,293,542 | 38 | Nebraska | 1,729,180 |
| 13 | Massachusetts | 6,427,801 | 39 | Idaho | 1,341,131 |
| 14 | Indiana | 6,159,068 | 40 | Maine | 1,294,464 |
| 15 | Washington | 6,068,996 | 41 | New Hampshire | 1,275,056 |
| 16 | Tennessee | 5,797,289 | 42 | Hawaii | 1,244,898 |
| 17 | Missouri | 5,672,579 |  | *Gabon* | *1,200,000* |
| 18 | Maryland | 5,458,137 | 43 | Rhode Island | 1,069,725 |
| 19 | Arizona | 5,456,453 | 44 | Montana | 909,453 |
| 20 | Wisconsin | 5,441,196 | 45 | Delaware | 807,385 |
| 21 | Minnesota | 5,019,720 | 46 | South Dakota | 761,063 |
| 22 | Colorado | 4,506,542 | 47 | Alaska | 643,786 |
|  | *Norway* | *4,500,000* | 48 | North Dakota | 634,110 |
| 23 | Alabama | 4,486,508 | 49 | Vermont | 616,592 |
| 24 | Louisiana | 4,482,646 | 50 | Wyoming | 498,703 |

SOURCE: U.S. Bureau of the Census at http://eire.census.gov/popest/data/states/tables/ST-EST2002-01.php; Population Reference Bureau 2002.

Some less populous states are also the size of major foreign countries. New York, for instance, ranks third in U.S. population and is about the size of Australia. Louisiana is a medium-sized state by U.S. standards, ranking twenty-second in population; yet it is the same size as Norway. We must appreciate the fact that American state governments are large enterprises.

There are also some small states; and again, size has its consequences. Alaska and Wyoming are among the most sparsely populated states, but they are huge in the number of square miles. Thus the unit cost of building highways and providing other services is high. Alaska and Wyoming cannot achieve economies of scale. Smaller democracies have difficulties and opportunities not found in California and New York.

### Population Growth

Whatever the population size, a state's leaders develop ways to cope with that size. More difficult to manage in the short run are changes in population. States experiencing sudden population growth have difficulties providing schools, roads, bridges, waste management, law enforcement, and the housing needed for an expanding population. States experiencing population decline, on the other hand, have a different set of concerns. As people leave the state and businesses die, the tax base erodes; if a state government adjusts by raising taxes, more people may leave and initiate a vicious cycle. Obviously, states would rather be growing than shrinking.

Changes in population between 1990 and 2000 are shown in Figure 1-1. During this decade when the national increase was 13.2 percent, the West experienced the highest growth (19.7 percent), followed by the South (17.3 percent), with much lower rates in the Midwest (7.9 percent) and Northeast (5.5 percent). Nevada grew by two-thirds, the highest increase of any state; next were Arizona (40 percent), Colorado (31 percent), and Utah (30 percent). Population shifts among states are a result of different fertility rates and different rates of net migration (in other words, the difference in the number of people moving into a state and the number moving out of that state). Migration patterns, in turn, are a function of economic opportunities: people usually move to find better jobs and a better quality of life. State leaders, therefore, focus on economic growth and full employment as a means to retain old citizens and attract new ones.

The 1990s were the only decade in the twentieth century in which all states gained population. But some had tiny gains: North Dakota's was the smallest at 0.5 percent, followed by West Virginia (0.8 percent), and Pennsylvania (3.4 percent) (Figure 1-1). In the stagnant states it is often necessary to consolidate schools in sparsely populated rural areas. A school and its sports teams are often the focal point of a community, so their loss is a blow to community pride and identity.

North Dakotans are full of inventive ideas to attract new residents: in 2001 a state booster group floated the idea of changing the state's name to simply "Dakota." Their theory was that "North Dakota" conjured up an image of remote, cold, windy plains; dropping the "North" part would improve the state's image and make it more inviting to outsiders, they reasoned. The idea was quietly abandoned after it proved to be a popular target for comedians on late-night TV shows.

These descriptions point up the differences among states associated with the pace of population growth. Nevada is illustrative of those states struggling to keep up with an expanding population and struggling to cope with the political values of new residents. Most states are in the middle of the two extremes, growing at a moderate rate. Even in cases of moderate population growth, state governments need to plan ahead to meet the needs of a growing population, because schools and roads are not built overnight.

Depending upon who moves into the state and who moves out, population growth and decline can have electoral consequences. In general, national surveys show that people who are more mobile are more likely to identify with the Republican party (Gimpel and Schuknecht 2001, 211), thus offering the possibility that if sufficient movers settle in Democratic areas and if sufficient numbers of them vote Republican in their new locations, they will change electoral outcomes in a Republican direction. Gimpel and Schuknecht (2001), using the technique of ecological

**Figure 1-1**    State Population Growth, 1990–2000

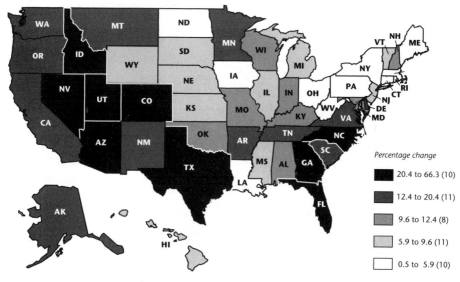

Percentage change

- 20.4 to 66.3 (10)
- 12.4 to 20.4 (11)
- 9.6 to 12.4 (8)
- 5.9 to 9.6 (11)
- 0.5 to 5.9 (10)

SOURCE: Perry and Mackun 2001.

inference in studying elections in twelve states over a 44-year period, confirmed that this generalization held firmly in six states (Florida, Georgia, Texas, Connecticut, Minnesota, Oregon), and held in some eras in three states (California, Colorado, Illinois); however, Michigan, Maryland, and New York were exceptions to the rule as cross-state migrants to these states were heavily Democratic. Population mobility makes the biggest difference to state politics when the gap between migrant and native voting is wide and where the influx of migrants is large.

*Population Density*

States also vary in the extent to which citizens live in densely populated urban areas or in more sparsely populated rural areas. As the U.S. population has grown, it has become more urbanized and less rural. Eighty percent of Americans live in metropolitan areas; 44 percent live in large metropolitan areas with more than 2 million residents. The cities between 2 and 5 million grew the fastest in the 1990s, sustaining 20 percent growth (Perry and Mackun 2001, 5). The most populous states tend to be among the most urbanized. There is a regional pattern as well. States on the East Coast tend to be densely populated, and states in the Mountain West are the least metropolitan.

The different interests of rural and urbanized areas often furnish the basis for sharp intrastate conflict. Illinois is a state with well-known metropolitan–downstate splits; about two-thirds of its population lives in the Chicago metropolitan area. As governed by the late mayor Richard J. Daley from 1955 to 1976, Chicago was the classic Democratic city machine. Its fiscal interests were often at odds with those in the rest of the state. In fact, columnist Mike Royko once suggested facetiously that the city secede from the state in order to free itself from the control of "downstate hayseeds and polyester-leisure suit suburbanites" (quoted in Peirce and Hagstrom 1984, 225).

Many other states manifest urban-rural splits or other sectional divisions. In heavily urbanized Florida, for example, there is a split between northern Florida and southern Florida. In the northern part of the state the traditional "southern" flavor lingers, whereas in southern Florida northern migrants furnish a "Yankee" flavor, and Latino immigrants provide their own flavor. In California disputes over the use of water reached such an impasse that northern residents wanted to secede and form a fifty-first state. In 1993 an advisory referendum on secession was held in 31 of the state's 58 counties; voters in 27 counties preferred secession. Such intrastate sectional differences influence and structure voting patterns and electoral outcomes.

*Population Composition*

States also differ in the composition of their populations—that is, in the types of demographic groups that are typical. States vary in the proportion of old people to young people, in the number of poor people, in the number of foreign-born people, and in the number of minorities. The increasingly diverse population mix presents challenges to government and often provides a basis for political conflict.

*Age.* Although the U.S. population as a whole is aging, the growth and concentration of seniors is quite variable at the state and local level. Retirement magnets in the South and West attract relatively affluent retirees; other locations in the Midwest and Northeast have large elderly populations because of "aging in place" and the out-migration of younger persons. In 2000 Florida had the highest percentage of people over age 65 (17.6 percent), illustrative of the retirement magnets. A recent report estimating the economic impact of Florida's residents over age 50 demonstrates why state officials continue to court retiring seniors: due to senior Floridians' spending habits and their tax payments, even after health and other services are factored in, they provide the state a net economic benefit of $1.4 billion ("Study: Seniors mean $1.4-billion to the state" 2002).

However, the other states in the top five on percent seniors (Pennsylvania, West Virginia, Iowa, and North Dakota) are illustrative of "aging in place" (U. S. Bureau of the Census 2000). In all of these states there will be increasing demand for the number of nursing homes, doctors, mass transportation, and senior centers.

Faced with an aging population, Iowa's governor Thomas Vilsack announced in 2000 that the state must encourage immigration to avoid economic decline. Marshalltown, Iowa, with a population of 29,000, was one of three communities to receive funds under the governor's program. Marshalltown in fact had already experienced a surge in its Hispanic population, up to 12 percent in the 2000 census

(Conte 2002, 33). Nearly all of its Latinos hail from one town in central Mexico; they hold about half the jobs in the local meatpacking plant, and their children account for a quarter of the enrollment in the public schools. Though the governor's immigration initiative stirred up trouble in parts of Iowa, Marshalltown's mayor welcomed the newcomers and even traveled to their hometown in Mexico to foster understanding. As he put it, "We need people."

Other states, especially those growing rapidly, have a high proportion of children. Generally speaking, the southern and western states have more young people: Utah ranks highest, with 26.6 percent of its citizens under age 15, followed closely by Alaska, Texas, Idaho, and New Mexico (Hobbs and Stoops 2002, 61). These states have to worry about the demand for school classrooms, day care centers, and youth services. Intergenerational stress is felt in some areas, particularly in Utah, Texas, and New Mexico, which have become retirement meccas in recent years. Their state leaders have to wrestle with questions of fairness and equity in making trade-offs between different age cohorts.

*Poverty.* Altogether about 33 million people in the United States fall below the U.S. government's poverty line, but poverty is not equally distributed among the states. New Mexico's population is the poorest (18.8 percent in 1999–2001), and New Hampshire's the least poor (6.2 percent). In general, the rate of poverty is highest in the South and Southwest.

The size of the poverty population presents a direct challenge and burden to state governments. States, even with aid from the federal government, struggle to provide cash benefits, medical care, and housing to the poor within their borders. The states, such as New Mexico, Arkansas, Louisiana, and Mississippi, that can least afford it are the states with the largest number of potential recipients. The states that can more easily afford to support the poor may exercise restraint because they fear generous benefits will attract poor people from out of state. The "welfare magnet" concept has been a popularly accepted one, although it receives only mixed support in scholarly literature. The perception by policy makers, however, that high welfare benefits act as a magnet can constrain the level of benefits. Chapter 11 explains this dynamic in more detail.

*Foreign-Born.* The United States is a nation formed by immigrants. Much of our nation's history can be told by reviewing the arrival of the different waves of immigrants—the Italians, the Irish, the Scandinavians, and so forth. Indeed, the entry of these ethnic groups into the political system formed the basis of many political cleavages. Today about half of the immigration stream comes from Latin America, a quarter from Asia, and only one-seventh from Europe (Schmidley 2001, 2). In the long run the country will reap substantial benefits from their arrival, just as it did from earlier immigrants. But in the short run the states in which refugees, "regular" immigrants (in other words, those who are not fleeing to this country for political asylum), and illegal immigrants locate experience difficulties in absorbing them. In 2000, 70 percent of the total foreign-born population lived in just six states: California, Florida, Illinois, New Jersey, New York, and Texas (Schmidley 2001, 2). Within those states the foreign-born population tends to concentrate in metropolitan areas: in the Los Angeles-Riverside-Orange County CMSA,[1] for example, the foreign-born constituted roughly 30 percent of the population in 2000.

There are two streams of immigrants arriving: one stream needs social services and language training and the other stream provides valuable workers for high-tech industries. For states the problem is that immigrants (and natives) pay most of their taxes to the federal government, whereas more of the costs of caring for immigrants falls to state and local governments. For example, a study by Los Angeles County showed that immigrants paid a great deal more in taxes than they received in social services. However, so much of the taxes went to Washington, D.C., that Los Angeles County was left with an $808 million "immigration deficit" (cited in Martin and Midgley 1994, 33).

The magnitude, geographic concentration, and type of immigration has affected many state governments, even provoking a backlash in some states. One obvious impact is that many new arrivals do not speak English or do not speak it well: 21 million people admitted they spoke the language "less than very well" in the 2000 census. The prevalence of non-English speakers has provoked more than twenty states to enact laws making English the official language. It is unclear what practical effect such laws have because most immigrants want to learn English.

The task of teaching English falls to the public schools, particularly to the large urban districts. Nearly all of the cost of English instruction comes from state and local coffers; very little funding is given by the federal government. Los Angeles had a herculean task: it had to educate more than 300,000 students with limited English proficiency in 1996–1997, just about half of its total school population. They spoke more than eighty different languages (Bathen 1998, 32). The success of California schools in teaching English became a divisive political issue, culminating in the adoption of Proposition 227 in 1998, which ended bilingual instruction in the public schools. Arizona voters adopted a similar proposition in 2000.

Language proficiency also affects immigrants' ability to access health care. Under a nondiscrimination directive issued by the Clinton Administration all providers who receive federal funds must offer non-English-speaking patients free assistance (interpreters, translators) in their language. This covers state, county, and local health and welfare agencies, hospitals, clinics, emergency rooms, nursing homes, and so forth. There is some federal financial help available through Medicaid and other funds, but much of the money has to come from state government.

Though some newcomers need public assistance upon arrival, relatively soon most obtain jobs and become taxpayers; within 10 to 15 years their employment rates are quite similar to those of natives. According to a National Academy of Sci-

---

1. A CMSA (Consolidated Metropolitan Statistical Area) has a population of one million or more with separate component areas (PMSAs, or Primary Metropolitan Statistical Areas) that meet statistical criteria and are supported by local opinion.

ences study (Smith and Edmonston 1997), the net fiscal impact of immigration is positive under most long-term economic scenarios. Certainly, immigrants who arrive in this country before age 25 pay more in taxes than they receive in government benefits. But, as noted, the political problem is that the federal government gets about two-thirds of their tax revenues, while the states provide the bulk of the services. The nation is reaping a great economic and societal benefit from immigration while a handful of states are incurring a net fiscal burden.

*Minorities.* Because of immigration and differential birth rates, the United States has gradually evolved from a largely white, European society to an increasingly diverse one; today one in four Americans is a member of a racial or ethnic minority. By the middle of this century minorities will equal the majority; this has already happened in California and New Mexico where minorities constitute over half the population. And it will happen soon in Texas where white non-Hispanics hold a slight numeric edge. In Hawaii whites have long been in the minority. The Hispanic and Asian populations are growing the fastest; indeed, in 2001 Hispanics became the country's largest minority group, surpassing blacks.[2]

As our previous discussion of immigration would suggest, each minority population tends to be concentrated in certain states. More than half of all African Americans live in the South. Historically, the politics of individual southern states have varied according to the proportion of blacks. The Deep South states—Alabama, Georgia, Louisiana, Mississippi, and South Carolina—with the highest concentration of blacks were much more conservative than the peripheral South—Virginia, Tennessee, Florida, Arkansas, North Carolina, and Texas. Political behavior varied because where there were more blacks, whites were more likely to unite behind racial conservatism. Today blacks constitute from a quarter to a third of the population in those five Deep South states.

Hispanics, in contrast, are concentrated primarily in the Southwest, totaling about a third of the population in California and Texas and 42 percent in New Mexico. There is also a significant Hispanic presence of more than 10 percent in Arizona, Colorado, Illinois, Nevada, New Jersey, New York, and Florida. But there are differences within these communities: in New York the population is mostly Puerto Rican and in Florida, Cuban. Like blacks, Hispanics are a disadvantaged minority, but unlike blacks many Hispanics lack fluency in English, which provides an additional obstacle in obtaining jobs.

More than half of all Asian Americans live in the West, primarily in California, Washington, or Hawaii, with another significant portion in New York and New Jersey. As their numbers are much smaller than those of Hispanics or African Americans, Asian Americans do not constitute a significant fraction of the total

---

2. Hispanics are an ethnic group, not a racial group; Hispanics can be white, black, or other. The term "Hispanic" is a Census Bureau label that applies to all people from Spanish-speaking countries—that is from Spain or Latin America. Many Hispanics born in the United States prefer to be called Latino, which refers to people of Latin American descent living in the United States. Or they prefer to be known by their national origin—for example, Cuban or Mexican.

population except in Hawaii. There the Asian American population is the majority. Hawaii has been successful in race relations for a long time and may provide a model for other states.

Native Americans are the smallest minority group; they primarily reside in the Southwest, especially New Mexico, South Dakota, Oklahoma, Arizona, and Montana, where their proportions range from 5 to 10 percent. About half live on tribal lands and about half are urbanites. In Alaska, Alaska Natives constitute about 15 percent of the population.

The rapid growth of minorities—88 percent increase from 1980 to 2000—has increased their political clout, though they are still underrepresented among elected officials. Thus far Hispanics have achieved the governorship in Florida, Arizona, and New Mexico. Douglas Wilder in Virginia is the only African American to attain this office, and Gary Locke, elected governor of Washington in 1996, is the first Chinese American governor.

The close proximity of minority groups sometimes creates racial tensions over political issues. Several states have had challenges to congressional districts drawn along racial lines, and the U.S. Supreme Court is dealing with those affirmative gerrymandering cases. Chapter 6 describes in more detail the racial issues involved in legislative reapportionment. In California backlash against minorities was expressed in 1996 by voters' adoption of Proposition 209, which says that state government cannot use racial quotas or preferences in education, contracting, and employment. Chapter 5 examines this and other states' use of the initiative vis-à-vis minorities.

Overall the states' diversity in population composition—whether racial, age, foreign-born, or poor—leads to political diversity. Political parties are likely to be different in California than in Iowa. They will be based on different political cleavages and different opinions about public policy needs. There are likely to be more groups representing a wider spectrum of interests in Florida than in Mississippi. In subsequent chapters we will see the consequences of states' population diversity.

## THE PLACE

States also differ in terms of their physical characteristics. Some of these attributes are fixed and cannot be changed: the land area, the location, and the climate. State leaders can try to compensate for the effects of a remote location, a cold or unpleasant climate, or small size, but for the most part they are constrained by nature. Similarly, states are constrained by their natural resource endowments: some states have rich soil; others cannot grow much. Some states have plenty of water, forests, minerals, oil, or coal. Others have to get their water from other states and must rely on imported oil and coal. The net effect of the maldistribution of natural resources is that states vary in the types of economic activities that can be conducted in them. The overall wealth of states, in turn, depends on the vigor of the economy.

*Land*

States vary enormously in their land area. We all know that Alaska is the largest state, followed by Texas. What is less well known, however, is how big Alaska is in relation to other states. It is more than twice the size of Texas. In fact, the twenty-two smallest states could be combined before an area as large as Alaska is reached.

What difference to a state does its geographic size make? First, there are distinct differences in a state's political style. In larger states legislative districts are by necessity quite large. In wide-ranging districts it is hard for legislators to keep in touch with constituents; airplanes are frequently used for campaigning in Alaska, for instance. In rural Texas districts are vast. Moreover, legislators must travel hundreds of miles from their homes and jobs to Austin, the state capital. The travel burden affects the type of people who can afford to serve in the legislature. In Arizona the prospect of serving in one legislative district stretching for 300 miles was so uninviting that no one filed to run for the office in 1998!

In smaller states, such as New Hampshire and Vermont, districts are small and compact. Legislators can run personal, almost one-on-one campaigns. Once in office, they can commute to the capital on a daily basis, continuing in their regular occupations. The result is more of an amateur, small-town flavor in politics.

Second, geographic size has policy implications. In the provision of highways, for instance, geographic area and population density determine expense. Alaska, Montana, and Wyoming are large and sparsely populated states; their per capita highway expenditures are among the highest in the nation. Rhode Island is a small state with a compact population; its expenditure is among the lowest. The state's size affects the delivery of services in many other policy areas as well.

Third, land can be the basis of political conflict. Among the most divisive issues in the western states is that the federal government owns much of the land. Eighty-two percent of Nevada is owned by the federal government; more than 60 percent of Alaska, California, Idaho, and Utah is federal domain. This means that vast areas of the West are not under state jurisdiction; this land can be put only to the uses allowed by the federal government. Federal ownership, therefore, constrains urban growth and economic development in many western cities. Federal lands are often rich in mineral and other natural resources, assets unavailable to state governments. The federal government does, however, pay state royalties for the lost tax revenues.

Occasionally, unrest over federal landholding rises, and outbreaks occur, such as the Sagebrush Rebellion in 1979. This symbolic revolution began when Nevada passed a law requiring the U.S. government to turn much of its land over to the state; several other states passed similar laws. Naturally, the federal government ignored these laws, and the rebellion gradually died out. Now the state of Nevada has a new beef with the federal government. In July 2002 the U.S. Congress, upon recommendation of the U.S. Energy Department and President Bush, designated a six-mile strip of federal land at Yucca Mountain as the nation's nuclear waste repository. Nevada officials have repeatedly filed lawsuits to stop the federal project; they argue that the site, located 80 miles north of Las Vegas on a volcanic ridge, is unsafe due to its geologic features. In reality, some state had to be chosen as the unlucky recipient; being a small state with few congressional allies was probably Nevada's downfall.

*Natural Resources*

Natural resources such as soil, water, minerals, and energy are attached to the land. The distribution of natural resources has great economic consequences: it allows states blessed with abundant water and rich topsoil to concentrate on crop production. Less fortunate states must import their water and some of their food. Some states receive income from the coal, oil, and minerals extracted from the land. Not only do these states have access to these nonrenewable resources, they can also derive tax revenue from the companies who mine the coal or pump the oil and natural gas. Those companies then refine the natural resources and sell them to customers at prices sufficient to cover the severance tax and make a profit. In essence, resource-rich states can shift some of their tax burden onto citizens of other states, at least as long as there is a demand for oil, coal, and natural gas.

To begin, first consider the rich topsoil that makes some states substantial agricultural producers. California is the top farm producer, as measured by gross state product (GSP),[3] followed by Texas, Florida, North Carolina, and Iowa. Most of the other states in the Midwest rank fairly high, and the New England states rank low. Their state economies produce few agricultural products. In no state, however, is agriculture the largest sector of the state's GSP. But agriculture looms large in other ways. In the rural states there is a sense of pride and identification with the land. Iowa, for example, had on its billboards the slogan "Iowa, a Place to Grow," suggesting simultaneously the growth of crops and the growth of sturdy young children.

In addition to fertile topsoil, agriculture requires the availability of water. The Midwest is blessed with sufficient water, but the West is not. Nowhere is water a more important issue than in the Southwest and West. On the wall of the Colorado state capitol an inscription reads, "Here is the land where life is written in water." The battle over use of the water from the Colorado River is illustrative. California and six other states—Arizona, Colorado, New Mexico, Nevada, Utah, and Wyoming—share the river's water according to an interstate compact adopted in 1922, with California receiving by far the largest share. Historically, most of the water was consumed by agriculture. But economic development, the rapidly increasing population, and some energy projects all require water. The allocation of water between states, and within states between agriculture and other competing purposes, are ongoing battles. In early 2003 the Interior Department, which manages the flow of the Colorado River, intervened to limit California's use of the river's water; the feds deemed the Golden State's usage excessive because too much

---

3. GSP is the gross market value of the goods and services attributable to labor and property located in a state. It is the state equivalent of gross national product (GNP).

water was going into irrigation of crops in southern California rather than to the city of San Diego.

Finally, nonrenewable natural resources are unevenly distributed across the states. Minerals, coal, and petroleum are found only in some locations. Coal is found in large quantities in Kentucky, Pennsylvania, West Virginia, and the surrounding states, and in the West, particularly in New Mexico and Wyoming. Oil is located in the South and Southwest, primarily Louisiana, Oklahoma, and Texas, and in Alaska. The unequal distribution of natural resources has at least two major consequences for state governments. One favorable consequence for a state that has such resources is that the resources can be taxed. This tax is called a "severance tax."

The states in which the severance tax looms largest are Alaska and Wyoming. Wyoming has no income tax; interest from a mineral trust fund and severance taxes on natural gas, coal, and oil furnished nearly half of state tax revenues in 2001 (Barrett et al., 2003, 97). Alaska is even more dependent upon its oil reserves: nearly 60 percent of state tax revenues in 2001 came from severance taxes on oil and natural gas (Barrett et al. 2003, 39). The state has no individual income tax or general sales tax and has even been able to grant each citizen an annual dividend, amounting to $1,500 in 2002.

Reliance on the severance tax to the exclusion of other taxes, however, can have undesirable consequences. When the price of the nonrenewable resource drops, tax revenue plummets. Wyoming has found natural gas prices to be extremely volatile and thus tax revenue difficult to predict. Alaska state officials believe that by 2006 the revenue from the severance tax will no longer be adequate (Barrett et al. 2003, 39). Thus the state needs to shift onto a more stable taxation base, such as the income tax or sales tax. But in a state of rugged individualists who have not paid taxes in more than two decades, the tax collector will have a tough job. Chapter 10 explores the range of tax choices that states have.

## THE ECONOMIC CONTEXT

States' economic performance depends on their natural resources, available human capital, and national and international economic trends.

### State Economic Activities

The land and its natural resources initially determine the type of economic activities that will prosper in different regions of the country. The regions' different resource bases mean they concentrate on different economic activities, and they enjoy different levels of prosperity. Table 1-3 relates some of these differences. As you see, California has by far the largest economy as measured by Gross State Product, followed by New York, Texas, Florida, and Illinois.

States' economies vary in size, in which economic sector is most important (manufacturing, services, finance, and so on), and in the major goods produced. Many of these variations result from the natural resources of each state—that is, minerals, timber, soil, and access to waterways. Over time the sectors of the economy based on

**Table 1-3** Value of Gross State Product (in $ millions) and Size of Dominant Economic Sector, 2000

| Rank | State | GSP | Dominant sector | Percentage of GSP |
|------|-------|-----|-----------------|-------------------|
| 1 | California | $1,344,623 | Services | 24 |
| 2 | New York | 799,202 | Finance, insurance, real estate | 33 |
| 3 | Texas | 742,274 | Services | 20 |
| 4 | Florida | 472,105 | Services | 25 |
| 5 | Illinois | 467,284 | Services | 23 |
| 6 | Pennsylvania | 403,985 | Services | 23 |
| 7 | Ohio | 372,640 | Manufacturing | 24 |
| 8 | New Jersey | 363,089 | Finance, insurance, real estate | 24 |
| 9 | Michigan | 325,384 | Manufacturing | 26 |
| 10 | Georgia | 296,142 | Services | 20 |
| 11 | Massachusetts | 284,934 | Services | 28 |
| 12 | North Carolina | 281,741 | Manufacturing | 24 |
| 13 | Virginia | 261,355 | Services | 24 |
| 14 | Washington | 219,937 | Services | 24 |
| 15 | Indiana | 192,195 | Manufacturing | 31 |
| 16 | Maryland | 186,108 | Services | 25 |
| 17 | Minnesota | 184,766 | Services | 21 |
| 18 | Missouri | 178,845 | Services | 21 |
| 19 | Tennessee | 178,362 | Services | 21 |
| 20 | Wisconsin | 173,478 | Manufacturing | 25 |
| 21 | Colorado | 167,918 | Services | 24 |
| 22 | Connecticut | 159,288 | Finance, insurance, real estate | 30 |
| 23 | Arizona | 156,303 | Services | 22 |
| 24 | Louisiana | 137,700 | Services | 17 |
| 25 | Alabama | 119,921 | Manufacturing | 19 |
| 26 | Oregon | 118,637 | Manufacturing | 26 |
| 27 | Kentucky | 118,508 | Manufacturing | 27 |
| 28 | South Carolina | 113,377 | Manufacturing | 21 |
| 29 | Oklahoma | 91,773 | Services | 18 |
| 30 | Iowa | 89,600 | Manufacturing | 22 |
| 31 | Kansas | 85,063 | Services | 17 |
| 32 | Nevada | 74,745 | Services | 32 |
| 33 | Utah | 68,549 | Services | 21 |
| 34 | Arkansas | 67,724 | Manufacturing | 22 |
| 35 | Mississippi | 67,315 | Manufacturing | 20 |
| 36 | Nebraska | 56,072 | Services | 20 |
| 37 | New Mexico | 54,364 | Services | 18 |
| 38 | New Hampshire | 47,708 | Finance, insurance, real estate | 24 |
| 39 | Hawaii | 42,364 | Finance, insurance, real estate | 22 |
| 40 | West Virginia | 42,271 | Services | 18 |
| 41 | Idaho | 37,031 | Manufacturing | 23 |
| 42 | Rhode Island | 36,453 | Finance, insurance, real estate | 30 |
| 43 | Delaware | 36,336 | Finance, insurance, real estate | 38 |
| 44 | Maine | 35,981 | Services | 21 |
| 45 | Alaska | 27,747 | Mining | 22 |
| 46 | South Dakota | 23,192 | Finance, insurance, real estate | 20 |
| 47 | Montana | 21,777 | Services | 21 |
| 48 | Wyoming | 19,294 | Mining | 24 |
| 49 | Vermont | 18,411 | Services | 22 |
| 50 | North Dakota | 18,283 | Services | 19 |

SOURCE: U.S. Bureau of Economic Analysis at http://www.bea.doc.gov/bea/regional/gsp.

natural resources have declined in dollar value and in employment relative to the rest of the economy, however.

In nearly all states the manufacturing sector is still important, even though no longer the dominant economic sector. Each state's natural resources heavily determine the type of manufacturing base. Midwestern states such as Illinois and Ohio focus on the production of machinery, while Michigan, Indiana, Ohio, and Kentucky lead in production of automobiles. In parts of the South—Georgia, North Carolina, and South Carolina—the manufacturing base has rested on the textile industry, but some of that activity is moving overseas. Food and food processing is a major manufacturing activity in other parts of the South—Arkansas, Florida, Georgia—and in the Midwest—Nebraska and Iowa. The chemical industry is crucial to the economies of Alabama, Delaware, Louisiana, New Jersey, and Tennessee.

Manufacturing is no longer the dominant sector of the national economy, however. Manufacturing's share of employment shrank from 26 percent in 1970 to 15 percent in 2000 (U.S. Bureau of the Census 2001b, 384). This is referred to as the "deindustrialization of America." As can be seen in the table, in thirty-seven states manufacturing is now surpassed in value by some other economic sector.

The services sector is now the single largest sector in twenty-seven states, including the previously industrial states of Illinois, Massachusetts, and Pennsylvania. This sector's major components are business services and health services, but it also includes a variety of other things such as hotels and lodging; thus the services sector is critical in tourist meccas like Florida and Nevada. In eight other states the financial sector is the most important: New York, the established financial capital, has been joined in financial circles by seven other states, including New Jersey, Connecticut, New Hampshire, Hawaii, Delaware, Rhode Island, and South Dakota. The last state offers especially favorable regulatory conditions to the banking and insurance industries, so banks locate their subsidiary operations there.

In the nation as a whole, the services sector's share of employment has increased from 26 percent to 38 percent since 1970. These tend to be more mobile occupations, which can be carried on anywhere. Your credit card's customer service center is likely to be located in Sioux Falls, South Dakota, or Fargo, North Dakota; your airline reservation agent may be in Chisholm, Minnesota. These occupations do not depend on particular natural resources, although they do depend on business activity in general.

These changes in economic circumstances are a part of larger changes in the national and international economies. The "globalization of capitalism" means that states increasingly feel the effects of surges and declines in prices, labor markets, and exchange rates thousands of miles away. States' economic fortunes in a global economy depend on their ability to export products abroad and their capacity to attract direct foreign investment. Although Chapter 14 describes states' effort to attract foreign investors, as well as domestic investors, let us say a bit about exports here.

Exports account for about 11 percent of the U.S. economy, but states vary in their success in finding export markets. Michigan, for example, ranks high (fourth) among the states in GSP generated by exports, probably due to export of automobiles. Other states' economies are buoyed by their agricultural exports, e.g., California, Illinois, Iowa, Kansas, Minnesota, Nebraska, and Texas. Amidst the political discussion of jobs lost to cheap foreign labor, the U.S. jobs created by exports to foreign markets are often overlooked. A 1997 U.S. government study (International Trade Administration) showed that exports of manufactured goods supported 7.7 million U.S. jobs or about 20 percent of all manufacturing jobs; in over half the states exports contributed more than 100,000 jobs to the local economy. Many states' economies are being helped by the buying power of consumers far away.

In recent years states have greatly increased their budgets for export promotion, for example establishing more trade offices overseas or sending governors abroad on trade missions. One of the most amazing events took place in the fall of 2002 when 300 U.S. firms pitched their products at a food fair in Havana, Cuba. Several governors from agricultural states—good Republican governors—attended the exhibition hosted by President Fidel Castro, a communist; Minnesota's flamboyant governor Jesse Ventura got the most attention. Even though the U.S. government still has an economic embargo against Cuba, there is growing sentiment in the U.S. Congress to lift the ban. This exhibition was designed to apply political pressure on the national government. The governors from farm states know a potential market when they see one. The 11 million people in Cuba need more eggs, meat, chicken, rice, beans, and dairy products, products midwestern farmers will be happy to export when it is legal. One Republican governor who stayed home was Florida's Jeb Bush, running for re-election and counting on votes from anti-Castro Cuban Americans. In fact, he wrote a letter to Governor Ventura urging him not to attend the trade fair.

States along the borders of Mexico and Canada have special ties to the international economy. Obviously, immigration is a longstanding issue affecting local labor markets as well as reliance on social services. As explained further in Chapter 2, trade relations are affected by NAFTA, the North American Free Trade Agreement; a series of other international agreements attempt to coordinate border policies on pollution, wildlife, fishing, disease, law enforcement, and so on. Mexico is particularly important to Texas; on being elected, new Texas governors often visit Mexico even before they visit Washington, D.C. In fact, in the past thirty years all Texas governors have visited Mexico in the first ninety days of their administration (Don Lutz, September 1997, personal communication). Several international commissions and banks are located in south Texas, demonstrating the volume of international economic activity taking place along the border.

The globalization of the economy will continue, and experts think that the nation–state will become less relevant as an economic actor. The national economy may fracture into regional economies or smaller subnational economies, which is where the American states come in. One author even went so far as to say the fate of the United States depends on what the fifty states do in the international economy: "To a great extent, it will be state strategies and state alliances across a broad range

**Table 1-4** Per Capita Personal Income (PCPI) by State, 2001

| Rank | State | PCPI | Rank | State | PCPI |
|------|-------|------|------|-------|------|
| 1 | Connecticut | $42,435 | 26 | Vermont | 28,594 |
| 2 | Massachusetts | 38,907 | 27 | Texas | 28,581 |
| 3 | New Jersey | 38,509 | 28 | Kansas | 28,565 |
| 4 | New York | 36,019 | 29 | Missouri | 28,226 |
| 5 | Maryland | 35,188 | 30 | Oregon | 28,165 |
| 6 | New Hampshire | 34,138 | 31 | Indiana | 27,783 |
| 7 | Colorado | 33,470 | 32 | North Carolina | 27,514 |
| 8 | Minnesota | 33,101 | 33 | Iowa | 27,331 |
| 9 | Illinois | 33,023 | 34 | Tennessee | 26,988 |
| 10 | California | 32,702 | 35 | Maine | 26,723 |
| 11 | Delaware | 32,472 | 36 | South Dakota | 26,664 |
| 12 | Virginia | 32,431 | 37 | North Dakota | 25,902 |
| 13 | Washington | 32,025 | 38 | Arizona | 25,872 |
| 14 | Alaska | 30,936 | 39 | Oklahoma | 25,071 |
| 15 | Pennsylvania | 30,720 | 40 | Kentucky | 24,923 |
| 16 | Rhode Island | 30,215 | 41 | South Carolina | 24,886 |
| 17 | Nevada | 29,897 | 42 | Idaho | 24,621 |
| 18 | Michigan | 29,788 | 43 | Alabama | 24,589 |
| 19 | Wyoming | 29,416 | 44 | Louisiana | 24,535 |
| 20 | Wisconsin | 29,270 | 45 | Utah | 24,180 |
| 21 | Hawaii | 29,002 | 46 | Montana | 23,963 |
| 22 | Florida | 28,947 | 47 | New Mexico | 23,155 |
| 23 | Nebraska | 28,886 | 48 | Arkansas | 22,887 |
| 24 | Ohio | 28,816 | 49 | West Virginia | 22,881 |
| 25 | Georgia | 28,733 | 50 | Mississippi | 21,750 |

SOURCE:  U.S. Bureau of Economic Analysis at http://www.bea.doc.gov/bea/regional/spi

of international issues that will determine our nation's relative success in the global marketplace of the future" (Ryen 1996, 525).

*State Personal Income*

The net effect of states' natural resources, national and international economic trends, and the flow of federal funds (discussed further in Chapter 2) is reflected in state wealth, usually measured in political science research by per capita personal income. This figure includes the income of individuals from all sources; a state's growth in personal income over time is a good index of how well its economy is doing. In Table 1-4 I list the average personal income per person in 2001 for each state. It is clear that there are significant disparities in income between states and between regions: Connecticut at $42,435 is significantly ahead of Mississippi at $21,750. In general, the southern states cluster at the bottom; the New England and Middle Atlantic states toward the top. The disparity, however, has lessened over the years, so the South does not lag as far behind the rest of the country as it once did.

Personal income is an important constraint on state programs because wealth determines what a state can afford to do on its own and what its people need or want from the state. States such as Mississippi do not have a lot of taxable income. States at the top of the income ranking, such as Connecticut, have a larger tax base and can afford to offer more generous benefits to their citizens. The irony is, of course, that Mississippi's needs are greater than Connecticut's. Federal aid reduces these interstate disparities to some extent. How states make their decisions in regard to taxing and spending is described in Chapter 10.

State leaders do not, however, simply "convert" economic wealth into expenditures for public programs. There are too many anomalies in state wealth and expenditure rankings for simple conversion to be a convincing explanation. Moreover, as we have seen, the economic performance of states changes over time. Some develop new fiscal capacities that might be tapped by government; the fiscal capacity of others shrinks, leaving them with overdeveloped public sectors. Politics shape how economic resources will be translated into public policies. In the next section I introduce some of the political dimensions that structure how states use their economic resources.

## THE POLITICAL CONTEXT

The broader political context that influences state policy making includes long-standing historical and cultural patterns, contemporary public opinion and ideology, and national political trends.

### Historical Differences

Many of the political differences in states today—differences in voter turnout and party competition, for example—are longstanding ones. The South in particular has had a different political history than the rest of the country. Some of the South's differences from other regions of the country are rooted in distinct economic interests. But another important historical difference is the South's political culture. It shapes the habits, perspectives, and attitudes that influence present-day political life.

Daniel Elazar (1984) has written extensively on how state political cultures have shaped the operations of state political systems. He has argued that the United States shares a general political culture that is, in turn, a synthesis of three major subcultures—individualist, moralist, and traditionalist. The values of each subculture were brought to this country by the early settlers and spread unevenly across the country as various ethnic and religious groups moved westward. These migration streams have deposited their political values much like the Ice Age left permanent geological traces on the earth. Today's differences, according to Elazar, can be traced to the political values and perspectives of the earliest settlers.

The individualist subculture emphasizes the marketplace. Government has a limited role, primarily to keep the marketplace working properly. Bureaucracy is viewed negatively as a deterrent to the spoils system. Corruption in office is tolerated because politics is conceived of as a dirty business. Political competition tends to be partisan and oriented toward gaining office rather than toward dealing with issues. The individualist view of politics, Elazar has maintained, originated with English and German groups who settled the Middle Atlantic colonies.

In distinct contrast is the moralist subculture that emphasizes the commonwealth. In this view government's role is to advance the public interest or the good of the commonwealth. Thus government is a positive force in the lives of citizens. Politics revolve around issues; corruption is not tolerated. Politics are a matter of concern to all citizens; it is therefore a citizen's duty to participate in elections.

The moralist view was brought to the New World by the Puritans, who settled New England in a series of religious communities. Their Yankee descendants transported these values as they moved westward across the upper Great Lakes into the Midwest and across the Northwest; later waves of Scandinavian and northern European groups with similar values reinforced their moralism.

The third subculture, the traditionalist, is rooted in an ambivalent attitude toward the marketplace and the commonwealth. The purpose of government under this philosophy is to maintain the existing social and economic hierarchy. Politicians come from society's elite, who have almost a familial obligation to govern. Ordinary citizens are not expected to participate in political affairs or even to vote. The traditionalist values were brought to this country by the people who originally settled the southern colonies. They were seeking economic opportunity through a plantation-centered agricultural system. Their descendants moved westward throughout the southern and border tier of states.

Elazar classified the dominant political subcultures of each state, using the settlement patterns completed by the early twentieth century (Figure 1-2). Few states are pure examples of one subculture, but usually there is a dominant culture that gives the state its particular political style. In general, the states of the South are dominated by the traditionalist subculture. The individualist states stretch across the country's middle section. The states of the far North, Northwest, and Pacific Coast are dominated by the moralist culture.

Contemporary migration patterns between regions may either reinforce or override the cultural base laid by the first settlers. For example, if people leave individualist states such as Pennsylvania and Ohio to seek better jobs in Texas, they will reinforce the individualism within the Texas political culture and move it away from traditionalism. Or if the population influx is quite large, as in Florida, the cultural base may be eroded. States with stable populations, such as Minnesota, North Dakota, and Wisconsin, remain relatively pure examples of moralism.

Elazar's cultural theory has intuitive appeal as it is consistent with general impressions about state differences in political values, style, and tone. It also provides a historical explanation for differences. Many researchers have subjected his thesis to empirical investigation—that is, they have tested his predictions about political and policy differences between the three subcultures and found some support for them. Fitzpatrick and Hero (1988), for example, confirmed many of Elazar's hypotheses. They found that the competition between parties was stronger in moralist states than in other types of states and that this competition had greater relevance to public policy. Moralist states made greater use of merit systems than did other states. They demonstrated greater policy innovation and greater economic equality.

**Figure 1-2**  Dominant Political Culture by State

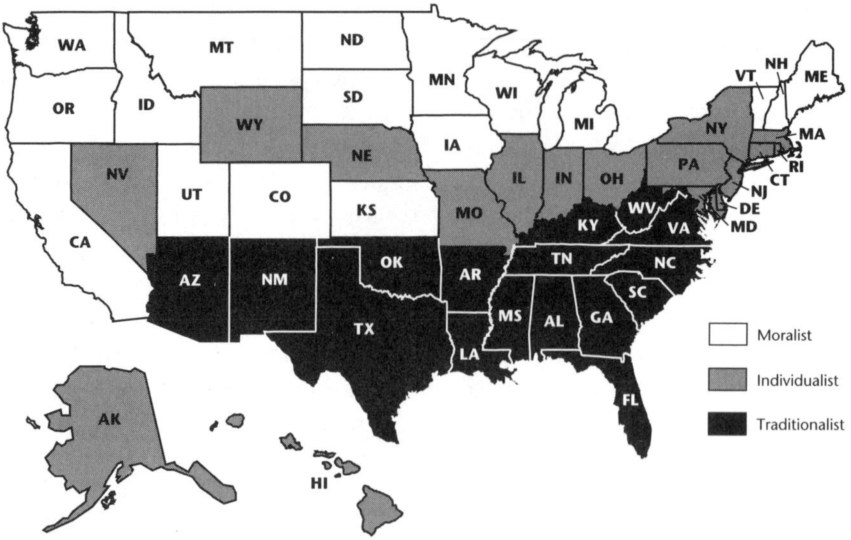

SOURCE: Adapted in part from Elazar 1984, 136.

One interesting question is what happens to people who move from one political culture to another. Russell Hanson (1992) found that migrants' adjustment to different norms of citizen duty depended on their culture of origin. Persons raised as moralists were dutiful wherever they lived; traditionalists and individualists conformed to their new surroundings, becoming either more or less dutiful, depending on the new culture.

Further evidence that political attitudes are conditioned by local political culture or context is provided by Erikson, Wright, and McIver (1993). Because their *Statehouse Democracy* is a significant study that we refer to throughout the book, it is worthwhile to explain their methods. To get around the problem that there are no public opinion polls that are comparable across all states, they pooled 122 CBS News/*New York Times* telephone surveys from 1976 to 1988 to obtain measures of ideology and party identification by state.

They are able to show that state political context has a dramatic effect on individual attitudes. They control for the obvious demographic variables that explain individuals' attitudes (education, income, age, race, religion, gender, and size of place) and still find that the state of residence has a significant effect, approximately equal to the demographic effects. For example, the difference in party identification produced by living in Democratic Arkansas as opposed to living in Republican New Hampshire approaches the magnitude of the partisan differences produced by being Jewish instead of Protestant or being black instead of white.

Although the authors cannot account for the source of these state effects (cultural or otherwise), they conclude that "the political attitudes of American citizens vary in important ways on the basis of where in the United States they live" (Erikson et al. 1993, 72). In further analyses they find strong support for Elazar's particular categorization of culture. State boundaries do make a difference.

*Contemporary Differences*

Others argue that historical cultural differences are not as important as contemporary differences in explaining public policy. Rodney Hero and Caroline Tolbert (1996; Hero 1998) argue that present-day patterns of racial and ethnic diversity are more influential than political subcultures derived from settlement patterns of the past. What is valuable about the Hero-Tolbert work is that they include the extent of the minority population (blacks, Latinos, and Asians) as well as the proportion of white ethnics (particularly those from southern and eastern Europe). Hero and Tolbert show that states vary in their policy choices according to the heterogeneity of their populations, but their research needs to be confirmed and extended by other investigators before their categorizations will replace political subcultures as an explanation.

Another contemporary difference in states' political makeup is public opinion. Public opinion constitutes the attitudes of individual citizens toward public issues: Should their state spend more on welfare? Should their state allow abortions? Should a state lottery be established? The cultural thesis outlined previously suggests that public opinion on these and other issues should vary by state, and indeed it does. An even more important question is whether state policy differences are related to (or caused by) differences in public opinion.

Erikson, Wright, and McIver in *Statehouse Democracy* (1993) provided a method for comparing public opinion across states; on Wright's website <http://php.indiana.edu/~wright1/> they post the updated measure through 1999. They measured public opinion by the standard ideology question: "How would you describe your views on most political matters? Generally, do you think of yourself as liberal, moderate, or conservative?" Their scale is the percentage of liberals minus the percentage of conservatives in each state per year.

We can use this public opinion liberalism measure to predict policy differences among the states. Recall our policy liberalism index presented in Table 1-1 earlier in the chapter. It is composed of five indicators measured between 1995 and 2001, representing policies on which liberals and conservatives usually disagree. The index is constructed so that 1 indicates the state making the most liberal choices (California) and 48 indicates the state making the most conservative policy choices (South Dakota). Given the direction of the two scales, we expect public opinion liberalism, averaged over the years 1995–1999, and the policy liberalism index to be positively correlated.

In Figure 1-3 we see that indeed there is a positive relationship between the two measures: as states increase in opinion liberalism (move to the right along the x axis), they make more liberal policy choices (move upward along the y axis). The correlation is .78, slightly less than the .82 Erikson, Wright, and McIver (1993) reported for

**Figure 1-3** Public Opinion Liberalism and Policy Liberalism

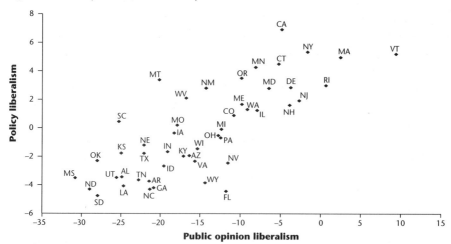

SOURCE: Policy liberalism index from Gray et al. 2002. The measure for public opinion liberalism was created using data aggregated by Gerald Wright, John McIver, and Robert Erikson based on CBS News/*New York Times* national polls, available at php.indiana.edu/~wright1/.

NOTE: In order to correspond to the time period covered by our policy index, we averaged the public opinion liberalism score for each state over the five-year time period, 1995–1999.

a different policy index measured in the 1980s. Of course, other factors besides public opinion must be included in a properly specified model, but the measure of public opinion liberalism holds up quite well statistically against other variables (Erikson, Wright, and McIver 1993; Gray et al. 2002).

In addition to public opinion, states' political organizations are crucial in policy making. In this book we examine in detail two types of organizations: political parties, treated in Chapter 3, and interest groups, discussed in Chapter 4. The chapter authors describe how parties and groups function and how they differ from state to state.

*National Forces*

The states' political context is also conditioned by national political trends. These external forces have an effect on the linkages between politics and policy within states. An article by John Chubb (1988) captures the statistical impact of external political and economic forces on state legislative and gubernatorial elections. Chubb found that presidential and senatorial coattails, voter turnout surges and declines, and national economic conditions have all affected the outcomes of state legislative races since 1940. Later research by Niemi, Stanley, and Vogel (1995) demonstrated that gubernatorial electoral outcomes are significantly affected by national political and economic forces. For example, after the 2002 elections when Republicans gained control of the U.S. Congress, they also improved their showing at the state level. Voters in 36 states went to the polls to elect governors: they selected 22 Republicans and 14 Democrats. Republican-controlled legislatures increased from 17 to 22. Thus national political and economic trends may indirectly affect state government through their impact on state elections.

Besides the electoral forces Chubb analyzed, other national political factors may affect the states. One such factor is the hierarchy of national offices that exists in the United States. As Schlesinger (1966, 1991) has documented, there is a regular career progression from state legislative and other entry-level offices to the governorship to Washington-based positions such as senator, vice president, and president. Most people who achieve high office in Washington have "worked their way up" through this office hierarchy. Former governors Jimmy Carter, Ronald Reagan, Bill Clinton, and George W. Bush are four examples of this phenomenon, which Chapter 7 describes in more detail.

These are but a few of the ways in which national political trends may affect state politics. Together with the historical and contemporary political differences among states, they structure how states handle their problems. Fiscal resources offer only the opportunity to solve problems; political means must still be used to confront the problems. In the final section of this chapter I examine these problems and discuss the capacity of states to face them.

## STATES' ABILITY TO GOVERN

Today the fifty states face a number of serious concerns. The most immediate is financial as the states enter 2003 in the worst fiscal shape since World War II. And the situation just seems to get worse: the budget gaps greeting newly elected governors in November 2002 had grown by 50 percent by February 2003 (National Conference of State Legislators 2003). It is not just that tax revenues were down; expenditures were over projections. Meeting federal mandates for homeland security and election reform proved to be expensive; health care costs were soaring. The options are not pretty—raise taxes or cut services—but state leaders know how to balance budgets. They have to because they have constitutionally required themselves to do so, unlike the federal government.

But the states also face a set of perennial issues that cannot be ignored for long. One is population growth; as noted, the 1990s were the only decade of the twentieth century in which all states gained population. Some states, primarily in the Sunbelt, struggle with the problems accompanying rapid population growth. They cannot pave new roads and build new schools fast enough. Other states such as West Virginia and North Dakota registered very tiny population gains; their citizens are among the nation's oldest. Thus their public coffers are likely strained to build nursing homes and pay for health care costs, not to build new public schools.

Another issue the states face is redistribution or taking resources from the rich to give to the poor. As discussed earlier, some states have demographic groups that require extra resources—the poor, some minorities, and recent immigrants. Yet the well-off in some states—moralist ones, for example—seem more willing to support redistributive programs than the rich in other states. Too great an emphasis on redistribution may lead affluent citizens to relocate to states where the tax burden is lower. Thus the balance between taxing and spending is tenuous in the face of interstate competitive pressures.

A third issue confronting the states is the growing diversity of the population. The United States has experienced a demographic revolution since the 1970s, which has altered the demographic composition of the population. The workforce is much more diverse, and the school-age population is more heterogeneous. Meeting the needs of diverse groups will continue to challenge the school system, the public health system, and the welfare system, all of which are ultimately state responsibilities. Assimilating immigrants into communities and minimizing social conflicts are also the province of state governments.

These broad issues, in turn, affect how states cope with their traditional responsibilities—education, welfare, hospitals, highways, corrections, and a myriad of smaller spending programs. As shown in Chapters 10 to 14, these responsibilities are the major objects of state expenditure. Population growth certainly affects the demand for and cost of public services. The presence of refugees and other immigrants affects the provision of many services. The issue of redistribution may come up in many policy areas but looms especially large in welfare. Therefore, all traditional areas of state responsibility will undergo scrutiny as the economy and society change.

The states and their leaders seem ready to take on these challenges. As documented in Chapters 6 to 9, the states have vastly improved their capacity for dealing with problems. In the legislative arena, increased staffing, longer sessions, better pay for members, new committee structures, and other changes allow a greater capacity for effective decision making than in the past. However, the introduction of term limits in seventeen states has restrained the capacity building. Similarly, state executive branches have undergone many dramatic changes during the past decade or two. Much of this reform has been directed toward enhancing the governor's authority and centralizing the executive functions within fewer agencies. The improvement in the capacity of executive and legislative branches to solve problems has been accompanied by an improvement in the caliber of people willing to serve in these institutions. Most observers agree that there is a "new breed" of legislators and governors. In addition, state judicial systems have been modernized and improved in the same time period. Thus state governments now have the institutional capacity to address the challenges of the twenty-first century. By taking a close look at smaller political systems such as the American states, ones that have undeniably improved their institutional capacities, we may be able to find cause for optimism about governance in general.

## REFERENCES

Barrett, Katherine, Richard Greene, Michele Mariani, and Anya Sostek. 2003. "The Way We Tax: A 50-State Report." *Governing.* February: 20–97.
Bathen, Sigrid. 1998. "Los Angeles Unified School District." *California Journal,* January: 32–38.

Chubb, John. 1988. "Institutions, the Economy, and the Dynamics of State Elections." *American Political Science Review* 82: 133–154.

Conte, Christopher. 2002. "Strangers on the Prairie." *Governing.* January: 29–33.

Elazar, Daniel J. 1984. *American Federalism: A View from the States.* 3d ed. New York: Harper and Row.

Erikson, Robert S., Gerald C. Wright, and John P. McIver. 1993. *Statehouse Democracy: Public Opinion and Policy in the American States.* Cambridge: Cambridge University Press.

Fitzpatrick, Jody L., and Rodney E. Hero. 1988. "Political Culture and Political Characteristics of the American States: A Consideration of Some Old and New Questions." *Western Political Quarterly* 41: 145–153.

Gimpel, James G., and Jason E. Schuknecht. 2001. "Interstate Migration and Electoral Politics." *Journal of Politics* 63: 207–231.

Gray, Virginia, David Lowery, Matthew Fellowes, and Andrea McAtee. 2002. "Public Opinion, Public Policy, and Organized Interests in the American States." Paper presented at the annual State Politics and Policy Conference, Milwaukee, May.

Hanson, Russell L. 1992. "The Political Acculturation of Migrants in the American States." *Western Political Quarterly* 45: 355–384.

Hero, Rodney E. 1998. *Faces of Inequality: Social Diversity in American Politics.* New York: Oxford University Press.

Hero, Rodney E., and Caroline J. Tolbert. 1996. "A Racial/Ethnic Diversity Interpretation of Politics and Policy in the States of the U.S." *American Journal of Political Science* 40: 851–871.

Hobbs, Frank, and Nicole Stoops. 2002. *Demographic Trends in the 20th Century.* Washington, D.C.: U.S. Bureau of the Census.

International Trade Administration. 1997. *U.S. Jobs From Exports.* Accessed at http://www.ita.doc.gov.

Martin, Philip, and Elizabeth Midgley. 1994. "Immigration to the United States: Journey to an Uncertain Destination." *Population Bulletin* 49: 1–47.

National Conference of State Legislatures. 2003. "State Budget Gaps Growing at Alarming Rate According to New NCSL National Fiscal Report." Accessed at http://www.ncsl.org/programs/press/2003/pr030204.htm.

Niemi, Richard G., Harold W. Stanley, and Ronald J. Vogel. 1995. "State Economies and State Taxes: Do Voters Hold Governors Accountable?" *American Journal of Political Science* 39: 936–957.

Peirce, Neal R., and Jerry Hagstrom. 1984. *The Book of America.* New York: Warner Books.

Perry, Marc J., and Paul J. Mackun. 2001. "Population Change and Distribution, 1990–2000: Census 2000 Brief." Washington, D.C.: U.S. Bureau of the Census.

Population Reference Bureau. 2002. "2002 World Population Data Sheet." Accessed at http://www.prb.org//Content/ContentGroups/Datasheets/wpds2002/2002_World_Population_Data_Sheet.htm.

Ryen, Dag. 1996. "State Action in a Global Framework." In *The Book of the States.* Vol. 31. Lexington, Ky.: Council of State Governments.

Schlesinger, Joseph A. 1966. *Ambition and Politics.* Chicago: Rand McNally.

———. 1991. *Political Parties and the Winning of Office.* Ann Arbor: University of Michigan Press.

Schmidley, A. Dianne. 2001. *Profile of the Foreign-Born Population in the United States: 2000.* Washington, D.C.: U.S. Bureau of the Census.

Smith, James P., and Barry Edmonston, eds. 1997. *The New Americans.* Washington, D.C.: National Academy Press.

"Study: Seniors mean $1.4-billion to the state." *St. Petersburg Times,* July 8. Accessed at http://www.sptimes.com/20...ws_pf/State/Study__Seniors_mean_1.shtml.

U.S. Bureau of the Census. 2000. *Population and Ranking Tables of the Older Population for the United States.* Accessed at http://www.census.gov/population/www/cen2000/phc-t13.html.

———. 2001a. *Census 2000 Summary File.* Accessed at www.census.gov/prod/cen2000.

———. 2001b. *Statistical Abstract of the United States, 2001.* Washington, D.C.: U.S. Government Printing Office.

## SUGGESTED READINGS

Erikson, Robert S., Gerald C. Wright, and John P. McIver. *Statehouse Democracy: Public Opinion and Policy in the American States.* Cambridge: Cambridge University Press, 1993. A sophisticated study of public opinion in the states and its effect on public policy.

Gimpel, James G. *Separate Destinations: Migration, Immigration, and the Politics of Places.* Ann Arbor: University of Michigan Press, 1999. Contrasts the mobility patterns of natives and newer immigrants to show their differential impacts on state politics.

http://www.stateline.org, "Your Source for State News." Funded by the Pew Charitable Trusts, provides in-depth coverage of state government and public policy. The content is updated daily; it is organized by state and by policy topic.

Newspaper Association of America Website, at http://newspaperlinks.com. Provides links to all machine readable newspapers in the country. Organized by state; click on the map for the state you want, then on the paper you want.

U.S. Bureau of the Census. *Statistical Abstract of the United States, 2002.* Washington, D.C.: U.S. Government Printing Office, 2002. The official source of statistics on many aspects of state demography, economy, and policy. Online editions, as well as other census data, are available at http://www.census.gov.

CHAPTER 2

 *Intergovernmental Relations*

RUSSELL L. HANSON

The national government is once again asserting leadership in domestic policy making. In the wake of September 11, 2001, Congress and the president are mobilizing state and local governments across the country to secure the homeland from terrorist attacks. This is a difficult undertaking, not least because every government has different security concerns and defensive capabilities. Each government also prizes its independence and sense of what is best for its people. Fashioning a partnership of domestic governments will test the capacity of our political officials and could transform our federal system of governance.

This has happened before (Walker 2000). During the Great Depression, a host of programs was established to provide income security. In the course of administering unemployment insurance, public assistance, public health, and many other programs, national government became deeply involved in state and local affairs. The trend continued with the War on Poverty and establishment of Medicaid. Civil rights legislation furthered the interdependence of government, as did policies for environmental protection. In both cases, agencies of the national government exerted influence in domains long dominated by subnational authorities.

In American history, expansions of national power often trigger reactions against the centralization of governance (Conlan 1998). The emergence of a "welfare state" was no exception. Ronald Reagan launched his 1980 presidential campaign with a promise to return power and responsibility to state and local governments. The promise was partially redeemed in 1996, when the "devolution revolution" achieved its biggest victory, the reform of public assistance. There was less success in other policy areas, and the revolution failed to halt the centralization of American governance (Kincaid 2001, 1998).

Security concerns will energize the national government, and this could accelerate the process of centralization. For constitutional and political reasons, though, Congress and the president cannot act unilaterally. In many domestic areas they must work through the states to accomplish policy objectives. Defense of the homeland will follow this pattern; it will be a federal concern, or joint undertaking by national and state governments. If states claim a prominent role in homeland security, the overall scope of government could grow without changing the balance of power between levels of government.

States will develop security measures in conjunction with local governments, which perform critical homeland functions. Local police are the initial line of resistance to terrorism, and local firefighters and hospitals respond first to emergencies caused by attacks. States want to boost the capacity of local governments in these areas and coordinate the activities of local governments on a regional scale. For that matter, states will try to develop security measures in cooperation with neighboring states, since no government commands all of the resources needed to address massive emergencies.

Thus national policies to improve homeland security will reverberate throughout our political system, which includes more than 85,000 governments. Precisely because we now have so many governments, relations between governments are crucial to policy making in the United States. These relations have different features, depending on which levels of government are involved in any particular venture. *Federalism* refers to the division of power between the national government in Washington, D.C., and state governments. It also describes the relation between the national government and tribal governments on Native American reservations. The two species of federalism are different in important respects, with states having more autonomy than tribes. However, both types of relation involve the division of authority that is characteristic of multilevel systems.

Relations between states are not federal. They are *confederal,* to use an older terminology that is still useful in conveying the importance of sovereignty in these interactions. As constitutionally recognized entities, states are on equal footing; none has a higher status than any other state in the Union. There are differences in political power and influence, to be sure, but the symmetry of constitutional authority means that state governments must negotiate their differences (although some disputes between state governments may be decided by agencies of the national government, including the Supreme Court).

Relations between states and their local units of government are *unitary.* Localities do not enjoy sovereignty; they are creatures of state government. The asymmetry of constitutional power is seldom displayed openly. Rather, it forms the backdrop for political relations that are much more balanced. The states vary tremendously in their treatment of local units of government, and so this set of intergovernmental relations is further distinguished by great diversity.

States also broker the relation between national and local governments, carrying the goals and concerns of one to the other, while adding the preferences and resources of governors and legislators to the mix. Similarly, states increasingly regulate interactions among local governments, mediating conflicts and creating regional agencies to coordinate the actions of neighboring localities (Cigler 1998). Thus state governments are at the center of an elaborate web of intergovernmental relations; they transmit political developments from one sector of the web to others, sometimes magnifying the impulses and sometimes dampening them.

### CONFEDERALISM

Federalism in the United States is a product of dissatisfaction with the Articles of Confederation (1781–1788). Alarmed by the weakness of Congress under the Articles, Federalists proposed a union of states with an "energetic" national government. Their plan went into effect in 1789, and states lost some of their autonomy. Nevertheless, states retained important powers, and it is useful to review the many ways in which states still behave like the sovereign entities they once were.

State governments frequently interact with other nations (Frye 1998). For example, American states and Canadian provinces joined to halt the spread of zebra mussels in the Great Lakes basin and eastern spruce budworms in northern forests. Similarly, the North American Clean Air Alliance of northeastern states and provinces is promoting the commercial development of zero-emission vehicles to reduce air pollution in that region. Along the Rio Grande, southern U.S. and Mexican states jointly monitor the spread of tuberculosis across the border, regulate the international trucking industry, and allocate water resources.

States also develop economic ties with other countries. In fact, every state now devotes considerable attention to foreign trade. States actively promote overseas markets, providing information and technical assistance to exporting firms, capitalizing their activities, and conducting trade missions (Saiz and Clarke, Chapter 14 in this volume). For many states, though, free trade is a one-way street. States and localities routinely enact protectionist legislation to staunch the flow of imported goods and services. This causes problems for a national government seeking fair trade on an international scale (Kline 1999). In the Uruguay Round of talks on the General Agreement on Tariffs and Trade (GATT), the European Community pressed the U.S. government to eliminate "buy American" requirements in forty states and 2,700 municipalities (Weiler 1993–1994). The North American Free Trade Agreement (NAFTA) brought similar requests from Mexico and Canada, over the objections of state and local officials who feared job losses in their jurisdictions.

States interact with each other too (Zimmerman 1996). Some of these interactions are expressed in formal compacts, wherein states agree to address common problems. Before 1920 only three dozen compacts were signed by states. Most were bilateral agreements involving the location of boundaries. Since then more than 150 compacts have been established—100 of them since World War II. The average state is now a member of 27 compacts, many of them regional or national in scope (Mountjoy 2001).

Modern compacts cover a host of issues: conservation and resource management, pollution control, transportation, navigation on interstate waterways, law enforcement, and metropolitan development, to name a few. Disaster relief is an emerging area of cooperation, with forty-eight states joining the Emergency Management Assistance Compact, formed in the wake of Hurricane Andrew. This compact or one very much like it will become a key element of homeland security as states pool their resources for responding to acts of terrorism.

Some interstate compacts include agencies of the national government as parties to the agreement, but most do not. Such compacts exemplify what Elazar (1984) called "federalism without Washington." The Delaware River Compact and the Colorado River Compact are two instances in which states make regional allocations of water without relying on Congress or the Supreme Court for direction. In fact, the upper-basin states in the Colorado River agreement have their own compact within a compact to allocate water from the Colorado River (Lord and Kenney 1993).

Compacts are not the only means of ensuring interstate cooperation. Many states have reciprocity agreements with other states. A state's public universities may offer in-state tuition to residents of adjacent states in exchange for similar discounts in those states' schools. Licensure of teachers, real estate agents, and other professions may be covered by reciprocal agreements. Several states now permit individuals to carry concealed weapons, and the permits are recognized by some other states too. Reciprocity agreements and other routines make up an important part of interstate relations.

States cooperate extensively in less formal ways. In recent years states have joined forces in challenging powerful corporations, for example. Attorneys general sued tobacco companies and won an estimated $246 billion settlement in 1998. They won modest regulatory relief in antitrust litigation against Microsoft. Now states are forming cooperatives to buy and distribute pharmaceuticals in order to reduce costs in Medicaid and other public health programs.

Such cooperation depends on communication by state officials, who regularly share information. Professional associations alert policy makers to emerging issues and political developments in Washington. Indeed, the National Governors Association, National Conference of State Legislatures, National League of Cities, U.S. Conference of Mayors, and National Association of Counties lobby Congress and the administration on matters of interest to state and local officials (Cigler 1995). For example, governors led the charge for welfare reform in 1996, when Congress replaced Aid to Families with Dependent Children with Temporary Assistance to Needy Families, giving states greater control over public assistance (Weaver 2000).

Associations of state officials zealously oppose national encroachments on "states' rights" (Cammisa 1995). Occasionally, the complaints lead to summit meetings on federalism and proposals for tipping the balance of power in favor of states and their localities (Council of State Governments 1997). Such gatherings make

Congress more attentive to the concerns of state politicians and their lobbyists in Washington, and occasionally lead to the elimination of regulations that states find particularly objectionable (Dinan 1997). Success depends on forming alliances with other interest groups, however. Public and private interest groups combined in support of the 1998 Transportation Equity Act for the 21st Century, which gave states more control over highway funds (Marbach and Leckrone 2002). On the other hand, in 1999 states failed to win passage of the Federalism Accountability Act, designed to curb federal preemption of states' authority. The bill was opposed by business organizations, which favor uniform national regulations over the "patch work" of regulations that states produce when acting on their own (Bowman 2002).

### FEDERALISM

In the United States the formal allocation of power between state and national governments is constitutionally prescribed. The Constitution gives some powers primarily or exclusively to the national government. Other powers are given to the states, which must exercise those powers within limits set by the Constitution and Bill of Rights. Still other, unspecified powers are reserved to the states or the people under the Ninth and Tenth Amendments. Then there are powers concurrently exercised by national and state governments, including the authority to tax and borrow money, make and enforce laws, and so forth. Within this group of concurrent powers there are some—for example, the power of amendment—that are exercised jointly.

The allocation of specific powers is imprecise and subject to change over time. All politicians want to control policies of vital interest to their constituencies. Frequently this produces a tug of war between state and national officials who want to dictate policy. The boundaries between governments are settled in this political competition, which is regulated by the Supreme Court (and ultimately the people, who have the power to amend the Constitution). Knowing where the Court stands on federalism is essential for understanding contemporary relations between national and state governments.

### National Power and States' Rights

During the nineteenth century, the doctrine of dual federalism retarded the activity of the national government in domestic affairs (Corwin 1934). This doctrine prescribed a sharp division of responsibilities between governments. Defense and foreign policy, regulation of currency, and, to a much lesser extent, interstate trade were the responsibility of national government. Property laws, civil rights, and basic services were the province of state governments and, through them, local communities. The two spheres of responsibility were considered distinct, and conflicts between governments over the right to make policy in specific instances were generally decided in favor of one or the other by the Supreme Court.

In the twentieth century, however, power gravitated to the national level in a series of decisions by liberal majorities on the Supreme Court. As the umpire of our federal system, the Court claimed the power of judicial review over state actions; increased the power of Congress to regulate interstate transactions, particularly those related to commerce; and enlarged executive powers it deemed necessary to the fulfillment of the Constitution. It even allowed some degree of national control over local affairs, especially in matters pertaining to civil rights and public employment.

Furthermore, the Court declined to interpret other passages in the Constitution, including the reserved powers clause of the Tenth Amendment, that uphold the authority of states. This began to change in the 1990s, when a more conservative Court narrowed the powers of Congress in domestic policy making, exempted state governments from some civil rights legislation, and eased some of the restrictions imposed on states by previous decisions of the nation's top tribunal. Grounded in a return to the doctrine of dual sovereignty, these decisions shifted the balance of power in American federalism in subtle, yet profound, ways.

The shift became apparent after Clarence Thomas joined the Supreme Court, giving conservatives a working majority on many issues. On a 5-4 vote in 1995 the Court struck down the Gun Free School Zones Act, which outlawed possession of a firearm within a thousand feet of a school. In the majority's opinion, Congress had no authority to impose such mandates in education, a traditional preserve of state and local governments. *United States v. Lopez* (514 U.S. 549 [1995]) was the first time since 1937 that the Court rejected Congress's invocation of the interstate commerce clause to justify domestic legislation.

Two years later, the Court challenged the expansion of congressional power under the necessary and proper clause. In *Printz v. United States* (521 U.S. 98 [1997]) the Court set aside the Brady Handgun Violence Prevention Act of 1993. (The act was named after an aide who was wounded and paralyzed in a near-fatal attack on President Ronald Reagan by the pistol-packing John Hinckley.) The majority of five said that Congress could not require state and local police to check the background of prospective handgun buyers as the Act mandated.

Section 5 of the Fourteenth Amendment confers upon Congress the power to ensure due process and equal protection for all; it is the basis for civil rights legislation that offers judicial remedies when state laws and local ordinances do not. Thus in 1994 Congress passed the Violence Against Women Act, allowing victims of rape, abuse, or other forms of gender violence to seek damages from perpetrators in federal court. However, the Supreme Court ruled in *United States v. Morrison* (120 S. Ct. 1740 [2000]) that the Act exceeded Congress's authority under Section 5. Despite substantial evidence that state justice systems were biased against the victims of gender-motivated violence, the Court noted that the Violence Against Women Act was actually aimed at the perpetrators of this type of violence, not state officials. The Fourteenth Amendment applies to the latter, but not the former, and states cannot be sued in federal court.

In other cases, the Supreme Court has immunized states from federal legislation that binds nonprofit organizations, corporations, small businesses, and indeed all private entities. *Seminole Tribe of Fla. v. Florida* (517 U.S. 44 [1996]) shielded states from lawsuits filed in federal court, based on Eleventh Amendment guarantees of sovereign immunity. Applying this precedent the Supreme Court ruled in *Kimel v. Florida Board of Regents* (120 S. Ct. 631 [2000]) that states could not be sued in federal court by state employees claiming to be victims of age discrimination, even though Congress outlawed age discrimination in 1967. Nor for that matter can states be sued in their own courts for violating federal laws: *Alden v. Maine* (527 U.S. 706 [1999]) shielded states from the Fair Labor Standards Act of 1938, and *Board of Trustees of the University of Alabama v. Garrett* ([99-1240] 193 F.3d 1214 [2001]) held that states could not be challenged under the Americans with Disabilities Act, either.

States have also benefited from decisions easing earlier Court restrictions. For example, states regained some latitude in regulating access to abortion after *Planned Parenthood of Southeastern Pennsylvania v. Casey* (505 U.S. 833 [1992]]). In that case, the Supreme Court ruled that states have legitimate interests in protecting the health of a woman and the life of a fetus from the onset of pregnancy, although regulations may not unduly burden a woman's constitutional right to obtain an abortion prior to the point of fetal viability. After the fetus becomes viable, states may restrict or even prohibit abortions so long as their laws contain exceptions for pregnancies endangering a woman's life or health. Some states have restricted access to abortions; others have not, as shown by Meier and Eshbaugh-Soha in Chapter 13 of this volume.

Although the "Federalism Five" on the Rehnquist Court are favorably disposed toward states' rights, Congress often uses grants-in-aid to "buy" cooperation from state policy makers who might otherwise be reluctant to endorse national legislation. Since states are not compelled to accept grants, the Supreme Court has no basis for invalidating conditions that Congress imposes on aid. So, for example, state officials must implement the No Child Left Behind Act according to regulations promulgated by the Department of Education, or forego some grants. Officials in Vermont and Nebraska have threatened to do just that, because they find the regulations too intrusive.

### Fiscal Federalism

The national government mandates compliance with some of its objectives, but more often it relies on inducements to achieve its ends. The inducements or incentives generally take the form of financial assistance to subnational governments willing to pursue national goals. States may refuse the inducements, but the amount of assistance attracts state and local participation in most cases—under the supervision of national agencies, and subject to national guidelines, of course.

Congress's use of incentives to obtain cooperation has generated a concomitant expansion of state activity. This is evident in patterns of government spending. Figure 2-1 shows spending as a proportion of Gross Domestic Product (GDP) by national, state, and local governments in selected years from 1927 to 2005. (To facilitate comparisons with state and local spending, only spending on domestic

**Figure 2-1**    Velocity of Federal, State, and Local Governments, 1927–2005

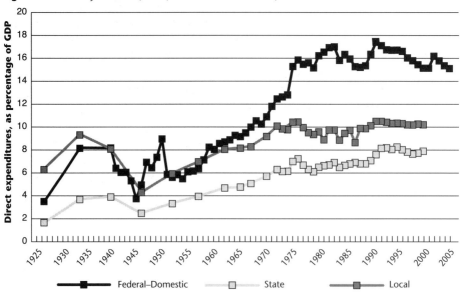

SOURCE: U.S. Advisory Commission 1993; U.S. Bureau of the Census, *Government Finances,* various years; and U.S.Office of Management and Budget, *Historical Tables,* various years.

programs by the national government is shown; it is calculated by subtracting outlays for defense and foreign aid from total national outlays.)

Domestic spending by the national government increased substantially in the twentieth century. Just before the Great Depression, direct spending by state governments was about 2 percent of GDP. This was only a little less than the national government spent on domestic matters. Local governments played a much larger role, spending twice as much as the national government and three times as much as state governments. Together, states and local governments were the most important policy makers before the New Deal.

During the Great Depression, the velocity of national government accelerated rapidly; as a proportion of the GDP, national spending on the home front tripled by the onset of World War II. Social security, unemployment insurance, and public assistance were all established at this time. Massive public works projects were also undertaken at the behest of President Franklin D. Roosevelt and advocates of the New Deal. The national government subsidized the construction of roads, dams, public buildings, and other projects undertaken by state and local governments. The attendant mixing of powers and resources has been described as "marble cake federalism," to distinguish it from the "layer cake" of dual federalism (Grodzins 1966).

The federal partnership continued after World War II as veterans' benefits were added to income security programs and new public works, such as the interstate highway system, were constructed. The expansion of activity by the national government accelerated in the 1960s during the War on Poverty, a period of "creative federalism." The activity of all governments rose steadily in this period, as is evident in Figure 2-1. Beginning in 1970, though, the national government began to out-pace state and local governments. Even the presidency of Ronald Reagan, which was generally characterized by reductions in the scope of federal regulation, saw a burst of speed unmatched by any corresponding increase in the pace of state and local governments. This was followed by another sharp upturn in 1990, when the "peace dividend" (the savings in defense spending after the Cold War ended) was used to finance new programs in health and education.

It is likely that national spending will surge again as Washington strives to im-prove homeland security. This will make subnational governments more energetic too, because a sizable portion of national domestic spending flows to state and local governments in the form of grants. Thus, Figure 2-1 shows an increase in the veloc-ity of state government during the 1930s, as states adopted New Deal programs. State spending as a proportion of GDP also expanded during the War on Poverty in the 1960s, and then settled around 7 percent in the mid-1970s. In the early 1990s it grew to about 8 percent, and stayed there. Homeland security will surely produce another growth spurt.

During the same period, local spending rose slowly and now represents about 8 percent of the GDP. The combined spending of state and local government now exceeds national domestic spending as a percentage of GDP. This is reflected in government employment, another measure of activism. The national govern-ment employed 4 million civilians in 2001, but state employment was 5 million, and local employment was 11 million workers. Clearly, state and local govern-ments are part of the "big government" we now have; in fact, they are the largest part of that government.

*Politics of Grants-In-Aid*

Grants-in-aid encourage state governments to enact programs and policies de-signed to achieve national objectives. They also generate fascinating political pat-terns (Brown 1984). The origins of grants, the different forms they assume, and the bureaucratic linkages they bring into existence are best described by Anton (1989), who views grants as the product of "vertical coalitions."

Vertical coalitions consist of widely dispersed individuals and groups who form national alliances to gain a favorable hearing in Congress. By responding to vertical coalitions, national policy makers address "societal needs and at the same time take credit for new program dollars that flow into their districts." Similarly, administra-tors "appear to be responsive while simultaneously expanding budget and staff to deliver the new benefits." And lower level officials "have new resources to be devot-ed in various ways to the problem or problems that originally motivated their search for assistance." Thus when vertical coalitions are successful, everyone seems to benefit (Anton 1989, 85).

Grant programs are well suited to the demands of vertical coalitions. Serious po-litical differences can be sublimated under general, unobjectionable statements about policy goals, whereas important details of program design and implementation are left to the discretion of state and local policy makers. Grants are also highly resistant to attack; clients who receive services, government employees who provide them, administrators who oversee programs, and politicians who claim credit for them regularly and effectively lobby to continue grants. Even in the face of rising deficits, created in part by the successes of many vertical coalitions, Congress and the president are reluctant to eliminate grant programs.

Aid programs typically originate as categorical project grants closely controlled by the national government. *Categorical grants* may be used only for narrow purposes approved by Congress. *Project grants* are awarded on a more or less competitive basis to governmental units that submit proposals for review and funding by an agency of the national government. A categorical project grant, then, allows the national government to determine which governments will receive money, and for which purposes.

Categorical grants spawn bureaucratic alliances across levels of government. Administrative subsystems form around each grant program, as program specialists and professionals from different levels of government develop routines that may be difficult to comprehend or influence, even for politicians who created the programs in the first place. This produces fragmentation of policy at the national level, because programs are both isolated and insulated from each other by the existence of distinct bureaucratic subsystems (Wright 1988). At state and local levels, it causes great consternation among elected officials when local agencies fall under the sway of patron agencies at the national level and either cannot or will not respond adequately to the preferences of subnational policy makers (Cho and Wright 2001).

This development has been called *picket fence federalism* because of the narrow ties that run between higher and lower levels of government (Wright 1988). State and local officials and their allies have long advocated reforms to eliminate the bureaucratic maze and reduce national control over the disposition of grant monies. This can be accomplished in two ways. Categorical grants may be combined or consolidated into block grants, which permit recipients to determine, within broad limits, how aid is used. Another way of reducing national control involves the distribution of aid according to a formula, so that national agencies have less control over which state or local governments receive aid.

When block grants are awarded according to a congressionally approved formula, national influence is minimized, and state and local discretion is correspondingly enhanced. That was the rationale behind the New Federalism of Richard Nixon's administration, which combined some categorical grants with block-formula grants (Conlan 1998). The latter were called *special revenue-sharing grants,* to distinguish them from general revenue-sharing grants, which awarded money to state and local governments on the basis of population, per capita income, levels of taxation, and several other factors. Subnational governments were virtually free to decide how funds would be used, and the amounts of money were not trivial: tens of billions of dollars were distributed between 1972 and 1986, when general revenue sharing ceased. Not coincidentally, block-formula grants and general revenue sharing bestowed greater assistance on fast growing cities in the Sunbelt, as well as suburbs, small cities, and rural areas integral to the emerging Republican presidential coalition (Brown 1984).

In 1980 the same coalition elected Ronald Reagan, who sought to replace many categorical grants with a much smaller number of block grants in education, health, social services, community development, and transportation (Conlan and Walker 1983). Reagan's proposals were defeated, but categorical grants came under renewed attack in 1995, when Republicans gained control of Congress. GOP leaders sought to consolidate existing grants, though the vertical coalitions stoutly resisted (Dilger 2000). Most new block grants were simply added to the long list of (mostly) categorical grants. Consequently, there are now more than 600 grant programs serving state and local governments.

The volume of grants-in-aid is charted in Figures 2-2 and 2-3, which show intergovernmental subsidies as proportions of all general revenues raised by state and local governments. During the late 1970s, grants provided more than half of local government revenues. When general revenue sharing expired, the flow of funds from the national government shrank to about 4 percent. Some of that decline was offset by additional state aid, which increased to 35 percent of local government revenues. Local governments made up the difference by exploiting their own revenue sources more intensively, adding user fees and the like.

A little more than 25 percent of all state revenues come from Washington, D.C., as may be seen in Figure 2-3. That will increase if Congress restores revenue sharing in order to help states balance their budgets over the next few years. Many states are experiencing a financial crisis that is partly their own doing (Johnson 2002). While their economies boomed in the 1990s, states reduced personal and corporate income tax rates and still reaped revenue windfalls. But when their economies stagnated, personal income tax receipts declined and corporate income tax receipts virtually collapsed. As a result, forty-one states collected substantially less revenue than they anticipated in FY2002, throwing state and local budgets into disarray (National Governors Association 2002).

Adjusting for inflation, state revenues declined $38.4 billion in FY2002. Responding to the problem, states used $17.1 billion of "rainy day funds," leaving balances at precariously low levels. Sixteen states enacted tax increases worth $8.4 billion, mostly from higher levies on cigarettes, liquor, and gasoline. Another $12.5 billion was offset by reductions in appropriations, with big cuts in child care, health care for the poor, and higher education. Other states froze or reduced aid to local governments, and some even paroled prisoners in order to ease the strain on budgets.

The projected deficits for FY2003 are even larger, and the preliminary estimates for FY2004 are discouraging. State governors and legislators are now calling on Congress to absorb a larger proportion of Medicaid costs or reestablish revenue sharing on an emergency basis to alleviate the crisis. Neither can be done without aggravating the national deficit, however. Responding to President George W. Bush

**Figure 2-2**   Intergovernmental Revenue Flows to Localities, 1955–2000

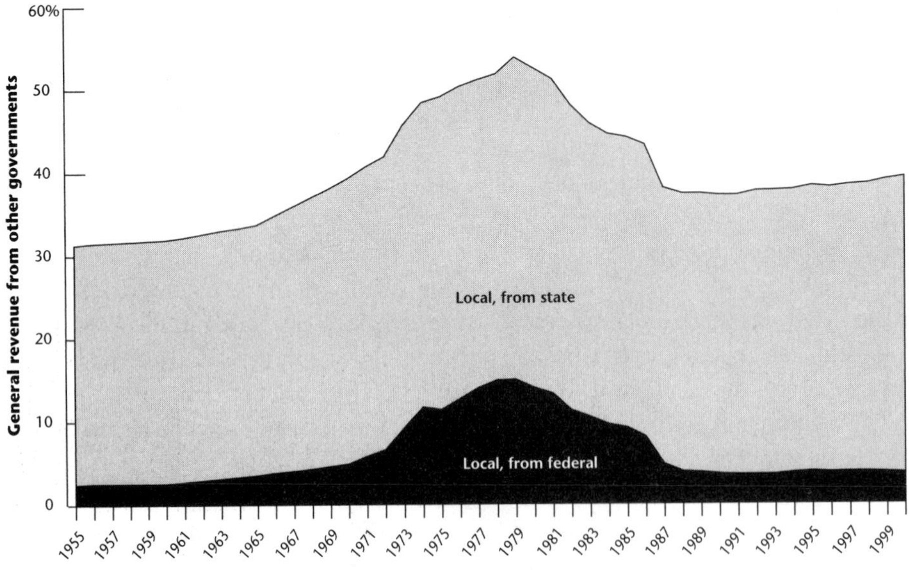

SOURCE: Calculated from U.S. Bureau of the Census, *State and Local Government Finances,* various years.

in 2001, Congress adopted a plan to lower tax rates over ten years. Consequently, revenues are not keeping pace with spending increases associated with the war on terror and homeland security. The national budget is in deficit, and will be for several years. Any additional assistance for state and local governments must therefore come from borrowing, which increases interest payments and dampens long-term economic growth. A Republican Congress cannot be enthused by that prospect.

*Distribution and Impact of Grants*

State and local governments received more than $260 billion from the national government in FY2000. The bulk of this money was passed on to individuals, or those who provided health and social services for them. A smaller (and declining) share went to state and local governments for public projects. In neither case were the funds distributed equally. Some states received much more "money for people" and "money for places" than others (Kincaid 1999).

The grant system is not geographically neutral, nor is it intended to be. One of its principal functions is to achieve some degree of equalization by redistributing resources to states and localities with great needs but few resources of their own. That is why a substantial portion of national grant monies goes to deprived areas, as measured by legislative formulas that incorporate various indicators of need and financial ability. To the extent that these formulas succeed in targeting aid, some states reap especially large shares of financial assistance from the national government, and other states receive smaller shares (Bahl 1990).

**Figure 2-3** Intergovernmental Revenue Flows to the State, 1955–2000

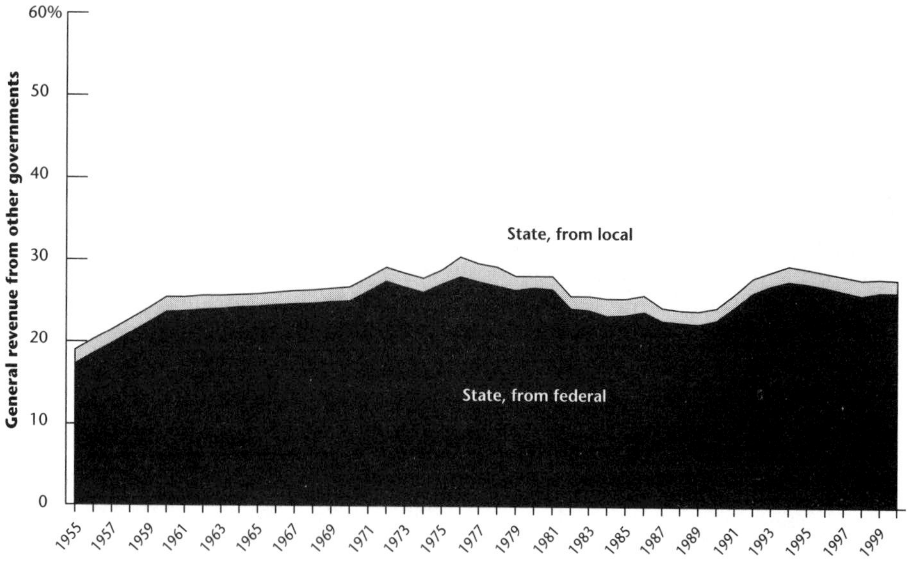

SOURCE: Calculated from U.S. Bureau of the Census, *State and Local Government Finances,* various years.

The extent of redistribution is measured by comparing the value of grants received by state and local governments to the amount of federal taxes needed to finance grants in each state (Moody 2002). These ratios are depicted in Table 2-1. In fiscal year 2001 a majority of states received more grant dollars than citizens paid in taxes for grants. Some of these states were big winners indeed: Alaska, New Mexico, North Dakota, Montana, West Virginia, and Mississippi obtained more than $2.00 in grants for every $1.00 in taxes paid for national grant programs. In contrast, state and local governments in Connecticut, Virginia, and New Jersey received less than $.70 for each $1.00 in federal taxes used for grants. Residents in these populous states are effectively subsidizing the operations of government in small, rural states (Peterson 1995).

Through grant formulas and administrative decisions about the distribution of grant funds, resources are redistributed on a rather large scale. Not surprisingly, losing states complain about this treatment; what counts as equalization for some is discrimination for others. This gives rise to pitched battles over the composition of formulas for distributing aid (Stanfield 1978). Representatives from states with divergent interests, each supplied with statistical analyses of the estimated impact of alternative formulas, must then resolve their differences (Dilger 1982). A dispute between northern and southern states delayed passage of welfare reform in 1996 until a compromise formula was discovered, one that did not disturb the existing distribution of matching funds. Similarly, the Census Bureau's methods for estimating

**Table 2-1** Federal Taxes and Spending, 2001

| State | Federal tax burden, 2001 (current millions) | | Federal expenditure, 2001 (current millions) | | Ratio of total federal expenditure to total federal tax burden (rank) | | Ratio of grants to state and local government to intergovernmental grant tax burden |
|---|---|---|---|---|---|---|---|
| | Total | Intergovernmental grants | Total | Grants to state and local government | | | |
| Alaska | 4,200 | 719 | 6,843 | 2,314 | 1.63 | (6) | 3.22 |
| New Mexico | 8,487 | 1,453 | 17,635 | 3,586 | 2.08 | (1) | 2.47 |
| North Dakota | 3,288 | 563 | 6,407 | 1,284 | 1.95 | (2) | 2.28 |
| Montana | 4,359 | 746 | 7,270 | 1,665 | 1.67 | (5) | 2.23 |
| West Virginia | 7,793 | 1,334 | 13,512 | 2,971 | 1.73 | (4) | 2.23 |
| Mississippi | 12,094 | 2,070 | 21,581 | 4,246 | 1.78 | (3) | 2.05 |
| Wyoming | 3,583 | 613 | 4,093 | 1,213 | 1.14 | (23) | 1.98 |
| South Dakota | 4,293 | 735 | 6,429 | 1,254 | 1.5 | (9) | 1.71 |
| Louisiana | 21,371 | 3,658 | 30,328 | 6,173 | 1.42 | (13) | 1.69 |
| Vermont | 3,731 | 639 | 4,192 | 1,069 | 1.12 | (26) | 1.67 |
| Arkansas | 12,476 | 2,135 | 18,143 | 3,448 | 1.45 | (11) | 1.61 |
| Maine | 6,904 | 1,182 | 9,025 | 1,905 | 1.31 | (15) | 1.61 |
| Kentucky | 20,509 | 3,510 | 28,247 | 5,100 | 1.38 | (14) | 1.45 |
| Oklahoma | 16,667 | 2,853 | 24,677 | 4,119 | 1.48 | (10) | 1.44 |
| Alabama | 22,437 | 3,840 | 34,282 | 5,298 | 1.53 | (8) | 1.38 |
| Rhode Island | 6,990 | 1,196 | 7,792 | 1,607 | 1.11 | (27) | 1.34 |
| South Carolina | 20,799 | 3,560 | 27,121 | 4,730 | 1.3 | (16) | 1.33 |
| Idaho | 6,683 | 1,144 | 8,309 | 1,505 | 1.24 | (19) | 1.32 |
| Hawaii | 6,903 | 1,181 | 10,610 | 1,514 | 1.54 | (7) | 1.28 |
| Tennessee | 33,225 | 5,687 | 39,930 | 7,027 | 1.2 | (20) | 1.24 |
| New York | 158,410 | 27,112 | 132,256 | 32,897 | 0.83 | (42) | 1.21 |
| Missouri | 33,718 | 5,771 | 43,345 | 6,865 | 1.29 | (17) | 1.19 |
| Oregon | 21,241 | 3,635 | 21,187 | 4,308 | 1 | (34) | 1.19 |
| Utah | 11,358 | 1,944 | 12,602 | 2,244 | 1.11 | (28) | 1.15 |
| Nebraska | 10,415 | 1,783 | 12,169 | 2,054 | 1.17 | (22) | 1.15 |
| North Carolina | 47,579 | 8,143 | 50,259 | 9,122 | 1.06 | (30) | 1.12 |
| Iowa | 16,725 | 2,863 | 19,595 | 3,079 | 1.17 | (21) | 1.08 |
| Maryland | 41,779 | 7,151 | 52,690 | 7,586 | 1.26 | (18) | 1.06 |
| Pennsylvania | 83,052 | 14,215 | 88,547 | 14,847 | 1.07 | (29) | 1.04 |
| Arizona | 30,057 | 5,144 | 33,803 | 5,190 | 1.12 | (25) | 1.01 |
| Ohio | 69,127 | 11,831 | 69,889 | 11,762 | 1.01 | (32) | 0.99 |
| Wisconsin | 34,609 | 5,923 | 30,829 | 5,843 | 0.89 | (37) | 0.99 |
| Kansas | 16,503 | 2,825 | 18,732 | 2,721 | 1.14 | (24) | 0.96 |
| Massachusetts | 59,779 | 10,231 | 50,001 | 9,718 | 0.84 | (41) | 0.95 |
| Texas | 134,809 | 23,073 | 124,580 | 21,675 | 0.92 | (36) | 0.94 |
| Michigan | 67,886 | 11,619 | 58,713 | 10,887 | 0.86 | (38) | 0.94 |
| Indiana | 36,733 | 6,287 | 36,363 | 5,850 | 0.99 | (35) | 0.93 |
| Delaware | 5,750 | 984 | 4,918 | 892 | 0.86 | (39) | 0.91 |
| Georgia | 52,225 | 8,938 | 52,638 | 7,929 | 1.01 | (33) | 0.89 |
| California | 264,344 | 45,243 | 215,916 | 39,797 | 0.82 | (44) | 0.88 |
| Minnesota | 36,519 | 6,250 | 29,451 | 5,260 | 0.81 | (45) | 0.84 |
| Washington | 49,651 | 8,498 | 41,564 | 6,794 | 0.84 | (40) | 0.80 |
| New Hampshire | 10,315 | 1,765 | 7,335 | 1,288 | 0.71 | (48) | 0.73 |
| Florida | 110,294 | 18,877 | 116,006 | 13,666 | 1.05 | (31) | 0.72 |
| Illinois | 96,686 | 16,548 | 75,757 | 11,883 | 0.78 | (46) | 0.72 |
| Colorado | 33,898 | 5,802 | 27,841 | 3,916 | 0.82 | (43) | 0.67 |
| Connecticut | 38,906 | 6,659 | 26,232 | 4,364 | 0.67 | (49) | 0.66 |
| Virginia | 52,858 | 9,047 | 76,832 | 5,908 | 1.45 | (12) | 0.65 |
| New Jersey | 80,769 | 13,824 | 53,886 | 8,478 | 0.67 | (50) | 0.61 |
| Nevada | 15,014 | 2,570 | 11,390 | 1,442 | 0.76 | (47) | 0.56 |
| United States | 1,953,312 | 334,313 | 1,953,312 | 334,313 | 1 | | 1 |

SOURCE: Computed from Moody 2002.

NOTE: Last two columns assume that tax burdens for grants are proportionately equal to overall tax burdens.

population at the state level are a matter of contention in the legislature. Different statistical techniques yield different population estimates, and hence different grant allocations, and the members of Congress know it (DeVaul and Twomey 1989).

The budgetary impact of grants-in-aid is significant. Most grants require matching funds from states, and depending on the stringency of these requirements, states may have to commit a substantial portion of their own revenues to purposes served by the grants. States may also exceed matching fund requirements in some policy areas, if they want to enlarge on national policy objectives. As a result, grants have leverage beyond their size, giving them broad influence over state and local spending patterns.

In part, this is what Congress intends, but grant programs skew the priorities of state policy makers who concentrate on obtaining grants with low matching fund requirements. These programs give a bigger "bang for the buck" than programs with high matching fund requirements, or when national funds are not available at all. Budget-conscious policy makers may neglect important state and local concerns, if those concerns are not sufficiently general to warrant attention by the national government. Clever state officials may discover methods that allow them to substitute national dollars for their own or those of local governments, however. This permits officials to divert state and local revenues to popular causes, or alternatively to avoid tax increases.

"Maintenance of effort" provisions are Congress's response to the strategy of substituting federal dollars for state outlays. New grant programs often require state and local governments to continue spending at current levels in order to qualify for assistance from the national government. In this way, the politics of grants are like a chess game, with each side trying to anticipate and block the other's moves.

### Coercive Federalism

When national budgets are tight and money is not available for new grants, Congress uses mandates to impose its objectives on subnational governments. Four different kinds of mandates have been employed by Congress (and the executive branch), according to the U.S. Advisory Commission on Intergovernmental Relations (1984). A *direct order,* in the form of a law or regulation, may be issued in policy areas where national power is well-established under the supremacy clause of the Constitution. Subnational governments must abide by the Equal Employment Opportunity Act and the Occupational Safety and Health Act, for example, and they risk civil and criminal sanctions if they do not respond to orders of compliance.

*Cross-cutting regulations* are across-the-board requirements that affect all or most federal assistance programs. They involve provisions that prohibit the use of funds from any national source in programs that discriminate on the basis of race, ethnicity, gender, or religious practice, for example. Another familiar cross-cutting regulation requires the preparation of an environmental impact statement for any construction project involving national funds. State and local governments must provide evidence of compliance with these regulations, and they incur administrative costs for preparing the necessary scientific and technical reports.

National officials may terminate or reduce assistance in one program if state and local officials do not comply with the requirements of another grant-in-aid program. This is a *cross-over sanction*. National highway funds are often used in this way to pressure states into adopting policies preferred by Congress. Thus a recent act requires states to adopt .08 blood alcohol content laws to combat drunk driving, or lose 2 percent of their national highway funds in FY2004. The withholding escalates by two percentage points each year, reaching a maximum of 8 percent in FY2007. Already, thirty-two states have complied; the others will be able to recover the withheld funds if they act by FY2007.

The fourth type of regulation is *partial preemption,* and it often rests on the commerce clause of the Constitution. By engaging in this type of regulation the national government essentially sets national minimum standards by issuing appropriate regulations for, say, air or water quality, when a state refuses to do so. Should a state decline to enforce standards issued by an agency of the national government, the agency will assume jurisdiction for enforcement. States are entitled to adopt and implement more stringent standards, but weak or nonexistent standards are foreclosed by Congress (Zimmerman 1993).

Whatever the form, state (and local) government officials strongly resent mandates (Conlan and Beam 1992). They gained some relief after the Republican landslide of 1994. The GOP's Contract with America included a pledge to reduce unfunded mandates, and with the support of many Democrats, including President Bill Clinton, Republicans enacted legislation requiring the Congressional Budget Office to estimate the cost of all mandates proposed in Congress. Bills that impose new mandates in excess of $50 million on state and local governments must be approved by a majority of each chamber in a separate vote.

The Unfunded Mandates Reform Act of 1995 did not rescind any previous mandates, and it produced only a slight reduction in the number of mandates enacted in 1996. On the other hand, it has modified new mandates. They are less sweeping, less expensive, and less heavy-handed than before (Kelly and Gullo 2001). Furthermore, passage of the act has probably deterred lawmakers from proposing mandates that are popular only with some interest groups and congressional constituencies (Posner 1998). Indeed, the Congressional Budget Office (2001) charts a steady decline in the number of bills with mandates exceeding the $50 million threshold (which is adjusted for inflation).

Agencies of the executive branch are also bound by the Unfunded Mandates Reform Act, insofar as regulations impose costs on state and local governments. Many of these regulations fall below the $50 million threshold, however. Still others impose new conditions on existing grants-in-aid and are not considered "unfunded" mandates under the law. Congress shows little inclination to close this loophole. Evidently, it wants to preserve the option of coercion by regulation when legislative mandates are politically risky.

### FEDERALISM AND TRIBAL GOVERNMENTS

Relations between state and national governments dominate American federalism, but they do not exhaust this field of intergovernmental relations. Native American tribes also claim powers of self-determination, albeit not as successfully as state governments. That is because the constitutional status of tribes is ambiguous. In *Cherokee Nation v. Georgia* (30 U.S. [5 Pet.] 1 [1831]), Chief Justice John Marshall characterized tribes as "dependent domestic nations." The tribes are nations insofar as they were once sovereign, domestic insofar as they have been absorbed into the union, and dependent insofar as the U.S. government is entrusted with the protection of indigenous peoples and their ways of life.

In practice this means tribes are semisovereign entities, subject to the will of Congress but relatively independent of governments in states where reservations are located. Therein lie the seeds of conflict between tribal and state governments, on the one hand, and tribal governments and Congress, on the other.

There are more than 500 federally recognized tribal governments in the United States, many of them in the upper Midwest and western states. Most tribal governments operate under written constitutions delineating their powers, responsibilities, structure, and composition. They pass civil and criminal laws, which are enforced by tribal police and adjudicated in tribal courts. To finance these activities, tribal governments may impose taxes on Indians and non-Indians living or doing business on reservation lands. People on the reservation are not subject to most state laws or regulations, however, nor do they pay state taxes on property, sales, or income earned from activities conducted on the reservation. Thus states have little control over reservation affairs.

States are well-represented in Congress, though, and Congress exercises plenary power over tribal governments. In the past, Congress used its power to abrogate treaties, dilute tribal ownership of lands, and regulate tribal governance. Congress also limited the jurisdiction of tribal courts in criminal matters and obliged them to respect the rights of the accused. Thus major crimes defined in federal law are tried in U.S. courts, and Indians accused of lesser crimes in tribal courts are protected by the Indian Civil Rights Act, which affords guarantees similar to those in the Bill of Rights and Fourteenth Amendment.

With Public Law 280 Congress delegated to some states jurisdiction over certain types of crimes committed against Indians on the reservation. Non-Indians accused of committing crimes on reservation lands can only be prosecuted under state or federal laws, however, following *Oliphant v. Suquamish Indian Tribe* (435 U.S. 191 [1978]). Thus the rights of the accused take precedence over tribal autonomy for Congress and the Supreme Court.

The pattern is different in civil matters, where tribal governments enjoy sovereign immunity. Tribal governments may not be sued by states or their citizens for breaching civil laws. Nor are tribal members subject to state regulations, for example, laws governing the use and operation of motor vehicles on the reservation. Although Congress recognizes the validity of state laws governing contracts between individuals living on Indian reservations, it seems inclined to respect the autonomy of tribes in civil matters intimately related to the preservation of tribes' traditional ways of life.

The Supreme Court also recognizes the autonomy of tribes in civil affairs, with one important limitation. In *Montana v. United States* (450 U.S. 544 [1981]), the Court ruled that in the absence of any congressional authorization, Indian tribes lack authority over the conduct of non-Indians on privately owned land within a reservation, with two exceptions: when nonmembers have entered into consensual agreements with a tribe or its members, or when nonmembers' conduct threatens or directly affects the tribe's political integrity, economic security, health, or welfare. Thus the Navajo Nation cannot tax a trading post and hotel situated on privately owned land on its reservation, according to *Atkinson Trading Company, Inc. v. Shirley* (121 S.Ct. 1825 [2001]).

State governments are sometimes frustrated by the autonomy of tribal governments. Tensions have grown over tribes' development of the gambling industry. Until states rescinded laws against gambling, only reservations could offer bingo, lotto, pull tabs, and so forth. The stakes were raised in 1988, when Congress passed the Indian Gaming Regulatory Act. The Act preserved tribes' right to offer bingo and other Class II games on reservations and opened the door for Class III gaming (slot machines, casino gambling, parimutuel betting, etc.) States that did not explicitly prohibit Class III games were required to enter into good faith negotiations with tribes seeking to expand their operations by offering Class III games. The negotiations produced compacts between state and tribal governments defining the conditions under which Class III gaming must be offered and specifying the state's share of the proceeds from casino gambling (Mason 1998).

Compact negotiations between tribes and states are often contentious. Tribes view regulations as an infringement on their sovereignty, and they resent having to share the proceeds from an industry they developed—and it is an industry. Of the 562 federally recognized tribes, 201 now operate Class II or Class III games in 29 states. These operations employ more than 300,000 people (only a quarter of whom are Indians) and generate $13 billion annually, or 10 percent of all gaming revenues in the United States (National Indian Gaming Association 2003).

States, which cannot tax reservation gambling, want to recover the costs of upgrading state roads and municipal utilities serving reservations with popular casinos. They also want to use revenue from gambling for other purposes. Some politicians have gone so far as to suggest that states ought to sponsor their own casinos, but there is powerful religious opposition to gambling in many states. Indeed, the opposition to state-sponsored gambling is what allowed tribes to develop a near-monopoly on gaming in the first place.

*Seminole Tribe of Fla. v. Florida* (517 U.S. 44 [1996]) increased states' leverage in compact negotiations. The Supreme Court shielded states from lawsuits compelling them to enter into compacts under the terms of the Indian Gaming Regulatory Act. Any impasse between a state and tribe is now mediated by the U.S. Department of the Interior, which may impose a solution on the parties. The department's authority is being challenged in court by several states, whose representatives in Congress are also seeking amendments to the Indian Gaming Regulatory Act to increase states' control over reservation gambling.

## RELATIONS BETWEEN STATE AND LOCAL GOVERNMENTS

Except on tribal reservations, state governments wield power in accordance with their constitutions. Each state constitution identifies the rights of persons residing in that state, including rights that are not guaranteed in the Bill of Rights. (The right to an equal public education is a good example.) The state constitution also defines the structure of state government, the terms and qualifications for holding various state offices, and suffrage requirements. Some state constitutions establish local governments or processes for creating different types of local government; others leave such matters to the legislature. Policy directions are also issued in state constitutions, which often bristle with social, economic, or environmental prescriptions accumulated over time (Tarr 1998).

State governments are often viewed as smaller versions of national government in the United States, but there is an important constitutional difference. The authority of the national government is defined positively; Congress and the president can only exercise powers conferred upon them under the Constitution. State governments, on the other hand, enjoy plenary powers, which are negatively expressed: states have the power to enact laws and promulgate policy unless their constitutions prohibit it. The presumption is that states have the authority to act within their borders, and those who oppose state action must point to limitations expressed or implied in the relevant constitution.

The point is essential for understanding relations between state and local governments. Constitutionally speaking, local governments are creatures of the state; their terms of existence are spelled out in laws or the state constitution itself. The structure, powers, and responsibilities of local governments may be modified by the legislature in the course of exercising its plenary powers. In states where constitutions provide for local governments, amendments may alter their terms of existence. This is fairly common at the state level, where constitutional amendments are routine and wholesale replacement occurs periodically.

States reconfigure local governments when they create special-purpose districts, stripping existing governments of previously held authority to make policy in certain policy areas—for example, mass transit, fire protection, water and sewer services—and providing for libraries, hospitals, and parks. This happens frequently. According to the Bureau of the Census, 35,356 special districts existed in 2002, almost triple the number in operation fifty years ago (U.S. Bureau of the Census 2002). More than 90 percent of these districts perform a single function; as a consequence, the proliferation of districts has fragmented local policy making along narrow functional lines. The average citizen is now subject simultaneously to a half-dozen or more units of local government with taxing or regulatory authority—county government, city government, school district, transit authority, parks board, waste district, and so on.

When special districts improve services and reduce costs, citizens and local officials welcome their establishment, even if it confuses lines of responsibility. Other reductions in local control are conceded only grudgingly. Immediately after World War II, many state governments abolished small schools in rural areas and transferred their students to consolidated districts so as to provide education more efficiently and inexpensively. Localities objected, but the states' power to create—and destroy—was used to bring about consolidation. The number of school districts nationwide fell from 67,355 in 1952 to 13,522 in 2002, even though two new states were added to the Union and the number of children enrolled in public elementary and secondary schools climbed 40 percent during this same period. A declining rural population could trigger another round of school consolidation in some sparsely settled states.

### Political Relations Between State and Local Governments

The constitutional vulnerability of local governments is mitigated by political considerations. A commitment to local determination is central to Americans' political heritage. In the Northeast, state constitutions were adopted after the Declaration of Independence, when local governments were already a hundred years old or older. Other areas of the country too were settled, and towns established, long before territories became states. As a result, strong traditions of localism exist, particularly in northern states (Elazar 1998). In these states, communities may be legally powerless to prevent states from limiting their autonomy, but in practice they enjoy substantial independence because tradition favors delegation of authority to the local level. Once delegated, this authority may be difficult to recover; and, indeed, some state courts have begun to protect local prerogatives in such areas as land use.

Furthermore, the same forces that make Congress responsive to states also make states responsive to local government. Representation in the legislature is by locale, and elected representatives often have prior experience in local affairs. They are sensitive to the desire of local policy makers for autonomy and quickly learn of resentment over state mandating and other practices that infringe on local self-determination. Representatives are forewarned of opposition to pending legislation by lobbying associations of local governments and mayors, law enforcement officers, school superintendents, and the like. These associations are among the most powerful lobbies in the state capital, and members of the state legislature are not inclined to enact measures that localities find too objectionable.

The major political consideration, therefore, is not whether states will be responsive to local governments but rather to which set of local governments they will be most responsive. Historically, the malapportionment of state legislatures gave rural counties a disproportionate voice in state policy making. Reapportionment strengthened the representation of urban and suburban areas in state legislatures in the 1970s and 1980s. Now suburbs are growing faster than cities, and their representation is swelling in state legislatures (Rosenthal 1997).

The political influence of certain locales may result in favorable treatment from state government. For example, big central cities, particularly those in otherwise rural states, commonly enjoy home rule charters, designed to promote local autonomy. The amount of autonomy under home rule varies from state to state and even across cities within the same state, and home rule charters may be withdrawn or set aside when state interests are deemed paramount (Krane, Rigos, and Hill 2000).

A systematic examination of local autonomy in the American states shows that different local governments enjoy different kinds of discretion (U.S. Advisory Commission 1981). When the residents of a locale petition to establish a local government, they may in some states be able to draft their own charter of incorporation. In other states, they may be able to choose from a variety of alternative forms of government, depending on the size of the local population and type of government desired. Local powers to amend charters may also be broad, and local units may be given limited or broad powers of annexation, further affecting control over the structure of local government.

A second area of discretion involves the range of functions local units may undertake. The greatest discretion exists in states that devolve authority to local governments, which enjoy powers not specifically denied to them by the legislature or the constitution. At the other extreme are Dillon's Rule states, which insist on enumerating the powers and functions of local governments; powers not explicitly given are denied, although the legal understanding of granted powers may be fairly liberal. More subtle ways of affecting the level and kind of services provided by local governments include restricting revenues, earmarking to certain uses, and establishing performance standards.

Although garbage collection, fire protection, and even elementary education can be provided through contractual arrangements with private concerns, they are most often supplied by public employees, and the conditions of employment by local government are stipulated in detail by state governments. The most important requirements concern the extent to which merit informs hiring, promoting, and firing decisions. But states may also establish training, licensing, and certification standards for employees; define procedures for determining wage and salary levels (for example, collective bargaining and compulsory arbitration rules); set actual salary and wage levels for certain categories of employees; control hours of employment and working conditions; regulate disability benefits; and mandate retirement programs (MacManus 1983).

The exercise of local discretion in all three areas (structure, function, and personnel matters) is often limited by fiscal regulations. Although cities in Arizona, Illinois, Maine, and Texas have substantial latitude in fiscal matters, local units in other states do not. In most states the constitution or legislature determines which taxes may be levied by local units and what sort of exemptions must be granted. In addition, the magnitude of tax increases is often restricted by constitutional amendments enacted during the tax revolts of the late 1970s and early 1980s. Local borrowing is also tightly regulated in most states; overall debt loads are limited, and the type of debts that may be incurred, as well as the interest rates that may be paid on bonds, are typically controlled by the legislature. Similar restrictions affect spending practices, and in New Mexico cities and counties must submit their entire budgets to an agency of the state government for approval.

Variations in the autonomy of local governments are the result of many factors. The political culture of a state shapes beliefs about the most appropriate relation between state and local government. The length of legislative sessions and the number of local governments in a state have an effect too. Legislatures cannot closely supervise a large number of local units when state representatives meet infrequently and for short periods of time. Under these circumstances legislatures are more inclined to grant higher degrees of local autonomy, especially because the existence of a large number of governments is associated with strong associations of local officials capable of influencing legislators. (It is also associated with large public employee unions, which may persuade legislatures to mandate actions on their behalf, over the objections of local policy makers.)

Finally, the complexity of a state's constitution and the ease of amending it can influence the amount of discretion permitted local governments. The constitution of some states makes it extremely difficult for legislatures to exercise authority over local governments in a timely fashion, particularly if incorporation of the governments is by constitutional amendment; in that case, further amendments must be adopted for the legislature to have its way. The Alabama constitution is three times longer than any other state constitution, primarily because it spells out the status of specific county governments in detail. Constitutions in other southern states do the same, owing to the strength of political traditions that favor localism over centralism.

Even in states where constitutions are not an impediment to legislative control, trends since the mid-1970s favor the expansion of local discretion and home rule (Zimmerman 1981; Zimmerman and Clark 1994). State legislatures have granted more statutory authority to local governments, and voters in many states have approved constitutional amendments that expand local autonomy. The pace of change is particularly quick in states that allow ballot initiatives, but amendments are common in other states.

*Fiscal Relations Between State and Local Governments*

Although the discretionary power of local governments has increased in several states, many local governments lack resources to address problems independently. Economic instability, weak infrastructure, environmental degradation, and inadequate school systems pose great challenges to local policy makers, not just in older, central cities, but in many boom towns, suburbs, and rural areas as well. Local governments cannot cope with these problems on their own; their tax bases have stagnated, voters have imposed restrictions on taxing and spending powers, and the national government has decreased its support for grant programs aimed at local governments.

Unable to discharge all of the responsibilities assigned them by state government or demanded by constituents, local policy makers have turned to state leaders for assistance. As a result, policy making is becoming more interdependent at the subnational level. The degree of interdependence varies from state to state, and across policy areas within the same state. States generally take the lead in constructing highways, providing welfare, maintaining correctional institutions and mental health hospitals, and regulating natural resources. Municipal governments typically provide public safety, sanitation, and sewage disposal, and school districts manage educational services. Yet even these locally provided services are heavily influenced by state actions, insofar as many state governments provide huge sums of money to the responsible local units.

From 1980 to 2000, total state spending for local governments increased from $82.8 billion to $317.1 billion—two and a half times the rate of inflation during the same period. States became the principal financiers of many public services, even those provided by local governments. New legal requirements and general policy guidelines were imposed by state officials demanding greater accountability from local governments. As a result, state governments now control or influence areas of policy making long dominated by local governments.

Increased state aid is only one path to policy centralization, however. States can achieve the same result by providing goods and services directly, without involving local governments. This requires substantial outlays by state governments, but it does ensure control over the formulation and implementation of public policy. Under this method, no intermediaries are needed—or rather, the intermediaries are agencies and employees of state government, whose actions are easier to regulate than those of local government officials. Social services sometimes fall under this heading; higher education typically does.

States differ in the extent to which they rely on direct or indirect methods of centralizing control over the provision of public goods and services. These differences are apparent in Figure 2-4, in which states are listed by region according to their overall or combined level of fiscal centralization. The most centralized states are at the top of each region's listing, and the least centralized states are toward the bottom. Small, rural states tend to be most centralized: for instance, state governments directly and indirectly account for three quarters of all state and local spending in Vermont, Arkansas, and New Mexico. Near the other extreme are several large, diverse states—for example, New York and Illinois—where direct and indirect state expenditure amounts to a little more than half of all state and local outlays.

Among the more highly centralized states there are clear differences on the two dimensions of centralization. Hawaii and New Mexico are almost equally centralized, but they arrive at this destination by different routes. Hawaii provides almost no state aid at all; it funds services directly from the state treasury. In fact, Hawaii fully funds public education, and because education is the most expensive service

**Figure 2-4**   Centralization of State and Local Finances, 2000

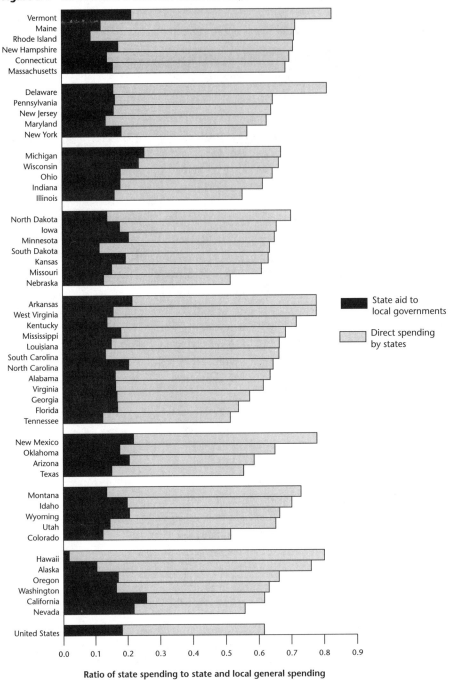

State aid to
local governments

Direct spending
by states

Ratio of state spending to state and local general spending

SOURCE: Calculated from U.S. Bureau of the Census, *State and Local Government Finances,* various years.

provided by state and local governments, the state ranks high on the index of fiscal centralization.

New Mexico, by contrast, augments direct spending with a significant amount of state aid, mostly for local school systems. The use of money is the same as in Hawaii, but the method of financing is indirect. In New Mexico the importance of state aid in funding education allows the state government substantial control over this vital service. Other states, including Vermont and New Hampshire, are moving in this direction as they comply with court orders to equalize school funding (see Wong's discussion in Chapter 12 of this volume).

Both state aid and direct spending by states have become more centralized over time (Stonecash 1995). States high on both dimensions have remained so, whereas those which emphasized state aid have begun to stress direct spending more. States with traditions of heavy direct spending have maintained them, but they have also shown more interest in indirect financing of services. Finally, states not originally centralized on either dimension have become more centralized on both—even in Nebraska, state spending now accounts for more than 50 percent of all state and local outlays, when state aid and direct spending are combined.

The continuing importance of state aid in this process of fiscal centralization, especially in California, Michigan, and Wisconsin, is significant. In simple terms, it represents a political determination of these state governments to work with, rather than without, local governments in fulfilling basic functions. In part this reflects political realities: in these and similar states, local governments are powerful enough to persuade legislatures to assist them financially. Many of them are also capable policy makers, with long histories of service provision and relatively high levels of citizen satisfaction with local government. The idea of a partnership between state and local government is particularly strong in such states (Stonecash 1998).

The form of aid is one measure of states' confidence in local governments. The lion's share of state aid goes to categorical grants for education and public welfare. But state revenue sharing is next in importance; some states return a portion of sales and income taxes to the jurisdiction in which they were collected. Others reimburse local governments for property tax exemptions mandated by the state, or replace tax revenues lost because of general limitations on increases in property tax rates. State revenue-sharing funds are also distributed in some states on a per capita basis, although states are turning toward more complex formulas based on differences in need and ability to raise revenue (Peliserro 1985).

State revenue-sharing funds are relatively unrestricted; local governments are free to decide how these funds will be used. The monies therefore preserve local discretion and serve local priorities. State policy makers do not control or strongly influence the use of revenue-sharing funds, as they often do where categorical grants are involved, and as they most certainly do when funds are spent directly by agencies of the state.

Aid is the carrot used by state officials to influence local decision making. Mandates are the stick. States resent mandates from Congress, and they have the capacity to resist national policy makers who depend on them for policy implementation (Derthick 1986). But local governments are administrative conveniences of the state, and they are vulnerable to state officials who insist on having their way. Consequently, local governments labor under hundreds or even thousands of mandates from state governments (Zimmerman and Clark 1994).

Mandates hold special appeal in states facing budgetary problems. When revenue is scare, legislatures delegate important responsibilities to local government without increasing state aid. Indeed, several states now facing deficits have actually reduced aid to localities in order to balance their budgets. Local governments and school corporations have had to make do with less, as "deficit sharing" percolates through state and local finances.

Local opposition to state mandating is spreading. More than half the states now have constitutional limits or statutory restrictions on mandating; the latter have become especially popular in the past ten years. A few of these measures require approval of mandates by local governments, but most prohibit mandating unless the state legislature provides funding for the activity in question, reimburses local governments for the cost of mandates, or provides them with a new source of funding to cover those costs (Zimmerman 1994). There are ways around these restrictions, however, and many state legislators would rather mandate than raise taxes and face the wrath of voters.

### INTERGOVERNMENTAL RELATIONS AND HOMELAND SECURITY

The terrorist bombing on September 11, 2001, revealed our nation's vulnerability to attack and highlighted significant weaknesses in our response to acts of war on home soil. The subsequent outbreak of anthrax underscored these problems, and a new, Cabinet-level department was created to improve domestic security. The Department of Homeland Security (DHS) combines all or parts of twenty-two agencies at the national level, including the Transportation Security Administration, Immigration and Naturalization Service, Customs Service, and Border Patrol, as well as the Coast Guard and Federal Emergency Management Agency.

Blending this many disparate agencies will be difficult and time-consuming, but policy coordination at the national level is essential for improving homeland security. Intergovernmental cooperation is no less important (Kettl 2002). Because the DHS's powers of preemption and regulation are limited, it depends on state and local governments for law enforcement, public health, and other services related to domestic safety. Hence the DHS cannot discharge its responsibilities without obtaining assistance from state and local governments and developing their capacity to combat terrorism.

For example, maintaining border security is a primary responsibility of the Department of Homeland Security. To carry out this responsibility, the department could ask the president to mobilize the National Guard. This is an emergency measure only; the Posse Comitatus Act of 1878 does not allow presidents to use the Guard for routine law enforcement. Governors enjoy more authority in this regard;

they can mobilize the Guard for many different reasons, including airport security, border patrols, and infrastructure protection. Lengthy mobilizations present political problems for governors, however, since Guard members are not available to their families and employers during the period of activation. It also costs money to equip and train the Guard for new duties, and governors have their own spending (or taxing) priorities. Accommodating the desires of all these actors is necessary to ensure gubernatorial cooperation over the long haul, and it will test the political skills of the secretary for Homeland Security.

Fighting terrorism involves more than border security, however. State and local law enforcement agencies need access to information and intelligence gathered by national agencies, including the FBI, Bureau of Alcohol, Tobacco and Firearms, Secret Service, and CIA. Information systems must be upgraded and integrated in order to counter terrorism. The deeper problem, though, is that national agencies do not always share information with each other on a timely basis. They are even less inclined to cooperate with state and local officials, as any American television viewer knows. "Connecting the dots" will be difficult unless subnational officials are regarded as strong partners and provided with security clearances and access to intelligence reports and raw information.

The Department of Homeland Security uses grants-in-aid to underwrite cooperation from state and local governments. The proposed FY2003 federal budget includes $10 billion for research on biological and chemical weapons and the development of vaccines, antidotes, and medical treatments. The budget includes another $1.6 billion to upgrade public health care systems, which are ill-prepared for emergencies triggered by terrorist attacks. Better public health care is an important aspect of homeland security, and a daunting one: the city of New York's system was almost overwhelmed on September 11, and it is one of the strongest in the nation.

Expanding the capacity of local governments is the goal of another grant-in-aid too. Preparedness assistance for "first responders" will be administered by the Office of Domestic Preparedness (ODP), an entity within the Federal Emergency Management Administration, which has been absorbed by the DHS. ODP will award $3.5 billion in FY2003 for training and equipping local police, firefighters, and emergency medical technicians called to the scene of attacks. Each state will receive an allocation of $15 million, with $3 million for each territory. The remaining funds will be awarded under a block formula based on population and risk, including proximity to nuclear power plants, military installations, international borders, and so forth.

Everyone endorses the goal of this grant, but that does not exclude politics from its administration. Congress expects states and localities to pay their share of the costs for boosting first responders' capability. Hence there is a 25 percent matching requirement for these grants. There is also a "maintenance of effort" provision to prevent states and localities from reducing their current outlays once federal funds become available. Finally, ODP will employ performance standards to assess the effectiveness of state and local policies before grants are renewed.

National defense strategists also want to promote mutual aid agreements between local communities, which generally require enabling legislation from state governments. For that reason the new grants flow to the states for distribution to local areas. Governors and state legislators prefer this method because it increases their policy-making leverage. On the other hand, local officials often want to bypass state officials and any conditions they might impose on the use of funds. Thus, the U.S. Conference of Mayors unsuccessfully lobbied Congress to "eliminate the middleman" by allowing ODP to award funds directly to local officials.

The first responders program encapsulates the difficulty of improving homeland security in a federal system. Congress and the president have formulated a national strategy for combating terrorism, but key elements of that strategy must be implemented by state and local officials elected to serve the people under their jurisdiction. Not every jurisdiction feels threatened by terrorists, however, nor are they equally willing to subordinate state and local priorities to the wishes of lawmakers in Washington. We may therefore expect challenges to antiterrorist policy and even deviations from it as implementation proceeds.

Security policy will undoubtedly vary from state to state, and locality to locality. If the variation is too great, it will undermine the effectiveness of policies for protecting the homeland. Conventional wars typically narrow the range of variation, as policy makers at all levels set aside their differences in the name of national security. The war on terror is a new kind of war, however. A protracted, low-level conflict with shadowy enemies may unite us for a while, but it will not sublimate our political differences indefinitely. They will be expressed, and the range of variation in policies will expand. Federalism insures it.

## REFERENCES

Anton, Thomas J. 1989. *American Federalism and Public Policy: How the System Works.* New York: Random House.

Bahl, Roy. 1990. "Changing Federalism: Trends and Interstate Variations." In *The Changing Face of Fiscal Federalism,* edited by Thomas R. Swartz and John E. Peck. Armonk, N.Y.: M. E. Sharpe.

Bowman, Ann O'Malley. 2002. "American Federalism on the Horizon." *Publius: The Journal of American Federalism* 32(2): 3–22.

Brown, Lawrence D. 1984. "The Politics of Devolution in Nixon's New Federalism." In *The Changing Politics of Federal Grants,* edited by Lawrence D. Brown, James W. Fossett, and Kenneth T. Palmer. Washington, D.C.: Brookings Institution.

Cammisa, Anne Marie. 1995. *Governments as Interest Groups: Intergovernmental Lobbying and the Federal System.* Westport, Conn.: Praeger.

Cho, Chung-Lae, and Deil S. Wright. 2001. "Managing Carrots and Sticks: Changes in State Administrators' Perceptions of Cooperative and Coercive Federalism During the 1990s." *Publius: The Journal of Federalism* 31(2): 57–80.

Cigler, Beverly. 1998. "Emerging Trends in State-Local Relations." In *Governing Partners: State-Local Relations in the United States,* edited by Russell L. Hanson. Boulder, Colo.: Westview Press.

———. 1995. "Not Just Another Special Interest: Intergovernmental Representation." In *Interest Group Politics,* 4th ed., edited by Allen J. Cigler and Burdett A. Loomis. Washington, D.C.: CQ Press.

Congressional Budget Office. 2001. *CBO's Activities Under the Unfunded Mandates Reform Act, 1996–2000.* Washington, D.C.: Congressional Budget Office.

Conlan, Timothy J. 1998. *From New Federalism to Devolution: Twenty-Five Years of Intergovernmental Reform.* Washington, D.C.: Brookings Institution.

Conlan, Timothy J., and David R. Beam. 1992. "Federal Mandates: The Record of Reform and Future Prospects." *Intergovernmental Perspective* 18(4): 7–11.

Conlan, Timothy J., and David B. Walker. 1983. "Reagan's New Federalism: Design, Debate, and Discord." *Intergovernmental Perspective* 8(4): 6–22.

Corwin, Edwin S. 1934. *The Twilight of the Supreme Court.* New Haven, Conn.: Yale University Press.

Council of State Governments. 1997. "State Leaders Unveil Federalism Plan." Press release, November 7. Available at http://www.csg. org/whatsnew/pr-07nov97pressrel.htm.

Derthick, Martha. 1986. "Preserving Federalism: Congress, the States, and the Supreme Court." *Brookings Review* 4(2): 32–37.

DeVaul, Diane, and Heather Twomey. 1989. *Federal Funding Formulas and State Allocations.* Washington, D.C.: Center for Regional Policy, Northeast Midwest Institute.

Dilger, Robert Jay. 2000. "The Study of American Federalism at the Turn of the Century." *State and Local Government Review* 32(2): 98–107.

———. 1982. *The Sunbelt/Snowbelt Controversy: The War over Federal Funds.* New York: New York University Press.

Dinan, John. 1997. "State Government Influence in the National Policy Process: Lessons from the 104th Congress." *Publius: The Journal of Federalism* 27(1): 129–142.

Elazar, Daniel J.1998. "State-Local Relations: Union and Home Rule." In *Governing Partners,* edited by Hanson.

———. 1984. *American Federalism: A View from the States.* 3d ed. New York: Harper and Row.

Frye, Earl H. 1998. *The Expanding Role of State and Local Governments in U.S. Foreign Affairs.* Washington, D.C.: Council on Foreign Relations Press.

Grodzins, Morton. 1966. *The American Political System.* Chicago: Rand-McNally.

Johnson, Nicholas. 2002. "The State Tax Cuts of the 1990s, the Current Revenue Crisis, and Implications for State Services." Washington, D.C.: Center on Budget and Policy Priorities.

Kelly, Janet M., and Theresa Gullo. 2001. "The Unfunded Mandates Reform Act: A Five Year Review." Paper presented at the annual meeting of the American Political Science Association, San Francisco, August 30–September 2.

Kettl, Donald F. 2002. "Promoting State and Local Government Performance for Homeland Security." Homeland Security Project Paper. New York: Century Foundation.

Kincaid, John. 2001. "The State of U.S. Federalism, 2000–2001: Continuity in Crisis." *Publius: The Journal of Federalism* 31(3): 1–30.

———. 1999. "De Facto Devolution and Urban Defunding: The Priority of Persons Over Places." *Journal of Urban Affairs* 21(2): 135–167.

———. 1998. "The Devolution Tortoise and the Centralization Hare." *New England Economic Review* (May/June): 13–40.

Kline, John M. 1999. "Continuing Controversies over State and Local Foreign Policy Sanctions in the United States." *Publius: The Journal of Federalism* 29(1): 111–134.

Krane, Dale, Platon N. Rigos, and Melvin Hill. 2000. *Home Rule in America: A Fifty-State Handbook.* Washington, D.C.: CQ Press.

Lord, William B., and Douglas S. Kenney. 1993. "Resolving Interstate Water Conflicts: The Compact Approach." *Intergovernmental Perspective* 19(1): 19–23.

MacManus, Susan A. 1983. "State Government: The Overseer of Municipal Finance." In *The Municipal Money Chase: The Politics of Local Government Finance,* edited by Alberta M. Sbragia. Boulder, Colo.: Westview Press.

Marbach, Joseph R., and J. Wesley Leckrone. 2002. "Intergovernmental Lobbying for the Passage of TEA-21." *Publius: The Journal of Federalism* 32(1): 45–64.

Mason, W. Dale. 1998. "Tribes and States: A New Era in Intergovernmental Relations." *Publius: The Journal of Federalism* 28(4): 111–130.

Mountjoy, John. 2001. "Interstate Compacts Make a Comeback." In *Eight State Trends: Spring/2001*. Lexington, Ky.: Council of State Governments.

Moody, J. Scott. 2002. "Federal Tax Burdens and Expenditures by State." Washington, D.C.: Tax Foundation.

National Governors Association. 2002. *The Fiscal Survey of States*. Washington, D.C.: National Governors Association.

National Indian Gaming Association. 2003. Library and Resource Center Webpage at www.indiangaming.org/library.

Peliserro, John P. 1985. "State Revenue Sharing with Large Cities: A Policy Analysis over Time." *Policy Studies Journal* 13: 643–652.

Peterson, Paul E. 1995. *The Price of Federalism*. Washington, D.C.: Brookings Institution.

Posner, Paul L. 1998. *The Politics of Unfunded Mandates Reform: Whither Federalism?* Washington, D.C.: Georgetown University Press.

Rosenthal, Alan. 1997. *Decline of Representative Democracy: Process, Participation, and Power in State Legislatures*. Washington, D.C.: CQ Press.

Stanfield, Rochelle L. 1978. "Playing Computer Politics with Local Aid Formulas." *National Journal*, December 9, 1977–1981.

Stonecash, Jeffrey M. 1998. "The Politics of State-Local Fiscal Relations." In *Governing Partners*, edited by Hanson.

———. 1995. *American State and Local Politics*. Ft. Worth, Texas: Harcourt Brace.

Tarr, G. Alan. 1998. *Understanding State Constitutions*. Princeton, N.J.: Princeton University Press.

U.S. Advisory Commission on Intergovernmental Relations. 1993. *Significant Features of Fiscal Federalism, 1993*. Washington, D.C.: U.S. Government Printing Office.

———. 1984. *Regulatory Federalism: Policy, Process, Impact, and Reform*. Washington, D.C.: U.S. Government Printing Office.

———. 1981. *Measuring Local Discretionary Authority*. Washington, D.C.: U.S. Government Printing Office.

U.S. Bureau of the Census. 2002. *2002 Census of Governments: Government Organization*. Washington, D.C.: U.S. Government Printing Office.

———. Various years. *Government Finances*. Washington, D.C.: U.S. Government Printing Office.

———. Various years. *State and Local Government Finances*. Washington, D.C.: U.S. Government Printing Office.

U.S. Office of Management and Budget. Various years. *Historical Tables*. Washington, D.C.: U.S. Government Printing Office.

Walker, David. 2000. *The Rebirth of American Federalism: Slouching Toward Washington*. New York: Chatham House.

Weaver, R. Kent. 2000. *Ending Welfare as We Knew It*. Washington, D.C.: Brookings Institution.

Weiler, Conrad. 1993–1994. "GATT, NAFTA, and State and Local Powers." *Intergovernmental Perspective* 20(1): 38–41.

Wright, Deil S. 1988. *Understanding Intergovernmental Relations*. 3d ed. Pacific Grove, Calif.: Brooks/Cole.

Zimmerman, Joseph F. 1996. *Interstate Relations: The Neglected Dimension of Federalism*. Westport, Conn.: Praeger.

———. 1994. "State Mandate Relief: A Quick Look." *Intergovernmental Perspective* 20(2): 28–30.

———. 1993. "Preemption in the U.S. Federal System." *Publius: The Journal of Federalism* 23(4): 1–13.

———. 1981. "The Discretionary Authority of Local Governments." *Urban Data Service Reports* 13(11).

Zimmerman, Joseph F., and Julie M. Clark. 1994. "The Political Dynamics of State-Local Relations, 1991–1993." In *The Book of the States, 1994–1995*. Lexington, Ky.: Council of State Governments.

## SUGGESTED READINGS

*The Book of the States.* Now an annual publication of the Council of State Governments, the "bible" of research on state politics contains a wealth of comparative data and information, along with reviews of trends in all aspects of state politics and policy.

*Publius: The Journal of Federalism.* A scholarly journal devoted primarily to research on American federalism, although comparative studies are occasionally included. It is published quarterly, and one issue each year centers on the state of American federalism in that year.

*Significant Features of Fiscal Federalism.* The Rockefeller Institute at SUNY-Albany replaces the U.S. Advisory Commission on Intergovernmental Relations as publisher of an indispensable reference for taxing and spending by all levels of government.

Wright, Deil S. *Understanding Intergovernmental Relations.* 3d ed. Pacific Grove, Calif.: Brooks/Cole, 1988. This is still the definitive treatment of intergovernmental relations in the United States. David C. Nice and Patricia Fredericksen provide a more recent treatment in *The Politics of Intergovernmental Relations,* 2d ed. Chicago: Nelson-Hall, 1995.

CHAPTER 3

 *Parties and Elections*

JOHN F. BIBBY AND THOMAS M. HOLBROOK

Political parties permeate every aspect of state governments, and political scientists have long stressed their crucial role in aggregating and mobilizing the interests of vast numbers of citizens, enhancing voters' capacity to hold public officials accountable, acting as agents of political socialization, and organizing the decision-making institutions of government. While political scientists' commitment to parties has remained relatively constant, public support has withered as the parties have been buffeted by a succession of threatening challenges: the loss of patronage traditionally used to sustain their organizations; surrender of control over nominations as states adopted primary elections to choose candidates; and competition from interest groups, candidates' personal organizations, and campaign consultants. These party-weakening challenges have caused American politics to become more candidate centered. Yet despite these challenges, parties have demonstrated amazing adaptability and durability. Unlike traditional patronage-based party organizations of the early twentieth century, parties have found their niche in the current candidate-centered era as institutions in service to their candidates (Aldrich 1995, 269–274).

## STATE PUBLIC POLICY TOWARD PARTIES

In most western democracies, political parties are considered to be private associations. As such they are permitted to transact business in private, largely unregulated by government. American political parties, however, are heavily regulated by state laws. They function in a manner similar to public utilities in that they provide essential public services (for example, nominating candidates, contesting elections, organizing the government) that have sufficient impact on the public to justify governmental regulation (Epstein 1986, 157).

State regulation of parties was encouraged by the introduction in the 1890s of the Australian ballot: secret general election ballots provided by the government with candidates designated by party labels. By granting official recognition to political parties on government-provided ballots, the states acquired a legal justification for engaging in the regulation of parties (Epstein 1986, 152–167).

*Ballot Access and Form*

State laws define what constitutes an officially recognized political party eligible for a line on the general election ballot. The requirements for parties retaining automatic ballot access normally involve winning a specified percentage of the vote for governor in the last election (the percentage ranges from 20 percent in Alabama to a low of 1 percent in Wisconsin). New parties or independent candidates seeking ballot access must secure signatures from a designated percentage of the voters. Whatever the specific form statutes governing ballot access may take, their general effect is to protect the dominant status of the two major parties and serve as barriers to independent candidacies and the emergence of third-party movements (Winger 1997, 165–172). Thus, in the almost sixty-year history of Georgia's ballot access law that requires a minor-party candidate to secure the signatures of 5 percent of the registered voters on the petition, no minor-party candidate for the U.S. House has ever been able to comply with the petition requirement and qualify for a place on the ballot (*Ballot Access News* 2002).

Through their regulation of the form of the ballot, states may either encourage straight-ticket party voting through use of the party column ballot or encourage voters to engage in split-ticket voting by using the office bloc ballot. The trend since the 1960s has been for states to switch from the party column ballot to the office bloc form of ballot. As a result, only a bare majority of states still use the party column ballot. A companion trend that eliminates the ability of citizens to vote for all of a party's candidates with a single action in the polling booth further encourages a candidate-centered style of politics. In 2002 only fifteen states retained a ballot form containing a provision for expedited straight-ticket voting.

The importance of state regulation and administration of elections was dramatically demonstrated by post-election vote-counting controversies that swirled around the 2000 presidential election in Florida. Confusion created by Palm Beach County's so-called butterfly ballot that appeared to cause some voters to cast their votes for a candidate other than the one intended was but one of the sources of controversy. There were also disputes over counting punch card ballots with "hanging chads" and absentee ballots from overseas, allegations that persons were denied the right to vote, and issues concerning the proper role of the secretary of state (Florida's chief election officer), the state legislature, and courts in determining whether George W. Bush or Al Gore won the state's electoral votes on which hinged the outcome of the national election. As a consequence of the 2000 election administration controversies in Florida and other states, Congress in 2002 passed an election reform act that authorized $3.86 billion to upgrade voting equipment, improve election administration, and train poll workers. The act also mandates the states to prepare computerized voter registration lists, provide provisional ballots to voters whose names do not appear on voter lists, and make voting machines accessible to the handicapped.

### Eased Procedures for Voting

As the states have eased the process of voting through more liberal absentee ballot rules, early voting, and mail-in ballots, the political parties' function of mobilizing voters has become more complicated, time consuming, and crucial. Approximately half the states now give absentee ballots to any voter who simply requests that option. No excuses or notarization are required. Thirteen states allow early voting; residents can vote 17 to 21 days prior to election day—a process that has been shown to have substantial public appeal. Thus more than half of Washington's voters in 2000 cast either absentee or early ballots, and one-third did so in Arizona, Colorado, Tennessee and Texas. In addition, Oregon has pioneered mail-in ballots and has eliminated the polling booth. The trend toward easing the voting process is dramatically changing the timetable under which parties operate and forcing them to reexamine their strategies.

### Party Membership

In all but a handful of states, statutes provide a description of the requirements for party membership—that is, who is eligible to vote in partisan primary elections. Normally requirements include minimum age, state or local residence, citizenship, and depending on the type of primary election system employed in the state, party affiliation. By limiting participation in primaries to registered Democrats or Republicans, as is done in closed primary states, the law is in effect defining party membership. Party bylaws sometimes define membership in the party organization by making more substantial demands on voters and party activists. For example, the Democratic party of West Virginia requires people to register as Democrats in order to participate in party organizational activities. On the other hand, there are also numerous state parties that automatically issue legally meaningless "sustaining membership" cards to small contributors as a fund-raising incentive.

### Organizational Structure

State regulations frequently extend to matters of internal party organization such as procedures for selecting officers, composition of party committees, dates and locations of meetings, and powers of party units. In each of the states, the two major parties have state central committees headed by a state chair. The state committees are normally composed of members elected by county committees, state and congressional district conventions, or party primaries. The state committee's duties vary from state to state, but normally include calling the state convention, adoption of party policies, fund-raising, assisting with campaigns, aiding local party units, and serving as a party public relations agency. Most state parties have vested an executive committee with the same powers as the parent state central committee and authorized it to act for the party between the infrequent meetings of the central body.

More than three-quarters (77 percent) of state party chairs are elected for two-year terms, and 23 percent have four-year terms. Turnover, however, is high. The average tenure of state party chairs in 1999 was two years with Republicans serving on average 2.3 years and Democrats 1.6 years (Aldrich 2000, 656). State chairs or the party executive directors act as the operational heads of state party organizations responsible for fund-raising, candidate recruitment, campaign activities, party publicity, and liaison with local and national party organizations and elected officials. Both Republican and Democratic state chairs serve on their parties' national committees. State chairs are frequently handpicked by their party's governor and, therefore, are expected to advance and protect gubernatorial interests within the party. For the party out of power—lacking control of the governor's office—the state chair may be the real party leader and its principal spokesperson.

Congressional district, legislative district, county, city, ward, and precinct organizations constitute the remainder of the formal party structure. Each level of party organization is controlled by a committee that is headed by an elected leader. In reality, the state party organization is much more encompassing than this description would suggest. The party can be viewed as a network of individuals and organizations with an array of resources on which party candidates can draw. Included in this network are allied interest groups (for example, unions, teachers, trial lawyers and environmental groups for the Democrats; business groups and evangelical Christians for the GOP), political action committees (PACs), fund-raisers, candidates' personal campaign organizations, political consultants, and the state legislative campaign committees controlled by legislative leaders.

*Campaign Finance*

States have long set at least some minimal limits on campaign spending and activities. Most ban election-day expenditures; all prohibit bribery and vote buying; and each imposes some form of public disclosure and reporting of campaign receipts and expenditures. Since the Watergate scandals of the 1970s campaign finance legislation has been the most rapidly growing body of election law. Thirty-five states have imposed some limits on individual contributions, the constitutionality of which was upheld by the U.S. Supreme Court in 2000 (*Nixon v. Shrink Missouri Government PAC*, 93 U.S. 963); forty-three have prohibited or placed limits on corporate contributions; thirty-eight have restrictions on direct labor union contributions; thirty-six limit PAC contributions; and forty-four prohibit or limit contributions from state-regulated industries (Council of State Governments 2000, 187–232; Malbin and Gais 1998, 14–19). However, there are states, such as Colorado, New Mexico, Texas, and Utah, with no restrictions on individual and PAC contributions or party spending. Despite the abundance of state campaign finance laws, the effectiveness of state regulation is severely limited by the fact that most enforcement agencies are understaffed and have inadequate resources.

In twenty-six states there are programs to provide some form of state financing of elections that channel public funds to candidates, political parties, or both. State funding, however, tends to be inadequate for financing campaigns at a level commensurate with candidates' needs. The evidence to date shows that public funding has not brought about the heightened electoral competition that was intended by this reform (Malbin and Gais 1998, 137).

One of the most interesting aspects of public funding occurs in states that permit minor parties and independent candidates to qualify for public funding. In Maine, Minnesota, and Vermont public funding has encouraged and strengthened third-party movements that are capable of challenging the traditional electoral dominance of the Republicans and Democrats. The most dramatic example occurred in the 1998 Minnesota gubernatorial election, which was won by the Reform party nominee, Jesse Ventura, a former professional wrestler. Under Minnesota law, Ventura qualified for $400,000 in public funding because the Reform Party won 5 percent of the vote in the previous election. With his public funds, Ventura moved beyond being a marginal candidate to become a real contender because public funding enabled him to run a media campaign that featured attention-getting radio and television ads. His major-party opponents had also accepted public funding, which imposed spending limits on their campaigns. Each spent heavily early in the campaign, and when they finally realized that Ventura was a serious threat, they had already nearly reached their spending limits and were unable to bombard the electorate with television ads designed to counter Ventura's media campaign. Thus public funding combined with spending limits placed upon major-party candidates and strategic budgetary decisions by the candidates contributed to Ventura being the first Reform party candidate to be elected to statewide office.

### The Changing Legal Status of State Parties

As state statutes have given parties legal standing and special benefits (for example, ballot access and public funding), stipulated functions they will perform, and regulated how those functions will be carried out, the parties have become quasipublic agencies. As adjuncts of state government, their existence has been practically mandated by state law and their continued existence virtually assured. The legal status of parties is, however, in the process of modification as a result of a series of U.S. Supreme Court decisions. These decisions have extended First and Fourteenth Amendment freedom of association rights to political parties and struck down a series of state-imposed restrictions on parties.

In *Tashjian v. Connecticut* (479 U.S. 20 [1986]), the Court held that Connecticut could not prevent voters registered as independents from voting in a Republican primary if the state GOP wanted to permit independents as well as registered Republicans to vote in its primaries. While this decision had potentially important long-term implications for limiting the states' regulatory power over parties, its short-term effects were limited because only a few states used the Court-granted power to open their primaries to independents. It was not until after California had enacted in 1996 a blanket primary law that state parties sought to use the *Tashjian* precedent to close rather than open their primaries. The blanket primary law permitted voters to participate in any party's primary and to vote in different party primaries as long as they voted for only one candidate per office. It was challenged on First and Fourteenth Amendment grounds by the parties in California, and in 2000 the U.S. Supreme Court declared California's blanket primary unconstitutional as "stark repudiation of political association" that denied parties the ability to control their own nomination processes and define their own identities (*Democratic Party v. Jones*, 530 U.S. 567 [2000]). To bring the state's statutes into conformity with the Court decision, California enacted a primary law that followed the formula set forth in *Tashjian*. That is, voters registered as partisans in order to vote in party primaries and unaffiliated voters could vote in party primaries if party rules permit them to participate.

The California case left open the question of whether or not open primaries are constitutional since two dissenting justices asserted that the decision cast serious doubt upon the constitutionality of various forms of open primaries. However, it is not at all clear that the states, parties, or the Court are prepared to throw out traditional open primary systems that have become established parts of the states' political culture.

Another instance in which the Court asserted the state parties' freedom of association rights to limit state regulatory power over parties occurred in 1989 when it threw out a California law that banned parties from endorsing candidates in primaries, limited the length of state chairs' terms, and required rotating the position between northern and southern California every two years (*Eu v. San Francisco Democratic Central Committee*, 49 U.S. 214 [1989]).

Although the Court has stated clearly that there are limits on the extent of regulation that states may impose on political parties, it has also demonstrated a willingness to allow the states considerable leeway in determining the nature of their electoral and party system. Thus in 1997 it held in *Timmons v. Twin Cities New Party* (520 U.S. 351 [1997]) that although parties have an unquestioned right to nominate their own candidates, the states also have the constitutional right to regulate elections and prevent manipulations of the ballot and factionalism among the voters. The Court, therefore, ruled that Minnesota had the power to prevent the left-leaning New Party from engaging in the practice of "cross-filing" or "fusion" by nominating a candidate for the state legislature who had already accepted the Democratic nomination. This decision, of course, struck a severe blow against a struggling third party and, in effect, gave the Court's blessing to state efforts to promote a two-party system.

STATE PARTY ORGANIZATIONS:
INSTITUTIONALIZED SERVICE AGENCIES

In the 1950s the leading student of American political parties, V. O. Key Jr., gave the following dismal assessment of state parties. The "general impression that most . . . [state party committees] are virtually dead is probably not far from wrong" (1956, 287). During the 1960s and 1970s prominent observers of American politics continued to express concern for the state of the parties. Although it is indeed true that voters—the party-in-the-electorate—are now less guided by partisanship in making their choices in the polling booth, state parties have not collapsed. Instead, state party organizations have become since the 1980s increasingly professional and stronger in the sense that most can provide campaign services to their candidates and assistance to their local affiliates. The once highly autonomous state party organizations are also now closely integrated with the national party organizations, which use them to implement their campaign strategies in presidential, senatorial, and congressional campaigns. The national party committees have even become a significant source of financing and campaign services in close gubernatorial races and state legislative contests in which party control of legislative chambers is at stake.

The institutionalization of state parties as campaign service organizations parallels the resurgence of the national party organizations, where a massive fund-raising capacity has transformed the once weak Republican and Democratic National Committees into major service agencies to candidates and state and local party organizations. There are also parallels between the substantial campaign roles being played by the parties' senatorial and congressional campaign committees at the national level with the emergence of state legislative campaign committees as a major party–based campaign resource for legislative candidates.

### The Passing of the Traditional State Party Organization

Although state party organizations have gone through a resurgence since the early 1980s, they bear scant resemblance to the traditional party organizations that dominated state politics, particularly in the Middle Atlantic, New England, and lower Great Lakes states of the early twentieth century (Mayhew 1986). These patronage-based organizations, which controlled nominations and ran their candidates' campaigns, had largely passed from the scene by the mid-1980s (Reichley 1992, 383–384). Patronage as a basis for building party organizations was severely weakened by civil service laws, strengthened public employee unions, and a critical public. In the 1970s the Supreme Court threw its might into the anti-patronage movement. In a series of cases the Court hit at the heart of large-scale patronage operations run by both Democrats and Republicans in Illinois. It ruled that the Cook County Democratic organization could no longer fire people on the basis of their party affiliations (*Elrod v. Burns,* 427 U.S. 347 [1976]), and it followed this decision with one declaring that the state GOP could not use "party affiliations and support" as a basis for filling state jobs unless party affiliation was an "appropriate requirement" for filling the position (*Rutan v. Republican Party* 488 U.S. 1872 [1990]). In this once patronage-rich state, the Democratic chair observed that "the party no longer functions as an employment agency. More and more we must rely on the spirit of volunteerism" (Reichley 1992, 385).

Even though patronage jobs no longer provide an important basis for party workers and money, other forms of governmental preferment remain important. Gubernatorial appointments to state boards and commissions that control professional licensing, gambling, higher education, hospitals, state investments, environmental and recreation policy, and cultural activities are assignments that are much sought after by persons seeking policy influence and recognition. Partisan considerations can also affect state decisions regarding state contracts, bank deposits, economic development, and purchase of legal and consulting services. However, these types of preferments are useful primarily for fund-raising and do not provide campaign workers in the same way that patronage jobs once did (Reichley 1992, 385).

### The Service-Oriented State Party Organization

Among the indicators of the strengthened nature of most state party organizations are permanent headquarters; professional leadership and staffing; and adequate budgets to maintain the organization and its programs of support for candidates, officeholders, and local units (Aldrich 2000; Appleton and Ward 1997; Cotter et al. 1984; Reichley 1992, 386–391).

*Permanent Headquarters Contains Modern Technology.* As late as the early 1970s state party organizations were frequently run out of the offices and homes of the state chairs. This ad hoc type of operation has now largely ceased to exist as the parties in the main now operate permanent headquarters stocked with high-tech equipment in modern office buildings located in state capitals. The degree to which headquarters use up-to-date technology depends upon the party's financial resources, but almost all have some form of computerized voter database that can be used for voter contact and registration, recruiting volunteers, mailings, and fund-raising (Aldrich 2000, 656). In the creation of these databases, national party committees have frequently provided technical assistance, especially in the case of the Republicans. Most state parties also operate web sites.

*Professional Staffing.* Even into the 1970s many state party headquarters operated with small staffs consisting of only an executive director, secretary, and a few volunteers. Today virtually all state parties have professional leadership with 54 percent having a state chair who works full time compared to one-third in 1984 (Aldrich 2000, 656; Reichley 1992, 389). There is a full-time executive director in nearly every state headquarters and a majority have a field staff, comptroller, research staff, public relations director, and fund-raising operation. The average headquarters has an election-year staff of nine full-time employees and seven working part time. The Florida parties reflect the trend toward professionalized and expanded headquarters staffing. The state GOP has regularly had a staff of over twenty-five plus part-time employees, and in 2000 had thirty temporary employees; the Democrats have had a somewhat smaller staff of about sixteen full-time workers (Nagourney and Barstow 2000; Appleton and Ward 1997, 62).

Although the state parties have been largely successful in professionalizing and expanding their staffs, they are plagued with high turnover in both leadership and staff positions. State chairs serve on average only two years (Aldrich 2000, 656), and professional operatives tend to be transients who move from job to job with party organizations, candidates, and consulting firms, often on leads provided by national party organizations.

To supplement their own headquarters staff, state parties now increasingly rely upon political consultants for such services as polling, direct mail, media production and buying, and fund-raising. In addition, state parties may pay for preferred consultants' services to selected candidates or maintain a list of preferred consultants that is given to candidates who then pay for the consultants' services (Kolodny 2000, 118–124).

*Finances.* Operating a professional headquarters requires an ability to raise significant amounts of money on a continuing basis. Most state parties have developed direct mail and telemarketing capabilities to reach small- and medium-sized contributors, while also having more traditional large-donor programs. Aldrich's 1999 survey reported that the average state party election year budget was $2.8 million. National averages, however, mask the extent to which some state parties (e.g., in New York and California) have the ability to raise money by the tens of millions. Nor do national averages reflect the millions that the national party committees transfer to state parties in an effort to use their state affiliates to implement national party strategies. Thus, in the 2000 election cycle, national-level Republican committees sent in excess of $10 million to their state parties in Florida, Michigan, and Pennsylvania; nine other GOP state units received more than $3 million. National-level Democratic committees were similarly active as they transferred $15 million to the Michigan Democratic party, $13 million to their Pennsylvania affiliate, and more than $3 million to nine other state Democratic parties. National party transfers to state parties totaled $150 million for the Democrats and $130 million for the Republicans (Federal Election Commission 2001b).

### Party Activities: Organization Building and Candidate Support

With enlarged and more professional staffs plus adequate financial resources, state parties have expanded their activities in the areas of candidate support and party building. The growth of campaign activity since the early 1980s has been especially noticeable in terms of providing financial support to party nominees. More than 80 percent of state parties contribute to gubernatorial, state constitutional, congressional, and state legislative candidates (Aldrich 2000, 656). Parties also aid their nominees by matching them up with appropriate PAC donors so that the organized groups become partners with the party. An array of campaign services is often provided—polling, fund-raising assistance, media consulting, research, and campaign seminars (Aldrich 2000, 656; Reichley 1992, 390). However, because their resources are limited, state parties must be selective in the services they offer, and there has been a tendency to engage in labor-intensive voter mobilization programs that have the potential to benefit party candidates up and down the ballot.

In addition, state parties also engage in party-building activities including publishing newsletters, recruiting candidates, sharing mailing lists with local units, and conducting joint county-state fund-raisers and get-out-the-vote drives.

Although state parties have been strengthened in terms of their ability to provide services to their candidates, it must be kept in mind that their role is to supplement the activities of the candidates' own personal campaign organizations principally in the areas of voter mobilization and fund-raising. This restricted campaign role is an adaptation by the parties to the candidate-centered nature of state electoral politics in which candidates rely primarily on their own organizations, set up personal headquarters, and have nonparty groups providing campaign assistance. The candidates also often hire campaign consultants to work exclusively on their behalf.

### Electoral Impact of State Party Organizations

Although in this era of candidate-centered politics, party organizations play a supplementary role to that of the candidates' own personal organizations, the level of party organizational strength can affect elections. Analyses of gubernatorial elections show that the state party with an organizational strength advantage gains increments of votes over the opposition party (Cotter et al. 1984, 100–101); and the parties' ability to turn out voters on election day is a factor in determining the extent of interparty competition within the states (Barrilleaux 1986; Patterson and Caldeira 1984). Thus southern Republican parties were initially unable to take advantage of the inroads made by GOP presidential candidates in the 1950s and 1960s because their organizations were weak. However, the spectacular gains by Republican candidates for congressional, state, and local office in more recent years are in large measure a product of much stronger Republican organization (Jewell and Morehouse 2001, 99). There is also evidence that strong and competitive party organizations within a state contribute to public attitudes supportive of parties (Coleman 1996).

The benefits of an organizational strength advantage were clearly in evidence during the post-election dispute in the 2000 Florida presidential election. In this crucial struggle, the organizationally stronger Florida GOP immediately converted itself into a full-fledged operative arm of the Bush campaign. The three-story party headquarters was turned over to Bush lawyers and strategists; thirty employees scheduled for post-election layoff "were put into round-the-clock service to the Bush organization to do everything from legal research to fetching food and laundry for Mr. Bush's team"; party workers observed court clerks' offices to serve as an early warning system for surprise motions and orders, and the state Republicans handed out disposable cameras to document questionable vote counting and evidence bags used to gather disputed chads (Nagourney and Barstow 2000).

The relationship between party organizational strength and electoral success, however, is complex, often indirect, and difficult to fully assess. Just because a state party develops itself into a sophisticated campaign service organization does not mean that it will automatically and simultaneously become successful electorally. Yet it is apparent that the maintenance of effective party structures has aided the continuing electoral success of the Michigan Democrats and the Ohio Republicans. Even so, in states where a party has long enjoyed electoral dominance, there may be little incentive to build a strong party structure—for example, the Democrats in the South during their time of hegemony. It appears, therefore, that the real significance of party organizational strength is not so much its impact in any given year, but rather that such strength provides the infrastructure for candidates and activists to continue to compete in the face of short-term defeats and even long-term minority status and to take advantage of favorable conditions when they occur (for example, an opposition incumbent's retirement, scandal, divisiveness within the other party, a shift in public mood).

With either party now capable of winning gubernatorial elections in each of the fifty states and with intense battles in many states for control of legislative chambers, there are powerful incentives for state parties to build and maintain strong organizations. Parties with organizations that fail to perform effectively can suffer electoral drought (Jewell and Morehouse 2001, 99).

*Party Differences and the Heightened Involvement of Party-Allied Groups*

Studies of state central committees have generally shown the Republicans to be organizationally stronger than their Democratic counterparts (Aldrich 2000, 655; Cotter et al. 1984). This reflects a key difference between the parties: Republican state organizations tend to be a more important source of campaign support than do Democratic party organizations. This does not mean that Democratic candidates are necessarily lacking or unequal in resources, but it does mean that Democrats tend to rely more heavily for assistance from allied nonparty groups such as labor unions, teachers, abortion rights advocates, environmentalists, and trial lawyers to help supply money, workers, media advertising, and in-kind services. Democratic state parties thus tend to be more labor intensive than the more capital intensive GOP organizations. Magleby and his associates (2003) have provided vivid documentation of the heavy involvement of allied groups in the 2000 elections. For example, in Michigan the United Auto Workers negotiated Election Day as a paid holiday in their contract enabling the union to have 2,000 poll workers in the Detroit area compared to 350 in 1998. The state's GOP governor, John Engler, described this as "the largest soft money contribution in American political history." The union also set up worker-to-worker telephone contacts, provided each member with four to seven pieces of literature, and ran phone banks as part of its get-out-the-vote operation (Traugott 2003, 103). Of course, allied groups are not the exclusive province of the Democrats. The Christian Right and business organizations are often active on behalf of Republican candidates, but on the whole the Democrats tend to be dependent upon campaign involvement by allied groups

The use that state parties and their candidates make of allied group assistance—indeed, oftentimes their dependence on it—demonstrates the need to view parties in an inclusive and comprehensive manner that encompasses more than the formal, legally sanctioned organizational structure. The state party organization is actually a network that includes the regular party structure, candidate organizations, party-allied groups, fund-raisers, campaign consultants and the army of incumbent legislators' staffers, who are frequently and heavily involved in advancing their bosses' electoral interests as well as those of the party.

*Parties as Networks of Issue-Oriented Activists*

An emerging feature of American parties is that they are increasingly networks of "issue based participatory activists" (Shafer 1996, 35). The sources for this trend are found in a complex set of interacting forces: the development of a postindustrial society in which noneconomic social–cultural issues have gained heightened salience (for example, abortion, environmentalism, crime, gun control, women's and gay rights); sociological and economic change that resulted in heightened educational attainment, reduced blue-collar employment, and an expanding white-collar workforce; and decline in the availability of patronage as an incentive for political participation. Changes in the rules governing presidential nominating politics that have diminished the influence of party leaders have also enhanced the role of issue-oriented activists.

Surveys of national and state convention delegates, financial contributors, campaign workers, and candidates have demonstrated that party activists are more ideologically motivated than in the past, and these persons come from the extremes of opinion distribution. Thus while rank-and-file voters are by and large moderates comfortable with compromises and trade-offs, many activists are "hard liners" who are not willing to compromise their strongly held views (Fiorina 1999, 408–413). These "true believers" with their advocacy style of politics have now become well ensconced in state and local organizational structures (Bruce et al., 1991). For example, *Campaigns and Elections* reported in the mid-1990s that eighteen Republican state organizations were dominated by the Christian Right and that it had substantial influence in thirteen more (Wilcox 2000, 76–77). As significant as the Christian Right's involvement in GOP politics is in several states, an in-depth analysis has shown that its influence is not as great as its enemies, like People for the American Way, fear or one of its leaders, Reverend Pat Robertson, claims. Its influence varies widely across the states and it faces internal party opposition (Green, Guth, and Wilcox 1999, 133).

The Democrats, too, have been afflicted with issue-oriented group influence that has made it difficult to maintain the support of rank-and-file voters. An analysis of Democratic party–interest group relations concluded that "many of the postmaterial issues advocated by liberal citizen groups and Democratic candidates are peripheral to the lives of middle-class Americans. . . . The Democrats' preoccupation with civil rights, women's rights, environmentalism, and other causes has surely contributed to the Democrats' gender gap with white males" (Berry and Schildkraut 1998, 155). Democrats became the advocates of these causes because they were lobbied effectively by groups engaged in traditional political organizing, just as the Republicans have been subjected to intense organizing efforts by conservative groups.

The mounting involvement in party organizations by individuals and groups whose motivation to participate in party affairs is based not on material rewards such as patronage but rather on issue-based concerns is creating conflicts between rank-and-file party voters and the activists. It is also causing rifts between office-holders and party organizations. Indeed, in some states an almost schizophrenic party structure has developed with elected officials needing broad-based electoral support to win existing side-by-side with a growing body of organizational activists mainly concerned about ideology and principles. The potential for conflict inherent in this mix was apparent within the Texas GOP when Governor George W. Bush in 1997 found himself in open conflict with the right-wing chair of the state Republican party over tax policy. To deal with this problem, Bush and his campaign chairman cut off a large chunk of the state party's funding by directing most large contributors to a separate fund controlled by Bush's personal organization (Morehouse 2000,16). Republican governors of Colorado and Kansas have also had intraparty conflicts similar to that of Bush. During the 1998 Colorado governor's race, the state GOP chairman, a social conservative, expressed doubts about even supporting the party nominee, Bill Owens, because of ideological disagreements; and in Kansas the Republican state chairman resigned in order to run in the 1998 primary against the incumbent governor, Bill Graves, whom he considered insufficiently conservative.

To the extent that state parties become increasingly networks of issue-oriented activists, elected officials' conflicts with party organizational and allied group activists are likely to proliferate. In addition, the increasing influence exerted by issue-oriented activists within the parties and on their candidates will in all likelihood widen the policy differences between the parties. Indeed, the traditional conception of parties as "vote maximizers" appears to require some revision. Like interest groups, parties now contain an enlarged element that is mainly interested in achieving policy objectives—that is, the party structures are heavily influenced by "policy maximizers."

## STATE LEGISLATIVE CAMPAIGN COMMITTEES

As is the case at the national level, the state party organizational structure is decentralized, with a variety of organizations focusing on different offices and activities. The state central committees tend to concentrate on state-wide races, and the state legislative campaign committees focus their resources exclusively in legislative races and have emerged as the major source of party assistance to legislative candidates.

*Reasons for the Emergence of State Legislative Campaign Committees*

Legislative campaign committees are autonomous from their parties' state central committees. They are composed of incumbent legislators in both chambers and usually headed by legislative party leaders. These committees emerged as party support agencies for legislative candidates in response to intensifying partisan competition for control of legislative chambers, rising campaign costs ($500,000 expenditures in targeted races are no longer unusual), increased uncertainty about election outcomes, and the inability of many state central committees in the 1970s to provide meaningful assistance to legislative candidates (Gierzynski and Breaux 1992, 11–14). In addition, the development of strong legislative campaign committees is linked to increased legislative professionalism—full-time legislators who are paid a reasonable salary and backed by ample staff. Professionalism increases the value of legislative service, especially when accompanied by majority-party status. Legislative leaders, therefore, created campaign committees to protect and further their own and their party colleagues' interests. At the same time, a legislatively based campaign organization requires institutional resources to operate—virtually full-time legislative leaders, legislative caucus staffs, and computer and media resources.

*Campaign Activities*

Legislative campaign committees began as mechanisms to raise and distribute funds to candidates. However, they have developed into full-service operations for individual candidates, particularly in states with professionalized legislatures. The committees' involvement in candidate recruitment is particularly crucial. Recruitment of quality candidates is directly related to being able to raise campaign dollars, gain volunteer workers, and run truly competitive races for legislative seats. As state politics expert Alan Ehrenhalt noted,

> Every other year, Democrats and Republicans battle for legislative control . . . in what is advertised as a debate about which party best reflects the views of the electorate. Within the corridors of the state capitol, however, the biennial legislative elections are recognized for what they really are: a competition to attract candidates who have the skills and energy to win and the desire and resourcefulness to stay in office. (1989, 29–30)

The scope of legislative campaign committee spending and services can be extensive. In Ohio, for example, the Republican Senate Caucus provides candidates with a structured package of in-house polling, campaign managers, telephone banks, media planning, and issues research that costs in excess of $3.5 million. However, party committees tend not to handle the actual management of campaigns. Instead, they play a supporting role in recommending consultants to legislative candidates. By entering into relationships with the consulting industry to assist them in winning elections, the state parties are functioning in a manner that is strikingly parallel to the way the national parties function as brokers between candidates and consultants (Francia and Herrnson 2001, 4–5). As the intricacies of campaign election laws have increased, the importance of party-supplied legal advice has grown steadily.

Both the state committees and the legislative campaign committees have also proven to be adaptable to the growing role of PACs in funding elections. This adaptation has involved working with the PACs to channel PAC money into races in which additional dollars are thought to have the potential to affect outcomes. The legislative leaders provide PAC directors with political intelligence about where their contributions will have maximum impact. In the process, candidates benefit by having the campaign committees give them a stamp of legitimacy as good PAC investments. An assistant to the Speaker of the Indiana House observed, "For every one dollar we [the legislative campaign committee] raise, we direct two dollars of interest group money" (Gierzynski and Breaux 1992, 55). By channeling PAC money to candidates, as well as by soliciting PAC funds directly, the parties have infused campaigns with additional money that carries "the imprimatur of the party at no direct expense to party coffers" (Jones 1984, 197). State party organizations and allied PACs have also coordinated their efforts to provide in-kind services to candidates.

*Electoral Strategies*

Legislative campaign committees concentrate their resources on close or competitive races—either to maintain or gain control of a legislative chamber. Party money tends to flow either to vulnerable incumbents, viable challengers, or open-seat candidates. A recent multistate study of legislative campaign finance revealed parties are particularly generous with nonincumbent candidates. Slightly fewer than 50 percent of Democratic party funds went to nonincumbents, whereas the amount going to nonincumbent Republicans was 80 percent. This interparty difference reflected the fact that Democrats controlled more legislative seats than did the GOP at the time of the study (Gierzynski and Breaux 1998, 195–196). Candidates, especially challengers, who assemble professional organizations and hire consultants to handle such functions as advertising, media relations, and polling are considered good investments by the parties and receive more financial assistance (Francia and Herrnson 2001, 8–9).

Although party money can play a critical role in legislative races, one should not overstate the parties' involvement. A multistate study found that since 1994 there has been a decline in the percentage of legislative candidates who report that they relied upon their parties for fund-raising. As campaign costs have risen, candidates who need to raise large sums have found that they are best served by hiring fund-raising professionals to work on their campaigns. Fund-raising in state legislative elections has become more a candidate-centered activity with parties playing supporting rather than primary roles. This pattern is similar to that in congressional elections (Francia and Herrnson 2001, 5).

Shared goals, party loyalty, and personal connections do encourage an element of cooperation and coordinated activity between legislative campaign committees and state committees. However, because legislative campaign committees are always led and dominated by legislative leaders, the committees tend to operate independently of state central committees. Campaign finance expert Frank J. Sorauf (1992, 120) observed that legislative campaign committees are built and maintained by incumbents to serve primarily the agendas and priorities of legislative partisans and "insulate them from the pressure of other parts of the party. Collective action has helped to bring legislative parties freedom from the agencies of . . . gubernatorial parties."

## THE IMPACT OF STRENGTHENED NATIONAL PARTY ORGANIZATIONS: NATIONALIZATION AND HEIGHTENED INTRAPARTY INTEGRATION

Until the 1970s, political scientists emphasized the decentralized and confederate nature of American party organizations. The Republican National Committee (RNC) and the Democratic National Committee (DNC) were considered so lacking in influence that a landmark study even characterized them as "politics without power" (Cotter and Hennessy 1964). Power within the party structure resided with state and local organizations, and the national committees were heavily dependent on the state organizations for their funds. The national committees, which once existed in a state of dependency on their state affiliates, have now been transformed into large-scale and well-heeled enterprises housed in party-owned modern office buildings. Through their ability to raise massive amounts of money the national committees have been transformed into institutions capable of playing a major role in providing significant assistance to candidates and to their state affiliates. In the 2000 election cycle, the DNC raised more than $259 million and the RNC total topped $361 million (Federal Election Commission 2001b). The increased resources and influence of the national party organizations has been accompanied by heightened integration and interdependence between national and state party organizations.

### Centralizing Power through National Party Rule Enforcement

Since 1968 the national Democratic party organization has intensified efforts begun in 1948 to use its rule-making authority to ensure the loyalty of state party organizations to the national ticket. Starting with the McGovern-Fraser Committee in the late 1960s, the national party has developed elaborate rules that state parties are required to follow in the selection of national convention delegates. In addition, the National Democratic Charter, adopted in 1974, contains stipulations concerning the organization and operation of state parties. The national party's authority has been backed up by a series of Supreme Court decisions that ruled that national party rules governing delegate selection take precedence over state party rules and state statutes (*Cousins v. Wigoda*, 419 U.S. 450 [1975]; *Democratic Party of the U.S. v. Ex rel. La Follette*, 450 U.S. 107 [1981]).

Unlike the Democrats, the national GOP has not sought to gain influence over its state affiliates through tough rule enforcement. Instead, it has maintained the confederate legal structure of the party, and the RNC has assumed a relatively passive role in delegate selection and internal party organization.

*National Party Assistance Programs to State Parties and the*
*Shift of Intraparty Influence to National Organizations*

The Republicans were the first to use their ability to raise massive amounts of money to institute programs of financial, technical, and staff assistance designed to strengthen their state affiliates during the 1960s and 1970s. By the 1980s the Democrats were quite consciously copying the RNC's state party assistance programs. Among the programs provided to state parties by the national committees are cash grants, professional staff, consulting services for organizational development, data processing, fund-raising, campaigning, media communications, and redistricting. Both parties operate special programs to assist state legislative candidates, and there have been major investments of money and personnel in the development and maintenance of voter lists and efforts to get out the vote. Because they have been more proficient in raising national party money, the RNC has had a more extensive array of programs than has the DNC, which has sought to make up for this deficiency by encouraging state parties, state-level candidates, and allied interest groups (particularly organized labor) to pool resources with the national party and engage in "coordinated campaigns."

By providing an array of services to their state and local party organizations, the national committees have gained unprecedented intraparty influence and leverage. These assistance programs operate in a manner similar to federal grant-in-aid programs for the states in that before the state parties can receive aid they frequently have to accept conditions—albeit usually quite flexible conditions—imposed by the national party. Through these national-to-state party aid programs, the state parties have gained campaign assets—professionalized staffs, money, current voter lists and telephone banks for get-out-the-vote operations, and computers. However, an additional consequence of these aid programs has been that the national party organizations have gained unprecedented intraparty influence and leverage over their state and local affiliates.

*Strengthened Intraparty Integration*

Using their considerable financial resources, the national party committees have been able to achieve an unprecedented level of intraparty integration as the state parties have become integral elements in implementing national campaign strategies. In this process, large-scale transfers of funds from the national committee have played a critical role. In the 1999–2000 election cycle, the RNC and DNC combined transferred $241.9 million ($155 million by the DNC and $126 million by the RNC) to their state parties.

As substantial as the RNC and DNC transfers were, they constituted only part of the total national party funds passed on to state parties. Both parties' congressional and senatorial campaign committees also have been heavily involved in transferring

**Table 3-1** Transfers from National Party Committees to State Parties, 1999–2000 Election Cycle

| National party transfers | Hard | Soft | Total |
|---|---|---|---|
| Republican | | | |
| National committee | $33,853,563 | $93,017,578 | $126,871,141 |
| National congressional committee | 10,957,743 | 15,852,920 | 26,810,663 |
| National senatorial committee | 10,689,700 | 20,485,179 | 31,174,879 |
| Total | | | 184,486,683 |
| Democratic | | | |
| National committee | 41,892,535 | 73,087,085 | 114,979,620 |
| Congressional campaign committee | 15,383,695 | 34,707,004 | 50,090,699 |
| Senatorial campaign committee | 24,388,338 | 37,444,869 | 61,833,207 |
| Total | | | 226,903,526 |

SOURCE: Federal Election Commission 2001b, 8–9.

funds to the state parties (see Table 3-1). Thus 2000 Democratic transfers to the states totaled $226.9 million, and Republican transfers were $184.5 million (Federal Election Commission 2001b). The national parties not only transfer money to state parties, but they also channel major donors to state party organizations that are considered crucial in the national parties' strategies. These donors are asked to send money directly to states in which there are highly competitive races.

Transferred funds are used to defray the general party overhead, help state candidates, and increasingly to pay for voter mobilization activities. These get-out-the-vote operations can provide crucial assistance to federal as well as state candidates. For example, the RNC in 2000, working through its state parties, invested $40 million in voter contact programs that sent out 110 million pieces of mail and made 65 million phone calls to get supporters to the polls (Republican National Committee 2000). After the DNC pioneered in 1996 the use of transferred money to parties in battleground states to pay for issue ads prepared by the national party, this technique was used extensively by both parties in the 1996–2002 campaigns.

National party organizations allocate funds to state parties in a highly strategic manner that is intended to implement a national campaign strategy geared toward winning key states in presidential contests and maximizing the party's seats in the House and Senate. Table 3-2 demonstrates the strategic nature of national party transfers to the states. In 1999–2000 both the RNC and DNC pumped large sums into the critical states of Florida, Michigan, Ohio, and Pennsylvania, while low-priority states got only token or small transfers.

Coordinated national-state party campaigns, which result in a flow of funds into state parties and creation of tangible assets such as voter lists, professional staff, and high-tech equipment, can strengthen state parties' campaign capacity.

**Table 3-2** Strategic Targeting of the National Party Fund Transfers to State Parties, 1999–2000 Election Cycle

| | Battleground states[a] | | | |
|---|---|---|---|---|
| State party | Republican National Committee (total transfers) | State party | Democratic National Committee (total transfers) |
| Florida | $12,753,385 | Michigan | $15,966,163 |
| Pennsylvania | 11,280,751 | Pennsylvania | 13,422,664 |
| Michigan | 11,098,933 | Florida | 9,073,616 |
| Ohio | 9,624,308 | Ohio | 8,506,657 |
| California | 9,043,243 | Missouri | 7,086,388 |
| Missouri | 8,733,054 | Wisconsin | 6,512,027 |
| Washington | 6,621,648 | Washington | 6,249,244 |
| Wisconsin | 5,294,030 | Oregon | 5,434,742 |
| Illinois | 4,603,717 | Iowa | 4,658,266 |
| Oregon | 4,580,561 | California | 4,589,434 |
| Iowa | 3,342,391 | Illinois | 4,377,179 |
| New York | 3,069,595 | Louisiana | 3,248,361 |

| | States with Low Priority in the Campaign[b] | | | |
|---|---|---|---|---|
| State party | Republican National Committee (total transfers) | State party | Democratic National Committee (total transfers) |
| Vermont | $  7,286 | Rhode Island | $  6,371 |
| Rhode Island | 15,000 | Mississippi | 21,573 |
| Kansas | 15,025 | Wyoming | 26,613 |
| South Dakota | 43,300 | Hawaii | 29,642 |
| Mississippi | 52,288 | North Dakota | 33,578 |
| Indiana | 53,500 | Alaska | 35,299 |
| Alaska | 55,000 | Indiana | 42,193 |
| West Virginia | 102,500 | Nebraska | 44,638 |
| Massachusetts | 143,000 | Vermont | 45,964 |
| Colorado | 207,000 | Utah | 47,763 |

SOURCE: Federal Election Commission, 2001b, 8.

[a] States receiving in excess of $3 million in national party fund transfers.

[b] States receiving less than $250,000 in national party fund transfers.

LaRaja's research has shown that there is a correlation between fund transfers to state parties and the parties' campaign activity (2001, 30).

*Implications of the Bipartisan Campaign Reform Act*

National-state party relations were put into flux by the passage of the 2002 Bipartisan Campaign Reform Act (BCRA, also known as the McCain-Feingold Act), which bans national parties from receiving soft money contributions (unrestricted funds raised outside of the contribution limits of the Federal Election Campaign Act—FECA). This means that state parties will be cut off from the massive soft money transfers to which they had become accustomed. However, national-to-state party transfers of hard money (money raised in compliance with FECA) will continue, probably at higher levels, because the BCRA now sets a biennial cap of $57,500 on individual contributions to all parties and PACs. The net effect is apt to be some diminution of national party support for state parties and therefore some loss of intraparty influence by national party committees. The national party committees, however, are busily seeking to exploit loopholes in the law that will enable them to continue collecting soft money by creating party entities that are technically separate from the official party committees (Stone 2002).

State parties will benefit from a provision in the BCRA that permits donors to give $10,000 per year in soft money to state parties for get-out-the-vote drives. This can be expected to increase the importance of state parties in both federal and state campaigns. With state parties eligible to receive limited amounts of soft money, the importance of having sophisticated state party organizations will increase. It is also likely that the national parties will steer soft money contributors to parties in states that are important to a national party campaign strategy. However, the full impact of the BCRA on the parties is not yet clear. Based upon experience with the 1974 FECA, which was designed to reform campaign spending, but which was subverted to permit massive contributions and spending, there is every likelihood that the BCRA will also have unintended consequences. Like the FECA, the 2002 act was immediately challenged in court; in May 2003 a three-judge federal panel found portions of it unconstitutional. From there it went to the U.S. Supreme Court for a decision during its 2003–2004 term.

While the large-scale transfers of national party money to the state parties has had organizational strengthening benefits, the state parties can suffer a loss of autonomy and become dependent on national party largess. In some instances, state parties' headquarters quite literally may be taken over by the national party or presidential campaign operatives as the state party becomes little more than a check-writing mechanism for the national party to avoid restrictions of the FECA. Moreover, when these takeovers occur, national party priorities prevail, often with resources devoted to the presidential or other high-profile races to the detriment of contests lower down on the ballot such as state legislative candidates. There also have been instances of tension and conflict between national and state/local staff personnel and times when national party resources were pulled out of a state mid-campaign when it appeared that these resources could be more effectively used in another state.

## PARTY NOMINATIONS

The nomination process is crucial for parties because selecting a quality candidate can bring victory on election day, whereas a weak nominee can doom the party to defeat. In addition, control of the party is at stake, because nominations go a long way in determining which party factions will gain ascendancy, who receives the rewards that elected offices bestow on their supporters, and a party's policy orientation.

In most Western democracies, party candidates are selected by party organization leaders. Operating largely without government regulation, these party leaders designate the party nominees and there is no appeal of their decisions to the voters. Rank-and-file voters participate only in the general election—a contest between parties—not in intraparty contests to select nominees. By contrast, the widespread use of the direct primary election in the American states involves not only party activists, but also ordinary voters in the nomination process. Because it gives rank-and-file voters a deciding voice in nominations, the direct primary has weakened the capacity of party hierarchies to control candidate selection. Among Western democracies, the American direct primary is unique not only for the amount of popular participation it permits but also for the wide variety and extensive state-level regulation that accompanies it.

Early in the twentieth century the direct primary gradually replaced nominations by party conventions and caucuses as a part of the Progressive era reform movement, whose leaders decried bossism and corrupt party machines and believed that ordinary voters should have a direct say in selecting party candidates. The absence of real two-party competition in much of the country also furthered the spread of the direct primary. In one-party states, nomination by leaders of the dominant party was tantamount to election. As a result, instituting primary elections to nominate candidates constituted a means of ensuring meaningful popular participation in election and "an escape from one-partyism" (Key 1956, 81).

### Types of Direct Primaries

The constitutional principle of federalism permits the states wide latitude in regulating the nominating process. They can specify the circumstances under which a primary must be used and the type of primary to be used for a party's candidates to secure a slot on the general election ballot. Thus state laws regulating party nominating procedures vary significantly in terms of the degree of public disclosure of party preference required of voters (see Table 3-3).

*Open Primary Systems.* Ten states have an open primary system, in which a public declaration of party preference is not required to vote in the primaries. In nine of these states, voters receive a ballot containing the names of all parties' candidates and then decide in the secrecy of the voting booth in which party's primary they wish to vote. An even more open system is Louisiana's "nonpartisan" primary. In this system all of the candidates for each office are placed on the ballot with candidates' party affiliation listed on the ballot. If a candidate receives a majority of votes cast in the primary, he or she is elected. But if no candidate receives a majority of the primary votes, the two top finishers, irrespective of party, must face each other in the general election. Louisiana's unique primary, instituted in 1975, was a project of a Democratic governor, the roguish Edwin Edwards, and was designed to aid his party's candidates because at the time of its adoption the Republican party was weak and its candidates were not assured of even making it into the general election runoff. However, as Macolm E. Jewell, a distinguished student of state politics, observed, "the major consequence of the nonpartisan primary has been to blur differences between the parties" (1997). Thus in 1991 the losing Republican guberna-

**Table 3-3** Party Affiliation Requirements for Voting in Direct Primaries

| Closed | Semiclosed | Semiopen | Open | Nonpartisan | Blanket |
|--------|------------|----------|------|-------------|---------|
| Connecticut [a] | Alaska [d] | Alabama [h] | Hawaii | Louisiana | Formerly used |
| Delaware | Arizona [c] | Arkansas [h] | Idaho | | in Alaska and |
| Florida | California [d] | Georgia [h] | Michigan | | California. |
| Kentucky | Colorado [e] | Illinois [h] | Minnesota | | Declared un- |
| Maine | Iowa [e] | Indiana [h] | Missouri | | constitutional |
| Nebraska [a] | Kansas [c] | Mississippi [h] | Montana | | by Supreme |
| Nevada | Maryland [d] | Ohio [h] | North Dakota | | Court in 2000. |
| New Jersey | Massachusetts | South Carolina [h] | Vermont | | Washington;[i] |
| New Mexico | New Hampshire [c] | Tennessee [i] | Wisconsin | | declared un- |
| New York | North Carolina | Texas | | | constitutional |
| Oklahoma | Oregon [d] | Virginia [h] | | | by Supreme |
| Pennsylvania | Rhode Island [c] | | | | Court in 2000. |
| South Dakota | Utah [f] | | | | |
| Wyoming [b] | West Virginia [g] | | | | |

SOURCE: Federal Election Commission, 2001a.

NOTE: *Closed:* party registration required; changes permitted within a fixed time period. *Semiclosed:* unaffiliated voters permitted to vote in a party primary. *Semiopen:* voters must publicly declare their choice or party ballot at polling place on election day. *Open:* voter decides in which party primary to vote in privacy or voting booth. *Nonpartisan:* Top two primary vote-getters, regardless of party, are nominated for general election. *Blanket:* voter may vote in more than one party's primary, but one candidate per office.

[a] At present, unaffiliated voters may not participate, but parties can adopt rules to permit participation by unaffiliated voters by party rule.
[b] Same day registration permits any voter to declare or change party affiliation at the polls and reverse the change after voting.
[c] Independent voters may choose either party ballot, which registers them with that party.
[d] Unaffiliated voters may vote in primaries, if permitted by party rule.
[e] Voters may declare party affiliation at the polls, which enrolls them with party.
[f] No public record kept of independent voters' choice of party primary.
[g] Independents may vote in Republican primary only.
[h] Voter's choice of party is recorded and parties have access to the lists.
[i] No public record kept of voter choice of party primary.
[j] Washington was in litigation over the constitutionality of its blanket primary as of 2003.

torial candidate had been elected to the post as a Democrat four years earlier; and the Republican governor elected in 1995 and reelected in 1999 had been a Democrat until six weeks before his first election.

*Blanket Primary Declared Unconstitutional.* Washington pioneered the use of the "blanket primary," which was later adopted by Alaska and California. The blanket primary permitted voters to switch back and forth between parties from office to office. Under this system, it was possible for an elector to vote in the Republican primary for governor, the Democratic primary for attorney general, and then to go back and vote in the GOP primary for the state legislature.

As previously noted, California's blanket primary was declared unconstitutional by the U.S. Supreme Court in 2000 on the grounds that it violated the parties' First Amendment rights of free political association. California and Alaska changed their primary laws to bring them into conformity with the Court's decision, while Washington entered into litigation to save its law.

In eleven mainly southern states, a semiopen system is used in which voters are not made to register with a party to vote but are required to declare openly at the polls in which party's primary they wish to vote. This system is only slightly less restrictive than the open primary.

*Closed Primaries.* Sixteen states operate closed primary systems, in which voters must be registered as party affiliates to vote in partisan primaries. They are permitted to vote only in the primary of the party in which they are registered. A voter who wishes to switch party registration must do so in advance of the primary, normally twenty to thirty days before the primary. As shown in Table 3-3, fourteen states have created loopholes in their closed primary laws that permit voters either to register or change party registration on election day. Several states permit unaffiliated voters to participate in party primaries either by statute or by state party rule. These arrangements tend to make these states' primaries into virtual open primaries.

*The Effect of Open and Closed Primaries.* Open primary systems encourage crossover voting—partisans of one party voting in the primary of the other party—whereas closed primary systems largely preclude this type of behavior. Crossover voting tends to occur in the party's primary in which there is a meaningful nomination contest, and those voters who cross over typically are engaging in sincere rather than strategic crossover voting. That is, they are voting for their most preferred candidate rather than crossing over to "raid" the opposition party's primary by voting for its weakest candidate. Because sincere crossover voting can affect primary outcomes, the candidates with policy positions closest to the median voter's views are more likely to be selected in open primary systems than in closed primaries (Gerber and Morton 1994).

*Runoff Primaries.* Usually the candidate who receives the most votes (a *plurality*) in the primary gains the nomination, even if that individual receives less than a majority of total votes cast. In eleven southern and border states, plus South Dakota, a majority of the vote in the primary is required for nomination (40 percent in North Carolina). If no candidate receives a majority, then a second, or runoff, primary is held between the top two finishers in the first primary. This system was instituted in the South when the Democratic party was so dominant that winning its primary was equivalent to being elected. To ensure that the person nominated in the Democratic primary and therefore "elected" had the support of a majority of Democrats, the runoff primary was instituted. It has been found that (1) runoffs are required in about 10 percent of the races; (2) the leader in the first primary goes on to win in the runoff 70 percent of the time, although the success rate falls to 50 percent for African American candidates; and (3) women are not at a disadvantage in the runoff system (Bullock and Johnson 1992).

### Nominating Conventions and Preprimary Endorsements

Although the direct primary is the predominant method of nomination, thirteen states either permit or require conventions for the nomination process. Four states (Alabama, Georgia, South Carolina, and Virginia) permit parties to nominate either by party convention or primary. There are also seven states that by law provide for preprimary endorsements by party conventions (Colorado, Connecticut, New Mexico, New York, North Dakota, Rhode Island, and Utah). In New Mexico, New York, and Utah, primaries are not mandatory and are held if two or more candidates receive a specified share of the delegate vote (30 percent in Colorado, 25 percent in New York, and 20 percent in New Mexico). A Connecticut law that required candidates to receive 15 percent of the votes at a party endorsing convention in order to qualify for a place on the primary ballot was declared unconstitutional on the grounds that it imposed undue burdens on party members seeking to participate in the nomination process. In Utah the convention designates for each office two candidates whose names are placed on the primary ballot, although if one receives 70 percent of the convention vote that person is automatically declared the nominee. Colorado law makes it possible for a candidate to become the nominee and avoid a primary by receiving the support of 50 percent of the convention delegates. In several of the states with statutorily required preprimary conventions, candidates may also get on the ballot by securing a requisite number of signatures on a petition.

Some state party organizations use informal or extralegal preprimary endorsement in an effort to influence the selection of nominees. For example, both parties in Massachusetts and Minnesota regularly endorse candidates at state party conventions; and in New Jersey county party committees endorse gubernatorial candidates in an effort to influence who will enter and win the primary. Behind the scenes, it is not at all unusual for party leaders to assist favored and quality candidates, while discouraging others from entering the race. The various methods that party organizations may use to influence primaries demonstrate that parties can be a critical factor in the nomination process. A frequent pattern in states that by law require preprimary conventions is for nonendorsed candidates to drop out of the race. However, the trend since the 1980s has been one of declining primary victories for party-endorsed candidates. Thus, while 89 percent of endorsed candidates for governor won contested nominations between 1960 and 1980, successful endorsees dropped to 53 percent between 1982 and 1998 (Jewell and Morehouse 2001, 109–110). Endorsed gubernatorial candidates had a particularly difficult time in 1994 as six of eleven were defeated in their parties' primaries, including the endorsed Democratic candidate in Connecticut, a state with a long tradition of party organizational control over nominations.

Although preprimary endorsements appear to have declined in influence in recent years, Morehouse, in a comprehensive study, has concluded that preprimary endorsements reduce the impact of money on the outcome of primary contests for governor. Candidates who succeed in securing party convention endorsements normally become as well known as their challengers because the endorsement process requires them to engage in face-to-face meetings with about a thousand party activist delegates from across the state. The public visibility achieved in the endorsement process helps to compensate for any campaign spending advantage their challengers may have. Further offsetting the impact of campaign spending in gubernatorial primaries are the resources of time and effort that parties confer on endorsed candidates. By contrast, in states that do not use preprimary endorsing conventions, candidate spending was the overwhelming predictor of the outcome of primary contests for governor (Morehouse 1998, 121, 199).

### Consequences of the Direct Primary

Just as the Progressive reformers had hoped, the direct primary has undercut the influence and control that parties can exert over nominations. With nominations ultimately in the hands of voters, party organizations cannot unilaterally designate party nominees. Primaries therefore encourage a candidate-centered style of politics, because without parties capable of controlling nominations, candidates have an incentive and need to set up their own personal campaign organizations. As the weak showing of endorsed candidates in 1994 demonstrates, endorsement by state or local party organizations does not eliminate the need for candidates to have an effective personal organization.

Although succeeding in breaking the party organization's grip on the selection of nominees, direct primaries have never fulfilled the expectations of their reform-minded sponsors. Voter turnout is typically much lower than in general elections. In addition, the extent of vigorous competition in primaries has been limited, with incumbents either running unopposed or with only token opposition. More than 90 percent of incumbent governors and U.S. representatives win renomination. Contests occur most often within the party that has the greatest opportunity of winning the general election and when there is no incumbent seeking renomination.

### Implications of the Primary for the General Election

The outcome of the primary, of course, has implications for the general election. In addition to narrowing the field of candidates and choices available to voters, the primary results can enhance or demolish a party's general election prospects, depending on which candidates are victorious. Party leaders frequently strive to avoid contested primaries on the assumption that divisive primaries will undermine the party's prospects in the general election. However, there is no consistent pattern demonstrating that contested primaries are necessarily damaging (Kenney 1988). Indeed, nominees emerging from contested primaries tend to do better in the general election than nominees that had no primary opposition (Hogan 2003). This is partly because primary contests more often occur in the electorally stronger party. In addition, contested primaries tend to produce seasoned candidates with battle-tested organizations as well as much needed candidate publicity and momentum.

#### POLITICAL COMPETITION

Since V. O. Key's seminal work on southern state politics (1949), scholars have recognized the importance political competition can have on the nature of politics in the states. First, it is generally recognized that competition can affect state public policy, with competitive states tending to spend more on social programs than states with weak interparty competition. Second, strong interparty competition is associated with higher levels of voter turnout.

*Competition for Control of Government*

A measure of interparty competition developed by Austin Ranney constitutes a widely used and long-standing indicator of competition for control of government (1976, 59–60). The Ranney index has several different components.

*Proportion of success:* the percentage of votes won by the parties in gubernatorial elections and the percentage of seats won by the parties in each house of the legislature;

*Duration of success:* the length of time the parties controlled the governorship and the length of time the parties controlled the legislature;

*Frequency of divided control:* the proportion of time the governorship and the legislature have been divided between the two parties.

Ranney used these three dimensions to calculate his index of interparty competition, which we have updated for 1999–2003.[1] The index is actually a measure of control of government, with a score of 0 indicating complete Republican control and a score of 1 indicating absolute Democratic control. At its midpoint (.5000), control of government is evenly split between the two parties, indicating a highly competitive environment. Ranney used this index to classify states by party control, using the following categories and definitions:

.8500 or higher: one-party Democratic;
.6500 to .8499: modified one-party Democratic;
.3500 to .6499: two party;
.1500 to .3499: modified one-party Republican;
.0000 to .1499: one-party Republican.

The values of the Ranney party control index calculated for the period 1999–2002 are presented in Table 3-4, where two important patterns emerge. First, the relative strength of the parties is nearly perfectly balanced: the vast majority of the states are competitive two-party states, and the number of modified Republican states is nearly equal to the number of modified Democratic states. Historically speaking, this reflects a real change in the balance of power. Prior to the early 1990s, the Democrats consistently held a distinct advantage over the Republicans, an advantage that was largely surrendered in the 1994 elections. Second, we also see some regional patterns to the parties' successes. The Democratic party is strongest in the South, whereas the Republican party is strongest in many Mountain West states (Arizona, Idaho, Montana, Utah, and Wyoming) and Plains states (Kansas, North

---

1. We calculated the average percentage of the popular vote won by Democratic gubernatorial candidates; the average percentage of seats held by Democrats in the state senate, in all legislative sessions; the average percentage of seats held by Democrats in the state house of representatives, in all sessions; and the percentage of all gubernatorial, senate, and house terms that were controlled by the Democrats. For each state we averaged these four percentages to create an index value representing the degree of interparty competition. Because of its use of nonpartisan state legislative elections, no index value was calculated for Nebraska.

**Table 3-4** States Classified According to Degree of Interparty Competition for Control of Government, 1999–2003

| State | Ranney party control index | Ranney competition index | State | Ranney party control index | Ranney competition index |
|---|---|---|---|---|---|
| | | *Modified one-party Democratic* | | | |
| Hawaii | 0.735 | 0.765 | West Virginia | 0.689 | 0.811 |
| Mississippi | 0.716 | 0.784 | Alabama | 0.684 | 0.816 |
| Maryland | 0.702 | 0.798 | California | 0.683 | 0.818 |
| Rhode Island | 0.700 | 0.800 | Arkansas | 0.657 | 0.843 |
| Massachusetts | 0.694 | 0.806 | | | |
| | | *Two-party competition* | | | |
| Kentucky | 0.629 | 0.871 | Oregon | 0.461 | 0.961 |
| North Carolina | 0.619 | 0.881 | Minnesota | 0.452 | 0.952 |
| New Mexico | 0.617 | 0.883 | Iowa | 0.435 | 0.935 |
| Georgia | 0.599 | 0.901 | New York | 0.435 | 0.935 |
| Vermont | 0.585 | 0.915 | South Carolina | 0.435 | 0.935 |
| Louisiana | 0.577 | 0.923 | Wisconsin | 0.424 | 0.924 |
| Tennessee | 0.576 | 0.924 | Colorado | 0.417 | 0.917 |
| Oklahoma | 0.570 | 0.930 | Nevada | 0.415 | 0.915 |
| Connecticut | 0.567 | 0.933 | Michigan | 0.389 | 0.889 |
| Washington | 0.557 | 0.943 | Virginia | 0.385 | 0.885 |
| Delaware | 0.551 | 0.949 | Texas | 0.378 | 0.878 |
| Maine | 0.537 | 0.963 | Nebraska | 0.365 | 0.865 |
| Missouri | 0.532 | 0.968 | New Hampshire | 0.358 | 0.858 |
| Illinois | 0.519 | 0.981 | Pennsylvania | 0.356 | 0.856 |
| Indiana | 0.514 | 0.986 | North Dakota | 0.354 | 0.854 |
| New Jersey | 0.479 | 0.979 | | | |
| | | *Modified one-party Republican* | | | |
| Arizona | 0.348 | 0.848 | Wyoming | 0.284 | 0.784 |
| Alaska | 0.340 | 0.840 | Kansas | 0.284 | 0.784 |
| Montana | 0.314 | 0.814 | Utah | 0.249 | 0.749 |
| Florida | 0.302 | 0.802 | South Dakota | 0.247 | 0.747 |
| Ohio | 0.289 | 0.789 | Idaho | 0.167 | 0.667 |
| Fifty-state average | 0.483 | 0.871 | | | |

SOURCE: Calculated by the authors.

Dakota, and South Dakota). This regional pattern, however, is not nearly as strong as it has been in the past.

The Ranney index can be recalculated to indicate the level of competition between the parties for control of government, rather than the degree of Democratic or Republican control.[2] Consider the most competitive states in Table 3-4, Illinois and Indiana, which have Ranney party control index values of .519 and .514, respectively. As you move away from Illinois and Indiana, in both directions, the states are less and less competitive. For instance, even though Vermont and Nevada display different partisan leanings, their party control values (.585 and .415, respectively) make

2. In the professional literature, this is called the *folded Ranney index.*

them equally competitive: Vermont is .085 units above and Nevada is .085 units below the point of perfect competition, .500.

The Ranney competition index is derived from the original Ranney index and represents how close the states are to perfect competition between the parties for control of government.[3] The Ranney competition index ranges from .500 (no competition) to 1.000 (perfect competition). The data in Table 3-4 indicate that the least competitive states are located in the South and, to some degree, in the Mountain West region. Although the states in the Midwest and Northeast have traditionally been the most competitive, the data in Table 3-4 do not show a clear regional pattern among the most competitive states.

While the classifications in Table 3-4 are useful, it is important to realize the limitations of such an index. First, the Ranney index is based exclusively on state offices and does not reflect the strength of the parties at other levels. For instance, until the 1992 election, the Democratic presidential ticket had not won more than a single southern state (Georgia in 1980) since 1976, when a southerner, Jimmy Carter, headed the ticket. This is exactly the opposite of what would be expected, based on the degree of Democratic party strength as measured by the Ranney index. Also, the significant gains made by Republicans in U.S. House and Senate elections in the South in recent years are not reflected in the Ranney index.

Second, the Ranney index gives more weight to some state offices than to others. The way the index is constructed, the state legislature is given much more weight than the governorship. This may also result in underestimating the strength of the Republican party in southern states, because many of the party's gains have been made in the governorships. It is also worth noting that the Ranney index does not include other state-wide offices, such as lieutenant governor (where separately elected), attorney general, state auditor, and state treasurer. Not all states elect these offices, but most of them do.

Third, this measure of interparty competition is "a snapshot of an object moving in time and hence does not always capture change that may be occurring when the measurement is taken" (Ranney 1976, 60–61).

Although interparty competition is a long-term phenomenon and, as such, should be relatively stable, significant change in the nature of competition for control of government has taken place. The changes from 1948 to 2002 in the mean level of Democratic control, as measured in Table 3-4, and the mean level of interparty competition, based on the Ranney competition index, are presented in Table 3-5. In these two measures there are signs of both stability and change. First, the mean score of Democratic control in the Ranney index tilted toward the Democratic side throughout most of the period, only to tip ever so slightly Republican since 1995. Second, the Democratic party grew in strength from 1948 to 1980 and has steadily lost strength since then. Much of the decline in Democratic strength in the

---

3. The formula for the Ranney competition index is 1 - |(.5 - Ranney)|. This index measures how close a state's level of interparty competition is to "perfect" competition on the Ranney index.

**Table 3-5** Changes in the Ranney Index of Interparty Competition, 1948–2002

|  | 1948–1960 | 1962–1973 | 1974–1980 | 1981–1988 | 1989–1994 | 1995–1998 | 1999–2003 |
|---|---|---|---|---|---|---|---|
| Mean level of Democratic control (Range: 0–1) | 0.56 | 0.58 | 0.64 | 0.60 | 0.55 | 0.49 | 0.49 |
| Mean level of interparty competition (Range: 0.5–1) | 0.78 | 0.83 | 0.81 | 0.84 | 0.87 | 0.86 | 0.87 |

SOURCES  Compiled from data in Patterson and Caldeira 1984; Bibby et al. 1990; Bibby and Holbrook 1996, 1999; and Table 3-4, this volume.

1980s and 1990s has occurred in southern states, where Republicans have made significant inroads. Third, in terms of the level of competition for control of government, the least competitive period was from 1948 to 1960, and the most competitive period has occurred from 1995 onward. Again, in large part, Republican gains in southern states account for the increase in competition in recent years.

Many of the recent changes in party control and interparty competition shown in Table 3-5 reflect the impact of the 1994 elections. Prior to the 1994 elections, the Democrats controlled 25 state legislatures and the Republicans controlled 8; following the 1994 elections the Democrats controlled 18 legislatures and the Republicans controlled 19. A similar change occurred in governorships: The Democrats went into the 1994 election with a 29-to-19 advantage in governorships and came out with 19 governorships to the Republicans' 30. Thus the 1994 elections represent a true reversal of fortunes for the two major parties. The picture has not changed much since: Following the 2002 elections, the Republicans controlled 21 state legislatures to the Democrats' 16, and 26 governorships to the Democrats' 24.

*Electoral Competition*

One of the limitations of the Ranney index is that because it is based on control of government, it is not an ideal measure of electoral competition. This is especially disconcerting because many of the hypotheses concerning the effect of competition on state politics are about how electoral competition affects state politics and policy making. To measure electoral competition in the states more accurately, an index based on district-level state legislative election outcomes from 1982 to 1986 has been developed by Holbrook and Van Dunk (1993).[4] The crucial difference between this index and the Ranney index is that the Holbrook–Van Dunk index is

---

4. The formula for the index is Competition = 1 - [(average margin of victory + average winning percentage + percentage uncontested + percentage safe seats)/4]. The original index is based on district-level state legislative election outcomes from 1982 to 1986 and does not include multimember free-for-all districts.

based entirely on election outcomes, whereas the Ranney index is based primarily on partisan control of state government.

Although there is wide variation in the level of *electoral* competition in the states, there is, to some extent, a familiar regional pattern: Most of the least competitive states are from the South, and there is no clear regional pattern among the most competitive states. This regional pattern bears some resemblance to the Ranney competition index. While the two are conceptually distinct, the relationship between the Ranney competition index from the late 1980s and the original Holbrook–Van Dunk index is moderately strong ($r = .68$; Bibby and Holbrook 1996).

*Consequences of Competition.* As mentioned earlier, it is widely expected that competition has an influence on public policy and voter turnout. Specifically, it is expected that competitive states will produce more liberal public policies and have higher rates of voter turnout than noncompetitive states. To a large extent, the data bear out these propositions, especially for the Holbrook–Van Dunk index (Holbrook and Van Dunk 1993).

Recent research on the impact of competition has blended the concepts of party control and electoral competition. Barrilleaux, Holbrook, and Langer (2002) examined welfare spending in the states from 1973 to 1992 and found that the most important role for electoral competition may not be its direct effect on public policy but the manner in which it conditions the impact of party control of the legislature. Barrilleaux, Holbrook, and Langer (2002) found that in states with low levels of electoral competition, party control of the legislature had relatively little impact on welfare spending. However, in states with a high level of electoral competition there were sizeable differences in welfare spending between Republican-controlled states and states where the Democrats controlled the legislature.

*Determinants of Competition.* As we pointed out earlier, competition follows a regional pattern; on both measures of competition, southern states are distinctly less competitive than the rest of the country. To a large extent, this demonstrates the long-lasting effect of the Civil War and Reconstruction on southern politics.

Beyond the effects of region, several other variables help explain state differences in competition. First, states with diverse populations have more competitive political systems than states with homogeneous populations (Barrilleaux 1986; Patterson and Caldeira 1984). Second, some states have lower levels of competition because they have higher levels of partisan bias in the electorate. If a state's electorate is overwhelmingly Democratic, then it makes sense that the Democrats would face little competition at the polls and would be able to establish control of state government (Barrilleaux 1986; Holbrook, Mangum, and Garand 1994). Finally, incumbency and the use of multimember districts have been found to suppress electoral competition, and large (in terms of population) legislative districts have been found to enhance electoral competition (Holbrook, Mangum, and Garand 1994; Van Dunk and Weber 1997). Note that both incumbency and district size can be manipulated to increase competition. Term limits, of course, could minimize the effect of incumbency, and reducing the size of the legislative body would result in larger electoral districts.

POLITICAL PARTICIPATION

Political participation in the United States takes many different forms: contributing to campaigns; attending rallies or protest events; writing letters to elected representatives; working for a campaign or community cause; attending town meetings or school board meetings; and, of course, voting in elections. Although voting is the most commonly practiced form of political participation, the degree to which citizens across the states take advantage of their right to vote varies widely.

*Patterns of Turnout across the States*

For a variety of reasons some people decide not to take advantage of their right to vote in elections. Although individual attributes have a lot to do with whether or not a person votes, turnout rates can also be affected by the type of election being held and by certain aspects of the state political environment. The traditional way of measuring turnout is to take the total number of votes cast as a percentage of the voting-age population in the state. In Table 3-6 this method is used to calculate the level of turnout in all states for presidential, gubernatorial, and congressional elections, 1997–2002. The first column in Table 3-6 presents the average rate of turnout across all four types of elections for each state. Once again, we see the emergence of a regional pattern: seven out of the ten lowest turnout states are southern or border states. At the other end of the scale we do not find a clear regional pattern, but most of the highest turnout states are small, sparsely populated states.

Besides differences across the states, there are substantial differences in turnout in different types of elections. The best way to examine differences across offices is to look at individual years, since most gubernatorial elections are held at the midterm when turnout is typically lower. As the data in Table 3-7 illustrate, turnout tends to be highest (controlling for year) in gubernatorial and presidential elections, then in U.S. Senate elections, and lowest in U.S. House elections. Table 3-7 can also be used to illustrate an important point: Turnout is always higher in presidential election years. Turnout was roughly 12 to 15 percentage points higher for all offices in the presidential years than in the midterm election years. This is because presidential elections are high-visibility events that generate a lot of interest and bring out a lot of voters who do not normally turn out to vote in elections for lower offices during midterm election years.

The turnout data in Tables 3-6 and 3-7 need to be interpreted with some caution. Because turnout is expressed as a percentage of the voting-age population, the numbers are probably different from what they would have been if turnout had been expressed as a percentage of the eligible voting-age electorate. The voting-age population of a state includes significant numbers of people who are not eligible to vote because they are not citizens or are institutionalized in correctional or mental health facilities.

Recent research by Michael McDonald (2002) bears directly on this issue. Mc-Donald calculates a measure of the voting-*eligible* electorate by accounting for the

**Table 3-6** Average Rates of Voter Turnout in the States, by Office, 1997–2002

| State | Total | President | Governor | U.S. Senate | U.S. House |
|---|---|---|---|---|---|
| Minnesota | 64.4 | 68.8 | 61.3 | 65.4 | 62.1 |
| Montana | 58.0 | 61.5 | 61.4 | 55.2 | 53.9 |
| Maine | 57.3 | 67.3 | 48.7 | 59.5 | 53.9 |
| Alaska | 57.2 | 66.4 | 52.9 | 52.9 | 56.5 |
| Vermont | 56.6 | 64.0 | 54.2 | 55.2 | 52.9 |
| North Dakota | 56.3 | 60.4 | 60.7 | 52.6 | 51.5 |
| South Dakota | 55.9 | 58.2 | 54.5 | 55.0 | 55.7 |
| Wyoming | 55.2 | 61.0 | 51.0 | 55.5 | 53.4 |
| Wisconsin | 54.0 | 66.1 | 45.2 | 55.0 | 49.5 |
| Missouri | 52.2 | 57.5 | 57.2 | 47.4 | 46.8 |
| Oregon | 51.3 | 60.6 | 47.2 | 47.5 | 49.9 |
| New Hampshire | 50.5 | 62.5 | 48.9 | 42.3 | 48.5 |
| Washington | 50.4 | 56.9 | 56.5 | 56.4 | 31.8 |
| Delaware | 50.4 | 56.3 | 55.6 | 48.0 | 41.6 |
| Iowa | 50.3 | 60.8 | 45.8 | 45.6 | 49.1 |
| Michigan | 49.4 | 57.5 | 43.2 | 50.3 | 46.5 |
| Massachusetts | 48.0 | 56.9 | 43.9 | 49.1 | 42.1 |
| Colorado | 48.0 | 56.8 | 44.2 | 44.4 | 46.4 |
| Nebraska | 47.9 | 56.5 | 41.9 | 47.7 | 45.7 |
| Connecticut | 47.6 | 58.4 | 41.7 | 45.8 | 44.3 |
| Utah | 47.2 | 52.6 | 52.0 | 43.6 | 40.6 |
| Rhode Island | 47.2 | 54.3 | 42.4 | 47.4 | 44.5 |
| Idaho | 46.9 | 54.5 | 43.4 | 43.1 | 46.5 |
| Ohio | 46.6 | 55.8 | 39.7 | 46.7 | 44.1 |
| Maryland | 45.6 | 51.6 | 42.4 | 44.5 | 43.8 |
| Indiana | 45.0 | 49.4 | 49.0 | 42.1 | 39.5 |
| Kansas | 44.3 | 54.1 | 40.5 | 38.6 | 44.1 |
| North Carolina | 44.3 | 50.2 | 50.8 | 36.8 | 39.4 |
| Illinois | 43.1 | 52.8 | 39.1 | 39.0 | 41.4 |
| Pennsylvania | 42.9 | 53.7 | 36.4 | 42.1 | 39.5 |
| Hawaii | 42.7 | 40.5 | 46.4 | 41.7 | 42.1 |
| Alabama | 42.6 | 50.0 | 40.8 | 40.2 | 39.5 |
| New Mexico | 42.2 | 47.4 | 39.0 | 42.3 | 40.2 |
| New Jersey | 41.8 | 51.0 | 37.6 | 41.6 | 37.0 |
| Oklahoma | 41.0 | 48.8 | 38.4 | 37.7 | 39.1 |
| Mississippi | 40.6 | 48.6 | 37.9 | 39.6 | 36.1 |
| Florida | 40.2 | 50.6 | 39.5 | 42.0 | 28.6 |
| West Virginia | 40.1 | 45.8 | 45.8 | 37.2 | 31.7 |
| New York | 40.0 | 49.4 | 34.8 | 41.7 | 34.2 |
| Virginia | 39.7 | 52.1 | 34.7 | 39.9 | 32.3 |
| Louisiana | 39.6 | 54.2 | 41.1 | 35.1 | 27.7 |
| Arkansas | 39.5 | 47.8 | 39.2 | 39.0 | 31.9 |
| South Carolina | 39.2 | 46.4 | 36.8 | 36.7 | 36.9 |
| Tennessee | 39.1 | 49.2 | 31.2 | 42.0 | 33.9 |
| California | 38.6 | 44.1 | 34.9 | 38.9 | 36.3 |
| Nevada | 37.8 | 43.8 | 33.5 | 38.2 | 35.7 |
| Kentucky | 37.1 | 51.6 | 19.4 | 37.3 | 40.2 |
| Georgia | 36.3 | 44.1 | 32.3 | 35.1 | 33.7 |
| Texas | 35.6 | 43.1 | 29.6 | 37.6 | 32.1 |
| Arizona | 35.1 | 42.3 | 30.8 | 33.6 | 33.6 |
| Fifty-state average | 46.1 | 53.9 | 43.5 | 44.6 | 42.2 |

SOURCE: Calculated from data in various sources, including data made available by the Center for the Study of the American Electorate.

**Table 3-7** Mean Percentage of Voter Turnout in the States, by Year and Office, 1989–2002

| Year | President | Governor | U.S. Senate | U.S. House |
|---|---|---|---|---|
| 1990 | — | 40.9 | 38.6 | 37.8 |
| 1992 | 58.3 | 59.2 | 55.2 | 54.3 |
| 1994 | — | 41.4 | 41.8 | 40.2 |
| 1996 | 50.8 | 52.6 | 51.5 | 48.9 |
| 1998 | — | 39.3 | 38.8 | 35.6 |
| 2000 | 53.9 | 55.9 | 52.0 | 50.5 |
| 2002 | — | 43.1 | 42.2 | 40.4 |
| Presidential year increase | 14.5 | 12.6 | 12.2 | |

SOURCE: Calculated from Table 3-6, this volume, and from Bibby and Holbrook 1996, 1999.

NOTE: The turnout rates for the 1989 and 1991 gubernatorial elections are included in the 1990 figure, the rates for the 1993 and 1995 gubernatorial elections are included in the 1994 figure, the turnout rates for the 1997 and 1999 gubernatorial elections are included in the 1998 figure, and the turnout rates for the 2001 gubernatorial elections are included in the 2002 figure.

number of noncitizens and ineligible felons living in the states, neither of which is reflected in the standard voting-age population measure of turnout. McDonald finds that reliance on the voting-age population tends to underestimate the true turnout rate in the states, sometimes by an especially large margin in states with large noncitizen populations and with prohibitions against convicted felons voting. For instance, California and Florida, both of which have large noncitizen populations and prohibit voting on the part of convicted felons, had voting-eligible population turnout rates that were twelve and ten percentage points higher, respectively, than their voting-age population turnout rates. Still, while some important differences emerge as a result of using the voting-eligible population, the *relative* turnout rate among the states is fairly similar across both measures. In the 2000 presidential election, for example, the correlation between the voting-age and voting-eligible measures of turnout was .94.[5]

*What Determines Turnout?*

Many factors help explain differences in voter turnout across states and individuals. For the individual voter, a variety of important demographic and attitudinal variables are related to turnout (Rosenstone and Hansen 1993; Wolfinger and Rosenstone 1980). For example, middle-aged people with high levels of income and education have a high probability of voting. People with a strong sense of political efficacy and strong ties to political parties are also very likely to vote. Many of these variables also help explain the pattern of turnout in the states. Socioeconomic differences across the states, for instance, are strongly related to differences in voter turnout; wealthy states and states with well-educated citizens generally have the highest rates of voter turnout (Kim, Petrocik, and Enokson 1975).

But state politics also have an effect on voter turnout. First, turnout is higher in states with high levels of electoral competition. In noncompetitive environments the elections are less likely to generate much interest and voters are less likely to vote. The

5. Based on data taken from McDonald 2002.

correlation between electoral competition and overall voter turnout ($r = .36$) demonstrates the strength of this relationship. Turnout can also be influenced by the level of campaign spending in particular races (Jackson 1997; Patterson and Caldeira 1983). As more money is spent in a campaign, voters are provided with more information about the candidates, which increases the likelihood that they will vote.

Another important determinant of turnout is the stringency of state voter registration laws (Wolfinger and Rosenstone 1980). In states in which it is difficult for voters to register or to stay registered, fewer people register, and voter turnout tends to be lower than it would be if registration laws made it easier to register. One example of such a law is the closing date for registration, or the number of days before the election that one must register to vote. The closing date ranges from zero (election day registration or, in North Dakota, no voter registration) to thirty or more days before the election. The difference in overall turnout (Table 3-5) between states with a closing date of ten or fewer days before the election and states with a closing date of thirty or more days before the election illustrates the effect registration laws can have: The average overall rate of turnout in the former is 54.3 percent, and the average turnout in the latter is 43.5 percent.

The 1993 National Voter Registration Act (NVRA) represents an attempt on the part of the national government to ease the burden of voter registration in the states by placing limits on purging of nonvoters, requiring states to register voters or renew voter registration as part of the driver's license application and renewal process, to make mail-in registration available, and to make voter registration materials available at other state agency (primarily welfare and social services) offices. It is difficult to judge the full impact of the NVRA, but early reports are not encouraging. Martinez and Hill (1999) found that the NVRA had little discernible impact on overall state turnout rates and may even have contributed to slightly higher class and racial inequalities in the active electorate. In a similar vein, Wolfinger and Hoffman (2001) found the motor voter component of the law made registration easier for those who might already be inclined to register and to vote, whereas the agency registration component tended to be used by those who were not inclined to vote. More to the point, Wolfinger and Hoffman found that those who registered to vote at an agency site were less likely to vote than those who registered at a motor voter site, and those who registered at a motor voter site were less likely to vote than those who registered via more traditional means.

### Class Bias in Turnout

Recent research on voter turnout has focused on the role of class bias in shaping public policies for the poor (Hill and Leighley 1992; Hill, Leighley, and Hinton-Anderson 1995). Class bias is defined in this research as the extent of overrepresentation (or underrepresentation) of higher (or lower) socioeconomic status voters in the electorate. The results of this research indicate that there is wide variation in the extent of class bias in state electorates and this bias is related to the provision of policies for the poor. Specifically, states in which the level of upper-class bias is relatively low (the poor are better represented in the electorate) tend to provide more generous welfare benefits than do states in which the level turnout bias is more severe. This research has also found that class bias tends to be most extreme in poor, racially diverse states (Hill and Leighley 1994). The findings of Martinez and Hill (1999) and Wolfinger and Hoffman (2001) suggest that class bias might actually increase as a result of government attempts to improve the position of low income voters via the NVRA.

## PARTY ADAPTABILITY AND DURABILITY IN AN ERA OF CANDIDATE-CENTERED POLITICS

The theme of change runs consistently through this survey of state political parties and elections. Since the 1960s and 1970s, state party organizations have developed into increasingly professional service agencies assisting candidates and local parties. State parties have also come into the orbit of the national party organizations, which, through massive transfers of funds plus supply of personnel and expertise, now use the state parties to implement national campaign strategies. This nationalization of the parties, with its heightened national–state party integration, has brought organizational benefits to the state parties but also some loss of traditional state party autonomy.

Within the states, autonomous state legislative campaign committees have emerged as major party support agencies for legislative candidates. Campaign costs have escalated as candidates have sought to take advantage of the latest techniques and technologies. State regulation of campaign finance has tightened, and an increasing number of states provide some form of public financing of elections. Candidates now rely primarily on their own personal campaign organizations rather than the party machinery. State electoral politics thus focuses more and more on the candidate rather than the party.

Parties, however, remain a major force in state electoral politics. Interparty competition has intensified since the 1970s, as intense battles rage for control of legislative chambers and governorships. On election day partisanship continues to be a major determinant of voter choice. In the face of an increasingly candidate-centered style of politics, both state central committees and legislative campaign committees have become more sophisticated and capable of providing an array of services to their clienteles. They have also adapted to the growth of PACs by soliciting and channeling this special interest money. The story of state parties since World War II is thus an impressive record of adaptability and durability. Although state parties neither control nominations nor run campaigns, they nevertheless remain the principal agencies for making nominations, contesting elections, recruiting leaders, and providing a link between citizens and their government.

## REFERENCES

Aldrich, John H. 2000. "Southern Parties in State and Nation." *Journal of Politics* 62: 643–670.
———. 1995. *Why Parties? The Origin and Transformation of Party Politics in America.* Chicago: University of Chicago Press.

Appleton, Andrew M., and Daniel S. Ward, eds. 1997. *State Party Profiles: A 50 State Guide to Development, Organization, and Resources.* Washington, D.C.: CQ Press.

*Ballot Access News.* 2002. February.

Barrilleaux, Charles. 1986. "A Dynamic Model of Partisan Competition in the American States." *American Journal of Political Science* 30: 822–840.

Barrilleaux, Charles, Thomas Holbrook, and Laura Langer. 2002. "Electoral Competition, Legislative Balance, and State Welfare Policy." *American Journal of Political Science* 46: 415–427.

Berry, Jeffrey, and Deborah Schildkraut. 1998. "Citizen Groups, Political Parties, and Electoral Coalitions." In *Social Movements and American Political Institutions,* edited by Anne N. Costain and Andrew S. McFarland. Lanham, Md.: Rowman and Littlefield, 136–158.

Bibby, John F., and Thomas M. Holbrook. 1999. "Parties and Elections." In *Politics in the American States,* 7th ed., edited by Virginia Gray, Russell L. Hanson, and Herbert Jacob. Washington, D.C.: CQ Press, 66–112.

———. 1996. "Parties and Elections." In *Politics in the American States,* 6th ed., edited by Virginia Gray and Herbert Jacob. Washington, D.C.: CQ Press, 78–121.

Bibby, John F., Cornelius P. Cotter, James L. Gibson, and Robert J. Huckshorn. 1990. "Parties in State Politics." In *Politics in the American States,* 5th ed., edited by Virginia Gray, Herbert Jacob, and Robert B. Albritton. Glenview, Ill.: Scott, Foresman.

Bruce, John M., John A. Clark, and John H. Kessel. 1991. "Advocacy Politics in Presidential Parties." *American Political Science Review* 85: 1089–1105.

Bullock, Charles S., III, and Loch K. Johnson. 1992. *Runoff Elections in the United States.* Chapel Hill: University of North Carolina Press.

Coleman, John J. 1996. "Party Organizational Strength and Public Support for Parties." *American Journal of Political Science* 40: 805–824.

Cotter, Cornelius P., and Bernard Hennessy. 1964. *Politics without Power: National Party Committees.* New York: Atherton.

Cotter, Cornelius P., James L. Gibson, John F. Bibby, and Robert J. Huckshorn. 1984. *Party Organizations in American Politics.* New York: Praeger.

Council of State Governments. 2000. *The Book of the States, 2000–2001.* Lexington, Ky.: Council of State Governments.

Ehrenhalt, Alan. 1989. "How a Party of Enthusiasts Keeps Its Hammerlock on a State Legislature." *Governing,* June, 28–33.

Epstein, Leon D. 1986. *Political Parties in the American Mold.* Madison: University of Wisconsin Press.

Federal Election Commission. 2001a. "Party Affiliation and Primary Voting 2000." Washington, D.C.: Federal Election Commission. Accessed at http:www.fec.gov/votregis/primaryvoting.htm.

———. 2001b. "Party Fund-Raising Escalates." Washington, D.C.: Federal Election Commission. January 12 press release.

Fiorina, Morris P. 1999. " Extreme Voice: A Dark Side of Civic Engagement." In *Civic Engagement in America,* edited by Theda Skopol and Morris P. Fiorina. Washington, D.C.: Brooking Institution, 395–425.

Francia, Peter L., and Paul S. Herrnson. 2001. "The Battle for the Statehouse: Party Campaigning in State Legislative Politics." Paper presented at the Conference on the State of the Parties, 2000 and Beyond, Ray C. Bliss Institute of Applied Politics, University of Akron, Akron, Ohio, October 17–19.

Gerber, Elisabeth, and Rebecca B. Morton. 1994. "Primary Elections Laws and the Nomination of Congressional Candidates." Paper presented at the annual meeting of the American Political Science Association, New York, September 1–4.

Gierzynski, Anthony, and David A. Breaux. 1998. "The Financing Role of the Parties." In *Campaign Finance in State Legislative Elections,* edited by Joel A. Thompson and Gary F. Moncrief. Washington, D.C.: CQ Press, 185–206.

———. 1992. *Legislative Party Campaign Committees in the American States.* Lexington: University of Kentucky Press.

Green, John C., James L. Guth, and Clyde Wilcox. 1999. "Less than Conquerors: The Christian Right in State Republican Parties." In *Social Movements,* edited by Costain and McFarland, 117–135.

Hill, Kim, and Jan Leighley. 1994. "Mobilizing Institutions and Class Representation in the U.S. State Electorates." *Political Research Quarterly* 47: 137–150.

———. 1992. "The Policy Consequences of Class Bias in State Electorates." *American Journal of Political Science* 36: 351–365.

Hill, Kim, Jan Leighley, and Angela Hinton-Anderson. 1995. "Lower-Class Mobilization and Policy Linkage in the U.S. States." *American Journal of Political Science* 39: 75–86.

Hogan, Robert E. 2003. "The Effects of Primary Divisiveness on General Election Outcomes." *American Political Research* 31: 27–47.

Holbrook, Thomas M., and Emily Van Dunk. 1993. "Electoral Competition in the American States." *American Political Science Review* 87: 955–962.

Holbrook, Thomas M., Maurice Mangum, and James Garand. 1994. "Sources of Electoral Competition in the American States." Paper presented at the annual meeting of the American Political Science Association, New York, September 1–4.

Jackson, Robert. 1997. "The Mobilization of the U.S. State Electorates in the 1988 and 1990 Elections." *Journal of Politics* 59: 520–537.

Jewell, Malcolm E. 1997. Personal correspondence.

Jewell, Malcolm E., and Sarah M. Morehouse. 2001. *Political Parties and Elections in American States,* 4th ed. Washington, D.C.: CQ Press.

Jones, Ruth S. 1984. "Financing State Elections." In *Money and Politics in the United States,* edited by Michael J. Malbin. Washington, D.C.: American Enterprise Institute.

Kenney, Patrick J. 1988. "Sorting out the Effects of Primary Divisiveness in Congressional and Senatorial Elections." *Western Political Quarterly* 41: 756–777.

Key, V. O., Jr. 1956. *American State Politics: An Introduction.* New York: Knopf.

———. 1949. *Southern Politics in State and Nation.* New York: Knopf.

Kim, Jae-on, John R. Petrocik, and Stephen Enokson. 1975. "Voter Turnout among the American States: Systemic and Individual Components." *American Political Science Review* 69: 107–123.

Kolodny, Robin. 2000. "Electoral Partnerships: Political Consultants and Political Parties." In *Campaign Warriors: Political Consultants in Elections,* edited by James A. Thurber and Candice J. Nelson. Washington, D.C.: Brookings Institution, 110–132.

LaRaja, Ray. 2001. "State Parties and Soft Money: How Much Party Building?" Paper presented at the Conference on the State of the Parties, 2000 and Beyond, Ray C. Bliss Institute of Applied Politics, University of Akron, Akron, Ohio, October 17–19.

Magleby, David B., ed. 2003. *The Other Campaign: Soft Money and Issue Advocacy in the 2000 Congressional Elections.* Lanham, Md.: Roman and Littlefield.

Malbin, Michael J., and Thomas L. Gais. 1998. *The Day after Reform: Sobering Campaign Finance Lessons from the American States.* Albany: Rockefeller Institute Press.

Martinez, Michael D., and David Hill. 1999. "Did Motor Voter Work?" *American Politics Quarterly.* 27: 296–315.

Mayhew, David R. 1986. *Placing Parties in American Politics.* Princeton: Princeton University Press.

McDonald, Michael P. 2002. "The Turnout Rate Among Eligible Voters in the States, 1980–2000." *State Politics and Policy Quarterly* 2: 199–212.

Morehouse, Sarah McCally. 2000. "State Parties: Independent Partners—The Money Relationship." Paper presented at the annual meeting of the American Political Science Association, Washington, D.C., August 31–September 3.

———. 1998. *The Governor as Party Leader: Campaigning and Governing.* Ann Arbor: University of Michigan Press.

Nagourney, Adam, and David Barstow. 2000. "GOP's Depth Outdid Gore's Team in Florida." *New York Times* (National Edition), December 22, A1, A22.

Patterson, Samuel, and Gregory Caldeira. 1984. "Etiology of Partisan Competition." *American Political Science Review* 78: 691–707.

———. 1983. "Getting out the Vote: Participation in Gubernatorial Elections." *American Political Science Review* 77: 675–689.

Ranney, Austin. 1976. "Parties in State Politics." In *Politics in the American States: A Comparative Analysis,* 3d ed., edited by Herbert Jacob and Kenneth Vines. Boston: Little, Brown.

Reichley, A. James. 1992. *The Life of the Parties: A History of American Political Parties.* New York: Free Press.

Republican National Committee. 2000. *Chairman's Report.* Washington, D.C.

Rosenstone, Steven J., and John Mark Hansen. 1993. *Mobilization, Participation, and Democracy in America.* New York: Macmillan.

Shafer, Byron E. 1996. "The United States." In *Postwar Politics in the G-7: Order and Eras in Comparative Perspective,* edited by Byron E. Shafer. Madison: University of Wisconsin Press, 12–46.

Sorauf, Frank J. 1992. *Inside Campaign Finance: Myths and Realities.* New Haven, Conn.: Yale University Press.

Stone, Peter H. 2002. "Hard Questions About Soft-Money Groups." *National Journal,* December 21, 36–38.

Traugott, Michael W. 2003. "The 2000 Michigan Senate Race." In *The Other Campaign: Soft Money and Issue Advocacy in 2000 Congressional Elections,* edited by David B. Magleby. Lanham, Md.: Roman and Littlefield, 97–110.

Van Dunk, Emily, and Ronald Weber. 1997. "Constituency-Level Competition in the U.S. States: A Pooled Analysis." *Legislative Studies Quarterly* 22: 141–159.

Wilcox, Clyde. 2000. *Onward Christian Soldiers: The Religious Right in American Politics,* 2d ed. Boulder, Colo.: Westview Press.

Winger, Richard. 1997. "Institutional Obstacles to a Multiparty System." In *Multiparty Politics in America,* edited by Paul S. Herrnson and John C. Green. Lanham, Md.: Rowman and Littlefield, 159–172.

Wolfinger, Raymond E., and Jonathon Hoffman. 2001. "Registering and Voting with Motor Voter." *PS* 34: 85–92.

Wolfinger, Raymond E., and Steven J. Rosenstone. 1980. *Who Votes?* New Haven, Conn: Yale University Press.

## SUGGESTED READINGS

Aldrich, John H. "Southern Parties in State and Nation." *Journal of Politics* 62 (2000): 643–670. Contains the results of a survey showing that state party organizational strength increased in the 1980s and 1990s and that the southern parties were the strongest organizationally.

Cotter, Cornelius P., James L. Gibson, John F. Bibby, and Robert J. Huckshorn. *Party Organizations in American Politics.* New York: Praeger, 1984. An analysis of the status, activities, and impact of state and local parties, based on a nationwide survey.

Esptein, Leon D. *Political Parties in the American Mold.* Madison: University of Wisconsin Press, 1986. A comprehensive treatise on American parties by a distinguished scholar, with significant insights concerning state parties in Chapters 5 and 6.

Mayhew, David R. *Placing Parties in American Politics.* Princeton, N.J.: Princeton University Press, 1986. An exhaustive survey of party organization in each of the fifty states, with an analysis of the factors influencing organizational development.

Morehouse, Sarah M., and Malcolm E. Jewell. *State Politics, Parties, and Policy.* Lanham, Md.: Roman and Littlefield, 2003. An up-to-date survey of state politics by leading authorities in the field.

# CHAPTER 4

*Interest Groups in the States*

CLIVE S. THOMAS AND
RONALD J. HREBENAR

Few aspects of American politics, including state politics, generate a more negative re-action from the public than do interest groups and the lobbyists who represent them. Yet Americans join interest groups by the tens of millions.

Much of this skepticism is based on a belief that "special" interests work to benefit certain segments of society at the expense of others, that they often undermine democracy, and that they use questionable, sometimes illegal, methods to achieve their goals. Even though the abuses of interest groups are probably far less than gener-ally believed, abuses of the past, such as that by the railroads in the late nineteenth and early twentieth centuries and scandals involving lobbyists in Arizona and South Car-olina in the early 1990s, are evidence to support this negative view. On the other hand, as one of the most efficient ways to aggregate the views or needs—the interests—of various segments of society and represent these positions to government, interest groups are indispensable to the democratic process in the American states. This is re-flected in the more positive attitude that state public officials, elected and appointed, have toward interest groups. In an attempt to deal with this paradox, that groups are both a necessity to democracy but can seriously undermine it, all states regulate the activities of interest groups.

Largely due to their indispensability to public officials and the public alike, from the time of the original thirteen states to the fifty states of today, interest groups have al-ways been a prominent and often the dominant force in state politics. In fact, in con-trast to national politics, which reflects the diverse socio-economic structure of the na-tion, the less diversified socio-economic systems in many states meant that interest groups were often the dominant force in their state. For instance, as late as the 1960s Montana was captive to the Anaconda Copper Company and Delaware to the DuPont Corporation. Today, however, while some states still have one or a few prominent interests (the Mormon Church in Utah, gaming in Nevada, agriculture and agribusiness in Arkansas, the coal companies in West Virginia, for example), states are no longer dominated by one single interest. However, as in the past, interest groups are still often able to determine what policies a state pursues and, often as important, those it does not pursue.

Politics across the states today is considerably different from what it was a hundred years ago or even at the end of World War II largely because many more and a much wider range of interest groups are now represented in state capitals promoting issues and causes such as gay rights, tax reform, compensation for crime victims, pro-life and pro-choice, among many others, that were unheard of even a few decades ago. And interest groups have always been among the first to detect changes in power relationships and direct their efforts toward these power points. Thus to study the activities of a state's most successful interest groups and their lobbyists reveals much about where power lies in that state and how it has changed over time. In this regard interest group activity is a bellwether of state politics past and present. In addition, although there are many similarities between interest group activities across the states, there are also many differences such as the range of groups active, the overall influence of groups, and the way that groups are regulated. Besides the value in comparing interest group systems, understanding the reasons for these variations provides insights into the broader question of why the politics in states differ.

This chapter explores the three elements of interest group activity outlined above: (1) their significance as a bellwether of state politics, including the types of groups operating past and present, their strategies and tactics, and their power in the public policy process; (2) how and why interest group systems vary from state to state and the consequences of this; and (3) the pros and cons of interest groups as they affect the democratic process in the states. First, however, we need to define some key terms.[1]

---

1. The data in this chapter come mainly from the Hrebenar-Thomas study of interest groups in all fifty states coordinated by the authors and involving ninety-six contributing researchers. The original study was conducted between 1983 and 1988, with three updates in 1993–1994, 1997–1998, and 2001–2002. The results of the original project can be found in Hrebenar and Thomas 1987, 1992, 1993a, and 1993b; syntheses can be found in Thomas and Hrebenar 1990, 1991, 1992, 1996 and 1999. Those contributing data to the 2002 update were, for Alabama, David L. Martin (Auburn University); Alaska, Clive S. Thomas (University of Alaska, Juneau); Arizona, David R. Berman (Arizona State University); Arkansas, Arthur English (University of Arkansas at Little Rock); California, John H. Culver (California Polytechnic State University); Colorado, John A. Straayer (Colorado State University); Connecticut, Sarah M. Morehouse, (University of Connecticut, Stamford); Delaware, Joseph A. Pika (University of Delaware); Florida, Eric Prier (Florida Atlantic University); Georgia, Scott H. Ainsworth (University of Georgia); Hawaii, Ira S. Rohter (University of Hawaii, Manoa); Idaho, James

## KEY TERMS AND CONCEPTS

There is no single agreed-upon definition of an interest group among scholars (Baumgartner and Leech 1998, 25–30). Often the term is narrowly defined in studies of state politics to include only those groups required to register under state laws and excluding those not required to do so. Yet many groups and organizations engage in lobbying but are not required to register. The most important are those representing the various levels and agencies of government itself. Most states do not require public officials at any level of government to register as lobbyists.

Therefore, to capture the gamut of interest group activity in a state the following broad definition is more appropriate:

An *interest group* is an association of individuals or organizations or a public or private institution that, on the basis of one or more shared concerns, attempts to influence public policy in its favor.

This definition embraces the three broad categories of interest groups represented in liberal democracies including the American states.

The first category, often referred to as the traditional membership group, promotes a host of economic, social, and political concerns and is made up of individuals such as senior citizens, environmentalists, schoolteachers, farmers, consumers, anti-tax advocates, and so on. The second, usually called organizational interests, is composed not of individuals but of organizations, such as businesses or trade unions. The third category is that of institutional interests, which are not really groups at all. As Salisbury (1984) points out for Washington, D.C., and Gray and Lowery (1995, 1996, 2001) for the states, a large percentage of the organized inter-

Weatherby (Boise State University); Illinois, Kent Redfield (University of Illinois-Springfield); Indiana, David J. Hadley, John C. Morgan, and Benjamin C. Tooley (Wabash College); Iowa, Arthur Sanders (Drake University); Kansas, Allan J. Cigler (University of Kansas); Kentucky, Penny M. Miller (University of Kentucky); Louisiana, Wayne T. Parent (Louisiana State University); Maine, Kenneth T. Palmer (University of Maine, Orono) and Rep. Jonathan R. Thomas (Maine Legislature); Maryland, James Gimpel (University of Maryland, College Park); Massachusetts, John C. Berg (Suffolk University); Michigan, William P. Browne (Central Michigan University); Minnesota, Craig H. Grau (University of Minnesota, Duluth); Mississippi, David A. Breaux (Mississippi State University); Missouri, James W. Endersby (University of Missouri, Columbia); Montana, Kenneth L. Weaver (Montana State University); Nebraska, Robert F. Sittig (University of Nebraska, Lincoln); Nevada, Eric B. Herzik (University of Nevada, Reno); New Hampshire, Michelle Anne Fistek (Plymouth State College); New Jersey, Stephen A. Salmore and Alan Rosenthal (Eagleton Institute, Rutgers University); New Mexico, Gilbert K. St. Clair (University of New Mexico); New York, David L. Cingranelli (Binghamton University, SUNY); North Carolina, Richard C. Kearney (East Carolina University); North Dakota, Theodore B. Pedeliski (University of North Dakota); Ohio, Frederick Older (University of Akron); Oklahoma, Jason F. Kirksey (Oklahoma State University); Oregon, William M. Lunch (Oregon State University); Pennsylvania, Patricia McGee Crotty (East Stroudsburg State University); Rhode Island, Maureen Moakley (University of Rhode Island); South Carolina, Robert E. Botsch (University of South Carolina at Aiken); South Dakota, Robert V. Burns (South Dakota State University); Tennessee, Anthony J. Nownes (University of Tennessee, Knoxville); Texas, Keith E. Hamm (Rice University); Utah, Nancy S. Lyon (University of Utah); Vermont, Anthony Gierzynski (University of Vermont); Virginia, John T. Whelan (University of Richmond); Washington, Stephen F. Johnson (Washington Public Utilities Districts Association); West Virginia, James R. Oxendale (West Virginia Institute of Technology); Wisconsin, David G. Wegge (St. Norbert College); Wyoming, James D. King (University of Wyoming).

ests represented before government are various private and public entities—businesses, think tanks, universities, state and federal agencies, and local governments. Today institutions constitute the largest category of organized interests operating in state capitals (Gray and Lowery 2001, Fig. 3).

It is also important to study interest group activity in the entire state capital—not just in the capitol building. Some studies focus only on the legislature, which is certainly the major target of lobbying for many groups. But the executive branch has always been lobbied, particularly the bureaucracy where major policy and regulatory decisions are made that affect a host of interests, and this target of lobbying is increasing (Nownes and Freeman 1998b, 96–97). Although less prominent, lobbying through state courts is also on the rise.

The terms *interest, lobby,* and *sector* are often used synonymously and interchangeably with the term *interest group;* but each is a more general term and they are used in a variety of ways. The term *lobby* always has political connotations (usually referring to a collection of interests of a similar type such as the business lobby); but *interest* and *sector* may or may not. They may refer to a part (a sector) of society with similar concerns or a common identity that may or may not engage in political activity, such as farmers or minorities. It is from these similar concerns and common identities of interests and sectors, however, that interest groups and lobbies are formed. Furthermore, the distinction between an interest or lobby and an organized interest group is sometimes difficult to make in practice. This is partly because organized groups such as environmental groups often act and are perceived as representing a broader political interest than their official membership.

Interest groups operate in the state public policy-making process by *lobbying,* which can be defined as the interaction of an individual, interest group, or interest with policy makers, either directly or indirectly, for the purpose of influencing current policy or creating a relationship conducive to shaping future policy to the benefit of that individual, group, or interest. Thus a *lobbyist* is a person who represents an interest group in an effort to influence government decisions in that group's favor. The decisions most often targeted by interest groups and their lobbyists are those concerning public policies; but they also include decisions about who gets elected and appointed to make those policies in an effort to create relationships conducive to their group's future interests. Lobbyists include not only those required to register by law but also those representing non-registered groups and organizations, particularly government.

Finally, we need to explain the concept of a *state interest group system.* This is the array of groups and organizations, both formal and informal, and the lobbyists who represent them working to affect public policy within a state. The idea of a state interest group system is an abstraction, of course, because even though there are relations between various groups and lobbyists representing various interests, never do all the groups in a political system act in concert to achieve one goal. However, for analytical purposes, as one element of the socioeconomic and political life of the state, it is the characteristics of the interest group system in a state—

size, development, composition, methods of operating, and so on—in its relationship to the economy, society, and government that is particularly important in determining such things as the political power structure, which public policies are pursued and which are not, and the extent of representation and democracy.

## TYPES OF GROUPS AND INTERESTS ACTIVE
## IN THE STATES PAST AND PRESENT

In the early 2000s increasing numbers and a wide range of membership groups, organizational interests, and institutional interests operate in the fifty states. Such numbers and diversity is a recent development, however. Before 1900 there were few and a very narrow range of organized interests operating in state capitals. By the 1930s five broad categories of interests had established themselves across the then forty-eight states: business, labor unions and professional groups, education, agriculture, and local government. These five interests have been called the traditional interests in state politics as they were the major ones active in the states for more than two generations (Zeigler 1983, 99). However, with the minimal role of state government, entire legislative sessions would go by without any activity by some of the groups that composed these interests.

All this began to change in the late 1960s. State interest group systems gradually became more pluralistic, a trend that continues today. Not only was there a marked increase in the number of groups lobbying in state capitals, the variety or range of groups operating also expanded. A host of new groups, organizations, and institutional interests, from individual businesses to social issue groups (for the poor, the handicapped, and so on) to minority and women's groups to religious organizations to governance groups (anti-tax, term limits, and so on), began to establish a presence as lobbying forces in the states.

Research from the Hrebenar-Thomas study and extensive work by Gray and Lowery reveals an expansion in both the numbers and variety of groups since the mid-1980s, especially institutional interests (Gray and Lowery 2001, Fig. 3). In particular, physicians and other healthcare groups, such as hospitals and nursing homes and medical insurance organizations (like Blue Cross/Blue Shield), utility companies (including telecommunications), lawyers, and various manufacturing groups have expanded their numbers considerably since 1980 (Gray and Lowery 2001, Table 1), largely because state governments increasingly regulate their activities.

The increasing prominence of several interests that are active in virtually all states is worthy of special mention. Of particular note is the increasing role of government and government-related groups. The most prominent of state agencies in all states are the departments of education, transportation, and health and welfare. State universities and colleges now also have a major presence. Associated with this rise in government lobbying has been the increased prominence of public sector unions, particularly unions of state and local employees, including police and fire fighters, as well as teachers' unions. More and more individual cities and towns are also lobbying on their own, although most still belong to their local government association such as a league of cities or county organization. Similarly, many individual businesses, like Microsoft and Hershey, have begun to lobby as individual corporations while still usually remaining a member of their state manufacturers' association, chamber of commerce, or specific trade association. Ideological groups, which are often single-issue groups, such as anti-abortionists and the Religious Right, have also become active in most states in recent years. Environmentalists, senior citizens, and sportsmen's groups (hunting, fishing, and anti-gun control, including state chapters of the National Rifle Association—NRA) are other forces that now have a significant presence in almost all state capitals.

Interests that do not have a presence across all the states tend to be newly formed groups, such as school choice (favoring vouchers or charter schools), children's rights groups, and family value groups, or those representing an interest concentrated in certain states, such as Native Americans, commercial fishing interests, and professional sports franchises. The general trend for most interests is to expand to more and more states. Since 1990 several interests have emerged that were not politically active before, such as victims' rights groups and organizations concerned with responding to environmental disasters. Still other groups, particularly gaming interests, Hispanics, and pro- and antismoking groups, have expanded their presence in the states. And more groups, senior citizens and Native Americans, for example, are active in virtually every legislative session.

Besides the greater number and variety of groups, interests are lobbying more intensively than was the case in the mid-1970s or even the mid-1980s. They have more regular contact with public officials and use more sophisticated techniques. In addition, more often than ever before ad hoc coalitions of groups, such as in the healthcare industry and the environmental community, come together to promote or fight issues.

According to work by Gray and Lowery, expansion of the number of interests in state capitals tells only one side of the story. Although many groups enter the lobbying scene, others leave it largely because these groups cease to exist. Mortality, the authors have argued, is much more likely to occur with membership groups and associations than with institutions. In general, they argue that the state interest group scene is more fluid in composition than has hitherto been believed (Gray and Lowery 1996, 124–125, 243; Lowery and Gray 1998).

This overview of changes in the number and types of interests active in state capitals is a good illustration of one way in which interest group activity is a bellwether of changes in state politics in recent years. The rise in the number of groups was both partly responsible for and a reflection of the increased role of state government, particularly from the 1970s onward. And the changing role of state government as the "Reagan revolution" of the 1980s affected the states also brought some groups into state capitals that had not been active before, such as anti-tax groups, individual local governments, groups promoting the arts, and the like. Similarly, the increase in the variety of groups both generated and reflected the much broader range of issues dealt with by state government, including issues about what responsibilities state government should shed as a result of the Reagan revolution.

Finally, a caveat is in order. Just because a group or interest is active in state politics and may even have high visibility does not ensure its success in achieving its goals. This will become clear below when we consider the power of interest groups.

## THE PRIVATE GOALS AND PUBLIC ROLES OF INTEREST GROUPS

Unlike political parties, which originate and exist primarily for political purposes, most interest groups are not primarily political organizations. They usually develop from a common economic or social interest, as, for example, businesses forming a trade association, gays forming a self-help association, or model railroad enthusiasts forming a club. Such organizations promote programs and disseminate information to enhance the professional, business, social, or avocational interests of their members. Much of this activity is nonpolitical, as when the American Medical Association publishes its journal or provides cut-rate life insurance for its members. However, many nonpolitical interest groups are forced to become politically active because there is no other way to protect or promote their interests, a situation that has been on the increase over the past thirty years. In promoting their private goals in the public arena, interest groups perform indispensable public roles that, for the most part, enhance the democratic process. The five most important of these are as follows.

### The Aggregation and Representation of Interests

Together with political parties, interest groups are a major means by which people with similar interests and concerns are brought together, or aggregated, and their views articulated to government. Interest groups act as major intermediaries between citizens and the government by representing the views of their members to public officials, especially between elections.

### Facilitating Government

Interest groups contribute to the substance of public policy by being significant sources of both technical and political information for policy makers. In most instances groups help to facilitate the process of bargaining and compromise essential to policy making in a pluralist system. And this is particularly important in the fragmented policy-making process that exists in many American states. Furthermore, in some cases groups aid in implementing public policies, as, for example, when the Illinois chapter of the National Federation of Independent Business distributes information about a state or federal small business loan program.

### Political Education and Training

To varying degrees, interest groups educate their members and the public on issues, particularly at election time. They also provide opportunities for citizens to learn about the political process and to gain valuable practical experience for seeking public office.

### Candidate Recruitment

Groups often recruit candidates to run for public office, both from within and outside their group membership.

### Campaign and Political Party Finance

Increasingly these days, groups help to finance political campaigns, both candidate elections and, at the state and local level, ballot measure elections (initiative, referendum, and recall). Since the 1970s many private interest groups, particularly businesses, trade associations, professional organizations, and trade unions have set up political action committees (PACs) to raise and distribute funds to candidates running for public office. Some groups also contribute money to political parties.

Certainly, each of these five functions is subject to abuse by interest groups, particularly campaign finance. But that does not make them any less essential to the working of democracy or lessen the importance of the public role of interest groups. What is contradictory about the relationship between these private political goals and public roles of interest groups is that the positive public roles are purely incidental. With few exceptions, in their private capacity interest groups do not exist to improve democracy or to improve the functioning of the political process. The positive public role of interest groups is a paradoxical byproduct of the sum of their selfish interests.

## EXPLAINING DIFFERENCES IN INTEREST GROUP SYSTEMS ACROSS THE STATES

Although there are many similarities in interest group activity across the states, there are also variations in all fifty group systems. Why do such differences exist and what are their lessons for understanding state interest group activity?

At the most general level, there is agreement among scholars that the socioeconomic and political environment shapes interest group systems and that differences in this environment produce variations in group system development and operation. There is both agreement and debate, however, as to the importance of the effects of the various elements in producing such variations. Wide agreement exists on the importance of the level of economic development and on the role of government. There is less agreement on such things as the role of political parties, political culture, and regional and interstate influences. One aspect of this debate revolves around whether the major factors that shape interest group systems are internal to the state, as Gray and Lowery in essence have argued, or whether there is a combination of internal and external factors as the Hrebenar-Thomas study has argued. In the absence of any definitive answers, it is most useful to combine the two perspectives to explain differences in group systems. This is done in the analytical framework set out in Box 4-1.

**Box 4-1** Five Major Factors Affecting the Development, Makeup, Operating Techniques, and Influence of Interest Groups in the American States

---

*Available Resources and Extent of Socio-economic Diversity*

---

*Key Elements*
   Level of economic development and state wealth
   Governmental expenditure and taxing levels
   Extent of social development and social/demographic diversity

*Significance*
The more resources available and the greater the level of social development and social and demographic diversity (e.g., higher percentage of the middle class and minorities), the wider the range or diversity of groups. The level of state economic development and wealth (measured by Gross State Product—GSP) and the level of government spending make more resources available for the organization and maintenance of groups, though high state taxation can restrain both. Generally, however, this factor produces a more diverse and competitive group system; a decline in the dominance of one or an oligarchy of groups; use of more sophisticated techniques of lobbying; and a rise in the professionalization of lobbyists.

---

*State Political Environment*

---

*Key Elements*
   Political attitudes: political culture, political ideology, and public opinion
   Political party–interest group relations
   Level of campaign costs and sources of electoral support

*Significance*
Political attitudes influence the types and extent of policies pursued; the strength/weakness of political parties; the level of integration/fragmentation of the policy-making process; what are and what are not acceptable influence or "lobbying" techniques; and the general context in which interest groups will operate and the attitudes toward them. Political party–interest group relations affect avenues of access and influence; group strategies and tactics; and, in the short run, the specific policies pursued and enacted, among other things. An increase in campaign costs puts increased pressure on candidates to raise funds. The more support coming directly to candidates from groups and their PACs, the more candidates are beholden to them.

---

*Governmental Institutional Capacity*

---

*Key Elements*
   State policy domain/areas of policy jurisdiction
   Level of integration/fragmentation of the policy process: extent to which this process is centralized or dispersed
   Level of professionalization of state government
   Stringency and enforcement of public disclosure laws, including lobbyist registration, ethics, and campaign finance laws

*Significance*
State policy domain will determine which interests will attempt to affect state policy. As the area of policy authority expands, the number and types of groups lobbying will increase. The level of integration/fragmentation of the policy process will have an impact on patterns of group access and influence. Generally, the more integrated the system (strong parties, strong executive including appointed cabinet, no or little provision for direct democracy, etc.), the fewer the options available to groups. Conversely, the more the system is fragmented, the larger the number of access points and available methods of influence. The level of professionalization (including state legislators, the bureaucracy, and the governor's staff) makes more varied sources of information available to policy makers. It also creates a higher demand for information by policy makers, including information from groups and lobbyists. Public disclosure laws increase public information about lobbying activities. This affects the methods and techniques of lobbying, which in turn affect the power of certain individual groups and lobbyists, though not necessarily system group power.

**Box 4-1** *Continued*

*Intergovernmental and External Influences*

*Key Elements*
  Intergovernmental spending and policy-making authority
  "Nationalization" of issues and intergovernmental lobbying

*Significance*
The distribution of intergovernmental spending and policy authority refers to the policies exercised and the amount of money spent by state governments versus policies and spending by federal and local governments. Changes in responsibilities between levels of government will affect the types of groups that lobby federal, state, and local governments and the intensity of their lobbying efforts. The "nationalization" of issues such as anti-smoking, term limits, and stiffer penalties for drunk driving have spawned similar groups across the states; increased out-of-state funding for group activity, especially on ballot propositions; and generally increased intergovernmental contact by all groups, including traditional interests.

*Short-term State Policy-making Environment*

*Key Elements*
  Political party effectiveness in government
  State public policy and spending priorities

*Significance*
Changes in party control of government, in either the legislative or executive branch, especially when this is accompanied by party and/or caucus and/or ideological cohesiveness, can affect the access and effectiveness of certain groups and interests. Spending and policy priorities, which may change as the result of an election or other event such as a financial crisis, refer to the policies and spending that state governments emphasize at a particular time, as opposed to their general constitutional/statutory responsibilities. Groups directly concerned with and affected by the areas of policy priority will often be given preferential access by government. The extent of this preferential access is related to the degree to which the group is needed by policy makers for advice in policy development and implementation. Thus shifts in policy and spending priorities will also affect both the access and influence capability of certain groups and the relative power of groups within specific policy areas.

S O U R C E :  Developed by the authors.

This framework sheds light on such key aspects of group activity as the development of state group systems; the types of groups that are active; the methods they use in pursuing their goals, including the increased intergovernmental activity of many interest groups; the power they exert; and short-term variations resulting from electoral changes and shifts in policy priorities. The five categories of factors and their components in this framework are very much interrelated. A change in one may reflect or lead to a change in one or more of the other factors. Not only can the framework be used to understand differences across interest group systems, it also sheds light on the operation of the system in an individual state.

## INTEREST GROUP STRATEGIES AND TACTICS:
## TIME-HONORED METHODS AND NEW TECHNIQUES

To achieve its goal of influencing government, an interest group develops a strategy and executes it through specific tactics. Group strategy and tactics involve a three-stage process: (1) gaining access to government decision makers; (2) building up relationships with them; and (3) influencing their actions in making public policy. However, much of a group's strategy and tactics do not involve contacting public officials directly but planning and organizing their campaign, monitoring what government is doing that might affect them, and, in many cases, working to get people sympathetic to their cause elected or appointed to office (Nownes and Freeman 1998b, 89).

### Direct and Indirect Tactics and Insider and Outsider Lobbying

Direct tactics are those that involve direct contact with public officials to influence their decisions, such as lobbying the legislature and executive and using the courts. In states where there are initiatives and referendum devices, groups often get involved in these campaigns. Indirect lobbying includes activities aimed at getting access to and influencing the environment in which officials make decisions. These include group members working on election campaigns and contributing money to them, not only for legislative and executive branch office seekers but also for judges in states where these are elected; mobilizing grassroots support through networking (sophisticated member contact systems); building coalitions with other groups; intergovernmental lobbying activities, as we will see below; trying to influence public opinion through public relations campaigns; and even mounting demonstrations, boycotts, and sit-ins.

Insider lobbying is the use of a narrow range of direct tactics centered around a lobbyist exploiting personal relationships with public officials by contacting them directly. Until the early 1970s this was the dominant, often the only form of lobbying used by most groups and is associated with the good ol' boy days of state politics. Outsider lobbying involves the use of indirect tactics, and although it is increasingly used by many establishment groups such as business and the professions, it is mostly associated with "outsider" groups—those that do not have insider access to public officials, such as social issue groups like gay and poverty action groups—to gain the attention of policy makers .

Today an increasing number of interest groups employ a much wider range of strategies and tactics, indirect and outsider as well as direct and insider, than they did in the 1970s or even the 1980s. However, although modern technologies such as computers and television have expanded their options, group strategy and tactics are still very much an art rather than a science. The essence of this art is interpersonal communications from an advocacy perspective between group members and leaders on one side and policy makers on the other. Effective personal contacts are the key to lobbying success and form an enduring element of any group's involvement in politics. In fact, the new techniques and indirect tactics are simply more sophisticated ways for increasing the effectiveness of group contacts in the policy arena. The success of a lobbying campaign ultimately depends on some form of direct (if not insider) tactics and this is likely to always be the case in the lobbying game.

*Choosing a Group Strategy and Deciding on Specific Tactics*

The essence of any group strategy is the ability to marshal group resources to achieve the goal at hand. Exactly how these resources should be marshaled and managed varies according to the nature of the group, its available resources, the way it is perceived by policy makers, the issue it is pursuing, and the political circumstances at the time. As a consequence, no one strategy is a guarantee of success for all groups or for any one group at all times. This is what makes lobbying an art and not a science and provides a continual challenge to lobbyists and group leaders and gives interest group politics its variety and fascination.

Two other basic factors about a group's choice of a strategy are important to bear in mind. First, particular strategies are largely determined by whether the group is currently involved in a defensive, maintenance, or promotional situation. A group trying to stop the passage of a law need only halt it at one point in its tortuous journey to enactment. Therefore, it is likely that the group will concentrate on a particular point in the system—such as a sympathetic committee chair. In contrast, to achieve enactment, the group must clear all the hurdles in the process, and thus a more broadly based strategy is required. Between these two situations are those groups that are simply working to maintain good relations with policy makers for the time when they will need to fight for their interests. Maintenance lobbying requires yet another strategy, which varies from group to group. Paralleling the increased activism of state government, one major change in state capital lobbying since 1960 has been the increase in the number of groups pursuing promotional strategies. Before 1960 most lobbying was defensive. In general, more resources and greater sophistication in their use are required to promote something than to kill it.

Second, most lobbying campaigns require a multifaceted approach. Few lobbyists today deal solely with the legislature. This is because a successful lobbying campaign, especially one that seeks to promote something, requires the cooperation and often the active support of one or more executive agencies. Without this support the chances of even partial success are considerably reduced. Moreover, passing legislation is only the first step in effective law making. Implementation of a law is the job of the bureaucracy, and in many cases, such as with health care and environmental legislation, this involves writing regulations before the law can be implemented. Lobbyists and group leaders must closely monitor this implementation process as it can make or break the effectiveness of a law.

*Modern Lobbying: Combining Direct and Indirect Approaches*

When it comes to direct involvement, by far the most common and still the most effective of group tactics is the use of one or more lobbyists. Since the 1960s, however, the changes in interest group activity detailed earlier, particularly the competition between groups for the ears of public officials, have forced groups to supplement the role of the lobbyist with other direct and indirect lobbying tactics. Particularly evident is the increased use of three tactics: money, the courts, and ad hoc issue coalitions.

Over the past twenty years or so there has been a significant increase in spending by certain interest groups both in their lobbying efforts in the state capital and in contributions of group members, lobbyists, and PACs to state-level candidates. PACs, in particular, have become major campaign fund providers in the states. Regardless of the significance of political parties in a state, the money triangle of elected official, lobbyist, and PAC is becoming increasingly significant.

Because of the role state courts play—like their federal counterparts—in interpreting their respective constitutions, some interest groups have increasingly turned to the courts to achieve their goals. The business community often challenges the constitutionality of regulations. And groups that cannot get the legislature to act or the administration to enforce mandated functions, such as certain mental health provisions, also often use the courts. One of the most publicized uses of the courts in recent years was their overthrow of a statewide initiative passed in Colorado in 1992 to limit the rights of gays and lesbians. More and more, too, interest groups—business groups, attorneys, and liberal cause groups—are getting involved in the selection and election of judges. A particularly rancorous campaign occurred in Ohio in 2000 when a number of business and conservative groups unsuccessfully tried to defeat Ohio Supreme Court Justice Alice Robie Resnick (Thomas, Boyer, and Hrebenar 2002).

Increasingly these days, the view of state lobbying efforts as being conducted by individual groups is misleading. Coalitions of groups and particularly ad hoc issue coalitions are increasingly important. To be sure, groups with long-term common goals and a similar philosophy have been natural allies for years—business and professional groups, social issue and public interest groups, and so forth—and have always used coalitions when it was to their advantage. But today certain issues, such as tort reform, economic development, healthcare costs, and education quality, affect a wide range of groups, sometimes cutting across philosophical boundaries and dividing traditional allies, and have produced a new type of coalition—the ad hoc coalition. This usually consists of a number of groups and may last for no more than the life of a legislative session or for the life of an initiative or referendum campaign. The campaign to deal with increasing healthcare costs is a good example. In many states it brought together business groups (particularly small business), farm groups, universities, local governments, and social issue and poverty groups.

*Lobbyists*

Although the image of the cigar-chomping good ol' boy lobbyist plying his clients with women, food, and liquor lingers on in the public mind, the reality has changed drastically. Fundamental changes in American government and politics since 1970 have had a significant effect on the types of people who make up the lobbying community, the skills required of them, and their styles and methods of doing business, as well as their gender. Overall, developments in the state capital lobbying community have been even more dramatic than those in Washington, D.C.

An in-depth understanding of the state capital lobbying community requires that we distinguish between categories or types of lobbyists. Different types of lobbyists have different assets and liabilities and are perceived differently by public officials. Such perceptions determine the nature and extent of the lobbyist's power base. In turn, the nature and extent of this power base affects the way a lobbyist approaches his or her job of gaining access to and attempting to influence public officials. Today's state capital lobbying community is composed of five categories of lobbyists: contract, in-house, government, volunteer, and private individual or self-appointed lobbyists. Details about these five types are set out in Box 4-2.

Although they constitute only about a quarter of the state capital lobbying community, it is the contract lobbyists, sometimes referred to derisively as "hired guns," about whom the public hears most through the press. This is partly because some of them earn six- or seven-figure incomes (although by our estimates these sorts of salaries make up less than 15 percent of the total) and partly because most of them represent the interests that spend the most money and have the most political clout—mainly business and professional associations.

In-house lobbyists are the executive directors, presidents, and employees of a host of organizations and businesses from environmental groups, state AFL-CIO affiliates, school board associations, and trade groups to telecommunications companies and large corporations such as General Motors and Safeway. These were the first type of lobbyists to appear on the political scene beginning in the mid-nineteenth century, when big business and especially the railroads became a significant part of the American economy. As a group they have probably always constituted the largest segment of the state capital lobbying community. Probably because of the negative connotations raised in the public's mind by the word *lobbyist,* in-house lobbyists are often given a euphemistic title by their organizations, such as representative, agent, advocate, government relations specialist, or, more often, legislative liaison. Possibly for the same reason that lobbyists have a negative image, in addition to the fact that governments attempt to maintain at least a facade of unity, no state officially refers to those lobbying for its agencies as lobbyists. Instead they also most often use the designation legislative liaison.

Citizen, cause, or volunteer lobbyists usually represent small non-profit organizations, social welfare groups, or community organizations such as a state group advocating charter schools, groups concerned about domestic violence, and local humane societies. The category of individual lobbyist has seen a "return of the moguls" in the mid- and late-1990s, as prominent, often very wealthy individuals such as Peter Angelos, owner of the Baltimore Orioles baseball franchise and a prominent trial lawyer, work state government to benefit their economic interests.

Technical knowledge is often not the greatest asset of contract lobbyists, who, as political insiders, are hired primarily for their knowledge of the system and their close contacts with public officials. What they usually possess is special knowledge of certain parts of the government—for example, the budget process or the work-

**Box 4-2** The Five Categories of Lobbyists, Their Recruitment, Gender, and Approximate Percentage of the State Capital Lobbying Community

---

*Contract Lobbyists*

---

Those hired on contract for a fee specifically to lobby. They often represent more than one client. Approximately 20 percent represent five or more clients.

*Recruitment*
Many, especially the most successful, are former elected or appointed state officials, usually legislators or political appointees. Some are former in-house lobbyists. An increasing number are attorneys from capital law firms and public relations and media specialists.

*Gender*
Predominantly male, ranges from 80 to 90 percent, higher in less developed state group systems.

*Percentage*
Make up from 15 to 25 percent of the state capital lobbying community, higher in more developed state group systems.

---

*In-house Lobbyists*

---

Employees of an association, organization, or business who, as part or all of their jobs, act as lobbyists. These represent only one client—their employer.

*Recruitment*
Most have experience in the profession, business, trade, and so forth that they represent (e.g., education, health care). Much less likely than contract lobbyists to have been public officials.

*Gender*
Approximately 75 percent male and 25 percent female.

*Percentage*
Constitute from 40 to 50 percent of the lobbying community—the largest category in almost all state capitals.

---

*Government Lobbyists and Legislative Liaisons*

---

Employees of state, local, and federal agencies who, as part or all of their jobs, represent their agency to the legislative and executive branches of state government. Thus these also represent only one interest. They include state government agency heads and senior staff members, both elected and appointed officials of local governments, and some federal officials. To specifically monitor their relations with the legislature, most state agencies and some local governments and federal agencies appoint a person designated as a legislative liaison.

*Recruitment*
Legislative liaisons are often career bureaucrats with broad experience in the agency or government unit that they represent. Some are political appointees and an increasing number are recruited from the ranks of legislative staffers.

*Gender*
Approximately 25 to 35 percent of legislative liaisons are female; higher in more economically and socially diverse states.

*Percentage*
Difficult to estimate as many states do not require government personnel to register as lobbyists. A rough estimate for all government lobbyists is between 25 to 40 percent. Tends to be higher in states where state and local government employment is highest, especially in the West.

---

**Box 4-2** *Continued*

---

*Citizen, Cause, or Volunteer Lobbyists*

---

Persons who, usually on an *ad hoc* and unpaid basis, represent citizen and community organizations or informal groups. They rarely represent more than one interest at a time.

*Recruitment*
Too varied for meaningful categorization; most are very committed to their cause.

*Gender*
Difficult to estimate as many are not required to register as lobbyists. However, it appears that the majority, and in some states as high as 75 percent, are female.

*Percentage*
An estimate is from 10 to 20 percent of the state capital lobbying community.

---

*Private Individual, "Hobbyist," or Self-styled Lobbyists*

---

Those acting on their own behalf and not designated by any organization as an official representative. They usually lobby for pet projects or direct personal benefits, or against some policy or proposal that they find particularly objectionable.

*Recruitment*
Other than self-recruitment, no common pattern.

*Gender*
Difficult to estimate as many are not required to or do not register as lobbyists. Most are probably male, but this will vary from time to time and from state to state.

*Percentage*
Difficult to estimate, but probably less than 5 percent.

---

SOURCE: Developed by the authors from the fifty state chapters of the Hrebenar-Thomas study (Hrebenar and Thomas 1987, 1992, 1993a, 1993b) and the four updates.

---

ings of a particular department—and so they may be used by legislators and other officials to assist in the policy-making process. In most cases they are facilitators of dialogue between their clients and public officials. Often they have a great influence on the disbursement of campaign funds on behalf of their clients. Many contract lobbyists organize fund-raisers for candidates and work to help them get elected or reelected. The fact that they usually represent clients with important economic influence is not lost on public officials.

The major political asset of most in-house lobbyists is their unequaled knowledge of their particular interest. This knowledge is often supplemented by campaign contributions from their association or business and by their ability to mobilize their membership. Government lobbyists, in contrast, have only one important tool—information—although they can, and often do, use their constituent groups to their advantage. For example, state departments of education often work, unofficially, with state parent-teacher associations and other client groups, such as those for handicapped or gifted children, to secure increased funding or to promote legislation. As voters and members of the public, these constituent groups can add political clout to the department's attempt to achieve its policy agenda. Volunteer lobbyists usually rely on moral persuasion to sell their causes to public officials, often coupled with the mobilization of their membership. They may also provide information not available elsewhere, but they usually lack the status of political insiders or access to big campaign contributions and sophisticated organizations. Self-appointed lobbyists have the fewest political assets of all, unless they have been major campaign contributors and are major economic forces in their state. These differing assets and liabilities very much shape the way that public officials view these lobbyists, and that view in turn partly determines their power base.

Overall, the state capital lobbying community has become much more pluralistic and has advanced greatly in its level of professionalism since the early 1960s. Although the level of professionalism varies from state to state, its general increase among contract lobbyists is evidenced by several developments. These include an increase in the number of those working at the job full time, the emergence of lobbying firms that provide a variety of services and represent as many as twenty-five clients, and an increase in the number of specialists among contract lobbyists in response to the increasing complexity of government. One California contract lobbyist, for example, specializes in representing California high-tech interests. Other contract lobbyists specialize in representing such interests as agriculture, health care, education, and local governments.

As mentioned earlier, lobbying is no longer a male-dominated occupation in state capitals. Women now make up about 20 percent of state capital lobbyists compared with less than 5 percent twenty years ago. Differences still exist, however, in the activities males and females perform as lobbyists. Women tend to have less experience than men at the job and are more likely to represent religious, charitable, or citizen groups and less likely to represent business and unions. Nevertheless, women use the same methods as men in trying to affect public policy. Furthermore, in many cases women are consulted more often by public officials on some policy issues—mainly social issues, because they offer a contrasting perspective (Nownes and Freeman 1998a).

Do all these developments mean that the old wheeler-dealer, good ol' boy has passed from the lobbying scene in state capitals? In the raw form in which he used to exist the answer is probably yes. Still, under a more sophisticated guise, wheeler-dealers do exist today and are very successful lobbyists. Like the old wheeler-dealers, they realize the need for a multifaceted approach to establishing and maintaining good relations with public officials. This includes everything from helping in election campaigns to aiding officials with their personal needs. In addition, the modern-day wheeler-dealer is aware of the greater importance of technical information, the higher degree of professionalism in politics, and the increased public visibility of lobbying. The result is a low-key, highly skilled, effective professional who is a far cry from the old public image of a lobbyist.

## INTEREST GROUP POWER: THREE PERSPECTIVES

Although the public and the press often hold a simplistic view of interest group power—such as the richest groups are the most influential or the good ol' boys always win—assessing group power is one of the most difficult and elusive aspects of interest group studies. The difficulty is due mainly to the fact that there are so many factors involved in determining group power, many of which change as political circumstances change.

Moreover, there are various ways in which group power can be defined. One way to view it is the ability of a group to achieve its goals as that group and its leaders define them, which we can term *single group power*. Alternatively, group power can be seen in terms of the most powerful groups in a society which we can call *overall interest power*. These first two perspectives are not the same. Some groups may be very successful in their own terms but those groups may never be seen as powerful in the political system overall. In contrast, a group that is seen as influential in the society overall may often lose political battles. A third way to view group power is *group system power*—the overall influence of interest groups in relation to political parties and other political institutions.

Despite the difficulties in definitively determining group power, research conducted in the American states is enlightening in explaining why some groups, interests, and group systems are more powerful than others.

### Single Group Power

As single group power is the ability of a group or coalition to achieve its goals as it defines them, the only important assessment of the degree of success is an internal evaluation by the group. There are several reasons why some groups can be very successful in achieving their goals but not be singled out as powerful by public officials. It might be because the group is only intermittently active when they have an issue, such as an association of billboard owners working to defeat restriction on the size of highway billboards. It could be an ad hoc group coming together on one issue and then disbanding when success is achieved, such as a coalition to defeat an anti-smoking ballot initiative. Or it could be that the group's issue is far from public view and of minor public concern, such as working with a department to write regulations as might be the case with chiropractors interested in the occupational licensing process. Rarely are chiropractors seen as among the most effective groups in a state; but they may be among the most successful groups in achieving their limited goals. Many groups involved in the regulatory process are very successful because they have captured their area of concern—acquired control of policy making—through dependence of bureaucrats on their expertise. The last thing most of these groups want is public attention and to be singled out as an "effective group."

### Overall Individual Interest Power

This is the aspect of group power that most interests the press and the public who are less concerned about the minutiae of government and more with high-profile issues and questions such as, "Who is running the state?" or "Who has real political clout?" Whereas the only important assessment of single group power is internal to a group, overall interest power is based on external assessments of informed observers.

Researchers have used three methods, singly or in combination, to assess overall interest power: sending questionnaires to public officials and sometimes conducting interviews with them; drawing on the expertise of political scientists; and consulting academic and popular literature on the states. The assessment in this chapter uses the Hrebenar-Thomas study, which combined quantitative and qualitative techniques employing the first two methods. This study has assessed overall interest power in all fifty states on five occasions (1985, 1989, 1994, 1998 and 2002). The 2002 assessment is set out in Table 4-1, with a comparison of interest rankings from the early 1980s. These five assessments, in addition to an earlier fifty-state assessment conducted in the late 1970s by Morehouse (1981, 108–112), enable us to compare trends over twenty-five years.

First, however, we must be clear on exactly what these assessments do and do not reveal. They do reveal the interests that are viewed by policy makers and political observers as the most effective in the states over a five-year period prior to the 2002 assessment. For this reason they tend to be the most active groups or those with a high profile. The assessment should not be viewed as indicating that the groups near the top of the list always win or even win most of the time; in fact, they may win less often than some low-profile groups not listed. The place of an individual interest in the ranking, however, does indicate its level of importance as a player in state politics over the period assessed and the extent of its ability to bring political clout to bear on the issues that affect it.

Comparing the listings over the years, what stands out is the relative stability both of the types of groups that make the list and their ranking. When changes in ranking do occur or new groups appear on the list, the changes appear to be influenced by the prominence of issues at the time, and by partisan control and the ideological persuasion of state government. Gaming, health, and insurance interests, for example, have steadily increased in perceived influence as lotteries and casinos, health care, and tort reform became issues in the states. Environmental and other liberal causes wax and wane in strength according to who is in power in government. Business and development interests have seen a boost in their rankings since the GOP successes in state elections in 1994.

Two interests far outstrip any others in terms of their perceived influence and continue to vie for the top ranking. These are general business organizations (mainly state chambers of commerce) and schoolteachers (mainly state affiliates of the National Education Association). Utility interests have also firmly established themselves in third place on a consistent basis. The top twelve interests as listed in 2002 are essentially those that were listed as most effective in the early 1980s. These top twelve interests are the only ones mentioned as effective (both of the first and second rank) in more than half the states. So despite the so-called advocacy explosion of the last thirty years it has not been paralleled by a broad range of groups

**Table 4-1** Ranking of the Forty Most Influential Interests in the Fifty States in 2002, with Comparison of Ranking in 1985

| Ranking (1985 ranking) | Interest | Number of States in which interest ranked among | | |
|---|---|---|---|---|
| | | Most effective | Second level of effectiveness | Less/not effective |
| 1 (2) | General business organizations (state chambers of commerce, etc.) | 40 | 12 | 5 |
| 2 (1) | School teachers' organizations (NEA and AFT) | 37 | 12 | 2 |
| 3 (6) | Utility companies and associations (electric, gas, water, telephone/telecommunications) | 24 | 26 | 6 |
| 4 (13) | Insurance: general and medical (companies and associations) | 21 | 19 | 15 |
| 5 (17) | Hospital/nursing homes associations | 21 | 18 | 13 |
| 6 (8) | Lawyers (predominantly trial lawyers, state bar associations) | 22 | 15 | 15 |
| 7 (4) | Manufacturers (companies and associations) | 18 | 20 | 19 |
| 8 (9) | General local government organizations (municipal leagues, county organizations, elected officials) | 18 | 17 | 17 |
| 9 (11) | Physicians/state medical associations | 17 | 16 | 19 |
| 10 (10) | General farm organizations (state farm bureaus, etc.) | 16 | 16 | 18 |
| 11 (3) | Bankers' associations | 15 | 15 | 22 |
| 12 (5) | Traditional labor associations (predominantly the AFL-CIO) | 13 | 16 | 22 |
| 13 (19) | Universities and colleges (institutions and employees) | 13 | 13 | 26 |
| 14 (12) | State and local government employees (other than teachers) | 11 | 15 | 26 |
| 15 (22) | Contractors/builders/developers | 13 | 11 | 26 |
| 16 (14) | Realtors' associations | 13 | 10 | 27 |
| 17 (16) | K–12 education interests (other than teachers) | 9 | 12 | 29 |
| 18 (15) | Individual labor unions (Teamsters, UAW, etc.) | 08 | 14 | 29 |
| 19 (27) | Truckers and private transport interests (excluding railroads) | 09 | 11 | 31 |
| 20 (35) | Sportsmen/hunting and fishing (includes anti-gun control groups) | 9 | 10 | 32 |
| 21 (36) | Gaming interests (race tracks/casinos/lotteries) | 9 | 10 | 31 |
| 22 (23) | Environmentalists | 6 | 15 | 30 |
| 23 (18) | Agricultural commodity organizations (stockgrowers, grain growers, etc) | 7 | 12 | 31 |
| 24 (21) | Retailers (companies and trade associations) | 8 | 9 | 34 |
| 25 (7) | Individual banks and financial institutions | 6 | 9 | 35 |
| 26 (29) | State agencies | 6 | 7 | 39 |
| 27 (34) | Religious interests (churches and Religious Right) | 6 | 7 | 38 |

**Table 4-1** *Continued*

| Ranking (1985 ranking) | Interest | Most effective | Second level of effectiveness | Less/not effective |
|---|---|---|---|---|
| | | | **Number of States in which interest ranked among** | |
| 28 (38) | Taxpayers' interest groups | 5 | 9 | 36 |
| 29 (25) | Liquor, wine and beer interests | 3 | 13 | 34 |
| 30 (37) | Tourist/hospitality interests | 5 | 6 | 39 |
| 31 (24) | Individual cities and towns | 6 | 5 | 39 |
| 32 (28) | Public interest/good government groups | 2 | 13 | 39 |
| 33 (26) | Mining companies and associations | 6 | 4 | 40 |
| 34 (39) | Tobacco interests | 4 | 7 | 39 |
| 35 (30) | Forest product companies/associations | 5 | 4 | 41 |
| 36 (20) | Oil and gas (companies and associations) | 4 | 5 | 41 |
| 37 (31) | Senior citizens | 2 | 9 | 39 |
| 38 (40) | Miscellaneous social issue groups (anti-drunk driving, anti-smoking, anti-poverty groups, child welfare, etc.) | 1 | 11 | 38 |
| 39 (0) | Criminal Justice lobby (victims' rights groups, etc.) | 2 | 8 | 41 |
| 40 (37) | Pro-life groups | 2 | 6 | 42 |

S O U R C E :  Compiled by the authors from the 2002 fifty-state update of the Hrebenar-Thomas study and the original 1985 study. See Note 1 for a list of the researchers who provided information.

N O T E :   Each researcher was asked to rank groups into two categories: a "most effective" and a "second level of effectiveness" category. Rankings were calculated by allocating 2 points for each "most effective" ranking and 1 point for each "second level" placement and adding the totals. Where a tie in total points occurs, where possible, interests are ranked according to the number of "most effective" placements or the overall number of states in which they are effective. In some cases the totals for an interest add up to more than fifty. This is because groups within an interest category sometimes appear within both the "most effective" and the "second level " category in a state. For example, utilities are ranked in both categories in Idaho and several other states. Therefore, they are counted once for each category.

being viewed as effective in most states. It is also worth noting that despite the advocacy explosion there is no public interest or citizen group ranked in the top twenty interests. Environmental groups come the closest at 22. This top twenty (and, indeed, the entire listing) has always been dominated by economic interests, especially business and labor (including the professions), with local governments, universities, and school boards the only interests approaching what might be considered the broad public interest. In short, the five surveys confirm what we have known since the first study of the power of state interest groups, conducted by Zeller (1954): Business and the professions remain the most effective interests in the states (as they do in Washington, D.C.).

The rankings of groups from 10 to 40 have also remained fairly stable, with universities having made the major gain from 19th to 13th in rank. The top twenty also now includes sportsmen, hunting, and fishing interests (including the NRA), which together with gaming (ranked 21) have made the major gain of fifteen places each over the twenty years of our survey. The three biggest losers since 1980 have been individual banks and financial institutions (dropping from 7 to 25), though banking associations have held their ranking in the top twelve; oil and gas (from 20 to 36), and railroads, which were ranked at 32 in the early 1980s but dropped off the list in 2002. Only one interest, criminal justice groups, was not on the list in 1985, while two besides railroads dropped off (newspapers and the media and women and minorities). These minor changes attest to the stability of this ranking over the years.

*Interest Group System Power in the States*

Whereas the power of single groups and the overall impact of individual interests is observed in their political mobilization and their ability to achieve their goals, group system power is much more abstract. The method most frequently used has been to garner the observations of political practitioners and political scientists regarding the importance of the players involved in the policy-making process in each state (Morehouse 1981, 107–117; Zeller 1954, chap. 13 and 190–193). This was the method used over the past twenty years by the Hrebenar-Thomas study, though this study fine-tuned the way of categorizing and understanding changes in group system power.

Earlier assessments of group system power used only three categories: strong, moderate, and weak (Morehouse 1981, 116–118; Zeller 1954, 190–193). These are rather general and do not convey the gradual movement between categories. The five categories developed by the Hrebenar-Thomas study improve on this categorization. Table 4-2 presents these new categories and lists the fifty states according to the strength of their group systems in the late 1990s/early 2000s with an indication of changes since the 1985 survey. States listed as dominant are those in which groups as a whole are the overwhelming and consistent influence on policy making. Groups in states listed as complementary tend to work in conjunction with or are constrained by other aspects of the political system. Most often this is the party system; but it could also be a strong executive branch, competition between groups, the political culture, or a combination of all these. A subordinate group system is one that is consistently subordinated to other aspects of the policy-making process. The fact that there are no entries in the subordinate column indicates that groups were not consistently subordinate in any state. There has, in fact, never been a state listed in this column during the entire Hrebenar-Thomas study. The dominant/complementary and the complementary/subordinate columns include those states whose group systems combine elements of or alternate between the two situations, or are in the process of moving from one to the other.

Comparisons between the first survey in the early 1980s and the latest one reveal three major points about group system power in the states over the past twenty years. First, changes are gradual. Sixty percent, or thirty, of the states have remained in the same category during this period. And the twenty that have moved have moved only one category at a time: only Connecticut moved among three categories over the past twenty years. Second, most activity involved the dominant/complementary category, which showed the only increase in the number of states

**Table 4-2** Classification of the Fifty States According to the Overall Impact of Interest Groups in 2002, with Comparison of Classification in 1985

| Dominant (5) | Dominant/ complementary (26) | Complementary (16) | Complementary/ subordinate (3) | Subordinate (0) |
|---|---|---|---|---|
| Alabama | - Alaska | Colorado | - Michigan | |
| Florida | Arizona | + Connecticut | Minnesota | |
| + Montana | Arkansas | + Delaware | - South Dakota | |
| + Nevada | California | - Hawaii | | |
| West Virginia | Georgia | Indiana | | |
| | Idaho | Maine | | |
| | + Illinois | Massachusetts | | |
| | + Iowa | New Hampshire | | |
| | + Kansas | New Jersey | | |
| | Kentucky | New York | | |
| | - Louisiana | North Carolina | | |
| | + Maryland | North Dakota | | |
| | - Mississippi | Pennsylvania | | |
| | + Missouri | + Rhode Island | | |
| | Nebraska | + Vermont | | |
| | - New Mexico | Wisconsin | | |
| | Ohio | | | |
| | Oklahoma | | | |
| | Oregon | | | |
| | - South Carolina | | | |
| | - Tennessee | | | |
| | Texas | | | |
| | Utah | | | |
| | Virginia | | | |
| | Washington | | | |
| | Wyoming | | | |

SOURCE: Compiled by the authors from the 2002 update and the original survey of the Hrebenar-Thomas study.

NOTE: + or - indicates movement one category up or down since the first survey in 1985.

(from 18 in 1985 to 26 in 2002). Overall, the general movement has been toward stronger but not dominant interest group systems. Third, over all five surveys the South has been the region with the most powerful interest group systems, though the gap with other regions has narrowed considerably. The Northeast remains the region with the least powerful interest group systems.

One final point needs to be made about interest group power in the states in general. Although there are some common influences across the states—some of which are identified in Box 4-1—the impact of groups in a particular state is a product of the unique ways in which these influences interact and change. In some states the power of certain single groups and the perception of the power of individual interests may hold firm or even increase at a time when the same groups and interests are declining in other states. The number of states that have seen increases in group system power in the past twenty years is close to the number in which group power has declined. So although some common denominators do exist across the states, changes in single group power, overall interest power, and group system power often depend on the individual circumstances in a state.

### CONCERNS ABOUT INTEREST GROUPS AND GROUP REGULATION

All political institutions can have both positive and negative effects on a political system and on the society at large. Nowhere is this more evident than with interest groups. The specific concerns about interest groups in the American states fall into four major categories. First, as vehicles of representation, interest groups are far from ideal as they do not represent all segments of the population equally—they are representationally biased. This bias is toward the better-educated, higher-income, majority culture (whites in most states), and male segments of the population. Minorities (including women) and the less-well-educated and lower-income segments of society are underrepresented by interest groups.

Second, resources—mainly money—do matter, and those groups that have the most resources, particularly business and the professions, tend to be more successful in gaining the all-important access as a prerequisite to influence than those groups with fewer resources. Third, extensive resources—including money, good lobbyists, and favored status with government officials—mean that some groups exert power out of all proportion to their number of members, and, in some instances, they can thwart the will of a much larger number of people favoring or opposing a cause. And fourth, because the stakes are so high, in the past some interest groups and lobbyists have used illegal means to gain their policy goals.

Over the years, a combination of concerns about undue influence and corrupt practices of interest groups plus a desire to reach an improved state of democracy has been at the root of moves to regulate interest groups. Today four types of legal provisions provide for the regulation and public disclosure of lobbying activity in the states. Lobby laws are the most important, but these are supplemented by three other types of provisions. Conflict of interest and personal financial disclosure provisions required of public officials are intended to make public the financial connections that government officials have with individuals, groups, organizations, and businesses (COGEL 1990, 129–148). Campaign finance regulations provide for public disclosure, to a varying extent, of campaign contributions from individuals and organizations (COGEL 1990, 87–128). The regulation of PACs is another aspect of campaign finance. All states now have laws regarding the activities of PACs.

State lobby laws vary considerably, however, in their inclusiveness, their reporting requirements, and the stringency with which they are enforced (Craine, Haven, and Horner 1995; COGEL 1990, 149–171; Opheim 1991). For example, although all states include contact with the legislature within their definition of lobbying, less than a third include contact with administrative officials within that definition. Similarly, some states require public officials (state or agency personnel) to register when they lobby, but most do not. States also vary in their reporting requirements and in the stringency with which they enforce lobby laws.

How do we explain such differences across the nation among lobby laws? Morehouse has argued that states with the most stringent lobby laws tend to be those with weaker interest group systems (Morehouse 1981, 130–131; see also Morehouse and Jewell 2003, 87–89). This is more or less confirmed by the Hrebenar-Thomas study.

It is ironic that these are the states that have suffered relatively few abuses at the hands of interest groups over the years, and thus have less need of such laws. The weakest laws exist in the South, where some of the greatest abuses have taken place.

Given variations among the states in the extent and in the stringency of enforcement of lobby laws, can we make any generalizations about their effect on interest group activity in the states? The greatest value of lobby laws and other lobby regulations is in providing information on who is lobbying whom. Disclosure increases the potential for public and, particularly, press scrutiny of lobbying. Increased public information has probably been the element of lobby regulation that has had the most significant effect on state politics and government.

According to regulatory officials, however, it is not the general public but rather the press, candidates seeking election, and interest group personnel and lobbyists who make the most use of lobby registration and related information. The bulk of the information about lobbyist expenditures and activities is disseminated by the press. So although the public has benefited from these provisions, the extent of these benefits is largely determined by the press. "Outsider interests" may also have benefited from lobby regulations because public information has made the activities of their entrenched opponents more visible and as a result more restrained in many instances.

This brings us to the effect that these regulations have had on the established interests and lobbyists in the states. Restraint in dealings with public officials, greater concern for their group's public image, and increased professionalism of lobbyists appear to be the three major effects. Lobbyists, especially those representing powerful interests, are much less likely to use blatant strong-arm tactics. This is, in part, the reason for the apparent disappearance of the old wheeler-dealer lobbyist from state politics and the increased professionalism of lobbyists in general. Even dominant interests, such as the Boeing Aircraft Company in Washington, prefer to use low-key approaches, buttressed by public relations campaigns. The more public is disclosure of lobbying activity in a state and the more stringently these laws are enforced, the more open is the process of group attempts to influence public policy.

## CONCLUSIONS: THE FUTURE OF STATE INTEREST GROUPS

How are state interest groups and group systems likely to develop over the next twenty years or so? And given that interest groups are often accused of thwarting the public will, how are these developments likely to affect the extent of democracy, in terms of representation and influence, in the public policy process? Based on past developments, particularly since the early 1980s, we can offer the following observations and speculations.

In regard to the types and numbers of groups and interests, there is likely to be continued expansion, particularly in the less-developed states like Wyoming and transitional states like South Carolina. In particular, there will likely be more out-of-state interests represented in state capitals and an increase in intergovernmental lobbying; plus, institutional interests are likely to continue to increase their overall percentage of state lobbying communities. However, based upon work by Gray and Lowery, the expansion of the numbers and types of groups and interests is likely to be much slower than over the past twenty years as interest group systems become more dense and competitive, particularly in developed interest group systems like that in New Jersey. Gray and Lowery (2001, Fig. 4) show that in the 1990s there was a marked slowing down of the expansion of membership groups, associations, and institutional interests, with institutions actually declining in overall numbers

Largely because of the increased competitiveness of interest group activity, it is likely that more and more groups will use an increasing range of strategies and tactics to get their points across to public officials. While the time-honored technique of using one or more lobbyists is always likely to be the major tactic, increasing use of PACs, grassroots lobbying, and coalitions with other groups is likely to expand to more and more states. These and other tactics will be considerably aided by development in technology such as e-mail and the Internet. These have already made access to state elected and appointed officials by lobbyists, group leaders, and members easier and much more efficient than ever before. In particular, the 2002 up-date of the Hrebenar-Thomas study indicates that electronic technology is changing the way that lobbyists operate. Many of them spend less time in the halls of government as they can do more monitoring and communicating from their offices.

What can be expected in terms of the power of individual interest groups and group systems? Judging by developments in the past twenty years, there is likely to be little change in the influence of individual interests. It has already been noted that the mere presence of a group does not mean that it will be effective. Moreover, the increase in the number of groups has likely undermined the chances of political success in some ways. The "hyperpluralism" that has developed in many states has made success in the policy process less predictable and even less likely for groups without substantial resources. Public disclosure laws cannot and do not restrict the power of "insider interests" or promote the power of "outsider interests." These laws have a much more modest effect—to create a more open scene for the lobbying game. And public opinion is still often thwarted by powerful interests. This was the case in 1997 when the Milwaukee Brewers baseball franchise was able to secure state aid to build a new stadium despite a statewide poll in Wisconsin showing that 70 percent of the public opposed such aid. Finally, if the major expansion that has occurred in the number and range of state groups seen in the past twenty-five years has had little effect on the groups considered powerful, then the near future is unlikely to see major changes in this regard.

As to the power of state interest group systems, the developments are likely to be mixed. The number of dominant group systems has certainly declined over the past twenty years. At the same time, groups that shared a complementary or complementary/subordinate relationship with other institution have also declined. There has been a general movement toward dominant/complementary group systems, particularly since the Republican victories of the mid-1990s, and this trend is likely to continue. Thus predictions of many writers in the 1980s that increased political

pluralism brought about by socioeconomic diversity and other advances would result in a general diminution of group power (and especially the power of business)
in the states have only partially materialized (Zeigler 1983, 129).

What, then, do all these likely developments (or lack thereof) in interest
group activity mean for the democratic process in the states? The answer is far
from definitive.

The expansion of group activity over the past twenty years has most likely resulted in more citizens involved in interest groups in the states than ever before, and
these groups cover the gamut from traditional conservative business interests to
newer, middle-of-the road and liberal interests such as senior citizen, environmental, women, minority, and poverty action groups. Development of networking and
grassroots techniques aided by new electronic technology has made access to state
elected and appointed officials much easier. Small groups with minimal resources
do sometimes succeed. Public disclosure laws give the press, the public, and potential candidates much more information about the activities of groups and make it
less likely that lobbyist–public official relations will involve or give the appearance
of corruption. And public opinion can and often does matter much more than it
did twenty-five years ago when it comes to affecting interest group goals, even when
a strong opposing interest is involved. This was the case across the country with
MADD (Mothers Against Drunk Drivers) in the late 1980s and early 1990s. Furthermore, a strong group or interest opposed to a majority stance among the public
may also lose on occasions. For example, most states have passed restrictions on
smoking despite the well-financed opposition of the tobacco lobby.

Against this we can list many points on the minus side. Interest groups, even in
the early 2000s, are still organizations that have a bias toward representing the
middle- and upper-middle classes. There has been little change in the groups that
are successful in state government during the past twenty years. The increasing
competition among groups makes it even more imperative that a group have extensive resources to play the lobbying game successfully. And in regard to ballot propositions, organized interests have greater access to the resources necessary to both
initiate and win ballot campaigns than unorganized citizen groups. Public skepticism of interest groups is justified: Money does count, and the more a group has
the more likely it is to be successful.

This last point illustrates the crux of why the contribution of interest groups to
the democratic process has and likely always will be riddled with contradictions. Resources are the major determinant of long-term success, and often short-term effectiveness, of interest groups, and resources are likely to remain unevenly distributed
in America. In this regard, business and other well-financed lobbies are unsur-
passed. In fact, in state after state our research indicates that business has consolidated and in many places expanded its power. An important reason for this is that it
has "the advantage of the defense" (Zeigler and van Dalen 1976, 125–127). Another
reason, however, is the political experience of business and the resources it can employ, which have enabled business groups to adapt more easily than the new inter-

ests to the changing circumstances and demands of state political systems. Although less so than it once was, the state political playing field is still tilted in favor of moneyed and insider interests.

## REFERENCES

Baumgartner, Frank R., and Beth L. Leech. 1998. *Basic Interests: The Importance of Groups in Politics and in Political Science.* Princeton, N.J.: Princeton University Press.

COGEL (Council on Governmental Ethics Laws). 1990. *Campaign Finance, Ethics, and Lobby Law Blue Book, 1988-89: Special Report.* Lexington, Ky.: Council of State Governments.

Craine, Susan, Russ Haven, and Blair Horner. 1995. *Taming the Fat Cats: A National Survey of State Lobby Laws.* Publication endorsed by the League of Women Voters of New York/New York Public Interest Research Group/Common Cause New York. August.

Gray, Virginia, and David Lowery. 2001. "The Institutionalization of State Communities of Organized Interests." *Political Research Quarterly* 54(2): 265–284.

———. 1996. *The Population Ecology of Interest Representation: Lobbying Communities in the American States.* Ann Arbor: University of Michigan Press.

———. 1995. "The Demography of Interest Organization Communities: Institutions, Associations, and Membership Groups." American Politics Quarterly 23(1): 3–33.

Hrebenar, Ronald J., and Clive S. Thomas. 1993a. *Interest Group Politics in the Midwestern States.* Ames: Iowa State University Press.

———. 1993b. *Interest Group Politics in the Northeastern States.* University Park: Pennsylvania State University Press.

———. 1992. *Interest Group Politics in the Southern States.* Tuscaloosa: University of Alabama Press.

———. 1987. *Interest Group Politics in the American West.* Salt Lake City: University of Utah Press.

Lowery, David, and Virginia Gray. 1998. "The Dominance of Institutions in Interest Group Representation: A Test of Seven Explanations." *American Journal of Political Science* 42: 231–255.

Morehouse, Sarah McCally. 1981. *State Politics, Parties, and Policy.* New York: Holt, Rinehart and Winston.

Morehouse, Sarah McCally, and Malcolm E. Jewell. 2003. *State Politics, Parties and Policy.* Latham, Md.: Rowman and Littlefield.

Nownes, Anthony J., and Patricia Freeman. 1998a. "Female Lobbyists: Women in the World of 'Good ol' Boys'. " *Journal of Politics* 60: 1181–1201.

———. 1998b. "Interest Group Activity in the States." *Journal of Politics* 60: 86–112.

Opheim, Cynthia. 1991. "Explaining the Differences in State Lobby Regulation." *Western Political Quarterly* 44: 405-421.

Salisbury, Robert L. 1984. "Interest Representation: The Dominance of Institutions." *American Political Science Review* 78: 64–76.

Thomas, Clive S., and Ronald J. Hrebenar. 1999. "Interest Groups in the States." In *Politics in the American States: A Comparative Analysis,* 7th ed., edited by Virginia Gray, Russell L. Hanson, and Herbert Jacob. Washington, D.C.: CQ Press.

——— . 1996. "Interest Groups in the States." In *Politics in the American States: A Comparative Analysis,* 6th ed., edited by Virginia Gray and Herbert Jacob. Washington, D.C.: CQ Press.

———. 1992. "Changing Patterns of Interest Group Activity: A Regional Perspective." In *The Politics of Interests: Interest Groups Transformed,* edited by Mark P. Petracca. Boulder, Colo.: Westview Press

——— . 1991. "Nationalization of Interest Groups and Lobbying in the States." In *Interest Group Politics,* 3d. ed., edited by Allan J. Cigler and Burdett A. Loomis, Washington, D.C.: CQ Press.

——— . 1990. "Interest Groups in the States." In *Politics in the American States: A Comparative Analysis,* 5th ed., edited by Virginia Gray, Herbert Jacob, and Robert B. Albritton. Glenview, Ill: Scott, Foresman/ Little, Brown.

Thomas, Clive S., Michael L. Boyer, and Ronald J. Hrebenar. 2002. "Interest Groups and State Court Elections, 1980–2000: A New Era and its Challenges." Paper presented at the annual meeting of the Western Political Science Association, Long Beach, Calif., March.

Zeigler, L. Harmon. 1983. "Interest Groups in the States." In *Politics in the American States: A Comparative Analysis,* 4th ed., edited by Virginia Gray, Herbert Jacob, and Kenneth N. Vines. Boston: Little, Brown.

Zeigler, L. Harmon, and Hendrik van Dalen. 1976. "Interest Groups in the States." In *Politics in the American States: A Comparative Analysis,* 3d ed., edited by Herbert Jacob and Kenneth N. Vines. Boston: Little, Brown.

Zeller, Belle. 1954. *American State Legislatures,* 2d ed. New York: Thomas Y. Crowell.

## SUGGESTED READINGS

Cigler, Allan J., and Burdett A. Loomis, eds. *Interest Group Politics,* 6th. ed. Washington, D.C.: CQ Press, 2002. A collection of essays presenting the latest thinking on interest group formation and influence in America.

Gray, Virginia, and David Lowery. "Interest Representation in the States." Chapter 11 in Ronald E. Weber and Paul Brace, eds. *American State and Local Politics: Directions for the 21st Century.* New York: Chatham House, 1999. The encapsulation of the findings from a major, ongoing empirical study on the development of interest communities in the states and how their composition influences politics.

Hrebenar, Ronald J., and Clive S. Thomas, eds. *Interest Group Politics in the Northeastern States.* University Park: Pennsylvania State University Press, 1993. This is one of four books that analyze interest group systems in each of the fifty states in the late 1980s and early 1990s.

Nownes, Anthony J., and Patricia Freeman. "Interest Group Activity in the States." *Journal of Politics* 60(1998): 86–112. Compares the types of interests operating, what groups do, and the techniques they use in three states (California, South Carolina, and Wisconsin) and extrapolates to provide insights on recent development in interest group operations across the states.

Rosenthal, Alan. *The Third House: Lobbyists and Lobbying in the States.* 2d ed. Washington, D.C.: CQ Press, 2001. A good descriptive account of the role and techniques of contract and in-house lobbyists in the states.

# CHAPTER 5

*The Initiative Process*

SHAUN BOWLER AND TODD DONOVAN

## INTRODUCTION AND OVERVIEW

About half the states, most of them in the West, have some type of direct democracy process that allows voters a direct say in shaping public policy. These states allow people to use the initiative process to draft laws and, if a sufficient number of signatures are collected from registered voters, place them on the state's ballot. Depending on the state, elected representatives may have little influence over the substance of what voters might decide on, as well as have limited ability to amend the measure if voters approve it. As we shall see, each state using initiatives has a unique set of rules regulating the process. In states where restrictions are minimal, politics and policies, at some levels, can be fundamentally different than in non-initiative states.

In recent decades, voters in states that use the initiative process have decided on many critical matters of policy—with battles over several of these setting the stage for major policy debates at the national level. Anti-tax initiatives from the late 1970s, for example, foreshadowed the Reagan-era federal tax cuts of the early 1980s. More recently, initiatives in California, Florida, and Washington targeting affirmative action set the tone for national debate on the policy in the late 1990s. That same decade, voters in over a dozen states decided the fate of proposals to limit state legislative terms. Indeed, initiative efforts in the states sometimes are part of larger campaigns designed to shape the national agenda as much as set policy in a particular state. Initiative activists with an eye to the national stage seek to place their proposals on the ballot in multiple states to promote their causes. As a result, measures backed by national groups advocating such things as a nuclear freeze, school choice, term limits, and the repeal of affirmative action can be found on the ballot in several different states.

Still, most of the proposals that reach a state's ballot are likely to be home-grown. This does not mean that all or even most initiatives are the product of the "average" citizen who rallies at the grassroots to challenge an established order. The initiative process is also used by political parties, incumbent politicians, candidates for office, wealthy individuals, and powerful interest groups (Smith and Tolbert 2001; Ellis 2002; Donovan et al. 1998). In addition, several initiative states have spawned individual policy entrepreneurs who, while never holding office, use multiple initiatives to re-shape their states' policy agenda (Smith 1998; Donovan et al. 2001). In this context, voters in initiative states have made decisions in the last decade on issues such as gun control, access to abortion, gay rights, services for immigrants, bilingual education, criminal sentencing, taxation, gambling, insurance reform, environmental protection, campaign finance reform, and term limits.

## ORIGINS OF INITIATIVES IN THE UNITED STATES

The initiative process was first introduced in South Dakota in 1898.[1] A series of other states followed South Dakota and adopted the initiative around the end of the nineteenth century as disaffected social movements such as labor groups, farmers (the Grange movement, the Farmers' Alliance), single-taxers, Prohibitionists, evangelists, and good government "goo goos" pressed for more direct say in their government. State governments that often seemed to these Populists and Progressives as too corrupt and too beholden to special interests were targeted for reform with the initiative and referendum devices. These direct democracy tools were part of a larger set of reforms, including direct election of U.S. senators, direct primary elections, and restrictions on political parties, that were designed to weaken the control that powerful economic actors had over government.

It is important to put these reformers in the proper context. At the turn of the twentieth century campaign contributions were unregulated, and bribery and graft were not uncommon in state legislatures (Schuman 1994; Sutro 1994). Given this context, powerful business interests were able to finance a political party or a coalition of legislators in exchange for favorable treatment. As one observer noted in the 1880s the Oregon legislature consisted of "briefless lawyers, farmless farmers, business failures, bar-room loafers, Fourth-of-July orators [and] political thugs" (in Schuman 1994, 949). To Populist and Progressive reformers of that era, legislators could not be trusted to serve the public interest (Sutro 1994).

Cain and Miller (2001) distinguish between the Progressive and Populists roots of the initiative process, both in terms of the different social bases of these movements and in terms of what each wanted from reforms. The Populists maintained that common people are trustworthy and competent but that elected legislators

---

1. Nebraska had allowed the use of the initiative in cities the year before, in 1897.

were neither (Cain and Miller 2001, 35). Their explicit intent was to take power away from incumbent politicians, vested interests, and party machines and give it to voters. Progressives, on the other hand, were more sympathetic to the legislative process but wanted to "liberate representative government from [the] corrupt forces so that it might become an effective instrument for social reform" (Cain and Miller 2001, 36). As one scholar put it, for legislatures intent on blocking popular policies, the initiative was the "spur in the flank," and for legislatures attempting to pass unpopular policies, it was the "bit in the teeth" (Johnson 1944).

## A WIDE VARIETY OF INITIATIVE SYSTEMS

Each of the twenty-four states that currently allow initiatives has its own unique version of the process. Eighteen of these states adopted the process between 1898 and 1914. Although South Dakota was the first state to place initiative provisions in its state constitution, it was in Oregon in 1904 that the initiative was first used. Initiatives are more common in the West, in part because many of these states formulated their constitutions when proponents of Populist and Progressive reforms were most influential.

Most western states that adopted the initiative early now allow citizens to draft constitutional initiatives as well as statutory initiatives.[2] Many of these states also require relatively few signatures to qualify measures. After 1914 the window of opportunity for the spread of wide-open direct democracy in the United States closed substantially. Alaska included the initiative in its constitution when it was admitted to the union (1959), but only Wyoming (1968), Illinois (1970), Florida (1970), and Mississippi (1992) have adopted it since. Being removed from the immediate context of the Populist zeal for direct democracy, each of these late-adopting states has a breed of initiative that is much more restrained than what is found in California, Oregon, and much of the rest of the American west.

Late-adopting states tend to have less extensive provisions for the use of initiatives. Three late-adopting states allow constitutional initiatives only, with severe restrictions on their subject matter or restrictive provisions for qualification (Florida, Illinois, and Mississippi). As such, initiatives are rarely used in these states—only 4 had appeared in Illinois by the year 2000, just 19 in Florida, 7 in Wyoming, and only 2 in Mississippi (National Conference of State Legislatures 2000). Although the public remains quite supportive of the initiative process in states where it is used, state legislators are less enthusiastic (Bowler et al. 2001), and recent proposals for expanding initiative use to additional states are less ambitious than were their early-twentieth-century Populist models. An initiative plan considered by the New Jersey legislature in 2002, for example, would limit subject matter and only permit petitions for statutory measures that would first be evaluated by the legislature (Holman 2002).

2. Statutory initiatives change the law, not the constitution, while constitutional initiatives change the constitution. Constitutional changes are typically much harder to amend. For that reason initiatives that seek to amend constitutions have higher qualification requirements.

In contrast, many of the early-adopting, Populist-inspired states have relatively liberal rules on qualification combined with provisions for constitutional and statutory initiatives. Over three hundred initiatives have appeared on Oregon ballots since it adopted direct democracy, with California not far behind. The five states with the most frequent use of initiative (Arizona, California, Colorado, North Dakota, Oregon) have averaged more than three initiatives per election since the Progressive era (Tolbert et al. 1998). This average understates how often the initiative has been used recently, however. There has been a steady increase in the number of ballot measures that have qualified in all states since the 1960s. After a decline in the 1940s and 1950s, use of initiatives reached a new peak in the 1990s, when there were nearly four hundred initiatives on state ballots—far more than any other decade (Ellis 2002). While most initiatives fail (Magleby 1994), they can nevertheless have a powerful effect on the design of state political institutions and on the political agenda.

### INITIATIVES AS A FORM OF DIRECT DEMOCRACY

Although we refer to "the initiative process" throughout this chapter, we should note that there are several distinct types of direct democracy that have been adopted in the United States. Although frequently lumped together, it is important to note the differences between them. The four main types of direct citizen voting on policy questions are direct initiative, indirect initiative, popular referendum, and legislative referendum. Under the legislative referendum, citizens vote on statutes and/or constitutional amendments that have previously been enacted by the state legislature or proposed by the legislature. Use of legislative referendums is quite widespread, with nearly every advanced democratic nation other than the United States (Butler and Ranney 1994) and nearly every American state having some provisions for them—particularly for state constitutional matters.

Initiatives and popular referendums are another matter, and may be thought of as forms of direct democracy because control over whether a public vote is held rests outside of the legislature. With popular referendums (also known as the popular veto), if enough voter signatures are collected a bill previously approved by the legislature is put before voters for a binding yes-or-no vote. With the exceptions of Florida and Mississippi, every state that adopted initiatives adopted popular referendums at the same time (Magleby 1984).

Initiatives are even more directly democratic in that the initiative's proponents, rather than the legislature, write the legislation that the public will vote on. With direct initiatives, qualified measures simply go straight to the ballot in the next election. A few states use indirect initiatives, which allow the state legislature to adopt a proposal once it qualifies but also gives it the option of coming up with an alternative measure to place on the ballot alongside the original initiative. Most states with initiatives have direct initiatives only; however, a few (Maine, Massachusetts, Wyoming) have indirect initiatives only. Five others have both.[3]

---

3. Michigan, Nevada, Ohio, Utah, Washington.

The distinction between direct and indirect initiatives is not always precise. Depending on the state, the "indirect" initiative question may go on the ballot if the legislature rejects it, submits a different proposal, or takes no action. Alaska's and Wyoming's initiative processes are usually considered indirect. However, instead of requiring that an initiative be submitted to the legislature for action, they only require that an initiative not be placed on the ballot until after a legislative session has convened and adjourned.

## INITIATIVES AND AGENDA SETTING

For our purposes we will treat direct and indirect initiatives as one category and one in which citizens or groups outside the legislature initiate policy proposals. We focus on the initiatives rather than popular referendums because they have the greatest policy impact and generate the most heated discussions among observers of state politics.

Under the initiative process, citizens, interest groups, and others who are outside of the government decide whether or not to place a question on the ballot, when to ask it, and what the details of the law will be. The initiative grants the power to make policy directly to the citizens and is a direct expression of both majority rule and popular sovereignty in a way quite distinct from a purely representative form of government.

## SUBJECT MATTER

What, then, can voters decide upon in initiative states? Although some states regulate initiative content, it is important to note that, generally speaking, any topic is a potential initiative subject.[4] The only major constraints on initiatives are constitutionality and single-subject laws. Half of the twenty-four initiative states do limit initiatives to a single subject. In the past, state courts were fairly tolerant of individual proposals with sweeping breadth, as long as their component parts could be seen as reasonably germane to one subject. Single-subject rules were adopted to ban egregious attempts at building coalitions of supporters via log-rolling. One famous, yet unsuccessful initiative proposal from California linked regulation of margarine; voting rights for Native Americans; gambling, fishing, and mining issues; and apportionment of the state senate into a single initiative question (Crouch 1943, 12). This sort of proposal is prohibited by single-subject laws.

Only Florida's court has been known to regularly nullify initiatives on single-subject grounds. The Florida State Supreme Court is the only court to overtly declare that single-subject evaluations should be applied more rigorously to initiatives than legislative bills (Lowenstein 1995, 282). Since 2000, however, state courts in California, Colorado, Nevada, and Oregon have become more rigid in the application of their state's single-subject rule. At times, this has meant that a

---

4. A few states prohibit measures dealing with the judiciary, bills of rights, or tax questions.

single initiative must be split into several questions that are put before voters (El-lis 2002, 144–146).

Although some states may review the proposal prior to circulating petitions to check for proper form, very few states' officials or courts are allowed to amend or revise the language of propositions without the proponent's consent. Of the twenty-four states, only six have much of a pre-election review at all. A few states have a largely advisory process (Colorado, Idaho, Montana, Washington).

Still, in most states there are few limits on the nature of contentious issues that reach the ballot—from taxation through issues such as the death penalty, regulation of euthanasia, abortion, drug use, rights for gays and lesbians, and prohibitions on the hunting of specific animals (e.g., horses, mountain lions). Other issues reach the ballot that are clearly designed to limit what legislators can do—for example, term limits, spending limits, and campaign finance reforms. Many of these are such polarizing matters that incumbent legislators may not wish to have floor votes on them, while others are often matters that many self-interested incumbents might resist.

Throughout the twentieth century a surprising degree of stability existed in the subject matter on which voters were asked to decide (Magleby 1994; see also Tol-bert et al. 2001). The most common types of initiatives since 1980 have been governmental reform measures such as term limits and campaign finance regulation (23 percent) and taxation questions (22 percent). Social and moral issues (17 percent) and environmental measures (11 percent) are the next most common type of question (Tolbert et al. 2001; Magleby 1994). Apart from an upsurge in the proportion of measures dealing with the environment and a slight decline in the proportion dealing with governmental reform, the general subject matter on ballots at the end of the 1990s was relatively similar to that appearing in the early decades of the twentieth century.

### GETTING ON THE BALLOT

An initiative's actual impact on state politics may depend on how easy it is to use, as well as on the nature of interest group demands in a state. As we will see, there is considerable variation in how easy it is for citizens to use the process across the twenty-four states that have some version of direct democracy. Independent of this, there is also considerable variation in the level of demand for initiatives in each state. Putting to one side for a moment the state-specific details of qualification procedures, there are four basic steps in the initiative process that most states share:[5]

1. A proposal is drafted by proponents.

2. The proposal is forwarded to a state office for review (usually for form, not legal content). An official title and summary of the measure are issued (a few states allow proponents to write the title).

---

5. For a more detailed discussion of California's initiative process, see http://www.ss.ca.gov/elections/elections.htm.

3. Proponents circulate petitions that include the title, a summary, and text of the law for registered voters to sign.

4. A state office verifies that the correct number of signatures has been gathered. If so, the proposal goes to the ballot.

Although these steps may sound relatively straightforward in principle, they can be tremendously costly in some states, and their actual practice can raise some quite difficult issues. These costs and the difficulty in obtaining enough signatures are affected by the states' rules regulating qualification and on the size of the state's population (Banducci 1998a).

Take, for example, the first two steps: the drafting and filing of a proposal. It is important to underscore that, at least in certain states, anyone with a few spare dollars can submit a proposal on just about any topic—in Washington anyone with just five dollars and a bee in his or her bonnet can start the initiative ball rolling. Far more proposals are thus submitted for title and summary than ever qualify for the ballot. While many commentators have expressed doubts about the advisability of a process in which anyone with a few dollars can make a policy proposal, in fact the costs and logistics of collecting signatures weed out all but the best-funded or best-organized proponents.

Important differences across states can be found in the qualification stage, when petitions are circulated for signatures. Most states require a minimum number of signatures, expressed in terms of a percentage of the votes cast for governor in the previous election. This percentage ranges from 3 percent in Massachusetts to 15 percent in Arizona. Other states also have distribution requirements that mean the signatures cannot come simply from one area or city but have to come from a broad area, usually defined in terms of counties. Nebraska requires that 5 percent of signatures come from at least two-fifths of the counties, while Wyoming requires signatures from two-thirds of all counties. States vary, too, in how much time is allowed to gather signatures. Although some states might allow over a year (Missouri, Utah), Oregon has a fairly stringent ninety-day time limit for collecting signatures.

Getting proposals onto the ballot can be quite arduous, but it is clear that it is harder to collect sufficient signatures in some states than others. In general the percentage thresholds for collecting signatures were put into place when the initiative process was first adopted, and as the population of states has grown over the past one hundred years, so too has the raw number of signatures required. But time limits for circulation have not changed. Thus where it might have taken fewer than 170 signatures per day to qualify in a state with 250,000 voters in 1900, it would require over 1,000 signatures per day if that same state has 1.6 million voters today.[6] In some states, the pace of signature collection now makes it difficult for anyone to reach the

6. This example reflects the situation in Oregon, assuming a 6 percent signature requirement and a ninety-day time frame.

ballot unless they pay professional petition firms to collect signatures for them. This leads some to argue that an "initiative industrial complex" has subverted the Populists' vision of who the initiative process would serve. In fact, the use of paid signature collectors (Beard and Schultz 1914) and professional initiative campaign staffs (McCuan et al. 1998) have been part of the process in some states since early in the twentieth century. Nevertheless, as qualification costs increase, many observers argue that only special interests and the wealthy are now able to get their measures on the ballot in many states (see Broder 2000; Schrag 1998; Haskell 2001; Ellis 2002).

Take, for example, California. Those who wish to get a constitutional initiative amendment onto the ballot have to gather signatures equivalent to 8 percent of the number of votes for governor (they need 5 percent for a statutory initiative). This means they must gather approximately 670,000 signatures (420,000 for statutory initiatives) within 150 days. This is a huge task. It is not surprising, then, that around 70 percent of initiative proposals fail to make it to the California ballot. That is, even after drafting a proposal, giving it to the secretary of state's office, paying California's $200 fee, and starting a petition drive, the overwhelming majority of proposals never obtain enough signatures to reach the ballot.[7]

It should also come as no surprise, then, that businesses expert in gathering signatures originated in California, and that they export their services to initiative proponents in other states. These companies, along with other, non-California firms, hire subcontractors who employ temporary workers to gather the signatures. Some of these "petition management" firms advertise that they will guarantee "instant" qualification—for a set price. A typical qualification effort might cost around $1 to $2 per signature.

One commonly made observation is that it costs over $1 million simply to put a proposal on the California ballot. Even in a smaller state such as Washington, the cost may easily exceed $300,000. Several states, including Washington and Colorado, passed laws banning the use of paid signature-gathering. However, the U. S. Supreme Court overturned these laws in 1988, arguing that the First Amendment protected paid petitioning as a form of political speech (*Meyer v. Grant*, 486 U.S. 414 1988). It is little wonder, then, that most proposals fail to make it to the ballot, and that those that do qualify require financial backing by wealthy groups (unions, professional associations, trade groups) or wealthy individuals who act as patrons for a group promoting some policy. Examples of the latter include Microsoft co-founder Paul Allen, who paid for a school-choice measure in Washington; hi-tech magnate Ron Unz, who bankrolled initiatives attacking bilingual education in Massachusetts; and movie director Rob Reiner, who funded a tobacco tax initiative in California.

Even accounting for the length of time that a state has had the initiative process, some states are much more frequent users of the initiative than others. In part, this

---

7. This holds for all states, as many proposals are filed by people who lack either the intent or the ability to mount a substantial petition effort. Many measures are filed simply as attempts to attract attention to an issue.

reflects limits placed on the use of initiatives. States that impose geographical restrictions on where signatures come from or that limit the scope of the initiative's subject matter—Illinois is especially restrictive—reduce the number of initiatives appearing on their ballots. Banducci (1998a, 117) demonstrates that signature-gathering regulations do matter. Even when several other factors are accounted for, there are significantly fewer initiatives in states that effectively require proponents to collect more signatures per day.

Table 5-1 provides a simple descriptive index of how difficult it is to qualify for the ballot in each state. The index accounts for whether only statutes or only constitutional measures are allowed, if the length of the qualifying period is limited, if requirements for a geographic distribution of signatures exist, if the proportion of voters' signatures required for qualification is relatively high, and whether or not there are limits on the substance of what can be decided by initiative. Oregon, having none of these limitations, tops the list with the most initiatives, while Mississippi, one of the most restrictive states, ranks near the bottom in initiative use. There is a modest correlation between this index and the number of initiatives qualifying in these states in the 1990s (Pearson's r = -.74).[8] The imperfect correlation reflects, in part, that items in the index are weighted equally despite the fact that some—like geographic requirements for signatures—may be much more of an impediment to qualification than others.

Liberal qualification rules are not the sole determinant of how many initiatives a state experiences. States with more people per state representative, with stronger interest group systems, and with more professionalized legislatures are also likely to have more initiatives (Banducci 1998a). Each of these factors probably reflects the fact that states that have greater demands on their political systems tend to have more initiatives, if they are allowed.

It is clear from Table 5-1 that initiative politics plays a much bigger role in western states, in particular the Pacific Coast states, where liberal access laws combine with relatively dense interest group demands.[9] Eastern states and midwestern states with initiatives tend to have more restrictive qualification rules, but they may also have political party organizations that play a larger role in structuring political competition, thus reducing demands for the use of initiatives (Dwyer et al. 1994). All this considered, many more initiatives reach state ballots west of the Mississippi.

## INITIATIVE CAMPAIGNS AND ELECTIONS

Getting onto the ballot is just the first major hurdle. Once qualified, a person or group sponsoring an initiative still has a campaign to fight. The campaign stage of the initiative process has attracted a considerable amount of attention from

8. Pearson's r reflects the degree of linear relationship between two variables. It ranges from -1 to +1 where +1 reflects a perfect positive relationship.

9. This means that much of our understanding of initiative politics comes from the Pacific Coast and Colorado. Much less is known about the initiative experience in, for example, the midwestern states of Missouri and Michigan.

**Table 5-1** Index of Qualification Difficulty and Initiative Use

| State | Year adopted | Qualification difficulty | Number from adoption to 2002 | Number from 1976 to 96 | Number from 1996 to 2002 |
|---|---|---|---|---|---|
| Oregon | 1902 | 0 | 339 | 86 | 50 |
| California | 1911 | 1 | 281 | 98 | 45 |
| Colorado | 1912 | 1 | 187 | 46 | 28 |
| North Dakota | 1914 | 1 | 167 | 34 | 6 |
| Arkansas | 1909 | 2 | 91 | 16 | 13 |
| Ohio | 1912 | 2 | 63 | 18 | 3 |
| Michigan | 1908 | 2 | 61 | 18 | 7 |
| South Dakota | 1898 | 2 | 52 | 24 | 8 |
| Idaho | 1912 | 2 | 25 | 13 | 6 |
| Arizona | 1912 | 3 | 156 | 29 | 18 |
| Washington | 1912 | 3 | 124 | 39 | 27 |
| Oklahoma | 1907 | 3 | 81 | 11 | 2 |
| Montana | 1904 | 3 | 73 | 27 | 12 |
| Missouri | 1906 | 3 | 71 | 18 | 9 |
| Massachusetts | 1918 | 3 | 59 | 25 | 11 |
| Utah | 1900 | 3 | 21 | 9 | 3 |
| Nebraska | 1912 | 4 | 43 | 13 | 8 |
| Maine | 1908 | 4 | 39 | 23 | 8 |
| Nevada | 1904 | 4 | 39 | 13 | 11 |
| Florida | 1972 | 4 | 25 | 14 | 10 |
| Illinois | 1970 | 4 | 4 | 1 | 0 |
| Alaska | 1959 | 5 | 38 | 17 | 13 |
| Mississippi | 1992 | 5 | 2 | 1 | 1 |
| Wyoming | 1968 | 6 | 7 | 4 | 1 |

SOURCES:  Magleby (1984); National Conference of State Legislatures (2000, 2002).

NOTE:  Higher scores equal more difficulty.  Points are added to the index if 1) only statutes or only constitutional measures are allowed, 2) the length of the qualifying period is limited, 3) geographic distribution of signatures is required, 4) the proportion of voter signatures that are required for qualification is between 7 and 10 percent, 5) the proportion of voter signatures that are required for qualification exceeds 10 percent, and 6) there are substantive limits on the subject matter of initiatives.

scholars. Since publication of the seminal works of David Magleby (1984) and Thomas Cronin (1989) on the initiative process, this has probably been the most studied aspect of American direct democracy. A common critique is that well-financed groups are advantaged in the campaign process. Some take this critique farther and argue that well-financed campaigns may manipulate voters into passing policies that they actually do not prefer. Criticism of the process at this stage thus falls into two broad categories: a critique of the role of special interests and a critique of the process for making too many demands upon voters. We can address each of these in turn.

The argument that special interests dominate the initiative process is a plausible one. After all, if it can take up to $1 million simply to ensure that a proposal appear on the ballot, even before campaigning begins, playing initiative politics obviously requires significant resources. Ordinary citizens are unlikely to have the necessary funds, but established, well-funded groups are not so disadvantaged.

The 1998 elections in California give some insight into how much spending is involved. In November 1998 there were twelve general election ballot measures.

Of these, seven measures (Propositions 4 through 10) were initiatives placed on the ballot by petitions signed by voters. The secretary of state reported that $196,823,595 was raised to qualify, support, and oppose all twelve measures. This was the most spent on initiative campaigns in any single election in California—and more than presidential candidates spent in the 2000 general election nationally. The most expensive measure on the November 1998 ballot was Proposition 5, with $92 million spent collectively to qualify, support, and oppose the ultimately successful initiative to legalize gambling on Native American reservations in California.

These enormous sums are possible because the U.S. Supreme Court views initiative campaigns differently than candidate contests. The Court recognizes that large contributions to candidates may create the appearance that a candidate for office may be corrupted (*Buckley v. Valeo*, 424 US 1 1976). This allows Congress and the states a limited ability to override First Amendment concerns and regulate the size of contributions given to candidates. Contributions to initiative campaigns, in contrast, are seen as attempts at direct communication with voters rather than attempts to influence elected officials. The Court reasoned that voters can't do any corrupt political favors for the donor, so they found no state interest in limits on contributions to initiative campaigns (*First National Bank of Boston v. Bellotti*, 1978 435 U.S. 765 1978). The *Bellotti* decision was the Court's first to explicitly extend free speech rights to corporations (Tolbert et al. 1998). Put simply, there are no limits on what can be spent on initiative campaigns.

Most initiative campaign spending funds TV advertising. How do voters respond? Since anyone with the money can bring an issue to the ballot, some initiatives may focus on the narrow concerns of a particular group or economic sector. Voters, furthermore, may be unfamiliar with issues of interest to such groups, issues such as HMO regulation, tort reform, securities litigation, car insurance regulation, or the status of tribal casinos. In such circumstances, they may find it difficult to decide. After all, voters are simply asked to vote yes or no on ballot initiatives—there are no party labels on the ballot and few other cues to guide them when they vote. To complicate matters, they may also be asked their opinion on several ballot initiatives in each election.

This would seem to be fertile ground for the impact of manipulative TV ad campaigns. Well-heeled special interests, the argument goes, can afford to get any issues they want onto the ballot. Once on the ballot these same interests can afford to buy spin doctors, campaign managers, and TV ads necessary to get voters to vote for things they do not really want or that even harm the public interest (for variants of this argument, see Broder 2000, Schrag 1998, and Smith 1998). It is, we should say, a very plausible argument and has to be taken seriously by supporters and opponents of the initiative alike. We can begin to address this argument by breaking it back down into its two component parts: first, that economic interests dominate the process (as opposed to broad-based citizen concerns) and, second, that voters are readily swayed by TV campaigns.

*Economic vs. Citizen Group Dominance*

One way to assess this is to ask whether narrowly focused economic interests (e.g., banks, trade and industry groups, corporations, professional associations) outspend other, broader-based citizen groups. Another way is to ask whether these economic groups tend to win the initiative contests they finance.

One of the most careful studies of the role of interest groups in the initiative process is Elisabeth Gerber's *The Populist Paradox* (1999). It is difficult, of course, to cleanly divide up the proponents and opponents of initiatives into "economic" interests and other, broad-based interests. Gerber defines economic groups as those whose members and donors are almost exclusively firms and organizations, rather than individual citizens. Examples include the Missouri Forest Products Association, the California Beer and Wine Wholesalers, the Washington Software Association (see Gerber 1999, 69–71), and specific business firms such as casino operators and tobacco giant Phillip Morris. Gerber's study of contributions from eight states found that over $227 million were contributed to ballot measure campaigns between 1988 and 1992, with 68 percent coming from narrowly based economic groups. Interestingly, Gerber found that a *negative* relationship exists between the amounts contributed by economic, professional, and business groups in support of an initiative and the probability that that initiative will pass (1999, 110).

In another study, Gerber (1998) found that while economic interests did outspend "citizen" groups, most of economic group spending was defensive. Nearly 80 percent of their contributions were spent trying to defeat measures, while nearly 90 percent of citizen spending was in support of measures. Economic group spending in opposition is often well spent. Banducci (1998a) estimates that a dollar spent by the "No" campaign has almost twice as much impact on eventual vote share than a dollar spent by the "Yes" side. Donovan et al. (1998, 90) also show that narrow economic groups regularly defeat initiatives supported by a broad, diffuse constituency. However, Gerber (1998, 18, 19) and Donovan et al. (1998, 90) found that measures supported by citizen groups and opposed by economic groups pass at rates higher than average.

When economic interest groups spend in favor of their own initiatives, they rarely win. Gerber concludes that economic groups are at a disadvantage in initiative contests because they "lack the resources required to persuade a statewide electoral majority" to vote yes on many things (Gerber 1999, 137). Another study looking at fifty-three California initiative contests in the years 1986–1996 found that the pass rate of propositions benefiting narrow interests was only 14 percent—a much lower figure than for propositions affecting broad-based groups (Donovan et al. 1998, 96). In short, while a high level of spending in support of an initiative does not appear to have a strong association with passage, a high level of spending against does. According to this evidence, then, "special" interests do not often write public policy via the initiative, but they are successful in blocking many proposals that might affect them. This is one of the more robust findings in all of the direct democracy literature.

*How (and What) Voters Decide on Initiatives*

It is more than plausible to suppose that voters are quite vulnerable to misleading advertising associated with initiative campaigns. Research suggests, however, that they may be able to make reasonable choices on initiatives. Their ability to do so rests on the availability of information, in the form of cues or shortcuts, that helps them make sense of complex issues (Lupia and McCubbins 1998; Lupia 1994; Bowler and Donovan 1998). One way they do this is by voting on the basis of elite endorsements (see, e.g., Karp 1998; Lupia 1994; Bowler and Donovan 1998). If, for example, voters see a prominent Democrat support a proposition, then Democratic voters are likely to support the proposition and Republicans oppose it. This kind of cue-taking can help explain the pattern of ideological consistency in votes observed across a range of initiatives on the same ballot (Banducci 1998b). Of course, voting on the basis of simple cues does not establish that citizens understand the details of the proposals they decide upon. It may explain, however, why there are so few examples of initiatives passing that are later found to be unpopular with the voters who approved them.

But how do voters receive the cues? In ten states the secretaries of state mail voters a ballot pamphlet that lists each ballot proposal and includes arguments for and against the proposition (Dubois and Feeney 1992, 126). In those states, key information cues are given to voters in the pamphlet; for many, finding out who signed the "pro" and "con" arguments is the single most important source of information they use when making their decisions (Bowler and Donovan 1998; 2002a). A second way that voters may find cues about an initiative is through TV ads paid for by the "Yes" or "No" campaigns. Surveys show that voters typically believe that initiative campaigns are attempts to mislead (Bowler et al. 2001, 370), and that voters discount the usefulness of political ads (Bowler and Donovan 2002a). However, these ads typically do provide useful cues to voters. One study of initiative campaign TV ads from several states shows that these ads often provide cues such as the names of sponsors or opponents, as well as the names of prominent groups, newspapers, and politicians who have taken positions on the measure. Voters in Washington and California report using multiple sources of information when deciding on initiatives, and less than 2 percent of those who used TV ads relied on that information source exclusively (Bowler and Donovan 2002a).

Spending on initiative TV ads and other campaign material probably increases public awareness of the initiatives that are the subject of the ads. Once an ad or series of ads is broadcast then general awareness of the initiative question is raised, and at that point citizens might pay a little more attention to the TV news, the newspaper, or the ballot pamphlet. This may explain, in part, why one study found higher levels of general knowledge about politics in states with prominent initiative campaigns (Smith 2002). Another study found that voters are more likely to have heard about an initiative when more was spent on the campaign, and that more citizens voted on initiatives that had higher campaign spending (Bowler and Donovan 1998).

Since voters are typically reluctant to alter the status quo (Bowler and Donovan 1998), and since most campaign spending in initiative elections is on the "No" side, the majority of initiatives fail. There are some variations across time and states, but overall fewer than half pass—around 40 percent. Multiple studies have established that initiatives are most likely to pass when supported by citizen groups (Gerber 1998; 1999) and when the initiative allocates broad, non-divisible benefits to a large, diffuse constituency (Donovan et al. 1998; Campbell 1997; Ernst 2001). Most initiatives that pass can be seen as a change that, for better or worse, taps into the preferences and concerns of the broader public.

### Initiatives and the Context of State Electoral Politics

Initiative campaigns can alter a state's political context. At one level, anec-dotes suggest that individual measures might mobilize different elements of the electorate at different times. A classic example of this is the 1982 California gu-bernatorial election. Los Angeles mayor Tom Bradley led in polls conducted im-mediately prior to the vote, but Bradley ended up losing to George Deukmejian. In this case, polls may have had difficulty estimating how an initiative would shape the participating electorate. The same ballot included a highly contested gun control measure, Proposition 15, which the National Rife Association (NRA) opposed. The NRA spent over $5 million against the measure and rallied pro-gun voters to the polls (Allswang 2000). Deukmajian, the Republican candi-date, probably benefited from this draw of voters. There is also systematic evi-dence that initiatives affect who participates in state elections. A number of re-cent studies (Tolbert et al. 2001; Smith 2001) have shown that initiative use increases turnout. Mark Smith's analysis (2001) suggests that highly salient ini-tiatives have the greatest effect, particularly in off-year (non-presidential year) state elections.

At times, political parties and politicians themselves become proponents of ini-tiatives—sometimes with an eye towards shaping the participating electorate. Ini-tiatives have also been used to promote the policy ideas of several gubernatorial candidates, and they are also used by political parties (Smith and Tolbert 2001). Daniel Smith shows how parties use initiatives to promote wedge issues they hope will split their opponents' base of support. Major examples of this from the past decade are affirmative action and immigration initiatives. Republicans adopted and promoted California initiatives to restrict affirmative action and another measure restricting services to illegal immigrants, hoping that Democrats across the nation would be forced to adopt policy positions that would harm their chances for re-election. Republican governor Pete Wilson of California as well as Democratic can-didate John Van de Kamp both raised money to put several policy questions on the ballot when they sought office.

This discussion has focused on initiative campaigns and elections and the direct effects initiatives have on a state's political context. Initiatives also shape state poli-tics in other ways, by changing how people see themselves as citizens.

## EFFECTS ON CITIZENS AND STATE POLITICS

A body of democratic theory proposes that people learn how to be citizens by making decisions in groups and by participating in politics (e.g., Pateman 1970). Greater democratic participation may have an educative role for citizens, and thus breed civic maturation. Some suggest that ballot initiatives, by forcing people to deliberate about public issues, might constitute a watered-down form of participatory democracy and lead to a more engaged, informed, and interested citizenry. Direct voting on policy matters, the logic suggests, may increase discussion about public policy and, at least at a minimal level, force voters to think more about policy issues put on the ballot.

A number of recent studies show that there might be some merit to these ideas. As noted, initiatives are associated with increased voter turnout. In fact, some voters will turn out and vote on an initiative contest when the candidate races on the ballot might otherwise have led them to stay at home. More votes were cast for California's anti-tax Proposition 13 in 1978 than for the governor's race on the same ballot.

The presence of highly visible initiatives on a state ballot may also be associated with higher levels of general knowledge about politics. Smith (2002) found that voters have higher levels of factual knowledge about politics where initiatives are used more frequently. Bowler and Donovan (2002b) found that citizens in states with frequent initiative use feel more competent when participating in politics, are more likely to think that they "have a say," and are more likely to think that public officials care about what they think. Similar results have been found for the case of Switzerland, the country of origin of the initiative and whose frequent use of the process matches that of the western United States (Frey 1997; Frey and Stutzer 1999).

## INITIATIVES AND MINORITIES

Many worry that the initiative process can be used to harm minorities—particularly groups such as gays and lesbians and racial, ethnic, linguistic, and religious minorities (see Gamble 1997; Hero and Tolbert 1996). Those who worry about repressive majorities can point to a series of anti-minority measures passed at the ballot box. Initiatives have emerged proposing the repeal of affirmative action in California, Florida, and Washington; immigration has been an issue in California; bilingual education in California and Massachusetts; and initiatives declaring English an "official language" have appeared in several states (Citrin et al. 1990). One key question, then, is whether on the whole the initiative process is repressive of minorities.

Hajnal et al. (2002) ask how often racial and ethnic minority voters are on the losing side when they vote on initiatives. If the initiative process is repressive, then ethnic minorities should be consistently in the voting minority. They find, however, that ethnic minority voters are no more likely to be supporting the losing side in an initiative contest than Anglo voters. The reason for this is quite straightforward: members of ethnic minorities are not simply one-dimensional characters but have a whole series of issues and concerns that may be addressed by the initiative process.

Gay rights have been both one of the more common and also more contentious areas of initiative politics, as politically conservative Christian activists have repeatedly sought to use the initiative to attack gay rights (Gamble 1997). In some cases they have succeeded at the local level, but for the most part these attempts have failed at the state level (Donovan and Bowler 1998). Voters in a number of states have refused to pass the most repressive anti-gay measures, with Colorado being the notable exception (Donovan, Bowler, and McCuan 2001). Having said this, we should not be too sanguine about the capacity of minorities to weather majority views under initiative politics. Cain and Miller (2001), for example, argue that the "limited evidence does suggest that the initiative process . . . is sometimes prone to produce laws that disadvantage relatively powerless minorities—and probably is more likely than legislatures to do so" (52).

Regardless of whether particular measures pass or fail, initiatives can still have major indirect effects on state politics and policy. By simply targeting a minority group, for example, public attitudes about the group (or about policies that benefit the group) can be changed, with mass opinion becoming less tolerant of the targeted minority group (Wenzel et al. 1998).

## INITIATIVES AND STATE POLICY

A number of scholars propose that the initiative causes public policy to better reflect the preferences of voters. The effect need not be due to an initiative passing, or even reaching the ballot. Rather, the mere existence of the initiative process can change how legislators behave. If legislators know that someone has a credible threat of passing a popular measure by initiative, they could have greater incentives to pass some version of it themselves in order to maintain some ability to shape the eventual policy. Initiatives can also send legislators signals about what the public wants done on key policy matters (Romer and Rosenthal 1979; Gerber 1996).

In states without initiatives, legislators face different pressures and may have fewer clear signals about what the public wants. Some studies find that certain public policies in initiative states—spending on certain state programs, abortion regulations, death penalty laws, and some civil rights policies—more closely match public opinion in those states than policies in non-initiative states (Arceneaux 2002; Gerber 1996; Gerber 1999; Matsusaka 1995). Others find no such effect (Lascher, Hagen, and Rochlin 1996; Camobreco 1998). Many of these studies examine different policy areas, however, and use different methods. Gerber (1996; 1999) finds that the presence of the initiative process in a state makes state death penalty and parental abortion notification laws better reflect that state's public opinion, while Lascher, Hagen, and Rochlin (1996) investigate a menu of different policies. Matsusaka (2001) argues that if proper statistical models are used, there is evidence that states with initiatives have policies that more closely match voter preferences.

One policy area where the initiative has a clear, direct impact is in what Tolbert, Lowenstein, and Donovan (1998) call "governance" policies. Voters in initiative states frequently pass measures that amend the political system itself. By giving groups outside the legislature a tool to craft policies, initiatives can advance policies that run counter to the self-interests of elected officials. States with the initiative process are much more likely to have adopted policies that constrain how legislators govern: term limits, supermajority requirements for new taxes, tax and expenditure limitations (Tolbert, Lowenstein, and Donovan 1998), and campaign finance reforms (Pippen et al. 2002).

The general effect of these reforms has been to give a different character to state politics in initiative states. Supporters of the initiative process say this is just as it should be. One of the original purposes of the initiative as an institution was to make policy that was more responsive to voter demands than what legislatures might produce. If, for example, legislatures kept increasing taxes beyond the willingness of voters to pay, then the initiative would allow someone to put in place mechanisms to restrain future tax increases—such as California's Proposition 13 of 1978, Oregon's Measure 5, Colorado's Taxpayer Bill of Rights (TABOR) amendment of 1991, or Washington's I-695 of 2000.

Similarly, if legislators do not allocate enough money to a particular program, then groups outside the legislature can demand those monies be allocated directly to specific programs. Education unions have been skilled at promoting such initiatives. The California Teachers' Association, for example, passed Proposition 98 in 1988 to mandate that a fixed percentage of state general fund revenues go to K-12 education. Washington's I-728 mandated smaller class sizes, while the Washington Education Association sponsored the successful initiative I-732 that mandated pay raises for Washington state's teachers. It is important to remember that these mandates for increased spending and limits on revenue can constrain legislatures both in the present and, potentially, in the future. Term limits are another example of initiative-induced constraints on legislators. Initiative states, for example, tend to have term limited legislatures, non-initiative states—with the exception of Louisiana—do not (Cain and Miller 2001, 49).

*Long-term Effects of Initiatives*

All of this creates the potential for initiative-fueled cycles of change. Initiatives may alter state policy directly by providing an additional point of access for groups seeking to change the substance of what government does. Thus advocates of decriminalization of drugs, physician-assisted suicide, minimum wage increases, or nearly any other policy have the potential to do an "end run" around the legislature and make their appeals straight to voters.

More important, initiatives also have effects on state policies that are less direct, but potentially more enduring. First, as we have discussed above, the existence of the initiative device may affect how legislators behave by increasing the likelihood that they will take note of the public's substantive policy preferences. That is, it allows groups an additional tool to pressure legislators into passing something that might be popular with voters. In the long run, then, in some policy arenas legislatures in initiative states may come to adopt policies more in line with public preferences.

But direct democracy provides more than just another access point to the legislative process. It allows those outside of the legislature, and those outside the traditional corridors of power, the ability to permanently change institutions of government that structure how policy may be made. As examples, initiatives have been used to re-write state rules about how judges sentence criminals, about how much a state may collect via existing taxes, and how much the legislature may spend in a given year. Initiatives have been used to change rules about how legislatures approve new taxes, and initiatives have placed limits on how often legislators may run for re-election. These rule changes have consequences in the long run. They limit the range of policy options available to future legislatures.

This is particularly evident in states that allow constitutional initiatives. To illustrate how radically different politics in initiative states are from, say, U.S. politics generally, consider who drives the process of amending the U.S. Constitution or other constitutions in non-initiative states. At the federal level, supermajorities of both houses of Congress are required to propose amendments that must then be approved by at least three-quarters of the states—usually by the state's legislatures. At both stages, incumbent representatives control the process. In non-initiative states, a state constitutional amendment may be referred to the voters for approval, but again, the amendment is written by the legislature. Under these conditions, changes in rules about how politics are conducted are largely shaped by actors who have to live with the consequences, and who also have experience with the routine business of making government work.

### Initiative Effects on State Fiscal Policy

In initiative states, however, these conditions need not hold. By opening lawmaking and constitutional amendment processes to those outside of the legislature, a state's political system can be re-engineered by the visionary, and the vindictive. Direct democracy has allowed outsiders—particularly anti-tax advocates—the opportunity to institutionalize rules that constrain taxing and spending. It also allows an additional point of access for groups seeking their slice of the budget pie. This means voters are asked to cut property taxes, increase tobacco taxes, guarantee a certain share of general funds for education, or authorize teacher pay raises and smaller class sizes. A single ballot may thus contain choices for cutting some taxes, raising others, issuing public debt for specific projects, and increasing spending on specific programs. If not on a single ballot, voters in initiative states may nevertheless make such budget choices over time. In most states, choices about increasing spending need not be linked to specific proposals about where the revenue will come from. Likewise, choices about cutting taxes typically need not be linked to specific programs that will lose funding.

Little is known about how voters reason about such choices over time. The electorates in several states have voted on fiscal matters in ways that may seem, on the surface, somewhat contradictory. Washington voted to limit revenues in 1992 and voted to cut taxes in 1999, then approved dramatic increases for spending on education in 2000. Californians voted to reduce property taxation in 1978 and in subsequent years, yet they did not approve a cut in their income tax in 1982. While continuing to support property tax limits, the California electorate later mandated funds for K–12 education and approved a sales tax increase to fund police and fire protection. Likewise, voters in other states can be found saying no to one kind of tax (usually property) while approving others (usually targeted sales taxes or lotteries). One reason for this may be that people tend to be more aware of, and hostile to, property taxes than sales taxes (Bowler and Donovan 1995).

The consequences of these fiscal initiatives—for example, on state budgets and bond ratings—may be more enduring than the effects of other initiatives that pass (Donovan and Bowler 1998). All of this presents several important questions about voters, initiatives, and state fiscal policies. That is, when given such a free hand in budgeting, do voters consider the fiscal tradeoffs implicit in such choices? Are they capable of budgeting, as a legislature would be expected to do?

Fiscal crisis may result if they are not. A unique mix of things only possible in initiative states complicates the legislature's task of writing state budgets. Many contemporary observers worry that initiative proponents can sell anti-tax measures to voters that promise "something for nothing"—essentially, continued service provision while taxes are cut (Sears and Citrin 1982). There is some evidence that, over time, the California electorate was much more likely to approve tax cuts than tax increases, and that they also preferred issuing debt much more than raising taxes (Donovan and Bowler 1998). Tax and expenditure limitations (TELs) are common throughout the fifty states, but initiative states are more likely to have adopted them (Tolbert 1998). Moreover, TELs in initiative states may be more restrictive than those in other states.

The fiscal position of initiative states is thus likely to be different from that in non-initiative states, with the former imposing more constraints on politicians than the latter. One problem with this is that legislators may have greater difficulty writing coherent budgets in initiative states. Peter Schrag (1998), one of the fiercest and also one of the most thoughtful critics of the initiative process, is especially scathing on this point. It may be the case that various initiative mandates and restrictions leave politicians with relatively little budgetary wiggle room, which may be especially problematic during economic downturns.

## THE LEGISLATURE'S ROLE: IMPLEMENTATION AND AMENDABILITY

There are, undoubtedly, constraints on elected officials imposed by the initiative. But some state legislatures are more insulated from the effects of initiatives than others. For example, if a state does not allow constitutional amendments, or does not allow some types of fiscal measures to be passed through the initiative, then their initiative measures are likely to place fewer constraints on a legislature. Statutory initiatives are more readily amended or repealed by the legislature in some states (such as Colorado, Maine, Idaho, Missouri), while other states require waiting periods, supermajorities, or both, before an initiative may be amended. California is the only state where the legislature can neither amend nor repeal an initiative statute. In contrast, where legislatures are more insulated from the initiative process, voters may pass a proposal only to have it changed by a legislature later on. Some states also restrict the number and type of subjects that may be covered by a single initiative.

We created a nine-item index reflecting factors that insulate a state legislature from the initiative process. Table 5-2 ranks states in terms of how much their legislature may be insulated from the effects of the initiative process. California—with constitutional amendments, no legislative ability to amend statutes, no restrictions on fiscal initiatives, no indirect initiatives, etc.—stands out as the least insulated. Wyoming, Maine, and Massachusetts rank as most insulated from the initiative's effects. In states at the opposite end of the continuum from California, the legislature has the discretion of ignoring, rejecting, or modifying initiatives that voters approve. The potential effects of initiatives on the legislature—and on policy—are better illustrated when Table 5-1 and Table 5-2 are considered together. For example, while the Arkansas legislature may have less formal control over initiatives that pass than the Oregon legislature (Table 5-2), it may be easier to qualify initiatives in Oregon (Table 5-1). Meanwhile, with relatively easy qualification processes, high initiative use, and limited legislative insulation from the effects of initiatives, California and Oregon appear as atypical cases of how the initiative process works in the United States.

Finally, even without the power of formal amendment, legislators may still find ways around fully implementing initiatives that they find too burdensome. Few states look like California, Colorado, or Oregon in terms of the ease of using initiatives and the formal limits placed on the legislature when it comes to amending initiatives. Indeed, California and Oregon may be at the extreme end of a continuum where the legislature is prevented from altering constitutional initiatives (in California, ever). Nevertheless, case studies suggest that even in California the legislature is able to avoid many of the more far-reaching effects of initiatives that pass. Since elected officials are in charge of implementing laws drafted by initiative, state political actors often have some discretion when it comes to avoiding many of the things that initiatives' proponents might have intended when they wrote their laws.

This is the theme of Gerber et al.'s book, *Stealing the Initiative*, whose authors take as a starting point the idea that "initiatives do not implement or enforce themselves" (2001, 109). Some initiatives try to build in enforcement provisions that make it harder for politicians to "cheat" the popular will. But most measures have to leave some discretion to politicians either wittingly or, in the case of badly drafted initiatives, unwittingly. Take, for example, Matsusaka's (1995) finding that spending in initiative states is lower at the state level but higher at the local level. One explanation for this is that state governments can avoid citizen-initiated tax and expenditure limitations (TELs) by establishing new local jurisdictions—spe-

**Table 5-2** State Legislature Insulation from the Initiative Process

| State | Legislative insulation index | State | Legislative insulation index |
|---|---|---|---|
| California | 1 | Illinois | 5 |
| Arkansas | 2 | Nevada | 5 |
| Arizona | 3 | Florida | 5 |
| Michigan | 3 | Alaska | 6 |
| North Dakota | 3 | Missouri | 6 |
| Oregon | 3 | Montana | 6 |
| Colorado | 4 | Nebraska | 6 |
| Idaho | 4 | Ohio | 6 |
| Oklahoma | 4 | Mississippi | 7 |
| South Dakota | 4 | Maine | 8 |
| Utah | 4 | Massachusetts | 8 |
| Washington | 4 | Wyoming | 9 |

SOURCES: National Conference of State Legislatures (2002); Gerber (1996).

NOTE: Higher scores reflect that the legislature has greater ability to affect initiatives and is more insulated from their effects. Points are added to the index if 1) the state has a single-subject rule, 2) if there are limits on the substance of initiatives, 3) if there are limits on fiscal initiatives, 4) if the legislature can amend or repeal initiative statutes, 5) if the legislature can repeal initiative statutes without a waiting period, 6) if the legislature can repeal initiative statutes without a supermajority, 7) if the state has no constitutional initiatives, 8) if the state has direct and indirect initiatives, and 9) if the state has indirect initiatives only.

cial service districts—that were not affected by earlier anti-tax initiatives (Bowler and Donovan 2001). In the 1990s initiative states saw a flowering of special governments such as sewer districts, water districts, fire districts, and the like, partly in response to TELs imposed at the state level. Thus one way around TELs at the state level is to push taxing and spending down to counties and special governments. The end result is that "the policy impact of most initiatives reflects a compromise between what electoral majorities and government actors want" (Gerber et al. 2001, 110).

Governing is different in initiative states, but this does not mean that the initiative process has supplanted the role of the legislature. Some journalists go so far as to suggest that initiatives have rendered some state legislatures meaningless. Yet the evidence suggests that the legislature is able to manage within the constraints imposed by the initiative process. According to one's view as either a supporter or opponent of the initiative process, this means that state legislatures can be seen as capable of either defending themselves or subverting popular wishes. After all, if most initiatives are defeated at the ballot box, or may be amended after they have passed, or not be fully implemented by state government, it is pretty clear that the critics of the process are greatly overstating the threat that initiatives offer to republican government. The potential effects of initiatives may seem even more muted when we consider ex post judicial review.

### THE COURT'S ROLE: LEGAL CHALLENGES

Legislatures, political parties, interest groups, and initiative entrepreneurs are not the only actors who influence the fate of initiatives. Initiatives are embedded in the system of checks and balances through the judicial process. Initiatives, like any other law, must be consistent with both the U.S. Constitution and the relevant state constitution, and must as well abide by the state's regulations on the initiative process.

As we noted above, nearly all states' courts play no role in evaluating measures before they are voted on. But they do play a substantial role once measures are approved by voters. Courts tend to reason that no one has legal standing to challenge an initiative—in terms of constitutionality, conformity with single-subject rules, and other matters—unless it has passed and actually begins to affect policy. Otherwise, state and federal courts fear, they would be over-stepping their role and affecting voter decisions if they provided a pre-election review of a measure's constitutionality. The result of this resistance to rule on initiatives before elections means that voters quite often approve of measures that are later invalidated by state and federal courts.

There is some conflict among observers of initiatives as to what the court's proper role should be. Advocates of the "juris-populists" approach argue that because initiatives are the direct, undiluted expression of popular will, the courts should give greater deference to initiatives than they might give to bills approved by legislatures (Cain and Miller 2001). In practice, however, state and federal courts treat initiative laws just like laws passed by legislatures. Ellis (2002) notes that some legal scholars argue that initiatives should be given even greater scrutiny than legislative bills since initiatives are not subject to the same checks and balances as other laws (i.e., no governor's veto threat) and because initiatives have not been vetted through the rigors of the legislative drafting process. Others argue for greater court activity prior to elections to prevent unconstitutional matters from being the subject of campaigns (see Ellis 2002; Haskell 2001).

Still other observers worry that some state courts, particularly those selected or re-appointed via popular election, might be reluctant to overturn voter-approved initiatives out of fear that voters will punish them when they stand for re-election (Eule 1990). One counter-argument to this is that courts should be especially keen to review voter-approved initiatives because the courts are the only institution that can exercise a counter-majoritarian force against direct democracy. In practice, courts have, for some observers, become too willing to strike down initiatives. Miller (1999) demonstrates that most state initiatives in a set of states he examined were challenged in court, with 40 percent overturned in whole or in part. This high level of litigation might reflect the willingness of those who lose at the ballot box to try and find a way to win through the courts and so give judges opportunity to exercise power. Holman and Stern (1998) show that plaintiffs challenging successful initiatives in court are able to "venue shop" —that is, they can file cases in different districts of either state or federal courts in order to find those judges most likely to grant them a favorable ruling.

As Qvortrup (2001) notes, the "courts increasingly are encroaching upon decisions made by the citizens themselves" (197). He notes that over half of recent initiatives in three states have been challenged by the courts, and over half of those challenges resulted in invalidation of the initiative.

## THE FUTURE OF THE INITIATIVE PROCESS:
## LIMITED BY REFORM, OR EXPANDED USE?

The explosion of the use of initiatives in many states has led to renewed calls for reforming the process. As we outlined above, critics—both from academia and from the media—have advanced sustained critiques against the initiative process as a kind of faux populism. Instead of making politics more democratic or more responsive to the will of the voters, they argue, the initiative process may simply give well-established interests yet another point of access to the system or tie up the policy-making system of the state. Most reforms to the process are generated from within the state's political institutions and are often couched in terms of a desire to protect the "integrity" of the process and prevent corruption or the appearance of corruption (see, e.g., Drage 2001). For the reformers, the question is whether or not the process can really provide for "an informed, deliberative discussion and debate on important issues" (Speaker's Commission on the California Initiative Process 2002). However, these reforms often have as a consequence the capacity to limit the scope of the initiative process. A recent commission on California's process, promoted by the speaker of the assembly, made nine specific recommendations for reforming what is among the nation's most open initiative process. Two of the nine proposals were aimed to allow an easing of some of the restrictions on signature-gathering while three sought to effect an increase in the amount of information being provided to voters about initiative proposals and their financial backers. The remaining proposals, however, sought to give existing political structures a greater say in the process by establishing an indirect initiative process, elaborating a stronger single-subject rule, or requiring greater pre-proposal review and including in the ballot pamphlet an assessment to the effect that any or all of the propositions may be ruled unconstitutional in whole or in part (Speaker's Commission on the California Initiative Process 2002).

Clearly, many of these proposals are hard to dispute. Who, for example, could be against integrity or against fighting corruption? But not all reform efforts are unalloyed Good Things. Some have other aspects. The reforms that seek to limit the role of paid activists (as Colorado sought to do; see Drage 2001, 230) or to give greater say to the politicians prior to a vote (as the California suggestions seek to do) also mean limits on propositions. They make it harder to propose issues and can, as the "warning language" proposal would surely do, make it harder to pass proposals. If voters are told as they vote, for example, that they are voting on a proposal that may well be unconstitutional, it seems reasonable to suppose that fewer people will actually vote on the proposal and that more people will vote "no." And so, while attempts at reform seem—and quite possibly are—driven by the purest of intentions, some of the consequences of proposed reforms are to raise the hurdles higher for those who would use the process. If these hurdles come in the form of increased costs, then it follows that the playing-field would be further skewed to advantage those who can raise large amounts of money. Although they might (slightly) limit the number of measures on ballots in some states, in fact many of the reform proposals offer few cures for the ills that supposedly ail the initiative process.

At the same time as politicians in states with the initiative process seek to limit it, politicians in other states have at least made claims to want to introduce the process. Recent governors of Louisiana and Minnesota (Murphy "Mike" Foster and Jesse Ventura) made public their support of the process. Even states such as New York, Texas, and Rhode Island have seen campaigners work to introduce the measure, and the first two of these at least have seen some favorable mentions by the governor.

On the one hand, then, we see a series of reforms aimed at limiting the process. On the other, we see at least some attempts at expansion of the process that may result in its wider use. Of the two trends it is likely that the second will win out. Not only have attempts to limit the initiative process met legal obstacles (Drage 2001), its appeal to voters remains high. When surveyed—whether in initiative or non-initiative states—voters typically show overwhelming support for the process. To be sure, voters have some concerns. In particular, they express concern over the role of money and special interests. But the popular appeal of the process remains deeply rooted. Indeed, how could it not? One of the main assumptions of the U.S. Constitution is that of popular sovereignty, and one has to try very hard not to see the initiative process as a logical consequence of that assumption. As Americans continue to work out the implications of their Constitution, it seems reasonable to expect a widening, not a narrowing, of the use of direct democracy.

## CONCLUSION

Critics of initiative politics in the American states find fault with applying the Populists' reasoning to the contemporary era. For one thing, overt corruption among legislators is no longer the norm, as state legislatures have been professionalized over the last several decades. Furthermore, Richard Ellis (2002), Daniel Smith (1998), and others have demonstrated that contemporary initiative proponents often fail to fit the Populist vision of concerned citizens who turn amateur politician in order to prod a state legislature toward adopting policies that reflect the public's concerns. If anything, a large number of the proposals that make the ballot now in states like Arizona, California, Colorado, Oregon, and Washington are promoted by individuals who make a career as initiative proponents. Ellis and others worry that their motivations may largely be self-promotional. Rather than any concern with promoting responsible public policy, these initiative entrepreneurs need a constant stream of content in order to attract media attention and campaign contributions. These kinds of behaviors seem to unduly worry state officials and prompt them to introduce reforms that would limit the process.

Although it is easy to say things are "different" in initiative states, it is more difficult to establish empirically what the exact effects of initiatives are. While voters consistently support the idea of the initiative process in those states that allow for direct democracy, legislators are much less enthusiastic about the initiative. The real, long-term impact of initiatives may be in changing rules about how legislators can govern. Hot topics that receive media attention—assisted suicide, the decriminalization of drugs, the expansion or reduction of gay rights, the regulation of immigration—may well have relatively small long-term effects. For all the sound and fury, the majority of proposals tend to fail, and those that do pass are subject to judicial review that may undercut the proposals further. Oftentimes the more successful proposals are rules that alter how elected officials seek office, raise revenue, and set spending priorities in state budgets. And these are the ones to which elected officials take greatest exception. But these are also the kinds of proposals that would seem most in keeping with the ideas of the Progressives, Populists, and, conceivably, the Founders. For American government is the people's government, and it is presumably for the people to decide how their government functions.

## REFERENCES

Allswang, John M. 2000. *The Initiative and Referendum in California, 1989–1998.* Stanford, Calif.: Stanford University Press.

Arceneaux, Kevin. 2002. "Direct Democracy and the Link Between Public Opinion and State Abortion Policy." *State Politics and Policy Quarterly* 2(4): 372–387.

Banducci, Susan. 1998a. "Direct Legislation: When Is It Used and When Does It Pass?" In *Citizens as Legislators: Direct Democracy in the United States,* edited by S. Bowler, T. Donovan, and C. Tolbert. Columbus: Ohio State University Press.

———. 1998b. "Searching for Ideological Consistency in Direct Legislation Voting." In *Citizens as Legislators,* edited by Bowler, Donovan, and Tolbert.

Beard, Charles, and Bril E. Schultz. 1914. *Documents on the State-wide Initiative, Referendum, and Recall.* New York: Macmillan.

Bowler, Shaun, and Todd Donovan. 2002a. "Do Voters Have a Cue? TV Ads as a Source of Information in Referendum Voting." *European Journal of Political Research* 41(6): 777–793.

———. 2002b. "Democracy, Institutions and Attitudes about Citizen Influence on Government." *British Journal of Political Science* 32: 371–390.

———. 2001. "Fiscal Illusion and State Tax and Expenditure Limitations." Paper presented at the State of the States Conference, Texas A&M University, College Station, March 2–3.

———. 1998. *Demanding Choices: Opinion and Voting in Direct Democracy.* Ann Arbor: University of Michigan Press.

———. 1995. "Popular Responsiveness to Taxation." *Political Research Quarterly* 48: 77–99.

Bowler, Shaun, Todd Donovan, Max Neiman, and Johnny Peel. 2001. "Institutional Threat and Partisan Outcomes: Legislative Candidates' Attitudes toward Direct Democracy." *State Politics and Policy Quarterly* 1(4): 364–379.

Broder, David S. 2000. *Democracy Derailed: Initiative Campaigns and the Power of Money.* New York: Harcourt.

Butler, David, and Austin Ranney, eds. 1994. *Referendums Around the World: The Growing Use of Direct Democracy.* Washington, D.C.: AEI Press.

Cain, Bruce E., and Kenneth P. Miller. 2001. "The Populist Legacy: Initiatives and the Undermining of Representative Government." In *Dangerous Democracy? The Battle over Ballot Initiatives in America,* edited by Larry J. Sabato, Howard Ernst, and Bruce A. Larson. Lanham, Md.: Rowman & Littlefield.

Camobreco, John F. 1998. "Preferences, Fiscal Policies, and the Initiative Process." *Journal of Politics* 60(August): 891–929.

Campbell, Anne. 1997. "The Citizen's Initiative and Entrepreneurial Politics: Direct Democracy in Colorado, 1966–1994." Paper presented at the Western Political Science Association Meeting, Tucson.

Citrin, Jack, Beth Reingold, and Evelyn Walters. 1990. "The Official English Movement and the Symbolic Politics of Language in the United States." *Western Political Quarterly* 43: 553–560.

Cronin, Thomas. 1989. *Direct Democracy: The Politics of Initiative, Referendum, and Recall.* Cambridge, Mass.: Harvard University Press.

Crouch, Winston. 1943. *The Initiative and Referendum in California.* Los Angeles: Haynes Foundation.

Donovan, Todd, and Shaun Bowler. 1998. "Responsive or Responsible Government." In *Citizens as Legislators,* edited by Bowler, Donovan, and Tolbert.

Donovan, Todd, Shaun Bowler, and David S. McCuan. 2001. "Political Consultants and the Initiative Industrial Complex." In *Dangerous Democracy?,* edited by Sabato, Ernst, and Larson.

Donovan, Todd, Shaun Bowler, David McCuan, and Kenneth Fernandez. 1998. "Contending Players and Strategies: Opposition Advantages in Initiative Elections." In *Citizens as Legislators,* edited by Bowler, Donovan, and Tolbert.

Donovan, Todd, Shaun Bowler, and Jim Wenzel. 2000. "Direct Democracy and Gay Rights Initiatives after *Romer.*" In *Politics of Gay Rights,* edited by Craig Rimmerman, Ken Wald, and Clyde Wilcox. Chicago: University of Chicago Press.

Drage, Jeannie. 2001. "State Efforts to Regulate the Initiative Process." In *The Battle Over Citizen Law Making,* edited by M. Dane Waters. Durham, N.C.: Carolina Academic Press.

Dubois, Philip L., and Floyd F. Feeney. 1992. *Improving the California Initiative Process: Options for Change.* Berkeley: California Policy Seminar, University of California.

Dwyer, Diane, M. O'Goorman, J. Stonecash, and R. Young. 1994. "Disorganized Politics and the Have Nots: Politics and Taxes in New York and California." *Polity* 27: 25–47.

Ellis, Richard. 2002. *Democratic Delusions: The Initiative Process in America.* Lawrence: University of Kansas Press.

Ernst, Howard R. 2001. "The Historical Role of Narrow-Material Interests in Initiative Politics." In *Dangerous Democracy?,* edited by Sabato, Ernst, and Larson.

Eule, Julian. 1990. "Judicial Review of Direct Democracy." *Yale Law Journal* 99: 1504.

Frey, Bruno. 1997. "A Constitution for Knaves Crowds out Civic Virtues." *Economic Journal* 107: 1043–1053.

Frey, Bruno, and Alois Stutzer. 1999. "Happiness, Economy and Institutions." Working Paper No. 15, Institute for Empirical Research in Economics, University of Zurich.

Gamble, Barbara S. 1997. "Putting Civil Rights to A Popular Vote." *American Journal of Political Science* 91: 245–269.

Gerber, Elisabeth R. 1999. *The Populist Paradox: Interest Group Influence and the Promise of Direct Legislation.* Princeton, N.J.: Princeton University Press.

———. 1998. "Interest Group Influence in the California Initiative Process." Background Paper No. 115. San Francisco: Public Policy Institute of California.

———. 1996. "Legislative Response to the Threat of the Popular Initiative." *American Journal of Political Science* 40: 99–128.

Gerber, Elisabeth R., Arthur Lupia, Mathew D. McCubbins, D. Roderick Kiewiet. 2001. *Stealing the Initiative: How State Government Responds to Direct Democracy.* Upper Saddle River, N.J.: Prentice Hall.

Hajnal, Zoltan, Elisabeth R. Gerber, and Hugh Louch. 2002. "Minorities and Direct Legislation: Evidence from California Ballot Proposition Elections." *Journal of Politics* 64(1): 154–177.

Haskell, John. 2001. *Direct Democracy or Representative Government? Dispelling the Populist Myth.* Boulder, Colo.: Westview Press.

Hero, Rodney, and Caroline Tolbert. 1996. "A Racial/Ethnic Diversity Interpretation of Politics and Policy in the American States." *American Journal of Political Science* 40(3): 851–871.

Holman, Craig. 2002. *An Assessment of New Jersey's Proposed Limited Initiative Process.* New York: Brennan Center for Justice at NYU School of Law.

Holman, Craig, and Robert Stern. 1998. "Judicial Review of Ballot Initiatives: The Changing Role of State and Federal Courts." *Loyola of Los Angeles Law Review* 31: 1239–1266.

Johnson, Claudius. 1944. "The Adoption of the Initiative and Referendum in Washington." *Pacific Northwest Quarterly* 35: 291–304.

Karp, Jeffrey A. 1998. "The Influence of Elite Endorsements in Initiative Campaigns." In *Citizens as Legislators,* edited by Bowler, Donovan, and Tolbert.

Lascher, Edward L., M. Hagen, and S. Rochlin. 1996. "Gun Behind the Door? Ballot Initiatives, State Politics, and Public Opinion." *Journal of Politics* 58: 760–775.

Lowenstein, Daniel H. 1995. *Election Law: Cases and Materials.* Durham, N.C.: Carolina Academic Press.

Lupia, Arthur. 1994. "Shortcuts versus Encyclopedias: Information and Voting Behavior in California Insurance Reform Elections." *American Political Science Review* 88: 63–76.

Lupia, Arthur, and Matthew McCubbins. 1998. *The Democratic Dilemma: Can Citizens Learn What They Need to Know?* New York: Cambridge University Press.

Magleby, David B. 1994. "Direct Legislation in the American States." In *Referendums Around the World: The Growing Use of Direct Democracy,* edited by Butler and Ranney.

———. 1984. *Direct Legislation: Voting on Ballot Propositions in the United States.* Baltimore: Johns Hopkins University Press.

Matsusaka, John. 2001. "Problems with a Methodology Used to Evaluate the Effect of Ballot Initiatives on Policy Responsiveness." *Journal of Politics* 63(4): 1250–1256.

———. 1995. "Fiscal Effects of the Voter Initiative: Evidence from the Last 30 Years." *Journal of Political Economy* 103: 587–623.

McCuan, David, Shaun Bowler, Todd Donovan, and Ken Fernandez. 1998. "California's Political Warriors: Campaign Professionals and the Initiative Process." In *Citizens as Legislators,* edited by Bowler, Donovan, and Tolbert.

Miller, Kenneth P. 1999. "The Role of Courts in the Initiative Process." Paper presented at the American Political Science Association Meeting, Atlanta.

National Conference of State Legislatures. 2002. *Final Report and Recommendations of the NCSL I&R Task Force.* Denver: National Conference of State Legislatures.

———. 2000. "Initiative States Ranked in Order of Use, 1898–1999." Accessed February 24, 2000, at http://www.ncsl.org/programs/legman/elect/inrank.htm. Denver: National Conference of State Legislatures.

Pateman, Carole. 1970. *Participation and Democratic Theory.* Cambridge: Cambridge University Press.

Pippen, John, Shaun Bowler, and Todd Donovan. 2002. "Election Reform and Direct Democracy: The Case of Campaign Finance Regulations in the American States." *American Politics Research* 30(6): 559–582.

Qvortrup, Mads. 2001. "The Courts v. the People: An Essay on Judicial Review of Initiatives." In *The Battle Over Citizen Law Making,* edited by Waters.

Romer, Thomas, and Howard Rosenthal. 1979. "The Elusive Median Voter." *Journal of Public Economics* 12 (February): 143–170.

Sears, David O., and Jack Citrin. 1982. *Tax Revolt: Something for Nothing in California.* Cambridge, Mass.: Harvard University Press.

Schrag, Peter. 1998. *Paradise Lost: California's Experience, America's Future.* New York: The New Press.

Schuman, David. 1994. "The Origin of State Constitutional Direct Democracy: William Simon U'Ren and 'The Oregon System.'" *Temple University Law Review* 67: 947–963.

Smith, Daniel A. 1998. *Tax Crusaders and the Politics of Direct Democracy.* New York: Routledge.

Smith, Daniel A., and Caroline Tolbert. 2001. "The Initiative to Party: Partisanship and Ballot Initiatives in California." *Party Politics* 7(6): 781–799.

Smith, Mark A. 2002. "Ballot Initiatives and the Democratic Citizen." *Journal of Politics* 64(3): 892–903.

———. 2001. "The Contingent Effects of Ballot Initiatives and Candidate Races on Turnout." *American Journal of Political Science* 45(3): 700–706.

Speaker's Commission on the California Initiative Process. 2002. Speaker Robert Hertzberg. Sacramento. January.

Sutro, Stephen. 1994. "Interpretations of Initiatives." *Santa Clara Law Review* 34: 945–976.

Tolbert, Caroline. 1998. "Changing the Rules for State Legislatures: Direct Democracy and Governance Policies." In *Citizens as Legislators: Direct Democracy in the United States,* edited by Shaun Bowler, Todd Donovan, and Caroline Tolbert. Columbus: Ohio State University Press.

Tolbert, Caroline, John Grummel, and Daniel Smith. 2001. "The Effects of Ballot Initiatives on Voter Turnout in the American States." *American Politics Review* 29(6): 625–648.

Tolbert, Caroline, Daniel H. Lowenstein, and Todd Donovan. 1998. "Election Law and Rules for Using Initiatives." In *Citizens as Legislators,* edited by Bowler, Donovan, and Tolbert.

Wenzel, James, Todd Donovan, and Shaun Bowler. 1998. "Direct Democracy and Minorities: Changing Attitudes about Minorities Targeted by Initiatives." In *Citizens as Legislators,* edited by Bowler, Donovan, and Tolbert.

## SUGGESTED READINGS

Bowler, Shaun, and Todd Donovan. *Demanding Choices: Opinion and Voting in Direct Democracy.* Ann Arbor: University of Michigan Press, 1998. Examines how voters decide on ballot initiatives; concludes that initiative campaigns are unlikely to dupe voters.

Ellis, Richard. *Democratic Delusions: The Initiative Process in America.* Lawrence: University of Kansas Press, 2002. Critical study of initiative politics in western states. Discusses role of courts and proposals to reform the initiative process.

Gerber, Elisabeth R. *The Populist Paradox: Interest Group Influence and the Promise of Direct Legislation.* Princeton, N.J.: Princeton University Press, 1999. Examines the role of groups in initiative campaigns; concludes that it is difficult for economic groups to sell most of their initiatives to voters.

Magleby, David B. *Direct Legislation: Voting on Ballot Propositions in the United States.* Baltimore: Johns Hopkins University Press, 1984. The first major contemporary study of direct democracy in the United States. The source of many research questions about the politics of initiatives.

Smith, Daniel A. *Tax Crusaders and the Politics of Direct Democracy.* New York: Routledge, 1998. Traces involvement of interest groups in "faux-populist" anti-tax campaigns in California, Colorado, and Massachusetts.

CHAPTER 6

 *Legislative Politics in the States*

KEITH E. HAMM AND
GARY F. MONCRIEF

State legislatures fascinate students of institutions as well as students of individual behavior. As institutions, state legislatures present an array of organizational and structural arrangements. It is probably safe to say there is more variation between state legislatures than any other institution of state government. For example, some legislatures are very large (the New Hampshire House, for example, consists of 400 members), and others are small bodies (there are twenty senators in the upper chamber in Alaska, and twenty-one in the Nevada and Delaware senates). The size of the districts represented by individual legislators is quite varied; each member of the Vermont House of Representatives has 4,000 constituents, whereas members of the Arizona, Florida, Illinois, New Jersey, New York and Ohio lower chambers each represent more than 100,000 people. A state senator in Texas has more than 670,000 people in his or her district, and each California state senator represents about 850,000 constituents.

Political scientists often categorize state legislatures by their degree of professionalization, based on session length, size of legislative operations, and salary. There are substantial differences between the state legislatures in regard to these and other dimensions (see Table 6-1 for some comparisons). For example, some state legislatures (California and New York) meet virtually full-time, much like the U.S. Congress. Others (North Dakota and Montana) meet only a few months every other year.

Obviously, compensation for legislators is likely to be tied to the time commitment required of those legislators. California state legislators receive a base salary of $99,000, plus a per diem expense that brings the total compensation package to at least $114,000. On the other hand, state legislators in New Hampshire receive $100 per year

**Table 6-1** Measures of Legislative Professionalization

| State | Potential compensation[a] | Session[b] Calendar | Session[b] Legislative | Permanent staff[c] | Squire's ranking[d] |
|---|---|---|---|---|---|
| Professional legislatures[e] | | | | | |
| California | $114,700 | 257 | 128 | 2,510 | 1 |
| Michigan | 79,600 | 337 | 87 | 1,360 | 2 |
| New York | 79,400 | 198 | 151 | 3,460 | 3 |
| Wisconsin | 73,800 | 363 | | 690 | 4 |
| Massachusetts | 50,100 | 362 | 147 | N/A | 5 |
| New Jersey | 49,000 | 361 | 36 | 1,460 | 6 |
| Ohio | 51,700 | 359 | 164 | 550 | 7 |
| Pennsylvania | 61,900 | 346 | 95 | 2,680 | 8 |
| Illinois | 67,300 | 135 | 55 | 970 | 11 |
| Hybrid legislatures[e] | | | | | |
| Hawaii | 32,000 | 108 | 62 | 260 | 9 |
| Florida | 27,900 | | 60 | 1,900 | 10 |
| Alaska | 43,700 | 133 | | 240 | 12 |
| Texas | 15,900 | 70 | | 1,960 | 13 |
| Washington | 38,900 | 84 | | 540 | 14 |
| Missouri | 40,800 | 133 | | 480 | 15 |
| Maryland | 31,500 | 91 | | 510 | 16 |
| Oklahoma | 45,200 | 72 | | 260 | 17 |
| Arizona | 24,000 | 110 | | 470 | 18 |
| Minnesota | 34,400 | 105 | 58 | 640 | 19 |
| Connecticut | 28,000 | 122 | 90 | 450 | 20 |
| Colorado | 30,000 | 121 | | 210 | 21 |
| Nebraska | 12,000 | 119 | 78 | 200 | 22 |
| Oregon | 23,900 | 104 | | 240 | 24 |
| Iowa | 29,800 | 105 | | 180 | 25 |
| Delaware | 33,400 | 170 | 106 | 60 | 26 |
| Virginia | 24,300 | | 55 | 470 | 27 |
| North Carolina | 31,600 | 173 | 114 | 170 | 28 |
| Louisiana | 23,800 | | 68 | 420 | 29 |
| South Carolina | 10,400 | 166 | 65 | 270 | 30 |
| Mississippi | 17,700 | 92 | | 130 | 31 |
| Tennessee | 21,200 | 136 | 38 | 210 | 32 |
| Kansas | 21,900 | 134 | 68 | 120 | 37 |
| Alabama | 30,600 | 120 | 39 | 320 | 45 |
| Kentucky | 12,900 | 50 | 30 | 320 | 42 |
| Citizen legislatures[e] | | | | | |
| Nevada | 7,800 | 60 | | 170 | 23 |
| Vermont | 23,300 | 145 | 79 | 40 | 33 |
| West Virginia | 22,900 | 71 | | 160 | 34 |
| Rhode Island | 11,200 | 258 | 82 | 220 | 35 |
| Idaho | 23,600 | 79 | | 60 | 36 |
| Georgia | 23,900 | 61 | 40 | 510 | 38 |
| Indiana | 27,300 | 138 | 42 | 180 | 39 |
| Arkansas | 12,800 | 45 | | 290 | 40 |
| Maine | 10,800 | 152 | 55 | 130 | 41 |
| Montana | 7,000 | | 75 | 50 | 43 |
| Utah | 12,200 | 45 | | 110 | 44 |
| South Dakota | 10,100 | 66 | 36 | 60 | 46 |
| North Dakota | 9,400 | 51 | 35 | 30 | 47 |
| Wyoming | 3,800 | 46 | 30 | 20 | 48 |
| New Mexico | 0 | 48 | | 50 | 49 |
| New Hampshire | 100 | 312 | 24 | 140 | 50 |

SOURCE: Council of State Governments 2002; Kurtz 1990; Squire 2000; and National Conference of State Legislatures Web site at www.nesl.org, especially various tables under "About State Legislatures"

[a] Computed as base salary plus unvouchered expenditures for those legislators outside the capital city area, as reported by the National Conference of State Legislatures or in the Council of State Governments, *Book of the States*. Does not include expenditures requiring vouchers. For states with biennial legislatures, or those with a mandated short and long session every other year, the compensation figures are averaged.

[b] Figures are averaged over the biennial period and include regular session and special sessions. Some states report session as calendar days, others report as actual legislative days in session. For those states that report legislative days, we have tried to calculate calendar days as well for purposes of comparison.

[c] Rounded to the nearest ten. We use permanent staff here as the benchmark because these are likely to be the professional, full-time staff. About three-quarters of all legislative staff members are in the category of permanent staff. However, in some states the session-only staff is a significant part of the workforce. States in which session-only staff comprise at least half of the total staff include Connecticut, Hawaii, Idaho, Kansas, Montana, Nevada, New Mexico, North Carolina, North Dakota, Utah, West Virginia, and Wyoming.

[d] Squire's index is based on comparisons to Congress for state legislative salary, staff, and session length. See Squire (2000) for his updated version of this index.

[e] Kurtz divides state legislatures into three categories based on resources and time commitments to the legislature (see Kurtz 1990).

for their work (New Mexico legislators receive no annual compensation but are reimbursed for daily expenses).

The magnitude of legislative operations also differs considerably. One commonly used measure is the number of legislative staff personnel. Although the New York and California state legislatures each employ several thousand people as staff, there are fewer than 100 full-time staff members in the New Mexico legislature.

All of these differences matter, in terms of state legislatures' effectiveness and independence in policy making. And they matter in terms of the types of people who are attracted to service in the state legislature. To put it another way, the incentives and the costs of legislative service are different in different states.

Although there is marked variation in the professionalization of state legislatures, most are more professional today than they were a generation ago. For example, many state legislatures met only every other year (in other words, they held biennial sessions) until the 1960s. Legislatures were then viewed as unrepresentative of the general public, controlled by "good old boys"—older, white males from rural areas. They met for only brief periods of time and were poorly staffed, ill-equipped, and were generally perceived as being dominated by the governor or a handful of powerful interest groups. Today all but five or six hold annual sessions, pay better salaries, and have bigger staffs. If one thinks of legislative professionalization as a continuum, almost all state legislatures have moved (some only slightly, some a great deal) in the direction of greater professionalization in the past thirty years.[1]

Just as there are important institutional differences today between legislatures, there are also significant differences that bear on the individual legislators state to state. The incentive structure for the individual legislator is different in a part-time, low-pay, low-staff legislature than in the more professional ones. There are also differences in what is known as the "opportunity structure."

The prospects for state legislators to advance to higher office vary significantly among the states (Squire 1988). For example, the eighty members of the California Assembly have an abundance of other electoral positions for which they may run, including forty state senate seats, fifty-three seats in the U.S. House, six state constitutional offices, and the mayor's office in several large California cities. Advancement prospects are much bleaker for the 400 members of the New Hampshire House of Representatives, because there are only twenty-four state senate seats, two seats in the U.S. House, and the only elected statewide office is that of the governor.

Although the individual costs and benefits of legislative service vary in different states, it is also true that almost all state legislators behave more like professional politicians today than they did a generation ago. At the same time, the extent of change is not uniform across all legislatures. As one might expect, the behavioral changes seem to be greatest in the more professional, careerist legislatures. Although many of the changes and improvements made to the state legislative insti-

---

1. James D. King's analysis identifies four states that actually *regressed* on the professionalism scores between 1964 and 1994. The four states are Georgia, Massachusetts, New Hampshire, and New Mexico. See King 2000, Table 1.

tutions in the past generation are positive, it is clear that legislatures are not held in particularly high regard by the general public. There are many reasons for this situation, including a lack of public understanding about how legislatures operate. They are, indeed, complex institutions, charged with solving very difficult societal problems.

Another reason for this lack of regard is that candidates who run for legislative office often find it easy to campaign against the legislature itself. Candidates for governor rarely attack the *office* of governor but instead focus on the other candidates who are running for governor. Candidates for judicial positions (in many states judges are elected) do not rail against the judicial system but instead promote their own qualifications for the office. But candidates for the legislature often campaign against the "do-nothing" legislature, characterizing it as "controlled by special interests" and urging the voters to "throw the bums out." Over time, this cannot help but drag down the public image of the state legislature.

Finally, Americans have never been fond of the idea that politics should be a career. It is clear that it *has* become more of a career in many state legislatures in the past twenty or thirty years. By the late 1980s, legislators in some states were staying in office for longer periods of time than ever before (although probably not for as long as the general public seems to think). The electoral system appeared to be so heavily biased in favor of incumbents that challengers seemed to have little chance to win. The public reaction in many states was to support the movement to limit the number of terms a legislator could serve. Term limits are now the law in sixteen states, and are discussed later in this chapter.

## THE ELECTORAL ARENA

The nature of the electoral system affects legislative politics. Two important characteristics of the electoral system are the *electoral formula* and *district magnitude*. All states use a plurality (also known as first-past-the-post) electoral formula for choosing legislators.[2] It is the simplest of all electoral formulas: Whoever gets the most votes wins. District magnitude (the number of legislators chosen from each district) varies a bit from state to state. Most states employ single-member districts (SMDs) exclusively. However, some states use multimember districts (MMDs) in the lower chamber. Within the multimember districting arrangement, there are further variations. The most common multimember arrangement is the two-member district, although there are a few states with three- or four-member districts.

Most of the MMDs are free-for-all districts, in which all candidates in the district run against one another and the two (in a two-member district) candidates receiving the highest vote counts are declared the winners. Some states employ *post-designate* (also known as *position-designate* or *seat-designate)* MMDs, in which the

---

2. This is true for general elections only. In some states primary elections require a candidate to receive a true majority of votes cast. If no candidate receives a majority in the primary, a second primary election, called a runoff, is held between the two top vote getters from the original primary.

candidates must declare for which seat in the district they are running (for example, seat A or B). In effect, such systems operate as a series of single-member elections within the same district.

To some extent, these characteristics of the electoral system make a difference. The role of political parties is probably greater in campaigns and elections in multimember districting systems, as members of the same party tend to run as a team. Historically, minorities (racial, ethnic, or the minority political party) were less likely to be elected in MMDs. Because of the potential to discriminate against minorities, many states (especially southern states, under court mandate) eliminated most of their free-for-all MMDs during the 1960s and 1970s. Today roughly 87 percent of all state legislators are elected in single-member (or seat-designate multi-member) districts, with a plurality rule. These conditions encourage candidate-centered campaigns and elections.

*Redistricting*

The terms *reapportionment* and *redistricting* are often used interchangeably in the United States, although technically they are not synonymous (Scher, Mills, and Hotaling 1997). *Apportionment* refers to the allocation of seats within the polity; *reapportionment* suggests a change in the number of seats allocated to subunits within the polity. *Redistricting* is simply the redrawing of the electoral boundaries, without a change in the actual number of seats or districts. At the congressional level, reapportionment does occur after each census, as the 435 seats in the U.S. House are reallocated so that some states gain House seats and some lose seats, based on population shifts within the country. Representatives in state legislatures are no longer allocated to political subdivisions, so the task is not one of reapportionment but rather one of redistricting.

The question of apportionment of legislative bodies is ultimately a question of how we view the concept of representation. In what way do we intend to represent the various interests and components of society?

With the exception of the U.S. Senate, the decision in this country has been resolved in favor of population equality as the basis of representation. The idea is that each person's vote should be of equal value, and in the context of the American system that has translated into equal populations per legislative district. Thus each district must contain roughly the same number of people.[3]

One of the most dramatic changes in the electoral system occurred in what has come to be known as the "reapportionment revolution" of the 1960s. Prior to 1962, the U.S. Supreme Court took a hands-off approach to the issues of state legislative reapportionment and redistricting. The constitutions of most states mandated that their lower chambers be apportioned according to equal population standards, but

---

3. The U.S. Supreme Court does permit some latitude at the state legislative level. Generally, an overall population deviation up to 10 percent between the most populous and least populous districts is permissible.

this requirement was simply ignored in some states. Moreover, many state constitutions provided for equal representation of counties in the state senates (usually one senator per county, regardless of population). The result of the county rule in the senates and the disregard for the population rule in many lower chambers was that many state legislatures were severely malapportioned according to population standards. For example, in both Connecticut and Florida in 1962, more than 50 percent of the seats in the lower chamber were controlled by a mere 12 percent of the state population. In Alabama, 26 percent of the total population could elect a majority of house members (Scher, Mills, and Hotaling 1997).

The situation changed dramatically when the U.S. Supreme Court decided a series of cases in the 1960s and early 1970s.[4] First, the Court reversed its previous position and decided that reapportionment issues were justiciable, and that the courts could (and would) intervene in reapportionment matters. This had the effect of forcing states to honor their own constitutional requirements that lower chambers be apportioned by population. Second, the Court determined that state senates also must be apportioned according to population standards, effectively eliminating the standard of county representation in state upper chambers. The effect of these decisions was dramatic; it greatly increased the number of state legislators from urban and suburban areas and sharply reduced the number of legislators from rural areas. Along with other changes in society (for example, the implementation of the Voting Rights Act of 1965 and the increasing political participation of women in the late 1960s), these reapportionment decisions helped pave the way for significant increases in the number of women and minorities serving in state legislatures today.

*The Issue of Minority Representation*

Although population equality among districts has been the principal concern of the courts, considerable attention has been given to the protection of racial and ethnic minority groups. During the 1960s and 1970s the concern of the U.S. Supreme Court was to ensure that minority voting strength was not diluted. In particular, the Court struck down some state districting plans that had included MMDs. In some places African American populations were sufficiently large and geographically compact so that the creation of SMDs would likely lead to the election of African Americans to the state legislature. However, by creating MMDs, states were able to undermine the voting strength of blacks, subsuming the minority population into larger multimember districts. This practice was particularly common in the southern states. Although never claiming that MMDs were by

---

4. There are many important cases bearing on state legislative reapportionment–redistricting issues, but early cases of significance include *Baker v. Carr* (369 U.S. 186 [1962]); *Reynolds v. Sims* (377 U.S. 533 [1964]); *Lucas v. Forty-Fourth General Assembly of Colorado* (377 U.S. 713 [1964]); *Whitcomb v. Chavis* (403 U.S. 124 [1971]), and *White v. Regester* (412 U.S. 755 [1973]).

nature unconstitutional, the Court rejected their use in cases in which MMDs would have the effect of reducing the potential influence of racial and ethnic minorities.[5]

During the 1980s and 1990s, however, the approach changed. Based in part on case law,[6] but largely on directives from the U.S. Department of Justice, emphasis was placed on maximizing the number of districts in which racial minorities constituted a majority. Many state legislatures engaged in "affirmative gerrymandering," drawing district lines in such a way as to maximize the number of districts in which minorities constitute a significant majority of district voters. This often led to the construction of oddly shaped districts.

However, the U.S. Supreme Court, in a series of cases in the mid- to late 1990s, indicated an unwillingness to continue the move toward "affirmative gerrymandering."[7] As of this writing, the redistricting cycle after the 2000 census has not yielded any surprises in judicial interpretation.

### The Legislative Consequences of the Electoral System

Electoral systems are often judged by their translation of electoral votes into legislative seats. The issue is the extent to which a particular percentage of votes (say, 40 percent) yields a commensurate percentage of seats in the legislative chamber. A system in which the votes-to-seats ratio is 1 (for example, 40 percent of the votes and 40 percent of the seats, or 40:40 = 1.00) is said to be proportional. The dominant system in the United States, SMDs with plurality, tends to be *disproportional* (Cox 1997). Specifically, the party that receives the most votes statewide will almost always receive an even higher percentage of seats in the legislature. Thus the party that receives, say, 55 percent of the popular vote statewide will usually command 60 to 65 percent of the legislative seats. Moreover, the relative weakness of party loyalty among American voters means that individual candidates have a strong incentive to cultivate a "personal vote" among the electorate. The upshot is that American elections, both at the national and state levels, are basically candidate-centered (rather than party-centered) contests. Running for the legislature puts a premium on personal ambition and drive, devotion to the local district and its needs, and attention to the political issues that can help mobilize voter support in the district.

On the other hand, the role of the legislature in governing the state requires a much different set of skills. First of all, it requires collective action, which in turn requires bargaining, negotiation, and compromise. This dilemma of legislative representation—serving the constituency and making policy for the state—provides the strain and conflict that make legislative life both interesting and frustrating. This tension between the electoral needs of individual legislators and the policy-

---

5. See, for example, *Whitcomb v. Chavis* and *White v. Regester.*
6. See, in particular, *Thornburg v. Gingles* (478 U.S. 30 [1986]).
7. See, for example, *Abrams v. Johnson,* (No. 95-1425 [1997]); *Shaw v. Hunt* (116 S. Ct. 1894 [1996]); *Johnson v. DeGrandy* (512 U.S. 997 [1994]).

making needs of the legislative institution appears to be particularly great today (Rosenthal 1998).

### RUNNING FOR THE LEGISLATURE

Beginning in the late 1960s, state legislatures underwent a modernization movement designed to increase their capacities to perform the tasks of policy making, oversight, and constituent service. These efforts led to "what is perhaps the most dramatic metamorphosis of any set of U.S. political institutions in living memory" (Mooney 1995, 47). Many assumed that as the *institution* of the state legislature changed, so would the *individuals* serving as legislators. Whether this is true or not is unclear. What is certain is that the cost-benefit structure for serving in the state legislature has changed in many states, and this probably has contributed to changes in the nature of recruitment.

Candidate recruitment is a product of many factors, including the nature of the state political system (systemic variables), the political conditions in the specific legislative district (district variables), and the individual attributes and decision-making calculus of the potential candidates themselves (personal variables). To varying degrees, all these factors affect who runs for state legislative office. For a detailed discussion of district and individual variables, as well as systemic variables, see Moncrief, Squire, and Jewell (2001).

### ELECTIONS

State legislative elections have been studied intensely in the past decade, and our understanding of state legislative electoral patterns has improved significantly. The following discussion focuses on the extent to which Democrats and Republicans contest elections, are competitive, and win. We then turn to explanations for these outcomes.

*Electoral Contestation, Competition, and Winning*

The first step in the electoral process involves selection of candidates by the major parties. In most states this decision is made in a party primary. Key issues involve who may vote in the primary and what percentage of the vote determines the winner. In most states, the primary winner is determined by a simple plurality. For example, if candidates *X, Y,* and *Z* contest the Republican primary for a specific state legislative seat, and they receive 25 percent, 36 percent, and 39 percent of the vote, respectively, then candidate *Z* would receive the Republican nomination. However, some states require the primary winner to receive a majority of the vote. In this example, a runoff primary would then be held between the two top vote getters *(Y* and *Z)* to determine who would receive the party's nomination for the general election contest.

The general election is typically a contest between Democrats and Republicans, although a smattering of third-party candidates (for example, the Libertarian Party) and independents are sometimes on the ballot. How frequently does a contest between Democrats and Republicans occur?[8] Table 6-2 provides information to help answer this question for two time periods (1968 to 1995 and 1996 to 2002) for forty-eight state legislative houses. The most striking aspect of the data in column 2 for the elections between 1996 and 2002 is the wide range in contestation within each level of professionalization. Overall, though, the Democrats and Republicans challenged each other in at least 75 percent of the general election races in roughly one fourth of the states, and this level of contestation was more likely to occur in the most professional legislatures.

Has contestation for state legislative office increased or decreased over time? We chronicled the development of political parties contesting for office from 1968 to 1995 in the previous edition of this volume. Comparing results from the 1996–2002 period with those from the earlier period (columns 2 and 3 in Table 6-2), contesting for state legislative office has declined in more states than it increased. Some states experienced very significant declines, exceeding 20 percent, with the most spectacular decline of over 30 percent occurring in Rhode Island. While increases in contesting for office happened less frequently during the latter part of the 1990s, significant increases did occur in states that were traditionally dominated by one party, including increases of 20 percent or more in Hawaii, Oklahoma, Alabama, Arkansas, Georgia, and Arizona.

It is one thing for a party to contest a legislative seat; it is quite another to be truly competitive—that is, to have a reasonable chance of winning the seat. Some legislative districts are so dominated by one party that the opposition party has little chance of winning even when they contest the election. Such a situation makes it more difficult to recruit quality candidates for the losing party. How competitive are the two parties in the states? If we define "competitive" as the case in which the loser received at least 40 percent of the vote, we can conclude that in general state legislative elections are not very competitive. Only in North Dakota did competitive races occur in 50 percent or more of the cases in 1996–2002; in ten states competition existed in less than 20 percent of the races. In contrast to our earlier findings on contestation, competition seems to be lowest in professional legislatures, a point addressed in the subsequent discussion on incumbency.

In a majority of states the percentage of competitive races declined from 1968–1995 to 1996–2002. While some of the decrease was relatively minor, in sixteen states it exceeded 10 percent, being greater than 20 percent in Connecticut and Indiana. Increases in competition were less frequent and in only five states did the change exceed 10 percent. In Arkansas and Alabama the change was greater than 20 percent.

Contestation and competition are important, but winning is ultimately what counts. An examination of the share of state legislative seats won by the two parties since 1960 underscores several trends. First, the greatest change has occurred in the

8. As defined in this study, a contested race is one in which the losing party received at least 10 percent of the vote.

**Table 6-2** Level of Two-Party Contestation and Two-Party Competition in State Legislative Houses, 1968–1995 and 1996–2002

| State | Two-Party Contestation | | Two-Party Competition | |
|---|---|---|---|---|
| | *1968–1995* | *1996–2002* | *1968–1995* | *1996–2002* |
| | Professional legislatures | | | |
| Michigan | 91 | 99 | 26 | 22 |
| New Jersey | 99 | 94 | 47 | 33 |
| California | 93 | 93 | 25 | 26 |
| Ohio | 90 | 87 | 27 | 24 |
| New York | 90 | 80 | 22 | 11 |
| Wisconsin | 76 | 64 | 32 | 31 |
| Pennsylvania | 82 | 61 | 27 | 12 |
| Illinois | 54 | 53 | 23 | 17 |
| Massachusetts | 44 | 30 | 17 | 10 |
| | Hybrid legislatures | | | |
| Minnesota | a | 93 | a | 39 |
| Hawaii | 63 | 83 | 22 | 33 |
| Oregon | 86 | 78 | 44 | 39 |
| Washington | 87 | 76 | 43 | 40 |
| Colorado | 78 | 73 | 41 | 36 |
| Connecticut | 92 | 67 | 44 | 23 |
| Iowa | 79 | 66 | 46 | 38 |
| Maryland | 63 | 66 | 26 | 28 |
| Alaska | 84 | 62 | 50 | 34 |
| Missouri | 46 | 62 | 19 | 26 |
| Oklahoma | 38 | 60 | 17 | 27 |
| North Carolina | 63 | 57 | 37 | 33 |
| Kansas | 71 | 53 | 37 | 21 |
| Alabama | 26 | 51 | 10 | 38 |
| Arizona | 56 | 51 | 29 | 32 |
| Virginia | 44 | 51 | 26 | 23 |
| Delaware | 74 | 49 | 38 | 19 |
| Florida | 37 | 46 | 20 | 24 |
| Tennessee | 33 | 44 | 17 | 18 |
| Kentucky | 33 | 43 | 17 | 22 |
| Texas | 29 | 37 | 13 | 16 |
| Mississippi | 22 | 36 | 10 | 29 |
| South Carolina | 36 | 33 | 16 | 15 |
| | Citizen legislatures | | | |
| North Dakota | 89 | 81 | 66 | 56 |
| Nevada | 77 | 80 | 37 | 44 |
| Maine | 77 | 79 | 39 | 43 |
| South Dakota | 80 | 74 | 56 | 40 |
| Utah | 82 | 74 | 43 | 32 |
| Montana | 77 | 68 | 47 | 36 |
| Vermont | b | 64 | b | 41 |
| New Hampshire | 58 | 64 | 30 | 38 |
| West Virginia | 69 | 61 | 40 | 28 |
| Indiana | 81 | 58 | 46 | 25 |
| New Mexico | 60 | 55 | 30 | 24 |
| Idaho | 64 | 52 | 35 | 25 |
| Wyoming | 73 | 50 | 47 | 30 |
| Arkansas | 8 | 42 | 3 | 28 |
| Georgia | 19 | 38 | 9 | 18 |
| Rhode Island | 70 | 38 | 27 | 13 |

SOURCES: Hamm and Hogan 2002; Anderson 1997, Tables 2:1a and 2:1b, used by permission of *Legislative Studies Quarterly.*

NOTE: Entries are percentages indicating frequency of Democratic versus Republican challenge.

[a] Minnesota did not hold partisan elections for part of this period.
[b] Data missing for some years during this period.

southern states. In 1960 the Democrats won 94 percent of all races in the South, but by 2002 this figure had fallen to 53 percent. In 2002 the Republicans claimed majority control in ten southern chambers. Second, in non-southern states the percentage of seats won by the two parties has fluctuated. Republicans won 62 percent of the seats in 1968, but claimed just 41 percent in 1974, probably as a result of the Watergate scandal. Third, since 1962 the president's party had always lost seats in mid-term elections until 1998, when Democrats actually gained about three dozen seats, and in 2002, when the Republicans gained around 200 seats. In the past ten presidential elections, the president's party has won seats in seven elections and lost them in three. President Bill Clinton's coattails were not long: the Democrats lost eighty-eight state house seats and sixty-two state senate seats in 1992; in 1996 they lost twenty-one senate seats but gained seventy-four house seats. In 2000 Republicans gained roughly seventy seats (National Conference of State Legislatures 1996a; Hansen 2000).

### What Affects Legislative Election Outcomes?

State legislative elections may be viewed in two ways. One perspective sees state legislative elections as battles between Democrats and Republicans; thus the focus is on trying to explain the percentage of the vote received by each party. A second perspective conceptualizes the battle as one between incumbents versus challengers. This view is more candidate-centered and focuses on what influences the percentage of the vote received by each type of candidate, regardless of party. From either perspective, election outcomes are conceptualized as a function of some combination of incumbency, campaign expenditures, past party strength, and, to a lesser extent, characteristics of the challenger (for example, quality of the challenger) and officeholder (for example, voting record).

*Party Strength.* In states in which political parties are competitive, election outcomes are often affected by the partisan makeup of the district. The impact of party strength, however, varies across the states. In addition, the electoral impact of district party strength is greater in some years than in others.

The tumultuous events of the 1994 election illustrate the potential volatility of the electorate and seemingly call into question the impact of party strength. In 1994 the Republicans captured not only the U.S. House of Representatives but took control of seventeen state chambers, gaining a total of 354 lower house seats and 106 state senate seats (Van Dunk and Holbrook 1994). Outside the South, the Democratic share of seats won was the lowest since the 1968 election. Nonetheless, an analysis of the pattern of control of lower house seats during 1992–1996 in eight states shows that 82 percent were won by the same party in all three elections (Frendreis and Gitelson 1997). Part of the reason for this outcome is that only one in three seats was contested in all three elections. At the same time we should not underplay the extent of change in some states.

*Incumbency.* State legislators, if they seek reelection, have a high probability of winning. In 1994, the last year for which we have complete data, incumbents won

92 percent of the time in the state senates and 90 percent of the time in the state houses. Even in the states in which incumbents were least successful, they won more than two-thirds of the races (National Conference of State Legislatures 1996b). The incumbency advantage has grown in recent years.

The probability of reelection varies across states. What factors account for this variation? Two studies (Berry, Berkman, and Schneiderman 2000; Carey, Niemi, and Powell 2000), covering elections from 1970–1989 and 1992–1994, respectively, find that the probability of reelection is higher when (1) the length of term is two years (as opposed to four years), (2) the legislator is a member of a more professional legislature, (3) redistricting is under the control of the incumbent's own party (rather than divided control or control by the opposite party), and (4) the incumbent was unopposed in the previous election (rather than being contested).[9]

Why is the level of legislative professionalism such a strong influence on incumbency, and thus on electoral outcomes? The argument is that by providing more institutional resources to members, professional legislatures serve to reduce the impact of other variables (for example, presidential coattails or a poor economy) on election outcomes. "Because members of a highly professional legislature should be able to take advantage of available resources to focus attention on themselves through both their legislative and campaign activities, they are more likely than members of less professionalized bodies to be able to shield themselves from external forces" (Berry, Berkman, and Schneiderman 2000, 863).

*Effects of Campaign Spending.* It is clear that money matters in American elections, including state legislative elections. Research convincingly shows that the candidate who spends the most money usually wins (Cassie and Breaux 1998). Incumbents generally have a substantial advantage over challengers in their ability to attract campaign contributions, and therefore incumbents enjoy a similar advantage in their ability to outspend challengers. This spending disparity between incumbents and challengers is particularly great in the states with more professional legislatures. The reason for this disparity is clear; it does not cost much to run for the state legislature in the rural states with citizen legislatures, and a challenger is more likely to be able to muster the $5,000 or so it takes to be competitive. On the other hand, it may cost $100,000 or more to run a competitive campaign in Illinois or California, and most challengers simply cannot raise that amount of money.

Does the amount of money spent on the campaign directly affect the share of votes that a candidate receives? Generally, the answer is yes. It seems to be especially true in primary elections, where candidates are able to increase their vote share by spending larger amounts of money (Breaux and Gierzynski 1991). In general elections, the impact of expenditures on the percentage of the vote won appears to vary from state to state and from year to year (Gierzynski and Breaux 1993).

---

9. The last two variables were included only in the Berry, Berkman, and Schneiderman (2000) study.

*State Legislative Campaigns.* Over the past few decades, electioneering practices in the United States have undergone dramatic changes. Political campaigns have become more candidate-centered as grassroots campaigning and party organizational support give way to mass media contact and professional consultants (Salmore and Salmore 1989). Modern electioneering practices are certainly used by some state legislative candidates who enlist the assistance of political consultants, conduct polls to gauge the preferences of voters, target tailored messages to specific segments of the population, and contact voters via radio and television. Although a growing number of state legislative candidates now employ such techniques, their use is not pervasive and is often conditioned by the level of available funds, the competitive situation of candidates, the congruence of district with television media markets, and a host of other constituency characteristics (Moncrief, Squire, and Jewell 2001; Hogan 1998).

## THE STATE LEGISLATORS

Obviously, institutions do not run themselves. They are social inventions, implying that they are created by and for people. In this section we take a look at the people who serve in legislatures.

### Who Are They?

The composition of most state legislatures is more diverse today than it was a generation ago. In this section we explore changes in three characteristics of state legislators (gender, race–ethnicity, and occupation) that have resulted in more diverse legislatures.

*Gender.* Although women make up a majority of the voting population, they have never been a majority in any U.S. state legislature. In 1894 the first three women to serve in a state legislature were elected to the Colorado House of Representatives (Cox 1996). In 1925, 141 women were serving in state legislatures (Cox 1996). By 1973 there were 424 women state legislators, and that number increased every electoral cycle for the next twenty years. But by the mid-1990s the percentage of legislative seats held by women leveled off (see Table 6-3). In 2003 women held at least 30 percent of the legislative seats in six states (Washington, Colorado, Maryland, Oregon, Vermont, and California) and 10 percent or less in only two states (Alabama and South Carolina). In general, higher percentages of women are found in the western state legislatures and lower percentages of women are found in the southern states.

Although it is important from the point of view of symbolic representation that more women now serve in legislatures, ultimately we want to know if their presence makes a difference behaviorally and in terms of public policy. Recent research suggests that it does, but only after the number of women who are elected reaches a critical mass. In those state legislatures with

**Table 6-3** Women in State Legislatures, Selected Years

| Year | Percentage of women |
|------|---------------------|
| 1973 | 5.6 |
| 1983 | 13.3 |
| 1993 | 20.6 |
| 1997 | 21.6 |
| 1999 | 22.4 |
| 2001 | 22.4 |
| 2003 | 22.3 |

SOURCE: CAWP 2003.

the highest proportion of female legislators, women are more likely to exhibit policy priorities related to issues of women, children, and family. In states with the lowest levels of female representation, these gender differences in terms of legislative priorities are absent (Thomas 1994).

Legislators have their greatest impact through the organizational positions they hold—the committee and leadership posts. In the 1970s women were typically assigned to and chaired committees dealing with those issues traditionally thought of as "women's concerns" (health and welfare), and they were underrepresented on rules, fiscal, and business affairs committees. By the late 1980s women were still frequently assigned to and chaired health and welfare committees, but they had significantly increased their representation on budget committees, although they were still underrepresented on business committees in most states (Thomas 1994, 66–67). In terms of chairing committees, by 1993–1994 women were overrepresented as chairs on education, health, and social and human service committees, and underrepresented on banking and financial institutions, energy, insurance, and rules committees (Darcy 1996). Nonetheless, one recent study concluded that "women are not discriminated against when committee chairs are selected" (Darcy 1996, 892). Increasingly, women are also assuming the most powerful positions in state legislatures. As of 2003, women were serving as the speaker in five state houses and as president in three state senates (CAWP 2003).

*Race-Ethnicity.* Another area of diversification involves racial-ethnic characteristics. Fifty years ago, there were almost no African Americans or Hispanics serving in state legislatures. By 1997 African American legislators constituted approximately 8 percent *(N =* approximately 600) of all state legislators. Hispanic legislators were a much smaller proportion, roughly 2.2 percent *(N =* 169). At least one African American was elected to serve in forty-five different state legislatures during the 1997–1998 sessions. In fifteen states (mostly in the South), at least ten African Americans were serving in the state legislature. Although at least one Hispanic is serving in twenty-six state legislatures, more than two-thirds are found in just five states: New Mexico, Texas, California, Florida, and New York.

The recruitment patterns for black and white legislators appear to be somewhat different. For example, black legislators received their start in politics outside of government (the civil rights movement, churches, or unions), whereas white legislators were more likely to start in state or local government (Button and Hedge 1996). African American legislators usually represent majority black urban districts, whereas white legislators tend to represent white rural or suburban districts. There is some disagreement as to whether or not African American state legislators face discrimination within the legislature. One recent study found that white legislators were less likely to perceive any discriminatory practices within the legislature, whereas the black legislators were more prone to believe that some discrimination did occur (Button and Hedge 1996). Black lawmakers report the greatest amount of discrimination in the Deep South legislatures, and the least amount of discrimination is perceived in the Rim South, probably because of the fact that blacks in this area represent a sizable number of white constituencies (Button and Hedge 1996). Comparable information for Hispanic legislators is not available. In a study of the perceived effectiveness of North Carolina legislators, race was a significant variable. African American legislators received lower effectiveness scores even after controlling for political party affiliation, seniority, and leadership status (Haynie 2001).

*Occupation.* Historically, the two largest occupation groups represented in the legislature were farmers and lawyers. This pattern has changed, however, during the twentieth century. A century ago, farmers constituted the largest group of state legislators, followed by lawyers. Lawyers remained a significant factor in state legislatures through the mid-1990s, making up 16 percent of all state legislators, whereas the proportion of farmers declined to just 8 percent (National Conference of State Legislatures 1996d).

A major change in the composition of state legislatures occurred with the emergence of the full-time legislator. When legislatures met for only a few months every other year, legislators could treat their office as a part-time vocation. The advent of longer sessions, higher pay, and more complex legislation, coupled with the availability of more technical and political information, has meant that legislators are forced to devote more time to their elected position. A former Washington state representative recently commented, "Anyone who thinks legislating anywhere in this country is a part-time commitment is nuts" (quoted in National Conference of State Legislatures 1996d, 3). As legislatures have professionalized, the number of members who claim their legislative occupation is a full-time job has also increased. According to the National Conference of State Legislatures, in 1972 fewer than 3 percent of the members listed their occupation as full-time legislator. By 1995, 14 percent reported they were full-time legislators (1996d).

As one might expect, the distribution of occupations is not the same in all state legislatures. In seven of the nine professional legislatures the largest occupation category is full-time legislator, reaching a high of 82 percent in Pennsylvania. Ironically, in the California legislature, often considered to be closest to the model of the U.S. Congress, only a handful of members considered themselves full-time legislators in 1995. How do we account for this anomaly? A significant part of the answer involves the impact of term limits. In 1993, two years before the implementation of term limits, roughly 38 percent of the members of the California legislature designated themselves full-time legislators. Today, given the short legislative career and the public's unhappiness with professional legislatures (Squire 1993), few legislators in California describe themselves this way. Attorneys and businesspersons are also well represented in most professional legislatures. A case can be made that as the percentage of full-time legislators increases, the percentage of businesspersons in the chamber decreases.

A greater mix of occupations exists in citizen legislatures. Business-related occupations are most consistently represented in these fifteen state legislatures. Farmers still constitute a sizable percentage of the membership in several citizen legislatures, such as North Dakota. Professionals other than lawyers—including accountants, consultants, doctors, clergy, and engineers or scientists—add to the mosaic of the citizen legislature, constituting more than 10 percent of all but one citizen legislature. Finally, in New Hampshire more than 40 percent of its members consider themselves retirees, students, or homemakers. This is quite a contrast to Pennsylvania or New York, where only 1 percent of the members designate themselves as fitting these categories.

The occupational structure of hybrid legislatures is more complicated to describe. Legislators who are in business-related occupations are represented reasonably well in the hybrid legislatures. Lawyers are quite prominent in some southern legislatures, but are a relatively small contingent in some western states. Full-time legislators constitute more than one in ten legislators in six hybrid legislatures. At the other end of the spectrum, less than 1 percent of the state legislators in Tennessee, Virginia, and Mississippi claim they are full-time legislators.

The chamber memberships include a smattering of doctors, accountants, consultants, engineers, and scientists. As expected, those with an agriculture occupation are most frequently seen in states in the Middle West region. Educators are more prevalent in Delaware, Maryland, Minnesota, Iowa, Arizona, and Alabama. In short, membership in the hybrid category of legislatures defies easy summation.

*Legislative Turnover and Legislative Careers*

Table 6-4 shows the average turnover for elections over the past seven decades. Several observations can be made from these data. First, turnover in state senates is generally slightly lower than turnover in the houses. In part, this is because state senators usually serve four-year terms, and they are staggered so that only one-half of the senate is elected at a time.

The second observation is that mean turnover dropped rather steadily in every decade until the 1990s. But note that the trend in average turnover in the 1990s actually increased slightly. This is almost certainly a product of the introduction of term limits in some states. Peverill Squire (1988) has shown that membership stability in the pre–term-limit period is best explained by two variables: pay and advancement prospects. In states where advancement from the lower chamber to higher office (for example, state senate, statewide office, or U.S. Congress) is unlikely and legislative pay is high, membership stability is also high (for example, in New York). Members in these legislatures are more likely to be career legislators, serving for longer periods in the same chamber. In "dead-end" legislatures, where both legislative pay and chances for advancement are low, membership is less stable. The greatest mem-

**Table 6-4** Average Turnover per Election in State Legislatures, by Decade (in percentages)

| Years | House | Senate |
| --- | --- | --- |
| 1931–40 | 59 | 51 |
| 1941–50 | 51 | 43 |
| 1951–60 | 45 | 40 |
| 1961–70 | 41 | 37 |
| 1971–80 | 32 | 29 |
| 1981–90 | 24 | 22 |
| 1991–2000 | 25 | 23 |

SOURCE: Moncrief, Niemi, and Powell 2003, 16.

bership instability exists in "springboard legislatures," in which the pay is comparable to that in a career legislature, but the chances for advancement to higher office are also high.

Some members leave office involuntarily. The obvious example is the legislator who is forced out of office as a result of electoral defeat. As noted earlier, most incumbents win reelection, but at least a few incumbents lose in each election. Death accounts for about one-fourth of those instances in which a legislator vacates the office before completing the term (Hamm and Olson 1992). The third reason for involuntary departure involves the individual being arrested, indicted, or convicted of a crime, or otherwise being forced from the legislature for some unethical behavior. Again, we are not accounting for the bulk of the departures, but in some states the effect is quite noticeable. The most extreme cases in the early 1990s occurred in South Carolina, where sixteen legislators went to jail in an FBI sting operation (Rosenthal 1998), and in Kentucky, where fifteen legislators were convicted on corruption charges (American Society of Legislative Clerks and Secretaries 1998).

State legislatures, through their state constitution, statute, or chamber rules, have a wide variety of options available to discipline members, including expulsion, censure, sanctions, and reprimands. The power to expel a member is rarely used. Only seventeen of ninety-one state legislative chambers that responded to a questionnaire indicated that they have taken this most serious action (American Society of Legislative Clerks and Secretaries 1998). This does not mean that state legislatures are unwilling to investigate serious charges. Rather, in the most serious cases members simply resign rather than be expelled. The upsurge in ethics laws and codes has not only clarified what actions are impermissible, but has also increased the frequency with which legislative chambers must investigate its members for a violation.

Another reason for involuntary departure now exists in many states: term limits. Until the early 1990s, legislators in the fifty states could serve as long as they wanted or until they were defeated. That situation began to change in the early 1990s when voters, using the initiative process, approved limitations on legislators' tenure in nineteen states.[10] In addition, legislators in Utah voted to place limits on themselves, and in Louisiana the legislature placed the term limit issue on the ballot and the voters approved it. Subsequent court actions have overturned term limits in Massachusetts, Oregon, and Washington. The Idaho state legislature repealed the term limit laws in 2002, and the Utah state legislature did likewise in 2003, leaving sixteen states with term limits. The term limit laws' main impact will be felt in the next few years.

Although a variety of states have term limits, the limits differ in two important respects: (1) the particular limit on the number of years of continuous service allowed, and (2) whether there is a lifetime ban on subsequent service. Based on

---

10. Only in Mississippi and North Dakota did a majority of the citizens vote no on term-limit legislation.

these criteria, term limits are most severe in the California Assembly, Arkansas House, and Michigan House, where a lifetime ban exists after serving six years. On the other hand, in both chambers in Utah and Louisiana members may serve twelve years of continuous service, sit out a term, and then return.

The adoption of term limits has led to numerous predictions about their potential impact on legislators and the legislative process. Early evidence, drawn from a survey of 3,000 legislators in 1995, indicates that term limits have not affected the overall composition of legislatures in terms of the background characteristics or ideology of those elected. But there is evidence of such changes in some individual states. For example, the number of Latino legislators in California grew substantially after term limits went into effect. It is likely that other factors contributed to this increase (see Clucas and Hatfield 2002), but there is little doubt that term limits facilitated the increase in minorities in some states. In terms of redistributing power, the major beneficiaries appear to be the governor, administrative agencies, and possibly legislative staff members and interest groups (Carey, Niemi, and Powell 1998; Moncrief and Thompson 2001). Because term limits are not yet fully in effect in most term-limited states, this evidence is preliminary. Further research will be necessary to document whether initial effects are long lasting.

*Representing Constituents*

In a representative democracy, legislators presumably represent their constituents. This simple statement hides a complex political phenomenon. What do the terms "constituency" and "representation" mean? Legislators use the term "constituency" in several different ways. From this perspective, one views the constituency not as a single entity but as a "nest of concentric circles" (Fenno 1978, 1). The largest circle represents the *geographical constituency*, the entire population living within the legal boundaries of the district. Occupying a smaller circle are the legislator's supporters, the *reelection constituency*. A subset of the reelection constituency is composed of the legislator's strongest supporters or the loyalists, their *primary constituency*. The smallest circle is confined to the political confidants and advisors, or those whom the legislator sees as good friends, otherwise known as the *personal constituency* (Fenno 1978). At any one time, a legislator may be focusing on one or more of these constituencies.

The concept of representation is also difficult to grasp. One useful way of conceptualizing representation is in terms of the legislator being "responsive" to the constituents in terms of policy, service, and allocation of public goods (Eulau and Karps 1977; Smith 2003).

Policy responsiveness involves the correspondence between the constituents' preferences and the behavior of the elected official. Alan Rosenthal (1998, 19) notes that "it is much more difficult, however, for representatives to act as agents of their constituency on policy matters." Why? First, some legislators, sometimes called *trustees*, use their own judgment because they lack confidence in the views of organized groups in their district or they believe that voters want their legislator to lead on critical issues (Jewell 1982). Second, as noted previously, the relevant constituency is not always obvious. Should the member be concerned with the total population, those who voted, or those who cast their vote for the legislator? Third, for those *delegates* or legislators who want to follow the wishes of their constituents, the problem is that most people do not have an opinion, save on the major issues (Rosenthal 1998). The result is that "most legislators are comfortable with the general policy viewpoints that they perceive as dominant in their districts; they believe that their own views are typical of those in the district. Consequently their role orientation does not usually lead trustees and delegates to vote differently on legislation" (Jewell 1982, 115).

Service responsiveness refers to the advantages and benefits that the representative is able to obtain for particular constituents (Eulau and Karps 1977). Legislators are, in effect, asked to help attain a divisible resource for particular individuals. Requests may cover an almost infinite number of subjects. For example, the legislator may be asked to help citizens obtain governmental assistance in the form of jobs or unemployment compensation, or help a business that has a disagreement with a state agency over licensing, taxes, or paperwork. The most common reasons constituents contact their state legislators are for information or help with bureaucratic red tape, and to a lesser extent in requests for jobs. Constituents contact their legislators less frequently about easing government regulations, intervening in local disputes, and helping with nongovernmental organizations (Freeman and Richardson 1996). The common term for this type of activity is *casework.*

What role does casework play in the job of the average legislator? Veteran legislators perceive that constituent demand for services has significantly increased and, as a consequence, they are spending more time on casework (Moncrief, Thompson, and Kurtz 1996). It is interesting to note that "legislators in all types of legislative institutions find tremendous increases in the pressures of the job, as well as in the demand for and time spent on constituent service" (Moncrief, Thompson, and Kurtz 1996). What affects the amount of time that a legislator and his or her staff devote to casework? The most recent research demonstrates that several factors appear to have an impact. At the individual level, legislators who place a high value on casework, who favor greater government spending, and who perceive that they will benefit electorally are more likely to devote more time, including that of the staff, to casework (Freeman and Richardson 1996). Conversely, legislators who place a low value on casework, who believe in a more limited role for government, and do not see any electoral benefit from casework are less inclined to devote time to these activities. The type of legislature in which one serves also has an impact. Legislators who serve in legislatures that have a tradition of supporting constituency service, offer career incentives for members, and provide personal staff or district offices are more likely to devote more time to casework (Freeman and Richardson 1994).

"Allocation responsiveness concerns the legislator's efforts to gain governmental goods and services for the district. They are general rather than individual benefits, but they frequently benefit one part of the district or one group more than others"

(Jewell 1982, 135). This type of responsiveness is often associated with "pork barrel" projects, which provide a benefit to a specific district but are paid for by everyone. Proponents of term limits argue that such limits will reduce allocational responsiveness, because legislators will not have the incentive to pursue pork barrel projects as a reelection tool. Preliminary results from one empirical study of term limits suggest that this may indeed be the case. Legislators in term-limited states report spending less time securing government money and projects for their district, and they report placing higher priority on the needs of the state as a whole rather than the narrower interests of their own district (Carey, Niemi, and Powell 1998).

### THE LEGISLATURES

While basic patterns of organization and leadership that are common to most legislatures, there are subtle differences that make each legislature unique. Below, we explore the commonalities and differences in the way state legislatures are structured.

*Organizational Features*

A comparative analysis of state legislatures reveals numerous differences in these organizations. Six important factors are the number of chambers, size, chamber leadership patterns, party caucuses, committees, and staff, each of which will be discussed in turn.

*Number of Chambers and Size.* In forty-nine of the fifty states, the legislature (also called the *general assembly* or *general court* in some states) is composed of two chambers. The upper chamber is called the *senate* in all states; the lower chamber is typically called the *house of representatives* (although in some states it is referred to as the *assembly, house of delegates,* or *general assembly*). The Nebraska legislature is a unicameral body with just one chamber, a senate. State senates range in size from a low of twenty members in the Alaska Senate to a high of sixty-seven in the Minnesota Senate. The lower houses evidence greater variability, the smallest being the Alaska House of Representatives with only forty legislators and the largest the New Hampshire House of Representatives with 400 members. The size of the legislative body affects both structural and procedural aspects of life in the legislature. For example, the greater the number of members in the chamber, the greater the degree of hierarchical organizational structure, the more limited the floor debate, and the greater the specialization among members (see Hedlund 1984).

*Chamber Leadership.* In the forty-nine lower houses the chamber leader, referred to as the *speaker,* is elected by the members of the house. Greater variation exists among the state senates. The membership elects a president in twenty-three state senates and a speaker in one. The lieutenant governor presides in twenty-six. However, as a member of the executive branch the lieutenant governor has limited power in the legislature; the real power resides with the president pro tempore, who is chosen by the senate members themselves.

Although examples exist of legislative leaders who have served in that capacity for a number of terms, a recent study found that 86 percent of senate presidents, house speakers, and majority and minority leaders changed between 1990 to 1997 (Hansen 1997). Until at least the early 1990s the career path to the top leadership position was becoming more institutionalized as the legislature itself institutionalized (Freeman 1995). Although the path to the top post varied, an apprenticeship in another leadership position (such as majority leader or chair of an important committee) was very common. This trend will probably continue to be the norm in those state legislatures not faced with term limits. If an apprenticeship norm is to be followed in the legislatures with term limits, future chamber leaders will have to be given major leadership positions (for example, committee chair or majority leader) early in their legislative careers—usually in their second or third terms at the latest (Hodson et al. 1995).

The job of the legislative leader is more complex today than in the past. Internal responsibilities include acting as the chief administrative officer, building legislative coalitions, and providing services and information to individual members, to name only a few. Leaders also have external responsibilities, including being party spokesperson, interacting with the executive, serving as the interchamber representative, holding press conferences, and preparing for campaigns (Little 1995).

Analyzing legislative leadership patterns in twenty-two states, Malcolm Jewell and Marcia Whicker (1994) provide a framework for research. They contend that legislative leadership is to a certain extent dependent on context. A key factor is the structure of the institution, including the power of the legislature relative to other key state political actors, its level of professionalization and representativeness, the nature of legislative rules, and the degree of party polarization. The legislative setting also affects the leader's power. For example, the fewer the restrictions on leadership tenure, the greater the leader's ability to affect policy. The larger the size of the party majority and the greater the degree of party cohesion and loyalty, the greater the impact of power of the leader. Leaders also have available to them a range of tools and techniques. For example, leaders find their power to influence public policy increases as their power to appoint committee members increases, as the size of the professional leadership staff increases, and as the techniques for controlling the party caucuses also increase. Finally, personal leadership style and goals are hypothesized to affect the leader's power.

In terms of the formal institutional powers of house speakers, a recent study indicates that speakers have potentially significant powers in five areas: appointing party leaders and committee chairs, controlling the committee system, providing campaign support and additional staff, controlling house procedures, and not being limited in the number of years that a speaker may serve (see Table 6-5). Speakers are more likely to have greater formal powers in states with higher levels of party competition and more likely to have lower powers in state legislatures which serve as a springboard for higher office. At the same time, greater professionalism of the legislature does not lead to weaker leadership (Clucas 2001).

**Table 6-5** Speakers' Institutional Power Index, by Level of Professionalism

| State | Appointment powers | Committee powers | Resource powers | Procedure powers | Tenure powers | Total index |
|---|---|---|---|---|---|---|
| | | | Professional legislatures | | | |
| Michigan | 3.0 | 4.0 | 5.0 | 4.5 | 5.0 | 21.5 |
| Wisconsin | 3.0 | 4.0 | 5.0 | 4.5 | 5.0 | 21.5 |
| Illinois | 5.0 | 3.5 | 5.0 | 2.5 | 5.0 | 21.0 |
| New York | 5.0 | 4.0 | 3.0 | 4.0 | 5.0 | 21.0 |
| Ohio | 3.0 | 4.0 | 5.0 | 3.0 | 5.0 | 20.0 |
| Pennsylvania | 3.0 | 1.0 | 5.0 | 4.0 | 5.0 | 18.0 |
| New Jersey | 3.0 | 5.0 | 3.0 | 4.5 | 2.0 | 17.5 |
| Massachusetts | 5.0 | 2.5 | 3.0 | 2.5 | 4.0 | 17.0 |
| California | 2.0 | 1.5 | 3.0 | 3.5 | 5.0 | 15.0 |
| | | | Hybrid legislatures | | | |
| Arizona | 3.0 | 5.0 | 5.0 | 4.5 | 5.0 | 22.5 |
| Oregon | 3.0 | 4.5 | 5.0 | 4.0 | 5.0 | 21.5 |
| Oklahoma | 4.0 | 4.0 | 5.0 | 4.5 | 3.0 | 20.5 |
| Iowa | 3.0 | 5.0 | 3.0 | 4.0 | 5.0 | 20.0 |
| Missouri | 3.0 | 2.5 | 5.0 | 4.5 | 5.0 | 20.0 |
| North Carolina | 3.0 | 5.0 | 3.0 | 4.0 | 5.0 | 20.0 |
| Minnesota | 3.0 | 5.0 | 3.0 | 3.5 | 5.0 | 19.5 |
| Texas | 4.0 | 1.0 | 5.0 | 4.5 | 5.0 | 19.5 |
| Tennessee | 3.0 | 4.0 | 3.0 | 4.0 | 5.0 | 19.0 |
| Virginia | 3.0 | 4.0 | 3.0 | 4.0 | 5.0 | 19.0 |
| Washington | 2.0 | 4.0 | 5.0 | 2.5 | 5.0 | 18.5 |
| Colorado | 3.0 | 2.5 | 3.0 | 4.5 | 5.0 | 18.0 |
| Delaware | 3.0 | 5.0 | 0.0 | 4.5 | 5.0 | 17.5 |
| Maryland | 4.0 | 4.0 | 0.0 | 4.5 | 5.0 | 17.5 |
| Connecticut | 4.0 | 4.5 | 3.0 | 3.5 | 2.0 | 17.0 |
| Louisiana | 3.0 | 4.0 | 1.0 | 4.0 | 5.0 | 17.0 |
| South Carolina | 1.0 | 4.0 | 3.0 | 3.5 | 5.0 | 16.5 |
| Alabama | 3.0 | 4.0 | 0.0 | 4.0 | 5.0 | 16.0 |
| Kansas | 3.0 | 4.5 | 3.0 | 3.5 | 2.0 | 16.0 |
| Florida | 4.0 | 5.0 | 0.0 | 4.0 | 1.0 | 14.0 |
| Kentucky | 2.0 | 1.0 | 3.0 | 3.0 | 5.0 | 14.0 |
| Alaska | 2.0 | 1.0 | 3.0 | 2.5 | 5.0 | 13.5 |
| Mississippi | 2.0 | 1.0 | 0.0 | 4.5 | 4.0 | 11.5 |
| Hawaii | 1.0 | 0.0 | 0.0 | 4.5 | 5.0 | 10.5 |
| | | | Citizen legislatures | | | |
| West Virginia | 5.0 | 4.0 | 5.0 | 4.5 | 5.0 | 23.5 |
| New Hampshire | 5.0 | 4.0 | 5.0 | 4.0 | 5.0 | 23.0 |
| Utah | 3.0 | 4.0 | 5.0 | 4.5 | 5.0 | 21.5 |
| New Mexico | 3.0 | 4.0 | 5.0 | 4.0 | 5.0 | 21.0 |
| Idaho | 3.0 | 5.0 | 3.0 | 4.0 | 5.0 | 20.0 |
| Indiana | 3.0 | 4.0 | 3.0 | 4.5 | 5.0 | 19.5 |
| Maine | 3.0 | 4.0 | 5.0 | 2.0 | 5.0 | 19.0 |
| Montana | 3.0 | 4.0 | 3.0 | 4.0 | 5.0 | 19.0 |
| Vermont | 3.0 | 4.0 | 3.0 | 4.0 | 5.0 | 19.0 |
| Rhode Island | 3.0 | 4.0 | 3.0 | 3.5 | 5.0 | 18.5 |
| Georgia | 3.0 | 4.0 | 3.0 | 3.0 | 5.0 | 18.0 |
| Nevada | 3.0 | 4.0 | 3.0 | 2.5 | 5.0 | 17.5 |
| North Dakota | 3.0 | 4.0 | 5.0 | 4.0 | 1.0 | 17.0 |
| Arkansas | 3.0 | 0.0 | 3.0 | 4.5 | 5.0 | 15.5 |
| South Dakota | 3.0 | 4.0 | 3.0 | 3.0 | 2.0 | 15.0 |
| Wyoming | 2.0 | 1.0 | 0.0 | 3.5 | 1.0 | 7.5 |

SOURCE: Clucas 2001, 326–327.

*Party Caucus.* In most state legislatures, members of the same political party belong to a party caucus. Although these groups dominated the state legislative process in the years after the Civil War and into the twentieth century (Campbell 1980), their role today is somewhat diminished. Caucuses may perform a multiplicity of functions: choosing the party leadership, keeping members informed, discussing policy to help leaders assess membership opinion, building cohesion, and mobilizing votes (Jewell and Whicker 1994, 100).

The importance of party caucuses varies among the state legislatures. In general party caucuses will be most important in the legislative process in small chambers with evenly matched parties. They are least important in large chambers with one dominant party (Francis 1989, 45). A recent analysis of party caucuses in formerly one-party legislatures, mostly in the South, found that when the minority party (in this case the Republican party) is more competitive in the electoral realm, the party caucuses become more complex in terms of meeting more frequently, having formal leadership and formal rules, providing information and acting in formulating policies (Anderson 1997).

*Committees.* State legislatures face a daunting problem. There is not enough time in a legislative session for the entire legislative membership to adequately discuss and debate each proposed bill. To solve this workload problem, legislatures create smaller working groups called *committees* to initially review, analyze, and rewrite bills that have been introduced. Because it is inefficient to assign a group of legislators to review only one bill or one specific issue and then break up, these small work groups usually exist for the life of the particular legislative session. To further enhance the division of labor, each committee generally has jurisdiction over a given policy area (for example, education or health). Jurisdiction is more likely set by the chamber leadership or a management committee rather than by rule (American Society of Legislative Clerks and Secretaries 1998). Membership on committees is usually restricted to just those legislators serving in the particular chamber. However, in at least twenty-nine state legislatures, and especially in Maine, Massachusetts, and Connecticut, some joint committees composed of members from both chambers exist (Hamm and Hedlund 1994).

Committee systems at the state level have changed extensively over time. A recent study chronicles the development of committee systems in thirty-eight chambers during the twentieth century (Hamm and Hedlund 1995). At the beginning of the century, the typical standing committee system in a state legislature consisted of a relatively large number of committees; the size of each committee was relatively small; and each legislator had a significant number of committee assignments. Committee names were stable from session to session and jurisdiction was generally quite narrow, sometimes limited to a single institution or problem. An extreme case was the Michigan House in which there was a standing committee for each specifically named state asylum, one for each state prison, a separate committee for the school for the blind and one for the deaf, plus one for the employment institution for the blind. Starting in the 1940s, though, the total number of committees, committee positions, and mean number of assignments per member declined to its nadir in the 1970s, and then increased slightly. Indications are that the number of committees or the average size of committees is a function of the size of the legislature, whereas the degree of committee specialization at the individual level is a function of the stability of the legislative membership (Francis 1989; Hamm and Hedlund 1995).

The role that standing committees play today in the legislative process varies among the ninety-nine state legislative chambers. In one set of legislative chambers, the key decision-making power is lodged mainly in the committees; in a second set of legislatures, the critical decisions are made by either the majority party leadership or the majority party caucus; in a third set power is shared between the standing committees and the leadership or the caucus. According to a study conducted in the early 1980s, in nearly two-thirds of the chambers, the shared committee–leadership/caucus model prevails (Francis 1989). It is interesting to note that committees are generally most important in chambers in which one party dominates (Francis 1989). An unexplored research question is whether committees remain important in chambers that moved in recent years from being one-party dominant to a more balanced two-party system (for example, the Georgia Senate).

The ability of committees to play a meaningful role in the legislative process can also be affected by the rules governing the operation of the legislature. These rules are found in state constitutions, state statutes, and the formal rules and regulations of legislative chambers. For example, committees in the Oregon House have significant influence over policy content because the rules permit them to introduce bills with the committee listed as the author; offer substitute bills in place of the original; have committee amendments automatically incorporated into the bill rather than have each amendment accepted or rejected by the floor; and make it very difficult to amend legislation on the floor by requiring unanimous consent to accept the amendment. The committees also are important in the law-making process because all bills must be referred to committee and bills reported from committee go directly to the calendar. In other words, the rules carve out a central role for committees in the legislative process. Committees do not have such favorable rules in most state legislatures.

*Staff.* A major change in state legislatures during the past thirty years has involved the growth of legislative staff. "State legislatures have moved away from dependence on external sources for information in favor of in-house staff resources" (Neal 1996, 24).

Legislative staff are not equally distributed among the state legislatures, however. During the 1995–1996 legislative session, 3,899 staff were employed in the New York legislature, whereas there were only fifty-eight staff positions in the Vermont legislature (National Conference of State Legislatures 1996c). Because staff is a component of professionalism, it is not surprising that in the mid-1990s professional legislatures had more staff (mean = 1,798) than either the hybrid legislatures (mean = 640) or the citizen legislatures (mean = 256). In professional legislatures there are, on average, eleven staff members for each legislator; this figure drops to fewer than five in hybrid legislatures and to two in citizen legislatures. The greatest difference is between California, with almost twenty-two staff members per legislator, and Vermont, with three legislators for each staff member.

Numerous types of legislative staff exist (National Conference of State Legislatures 1996c; Neal 1996). In all state legislatures, the chief parliamentary officers and staff are involved with the law-making and administrative processes of state legislatures. They deal with such issues as bill introductions, preparation of calendars, tracking amendments offered during debate, and posting hearing schedules. Leadership staff work directly for legislative leaders or for party caucuses. They are typically involved in policy research, constituent services, and administrative duties. In the most systematic treatment of state legislative leadership to date, Jewell and Whicker (1994, 97) argue that "the ability of leaders to be effective depends in no small part on the size, professional skills, and experience of their staffs."

Staff provide a variety of services, but the most important function is communication: staff are the eyes and ears of the leadership. They keep the leadership informed about the concerns and needs of the members. Staff members supplement the work of assistant leaders or party whips in keeping members informed about what is going on in the chamber and in committees. Prior to an important roll call, they help to poll the party membership. They keep the membership informed about the wishes of the leadership, the scheduling of legislation, and the status of members' bills. Staff members frequently represent the leadership in behind-the-scenes negotiations on bills, either in the committee stage or when bills are pending on the floor (Jewell and Whicker 1994).

Research staff compile background information on bills, respond to members' requests for information, and sometimes staff committees. The legal services staff, composed of individuals with legal experience, draft bills, conduct legal research, and may be involved in administration and enforcement of ethics codes. Legislative program evaluation staff engage in program evaluation and performance auditing. Legislative fiscal staff are involved in fiscal analysis, budget review, and revenue review for state legislatures. These staff usually examine budget requests made by state agencies and make suggestions to the state legislators about these requests. Personal staff who work for individual legislators are usually found in legislatures that are closer to full-time.

### Choosing Leaders and Subgroups

Once legislators have been chosen in district elections, the legislative chamber must be organized to conduct business. In effect, three processes, sometimes intersecting, are occurring: choosing chamber leaders, choosing legislative party leaders, and choosing committee chairs and members.

*Chamber Leaders.* In most state legislatures the majority party caucuses determine which of their members will serve as the presiding officer. In these state legislatures significant politicking takes place before the caucus meets as candidates try to line up votes. In some cases it becomes apparent that one candidate has captured a majority of the vote and the losing candidate withdraws before the caucus meets. Another variant is to have a short meeting at which only one ballot is necessary to elect the party's nominee. The third pattern is to have a protracted battle in which no one is initially able to assemble a winning coalition.

There is no guarantee that the members of the majority party caucus will abide by the caucus decision. In that case, at least five scenarios are likely, ranging from little or no impact to a complete restructuring of the legislature. First, a few members may vote for the minority party candidate, but their defection is not significant enough to change the outcome. A second possibility is that several party dissidents may simply withhold their support, making it impossible for the majority party candidate to win the position, and ultimately forcing the candidate to withdraw. A third scenario involves a dissident faction of the majority party teaming up with the minority party to elect one of the dissidents as speaker, without there being any long-term impact.

A fourth possibility has more lasting consequences, but still has a member of the majority party as speaker. The final scenario is more unusual in that the leadership is acquired by the minority party with the help of a few votes by disgruntled members of the majority party. Ralph Wright, the Democratic Speaker of Vermont from 1985–1991, came to power this way.

What happens if the two parties have an identical number of seats? This is a possibility in sixty-one chambers with an even number of seats, and it has actually occurred twenty-five times in the past thirty years. In the 2003 session, for example, Democrats and Republicans have an equal number of seats in the New Jersey and Oregon Senates. To resolve the situation, several solutions have been adopted. The most common is to have co-leaders, either alternating daily or monthly in running the floor session, and co-committee chairs. A variant of this approach involves chamber leadership changing partisan control at the end of the first year of a two-year session. Another way is to elect the leader from one party, but to give the bulk of the committee chairs to members of the other party. Sometimes the issue is settled by state law.

We have discussed the organization of the legislature as if it only involved the decisions of the members of that chamber. Although that is generally true today, in past years the governor, particularly in some southern states, was the kingmaker (Jewell 1962). In a most unusual occurrence, in 2002 the newly elected New Jersey governor, James McGreevey, convinced the newly elected Democratic majority in the assembly to accept his choice as speaker. The Democratic caucus acquiesced after sufficient threats to future political careers were made by members of the governor's team. As a result, a backbencher with only two years of legislative experience became what is considered to be the third most powerful politician in New Jersey government, bypassing those who had held key legislative positions in previous sessions (Diamond 2002).

*Party Leaders.* The second selection process involves choosing the political party leadership. The formal legislative party organization varies among the state legislative chambers. Legislative party organizations can be placed on a continuum from simple to relatively complex (Hamm, Hedlund, and Anderson 1994). At one extreme, there is no formal party organization (Mississippi). The simplest organization is where each party has a floor leader (majority or minority party) responsible for leading debate on the floor and working with the speaker in setting the agenda (Alaska Senate). More complex organizations (New York Assembly) have a more detailed leadership structure, including positions such as assistant majority leader, whip, and majority caucus chair.

The actual selection of the key party leaders usually takes place in the party caucus in which the legislators from that party vote for their officers. In essence, the leaders are chosen by their peers. This, however, is not always the case because the elected chamber leader, who is also the party leader, does appoint the majority leader and other party officials in a few chambers (Connecticut Senate). In addition, in a few legislative bodies the elected chamber leader also carries the title of majority leader, thus fusing power in one person (Illinois Senate and New York Senate). Another option is to forego a majority leader designation, having the elected chamber leader serve as the party chair. In the Ohio Senate, for example, there is no majority leader, and the Senate president, the elected chamber leader, presides over the majority party caucus.

*Committee Chairs and Members.* A third process, after the selection of the chamber and party leadership, involves designating the standing work groups for the legislature. The committee assignment process is a key organizational decision in which members are allocated for the duration of the legislative session to concentrate their time on certain policy areas. The leader's ability to control appointments is crucial to governing the chamber. As Jewell and Whicker (1994, 95) note, "The ability of the majority-party leadership to appoint, and if necessary to remove, committee chairs is one of its greatest sources of power." The elected chamber leader (speaker, president, or president pro tempore) selects committee chairs in about 70 percent of the state legislative chambers. In other states, committee chairs may be selected by the majority leader, by a chamber committee, by substantive committee members, by the entire chamber, by chamber seniority, or by committee seniority.

Across all state legislatures, the most frequent considerations in appointing committee chairs are political party, competency or talent of the member, and preference of the member, followed by seniority in the chamber, tenure on the committee, and support in the leadership election. Less important are occupation, geographic location of the member's district in the state, gender, and ethnic representation (American Society of Legislative Clerks and Secretaries 1998).

Legislators are appointed to committees in a variety of ways. In about one-half of the legislative chambers, legislators of the majority political party are appointed by the top leader (speaker, president), and in about one in four chambers this responsibility falls to the president pro tem, speaker pro tem, or majority leader. In roughly one in ten chambers, a committee-on-committees or a rules committee performs this task. Seniority is the rule in only a few chambers (Arkansas Senate, Utah Senate) (American Society of Legislative Clerks and Secretaries 1998). Even greater control is possible if the majority party leaders are able to dictate which minority party members will be appointed to specific committees. In several states, the minority leader has some influence over which members of her party will be assigned to the various committees (American Society of Legislative Clerks and Secretaries 1998).

### THE LEGISLATURE AT WORK

As governmental institutions, state legislatures perform several important functions. First, they *make policy.* Legislatures are not the only policy-making institutions in the states, but they are at the center of the process. Thus when most people are asked, "What do legislatures do?" their first response is usually "They pass bills" or "They make laws for the state."

But legislatures perform other tasks as well. One of the most important is *appropriation.* Legislatures must approve the budget for the state. Technically, this can be considered part of the law-making function, because budgets are constructed through appropriation bills passed by the legislature. But budget setting is such an important issue, and so dominates many state legislative sessions, that we treat it as a separate function from the regular, substantive law-making process. State budgets today are billion-dollar propositions. Not only does the state budget allocate funds for the various state agencies, but increasingly local governments (especially cities and school districts) receive substantial appropriations from the state budget.

Governors have a powerful influence over the state budgetary process, because in most states it is the governor's office that first makes revenue estimates and then submits a proposed budget to the legislature, based on the projected revenue. Moreover, the governor can claim to represent the fiscal interests of the entire state, whereas legislators have a natural tendency to look out for the budgetary interests of their individual districts first. Nonetheless, few legislatures today are willing to abdicate the appropriations function entirely to the executive branch. As Rosenthal (1998, 315) notes, "Over time legislative involvement has increased practically everywhere." Most legislatures have added their own revenue estimation and budget review staff to provide themselves with an independent analysis of the budget needs of the various state agencies.

A third function of state legislatures is *administrative oversight.* Because they have primary responsibility for passing legislation, but not for administering these laws, the legislature seeks a check on the way the various state agencies are operating. This is a difficult task for state legislatures, many of which meet only part-time and have limited staff assistance. Moreover, for most legislators, the personal incentive to invest vast amounts of time in oversight is generally not very great. Nonetheless, legislatures, in varying degrees, make an effort to perform oversight. One way legislators seek oversight of state agencies is through budget hearings. Most state legislatures also exercise some control by reviewing administrative rules and regulations. This review, which is now an institutionalized routine in many states, is a way to ensure that the administrative agencies are following legislative intent in the way the laws are executed.

Finally, legislatures perform *constituent service*. In truth, this function is more closely associated with the individual legislator than with the legislative institution, but legislators use institutional resources (for example, staff personnel) to perform this service. One form of constituent service is casework. Such service is often in the form of interceding on the constituents' behalf with a state agency, handling requests from constituents for information, or even helping them find a job (Freeman and Richardson 1996). In contrast to the oversight function, legislators have a strong incentive to perform casework and believe it aids in their efforts at reelection (Freeman and Richardson 1996).

Another form of constituent service is securing particularistic benefits for the district—a new road or airport, for example. Sometimes referred to as pork or pork barrel projects, these benefits are particularistic because they benefit a specific segment of the population (the legislator's district) but the costs are borne universally (the entire state foots the bill through the state budget). Obviously, this particular type of action is closely tied to the appropriations process.

*The Legislative Process*

The basic process of passing a bill into law is generally the same in all state legislatures (see Box 6-1 for a summary of the legislative process), but there are differences in the details from one state to another. Moreover, the formal process is only part of the story. Personalities, outside events, and timing are all factors that affect the likelihood that any particular proposal will wend its way through the process to become law.

Most bills do not become law. While the average for the fifty states is about 20 percent, the success rate varies greatly from one state to another. Many factors account for this variation, but one recent study finds that more professional legislatures and those chambers that do not impose a limit on the number of bills a legislator can introduce tend to pass lower proportions (Squire 1998). Another study found that both the number of bills and the proportion of bills enacted is inversely related to the number of interest groups in the state. In other words, the more interest groups, the more difficult it is to get legislation passed (Gray and Lowery 1995).

One reason that so many bills fail to become law is that the legislative process includes numerous obstacles, all of which must be overcome. To put it another way, the forces that oppose a bill only need to be successful at any one stage to block the proposed legislation, whereas the bill's proponents must win at each step. A bill can be effectively killed (and many are) in committee. It may be gutted through floor amendments. It might be defeated on the floor vote. It might even be passed on the floor and defeated on a reconsideration motion. The bill can lose at any of these stages, in either chamber. Or it may die because a conference committee cannot

**Box 6-1** The Legislative Process

---

*Bill is drafted*

---

The ideas for bills come from a variety of sources, including interest groups, administrative agencies, the governor's office, constituents, or the legislator herself. A bill may be drafted by an individual legislator, but more likely she will use the drafting service provided by the legislative staff. After the legislator approves the draft, she may seek cosponsors for the proposal.

---

*Introduction and first reading*

---

The draft becomes a bill when the sponsoring legislator "drops" the bill—that is, gives it to the clerk of the chamber, who assigns the bill a number. The bill is given its first reading at this point.

In an effort to keep the institutional workload manageable, a few state legislatures limit the number of bills an individual legislator can introduce each year. In most states with such rules, exceptions are permitted for certain types of bills (for example, local bills).

Another method of containing the workload is to impose bill introduction deadlines, which many state legislatures now employ. Under such rules individual legislators cannot introduce bills after a specified day (for example, the 25th day of the session).

---

*Committee referral*

---

The bill is assigned to one of the substantive standing committees of the chamber. Since different committees are comprised of different legislators, the decision as to which committee should get the bill can sometimes be an important determinant of the bill's ultimate fate. In most states the power of referral rests with the presiding officer.

---

*Subcommittee*

---

Some state legislatures make extensive use of subcommittees as a way to divide the workload within the committee. Some states make use of subcommittees only infrequently, usually to consider a particular issue such as reapportionment.

---

*Committee hearings*

---

Generally, the most extensive discussion and review of a bill occurs in hearings before the committee (or subcommittee). It is here that most public input will occur. This input, in the form of public testimony, is often dominated by lobbyists for interest groups, who testify in favor of or opposition to the bill, or who argue for specific changes in the bill. Control over the hearing process (including, in many states, the decision whether or not to schedule hearings) is usually in the hands of the committee chair. However, the rules of some state legislatures require all bills to receive a public hearing.

---

*Committee action*

---

After the bill has been reviewed and considered, the committee may report the bill out with one of several recommendations. The committee action at this stage is critical to the potential success of the bill. The possible recommendations include "Do Pass," "Do Not Pass," "No Recommendation," "Refer to Another Committee," "Withdraw from Consideration," "Amend," "Substitute," or "Table."

Perhaps 90 percent of the bills that receive a favorable ("Do Pass") recommendation from the committee will ultimately pass when the bill comes up for floor vote. An unfavorable recommendation ("Do Not Pass") is rare in most states; if the committee does not favor the bill it will simply not hold hearings, or it will vote to put the bill aside ("Table"). However, a few states require all legislation to be reported from committee to floor. In these states, a "Do Not Pass" recommendation is common, since the committee does not have the option of killing the bill through inaction.

Committees often recommend amendments to a bill. If substantial changes are needed, the committee may offer a substitute bill for the original one. In the case of committee amendments and substitute bills, the full membership of the chamber will have the opportunity to accept or reject the proposed changes in a separate vote prior to voting on passage of the bill itself.

**Box 6-1** *Continued*

### Committee action (continued)

Once the bill is reported from committee, it is placed on the second reading calendar. If committee amendments were reported, the legislature, operating as the Committee of the Whole, will consider whether or not to adopt the proposed amendments. Amendments offered by other members (floor amendments) are usually in order at this stage as well. If amendments to the bill are adopted, the bill must be rewritten to reflect the changes. This is known as engrossment.

### Third reading and floor vote

In most state legislative chambers, the floor debate and floor vote occurs at this stage. In order for a bill to pass, a simple majority of those present and voting is required in most states. Thus, if there are one hundred members, and on a given bill the vote is forty-five "yeas," forty "nays," and fifteen "not present" or "abstaining," the bill would pass. However, a few states require a true majority of the chamber to vote in favor of a bill in order for it to pass. If a true majority is required, the above vote of 45–40–15 would mean the bill fails, since a "true majority" in a chamber with one hundred members is fifty-one. Under these circumstances, "taking a walk" on a bill has the same effect on the vote outcome as voting "nay."

### Reconsideration

In keeping with the deliberative nature of legislatures, there is usually a provision that a vote on a bill can be reconsidered within twenty-four to forty-eight hours of the vote. Occasionally a bill will pass one day, be reconsidered, and fail the next day. Or it may fail and subsequently be reconsidered and passed.

### Action in the second chamber

The steps in the second chamber are generally identical to those listed above, from introduction through third reading and floor debate. Most states require sequential action, meaning that the bill is not referred to the second chamber until it has worked its way through the chamber in which it was originally introduced. However, some states permit concurrent introduction, meaning that the bill is introduced in both chambers at the same time.

### Conference committees

In order to become law, a bill must pass both chambers in precisely the same form. If a bill passes each chamber, but in different forms (for example, amendments were added in one chamber), a resolution of these differences is necessary. If neither chamber is willing to accede to the changes made by the other chamber, then a conference committee will be created in an effort to work out an acceptable compromise. In most cases the presiding officers appoint three or four members of each chamber to serve as the conferees. If a majority of the conference committee can negotiate an agreement, this new version of the bill is submitted for approval via floor vote in each chamber. If the conference report is accepted by the floor in both chambers, the bill passes. If either chamber rejects the conference report, or if the conferees cannot agree on a compromise version of the bill, the bill dies.

Conference committees are more prevalent in some state legislatures than in others. In some states they have become a very significant part of the legislative process.

### Governor's action

Once a bill is passed in identical form in both chambers, the bill is sent to the governor. He may sign it into law or veto the bill. Vetoes are most common under conditions of divided government (the governor is from one party and the legislative majority is from the other party), but they occur in almost all legislative sessions. The provisions for overriding a gubernatorial veto vary a bit from state to state; the most common rule is that a legislature must muster a two-thirds majority in each chamber to override the governor's veto. Only about 5 percent of gubernatorial vetoes are overridden.

SOURCE: Moncrief, Niemi, and Powell 2003.

produce an acceptable compromise. The governor may veto it. Some bills die simply because time runs out. It is not uncommon for a few bills to pass one chamber, be reported favorably out of committee in the second chamber, and yet be left to languish on the second or third reading calendar because the legislature adjourns the session.

Nor is it unusual for a specific piece of legislation to be introduced several years before it ultimately passes. Some proposals are so different from the status quo that it takes several years for the legislators to become "educated" about the issue, or for public opinion to become sufficiently solidified on a proposed solution. Interest groups, in particular, often take a long-term view, knowing a bill will not pass this year or perhaps even next year, but eventually "its time will come" (a common phrase in the legislative halls).

*Influences on Legislative Policy Making*

There are many factors involved in the policy-making process. Some of these factors have to do with the nature of the legislative institution. For example, the need to develop a majority coalition at both the committee and floor vote stages means that compromise is valued. Moreover, the bicameral structure of state legislatures (except Nebraska's) means that negotiation between the chambers is often necessary.

Another consideration is the time dimension (Loomis 1994). Time is important in state legislatures in several ways. First, most state legislatures meet in session only part-time (two to four months per year). As the end of the session approaches, time becomes a critical consideration. Because there is not enough time to process all the proposals, leadership often takes control of the legislative agenda in the last few weeks of the session, deciding which bills will come to the floor for a vote and which will die on second or third reading calendar.

Second, because it takes time for legislation to be drafted, introduced, and heard in committees, the workflow of legislatures is different in the beginning of the session than at the end. In the first month or so, legislators spend most of their time in committees and less time debating and voting on the floor. The pace appears to be slow and deliberative, even ponderous. As the session progresses, action on the floor picks up as more and more bills flow out of the committees. In the last few weeks, most of the committee work is complete and the floor activity often becomes frenetic, with perhaps dozens of roll-call votes occurring in a single day. Third, legislators (and legislation) are affected by electoral cycles. Some types of policies (for example, tax increases and perhaps highly emotional issues such as abortion) are less likely to be considered during an electoral year, as legislators fear the consequences for their own careers.

Most of the legislation that comes to floor vote is relatively non-controversial. These are often bills that make minor changes in existing law; the decision-making process on such legislation is routine and the roll-call votes are often unanimous or nearly unanimous. Over the course of the entire session, only 100 or so bills may generate considerable controversy at the floor stage. Of course, these are the bills that are most salient to the general public and the media and that may cause considerable angst for the legislators as they cast their votes.

The focus on how legislators vote on final passage of bills can mask the importance of behavior at earlier stages. Committee votes, for example, are less visible to the general public. There is evidence that roll-call votes on the floor (which are recorded) are not necessarily accurate predictors of the position taken by the legislator on the same bill in committee, where votes are often not recorded (Hamm 1982). Procedural votes (for example, a vote to recommit a bill to committee, or to hold a bill on second reading calendar) sometimes allow legislators to "kill" a bill without a formal roll call.

State legislators rely on "cues" from many sources in the policy-making process. Some of these sources, such as legislative staff, may be more influential at the bill formulation or the committee stage than at the floor vote stage. The committee report itself is often an important cue.

The extent of party voting varies by state legislature and circumstance. When a party holds a slim majority of seats in the chamber, legislators are more likely to feel pressure to "toe the party line" than when the party commands a large majority (more than 60 percent of the seats). In states where the party plays an important role in nominating candidates, members are also more likely to vote with the party on important votes.

Interest groups exert substantial influence over the legislative process in many states. In part this is because lobbyists are important sources of information for legislators, particularly in states with limited staff and time. In states in which there is a dominant economic interest (for example, agriculture in Kansas) legislators are often predisposed toward protecting that group. Recognizing the importance of the state legislature in policy making, many interest groups are increasingly active in state legislative elections. This often takes the form of campaign contributions to selected candidates who are supportive of a group's agenda.

Governors are also important players in the legislative process (Jewell and Morehouse 2001). Through the State of the State address and the budget message, both delivered at the beginning of the legislative session, the chief executive is able to help shape the policy agenda. The ultimate weapon in the gubernatorial arsenal, of course, is the veto.

Ultimately, the most important cue source for most legislators is their own perception of constituent opinion. When public opinion in the district is clearly on one side of a specific issue, the legislator will rarely vote against it. However, very few issues invite a clear and unified voice from one's constituency. On the vast majority of bills, legislators are relatively unconstrained by constituent opinion. They may, however, feel constrained by the opinion or wishes of specific segments of their constituency. Legislators are particularly attentive to those individuals or groups within their district who have the ability to mobilize enough voters to potentially affect the outcome of the legislator's next election.

## CONCLUSION

Legislatures are complex organizations. In part this complexity stems from the fact that to be productive legislatures must reach some consensus among a majority of members. But the members are elected from different electoral districts, representing constituencies that are often very different from one another. This is a fact of legislative life, but one not fully appreciated by the general public.

There are numerous similarities among the legislatures in the states. For example, all state legislatures are expected to carry out the same functions: policy making, budget appropriation, administrative oversight, and constituent service. But there are also many ways in which the legislatures differ from one state to another. Many of these differences are captured in the concept of professionalization, which reflects the differences in time commitment, monetary incentives, and staff support that one finds across the state legislatures. Other differences include the size of the legislative districts represented, the costs of campaigning for legislative office, and the degree of diversity among the legislators themselves. Further differences emerge when we examine the way the legislatures are organized and the specific rules under which they operate. It is these differences, and their consequences, that make state legislatures so interesting.

As a group, state legislatures face immense challenges in the years to come. Some of these challenges stem from the ongoing changes in federalism; states (and therefore state legislatures) are again emerging as important partners in the federal relationship. Other challenges stem from economic and social changes within the particular state—changes that bring both opportunities and problems that must be addressed by the legislatures. Still other changes, such as term limits, are aimed directly at the legislative institution itself. State legislatures under term limits will be forced to adapt in many ways.

This issue of adaptation and change in state legislatures will be a particularly interesting one to follow in the coming years. In the past thirty years, state legislatures have undergone many reforms aimed at modernizing the legislative institution. These reforms include an upgrade in physical facilities, larger staff, longer sessions, and increased salary for the legislators. Although these changes were important in extending the capacity of the legislative institution to do its job, they had the additional consequence of altering the incentive structure for those who serve in state legislatures. Because many legislatures now meet for longer periods, it becomes increasingly difficult for the individual legislator to juggle her private career and public service. Moreover, the increased staff and improved physical facilities have made the legislature a more attractive place to be.

Thirty years ago many legislators served only one or two terms and then left public service because the benefits (both psychological and economic) simply did not outweigh the costs (in terms of time away from family and business). This is no longer the case in many states. Thus the changes wrought to improve the legislature also had an effect on those who serve in the legislatures. Dissatisfaction with what the public increasingly perceives as "career" legislators has created a reaction against the legislators, which in turn affects the institution itself. This is one of the important dilemmas that legislators and the public must face in the years to come: Can we build effective legislative institutions while at the same time discouraging legislators from long-term service?

## REFERENCES

American Society of Legislative Clerks and Secretaries. 1998. *Inside the Legislative Process.* Denver, Colo.: National Conference of State Legislatures.

Anderson, R. Bruce. 1997. *Electoral Competition and the Structure of State Legislatures: Organizational Complexity and Party Building.* Unpublished Ph.D. dissertation, Rice University.

Berry, William D., Michael B. Berkman, and Stuart Schneiderman. 2000. "Explaining Incumbency Reelection." *American Political Science Review* 94: 859–874.

Breaux, David, and Anthony Gierzynski. 1991. " 'It's Money that Matters': Campaign Expenditures and State Legislative Primaries." *Legislative Studies Quarterly* 16: 429–443.

Button, James, and David Hedge. 1996. "Legislative Life in the 1990s: A Comparison of Black and White State Legislators." *Legislative Studies Quarterly* 21: 199–218.

Campbell, Ballard. 1980. *Representative Democracy: Public Policy and Midwestern Legislatures in the Late Nineteenth Century.* Cambridge, Mass.: Harvard University Press.

Carey, John M., Richard G. Niemi, and Lynda W. Powell. 2000. *Term Limits in State Legislature.* Ann Arbor: University of Michigan Press.

———. 1998. "The Effects of Term Limits on State Legislatures." *Legislative Studies Quarterly* 23: 271–300.

Cassie, William E., and David Breaux. 1998. "Expenditures and Election Results." In *Campaign Finance in State Legislative Elections,* edited by Joel A. Thompson and Gary F. Moncrief. Washington, D.C.: Congressional Quarterly.

Center for the American Woman and Politics (CAWP). 2003. "CAWP Fact Sheet: Women in State Legislatures 2003." Available at http:/www/rci/rutgers/edu/~cawp/.

Clucas, Richard A. 2001. "Principal-Agent Theory and the Power of State House Speakers." *Legislative Studies Quarterly* 26: 319–338.

Clucas, Richard, and Mark Hatfield. 2002. "California: The New Amateur Politics." In *The Test of Time: Coping With Term Limits,* edited by Rick Farmer, John L. Greene, and John David Rausch Jr. Lexington, Mass.: Lexington Books.

Council of State Governments. 2002. *The Book of the States, 2002.* Lexington, Ky.: Council of State Governments.

Cox, Elizabeth. 1996. *Women State and Territorial Legislators, 1895–1995: A State-by-State Analysis, with Rosters of 6000 Women.* Jefferson, N.C.: McFarland Press.

Cox, Gary W. 1997. *Making Votes Count.* Cambridge: Cambridge University Press.

Darcy, Robert. 1996. "Women in the State Legislative Power Structure: Committee Chairs." *Social Science Quarterly* 77: 889–898.

Diamond, Randy. 2002. "The Consensus Candidate." *State Legislatures* 28(April): 20–24.

Eulau, Heinz, and Paul D. Karps. 1977. "Representation: Specifying Components of Responsiveness." *Legislative Studies Quarterly* 2: 233–254.

Fenno, Richard. 1978. *Homestyle.* Boston, Mass.: Little, Brown.

Francis, Wayne. 1989. *The Legislative Committee Game: A Comparative Analysis of Fifty States.* Columbus: Ohio State University Press.

Freeman, Patricia. 1995. "A Comparative Analysis of Speaker Career Patterns in U.S. State Legislatures." *Legislative Studies Quarterly* 20: 365–375.

Freeman, Patricia, and Lilliard Richardson, Jr. 1996. "Explaining Variation in Casework among State Legislators." *Legislative Studies Quarterly* 21: 41–57.

———. 1994. "Casework in State Legislatures." *State and Local Government Review* 26: 21–26.

Frendreis, John, and Alan Gitelson. 1997. "Shifting Partisan Fortunes in Electoral Politics." Paper presented at the annual meeting of the Southern Political Science Association, Norfolk, Va., November 5–8.

Gierzynski, Anthony, and David Breaux. 1993. "Money and the Party Vote in State House Elections." *Legislative Studies Quarterly* 18: 515–533.

Gray, Virginia, and David Lowery. 1995. "Interest Representation and Democratic Gridlock." *Legislative Studies Quarterly* 20: 531–552.

Hamm, Keith E. 1982. "Consistency between Committee and Floor Voting in U.S. State Legislatures." *Legislative Studies Quarterly* 7: 473–490.

Hamm, Keith E., and Ronald D. Hedlund. 1995. "The Development of Committee Specialization in State Legislatures." Paper presented at the annual meeting of the American Political Science Association, Chicago, August 31–September 3.

———. 1994. "Committees in State Legislatures." In *The Encyclopedia of the American Legislative System,* edited by Joel J. Silbey. New York: Charles Scribner's Sons.

Hamm, Keith E., and Robert E. Hogan. 2002. "Testing the Effects of Campaign Finance Laws in State Legislative Elections." Project funded by the National Science Foundation. SES-0215450.

Hamm, Keith E., and David M. Olson. 1992. "Midsession Vacancies: Why Do State Legislators Leave and How Are They Replaced?" In *Changing Patterns in State Legislative Careers,* edited by Gary F. Moncrief and Joel A. Thompson. Ann Arbor: University of Michigan Press.

Hamm, Keith E., Ronald D. Hedlund, and R. Bruce Anderson. 1994. "Political Parties in State Legislatures." In *The Encyclopedia of the American Legislative System,* edited by Silbey.

Hansen, Karen. 2000. "The New Political Party." *State Legislatures* (December): 12–15.

———. 1997. "Living within Term Limits." *State Legislatures* (June): 13–19.

Haynie, Kerry L. 2001. *African American Legislators in the American States.* New York: Columbia University Press.

Hedlund, Ronald D. 1984. "Organizational Attributes of Legislative Institutions: Structure, Rules, Norms, Resources." *Legislative Studies Quarterly* 9: 51–121.

Hodson, Timothy, Rich Jones, Karl T. Kurtz, and Gary F. Moncrief. 1995. "Leaders and Limits: Changing Patterns of State Legislative Leadership under Term Limits." *Spectrum: The Journal of State Government* 68(Summer): 6–15.

Hogan, Robert E. 1998. *The Role of Political Campaigns in State Elections.* Unpublished Ph.D. dissertation, Rice University.

Jewell, Malcolm E. 1982. *Representation in State Legislatures.* Lexington: University of Kentucky Press.

———. 1962. *The State Legislature: Politics in Practice.* New York: Random House.

Jewell, Malcolm E., and Sarah Morehouse. 2001. *Political Parties and Elections in American States.* Washington, D.C.: CQ Press.

Jewell, Malcolm E., and Marcia Whicker. 1994. *Legislative Leadership in the American States.* Ann Arbor: University of Michigan Press.

King, James. 2000. "Changes in Professionalism in U.S. State Legislatures." *Legislative Studies Quarterly* 25: 327–343.

Kurtz, Karl T. 1990. "The Changing State Legislature (Lobbyists Beware)." In *Leveraging State Government Relations,* edited by Wesley Pedersen. Washington, D.C.: Public Affairs Council, 1990.

Little, Thomas H. 1995. "Understanding Legislative Leadership beyond the Chamber: The Members' Perspective." *Legislative Studies Quarterly* 20: 269–289.

Loomis, Burdett A. 1994. *Time, Politics, and Policies: A Legislative Year.* Lawrence: University of Kansas Press.

Moncrief, Gary F., and Joel A. Thompson. 2001. "On the Outside Looking In: Lobbyists' Perspectives on the Effects of State Legislative Term Limits." *State Politics & Policy Quarterly* 1: 394–411.

Moncrief, Gary F., Richard Niemi, and Lynda Powell. 2003. "Time, Turnover and Term Limits: Trends in Membership Turnover in State Legislatures." Paper presented at the Third Annual State Politics and Policy Conference, Tucson, Ariz., March 14–15.

Moncrief, Gary F., Peverill Squire, and Malcolm Jewell. 2001. *Who Runs for the Legislature?* Upper Saddle River, N.J.: Prentice-Hall.

Moncrief, Gary F., Joel A. Thompson, and Karl T. Kurtz. 1996. "The Old Statehouse, It Ain't What It Used to Be." *Legislative Studies Quarterly* 21: 57–72.

Mooney, Christopher. 1995. "Citizens, Structures, and Sister States: Influences on State Legislative Professionalism." *Legislative Studies Quarterly* 20: 47–67.

National Conference of State Legislatures. 1996a. "Fate of President's Party in State Legislative Elections, 1960–1996." Accessed at http:/www.ncsl.org/programs/legman.elect/presprty. html. November 11.

———. 1996b. "Incumbent Reelection Rates in 1994 State Legislative Elections." Accessed at http:/www/ncsl.org/programs/legman/elect/incumb.html. October 30.

———. 1996c. "Size of State Legislative Staff: 1979, 1988 and 1996." Accessed at http://www. ncsl.org/programs/legman/about/stf3.htm. June 30.

———. 1996d. *State Legislators' Occupations: 1993 and 1995.* Denver, Colo.: National Conference of State Legislatures.

Neal, Tommy. 1996. *Lawmaking and the Legislative Process: Committees, Connections, and Compromises.* Denver, Colo.: National Conference of State Legislatures.

Rosenthal, Alan. 1998. *The Decline of Representative Democracy: Process, Participation, and Power in State Legislatures.* Washington, D.C.: CQ Press.

Salmore, Stephen A., and Barbarba G. Salmore. 1989. *Candidates, Parties, and Campaigns: Electoral Politics in America.* 2d ed. Washington, D.C.: CQ Press.

Scher, Richard K., Jon L. Mills, and John J. Hotaling. 1997. *Voting Rights and Democracy.* Chicago: Nelson-Hall.

Smith, Michael A. 2003. *Bringing Representation Home: State Legislators Among Their Constituencies.* Columbia: University of Missouri Press.

Squire, Peverill. 2000. "Uncontested Seats in State Legislative Elections." *Legislative Studies Quarterly* 25: 131–146.

———. 1998. "Membership Turnover and the Efficient Processing of Legislation." *Legislative Studies Quarterly* 23: 23–32.

———. 1993. "Professionalization and Public Opinion of State Legislatures." *Journal of Politics* 55: 479–491.

———. 1988. "Career Opportunities and Membership Stability in Legislatures." *Legislative Studies Quarterly* 13: 65–82.

Thomas, Sue. 1994. *How Women Legislate.* New York: Oxford University Press.

Van Dunk, Emily, and Thomas M. Holbrook. 1994. "The 1994 State Legislative Elections." *Extension of Remarks, Legislative Studies Section Newsletter* (December): 8–12.

**SUGGESTED READINGS**

Loftus, Tom. *The Art of Legislative Politics.* Washington, D.C.: CQ Press, 1994. An anecdotal, "inside" look at politics in a state legislature, written by the former speaker of the Wisconsin State Assembly.

Moncrief, Gary F., Peverill Squire, and Malcolm Jewell. *Who Runs for the Legislature?* Upper Saddle River, N.J.: Prentice-Hall, 2001. A look at how candidates are recruited and how they campaign for state legislative office.

Rosenthal, Alan. *The Decline of Representative Democracy.* Washington, D.C.: CQ Press, 1998. A thoughtful review of the changes in state legislatures over the past generation.

Rosenthal, Alan, Burdett A. Loomis, John R. Hibbing, and Karl T. Kurtz. *Republic on Trial: The Case for Representative Democracy.* Washington, D.C.: CQ Press, 2003. A cogent defense of the legislative institution as the keystone to representative democracy.

Thomas, Sue. *How Women Legislate.* New York: Oxford University Press, 1994. Based on a survey of women legislators in twelve states, Thomas analyzes the increasingly important role of women in state legislatures.

CHAPTER 7

# The Governors

THAD BEYLE

At the top of each state's political and governmental hierarchy is the governor, who personifies the state to many. He or she is seen as the most powerful political personality in most states; the state's legislature, bureaucracy, press, politics, and policies are affected by or bear the imprint of the governor.

These major actors in our states are supposed to fill a long roster of roles. A handbook written just for governors lists the following: head of the executive branch, legislative leader, head of party, national figure, family member, and ceremonial chief (NGA 1978). Other roles are equally broad in responsibility, such as those of intergovernmental actor and policy leader, and some appear to be narrower in scope, such as those of manager and chief crisis manager (Morehouse 1981; NGA 1981). But after the 9/11 terrorist attacks, the crisis manager role has been growing in importance.

How a governor responds to and handles unexpected crises greatly influences how we perceive his or her overall performance as a governor. As former governor Scott M. Matheson (D-Utah, 1977–1985) argued, "[T]he public expects the governor to take a lead . . . and a governor found wanting in a crisis situation rarely recovers politically" (Matheson 1986, 200).

How a governor performs in day-to-day administrative actions can also influence how we perceive his or her performance in office. Most governors perform admirably and their administrations are well respected; others do not perform well and they struggle as they govern.

Governors have not always been at the top of the pecking order in their states, nor have they always been at the center of most state activities. The negligible powers and responsibilities given to the earliest state governors reflected the basic antipathy citizens felt toward executive power—a dislike carried over from their relations with imposed colonial governors. Over the next two centuries, the governors gradually gained more power, and many of the early restrictions placed on them were removed or greatly reduced. This did not happen in an orderly fashion; rather, it happened in a series of incremental steps and in varying degrees across the states. And in many states new restrictions or new problems and challenges faced the governors as state governments evolved.

Beginning with the democratization movement in the early nineteenth century, the selection of governors moved from the legislature to the people. This "pursuit of representativeness" also added new restrictions on the governor as other state administrative officials came to be selected by direct popular election (Kaufman 1963, 36). Thus some of the administrative functions were placed outside the control of the governor and into the hands of others directly responsible to the people.

It became apparent following the Civil War that legislative bodies could not run the states or administer programs, and as patronage and corruption increased, more changes occurred. Restrictions were placed on gubernatorial and legislative powers, and a drive to raise the competence of state government—in fact, governments at all levels—through the use of merit systems and civil service personnel procedures in which "what you know" became more important than "who you know" took firm root. Further, as new problems and responsibilities arose, agencies, boards, and commissions were established to handle them—again, often outside the direct control of any executive official. These efforts to obtain something called "neutral competence" in running government were an attempt to separate politics from administration. The governors and legislators were obviously on the political side, and these reforms were meant to maintain that separation.

In the twentieth century, constitutional revision and executive branch reorganization changed state governments and clarified lines of authority. Governors now have longer terms of office, can succeed themselves, and have more staff for assistance. In addition, they have been given considerable budget authority to help control the executive branch and more veto power to use in their legislative negotiations. At the same time, however, the strength and reach of the civil service and merit systems have increased, providing state employees with a degree of protection and even insulation from the governor.

In this chapter I examine the current status of the American governorship and discuss the following questions. First, who are the governors and how do they become governors? What is the nature of gubernatorial politics? Second, what powers do our states provide to governors so they may fulfill their roles? To what extent do these powers vary across the fifty states and by individual governors? Third, what are the major roles that all governors must perform? How do these roles provide governors with greater informal powers to achieve their goals? Fourth, what do governors do after the governorship? What are the options available to these key state actors following their tenure in office? In a sense, I follow the trajectory of the individuals who seek to be governor, win the election, serve as governors, and move on from the governorship. Each step influences what happens on the next, and as we shall see, these are not discrete steps.

Throughout the chapter I present the differences between states, governorships, and governors to point out the diversity inherent in the fifty-state federal union. This should not overshadow the larger point, however, that, despite this diversity, these actors, their offices, and their responsibilities are all quite similar.

## BECOMING GOVERNOR

In theory, anyone who meets the constitutional qualifications for office can become governor. In practice, some people are much more likely than others to occupy the governor's chair. In this section I consider why this is so.

### Where You Have Been Makes a Difference

A basic clue to what a particular public office is all about, and its position within any political power hierarchy, is who seeks and fills that office. Of interest are some of the career steps governors pursue prior to being elected governor. The first step of interest is their entry level onto the gubernatorial ambition ladder. Where did they start their elective political career? Table 7-1 indicates that more than half the governors serving between 1900 and 2003 began their political careers either as state legislators or in law enforcement.[1] This has been especially true since 1950 when nearly three out of five governors used these offices as their entry points. And the importance of the state legislature as the first step is increasing as nearly two of five governors elected since 1981 began their elective career there.

Note also the growing number of governors for whom the first elective office is the governorship itself—one of eight governors elected since 1981 had held no previous elected position. The ability to translate a well-known name from another part of society, combined with the "spend your way into office" type of politics so prevalent today, explains the rise. Also showing increasing importance as first steps are local elective positions[2] and service in the U.S. Congress.[3] On the other hand, starting out in administrative positions en route to the governorship has declined sharply since 1981.[4]

The second step of interest is the penultimate, or the last step prior to the governorship. Table 7-2 indicates that three-fifths of the governors' penultimate offices since 1900 were other statewide elective offices, the state legislature, or law enforcement—in about equal rates. Since 1981 there has been a considerable shift in

1. County and city attorneys, district attorney, U.S. attorney, judges at all levels, CIA and FBI personnel, and state attorney general (even if elected by statewide vote).
2. All elective offices at the local level except county and city attorneys or district attorneys.
3. Seats in the U.S. House of Representatives or U.S. Senate.
4. All public offices on local, statewide, and federal levels that are not elective. These are sometimes appointive and other times career positions. No law enforcement offices are included in this category. At the state level, elective offices in some states (such as the state auditor) are administrative in others.

**Table 7-1** Entry-Level or First Elected Office of a Governor's Career, 1900–2002 (in percentages)

| Office | 1900–1949 | 1950–1980 | 1981–2002 | 1900–2002 |
|---|---|---|---|---|
| n = | 501 | 324 | 154 | 979 |
| Legislative | 29 | 35 | 38 | 33 |
| Law enforcement | 19 | 23 | 16 | 20 |
| Administrative | 15 | 15 | 6 | 14 |
| Local elective | 10 | 11 | 16 | 11 |
| No prior office | 8 | 10 | 12 | 10 |
| Other | 13 | 1 | 3 | 7 |
| Statewide elective | 5 | 4 | 6 | 4 |
| Congress | 0.4 | 2 | 3 | 1 |

SOURCE: 1900–1949 and 1950–1980 data from Sabato 1983, 36–39; 1981–2002 and 1900–2002 data calculated by author.
NOTE: Percentages do not add to 100 because of rounding.

**Table 7-2** Penultimate Office of a Governor's Career, 1900–2002 (in percentages)

| Office | 1900–1949 | 1950–1980 | 1981–2002 | 1900–2002 |
|---|---|---|---|---|
| n = | 501 | 324 | 154 | 979 |
| Statewide elective | 19 | 22 | 27 | 21 |
| Legislative | 18 | 24 | 18 | 20 |
| Law enforcement | 19 | 19 | 11 | 18 |
| Administrative | 14 | 10 | 6 | 11 |
| Congress | 10 | 9 | 16 | 11 |
| No prior office | 8 | 10 | 14 | 10 |
| Local elective | 7 | 5 | 8 | 7 |
| Other | 6 | 0 | 1 | 3 |

SOURCE: 1900–1949 and 1950–1980 data from Sabato 1983, 36–39; 1981–2002 and 1900–2002 data calculated by author.
NOTE: Percentages do not add to 100 because of rounding.

launching pads. Other statewide elective offices now account for just over one in four penultimate positions while law enforcement has declined considerably to only one in nine. Also rising in importance are U.S. congressional and senatorial seats and, as noted previously, positions unrelated to previous elective office.

Elective statewide positions—whether lieutenant governor, secretary of state, state treasurer, state attorney general, or state auditor—obviously can provide strong jumping-off points for candidates for the governorship. Also included in this category are former governors who run and win the office again.

Of the 2003 incumbent governors, seventeen moved up from a statewide elective position, and two were former U.S. senators. Eight of the other incumbents had no prior elective office experience, seven were former U.S. congressmen, seven moved up from the state legislature and six from local government positions. Two of the 2003 incumbent governors initially succeeded to office on the removal or resignation from office of the elected governor.[5] In effect, they were "accidental" governors, but both subsequently won their own term as governor.

There has been a change in the number of individuals moving from the U.S. Congress to the governorship, from about 10 percent between 1900 and 1980 (Sabato 1983, 40) up to 16 percent between 1981 and 2003. In the most recent period, those candidates using this avenue tended to be in the South and the Northeast, with 50 of the 71 congressional candidates who ran (70 percent). Their success rate in these two regions was 24 percent, whereas only 2 of the 21 congressional candidates running in the Midwest and West won (10 percent). It is better to run from the base of a U.S. Senate seat, as 6 of the 9 U.S. senators running gubernatorial campaigns in this period succeeded.[6]

A part of the political calculus involved in making this type of move is the ability to do so without jeopardizing one's current congressional seat. Some states have off-year gubernatorial elections, which allow some members of Congress to campaign while retaining their federal seat. In some other states, such as Connecticut, the timing of the party nominations permits a member of Congress to hold the congressional seat until the nomination is won and then resign in time for the election campaign (Sabato 1983, 41).

By and large, the evidence suggests that previous electoral experience (with the attendant visibility) at the statewide, congressional, or state legislative levels is one of the most important steps to the governorship. Most governors have had such electoral experience as their penultimate office. But what of those who ran and failed to win the governorship? Have their paths to defeat substantially differed from the paths of those who won? It is an interesting question to consider.

There are a few hints if we look at the unsuccessful rates for some specific elective positions in the 1981–2001 elections. In that period 69 percent of the lieutenant governors who ran for governor lost. Other candidates seeking the governorship from other statewide offices experienced similar rates of defeat: attorney general (82 percent non-success rate); state auditor (75 percent non-success rate); secretary of state (70 percent non-success rate); and state treasurer (63 percent non-success rate).

*The Election Campaign: It Costs Money*

Will Rogers once said, "Politics has got so expensive that it takes a lot of money to get beat with." During the past few decades, the costs of running for and winning the governor's seat have escalated rapidly.[7] In 1956 the average cost of a gubernato-

---

5. In Arkansas Lt. Gov. Mike Huckabee became governor in 1996 on the conviction of incumbent governor Jim Guy Tucker on fraudulent business practices, and in Texas Lt. Gov. Rick Perry became governor in December 2000 upon the resignation of soon-to-be president George W. Bush.

6. Henry Bellman in Oklahoma (1986), Pete Wilson in California (1990), Lowell Weicker in Connecticut (1990), Lawton Chiles in Florida (1990), Dirk Kempthorne in Idaho (1998), and Frank Murkowski in Alaska (2002).

7. All dollar figures and amounts in this section are in 2002 equivalent dollars based on the Consumer Price Index (CPI-U). The CPI-U is based on 1982–1984 = 100. The 1977 CPI-U was equal to 60.6 of that index base; the 2002 CPI-U was equal to 179.9 of that index base.

**Figure 7-1** Gubernatorial Elections Expenditures, 1977–2002

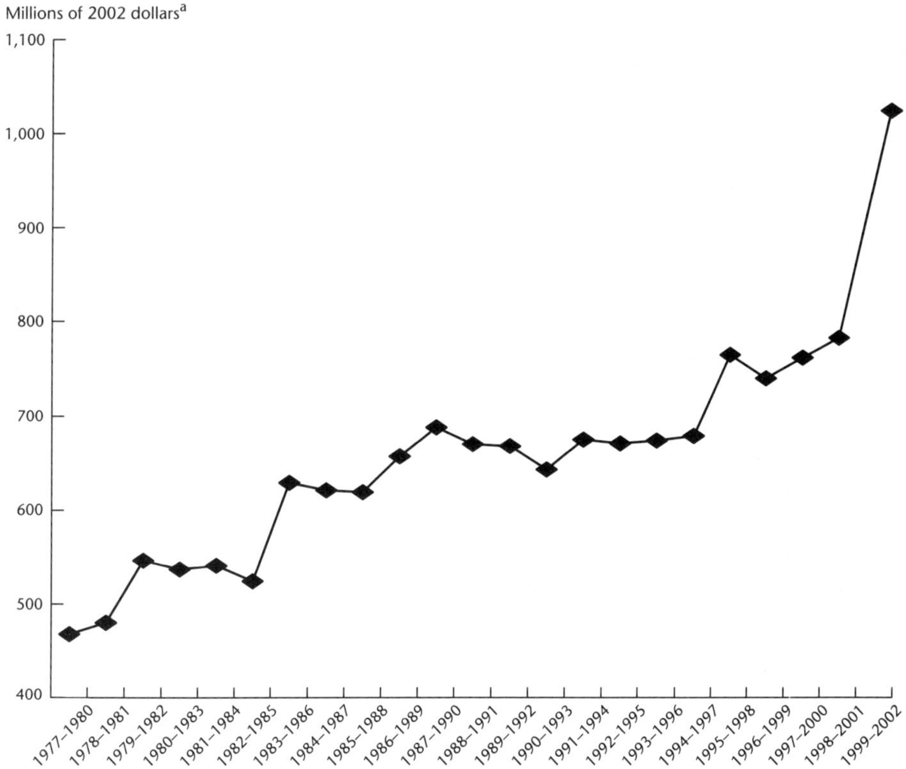

Millions of 2002 dollars[a]

SOURCE: Calculated by the author.

[a] All dollar figures are in equivalent 2002 dollars.

rial campaign was estimated to be $100,000, and up to $300,000 in the more populated states; any "political skull-duggery" would be on top of that (Ransone 1956,
105–106). Those 1956 dollars would be equal to just over $650,000 and just under
$2 million, respectively, in 2002 dollars.

The rise in the costs of gubernatorial elections is clearly demonstrated in Figure
7-1. Each data point represents all candidates' expenditures in the four-year bank of
elections noted, normalized into 2002 dollars for comparison purposes. In this way
we are able to see the comparative costs of gubernatorial elections across all fifty
states between 1977 and 2002. The year 1977 serves as the starting point because
that is when the reporting of such campaign data began to be required across the
states.

As can be seen, the cost of gubernatorial elections rose steadily, and at times
sharply, over the twenty-five-year period. In the earliest 1977 to 1980 bank of
elections, the total cost was $468 million; in the most recent 1999 to 2002 bank
of elections, the total cost was $1,024 million, a 119 percent increase. The largest
jumps in the level of expenditures occurred in those years in which thirty-six states

held their gubernatorial elections (1982, 1986, 1990, 1994, 1998, and 2002). In the 1980s these jumps were probably tied to the adoption of new and expensive campaign techniques and technologies. By the late 1980s, the cost of gubernatorial campaigns had leveled off in the mid-$600 million range, but in the late 1990s the costs of these elections escalated once again.

Some of the most expensive gubernatorial races have been where you would expect them to be—in the largest states. The past five gubernatorial races in California through 2002 averaged $86 million per election, and in Texas the average was $57.6 million. The 2002 race in New York, where incumbent governor George Pataki won his third term, was the most expensive governor's race ever—$146 million. The second most expensive governor's race took place in California in 1998, costing $136.6 million. In that election, control of the governorship shifted to the Democrats.

Although large states might be expected to have expensive gubernatorial races, some of the most expensive races have been in southern states, where one-party Democratic dominance is being replaced by costly, candidate-oriented campaigns in a two-party setting. As noted, the five most recent elections in Texas averaged $57.6 million, while those in Florida ($28 million), Virginia ($23 million), and North Carolina ($22 million) also proved expensive.

If we control for cost per general election vote in each state, however, another picture appears. The state boasting the most expensive general election per vote cast in the past five general elections is Alaska ($32.63 per vote cast), followed by Hawaii ($24.49), Kentucky ($23.41), Virginia ($15.40) and Texas ($14.52). Three of these five states are southern states, but the other two—Alaska and Hawaii—have uniquely situated populations. In these states, where it costs more to reach the voters, geography plays a considerable role in the cost of gubernatorial elections.

The reasons for the continuing escalation of election costs are many. Changes in the style of campaigning are the most significant. With the transformation of state political parties and the decline of party identification among voters, candidates cannot afford to sit back and work with the party regulars to deliver the votes needed for winning. Going from county to county and meeting with the local politicos may solidify some votes and bring together part of a winning coalition, but doing so takes time, hits too few people, and does not deliver enough votes.

The old "ground war" approach has been replaced by the newer "air war" campaigns. The most direct path to potential voters is through the mass media, and that costs a lot of money. Opinion polls, political consultants, media consultants, direct-mail persuasion and fund-raising, telephone banks, and rapid travel throughout the state are all expensive, but all are necessary to contemporary campaigns. The 2000 gubernatorial election in North Carolina provides a good example of the role and cost of media in a campaign. The two major candidates spent less than 1 percent of their money on travel. The winner, Democrat Mike Easley, spent 74 percent of his $11 million campaign on ads, while the loser, Republican Richard Vinroot, spent 62 percent of his $8.2 million campaign on ads (Beyle and Guillory 2002). For the not-so-well-known candidate in a party primary or the general election, "electronic advertising [television and radio] is the only way to gain visibility" (Morehouse 1987). But, as one political consultant noted, "Everyone knows that half the money spent in a political campaign is wasted. The trouble is that nobody knows which half" (North Carolina Center for Public Policy Research 1989).

What, in effect, all this money adds up to is the cost of building a winning coalition. As Sabato (1978) has suggested, this involves the creation of a party "substitute," through which the candidate constructs his or her own campaign organization for his or her gubernatorial race.

Why do so many candidates spend so much of their own and other people's money to become governor? One reason might be the salary a governor receives, a proposition suggesting that a candidate seeks office for the money he or she can make while governor. In 2002 gubernatorial salaries averaged more than $107,000, ranging from $179,000 in New York to $65,000 in Nebraska (CSG 2002, 148). Adjusted for inflation, this average is not too different from the average salary governors made in 1955 (Beyle 1995). These may be goodly sums, but they scarcely warrant the amounts spent in the campaign to become governor.

Salary is not the only monetary reward a governor can receive, however. On leaving office, some governors obtain high-paying positions in the private sector. Those who are lawyers often open or join a law firm in the state capital and receive large retainers to serve as legal representatives or lobbyists for various interests looking to purchase the former governor's unique access to state officials and agencies. Thus some candidates may spend the money in campaigns in anticipation of the money they can make after their term has ended.

A third reason is tied to the political ambitions of gubernatorial candidates. The governorship can serve as a launching pad to other, arguably more prestigious offices, such as a seat in the U.S. Senate or even the presidency. In the twentieth century, more than 120 governors moved on to the U.S. Senate; in the 108th Congress (2003–2004) 11 former governors held a seat in the U.S. Senate. Eighteen former governors have become president, and governors have been candidates for either the presidency or the vice presidency in 47 of the nation's 54 presidential elections. Most governors, however, go no further than the governorship: More than 2,000 have served in the office, and for most it is the final elective office they hold (Beyle 1988, 134–135).

Of course, any listing of the reasons for spending large amounts of money in a political campaign must include the desire to perform public service for the good of the state and its citizens. Even so, it costs a great deal to become a statesperson.

Which of these factors is the most significant probably varies not only by state but also by candidate and by circumstances. Individual governor's races are generally more expensive when political parties are weak, an open seat is up, the race is highly contested from nomination to general election, there is a partisan shift as a result of the election, or an incumbent is unseated (Beyle 1996, 10–14; 1998, 26–30).

*Opportunity to Become Governor*

Another constraint on individuals wishing to become governor is the availability of opportunities to do so.[8] Just how often do the governors' chairs have new occupants? The twentieth century has seen a decline in the number of such opportunities. One of the causes is obviously the executive reform movement, which has increased most gubernatorial terms from two years to four and has allowed more governors to seek reelection. In fact, several recent governors have effectively made the office their career, thereby closing off opportunities for others for more than a decade.

To demonstrate this change, the data in Table 7-3 indicate that there was a much greater opportunity to become governor after the Civil War, when the 37 states averaged 4.2 governors per state in the 1870s. This compares with the 1980s and 1990s when the 50 states averaged 1.4 new governors per state in each decade. However, if we look at the most recent elections since 1999, we find that 33 of the 52 states holding elections elected a new governor. So, around the turn of the twenty-first century, the states are electing new leadership. This is in contrast to the recent past when longer terms, the ability to succeed oneself to another term, and former governors reentering the office had greatly reduced the opportunities for outsiders to be elected to governorships. But some of these new governors may wind up wondering why they wanted the job, considering the difficult economic times the states are facing.

This state of affairs is significant for politically ambitious individuals in various states, because it suggests a further tightening of electoral opportunities at the top of the states' political ladders. An early study by Schlesinger (1966) indicated that only the U.S. Senate seats tended to be career offices and that congressional seats and the offices of state attorney general, secretary of state, and state auditor were intermediate offices (held for more than four years). Now, with the governorship in some states becoming, at a minimum, an intermediate office, if not a career office, political opportunities are being restricted.

Important is the concept of *political time* or *window of opportunity*—that moment in a person's political career when he or she can or should move to run for a higher office. It is not easy to define exactly when one's political time occurs, how long it lasts, or for whom it really does exist. It is much easier to define when it is not the right political time for someone to seek a higher office: The person is too young and his or her time will come, or the person is too old and his or her time has passed. For some, there will be a time for such an upward political move, for others there may never be. Clearly, the concept of an individual's political time varies from state to state and from individual to individual.

In general political time is relatively short from the individual's perspective. There are several reasons for this. As already noted, longer terms and succession have cut back the number of times available. Term limits on how long someone can

---

8. Portions of this section are taken from Beyle 1992b.

**Table 7-3** Number of New Governors, Selected Decades, 1800–2002

| Decade | States | New governors | Average number per state |
|---|---|---|---|
| 1800–1809 | 17 | 56 | 3.3 |
| 1820–1829 | 24 | 92 | 3.8 |
| 1850–1859 | 31 | 124 | 4.0 |
| 1870–1879 | 37 | 154 | 4.2 |
| 1900–1909 | 46 | 154 | 3.3 |
| 1920–1929 | 48 | 185 | 3.9 |
| 1950–1959 | 48 | 108 | 2.3 |
| 1960–1969 | 50 | 102 | 2.0 |
| 1970–1979 | 50 | 88 | 1.8 |
| 1980–1989 | 50 | 69 | 1.4 |
| 1990–1999 | 50 | 71 | 1.4 |
| 2000–2002[a] | 50 | 32 | 0.6 |

SOURCE: Adapted from Beyle 1998, 200; revised and updated through 2002 elections.

NOTE: Included are some former governors who decided to seek the governorship again and won after being out of office for a period of time.

[a] Results of the 2000–2002 elections only.

hold an office, where they exist, create periodic openings for those seeking an office and a time schedule of when these openings will occur. But the political time of others on the ladder may conflict with a person's own political time. In addition, the new variable of money in the political process allows political interlopers to interrupt an otherwise ordered process of political advancement by buying their way into the system at the very top.

With the average number of new governors per state per decade dropping to 1.4, there are very few openings. What do ambitious politicians do when this happens? Many move their ambitions elsewhere, even if it means leaving the political arena. The reform goal of longer terms for governors, with governors being able to succeed themselves for another term, may have led to the unanticipated result of shunting off into other careers potential candidates for governor or some other higher office. This shift is difficult to measure, but the oft-heard complaint that there are too few good candidates in many states suggests that something like this may be happening (Beyle 1992b, 172–173).

Although the term limits movement of the 1990s has been aimed mainly at state legislatures and Congress, some of the states have also included provisions restricting how long their governors may serve. Of the twenty-one states that adopted term limits in the past decade, fourteen placed limits on their governors. All went from no limits on how long a governor might serve to either two four-year terms or eight years in a specific time period (Beyle 1995; Beyle and Jones 1994). These limits should now produce more openings in these states.[9] And, in some states, idiosyn-

9. State supreme courts in Massachusetts, Oregon, and Washington invalidated term limits, and Idaho and Utah subsequently repealed them. New limits still apply to governors in Arizona, Arkansas, California, Maine, Michigan, Montana, Ohio, South Dakota, and Wyoming.

cratic political situations can either severely restrict an individual's access to office or overly enhance it.

In addition to the rule that money can buy the best campaign for the winners (it is obviously wasted or ill-spent in the campaign of a loser), another political rule has gained importance in the past decade: incumbency provides the best campaign platform. Even in the anti-incumbent mood of the 1994 elections, 17 of the 23 incumbent governors running won, and in the eight election years since then, 51 of the 58 incumbents seeking reelection won (88 percent).

### From Campaigner to Governor

A major hallmark of our political system is the concept of an orderly transition of power from one elected official to another once the election results are known. Even when an incumbent governor is beaten in a bitter and personally acrimonious campaign, the reins of power are turned over at the appointed time—although not always easily or with complete grace. There are no *coups d'etat* led by colonels of the state's highway patrol or members of the state National Guard; the vehicle of change in our executive chairs is the vote of the electorate.

The keys to a successful transition are planning and communication. When both sides have thought ahead to the transition period and the potential problems of leaving or entering office, many of the difficulties can be reduced. When both sides strive to communicate rather than continue the election campaign or start another conflict, we seldom hear of difficulties during this period (NGA 1990a, 1990b). The National Governors Association has developed a series of materials to assist in gubernatorial transitions and holds a "New Governors' Seminar" in the even years to let incumbent governors pass on their accumulated wisdom to those who are about to enter office (NGA 1978, 1990b).

But there are always some deviations from any general rules, and the Blanton-Alexander transition in Tennessee in 1978–1979 is an example. Federal law enforcement officials had reason to believe that outgoing Democratic governor Ray Blanton was "about to release some state prisoners who [were believed to have] bought their way out of prison." One of the prisoners allegedly involved in the governor's pardon-selling scheme was James Earl Ray, the convicted assassin of Martin Luther King, Jr. Newly elected Republican governor Lamar Alexander agreed to be sworn in three days early without the knowledge of the incumbent Blanton and the locks to the governor's office were changed so that Blanton could not gain access. Blanton was later convicted of selling pardons and served time in prison (Alexander 1986, 22, 24).

When a governor is forced from office by an adverse judicial decision, planning for a gubernatorial transition is more difficult. First, the incumbent is being forced from office and the new governor was not elected by the vote of the people to be governor. Second, the timing for such a transition is not written into the constitution or statute as being date specific—it just happens on the verdict of a judge or jury in a criminal trial. For example, we can cite the 1996 Arkansas transition between Gov. Jim Guy Tucker (D), convicted of two felony counts in federal court, and Lt. Gov. Mike Huckabee (R). This quick transition was thrown into momentary chaos when Tucker refused to give up the office until the question of whether he had received a fair trial was answered. Huckabee then called for Tucker's impeachment if he refused to resign, which Tucker did four hours after his earlier refusal to do so (English 1997, 18).

## THE POWERS OF THE GOVERNORS: A COMPARISON

As Schlesinger (1965, 1971) has shown, some governors are strong, some are weak, and some fall in between. Reasons for strength can derive variously from personality, personal wealth, electoral mandate, party or interest group structure, state statute, or the formal powers of the office itself. The ability to be strong can vary within a particular state; for example, a governor may have considerable power over the executive branch but little in working with the legislature. A governor may have little power with either of these but have a close relationship with the president, which confers significant power in the intergovernmental arena and even in the state.

The governors of the most populous states—California, New York, Texas—are important and powerful in political circles. They have greater influence in national political conventions with their large state delegations and in Congress with their larger congressional delegations. They are often elevated to potential presidential candidacy just because they are the governors of these states. The national press covers them closely, giving their state activities a national tinge. In short, these governors have national power because of the states they head. In the 1980s a former governor of California, Ronald Reagan, won the presidency twice while in 1996 then-governor Pete Wilson tried but failed. Texas governor George W. Bush was declared the winner of the 2000 presidential race.

In this section we will look at the powers the governors have within their own states: those powers they bring to the office themselves and those provided them by state constitution, state statute, and the voters. Let us turn first to those powers the governors bring with them.

### The Personal Power of Governors

Each individual serving as governor has his or her own set of personal attributes that can be turned into either strength (power) or weakness, depending on the situation. We will look at four separate indicators of the personal strength of the governors serving in 2003.

*Electoral Mandate.* The margin of victory by which the governor won the seat is an indicator of the size of the electoral mandate. The premise is that the larger the margin of victory, the stronger the governor will be in the view of other actors in the system. Governors with a wide margin can use that margin politically by declaring that the people overwhelmingly wanted him or her in office so that a particular goal could be achieved. Governors who won by a narrow margin or by a plurality in a three- or four-way race and those who succeeded to office on the death, removal, or resignation of the elected governor cannot use this argument.

In the calculations of the extent of a governor's mandate, a five-point scale is used, ranging from those governors who won in a relative landslide on the high side to those who succeeded to office and thus were not elected on the low side. As indicated in the EM (electoral mandate) column of Table 7-4, twenty of the governors won their most recent election rather handily, another nine comfortably. At the other end of the spectrum are the seven governors who won by less than 2 points or were plurality winners. The average score for the 2003 governors is 3.8 on the five-point scale.

*Position on the State's Political Ambition Ladder.* The political ambition indicator places the 2003 governors on the state's political ambition ladder in relation to their previous positions. The premise is that a governor progressing steadily up from substate to statewide elective office to the governorship will be stronger than those who start at the top with the governorship as their first office. They have worked their way through each level and have learned en route what to expect and what is expected of them. They also have cultivated friends and allies who will support them (as well as enemies and ingrates who will not). The governor for whom it is the first elective office must build such understanding and relationships on the job.

A five-point scale is used, running from those who moved upward in a steady progression from substate to statewide office to governor on the high side, to those for whom the governorship was their first elective office on the low side. As shown in the AL (ambition ladder) column in Table 7-4, nineteen of the governors did follow a steady progression up the rungs on their state's political ambition ladder, and at the other extreme nine of them started at the top. Former governors, those who moved up from legislative leadership or congressional posts, and those moving up from substate positions (mayors and legislators) fall between these two end points. The average score for the 2003 governors is 3.3 on the five-point scale.

*The Personal Future of Governors as Governors.* Governors who are near the beginning of their terms and who have the ability to run again have more power than do governors who are nearing the end of their terms in office or are retiring or are term-limited. Governors up for reelection are able to go out to the voters again and seek the electoral mandate voters can provide and at the same time possibly help supporters and hurt detractors. Governors who cannot run again become lame ducks with little political potential remaining.

A five-point scale—ranging from those on the high side, who are early in their terms and can seek reelection, to those on the low side, who are late in their final terms—indicates the personal future of governors as governors. As shown in the PF (personal future) column in Table 7-4, in 2003 thirty-seven governors will be able to run again and therefore still have some political potential. However, thirteen are lame ducks in their final terms, three of them late in those terms. The average score for the 2003 governors is 4.2 on the five-point scale.

**Table 7-4** Governors' Personal Powers, 2003

| State | EM | AL | PF | GP | GPP |
|---|---|---|---|---|---|
| Alabama | 2 | 3 | 5 | 5 | 3.8 |
| Alaska | 5 | 3 | 5 | 2 | 3.8 |
| Arizona | 2 | 5 | 5 | 3 | 3.8 |
| Arkansas | 4 | 5 | 3 | 4 | 4.0 |
| California | 3 | 5 | 3 | 1 | 3.0 |
| Colorado | 5 | 5 | 3 | 5 | 4.5 |
| Connecticut | 5 | 3 | 5 | 2 | 3.8 |
| Delaware | 5 | 5 | 4 | na | 4.7 |
| Florida | 5 | 1 | 3 | 4 | 3.3 |
| Georgia | 3 | 3 | 5 | 5 | 4.0 |
| Hawaii | 3 | 2 | 5 | na | 3.3 |
| Idaho | 5 | 3 | 3 | 3 | 3.5 |
| Illinois | 4 | 3 | 5 | na | 4.0 |
| Indiana | 5 | 5 | 3 | 3 | 4.0 |
| Iowa | 4 | 5 | 5 | 3 | 4.3 |
| Kansas | 4 | 5 | 5 | na | 4.7 |
| Kentucky | 5 | 5 | 1 | 2 | 3.3 |
| Louisiana | 5 | 3 | 1 | 5 | 3.5 |
| Maine | 3 | 3 | 5 | 5 | 4.0 |
| Maryland | 3 | 3 | 5 | na | 3.7 |
| Massachusetts | 3 | 1 | 5 | 4 | 3.3 |
| Michigan | 3 | 5 | 5 | 5 | 4.5 |
| Minnesota | 4 | 3 | 5 | 4 | 4.0 |
| Mississippi | 2 | 5 | 4 | 3 | 3.5 |
| Missouri | 2 | 5 | 4 | na | 3.7 |
| Montana | 3 | 5 | 4 | 1 | 3.3 |
| Nebraska | 5 | 2 | 3 | 5 | 3.8 |
| Nevada | 5 | 1 | 3 | 4 | 3.3 |
| New Hampshire | 5 | 1 | 5 | 2 | 3.3 |
| New Jersey | 5 | 2 | 5 | 2 | 3.5 |
| New Mexico | 5 | 3 | 5 | na | 4.3 |
| New York | 5 | 3 | 5 | 2 | 3.8 |
| North Carolina | 3 | 5 | 4 | 3 | 3.8 |
| North Dakota | 4 | 1 | 4 | 5 | 3.5 |
| Ohio | 5 | 5 | 3 | 3 | 4.0 |
| Oklahoma | 2 | 3 | 5 | na | 3.3 |
| Oregon | 3 | 5 | 5 | na | 4.3 |
| Pennsylvania | 4 | 2 | 5 | 4 | 3.8 |
| Rhode Island | 4 | 1 | 5 | na | 3.3 |
| South Carolina | 4 | 3 | 5 | na | 4.0 |
| South Dakota | 5 | 3 | 5 | na | 4.3 |
| Tennessee | 3 | 2 | 5 | na | 3.3 |
| Texas | 5 | 5 | 5 | 3 | 4.5 |
| Utah | 5 | 1 | 4 | 5 | 3.8 |
| Vermont | 2 | 5 | 5 | na | 4.0 |
| Virginia | 3 | 1 | 3 | 4 | 2.8 |
| Washington | 5 | 2 | 1 | 2 | 2.5 |

*(Table continues on next page)*

**Table 7-4** *Continued*

| | | | | |
|---|---|---|---|---|
| West Virginia | 3 | 3 | 4 | 4 | 3.5 |
| Wisconsin | 3 | 5 | 5 | 2 | 3.8 |
| Wyoming | 2 | 1 | 5 | na | 2.7 |
| Fifty-state average | 3.8 | 3.3 | 4.2 | 3.4 | 3.7 |

SOURCE: For EM, author's calculations; AL, individual governor's Web sites; PF, CSG 2002 and author's calculations; GP, author's calculations; GPP, author's calculations.

EM: Signifies governor's electoral mandate: 5 = landslide win of eleven or more points; 4 = comfortable majority of six to ten points; 3 = narrow majority of three to five points; 2 = tight win of zero to two points or a plurality win of under 50 percent; 1 = succeeded to office.

AL: Signifies governor's position on the state's political ambition ladder: 5 = steady progression; 4 = former governors; 3 = legislative leaders or members of Congress; 2 = substate position to governor; 1 = governorship is first elective office.

PF: Signifies the personal future of the governor: 5 = early in term, can run again; 4 = late in term, can run again; 3 = early in term, term limited; 2 = succeeded to office, can run for election; 1 = late in final term.

GP: Signifies gubernatorial job performance rating in public opinion polls: 5 = over 60 percent positive job approval rating; 4 = 50 to 59 percent positive job approval rating; 3 = 40 to 49 percent positive job approval rating; 2 = 30 to 39 percent positive job approval rating; 1 = less than 30 percent positive job approval rating; na = no polling data available.

GPP: Signifies governor's personal powers' index score, the sum of the scores for EM, AL, PF, GP divided by 4 and rounded to the nearest decimal, except for those states without a governor's job performance rating, where the sum is divided by 3 and rounded to the nearest decimal.

Being a lame duck is frustrating. While governors in this position enjoy the trappings and formal powers of office, they lack the political power and wallop they once had. You not only lose the potential wallop needed to convince those who are not necessarily your friends and allies, you also lose the support of your friends and allies.

*Gubernatorial Performance Ratings.* Their performance as governor is another aspect of the personal power of governors. There are several ways to measure the performance of the governors of the fifty states. Two of them rely on asking people—involved observers and the public—just how well they think the governor of their state is performing. The premise is that those governors who are seen as performing in a relatively positive way add to their own personal power and will be more effective than will those who are viewed as not performing well. But what constitutes a good performance by a governor? On what basis do observers make their judgments?

One factor in some evaluations is whether or not the governor is deemed to have achieved some level of success in economic development efforts. This can be especially important when a state has experienced a weak economic period during or just before the governor's term in office. Under such circumstances, successes in seeking and obtaining new businesses and new jobs is important. It could be, however, that the governor reaps the benefit of serving during good economic times and receives positive marks simply on the basis of this good timing.

A second factor in assessing a governor's performance involves comparisons with his or her predecessors. Clearly, if a governor is under some type of dark cloud for what he or she may have done (or not done), or what someone in his or her administration has done, this comparison will be negative. Another factor concerns the governor's ability to keep things on an even keel and to be in tune with what the voters want.

Gubernatorial performance can also be measured on the basis of state-level public opinion polls, which have proliferated in recent years. These polls, which measure how well the citizens, registered voters, or likely voters in a state feel their governor is performing, have yielded fairly consistent results. The results are usually made public by whichever media is paying for the polls or by the university center that is conducting the polls.

In such polls the reasons for the respondents' assessments are obscure, but how they rate their governor's performance becomes part of the politics around the governor. The categories of responses used vary from "approve, disapprove" to "excellent, good, average, fair, poor." What everyone looks for is the percentage of positive responses in the ratings of the governor, although most political consultants believe that the negative assessments are more meaningful in political terms.

To compare these job performance poll ratings across the fifty states, we use a five-point scale, ranging from those governors with a positive rating of 60 percent or higher to those who had a rating of less than 30 percent. These are all snapshot ratings taken at one point in time and are the most recent readings available. Most of these polls were taken during the governor's current term.[10] The results presented in the GP (gubernatorial job performance) column in Table 7-4 indicate that seventeen governors had a positive job approval rating of 50 percent or higher, with nine of these rated at above 60 percent and eight between 50 and 59 percent. At the lowest end of the scale were seven governors rated at between 30 and 39 percent and two governors with performance ratings below 30 percent. The two governors with the lowest ratings were Gray Davis (D-Calif.) and Judy Martz (R-Mont.). In 2003 Davis faced the beginnings of a recall effort as some citizens sought to remove him from office even though he just won reelection in 2002—albeit with just 47.7 percent of the vote.

The average score for the 2003 governors is 3.4 on the five-point scale. The impact of the early 2000s' faltering economy on the governors' job approval ratings is evident in this average score. In the "good" times of 1998, when the economy was booming across most states, the governors' average job approval ratings score was 4.3. This indicates there has been a 21 percent decline in the public's perception of how well their governors are performing in "hard" times.

Whatever the reasons for these ratings, their impact is clear. For those at the low side of the scale the outlook is gloomy. Their administrations are jarred and their political futures unclear, if not damaged beyond repair. For those at the high end of the scale, positive public opinion poll ratings become part of their political and personal arsenal in their efforts to achieve results.

*The Personal Power of Governors: Summary.* To make an assessment and comparison of how the fifty state governors fare in their personal power, the scores of each of the previously mentioned indicators were brought together into one index. Each

---

10. Two incumbent governors elected in 2000 (Delaware, Missouri) and the thirteen elected in 2002 have not had any reported job approval ratings from a state level poll as of May 2003. So, in this measure there are only ratings for thirty-five incumbent governors.

state's scores in the four separate indicators were totaled and then divided by four to keep within the framework of the five-point scale, except for the fifteen governors for whom there were no job approval ratings in polls; those states' scores were divided by 3.

As indicated in the GPP (governor's personal power index) column in Table 7-4, the overall average score of the governors was 3.7, with thirty of them falling in the 3.7 to 5.0 range. Two governors sit atop this index of personal power with scores of 4.7 or more. They are Ruth Minner (R-Del.), midway through her first term, and newly elected Kathleen Sebelius (D-Kan.). At the other end of the index are three governors with scores of 2.8 or lower. They are Gary Locke of Washington, who is midway through his second and final term; newly elected Dave Freudenthal (D-Wyo.); and Mark Warner (D-Va.), in his first and only term.

In summary, it appears that most governors bring, and continue to hold onto, their own brand of personal power to the governorship. Although there are some who fall toward the weaker side, there are considerably more on the stronger side.

### The Institutional Powers of Governors

The institutional powers of the governorship are those powers given the governor by the state constitution, state statutes, and the voters when they vote on constitutions and referenda. In a sense, these powers are the structure into which the governor moves on being elected to office.

*Separately Elected State-Level Officials.* The concept of a plural executive is alive and well in many of the states. Instead of following the presidential model, which we see at the national level with a president and vice president as the only elected executive branch officials, the states have opted to allow voters to select a range of state officials.[11] Over the course of the twentieth century, however, one of the most consistent reforms advocated for the states has been to reduce the number of separately elected executive branch officials. The likelihood of such reforms is low and unlikely to improve in the future. In 2000 there were 300 separately elected executive branch officials covering 12 major offices in the states (Hovey and Hovey 2003, 107). Ten states also have multi-member boards, commissions, or councils whose members are elected either statewide or from districts.

Each of these separate offices has its own political support network that is quite resistant to any changes in how leadership is selected. And as noted earlier, some of these offices serve as launching pads for individuals seeking higher elective offices, such as the governorship, and are tightly woven into the state's political ambition ladder. It is often just not worth the struggle to change how they are selected; too much political effort and capital would be expended for too little real political gain all in the name of reform.

---

11. Some still argue for the plural executive model in the states. See Robinson (1998) for a recent argument based on a study of several of these separately elected officials in Wyoming.

As shown in the SEP (separately elected executive branch officials) column of Table 7-5, only five states come close to mirroring the presidential model. The remaining states have a variety of other elected officials, ranging from a few process-type offices (attorney general, secretary of state, treasurer, and auditor) to some major policy offices (K-12 education, university boards, and public utility authorities). On this five-point scale, the average score is 2.9.

For the governor, this means working with other officials who have similar claims to a statewide political constituency. And although process-type officials seem to be more innocuous by definition, they can cause a governor considerable problems. For example, tensions between governors and lieutenant governors have led to bizarre political situations in which governors have been wary of leaving their states lest the lieutenant governor sabotage their programs while serving as acting governor. In another situation, the Republican governor of North Carolina once found himself being sued by the separately elected Democratic attorney general in one case while nearly simultaneously being represented by the same attorney general in another case (CSG 1992, 29).

*Tenure Potential.* How long governors can serve and whether they can succeed themselves for more than one term are important factors in determining just how much power they have. One argument is that those who enjoy the possibility of a longer stay in office are able to carry out their programs. But this can cut both ways: If limits were put on gubernatorial terms, governors might move faster and more decisively to achieve their goals and not be afraid of the voters' retribution at the ballot box when a necessary yet unpopular decision has to be made.

Initially, ten of the governors of the thirteen original states had one-year terms, another a two-year term, and two had three-year terms. Gradually, states moved to either two- or four-year terms, and one-year terms finally disappeared early in the twentieth century.

Another significant shift has been taking place since 1960: the borrowing by the states of the presidential succession model, as embodied in the Twenty-second Amendment to the U.S. Constitution, adopted in 1951, which states, "No person shall be elected to the office of President more than twice." This was a direct reaction to the four terms to which President Franklin D. Roosevelt was elected. In 1960 only six states restricted their governors to two four-year terms (Schlesinger 1965, 220). By 1969 this number had increased to eleven states (Schlesinger 1971, 223), and by 1988 to twenty-five states. With the rise of the term-limits movement, more states have acted to impose such a restriction, and by 2003 a total of thirty-eight had done so (see the TP, tenure potential, column of Table 7-5). On this five-point scale, the average score is 4.1.

*The Power of Appointment.* One of the first sets of decisions facing governors-elect on the morning after their election is the appointment of personnel to key positions in their administration. This power of appointment is fundamental to a governor's administration, especially in relation to the state bureaucracy. But the appointive power is also part of the governor's legislative role; promises of

**Table 7-5** Governors' Institutional Powers, 2002

| State | SEP | TP | AP | BP | VP | PC | Total[a] | GIP Score[b] |
|-------|-----|-----|-----|-----|-----|-----|-------|-----------|
| Alabama | 1.0 | 4.0 | 2.0 | 3 | 4 | 2 | 16.0 | 2.7 |
| Alaska | 5.0 | 4.0 | 3.0 | 3 | 5 | 4 | 24.0 | 4.0 |
| Arizona | 2.0 | 4.0 | 2.5 | 3 | 5 | 1 | 17.5 | 2.9 |
| Arkansas | 2.5 | 4.0 | 2.5 | 3 | 4 | 2 | 18.0 | 3.0 |
| California | 1.0 | 4.0 | 3.5 | 3 | 5 | 4 | 20.5 | 3.4 |
| Colorado | 4.0 | 4.0 | 3.0 | 3 | 5 | 4 | 23.0 | 3.8 |
| Connecticut | 4.0 | 5.0 | 3.5 | 3 | 5 | 2 | 22.5 | 3.8 |
| Delaware | 2.5 | 4.0 | 3.5 | 3 | 5 | 3 | 21.0 | 3.5 |
| Florida | 3.0 | 4.0 | 1.5 | 3 | 5 | 4 | 20.5 | 3.4 |
| Georgia | 1.0 | 4.0 | 1.0 | 3 | 5 | 3 | 17.0 | 2.8 |
| Hawaii | 5.0 | 4.0 | 3.0 | 3 | 5 | 2 | 22.0 | 3.7 |
| Idaho | 2.0 | 4.0 | 2.0 | 3 | 5 | 5 | 21.0 | 3.5 |
| Illinois | 4.0 | 5.0 | 3.5 | 3 | 5 | 4 | 24.5 | 4.1 |
| Indiana | 3.0 | 4.0 | 3.5 | 3 | 2 | 3 | 18.5 | 3.1 |
| Iowa | 3.0 | 5.0 | 3.5 | 3 | 5 | 2 | 21.5 | 3.6 |
| Kansas | 3.0 | 4.0 | 3.5 | 3 | 5 | 2 | 20.5 | 3.4 |
| Kentucky | 3.0 | 4.0 | 3.5 | 3 | 4 | 3 | 20.5 | 3.4 |
| Louisiana | 1.0 | 4.0 | 3.5 | 3 | 5 | 2 | 18.5 | 3.1 |
| Maine | 5.0 | 4.0 | 4.5 | 3 | 2 | 4 | 22.5 | 3.8 |
| Maryland | 4.0 | 4.0 | 3.0 | 5 | 5 | 2 | 23.0 | 3.8 |
| Massachusetts | 4.0 | 4.0 | 3.5 | 3 | 5 | 1 | 20.5 | 3.4 |
| Michigan | 4.0 | 4.0 | 3.5 | 3 | 5 | 2 | 21.5 | 3.6 |
| Minnesota | 4.0 | 5.0 | 4.0 | 3 | 5 | 3 | 24.0 | 4.0 |
| Mississippi | 1.5 | 4.0 | 3.0 | 3 | 5 | 4 | 20.5 | 3.4 |
| Missouri | 2.5 | 4.0 | 2.5 | 3 | 5 | 2 | 19.0 | 3.2 |
| Montana | 3.0 | 4.0 | 2.5 | 3 | 5 | 4 | 21.5 | 3.6 |
| Nebraska | 3.0 | 4.0 | 3.0 | 4 | 5 | 3 | 22.0 | 3.7 |
| Nevada | 2.5 | 4.0 | 3.5 | 3 | 2 | 3 | 18.0 | 3.0 |
| New Hampshire | 5.0 | 2.0 | 3.0 | 3 | 2 | 4 | 19.0 | 3.2 |
| New Jersey | 5.0 | 4.0 | 3.5 | 3 | 5 | 3 | 23.5 | 3.9 |
| New Mexico | 3.0 | 4.0 | 3.0 | 3 | 5 | 4 | 22.0 | 3.7 |
| New York | 4.0 | 5.0 | 3.5 | 4 | 5 | 3 | 24.5 | 4.1 |
| North Carolina | 1.0 | 4.0 | 3.5 | 3 | 2 | 3 | 16.5 | 2.8 |
| North Dakota | 3.0 | 5.0 | 3.5 | 3 | 5 | 4 | 23.5 | 3.9 |
| Ohio | 4.0 | 4.0 | 3.5 | 3 | 5 | 4 | 23.5 | 3.9 |
| Oklahoma | 1.0 | 4.0 | 1.5 | 3 | 5 | 4 | 18.5 | 3.1 |
| Oregon | 1.5 | 4.0 | 3.0 | 3 | 5 | 3 | 19.5 | 3.3 |
| Pennsylvania | 4.0 | 4.0 | 4.0 | 3 | 5 | 2 | 22.0 | 3.7 |
| Rhode Island | 2.5 | 4.0 | 4.0 | 3 | 2 | 1 | 16.5 | 2.8 |
| South Carolina | 1.0 | 4.0 | 2.5 | 2 | 5 | 4 | 18.5 | 3.1 |
| South Dakota | 3.0 | 4.0 | 3.5 | 3 | 5 | 4 | 22.5 | 3.8 |
| Tennessee | 4.5 | 4.0 | 4.0 | 3 | 4 | 4 | 23.5 | 3.9 |
| Texas | 1.0 | 5.0 | 1.5 | 2 | 5 | 4 | 18.5 | 3.1 |
| Utah | 4.0 | 4.5 | 3.0 | 3 | 5 | 5 | 24.5 | 4.1 |
| Vermont | 2.5 | 2.0 | 5.0 | 3 | 2 | 2 | 16.5 | 2.8 |
| Virginia | 2.5 | 3.0 | 3.5 | 3 | 5 | 2 | 19.0 | 3.2 |
| Washington | 1.0 | 4.0 | 3.0 | 3 | 5 | 3 | 19.0 | 3.2 |
| West Virginia | 2.0 | 4.0 | 4.0 | 5 | 5 | 4 | 24.0 | 4.0 |

**Table 7-5** *Continued*

| | | | | | | | | |
|---|---|---|---|---|---|---|---|---|
| Wisconsin | 3.0 | 5.0 | 3.5 | 3 | 5 | 2 | 21.5 | 3.6 |
| Wyoming | 2.0 | 4.0 | 3.5 | 3 | 5 | 2 | 19.5 | 3.3 |
| Fifty-state average | 2.9 | 4.1 | 3.2 | 3.1 | 4.5 | 3.0 | 20.7 | 3.5 |

SOURCES: For SEP, CSG 2002, 161–168; TP, CSG 2002, 145–146; AP, CSG 2002, 34–37; BP, CSG 2000, 20–21 and NCSL 1998; VP, CSG 2002, 104–105 and 150–151; PC, NCSL 2003.

SEP:  Separately elected executive branch officials: 5 = only governor or governor/lieutenant governor team elected; 4.5 = governor or governor/lieutenant governor team, with one other elected official; 4 = governor/lieutenant governor team with some process officials (attorney general, secretary of state, treasurer, auditor) elected; 3 = governor/lieutenant governor team with process officials and some major and minor policy officials elected; 2.5 = governor (no team) with six or fewer officials elected, but none are major policy officials; 2 = governor (no team) with six or fewer officials elected, including one major policy official; 1.5 = governor (no team) with six or fewer officials elected, but two are major policy officials; 1 = governor (no team) with seven or more process and several major policy officials elected.

TP:  Tenure potential of governors: 5 = four-year term, no restraint on reelection; 4.5 = four-year term, only three terms permitted; 4 = four-year term, only two terms permitted; 3 = four-year term, no consecutive election permitted; 2 = two-year term, no restraint on reelection; 1 = two-year term, only two terms permitted.

AP:  Governor's appointment powers in six major functional areas (corrections, K-12 education, health, highways/transportation, public utilities regulation, and welfare); the six individual office scores are totaled and then averaged and rounded to the nearest .5 for the state score: 5 = governor appoints, no other approval needed; 4 = governor appoints, a board, council or legislature approves; 3 = someone else appoints, governor approves or shares appointment; 2 = someone else appoints, governor and others approve; 1 = someone else appoints, no approval or confirmation needed.

BP:  Governor's budget power: 5 = governor has full responsibility, legislature may not increase executive budget; 4 = governor has full responsibility, legislature can increase by special majority vote or subject to item veto; 3 = governor has full responsibility, legislature has unlimited power to change executive budget; 2 = governor shares responsibility, legislature has unlimited power to change executive budget; 1 = governor shares responsibility with other elected official, legislature has unlimited power to change executive budget.

VP:  Governor's veto power: 5 = governor has item veto and a special majority vote of the legislature is needed to override a veto (three-fifths of legislators elected or two-thirds of legislators present; 4 = has item veto with a majority of the legislators elected needed to override; 3 = has item veto with only a majority of the legislators present needed to override; 2 = no item veto, with a special legislative majority needed to override a regular veto; 1 = no item veto, only a simple legislative majority needed to override a regular veto.

PC:  Gubernatorial party control: 5 = governor's party (gp) has a substantial majority (75 percent or more) in both houses of the legislature; 4 = gp has a simple majority in both houses (under 75 percent) or a substantial majority in one house and a simple majority in the other; 3 = split party control in the legislature or a nonpartisan legislature; 2 = gp has a simple minority (25 percent or more) in both houses or a simple minority in one and a substantial minority (under 25 percent) in the other; 1 = gp has a substantial minority in both houses.

[a] Sum of the scores on the six individual indices.

[b] Total divided by 6 to keep five-point scale.

appointment to high-level executive positions or to the state judiciary are often the coin spent for support for particular legislation.

The history of state governors' appointment powers is one of growth from weak beginnings. The increase of separately elected officials during the nineteenth century and the ad hoc proliferation of state agencies, often headed by boards and commissions, added to the problem of gubernatorial control. This diluted gubernatorial power was the background for twentieth-century reforms to increase gubernatorial appointive power. The assumption underlying these reforms is that governors who can appoint officials without any other authority involved can be held accountable for these officials' actions. Such governors are more powerful than those who must have either or both houses of the legislature confirm an appointment. Governors who only approve appointments rather than initiate them have even less appointive power. Weakest are those governors who neither appoint nor approve but have a separate body do so and those who have no opportunity to appoint because the officials who head agencies are separately elected.

The AP column in Table 7-5 presents the scores for the governor's appointment power. To assess this measure we establish who selects the heads of the agencies providing the six major functions in each state—corrections, K-12 education, health, highways or transportation, public utilities regulation, and welfare—and then average the score for all six. Obviously, governors face constraints in their appointment power. A majority of the states are in the middle of the scale—that is, someone other than the governor appoints these individuals to their positions with either gubernatorial or legislative approval, or both. On this five-point scale, the average score is 3.2.

One caveat on the appointive power index: A politically shrewd governor with an efficient political operation in the governor's office can probably orchestrate many of the selection decisions made by boards, commissions, and department or agency heads. Thus such governors might not be as powerless as their state's constitutional or statutory language suggests.

*Control Over the Budget.* The executive budget, centralized under gubernatorial control, is a twentieth-century response to the chaotic fiscal situations found in state government at the turn of that century. An executive budget in one document seeks to encompass under the chief executive's control all the agency and department requests for legislatively appropriated funds; it also reflects the governor's own policy priorities. This document is then transmitted to the legislature for its consideration and ultimate passage. By placing governors at the head of this process and making them the chief lobbyist for the budget in the legislature, the centralized budget puts much power in governors' hands.

What the governor can do is develop and present the state budget as the fiscal road map for the next fiscal year or biennium. However, the legislature can often undo much of this as the budget bill works its way through the legislative process. In some states the governor's proposed budget is described as DOA (dead on arrival) because the legislature intends to build the state's next budget on its own. Moreover, when there are conflicts over the budget within the executive branch agencies and between the agencies and the governor, the legislature is where agency grievances can be heard and gubernatorial decisions changed. The greater the power to make changes in the governor's proposed budget and the willingness of the legislature to do so, the less potential budget power for the governor. I use the word *potential* advisedly, because not all gubernatorial-legislative relationships are adversarial in nature, and what the governor proposes usually does set the agenda for debate and decision.

State legislatures have been seeking even more involvement in the budgetary process to regain some of the budgetary powers lost to governors. They have developed legislative oversight procedures, tried to require legislative appropriation or approval of federal grant funds flowing into the state, and sought to have legislative committees involved in administrative budgetary shifts made during the fiscal year.

But there are some limitations on the budgetary powers of both these executive and legislative branch actors. For example, most states earmark their gasoline taxes for highway or mass transportation uses, and some earmark taxes on alcohol for various purposes or allot a fraction of their sales taxes to local governments. Tolls and fees for bridges, highways, and other state-established public authorities are retained by the agencies collecting them to finance their activities and projects. In recent decades, states have been facing more and more federal mandates on how much they should be spending on Medicaid, certain environmental problems, prisons, and disabled individuals. A governor's budgetary power is thus reduced when appropriated funds are earmarked or otherwise diverted by legislative prescription, when public authorities raise or expend independent income, or when federal mandates direct state expenditures.

A five-point scale is used to measure the budgetary power given to each governor. It consists of two measures: the extent of the governor's responsibility to develop the budget and the extent of the legislature's power to change the governor's budget once it is sent to the legislature. At the top of the scale are the states whose governors have full responsibility for the executive budget and the legislature is constrained in how much change it can make in the governor's proposed budget. At the bottom of the scale are the states whose governors share responsibility for developing the executive budget with others and whose legislatures have unlimited power to change any proposed budget.

It is evident in the BP (budget power) column in Table 7-5 that most states provide their governors with full budget power; interestingly, they also award their legislatures with unlimited power to change a governor's proposed budget. The average score for the fifty states is 3.1.

*The Veto Power.* Governors have been provided the formal power of being able to veto bills and, in most states, parts of bills passed by the legislature. This is the most direct power the governor can exercise in relation to the legislature. There are many differences in the veto power extended to governors: total bill veto, item veto of selected words, and item veto to change the meaning of words (NASBO 1997, 29–31).

The veto, although a direct power over the legislature, also provides governors with some administrative powers because it gives them the ability to stop agencies from gaining support in a legislative end run around their governor's or their budget office's adverse decision. As noted earlier, this is especially true in those forty-three states in which the governor can veto particular items in an agency's budget without rejecting the entire bill (Benjamin 1982, 11; Moe 1988, 4). Several states have gone further by allowing the governor to condition his or her approval of a full bill with amendments to the bill or rewording of the lines (Moe 1988, 3–5).

The veto and its use involve two major actors: the governor and the legislature. It is a legislative act that a governor must sign or veto; however, the legislature has the opportunity to vote to override the veto and thus make a law without the governor's signature. In fact, more than a few states even allow their legislatures to recall bills from the governor prior to his or her action, thereby creating a negotiating situation—sort of an informal alternative to the veto (Benjamin 1982). This latter tactic can allow the governor to become part of the legislative process with de facto amendatory power as the governor and the legislature negotiate over the bill's contents (Benjamin 1982, 12; Moe 1988, 13–14).

The requirements for legislative override range from only a majority of members present and voting to a special majority, such as a three-fifths vote. Although the threat of a legislative override has not been great in the past, the number of gubernatorial vetoes overridden by legislatures has grown somewhat. In 1947 governors vetoed approximately 5 percent of the bills passed by legislatures and were overridden on only 1.8 percent of them (Wiggins 1980, 1112–1113). In the early to mid-1990s, governors vetoed about 3.7 percent of the bills and resolutions passed by legislatures and only saw 2.3 percent of these vetoes overridden (CSG 1996, 105–106). But this overall rate masks some of the extremes. In 1992–1993 Gov. Ned McWherter (D-Tenn.) signed all 1,262 bills presented to him into law, whereas Gov. Wilson of California vetoed more than 21 percent of the 2,681 bills presented to him—and none of these vetoes were overridden (CSG 1994, 148–150).

Some would argue that the use of the veto is a sign of gubernatorial weakness rather than strength because strong governors win the battle through negotiation rather than confrontation with the legislature. In a slightly different vein, one governor argued that a governor should "avoid threatening to veto a bill. You just relieve the legislature of responsibility for sound legislation" (Beyle and Huefner 1983, 268–269). Moreover, a governor using a veto risks embarrassment at the hands of the legislature. It is a power to be used sparingly (NGA 1987, 8).

A study done in the late 1980s suggests that there are at least four consequences following the use of a line-item veto in any of its variants. These are (1) profoundly altering the relationship of the legislature to the governor to the benefit of the latter; (2) increasing the number of formal confrontations between the two branches; (3) spawning procedures to neutralize its impact; and (4) precipitating litigation between the two branches. The last introduces the third branch of state government, the courts, into the law-making process at an early stage in its role as umpire (Moe 1988, 1–2).

The battle in Wisconsin over the governor's partial veto demonstrates most of these points. Republican governor Tommy Thompson startled the Democratic legislature in 1987 by creatively using the partial veto to change legislative intent. He excised isolated digits, letters, and words to the point of creating new words and meaning. The legislative leaders sought relief from the state's supreme court, only to have the court back the governor's actions in a four-to-three decision (*State ex. rel. State Senate v. Thompson* 144, Wis.2d 429, 424 N.W.2d 385, 386, n.3 [1988]; see also Hutchison 1989). The legislature placed a constitutional amendment on the ballot in 1988 prohibiting such vetoes, and it was approved by a 62-percent vote. In 1991 a federal appeals court, in upholding a lower court decision, found the partial veto "quirky" but not unconstitutional. By mid-1993 Thompson had executed more than 1,300 vetoes (Farney 1993).

The governors' veto power is measured on a five-point scale, with the high side having governors with an item veto requiring an extraordinary legislative vote to override it (three-fifths or two-thirds). The low side has governors with no item veto power and the legislature only needing a simple majority vote to override a veto. In between are variations on the type of veto and the size of the majority needed to override a governor's veto. As indicated in the VP (veto power) column in Table 7-5, most states do provide their governors with considerable veto power, with nearly four-fifths of the states in the top category. No states are in the lowest category, although in seven states the governor has no item veto at all. On this five-point scale, the average score is 4.5.

The veto can also be used in what might be called an affirmative way. During the 1991 legislative session, Connecticut governor Lowell Weicker (Ind.) had no one of his party in the legislature; yet he was able to use the veto over the state's budget as a positive weapon. He continually vetoed the budget bill because it did not contain an income tax. In doing this, he assisted those who favored the imposition of a state income tax and opposed those who would rather have turned to an increase in the state sales tax as a way to balance the state's growing budget deficit. In the end, an income tax was adopted, the first in the state's history (Murphy 1992, 69).

*Party Control.* Partisanship is a key variable in the governors' relationship with the legislatures. If the governor's party also controls the legislature, then partisan conflicts can be minimized and the governor's ability to achieve his or her agenda is more likely to be successful. Cooperation should be the style of their relationship. If the governor and the legislative leadership are not of the same party, then partisan conflicts all too often become the style of the relationship, and the ability of the governor to achieve his or her goals is diminished. Because there are two houses in the legislatures of each state except Nebraska, it is quite possible that at least one house will be controlled by the opposition party.

Recent decades have seen a growing trend toward a "power split" in state governments (Sherman 1984). In 1984 sixteen states had a power split; in 2003 there are thirty. V.O. Key Jr. called this power split a "perversion" of separation of powers allowing partisan differences to present an almost intractable situation (Key 1956, 52), but not all view this situation with alarm. In 1984 Gov. Alexander of Tennessee indicated that "it makes it harder, sometimes much harder; but the results can be better, sometimes much better" (Sherman 1984, 9). But, as in many things, it depends on how individual leaders handle a power split (Van Assendelft 1997).

At least three factors help to determine just how harmonious the power-split relationship will be: how great a majority the opposition party has in the legislature; the style and the personalities of the individuals involved—the governor and the legislative leaders; and whether an election year is near (Sherman 1984, 10).

When the governor's party is in the minority but controls a sizable number of seats, it is more difficult for the opposition majority to change the governor's budget or override his or her veto. However, open and easy-going personalities can often overcome partisan differences or, as Alexander said, "If you have good, well-meaning leaders, it's likely to be much better than any other process" (quoted in Sherman 1984, 12). A recent study of the spending patterns in the states between 1997 and 2002 found that when one party controls both the governorship and the state legislature, spending is greater than when there is a power split in the control (Cauchon 2003).

These variations in the governor's party control were measured on a five-point scale. The highest score is for states in which a governor's party controls both houses by a substantial majority, and the lowest score is for states in which the governor faces a legislature controlled by a substantial majority of the opposing party in both houses. On this five-point scale, the average score is 3.0.

Given the fact that there are thirty states in which a power split exists in 2003, it is no surprise to see in the PC (party control) column in Table 7-5 that only two governors have a legislature in which their party has a substantial majority. Nebraska's governor faces a unicameral (one-house) legislature elected on a nonpartisan basis. Three governors, two Republicans and one Democrat, faced a legislature controlled by a substantial majority of the opposition party.

*The Institutional Powers of the Governors: Summary.* To make an assessment and comparison of how the fifty governors fare in their institutional powers, the scores of each of the previously mentioned indicators were brought together into one index. The six indicator scores for each state governor were totaled and then divided by six to keep within the framework of the five-point scale. As can be seen in the GIP (governors' institutional power) score column in Table 7-5, the average score was 3.5. The six governorships with the most institutional power on this scale at 4.0 or higher were spread around the country, with no regional pattern evident.

At the lower end of this index were six governorships scoring 2.9 or less, located mainly in the South (three) and New England (two). The main weaknesses in the formal, institutional powers for these states lay in the presence of other statewide separately elected officials, reduced appointive power, and restricted veto power.

*Overall Gubernatorial Powers in the Fifty States.* Finally, the two sets of gubernatorial powers were combined into one overall ten-point index of gubernatorial power. The results, presented in Table 7-6, show an average score of 7.2. At the high side of this combined index, with scores of 8.0 or greater, are eight states—five in the Midwest, two in the West, and one in the East. At the low end of the scale, with scores of 6.1 or less, are four states, with two in the West and one each in New England and the South. Of course, these ratings change as incumbents are replaced with a new group of men and women carrying with them their own personal styles and strengths or weaknesses.

## BEING GOVERNOR

The true measure of governors and their administrations is how well they actually perform the various roles for which they are responsible. Are they able to translate their potential powers into effective action? What additional informal powers

**Table 7-6** Summary of Personal and Institutional Powers of Governors, by State, 2003

| State | Score | State | Score |
|---|---|---|---|
| Colorado | 8.3 | Indiana | 7.1 |
| Delaware | 8.2 | South Carolina | 7.1 |
| Illinois | 8.1 | Arkansas | 7.0 |
| Kansas | 8.1 | Georgia | 7.0 |
| Michigan | 8.1 | Hawaii | 7.0 |
| South Dakota | 8.1 | Idaho | 7.0 |
| Minnesota | 8.0 | Mississippi | 6.9 |
| New Mexico | 8.0 | Missouri | 6.9 |
| Iowa | 7.9 | Montana | 6.9 |
| Ohio | 7.9 | Vermont | 6.8 |
| Texas | 7.9 | Arizona | 6.7 |
| Utah | 7.9 | Florida | 6.7 |
| Alaska | 7.8 | Kentucky | 6.7 |
| Maine | 7.8 | Massachusetts | 6.7 |
| Connecticut | 7.6 | Louisiana | 6.6 |
| Oregon | 7.6 | North Carolina | 6.6 |
| Texas | 7.6 | Alabama | 6.5 |
| Maryland | 7.5 | New Hampshire | 6.5 |
| Nebraska | 7.5 | California | 6.4 |
| Pennsylvania | 7.5 | Oklahoma | 6.4 |
| West Virginia | 7.5 | Nevada | 6.3 |
| New Jersey | 7.4 | Rhode Island | 6.1 |
| North Dakota | 7.4 | Virginia | 6.0 |
| Wisconsin | 7.4 | Wyoming | 6.0 |
| Tennessee | 7.2 | Washington | 5.7 |
| Average | 7.2[a] | | |

SOURCE: Calculated from Tables 7-4 and 7-5.

NOTE: Each state's summary score is the sum of its overall scores in Tables 7-4 and 7-5.

[a] 359.9 divided by 50.

must they use to achieve the goals of their administrations?

As governor of Tennessee, Lamar Alexander argued that a governor's role was to "see the state's few most urgent needs, develop strategies to address them, and persuade at least half the people that he or she is right" (Alexander 1986, 112). To Alexander, the governor's main role concerned policy. A former governor of Vermont, Madeleine Kunin (D, 1985–1991), agreed and asserted that "the power of a governor to set the tone and define the values of a state administration is enormous." She also felt that "as governor, I had the incredible luxury to dream on a grand scale" (Kunin 1994, 11–12).

*The Governor as Policy Maker*

The goals of a gubernatorial administration are those policy directions a governor wishes to emphasize during his or her tenure in office. The types of policy priorities vary greatly across the activities of state government and depend on several factors, including the governor's own personal interests and outside events.

In a series of interviews with former governors, several themes emerged concerning how they believed they exerted policy leadership. Most saw their role as that of an issue catalyst, picking the issue up from the public, focusing it, and seeking to take action on it. Some others saw their role as that of a spectator viewing policy issues arising out of conflicts between actors on the state scene, whether they were special interest groups, the bureaucracy, or the mayor of the state's largest city. Finally, a few saw the governor as a reactor to accidents of history and other unanticipated events. In the eyes of these governors, leadership was more a process of problem solving and conflict resolution than agenda setting (NGA 1981, 1).

Obviously, issues and policy needs flow from many sources and provide governors with both flexibility and restrictions on the choices available. The events of the late 1980s and the early 1990s demonstrated just how governors can be forced to address issues and concerns not of their own choosing. The national recession of those years hit almost every state budget hard and some states, such as California, extremely hard. The main issues facing governors then were how to keep the state budget balanced in the face of falling revenues and how to provide the services people needed in such a down economy and that were normally provided in the states. The options available to the governors, and by extension the state legislatures, were to increase taxes, cut services, or both. Many states had to follow the third option, which was not a pleasing prospect for these leaders and the citizens of the states (Beyle 1992a).

During the mid-1990s, the economy recovered in the country and in most every state, and governors were freer to post their own agendas on the wall. Among the issues on their agendas were economic development, education quality and reform, health cost containment, welfare reform, children's policies, and crime control. In fact, because some of the issues that seemed to bedevil our national leaders threatened to bankrupt the states or cause even greater problems, governors and other state leaders in many of the states were already taking steps to address them.

The results of the 1994 elections served to place some Republican governors in a position to push the new national Republican congressional leadership to help the states. Some state leaders feared this new national leadership might seek to balance the federal budget at the expense of the states. But it was some of the long-serving Republican governors who took a leadership role in trying to shape new federal initiatives to benefit the states, or at least not to hurt the states.

In the late 1990s everyone involved in state policy making was helped by a very strong economy that provided almost every state with a surplus of tax revenues. From the dark fiscal days of the early 1990s, the states moved into the gravy days of the late 1990s when the policy questions revolved around what to do with all those excess revenues: spend it (where?); save it for a rainy day; or cut taxes (which?). Then came a return of the dark days of a faltering economy, falling revenues, and greater demand for services as the country moved into the twenty-first century. The governors and state legislatures of the first decade of the new century were facing the same problems that their counterparts did a decade earlier. Serving as governor was not as pleasant as it had been several years before.

But some other basic changes have aided governors in exerting policy leadership. The first level of change has taken place in the governor's office itself. In recent years the office has increased greatly in size, ability, functions, and structure. What used to amount to a few close associates working together with the governor has now been transformed into a much larger and more sophisticated bureaucratic organization in many of the states.

There have also been changes in the governor's extended office, the budget and planning agencies, which are increasingly being moved closer to the governor. In the most recent changes, governors have developed more aggressive offices of policy management, often following the federal model by creating a state-level Office of Management and Budget. One of the most critical roles of these agencies is "to provide the governor an independent source of advice on a broad range of state policy issues" (Flentje 1980, 26). They can also assist by reaching into the departments and agencies to help them implement policy directions and decisions.

These changes, and others, highlight the basic fact that governors have had to improve their policy capacity substantially to govern, especially in administering their state's executive branch. But governors can vary on how they use this capacity, how much they believe it really helps them, and how well they perform in this role, as we just saw in the "Personal Powers of the Governors" index.

### The Governor and the Legislature

A governor's relations with the legislature and success in dealing with legislators often determine how successful his or her administration will be. Although the governor takes the lead, it is still the legislature that must adopt the state budget, set or agree to basic policy directions, and, in many cases, confirm major gubernatorial appointments. A governor and legislature at loggerheads over a tax proposal, budget, policy direction, or a major department head's confirmation can bring part or all of state government to a standstill.

Added to the constitutional separation of powers are the political facts of life in many states in which the governor is of one party and another party controls one or both the legislative houses. Ideological factions can splinter a majority party's control of the legislature and be just as debilitating to a governor. Gov. Michael Dukakis (D-Mass.) found himself under greatest fire from his own party members. "And when you've got majorities of four to one in the Legislature—I'm sure you recognize that is by no means an unmitigated blessing—you've got conservative Democrats, you've got liberal Democrats, you've got moderate Democrats, you've got suburban Democrats, you've got urban Democrats, and you don't have any Republicans." He also noted that he was beaten in his 1978 reelection bid by a Democrat who was "philosophically miles away from him" (NGA 1981, 65).

The members of each of these two major branches bring quite different perspectives to state government. In terms of constituency, the governor represents the whole state; the legislature is a collection of individuals representing much smaller parts of the state. The governorship is a full-time job, and complete responsibility is placed on the shoulders of one person; the legislature is not a full-time job, although the time involved varies among states, as shown in Chapter 6 of this volume. The governor's chair sits atop the state's political ambition ladder; legislative seats are some of the rungs available in climbing the ladder.

Most new governors face their legislatures within the first month of their administration. The state of the state address, the governor's budget message, specific programmatic legislation, special messages on high-priority programs, oversight of agency bills, and responses to bills introduced by individual legislators are high on the governor's agenda. Over the course of an administration, the governor gradually reduces his or her relations with the legislature to a routine to lessen the personal burden and the burden on the governor's office in general.

The resources available to governors in their relations with the legislature can be formidable. Gubernatorial patronage appointments can be attractive to legislators either for themselves or for an important ally or constituent. Attractive, too, can be the allocation of certain state contracts for services and facilities or support for local projects. These political plums or "gifts" can be provided by a governor as payment for support, either already rendered or anticipated later, in the form of legislative votes for gubernatorial priorities.

Many governors develop elaborate legislative efforts under the direction of a legislative liaison. The governor's program is watched over by the liaison from its formative stages through its introduction as a bill or bills, legislative consideration in committee and on the floor, debate, and vote. Meetings with individual legislators and breakfast sessions at the governor's mansion with the governor serve to keep legislators aware of the governor's position and interest in issues.

But the governor should never try to be the chief legislator, according to those who have sat in the chair. This advice captures a very simple point: The governor can do much to set the agenda of the legislature, can try to direct the legislature's consideration and action on bills of concern to him or her, and can use the veto and other tools to redirect a legislative decision. But the governor should never intervene in purely legislative political processes such as leadership selection.

First, if the governor attempts to do this and loses this key legislative political decision at the outset of the legislative session, the governor's political power is often irretrievably diminished well before the key policy and budgetary issues are considered. Thus this step should never be taken unless the governor is certain to win. Second, such an intrusion is perceived as a step across the separation of powers line set in most state constitutions and in most state government practices. Third, and most important according to those who have been there, "a governor successful in managing the leadership selection gains a Pyrrhic victory" (Beyle and Huefner 1983, 268). All those on the losing side will be looking for a chance for revenge, and those on the winning side will not have their own strong political coalition on which they can count to run the legislature without the governor's support. Fourth, whatever negative situations occur in the legislature can be traced back to the governor and that political intrusion. Most governors find there are enough problems and explosive issues in the executive branch and elsewhere for them to cover and there is no need for the added burden.

### In the Middle of Intergovernmental Relations

The world that a governor must address is not constrained by the boundaries of the state. In an earlier time, out-of-state efforts made by governors were limited to occasional trips to attract industry, to attend the more socially oriented governors' conferences, and to participate in the presidential nominating conventions every four years. In recent decades, however, the states and the governors have found a need to focus on the issues, problems, and governmental activities that are part of the larger intergovernmental system in which individual states are lodged. Some of these issues concern several states at once, such as a pollution problem with a common river. Others are regional in scope, such as higher education in the South following World War II. Still others, such as health and welfare reform, are national in scope, and thus all states and governors have a stake in the actions of Congress and the national executive branch as noted earlier.

Governors were slow to move in these circles, tightly limiting their concerns and interests to their own states and leaving national government concerns to the state's congressional delegation. But since the 1960s, governors and states have been forced to develop relations with: national, regional, state, substate, and local governments. This development has generally coincided with the rapid expansion in national programs since the administration of President Lyndon B. Johnson (1963–1969), and it is also tied to the increasingly articulated demands of state citizens and interests for the government to do more about a wider range of concerns. Most recently, in the face of a reduced federal domestic effort, governors have worked to lessen or cushion the impact of federal cutbacks, unfunded federal mandates, and the devolution of federal programs down the federal system on their states and citizens. Why? The consequences of such cutbacks and programmatic shifts often land on their own desks as problems to be solved.

During the past few decades, governors have taken several significant steps to enhance their intergovernmental role. One was the establishment of a joint gubernatorial presence in Washington in the form of the National Governors Association (NGA). By the mid-1980s the NGA was considered one of the major public interest associations on Capitol Hill, with a lobbying, research, and state service staff of ninety—a marked increase from its staff of three in the late 1960s (Weissert 1983, 52). It is ironic to note that governors and other state officials had to increase their representation on Capitol Hill as it became increasingly clear that state congressional delegations often did not have the state government's overall interest in mind as they passed budgets and policy initiatives. So the states joined the crowd of interest groups pressing their needs on their own states' representatives.

Gubernatorial relations with a state's congressional delegation are complex and subject to different types of difficulties. At the purely political level, a governor can be seen as a potential challenger for a U.S. senator's seat or even a congressional seat, and we have seen that more members of Congress are eyeing gubernatorial chairs. On policy matters, a governor may have interests in particular issues for his or her own state or for states in general. Congressional delegation members also have interests of a national, specific, or constituent nature that may or may not coincide with the governor's expressed interests. Therefore, the degree of cooperation between these two sets of political actors can vary greatly; some governors find their delegations remote, inaccessible, and suspicious of any joint venture, and others find camaraderie.

But in politics changes can occur almost without warning. Following the election of 1994, the partisan ratio of the governors who are the constituency and bosses of the NGA shifted from a long period of Democratic dominance to Republican dominance. Ray Scheppach, the executive director of the NGA, indicated that "when you get a two-thirds change in your membership after an election, it changes things dramatically" (Mahtesian 1997, 24). The NGA staff, long attuned to working with the federal agencies to increase federal programs and largess to the states, suddenly found themselves being directed by a strong majority of governors wanting less government. It was an ideological shift of considerable proportions.

Suddenly the common cause of all governors represented by the NGA was shaken deeply as governors took a different look at their joint organization and its goals. Scheppach observed that "(s)ome Democrats think we're conservatives and some Republicans think we're liberals" (quoted in Mahtesian 1997, 24). And as already noted, some of the longer-serving Republican governors began working directly with the new Republican congressional leadership on major policy concerns, leaving the NGA—and the Democratic governors—shut out of the negotiations. Republican governor Fob James of Alabama decided to leave the NGA with its $100,000 annual dues because it "is useless, irrelevant and ideologically out of sync with the Republican ideal of smaller government" (Mahtesian 1997, 23).

In recent years a new factor entered the politics of intergovernmental relations. Longer tenure is important in the governor's intergovernmental role. The relations need time to mature, and the activities undertaken are complex and require time to be effective. Furthermore, leadership in intergovernmental organizations provides a platform for views to be made known and the opportunity for governors actually to affect policy. Term limitations, therefore, restrict governors in their ability to fulfill this intergovernmental role, especially in holding leadership positions. Thus states may be shortchanging themselves by limiting the tenure they allow their governors (Grady 1987). As one observer suggested, "Our state changes the team captain and key players just about the time we get the opportunity and know-how to carry the ball and score" (Farb 1977, 18). If the movement to limit terms of public officials grows and succeeds, this particular role of governors may also be curtailed.

*Working with the Media*

Probably the most significant source of informal power available to governors is their relationship with the public through the media and through other modes of contact. Most of the governors used media contact with the people to gain election to office, so they are well aware of the potency of this informal power. However, once in office the governor's relationship with the press undergoes a subtle yet important change. The governor is no longer the head of the army of attack but is the head of the army of occupation, the new administration in the state capital.

Although the media's attention to state government and its activities has waned in recent years, the media still watches the governor with a keen eye, often evaluating his or her performance not only against the promises but against previous gubernatorial efforts and the needs of the state. Furthermore, the media can suddenly become very interested in the activities and conduct of some of those whom the governor has brought into the administration. Stories of official misconduct sell newspapers and make the evening news more exciting—or so many in the media believe.

Governors have the opportunity to dominate the news from the state capital by carefully planning when press conferences are held during the day and when press releases are distributed. If they time it right, their story is on the evening television news programs and in the morning papers, where there are larger audiences to reach. A governor's communications or press relations office can in large part determine a portion of the news the citizens of a state receive about a gubernatorial administration.

Governors do vary, however, in their approach to and openness with the media. Some hold press conferences routinely and others hold them only on specific occasions. Individual interview sessions with members of the press are regular fare for some governors, whereas others are more protective of their time and interactions with the media.

The advice provided new governors by incumbents indicates just how sensitive they are to this relationship: "The media expects you to do well. Thus, doing well isn't news." "When you hold a press conference and are going to face the lions, have some red meat to throw them or they'll chew on you." "Never make policy at a news conference." And "Never argue with a person who buys ink by the barrel" (Beyle and Huefner 1983, 268).

How well do governors actually do in this relationship? Do the new governors heed the advice of their more experienced peers? Are they able to make that switch from campaigner to governor in a manner that helps to continue their relationship with the media, voters, and other constituencies? Obviously the answer is that it varies by individual governor. But governors seeking reelection can ill afford poor media relations, which are hard to overcome. After all, the media is one of the primary vehicles by which voters get a reading on how their governor is performing.

Another part of a governor's public role is primarily reactive. The governor's office receives many letters, visits, and telephone calls, each with a request, a critical comment, or question of some kind. Most of these must be answered. Each response probably affects two to five people among the extended family and friends of the recipient. Thus the number of direct or indirect contacts between the governor or governor's staff and the public is very high. How well the governor's office handles these letters and requests can become an important part of the public's perception of the governor's performance.

Some governors take an activist stance with regard to the public and generate citizen contacts through a variety of approaches. Some capitalize on their ceremonial role by appearing at county fairs, cutting ribbons at shopping centers, attending dedication ceremonies, and crowning beauty queens. These activities often can require a considerable investment of time.

Not the least of a governor's relations with the media and their statewide constituency is responding to an emergency situation. This can range from calling out the National Guard to helping maintain control when a disaster such as an earthquake, hurricane, or tornado has occurred. It is clear that when the governor makes a personal visit to the site of a disaster to see the damage and talk with the people who have suffered in the calamity it is a necessary step to be taken—and one that can also reap political rewards. In fact, it is probably a liability for any governor to fail to appear under such circumstances.

The governor, through this public role, has the potential to set the state's public agenda and focus attention on it. A governor's priorities can become the state's priorities unless unforeseen crises or problems arise or the media itself is inadequate to the task.

*Priorities on the Job: The Personal Factor*

Being governor is a time-consuming and busy undertaking. Many who have been governors or served with governors find that discussions and analyses of gubernatorial roles, power, and responsibilities do not provide the sense of what being a governor really means. In an attempt to capture the pace of a governor's life and show how time, or lack of time, affects gubernatorial actions, the NGA developed a case study called "A Day in the Life of a Governor" for newly elected governors (Beyle and Muchmore 1983, 32–42). That case cannot be recreated here, but based on a survey of those who scheduled gubernatorial time and from the estimates of sixteen incumbent governors, some indication can be given about where they spend their time (Beyle and Muchmore 1983, 52–66). And time "is one of the Governor's scarcest and most valuable resources" (NGA 1990c, 1).

Both governors and their schedulers basically agreed on how much time was allocated to the various roles a governor performs. Including recruiting and appointing personnel to positions in the executive branch, half their time was taken up just in running state government and working with the legislature. Another large segment of time was spent in their public roles, either directly interacting with the public, participating in ceremonial functions, or indirectly working with the media. Their schedulers estimated that more than one-third of the schedule was devoted to these public roles; the governors had a lower estimate of one-fifth of their time. The governors' intergovernmental activities, divided equally between federal and local governmental issues, took up slightly more than one-eighth of their time (Beyle and Muchmore 1983, 52–66).

In sum, we find what most of us would hope to find—governors serving primarily as chief executives and working with the legislature, relegating their public roles to second place, and giving their intergovernmental concerns less but not inconsiderable attention. They spend less time on politics by these estimates, although much that is politics is present in ceremonial, legislative, and other activities.

What gets squeezed in these official priorities is the governor as a person and his or her ability to maintain some semblance of a private life. As the NGA case study suggests, a governor in those few, short moments of reflection when alone with family "may find that his campaign did not result in his capturing the office, but in the office capturing him" (NGA 1978, 115). Nearly half of the fifty-one former governors responding to a 1976 NGA survey cited interference with their family life when asked what they considered the most difficult aspects of being governor. Being governor exacts a personal toll on the individual (Beyle and Muchmore 1983, 23–27).

## LEAVING THE GOVERNORSHIP

Former Vermont governor Kunin suggested that "[t]here are two climaxes in political life: rising to power and falling from it" (Kunin 1994, 19). At the end of a gubernatorial term, a governor usually has several options available for the future. Many can and do choose to seek reelection to the governor's chair. In recent decades we have seen some governors virtually turn a gubernatorial chair into their own private property as they served for several terms. Although seeking reelection as an incumbent usually provides a major campaign advantage, winning reelection (sometimes renomination) is not always an easy task, as was noted earlier.

### The Unplanned Departure

Why do incumbent governors lose? In a few situations a single issue can be pinpointed as the cause of a governor's defeat, and that issue may be something that the governor has little control over, such as a souring economy. In other cases, a defeat is the result of an accumulation of several issues and concerns about the governor's administration. Scandals and incompetence—administrative, political, or personal—are also significant factors in the defeat of an incumbent governor.

There have been situations in which incumbents just overstayed their welcome and were blocking others from the office; or the voters in the party primary or general election wanted someone new in the office. And as we have watched the Republican resurgence across the nation and in the South specifically, changing politics and voter preferences can be the cause.

Between 1970 and 2002, there were 466 separate gubernatorial elections, and 275 incumbent governors sought reelection to another term. Although most of these incumbents won (78 percent), 67 of them did lose: 15 in their own party primary and 52 in the general election. Several governors have not had the luxury to seek reelection as they were removed from office by a criminal court decision or impeachment (or the threat of it).

In sum, governors seeking to stay in office, or to regain office, are vulnerable to the ambitions of others within their party and the state; to a desire on the part of voters for a change to someone new; to issues directly affecting the electorate's wallets (taxation) or lives (jobs, the economy, the environment); and to allegations of misconduct or poor performance.

### Onward and Upward

Staying in office is only one of several options that an incumbent governor may weigh. As already noted, for some governors the position is one step on a ladder that they hope leads to a higher office, such as the U.S. Senate or even the presidency—four of our past five presidents had been governors—Jimmy Carter, Ronald Reagan, Bill Clinton and George W. Bush.

Some move on to appointed national-level positions, such as cabinet offices, as Health and Human Resources Secretary Tommy Thompson (R-Wis., 1986–2001), Director of the Environmental Protection Agency Christie Whitman (R-N.J., 1994–2001) and Director of the Office of Homeland Security Tom Ridge (R-Penn., 1995–2002) did in the G. W. Bush administration. Two New Hampshire governors became the president's chief of staff: Sherman Adams (R, 1949–1953) for Dwight Eisenhower and John Sununu (R, 1983–1988) for George H. W. Bush. Why did New Hampshire governors do so well in these presidential administrations? The early New Hampshire presidential primary is crucial to the presidential nomination process, and winning candidates remember the help given them by the governor.

Some other governors move into leadership positions in the corporate world or in higher education: former North Carolina governor Terry Sanford (D, 1961–1965) became president of Duke University; former Tennessee governor Lamar Alexander became president of the University of Tennessee; and former New Jersey governor Tom Kean became president of Drew University. However, we must be impressed most with the large number of governors for whom the governorship was their ultimate elected public office. They sought the office, served, and returned to their private lives—often to a lucrative law practice that may have included representing clients before the state legislature, state agencies, or state courts. Unfortunately, some governors were prosecuted for their misconduct while in office or prior to becoming governor, and some later served terms in prison.

*Leaving*

Most governors enjoy a satisfying life after their tenures as governor. But as former Michigan governor William Milliken (R, 1969–1983) observed, they must take pains in planning their departure and "take advantage of the lessons learned by those who have already gone down the path." This means taking steps to prepare for the new administration while winding down the old and preparing for their own new life (Weeks 1984, 77). The NGA has developed a "worst case scenario" to alert them to what can happen without such planning and suggest some strategies to follow to avert such problems (NGA 1990a).

This sounds most rational, but in the white heat of politics, and especially in the worst of all situations—being unseated as governor—these steps are not easy to take, nor does there seem to be enough time to plan them. Although states generally make provisions for their incoming governors, they tend to ignore their outgoing governors. The exiting governors suddenly lose all the perquisites of being governor: staff, cars, drivers, schedulers, office equipment, telephones, and so forth. This is seen in the lament of former governor Calvin L. Rampton (D-Utah, 1965–1977): "I never realized how much of a man's life he spends looking for a parking place" (quoted in Weeks 1984, 73).

CONCLUSION

The American state governorship is the highest elective office in a state and, in some cases, the stepping stone to an even higher office. The governor symbolizes the state to many, and when state government falters or errs, the public often holds the governor accountable. The states have refurbished their governments, bidding "Goodbye to Goodtime Charlie," and in doing so have generally obtained a new breed of very capable people to serve as governor (Sabato 1978). But there are signals that although there are few "Goodtime Charlies," there are still a few who have lost their moral or ethical compass either in seeking or in holding the office.

This chapter has provided a view of the governorship through the eyes of the governors themselves and of those who watch what governors do. In it we have looked at the politics of becoming governor, the tools available to the governor—both personal and institutional—the major roles now being performed by governors, and how, in performing these roles, governors have informal powers of considerable magnitude. Governors not only sit atop the state governments and the state political system, but through their informal powers, they can set and dominate the state's policy agenda and have an impact on regional and national agendas as well.

REFERENCES

Alexander, Lamar. 1986. *Steps Along the Way: A Governor's Scrapbook*. Nashville, Tenn.: Thomas Nelson.

Benjamin, Gerald. 1982. "The Diffusion of the Governor's Veto Power." *State Government* 55: 99–105.

Beyle, Thad L. 1998. "Reading the Tea Leaves?" *State Government News* 41(8): 26–30.

———. 1996. "Governors: The Middlemen and Women in Our Political System." In *Politics in the American States*, 6th ed., edited by Virginia Gray and Herbert Jacob. Washington, D.C.: CQ Press.

———. 1995. "Enhancing Executive Leadership in the States." *State and Local Government Review* 27(1): 18–35.

———. 1992a. *Governors and Hard Times*. Washington, D.C.: CQ Press.

———. 1992b. "Term Limits in the State Executive Branch." In *Limiting Legislative Terms*, edited by Gerald Benjamin and Michael Malbin. Washington, D.C.: CQ Press.

———. 1988. "The Governor as Innovator in the Federal System." *Publius* 18(3): 131–152.

Beyle, Thad, and Ferrel Guillory. 2002. "Follow the Money: Campaign Spending in Governor's Race 2000." *North Carolina DataNet* No. 30 (March): 1–2.

Beyle, Thad L., and Robert Huefner. 1983. "Quips and Quotes from Old Governors to New." *Public Administration Review* 43: 268–270.

Beyle, Thad, and Rich Jones. 1994. "Term Limits in the States." In *The Book of the States, 1994–1995*. Lexington, Ky.: Council of State Governments.

Beyle, Thad L., and Lynn Muchmore. 1983. *Being Governor: The View from the Office*. Durham, N.C.: Duke University Press.

Cauchon, Dennis. 2003. "GOP Outspends Democrats in States." *USA Today*, May 19, 1A.

CSG (Council of State Governments). 2002. *The Book of the States, 2002*. Lexington, Ky.: Council of State Governments.

———. 2000. *The Book of the States, 2000–2001*. Lexington, Ky.: Council of State Governments.

———. 1996. *The Book of the States, 1996–1997*. Lexington, Ky.: Council of State Governments.

———. 1994. *The Book of the States, 1994–1995*. Lexington, Ky.: Council of State Governments.

———. 1992. *The Book of the States, 1992–1993*. Lexington, Ky.: Council of State Governments.

English, Arthur. 1997. "The Political Style of Jim Guy Tucker." *Comparative State Politics* 18(2) (April): 18–28.

Farb, Robert L. 1977. *Report on the Proposed Gubernatorial Succession Amendment, 1977.* Chapel Hill, N.C.: Institute of Government.

Farney, Dennis. 1993. "When Wisconsin Governor Wields Partial Veto, the Legislature Might as Well Go Play Scrabble." *Wall Street Journal,* July 1, A16.

Flentje, H. Edward. 1980. *Knowledge and Gubernatorial Policy Making.* Wichita, Kansas: Center for Urban Studies, Wichita State University.

Grady, Dennis. 1987. "Gubernatorial Behavior in State-Federal Relations." *Western Political Quarterly* 40: 305–318.

Hovey, Kendra A., and Harold A. Hovey. 2003. *CQ's State Fact Finder, 2003.* Washington, D.C.: CQ Press.

Hutchison, Tony. 1989. "Legislating via Veto." *State Legislatures* 18 (January): 20–22.

Kaufman, Herbert. 1963. *Politics and Policies in State and Local Governments.* Englewood Cliffs, N.J.: Prentice-Hall.

Key, V.O., Jr. 1956. *American State Politics.* New York: Knopf.

Kunin, Madeleine. 1994. *Living a Political Life.* New York: Knopf.

Mahtesian, Charles. 1997. "Ganging up on the Governors." *Governing* (August): 23–25.

Matheson, Scott M. 1986. *Out of Balance.* Salt Lake City, Utah: Peregrine Smith Books.

Moe, Ronald C. 1988. *Prospects for the Item Veto at the Federal Level: Lessons from the States.* Washington, D.C.: National Academy of Public Administration.

Morehouse, Sarah M. 1987. "Money Versus Party Effort: Nominating the Governor." Paper presented at the annual meeting of the American Political Science Association, Chicago, September 4–7.

———. 1981. *State Politics, Party, and Policy.* New York: Holt, Rinehart and Winston.

Murphy, Russell D. 1992. "Connecticut: Lowell P. Weicker, Jr.: A Maverick in 'The Land of Steady Habits.' " In *Governors in Hard Times,* edited by Thad Beyle. Washington, D.C.: CQ Press.

NASBO (National Association of State Budget Officers). 1997. *Budget Procedures in the States.* Washington, D.C.: NASBO.

NCSL (National Conference of State Legislatures). 2003. "Report on 2001 Legislative Elections." Accessed at www.ncsl.org. March 1.

———. 1998. *Limits on Authority of Legislature to Change Budget.* Denver, Colo.: NCSL.

North Carolina Center for Public Policy Research. 1989. *Report on Campaign Financing in North Carolina.* Raleigh: North Carolina Center for Public Policy Research.

NGA (National Governors Association). 1990a. "The Governor's Final Year: Challenges and Strategies." *State Management Notes.* Washington, D.C.: NGA.

———. 1990b. "Organizing the Transition Team." *State Management Notes.* Washington, D.C.: NGA.

———. 1990c. "Use of the Governor's Time." *Management Brief.* Washington, D.C.: NGA.

———. 1987. "The Institutional Powers of the Governorship, 1965–1985." *State Management Notes.* Washington, D.C.: NGA.

———. 1981. *Reflections on Being Governor.* Washington, D.C.: NGA.

———. 1978. *Governing the American States.* Washington, D.C.: NGA.

Ransone, Coleman B. 1956. *The Office of Governor in the United States.* Tuscaloosa, Ala.: University of Alabama Press.

Robinson, Julia E. 1998. "The Role of the Independent Political Executive in State Governance: Stability in the Face of Change." *Public Administration Review* 58(2): 119–128.

Sabato, Larry. 1983. *Goodbye to Good-Time Charlie: The American Governorship Transformed.* 2d ed. Washington, D.C.: CQ Press.

———. 1978. *Goodbye to Good-Time Charlie: The American Governorship Transformed.* Lexington, Mass.: Lexington Books.

Schlesinger, Joseph A. 1971. "The Politics of the Executive." In *Politics in the American States ,* 2d ed., edited by Herbert Jacob and Kenneth N. Vines. Boston: Little, Brown.

———. 1966. *Ambition and Politics: Political Careers in the United States.* Chicago: Rand McNally.

————. 1965. "The Politics of the Executive." In *Politics in the American States*, edited by Herbert Jacob and Kenneth N. Vines. Boston: Little, Brown.

Sherman, Sharon. 1984. "Powersplit: When Legislatures and Governors Are of Opposing Parties." *State Legislatures* 10(5): 9–12.

Van Assendelft, Laura A. 1997. *Governors, Agenda Setting, and Divided Government*. Lanham, Md.: University Press of America.

Weeks, George. 1984. "Gubernatorial Transitions: Leaving There." *State Government* 57(3): 73–78.

Weissert, Carol S. 1983. "The National Governors' Association: 1908–1983." *State Government* 56(3): 44–52.

Wiggins, Charles W. 1980. "Executive Vetoes and Legislative Overrides in the American States." *Journal of Politics* 42: 1110–1117.

## SUGGESTED READINGS

Beyle, Thad L., ed. *Governors in Hard Times*. Washington, D.C.: CQ Press, 1992. A multi-authored, ten-state set of case studies on how the governors of those states coped with the economic downturn of the late 1980s/early 1990s, with some lessons learned that could be useful in our current economic situation.

Herzik, Eric B., and Brent W. Brown, eds. *Gubernatorial Leadership and State Policy*. Westport, Conn.: Greenwood Press, 1991. A multi-authored book focusing on the governors' policy roles. Case studies focus on both the policy processes around the governor and specific policy areas that concern governors.

Hovey, Kendra A., and Harold A. Hovey. *CQ's State Fact Finder, 2003*. Washington, D.C.: CQ Press, 2003. An annual compendium of a wide range of demographic, economic, governmental, political, and policy data on the fifty states presented in several different ways for the reader to use.

Thompson, Tommy G. *Power to the People: An American State at Work*. New York: Harper Collins, 1996. The longest serving governor's perspective on his administration and successes.

Van Assendelft, Laura A. *Governors, Agenda Setting, and Divided Government*. Lanham, Md.: University Press of America, 1997. A four-state case study of the problems governors have in setting and achieving their policy agendas when there is divided partisan control of government.

# CHAPTER 8

*Courts: Politics and the Judicial Process*

HENRY R. GLICK

Courts rarely come to mind when people think about state politics. Most judicial elections are invisible, and we expect courts to be governed by law and to avoid partisanship. Rather than analysis, most news reports entertain us with lurid crimes, jury trials, or occasional "ridiculous" lawsuits. But state courts frequently decide cases that are of equal or even greater consequence to our everyday lives than the policies of legislatures and governors. Courts render decisions involving the death penalty and sentencing laws, the liability of tobacco companies for cigarette-caused illnesses, taxation and spending on public education, regulation of businesses, professions and labor unions, employment discrimination, abortion, child custody and support and grandparents' visitation rights, the rights of individuals to end life-prolonging medical treatment, the rights of crime victims, gay and lesbian marriages and claims for public and employee benefits, the rights of biological and adoptive parents and more.

Courts also rule on the political process, weighing in on disputed elections, term limits, conflicts among government agencies, removal of corrupt officials, the wording of state constitutional amendments, and other issues. In the 2000 presidential election, when Florida ballot recounts were crucial, the Florida Supreme Court twice made decisions—overturned by the U.S. Supreme Court—that probably would have tipped the election to Democrat Al Gore rather than Republican George Bush.

The policy-making importance of state courts is growing because the U.S. Supreme Court recently has limited the power of the federal government to require the states to take on new administrative responsibilities or enforce federal regulations, and the

Court has curtailed the federal government in policies that traditionally have been the responsibilities of the states, including public education, crime and handgun control, employment discrimination, aspects of religion, and others. Some litigants probably will have to rely on state law and state courts to press claims that previously were heard in the federal courts. The states also pay a growing share of the cost of domestic policy and draw on state taxes rather than federal grants-in-aid to fund programs. State courts become the arbiters of disputes over these policies, which leads interest groups, political parties, and politicians to pay increasing attention to courts.

State courts also make millions of less visible decisions annually that settle the problems and disputes that most people are likely to encounter, such as divorce, traffic accidents and personal injury, and crime. Since courts often make similar rulings in like cases, numerous repeated decisions add up to policies for managing many common social problems.

## DUAL IMAGES OF COURTS: LEGAL AND POPULAR POLITICAL CULTURE

*Culture* refers to basic values and beliefs and expectations that people hold about social institutions. Our views of courts are ruled by two seemingly incompatible images: legal and popular political culture (Richardson and Vines 1970).

### Legal Culture

Legal culture maintains that courts *ought* to be separated from partisan politics and personality as much as possible and that "equal justice under law," not politics, should govern judicial decisions. Persons (litigants) have the right to a trial and to one appeal. In trials, attorneys for each side lay out competing views of the facts by closely questioning their own and opposing witnesses, and a judge or jury "renders a verdict," determining guilt or innocence in a criminal case or liability and costs in a civil case, such as a disputed auto accident. Appeals allow for no witnesses and rarely any discussion of the facts. Instead, attorneys for each side submit written presentations (briefs) and often have a little time to orally summarize their position on the law and proper trial procedure. Judges behave as neutral umpires unaffected by their own beliefs or public opinion, and they refrain from using cases as opportunities to expand the law or insert the courts into policy making.

To ensure that judges are neutral and keep to the law, legal culture maintains that we must carefully select the best qualified judges based on quality education and achievement, significant prior legal and judicial experience and knowledge, and possession of personal fairness and a calm judicial temperament.

In sum, the legal culture underscores the need to remove and insulate courts from the political and policy-making process. Legal culture affects the way that courts are organized, their procedures, assumptions about the proper way to select judges, law-based decision making, and views on the proper scope of judicial decisions.

*Popular Political Culture*

Legal culture distinguishes courts from other governmental institutions, but it overlooks how courts also are affected by state and local politics and that law itself guarantees that politics affects courts. Besides judicial elections, state and local politics affect court organization. Elected state legislatures, state constitutional conventions, and popular referenda all are used to create new courts or to modify older ones, and determine the kinds of cases courts may hear. The social and economic context in which courts are embedded also affects opportunities they have to decide cases. For example, courts in big cities decide many more cases involving big businesses and corporations and more serious cases of crime than courts in rural areas, and appellate courts in populous, urban states face many more controversial cases containing novel issues. Finally, the influence of state and local politics is paramount because nearly all state court cases begin and end in the states. State supreme courts decide about 90,000 cases annually, but U.S. Supreme Court review occurs in fewer than 1 percent of them.

Judges and courts also are linked to state politics through law, which seems like a contradiction, but there are many sources of law and no two cases are identical, so trial and appellate judges always have leeway to interpret and apply law in particular cases. Most trials are held before judges alone (bench trials), so they determine the facts *and* apply the law. In jury trials, juries decide the facts and judges instruct the jury on applying the law. Fact finding seems straightforward, but there are many facts that might be relevant. For example, a father who does not pay required child support states that he cannot find a job, is partially disabled, and has other financial responsibilities. But the other side asks how hard he has looked for a job; has he refused jobs; does he drink alcohol or take drugs. In addition, the judge asks if the father owns a car or has money in his wallet.

Connecting facts to law appears easy, especially because judges usually give juries limited options to decide what crime has been committed (for example, first- or second-degree murder or manslaughter), but juries often consider whether applying the law would be fair in their particular case, and jury nullification—deciding to acquit defendants or convict on lesser charges, despite a cold reading of the facts and the law—is fairly common. Sometimes, despite clear evidence, juries have acquitted police and prison guards of beating blacks or prisoners, and other juries have freed political protestors and drug users. Therefore, law and facts become mixed together to produce distinctive brands of local, popular justice (Abramson 1994).

Losers in the trial courts may ask appellate courts to review decisions for legal errors. Review may involve four main bodies of law: previous court decisions (precedents), also known as common law; legislative law (state statutes and city and county ordinances); administrative rules of various government agencies; and state and federal constitutions.

But problems develop quickly in using these sources of law. Regarding precedents, judges may choose among recent or old cases, cases from their own or other states, cases in which similar facts or legal principles seem most compelling, or they may reject all precedents and impose their own judgment.

Relying on the intentions of a legislature or the writers of an amendment to a state constitution is equally confounding because legislators often do not agree on a single clear intent, or they mask their intent in lofty, general rhetoric to avoid political controversy and opposition. Some laws intentionally allow judges to make choices, such as state criminal codes that provide a range of sentences that can be imposed in each case according to the facts and defendants' history and prospects. Therefore, sentences for similar crimes vary within and among states.

Constitutions are the most general sources of law. The U.S. Constitution is a short document filled with broad, general principles and rights that courts have interpreted differently since the nation's early history. State constitutions are much longer and more specific. In addition to outlining the structure and basic powers of state governments, they impose precise limitations on state legislatures regarding, for example, taxation, regulation of businesses, powers of local governments, as well as individual rights that are not mentioned in the national constitution, such as a right to privacy and gender equality. State constitutions would appear to be concrete guides for state courts, but provisions frequently become outdated, and many amendments added over the years sometimes are inconsistent and contradictory, which gives state courts great powers of interpretation and law making (Tarr 1997).

These many sources of law and their different possible meanings make it inevitable that courts have substantial leeway or discretion to select and interpret law. In turn, discretion guarantees, first, that judges on many state supreme courts disagree on decisions, leading them to produce a binding majority decision as well as dissenting votes and opinions cast by those who come to the opposite conclusion. Second, discretion guarantees that the states have different judicial policies regarding similar issues. State supreme courts currently disagree on the many important and sensitive public policies discussed earlier. The discretion to fit facts to law and to choose, interpret, or create new law means that many forces other than formal law—in other words, politics—are at work in the courts.

## COURT ORGANIZATION

Unlike the legislature and the governor's office, there are many state courts with authority to hear different cases. They are arranged in levels or a hierarchy from the highest appellate to the lowest trial courts and are distributed throughout a state.

### Types of Courts

Most of the states have four types of courts at different levels. At the top of the hierarchy are state supreme courts located in the capital city. Intermediate courts of appeal are located in the capital or are composed of several regional divisions. And at the local level there exist one or two trial courts of general (major) jurisdiction and one or more trial courts of limited (specialized) jurisdiction. Appeals from trial courts of limited jurisdiction get a new trial in a trial court of general ju-

**Figure 8-1**   Florida Court System

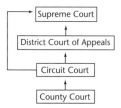

SOURCE: Derived from *State Court Caseload Statistics* 2001.
Williamsburg, Va.: National Center for State Courts.

risdiction, and appeals from trial courts of general jurisdiction go to intermediate appellate courts or state supreme courts, depending on the subject of the case. A single judge presides over a trial court, intermediate appellate courts generally are composed of three or more judges, and state supreme courts have from five to nine members.

Each state has its own distinctive set of courts. A few states have two intermediate appellate courts rather than one, and Texas and Oklahoma each have two supreme courts, one for criminal and another for civil cases. Populous, urban states frequently have hundreds of trial and dozens of intermediate appellate court judges. In contrast, a dozen less populous states in New England and the northern plains do not have intermediate appellate courts, so supreme courts hear all appeals in these states. Not only does structure vary, similar courts often have different names.

Court systems range from very simple and streamlined sets of a few courts to very complex and confusing arrangements of many courts. Consider the differences between the Florida and Indiana court systems (Figures 8-1 and 8-2). Florida has a few courts at each level and clear avenues of appeal. Indiana's complicated system includes two types of trial courts of general jurisdiction (superior and circuit) and six trial courts of limited jurisdiction, including a special tax court, all with various avenues of appeal. More states are moving toward more simplified systems, as in Florida.

It is difficult to account fully for why certain states have complex or simple court systems. State size matters, but probably equally or more important is partisan and interest group conflict leading to political deadlock. First, lawyers in many states divide into two general camps: plaintiffs' lawyers (often Democrats) who represent individuals who sue insurance companies, hospitals, and other businesses and organizations for injuries or other damages, and defendants' lawyers (often Republicans) who defend these organizations from lawsuits. Defendants' lawyers and their business clients generally believe that reorganized courts are more efficient, easier to use, and achieve a better public image. But many plaintiffs' lawyers resist change because the lawyers find an advantage in knowing how a complex court system works. Appellate judges also tend to prefer streamlined systems, but local court workers and trial judges frequently are satisfied with courts and their jobs as they are. Efforts to change court structure sometimes have been tied to proposed changes in judicial selection, but local politicians usually are wary about giving up their influence in electing or appointing judges, so comprehensive court reform proposals do not gain acceptance. New York state, for example, has one of the most

**Figure 8-2**   Indiana Court System

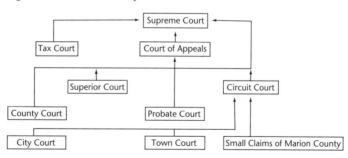

SOURCE: Derived from *State Court Caseload Statistics* 2001. Williamsburg, Va.: National Center for State Courts.

complicated court systems in the country, and political battles have been fought for decades to simplify it.

*Jurisdiction*

Jurisdiction refers to district boundaries and the subject matter of cases that courts are permitted by state law to hear. State supreme courts have authority over an entire state, and intermediate appellate courts may cover a state, or several identical courts hearing cases from a particular region. Trial court districts may include a single city or county or a few counties in rural parts of a state. Subject matter jurisdiction is more complex. Cases are either criminal or civil matters. Criminal cases involve a violation of state law punishable by a fine payable to the government or imprisonment. Civil cases concern all other disputes. They sometimes involve individuals or groups versus government, as in government regulation of particular businesses or professions, but most civil cases are conflicts between private parties involving traffic accidents, divorces, contract disputes, property and landlord–tenant disputes, personal injury, inheritance, and others.

Trial courts of general jurisdiction hear cases involving the most serious crimes (felonies) and civil disputes involving large amounts of money—for example, $15,000 or more. Minor criminal offenses (misdemeanors), such as traffic violations and public drunkenness, and smaller civil disputes, for instance landlord-tenant conflicts and complaints against businesses regarding poor service or products, go into one or more specialized trial courts of limited jurisdiction, such as small claims or county court.

States frequently create or eliminate courts with specialized jurisdiction in response to political demands for new solutions to social problems. For example, spurred by federal grants-in-aid and innovative policies, various states have created special urban drug and mental health courts that impose probation and rehabilitation and therapy rather than incarceration on defendants facing minor charges and with few or no previous convictions. Also, faced with economic recessions and budget cutbacks, states occasionally eliminate courts or consolidate judicial districts.

Appellate courts also have varying jurisdictions. In thirty-nine states with intermediate appellate courts the supreme courts have considerable discretion or latitude to decide for themselves which cases to hear, although they have some mandatory jurisdiction as well—for example, over all death penalty appeals and complaints that require disciplining attorneys or other judges. Generally, state supreme courts with intermediate appellate courts below decide criminal cases carrying the most severe penalties, civil cases involving the greatest amounts of money, and appeals from government agencies. Two-thirds of their cases come via discretionary jurisdiction, but supreme courts turn down 90 percent or more of requests for hearings. Intermediate appeals courts hear approximately two hundred thousand other appeals involving divorce judgments, criminal cases carrying sentences of a few years in prison, and smaller financial claims.

Important consequences flow from the organization and powers of state courts. Complex court systems frequently have confusing overlapping jurisdictions, which means that more than one type of court may hear the same case. This may encourage court shopping for the best predicted outcome.

But the most important political impact of court structure and jurisdiction concerns the policy-making role of state supreme courts. Reducing the types of cases that supreme courts are required to hear frees them to select cases they believe are the most important, and the judges acquire the time to evaluate legal arguments and write opinions that explain the interpretation and direction that the court gives to the law—in other words, they can make judicial policy. Since the U.S. Supreme Court decides very few cases, state supreme courts have the final word in nearly every important conflict they are asked to decide. Therefore, state supreme courts are becoming more and more important policy-making institutions.

### SELECTING STATE JUDGES

Because state courts, especially supreme courts, have increasing opportunities to make policy, determining who becomes judges also is becoming more important. Except for the occasional drama that surrounds the selection of a new justice for the U.S. Supreme Court, most Americans pay little attention to how lawyers become judges. But the stakes are very high. There are nearly thirty thousand trial appellate court positions in the fifty states, and many pay annual salaries close to $100,000 or more. There is no lack of qualified applicants for these secure and prestigious jobs.

Representing the legal culture, most judges, bar association leaders, and elite lawyers believe that judges ought to be chosen for their legal skills and distance from partisan politics. They prefer merit selection, which provides lawyers and judges special influence in choosing new judges. However, many politicians and various interest groups believe that judicial selection is precisely the place where the

**Table 8-1** Judicial Selection in the Fifty States

| Partisan election | Nonpartisan election | Gubernatorial appointment | Legislative appointment | Merit selection (Missouri plan) |
|---|---|---|---|---|
| *All or most judgeships* | | | | |
| Alabama | Florida | California | Connecticut | Arizona |
| Arkansas | Georgia | Maine | South Carolina | Alaska |
| Illinois | Idaho | New Hampshire | Virginia | Colorado |
| New York | Kentucky | New Jersey | | Delaware |
| North Carolina | Louisiana | | | Hawaii |
| Pennsylvania | Michigan | | | Indiana |
| Tennessee | Minnesota | | | Iowa |
| Texas | Mississippi | | | Kansas |
| West Virginia | Montana | | | Maryland |
| | Nevada | | | Massachusetts |
| | North Dakota | | | Missouri |
| | Ohio | | | Nebraska |
| | Oklahoma | | | New Mexico |
| | Oregon | | | Rhode Island |
| | South Dakota | | | Utah |
| | Washington | | | Vermont |
| | Wisconsin | | | Wyoming |
| *Some judgeships* | | | | |
| Connecticut | Arizona | Montana | Rhode Island | Florida |
| Georgia | California | New York | | New York |
| Indiana | | North Carolina | | Oklahoma |
| Maine | | | | South Dakota |
| Missouri | | | | Tennessee |
| South Carolina | | | | |

S O U R C E:   Derived from Table 4.4 of Council of State Governments 2000.

popular political culture should apply: because judges' personal values or attitudes influence decisions and judicial selection has policy-making implications, judges ought to be held directly accountable to the people through elections.

The fifty states use five methods to select judges. They are *partisan election, nonpartisan election, gubernatorial appointment, legislative appointment,* and *merit selection* (also known as the *Missouri Plan* after the first state that adopted it more than a half century ago). Table 8-1 presents the methods of selection generally used in the fifty states. The choice of a particular method has followed broader political trends throughout U.S. history. In the 1800s partisan election became popular as democratic ideals spread, but in reaction to political corruption, nonpartisan elections for many offices, including courts, became popular in the early twentieth century. Recently, merit selection has become prominent as part of the effort to make courts more professional and removed from politics. Because each method emphasizes different ideals and goals, we might expect them to operate very differently, but the five methods have more in common than we might think.

*Judicial Elections*

About half the states use either partisan or nonpartisan elections to choose all or most of their judges. But most of these elections are uncontested, with incumbents easily winning reelection. Winning against incumbents is difficult in any election, but especially in judicial elections in which the legal culture dissuades potential challengers from campaigning against judges who are doing an adequate job. Judicial vacancies draw many candidates, but even then most campaigns are sedate and cordial. As a consequence, voting in most judicial elections is low, with turnout of 10 or 15 percent or heavy ballot fall-off when judges are elected with other officials (Dubois 1980).

An important consequence of uncontested judicial elections is that half or more "elective" judges actually are appointed initially by governors. Usually incumbents hold office term after term until they resign, often in midterm, in order to give a governor of their own political party the chance to appoint another loyal party supporter to fill the vacancy. By the next scheduled election, the appointed judge is the incumbent who faces no serious opposition.

Court reformers oppose election of judges as improper, but they also claim that elections do not fulfill their purpose of offering the voters much choice since there are so few challengers. But many other elective positions in the United States also are safe for incumbents. For example, while members of the U.S. House of Representatives are more likely than state supreme court judges to face election challengers, nearly all House members win reelection with margins of victory that are about the same as for incumbent state judges. Interestingly, from 1980 to 1995, slightly more judges than House members were defeated for reelection (Hall 2001a).

The least secure judges are those who run in partisan elections in two-party competitive states. There, judicial elections are held in November along with elections for many other offices, and each party has a good chance of winning these contests. Voters frequently take cues from party leaders and interest groups, and if the out party sweeps elections for governor, legislature, or president, incumbent judges may lose too. Judges in these states who retire sometimes do so because they sense a threatening political climate in an upcoming election (Hall 2001b).

Heavily contested judicial elections still are the exception, but the trend points toward more competition and intense political campaigns. Most contributors to judicial elections are lawyers who probably hope to maintain good rapport with sitting judges, but big business political action committees increasingly make significant contributions totaling in the millions of dollars in a single election, sometimes even to candidates who face no opposition and have no need for the money. Some large contributions have been made just before big cases involving millions of corporate dollars are to be argued before the courts. There is some evidence too that candidates raising the most money win more elections (Cheek and Champagne 2000; Eisenstein 2000).

This trend worries many who fear that big contributors can buy favorable judicial decisions, for there is a distinction between judges responding generally to broad public sentiment and making specific decisions in response to large donations. But imposing contribution limits is difficult because giving money is considered a form of free speech, and laws place few limits on contributions for issue-oriented advertising. Certain states also do not limit direct contributions to candidates.

*Legislative and Executive Appointment*

The key to winning a judicial appointment in the few states that use legislative appointment is to have been a member of the state legislature, which generally rewards its own members. Getting appointed by the governor is more complicated mainly because the governor cannot personally know everyone who might be appointed to dozens of vacant judgeships. In general, governors place members of their own political party on the courts, particularly as patronage to reward people who have contributed money or other support to political parties and campaigns or who have held other offices. Also, awarding court positions to members of particular groups—for example, women, minorities, prosecuting attorneys (law enforcement)—attracts broader political support to a politician's or political party's voting base. Governors also sometimes use appointments as trade-offs with key legislators to get support for their programs. For trial and intermediate appellate courts, governors often rely on political allies for recommendations, including legislators, mayors, and local leading lawyers and friends. For the supreme court, governors are more likely to choose lawyers they know personally. Gubernatorial appointment is more prevalent than the distribution of states in Table 8-1 suggests because, as discussed earlier, many elective judges also are appointed initially. Governors also play an important role in merit selection.

*Merit Selection*

Merit selection is the most recent innovation in choosing judges. It is designed to reduce the influence of partisan politics by having local, regional, and statewide panels of lawyers, nonlawyers and, in some states, senior judges screen and nominate several candidates for each trial and appellate court vacancy. Governors make the final choice, but they usually are limited to three nominees put forward by each selection panel. Once the governor makes an appointment, the new judge typically serves for one or a few years and then runs in a retention election in which there is no other candidate. The voters are asked only whether Judge X should remain in office. If retained, the judge serves for life or a very long term.

Lawyers are expected to play a major role in influencing panel decisions because presumably they know what it takes to be a good judge. Local bar associations sometimes organize the election of lawyers to the panels, and the lawyer members tend to come from larger partnerships and law firms. The nonlawyers are appointed by the governor and generally are business and professional people such as doctors, accountants, and teachers (Henschen, Moog, and Davis 1990).

Although merit selection is designed to protect courts from partisanship and interest group influence, the process produces outcomes that are not far different from the results of elections or appointment by the governor. First, plaintiffs' and defendants' lawyer groups work to elect allies and supporters to the nominating panels. Then, both sides tend to disagree on who would make the best judge, and group and party loyalties shape their choices. Partisanship occurs too because governors appoint nonlawyer commissioners with political and civic group experience who also are aligned with governors and their party. As a consequence, panels usually give governors lists of names that include at least one person the governor wants to appoint to the court vacancy (Watson and Downing 1969).

Because merit-appointed judges face no opposition during their retention election, almost all of them are retained by very wide vote margins (Aspin 1999). Exceptions occur when judges are involved in personal scandals or make visible and controversial court decisions, particularly when state supreme courts reverse death penalty sentences. Increases in local murder rates also tend to decrease the margin of victory in merit retention elections, and, like their partisan elected brethren, some merit judges retire prior to a retention election if the state partisan and ideological climate has shifted away from the policy positions they have taken on the supreme court (Hall 2001b).

Despite claims for the superiority of merit selection, there is no evidence that a particular method of selection makes much difference in producing judges with different personal characteristics or abilities (Glick and Emmert 1987). This probably is due to the similar influence of governors, political parties, and various groups in all selection systems. In addition, few politicians are motivated to choose unqualified people for the courts, because that would reflect badly on them. Therefore, most state judges have credible educations and relevant legal, judicial, civic, and governmental experience.

Overall, white males still hold most judicial positions, but the number of white women on state supreme courts has increased substantially from ten in 1980 to about eighty just twenty years later. Their numbers on intermediate courts of appeals have tripled from fewer than fifty in 1985 to well over 150 in 1999. Non-whites, however, have not made big gains, and their percentage of the total number of judges is slim. A few black and Hispanic women and fewer than twenty black and Hispanic males sit on state supreme courts (Hurwitz and Lanier 2001).

The number of minorities on state courts may not increase rapidly since judicial and other official support for affirmative action is weakening, and fewer minorities recently have been admitted to various law schools. In the 1990s a few states facing legal challenges created smaller election districts with black majorities to guarantee the election of black trial judges. But the U.S. Supreme Court has banned specially created majority black voting districts in which race was the only consideration, so it is less likely that black judges will be elected under these arrangements. Moreover, because appellate judges are chosen statewide or in larger districts, where blacks rarely constitute a majority, few blacks are elected. Overall, blacks and other minorities in elective states may find that their chances of getting court positions are greatest when governors make interim appointments to cement their links to minority voters.

## LAWYERS, LITIGANTS, AND INTEREST GROUPS

Courts are passive institutions, which means they do not create their own work-load but must wait for others to bring cases to them. Therefore, lawyers and their clients are crucial for determining which disputes or cases of crime get to court and how they shape the issues for judges and juries. However, all but a few cases are dropped or settled through negotiation before they reach the trial stage, which makes lawyers and litigants doubly important for determining how disputes are resolved.

### Lawyers

Except for small claims courts, where litigants might try to go it alone, lawyers are essential in the judicial process. Lawyers know the procedure and the proper legal language, and they know the clerks and judges who run the courts, the informal workaday routines for processing paperwork and the attitudes and inclinations of judges and opposing lawyers. No one else has this kind of knowledge and access.

*Law Work.* Although we usually connect lawyers with trials, most people are anxious to avert trouble, and law work consists mainly of researching law and advising clients on how to avoid expensive and time-consuming lawsuits through negotiation, clear contracts, and cooperating with government regulators. Only a tiny fraction of disputes—often only one percent—go all the way to trial.

Other lawyers work for government and have a wide variety of jobs, for example, auditing the budgeting and spending practices of state agencies, gathering and analyzing information for legislative committees, and advising university administrators. Others work for the attorney general, the state's leading lawyer, and represent the state when an agency is involved in litigation.

The most visible government attorneys are prosecutors and public defenders. The prosecutor represents "the people" or the state in criminal cases, and public defenders represent criminal defendants who are too poor to hire their own lawyers. Chief prosecutors and public defenders employ a number of lawyers as assistants who directly handle the caseload. Prosecutors have almost unlimited power to decide whether to charge a defendant and what charges to bring, negotiate guilty pleas and the terms of settlements, or go to trial. Prosecutors drop as many as a quarter or more of all cases, and about 90 percent of the remainder are settled through negotiated guilty pleas. In most cities, particular prosecutors, defense attorneys, and judges interact regularly in stable work groups, so they soon reach understandings about acceptable sentences for different types of crimes (Eisenstein and Jacob 1977). Reelection politics may influence prosecutors' decisions as well, and they sometimes seek publicity for temporary crackdowns against writers of bad checks, X-rated video shops, or they ask for the death penalty in high-profile cases.

Most criminal defendants are poor and are represented by public defenders. Some communities also use court-appointed lawyers who are paid a set fee for each case. Other defendants usually obtain a lawyer whose practice consists mostly of handling a large volume of criminal cases for modest fees. Given their large caseloads and the high odds that their clients are guilty of some violation, defense attorneys usually advise their clients to plead guilty to a negotiated settlement that will get defendants probation or shorter sentences than if they are convicted at a trial. However, public defenders go to trial when they believe their clients are innocent or face charges that do not fit the facts.

Lawyers in private (nongovernment) practice generally specialize either in business or personal law, and they opt either for law office work (research, communications, and negotiation) or a trial or appellate court practice. There is little overlap between each of these fields. However, lawyers in small towns and rural states usually cannot specialize (Curran 1986; Heinz and Laumann 1982).

There is an important link between law work and politics. Highly paid business lawyers have the most prestige because their work brings them into regular and long-term contact with wealthy, upper-class individuals, and the work avoids overt human conflict and distasteful personal problems such as divorce, crime, and injuries. These lawyers also usually have high-status backgrounds themselves, and some of them become presidents or officers of large corporations. As discussed earlier, because these lawyers are closely connected to business, they are likely to be conservatives and Republicans and allied with defendants' lawyers who represent businesses and professions in court.

Prosecuting attorneys frequently become business lawyer allies because of their shared conservative and law-and-order posture. Less prestigious are lawyers who usually earn much less and handle the personal problems of clients who need lawyers only occasionally. These lawyers often have to search for new clients to maintain a stream of income, and they are more likely than others to favor lawyer advertising to bring in new business. Personal plight lawyers represent people with modest or low incomes who sue businesses for injuries, and these lawyers are likely to be liberals and Democrats. As we have seen, divisions among lawyers affect the politics of court reorganization and judicial selection, but they also divide lawyers in state legislatures on lawyer advertising and solicitation of clients, limits on the opportunities to sue (tort reform), liability law involving manufacturers of retail goods, hospitals and nursing homes and insurers, and similar issues.

*Getting Representation.* It often seems that we have enough or even too many lawyers. The number of lawyers has greatly increased during the past four decades. In 1960 the total number of lawyers in the United States was about 286,000, or one lawyer for each 627 people. By 1997 the number of lawyers had increased to nearly 925,000, or one lawyer for each 278 people (American Bar Association files).

With so many lawyers and a variety of practitioners, it would seem that no one would have trouble finding a lawyer. But lawyers are not so widely available as one might think. First, lawyers are not distributed equally throughout the country. New York state has more than 100,000 lawyers—one for every 172 people—but Arkansas and North Dakota have approximately 6,500 and 1,300 lawyers, or one lawyer for every 373 and 474 people, respectively. Lawyers also are concentrated in large cities and state capitals. Second, few people have legal insurance, so hourly fees of $100 or much more are steep for most individuals. Also, because few people use lawyers regularly or move in business circles, they have fewer ways of finding a suitable lawyer.

The very poor have some opportunities to get free legal help through clinics supported by various law schools and local charities, but most legal aid societies are connected to the Legal Services Corporation, a nonprofit organization supported by federal, state, and local government grants-in-aid. Legal services lawyers were especially aggressive regarding public policy during the 1960s when they took on local governments and businesses to try to improve housing, working conditions, and hospital and jail conditions for the poor. Conservative congresses and Republican presidents have since reduced the program's budget and generally have been able to limit these organizations to helping the poor only in individual personal disputes. Even so, many of the poor are unaware of legal aid or are reluctant to seek help. Legal aid lawyers, especially in small towns and rural areas, also have felt pressured to get along with local business and law elites and to settle disputes without litigation (Kessler 1986; Lawrence 1990). As a consequence, both the poor and the middle class have less access to lawyers than the sheer number of lawyers would indicate.

### Litigants

Most people try to avoid litigation, so the main way that civil disputes are settled is through private negotiation, mediation, or arbitration. In successful negotiation, individuals try to put their emotions and disappointments aside and narrow their complaints to specific issues to which the other side can respond. Individuals often fare much better with lawyers than they could on their own because they have no clear idea what their injuries "are worth," or because the law on which they rely is complicated (Ross 1970).

Mediation occurs when opposing sides voluntarily ask a neutral third party to attempt to bring opponents to an agreement. Mediation is available through various volunteer and social agencies. It is informal and may cover the pertinent facts and the law as well as the personal relationship among the parties. In an effort to reduce caseloads, many courts, especially small claims and family (divorce) courts, *require* litigants to try mediation as an alternative to trial. Although the benefits to judicial administration are unclear, litigants generally are satisfied with being able to vent their feelings and with mediation's informality, and lawyers like it because mandatory mediation structures and speeds negotiations while allowing attorneys to retain control (Gordon 1999). Arbitration is more formal—like a mini-trial—and decisions of an arbitrator are legally binding. Arbitration is preferred and required by various businesses, for example, professional sports and securities sales. But individuals sometimes bridle at signing agreements containing mandatory arbitration clauses because the agreements disallow opportunities to go to court. The courts generally have upheld arbitration agreements, however.

Most individuals appear in court as defendants. Other than divorce, most civil cases involve businesses and organizations, such as banks, loan companies, hospitals, and home construction firms, filing cases against individuals to collect debts and unpaid bills. Governments file similar suits for nonpayment of taxes. When individuals file suits against other individuals, they too are generally attempting to collect debts or compensation for accidents and other property damage and contract violations.

Business plaintiffs have advantages in these cases because there usually is no doubt that the debt is owed and, unlike defendants, they have the money, lawyers, and experience necessary for using the courts. Businesses win many of their cases by default because defendants do not appear for trial. Similar problems plague some individuals who have valid financial claims against others, but who are reluctant to file cases because they are inexperienced and wary of court procedures or they cannot afford to pursue collection of relatively small amounts of money (Yngvesson and Hennessey 1975).

Criminal cases also involve particular groups of individuals. Most crimes are committed by young men: more than 80 percent of those arrested are males and about the same percentage are younger than thirty-four; nearly half are younger than twenty-four. Whites account for nearly 70 percent of those arrested, but because blacks are a small percentage of the total population they are very disproportionately represented among criminal defendants and prisoners. Most arrests are for drunk driving and public drunkenness or disorderly conduct, larceny and theft, possession of drugs, and assaults. Arrests for the most serious offenses such as murder, rape, and manslaughter are less than 1 percent of all arrests, but these crimes receive the most attention because they inflict much more damage on victims and the public psyche. Crimes involving black assailants and white victims arouse the greatest interest.

### Interest Groups in Court

In addition to individuals and particular businesses, organized groups use courts to pursue decisions that further group goals. The growing attention that interest groups give state courts also attests to the courts' policy-making importance. Lobbyists are unlikely to contact a judge about a pending case because legal culture expects judges to wall themselves off from groups and individuals who are involved in litigation, but there are other ways to exert influence.

One of the best ways to influence government policy is through the selection of decision makers. Therefore, various interest groups, particularly lawyers and businesses, try to influence judicial recruitment. As discussed earlier, they appear to be making substantial campaign contributions to various court candidates, and they undoubtedly try to get the attention of key legislators or the governor's office to influence appointments.

Influencing the courts through decision making is more complicated. Cases must be filed by those who directly have suffered some wrong or damage, which prevents groups or associations from routinely filing cases themselves. But groups sometimes look for promising cases and pay the expenses and provide lawyers to individuals whose lawsuits closely represent the group's policy designs. Examples include cases filed by citizens who object to new types of taxes, claim they have suffered discrimination in obtaining a job or getting admitted to a university program, or object to government-approved construction of radio towers, incinerators, and garbage dumps or planning for new residential subdivisions.

But the major way that groups become involved in the courts is by filing *amicus curia* or friend of the court briefs, mostly in state supreme courts. These are formal, written documents that make legal and policy arguments similar to those submitted by one or the other main litigants in a case. Judges can be expected to give the briefs some level of consideration. Cases that attract several *amicus* briefs on both sides project the real taste of interest group conflict in court.

Interest group lobbying has been important in the federal courts for many decades, but groups are becoming more active in state courts as well. Group participation as *amici* has increased since 1980, with a sharp upward trend into the 1990s (Epstein 1994). The variety of groups filing briefs also has grown. Now government and groups representing business, civil liberties and education organizations, and lawyers' associations are the most active. It appears that large, urban, socially complex states such as California, New Jersey, Illinois, and Michigan have the largest amount of interest group involvement.

### Is There Too Much Litigation?

The amount of litigation has increased sharply during the past fifty years, leading to what many have termed a "litigation explosion" and a tendency of Americans to react with lawsuits whenever they feel they have been wronged by some person, business, or public institution. In the late 1970s the total number of cases filed in the fifty states was about 67 million, increasing to about 100 million in the early 1990s, but declining recently to about 90 million. Certain states have had even steeper climbs, such as Michigan, which went from 167,000 to nearly 750,000 cases per year (*State Court Caseload Statistics*, 2001).

To some extent increases in litigation parallel population growth, but that does not explain all of it. Are Americans litigation crazy? We need to consider some other facts as well. First, rates of litigation (number of cases per 100,000 people) are not much different from rates in other industrial countries. Second, amounts of litigation vary widely among the American states and from year to year, as shown in Figure 8-3, which portrays the rates of tort (mostly personal injury) filings in eight states over twenty years. Most states experienced huge increases in litigation after World War II (not shown in Figure 8-3), but since 1975 some states continue to have increases while others have leveled off or decreased except for a spike or two up or down.

Differences also occur in particular types of cases. For example, automobile liability cases are up in many states, but other liability cases, such as lawsuits against doctors and businesses, have decreased. There also is evidence that doctors are not sued routinely, as many believe, but face lawsuits only in the most grievous cases

**Figure 8-3**  Rates of Tort Litigation Filings in Eight States, 1975–1995

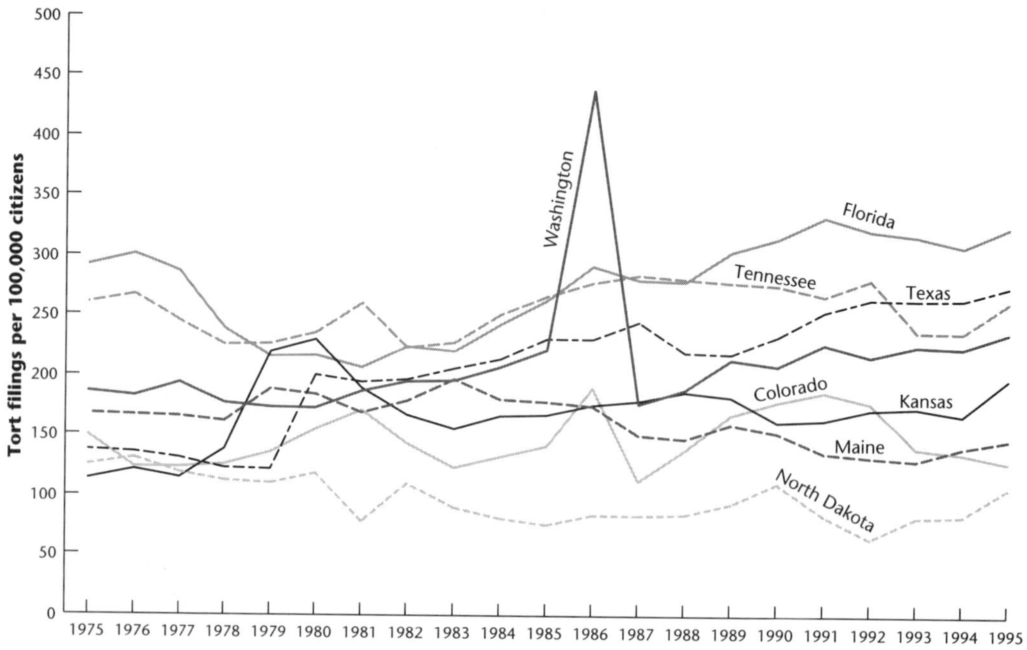

SOURCES: Derived from Yates et al. 1998, and National Center for State Courts.

of negligence and injury, and they win about three-quarters of these cases. Trial lawyers also turn away as much business as they accept because many potential clients do not have good cases (Galanter 1993; Kritzer 1997; Sloan and Hsieh 1995).

Population density (the number of people per square mile) is the most powerful explanation for differences in rates of litigation, which reflects the fact that most people now live in large and growing cities where relationships with neighbors, employers, and businesses are likely to be much more complex, remote, and temporary, and where strangers, rather than friends and family, are more likely to go to court. The size and scope of commerce and government also have expanded tremendously in the past fifty years. New and more consumer products and services improve life but also sometimes cause harm or loss with legitimate claims for compensation. Government policies regulate business and labor practices but also have greatly expanded individual rights and liberties that give people lawful opportunities to challenge the behavior and policies of government and public organizations.

Even policies that seem to have no direct connection with litigation may have an effect. For instance, research on the eight states in Figure 8-3 suggests that, in addition to population density, large gaps between rich and poor (income inequality) are related to higher rates of litigation, as are state government welfare policies that keep payments low. This does not mean that the poor use the courts to get money; rather, it suggests that wide economic differences may reflect a conflictual and strained social environment with a greater likelihood for people generally to use courts. However, various tort reform strategies have no effect on reducing litigation. Finally, increases in the overall workload of state courts are partly a result of rising crime rates and the increasing amount of criminal law produced by the states. Consequently, caution is needed before making sweeping statements about American litigiousness or concluding that litigation forever increases.

## MAKING JUDICIAL DECISIONS

For lawyers, politicians, and litigants, making decisions is the crux of the judicial process. Legal culture expects judges to be limited by the facts and the law, but the popular political culture conceives that many forces influence decisions, including the social and political context in which courts are embedded, the structure and operating rules of court systems, judicial selection and judges' personal backgrounds, experiences, and political attitudes. Studying appellate courts that are comprised of several judges is especially informative because each judge has access to the same facts and law and each decides the same case. When the judges disagree on decisions, we can establish who is in the majority and who is in dissent and analyze why.

The most important impact on judges' decisions is their political party affiliation (Dubois 1980). When law is unclear and there are many facts that could be considered, Democratic judges, like their fellow partisans elsewhere, tend to favor labor unions, poorer litigants, women, racial minorities, those who have been injured by the negligence of others, and social underdogs in general. Republicans favor business interests and social upperdogs. Additional personal characteristics also affect judges' decisions. For instance, women judges more heavily support women's rights involving sex discrimination and child support collection; they are also more likely to impose longer sentences on rapists. Women judges are more liberal on various other issues as well. Similarly, Evangelical Protestants are significantly more conservative than other Protestant, Catholic, or Jewish judges on visible, controversial, moral issues (Songer and Tabrizi 1999; Songer and Crews-Meyer 2000).

Political environments also impinge on judges' freedom to make decisions. In death penalty cases, for example, Republican and older judges and judges who have served previously as prosecuting attorneys are more likely to uphold death sentences. However, judges of both parties in states that use partisan judicial elections are especially sensitive to public opinion and the ideological leanings of their state legislatures when the courts confront capital punishment and abortion cases. Overall, it appears that judges who are most easily held accountable are most likely to respond to public opinion in these most visible cases (Brace, Hall, and Langer 2001). In states that do not use elections, ideologically oriented governors influence decisions indirectly by appointing liberal Democrats or conservative Republicans who frequently take different partisan positions on the courts.

What is the influence of law? Various research shows that case facts, such as the gender or age of crime victims, and legal issues make some difference; but since Democratic and Republican judges often rate the importance of certain facts and law differently, their legal evaluations often parallel their personal ideologies (Traut and Emmert 1998).

This research has important implications for understanding and evaluating state courts. It shows that a combination of familiar political forces is crucial in judicial decision making. For example, whether or not a defendant will be executed is significantly contingent on which state supreme court makes the decision, who the judges are, and the method of judicial recruitment. Earlier we saw that the method of selection made little difference in who became a judge; but seeking reelection seems to make some judges vulnerable to public preferences on hotly contested issues. As a result, some critics argue that judges ought to be further removed from politics; but others maintain that judges should in fact be responsive to issues on which the public feels very strongly. However we evaluate the meaning of this research for debate over the proper role of courts, it clearly shows that judicial decision making is a political process.

## JUDICIAL POLICY MAKING

Supreme courts have many more opportunities than other state courts to make policy. The most visible way is when courts innovate or produce new solutions to emerging social problems in a single prominent case. Because law frequently is unclear or contradictory, appellate judges inevitably must innovate to deal with new issues or new twists on old problems.

Supreme courts have some opportunities to make policy in addition to deciding cases. First, many supreme courts may issue advisory opinions about proposed or unclear law when asked by the governor, attorney general, or other high-level state officials. Supreme courts also make legal rules of procedure for other state courts, and they oversee the practice of law, including disciplining and disbarring attorneys.

State court policy that affects the structure and operation of government sometimes includes deciding cases and reviewing other state government decisions. A prominent example is state legislative redistricting. After each census, state legislatures must redraw the boundaries of the state's congressional districts and state house and senatorial legislative districts to produce equal representation throughout the state. Earlier discussion of state legislatures portrays the massive political wrangling that accompanies this process (see Chapter 6). Some states allow legislatures to redistrict themselves while others appoint special commissions to redraw the maps. In various states, the supreme court chief justice appoints some of the members to these commissions, and supreme courts review their final work. Where legislatures do redistricting, leaders of the minority political party or various groups of voters, such as urban residents who claim rural areas are overrepresented or racial minorities who have faced voter discrimination, frequently file court cases to overturn the new maps. Litigants also may sue in federal court since both state and federal statutes and constitutions govern redistricting. Courts are required to give commissions and legislatures ample opportunities to produce equitable redistricting plans, and federal judges are required to defer to state courts, but both sets of courts may set deadlines and ultimately produce their own redistricting plans.

It has been reported that after the 1990 census, 20 states were involved in state lawsuits, 28 were in federal court, and 11 states were in both state and federal courts. Early in 2002, after the 2000 census, about ten states were responding to lawsuits in state courts and several others were in federal court or both state and federal courts. Illinois had fourteen different lawsuits. In Florida the Republican-controlled state legislature and Republican governor Jeb Bush defended the legislative redistricting plan, but the independently elected Democratic attorney general claimed it violated state law. Suits are currently pending in both state and federal court. Decisions to sue in state or federal courts frequently depend on where litigants guess they will be most successful. For example, Democrats and black voters in some states sue in state court because they believe that Republican federal judges serving in their areas will support Republican redistricting plans. But where Republicans have a majority on state supreme courts, Democrats may go to federal court. Some courts operate in a bipartisan fashion, but many others reveal judges' partisanship in these intense and high stakes contests for party control of state government.

In contrast to supreme courts, trial and intermediate appellate courts deal with thousands of similar cases annually, which provide judges on these courts little time for developing innovative policy or writing opinions. Therefore, some observers see lower-level courts as litigation factories in which judges apply or enforce locally accepted values and law in routine civil disputes and cases of crime (Jacob 1984). However, because they repeatedly make decisions in factually similar cases, particular lower court judges often reveal a consistent pattern for dealing with certain kinds of problems. This constitutes a *cumulative* form of policy making because it builds up gradually over time and reveals how courts contribute to the way that states and communities respond to particular problems and groups of litigants. Examples abound in reports on racial discrimination in criminal sentencing or the power and success of businesses in commercial cases against individuals.

A recent controversial cumulative policy is the judicial response to three-strikes-and-you're-out sentencing laws enacted in about half the states. Although each law varies, the general purpose is to heavily punish, up to life in prison, persons convicted of a third offense. It has become extremely controversial in California, which was an early adopter in the early 1990s. There, legislative and other opponents now claim that the law was intended to apply only to those who committed very serious, violent felonies, but that hundreds of people have received very long sentences for a minor third strike, such as drug possession. Others claim the law is applied unevenly and unfairly because prosecutors often drop the threat of using the third strike law in exchange for defendants' pleading guilty to the third crime. Defendants who agree receive much lighter sentences than those who resist and lose in a trial.

California trial courts also are seen as applying the law differently in various parts of the state; for example, liberal San Francisco judges frequently dismiss the third strike charge for minor offenses while judges in more conservative San Diego hand down stiff sentences for similar minor third strikes. Although each case of crime attracts little notice, the cumulative judicial output in these decisions has attracted considerable scrutiny. A federal court of appeals recently ruled that a fifty-year sentence for shoplifting constituted cruel and unusual punishment, but the U.S. Supreme Court disagreed, accepting the constitutionality of California's law in 2003.

Because the trend in state government is to reduce the mandatory jurisdiction of state supreme courts, the policy-making role of these courts likely will increase. Therefore, this chapter concludes by examining the policy-making role of state supreme courts further. This includes illustrations of innovative judicial decisions, policy making through judicial review of legislation, and possible shifts in policy-making opportunities from the U.S. Supreme Court to the state courts—termed the new judicial federalism.

*Innovation*

Examining policy innovation identifies those states and government institutions that produce new solutions to thorny problems. In general, the most populous and socially complex states produce greater amounts of new litigation and opportunities for judicial innovation. Certain state supreme courts have attained national reputations for being leaders in creating new solutions to society's modern problems, and they frequently provide the policy models that other state supreme courts embrace. Judicial innovation encourages additional litigation on novel issues as well as additional policy making throughout the state political system as groups arrayed on both sides of an issue seek to expand or limit the policy through legislation and administrative rules. Therefore, judicial innovation can have far-reaching consequences beyond a court's decision in a single case.

The state supreme courts likely to be leaders in policy innovation are listed in Table 8-2. The California, New Jersey, and New York supreme courts stand out from the rest and rank very high in all estimates of judicial policy leadership, followed by others mostly in large and growing states in the Midwest and Northeast. Three other courts (in New Hampshire, Florida, and Michigan) are policy leaders somewhat less often.

An illustration of innovation and the intricate policy relationships it engenders in state politics is recent "right to die" litigation (Glick 1992). A modern social problem is that high-tech medicine has the ability to prolong the lives of terminally ill individuals and those in a permanent unconscious or vegetative state. Traditional medical ethics encourages preserving life, and physicians sometimes worry about legal liability if they do not do everything possible to save a patient. Conflicts occur when individuals or their families do not want such treatment, family members disagree among themselves, or patients' wishes are unclear but they no longer can communicate their desires.

The first innovative government decision in this policy area was made by the New Jersey Supreme Court in 1976, which ruled that the parents of a young

**Table 8-2** The Top Innovating State Supreme Courts

| Rank[a] | State |
|---|---|
| 1 | California |
| 2 | New Jersey |
| 3 | New York |
| 4.5 | Massachusetts; Washington |
| 6 | Pennsylvania |
| 7.5 | Illinois; Minnesota |
| 9 | New Hampshire |
| 10.5 | Florida; Michigan |

SOURCES: Composite rankings constructed from Canon and Baum 1981; Caldeira 1983; Domino 1989; Glick 1992.

[a] States are rank-ordered according to their composite innovation scores. States with the same scores receive a ranking midway between the ranks determined by their scores.

woman in a permanent vegetative state could act as guardians and order nursing home staff to remove their daughter's respirator (*In re Quinlan* [355 A.2d 647]). Subsequently, many other state supreme courts received similar cases and most followed New Jersey's lead. Most of these decisions were made before state legislatures had made new laws, mainly because state Catholic Conferences had lobbied legislatures not to enact laws that would expand individual rights to curtail medical treatment at the end of life. In time, however, the rising volume of court cases and favorable public opinion convinced many legislatures that new laws were needed. Then, Catholic lobbyists worked for law and nursing home regulations that limited supreme court rulings, which in turn often stimulated advocates of the right to die to go back to court. In some states, neither the supreme court nor the legislature nor the executive branch has had the last word.

In a 1990 case appealed from the Missouri Supreme Court, the U.S. Supreme Court upheld the right to withdraw treatment but supported Missouri's unusually stringent policy that a patient's wishes must be very clearly expressed, preferably in writing (*Cruzan v. Director, Missouri Department of Health* [110 S.Ct 2841]). However, the Supreme Court did not require other states to adopt Missouri's policy. The responses of other state supreme courts following this decision highlight the power that courts have to create new policy. Supreme courts that had fashioned more lenient policies before the Supreme Court's decision continued to follow their own rulings, but others that had not yet ruled on the right to die were inclined to follow the U.S. Supreme Court.

Now, the "right to die" has expanded to include a "right to assisted suicide," and the issue has involved state courts, legislatures, public referenda, as well as the U.S. Supreme Court. For decades, about half the states had criminalized assisting in a suicide. Nearly a dozen more adopted similar laws in the 1990s, following the highly publicized assisted suicides by Dr. Jack Kevorkian, a retired Michigan pathologist. In 1997 the U.S. Supreme Court ruled that assisted suicide is not a constitutional right (*Washington v. Glucksberg* [521 U.S. 702]; *Vacco v. Quill* [521

U.S. 793]), but it also permitted the states to consider their own policies. Only the Alaska and Florida Supreme Courts have heard a case on assisted suicide since then, and both adopted the Supreme Court's position. Public opinion is sharply divided, and the policy is much too controversial to get through most legislatures where conservative religious groups are prominent. Oregon is currently the only state with legalized assisted suicide, enacted by voter referendum. In 2001 U.S. Attorney General John Ashcroft tried to prevent doctors there from prescribing the necessary drugs, but he has been blocked by a federal district court.

A second illustration of judicial innovation concerns state taxing and spending for public education, which is the largest public program in most states. It has been common in the fifty states since the early 1900s for government to pay for public education largely with money raised locally through taxes on real estate property. Early in the 1970s, several state supreme courts ruled that since local property taxes produce unequal amounts of revenue because of variations in value, the tax also produces inequality in public education and is forbidden by the U.S. Constitution. However, in 1973 the U.S. Supreme Court disagreed, saying that tax and education policies were unrelated (*San Antonio School District v. Rodriguez* [411 U.S. 1]). Nevertheless, citizens continued to bring cases to state courts relying on provisions in state constitutions. With both state and federal constitutions and a U.S. Supreme Court precedent available to them, approximately four-fifths of the state supreme courts have made education policy decisions. About half, many in states with liberal political cultures, have ruled that relying on the property tax to fund public education is unconstitutional, requiring state legislatures to enact new law to equalize funding (see chapter 12). The few courts without cases are mostly in conservative and sparsely populated states.

Courts that have ordered a change in policy have led state legislatures to redistribute property tax revenues from rich to poor districts, reduce reliance on property taxes, and create other new state taxes. Legislatures often have acted reluctantly and in piecemeal fashion, sometimes requiring additional litigation to get them to comply with state supreme court rulings, but it appears that the state supreme court rulings have promoted more equal funding for public schools (Reed 1998).

*Judicial Review of Legislation*

Judicial review is the most visible part of a two-hundred-year debate over the proper role of courts, particularly whether they should be activist by overturning legislation judges see as unconstitutional or exercise restraint by supporting laws passed by democratically elected legislatures. Like the U.S. Supreme Court, state supreme courts also have the power to review state legislation, and together they examine more than six hundred laws each year (Emmert and Traut 1992).

State judicial review cases involve a wide range of issues. The largest percentage (40 percent) concerns rules of criminal procedure brought by defendants hoping to get out of jail, but courts overturn laws in fewer than 10 percent of these cases. Additional cases involve government regulation of businesses, professions and labor, civil rights and liberties, relationships among agencies of government, and various private disputes. In contrast to the criminal cases, courts overturn a quarter or more of the laws contested in these cases.

The volume of judicial review cases depends heavily on the structure of legal and political systems that present supreme courts with opportunities to review cases (Emmert 1992; Wenzel, Bowler, and Lanoue 1997). Supreme courts with heavy caseloads and little control of their dockets and where constitutions are long and complex (mostly in the South) generally have many more cases involving constitutional questions than courts in other states, and they overturn a larger number of state laws. However, courts that have greater control of their dockets and fewer cases often overturn a similar or greater percentage of laws than other courts. For example, Georgia led the states with 165 laws challenged over five years, of which 25 (15 percent) were overturned by the supreme court. New York had fewer (80) challenged laws, but the court overturned about 25 percent, and California had 50 challenges, with the court overturning 13 laws, or about 26 percent. Therefore, judicial review can be an important component of supreme court policy making in all states, even those with fewer cases. Like the U.S. Supreme Court, state supreme courts with discretionary jurisdiction probably carefully select cases with a greater likelihood of overturning a law.

### New Judicial Federalism

An important issue regarding state supreme court judicial review concerns whether state courts are striking out on their own to create new constitutional rights. Since the 1950s the U.S. Supreme Court has been perceived as preeminent in judicial policy making primarily through its liberal decisions expanding civil rights, civil liberties, and the rights of criminal defendants. However, with the appointment of conservative justices since the Reagan presidency of the 1980s and the general cooling of support for liberal policies, the justices appointed since 1986 have reversed more state supreme court cases in the conservative direction (Brisbin and Kilwein 1994). The Court also is hearing fewer cases and allowing state governments more freedom to deal with social problems.

Some analysts believe this trend creates a new Supreme Court relationship with the states—a new judicial federalism—that will lead state supreme courts to become more active and independent policy makers. Under settled law, the states may create more, but not less, expansive interpretations of rights than those given by the U.S. Supreme Court. Believers in a new judicial federalism speculate that because minority and other underdog groups have lost much of their favorable access to the U.S. Supreme Court, they will persuade state supreme courts to rely on Bill of Rights–type provisions in state constitutions to continue the expansion of individual rights.

From time to time, particular state supreme court decisions give the impression that the new judicial federalism is on the march. For example, in the 1970s supreme courts, most prominently in California, New Jersey, Alaska, and Michigan, as well as in a few other states, created standards for police interrogation and search and seizure that went beyond the weakened requirements produced by the increasingly conservative Supreme Court, as did the supreme courts of Illinois and Pennsylvania regarding sexual discrimination. In 1980 the California Supreme Court expanded the right to free speech on business premises that went beyond previous U.S. Supreme Court rulings, and Justice William Rehnquist and other Supreme Court justices lauded the state court's use of state constitutions to support the decision (Stumpf and Culver 1992).

But more comprehensive study of state supreme court decisions leads to a different conclusion. First, state supreme courts rely on state constitutions as the sole basis of their decisions in one-sixth or fewer of their cases involving state legislation, preferring mostly U.S. Supreme Court precedents or a combination of state and national constitutions in these cases (Emmert and Traut 1992; Kramer 1996). State constitutions are used least often in criminal and civil liberties cases, under 10 and 15 percent, respectively, with some states *never* relying on state law of any sort (Emmert and Traut 1992; Esler 1994). Also, many state supreme courts that rely on state constitutions or other state law do not use them to advance civil liberties but interpret rights about the same way as the U.S. Supreme Court, and a few state supreme courts that moved in a liberal policy direction in the 1980s were curtailed by state constitutional amendments that required the courts to conform to more conservative federal interpretations (Tarr 1997). Finally, judicial review cases mostly involve state government issues to which the U.S. Constitution does not apply, including, for example, jurisdictional disputes among government agencies in state administration and rule making and various state taxing and spending issues.

There are several reasons why state supreme courts have not led the way toward a new judicial federalism. First, the U.S. Supreme Court is the preeminent court in the nation, and it has a long history of policy making in civil rights and liberties and provides many precedents for the state courts. Second, many state constitutional provisions are similar to federal law, and few law school courses emphasize state constitutions. Third, most state political environments are conservative, and judges have few incentives to make liberal policies in the face of judicial elections or conservative public opinion and police, prosecutors, and other law and order interest groups that oppose greater constitutional protections (Esler 1994; Kilwein and Brisbin 1997). The few states that have been leaders in the new judicial federalism generally are in ideologically liberal states where public opinion and other political groups and institutions are more likely to promote or accept expansive decisions.

If the new judicial federalism means only that state supreme courts will expand personal liberties beyond U.S. Supreme Court rulings, there does not seem to be much to this anticipated trend. However, this definition of the new judicial federalism is too narrow. First, state supreme courts rely on their own constitutions not only to rule on state legislation but to review actions of the executive branch and local government as well. Some involve salient issues. For example, the Florida Supreme Court upheld as constitutional a Miami ordinance requiring job applicants to swear they had not used tobacco products during the previous year. The court said there is no constitutional right to smoke. State courts also have opportunities to rule on matters where state and federal statutes could apply, but litigants choose to file cases in state court. An example concerns state fair-employment practices laws, which ban employment discrimination. Compared to federal law, many state employment discrimination laws allow much broader definitions of bias, have more generous or no caps on the amount and types of damages (compensatory and punitive) that can be awarded, and do not require plaintiffs to use preliminary administrative hearings before they may file lawsuits. In addition, state judges appear less likely than their federal counterparts to dismiss such cases. Therefore, there appears to be a shift of litigation from federal to state court (Wolff 1997). Many of these cases recently have reached state supreme courts.

Recent tobacco litigation also demonstrates the importance of state law and courts as alternatives to federal jurisdiction in litigation with potentially enormous impacts on policy. The U.S. Supreme Court has ruled that federal regulations do not exempt tobacco companies from lawsuits based on state products liability statutes and other long-standing state common law. Lower federal court judges have ruled that a national class action suit, in which thousands or millions of people would be represented at the same time, is much too unwieldy. But state judicial procedure has long permitted class actions for personal injuries, and the tobacco liability cases qualify.

Tobacco companies have been sued for decades, but not until the mid-1990s when industry documents acknowledging the harmful effects of smoking were made public did more juries begin to find the companies liable, awarding many millions of dollars in compensation. In 1999 the state attorneys general settled cases in state courts worth approximately $246 billion over twenty years for government costs in treating thousands of smoking-related illnesses. This has not ended state litigation, however, because individuals and other organizations, such as labor union insurance funds, may continue to sue to recover compensation for illnesses and the costs of medical treatment. The largest award in a state class action case is a Miami jury's decision in 2000 to impose $145 billion in punitive damages. State supreme courts so far have heard few appeals involving the dollar amounts awarded, but recent supreme court cases concern related issues, including disputes over state plans to use the attorneys generals settlement money for particular healthcare programs; directing settlement money to particular groups, organizations, or local governments; attempts to hold tobacco companies partially liable for lung diseases of industrial workers who smoke; and liability for second-hand smoke. Many other cases are pending throughout the country, and the policy-making role for state supreme courts is just beginning in these controversial cases.

However we might expand the definition of the new judicial federalism, searching for signs of a rebirth of state judicial power may lead us to undervalue the independent policy-making role that state supreme courts always have had. State judges are not mere subordinates in a hierarchical federal system; rather, they interpret state and federal law by applying their own values and assessments of state political conditions to their decisions. As it happens, most of their recent conservative civil liberties and criminal justice decisions parallel recent Supreme Court policy, so the state courts do not stand out as innovators. But in years past, conservative state court decisions ran contrary to liberal Supreme Court policy and provided the High Court with many cases that allowed it to vastly expand personal freedoms and individual rights. And as discussed, judicial decisions include more than individual rights and protections from unlawful police conduct, and state courts rely mainly on state constitutions in many areas of state government administration, taxation, and spending, where the U.S. Constitution and the U.S. Supreme Court have little to say or have deferred to the states. These are important areas of state politics and policy, as other chapters in this volume attest. Certain innovative state supreme court decisions based on state constitutions have been crucial in various areas of policy, notably equalizing state spending for education, the right to die, zoning and land use, as well as the right to an abortion in the face of limiting state legislation. Finally, state supreme courts may achieve even greater importance in interpreting and applying state statutes in cases where litigants choose to use state rather than federal courts.

## CONCLUSION

This chapter began by suggesting that courts usually are not seen as important governmental or political institutions. But state supreme courts have many opportunities to make important innovative policy decisions, and all state courts have substantial impacts on many people because they deal with most of the disputes and crime that people are likely to encounter. The patterns of decisions or cumulative policies courts produce and relations between their decisions and the policies of other government institutions place courts at the center of government and politics. Politics also affects other aspects of courts, including their organization and jurisdiction, judicial selection, and the effects of ideology and partisan politics on judicial decision making. As society becomes more complex, state courts will have an ever-widening impact on social, economic, and political issues.

## REFERENCES

Abramson, Jeffrey. 1994. *We, the Jury.* New York: Basic Books.
Aspin, Larry. 1999. "Trends in Judicial Retention Elections, 1964–1998." *Judicature* 83: 79–81.
Brace, Paul, Melinda Gann Hall, and Laura Langer. 2001. "Placing State Supreme Courts in State Politics." *State Politics and Policy Quarterly* 1: 81–108.
Brisbin, Richard A., Jr., and John C. Kilwein. 1994. "U.S. Supreme Court Review of State High Court Decisions." *Judicature* 78: 33–46.
Caldeira, Gregory A. 1983. "On the Reputation of State Supreme Courts." *Political Behavior* 5: 83–108.
Canon, Bradley C., and Lawrence Baum. 1981. "Patterns of Adoption of Tort Law Innovations: An Application of Diffusion Theory to Judicial Doctrines." *American Political Science Review* 75: 975–987.
Cheek, Kyle, and Anthony Champagne. 2000. "Money in Texas Supreme Court Elections." *Judicature* 84: 20–25.

Council of State Governments. 2000. *The Book of the States, 2000–2001.* Lexington, Ky.: Council of State Governments.

Curran, Barbara A. 1986. "American Lawyers in the 1980s." *Law and Society Review* 20: 19–49.

Domino, John C. 1989. "State Supreme Court Innovation in the Policy Area of Privacy: A Comparative Analysis." Paper presented at the annual meeting of the Law and Society Association, Madison, Wisconsin, June.

Dubois, Philip. 1980. *From Ballot to Bench.* Austin: University of Texas Press.

Eisenstein, James. 2000. "Financing Pennsylvania Supreme Court Candidates." *Judicature* 84: 10–19.

Eisenstein, James, and Herbert Jacob. 1977. *Felony Justice.* Boston: Little, Brown.

Emmert, Craig F. 1992. "An Integrated Case-Related Model of Judicial Decision Making." *Journal of Politics* 54: 543–552.

Emmert, Craig F., and Carol Ann Traut. 1992. "State Supreme Courts, State Constitutions, and Judicial Policymaking." *Justice System Journal* 16: 36–48.

Epstein, Lee. 1994. "Exploring the Participation of Organized Interests in State Court Litigation." *Political Research Quarterly* 47: 335–351.

Esler, Michael. 1994. "State Supreme Court Commitment to State Law." *Judicature* 78: 25–32.

Galanter, Marc. 1993. "News from Nowhere: The Debased Debate on Civil Justice." *Denver University Law Review* 71: 77–103.

Glick, Henry R. 1992. *The Right to Die.* New York: Columbia University Press.

Glick, Henry R., and Craig F. Emmert. 1987. "Selection Systems and Judicial Characteristics." *Judicature* 70: 228–235.

Gordon, Elizabeth Ellen. 1999. "Why Attorneys Support Mandatory Mediation." *Judicature* 82: 224–231.

Hall, Melinda Gann. 2001a. "State Supreme Courts in American Democracy." *American Political Science Review* 95: 315–330.

———. 2001b. "Voluntary Retirements from State Supreme Courts." *Journal of Politics* 63: 1112–1140.

Heinz, John P., and Edward O. Laumann. 1982. *Chicago Lawyers.* New York: Russell Sage Foundation and American Bar Foundation.

Henschen, Beth, Robert Moog, and Steven Davis. 1990. "Judicial Nominating Commissions: A National Profile." *Judicature* 73: 328–343.

Hurwitz, Mark S., and Drew Noble Lanier. 2001. "Women and Minorities on State and Federal Appellate Benches, 1985 and 1999." *Judicature* 85: 84–92.

Jacob, Herbert. 1984. *Justice in America.* 4th ed. Boston: Little, Brown.

Kessler, Mark. 1986. "The Politics of Legal Representation: The Influence of Local Politics on the Behavior of Poverty Lawyers." *Law and Society Review* 8: 149–167.

Kilwein, John C., and Richard A. Brisbin. 1997. "Policy Convergence in a Federal Judicial System: Application of Intensified Scrutiny Doctrines by State Supreme Courts." *American Journal of Political Science* 41: 122–148.

Kramer, Paul A. 1996. "Waiting for Godot?—The New Judicial Federalism 1987–1992: Reality or Hoax?" Paper presented at the annual meeting of the American Political Science Association, San Francisco, August 29–September 1.

Kritzer, Herbert M. 1997. "Contingency Fee Lawyers as Gatekeepers in the Civil Justice System." *Judicature* 81: 22–29.

Lawrence, Susan. 1990. *The Poor in Court.* Princeton, N.J.: Princeton University Press.

Reed, Douglas. 1998. "Twenty-five Years after Rodriguez." *Law and Society Review* 32: 175–220.

Richardson, Richard J., and Kenneth N. Vines. 1970. *The Politics of Federal Courts.* Boston: Little, Brown.

Ross, H. Laurence. 1970. *Settled Out of Court.* Chicago: Aldine.

Sloan, Frank A., and Chee Ruey Hsieh. 1995. "Injury, Liability, and the Decision to File a Medical Malpractice Claim." *Law and Society Review* 29: 413–435.

Songer, Donald R., and Kelly A. Crews-Meyer. 2000. "Does Gender Matter?" *Social Science Quarterly* 81: 750–762.

Songer, Donald R., and Susan J. Tabrizi. 1999. "The Religious Right in Court." *Journal of Politics* 61: 507–526.

*State Court Caseload Statistics: Annual Report 2001.* 2001. Williamsburg, Va.: National Center for State Courts.

Stumpf, Harry P., and John H. Culver. 1992. *The Politics of State Courts.* White Plains, N.Y.: Longman.

Tarr, G. Alan. 1997. "The New Judicial Federalism in Perspective." *Notre Dame Law Review* 72: 1097–1118.

Traut, Carol Ann, and Craig F. Emmert. 1998. "Expanding the Integrated Model of Judicial Decisionmaking: The California Justices and Capital Punishment." *Journal of Politics* 60: 1166–1180.

Watson, Richard A., and Rondal G. Downing. 1969. *The Politics of the Bench and the Bar.* New York: John Wiley Sons.

Wenzel, James P., Shaun Bowler, and David J. Lanoue. 1997. "Legislating from the Bench: A Comparative Analysis of Judicial Activism." *American Politics Quarterly* 25: 363–379.

Wolff, Robert M. 1997. "Making the Leap to State Courts." *National Law Journal* (June): 38.

Yates, Jeff, Richard Fording, Belinda Davis, and Henry R. Glick. 1998. "State Litigiousness: An Empirical Examination of State Tort Litigation Rates." Paper presented at the annual meeting of the Law and Society Association, Aspen, Colorado, June 4–7.

Yngvesson, Barbara, and Patricia Hennessey. 1975. "Small Claims, Complex Disputes: A Review of the Small Claims Literature." *Law and Society Review* 9: 235–243.

## SUGGESTED READINGS

Baum, Lawrence. *American Courts: Process and Policy.* 5th ed. Boston: Houghton Mifflin, 2001. An accessible text on the politics of the judicial process that includes deep coverage of local justice and state appellate courts.

Dubois, Philip L. *From Ballot to Bench.* Austin: University of Texas Press, 1980. A comprehensive analysis of state judicial elections that also considers the major criticisms of electing judges.

Eisenstein, James, and Herbert Jacob. *Felony Justice: An Organizational Analysis of Criminal Courts.* Boston: Little, Brown, 1977. A classic in the study of criminal courts that provides basic theory and in-depth understanding of the informal workings of local justice and the content of judicial decisions.

Glick, Henry R. *The Right to Die: Policy Innovation and Its Consequences.* New York: Columbia University Press, 1992. Illustrates the innovative policy-making role of state supreme courts and the dynamic interaction of courts, legislatures, and the state policy-making process.

Tarr, G. Alan, and Mary Cornelia Aldis Porter. *State Supreme Courts in State and Nation.* New Haven, Conn.: Yale University Press, 1988. An introduction to the political role of state supreme courts with detailed illustrations drawn from three states.

CHAPTER 9

# Administering State Programs: Performance and Politics

RICHARD C. ELLING

After the governor's "State of the State" messages, bill signings, and vetoes, there is the state bureaucracy. After the legislative committee hearings, floor debate, and roll-call votes, there is the administrative apparatus of state government. With responsibilities ranging from A (agriculture, the arts) to Z (zoos), state bureaucracies do much of the work of state governments.[1] The ability of state elected officials to achieve their goals can be significantly affected by what such organizations do, or what they fail to do.

For most Americans, state government is as much a state agency and its employees as it is the governor or the state legislature. Citizens interact most frequently with lower-level state bureaucrats. Welfare caseworkers, conservation officers, college financial aid officials, public health inspectors, state police officers, unemployment compensation clerks, probation and parole agents, tax collection officials, even state university professors, can significantly affect the fortunes of those with whom they deal. Higher-level administrators make less routine decisions, determine standards to guide the actions of subordinates, and supervise the performance of those subordinates. They also interact with numerous external institutions, officials, and groups.

State administrative agencies matter because they implement state programs. The model of an agency receiving the authority and the funding from the legislature to employ the personnel it needs to carry out various responsibilities on its own is, however,

---

1. Here I use the term *bureaucracy* as a synonym for a large, complex organization such as a government agency. Later in the chapter I provide a more precise definition of the concept of bureaucracy. In this chapter I use the terms *administer* and *implement* as synonyms that refer to the processes by which formal policies and programs are applied to the problems that those policies or programs were designed to address.

less and less common. Implementing state programs increasingly involves several state agencies working together, sometimes in collaboration with nonprofit or for-profit organizations. Moreover, the federal government increasingly relies on state bureaucracies to achieve the purposes of federal programs funded to varying degrees by its several hundred grant-in-aid programs. Changes in federal programs for poor families that gave states and their public welfare agencies much greater responsibility are but one example of increased federal reliance on state bureaucracies (see Chapter 11). State governments may, in turn, forge linkages with local units of government and, increasingly, with either for-profit or nonprofit entities to carry out programs funded in part by federal grant dollars.

State bureaucracies also matter because their role extends well beyond "administration" narrowly defined. After a policy has been established, many questions remain about how best to deliver services, or how to secure the compliance of those affected by a policy. Decisions on these matters are largely in the hands of state bureaucrats. Elected officials are made aware of shortcomings in existing programs by administrators who regularly deal with those programs. Administrators also help develop solutions to problems on the policy agenda and advise the elected officials who formally adopt policies as they debate the merits of various policy options.

## THE CHALLENGING AND DYNAMIC ENVIRONMENT OF STATE ADMINISTRATION

How states implement programs and deliver services is in a state of flux as new management approaches have emerged, as the state role in the American federal system evolves, as the line between what is "public" and "private" blurs, and as new information technologies are developed. These factors, combined with a public mood that is skeptical of government and resists higher taxes, have forced state administrative agencies to reconsider how to best accomplish their goals.

State administrative structures reflect the emergence of new problems and the response of state governments to those problems. Jenks and Wright (1993) think about the evolution of state bureaucracies in terms of the emergence of several different "generations." The more than fifty types of agencies present in at least thirty-eight states by the end of the 1950s constituted a first generation. Included here are agencies that administer programs in areas such as agriculture, banking, corrections, education, fish and wildlife management, health, higher education, highways, mental health care, parks, tax collection, unemployment insurance, welfare, and workers' compensation. Concern over issues such as civil rights, environmental protection, consumer protection, poverty, workplace safety, vocational rehabilitation, mass transit, medical care for the poor, and urban distress during the 1960s and early 1970s resulted in the emergence of a second, and then a third, generation of state administrative agencies that included more than forty new entities between them.

The scope of state administration is reflected in the size of the state workforce. In 2000 the fifty states employed 3.6 million people on a full-time basis and 1.3 million on a part-time basis, for a full-time equivalent workforce of roughly 4 million (see Table 9-1). More populous states have more employees, although the ratio of state employees to state population is generally lowest in such states, as the fifth column of Table 9-1 indicates. The balance of responsibilities between a state and its local governments also impacts state employment. More sparsely populated, geographically smaller, and poorer states all tend to rely more heavily on state government for the delivery of services. Thus, while Arkansas ranks thirty-third in population, it is tied for eighteenth in state government employees per 10,000 state residents. Some states have more employees because they do more in certain program areas. While roughly one-third of all state government employees work in higher education, this percentage ranges from less than 20 percent in three states to more than 50 percent in three others (see the fourth column of Table 9-1).

The more constrained circumstances of contemporary state administration are evident in the slower rate of growth in state government employment in the 1990s (6.3 percent) than in the 1980s (24 percent), despite the nation's population increase of 13.2 percent in the 1990s. Growth was also uneven across states. Employment increased by 25 percent or more in eight states—most of which had high rates of population growth during the decade—while it shrank in eleven states (see column 7 of Table 9-1). The number of state government employees as a percentage of a state's population declined in thirty-eight states.

Moreover, state government employment growth during the 1990s was concentrated in a few programmatic areas. Seeking to "get tough" on crime, beginning in the 1980s states built more correctional facilities and had to staff them. Thus employment in the corrections field grew by 40 percent during the 1990s on top of a 77 percent increase during the 1980s, in the process expanding job opportunities for college students majoring in fields such as sociology and criminal justice studies. The remaining growth in state government employment during the 1990s was concentrated in the areas of higher education (up 9.8 percent) and health services (up 7.7 percent).

### PERSPECTIVE ON STATE BUREAUCRATIC PERFORMANCE

Although the bureaucratic "horror story" is a journalistic staple, the more systematic evidence we have suggests that such stories are the exception and not the rule. For example, more than 80 percent of a sample of Wisconsin residents described their contacts with state transportation employees (highway patrol officers and driver's license examiners) as being either "good" or "excellent" as far as "courtesy of treatment" and "helpfulness of employees" were concerned (Goodsell 1985). Other client surveys paint a similar picture (Goodsell 1994, esp. 25–39; Michigan Department of Civil Service 1987). Recorded statistics on agency operations also suggest satisfactory performance. Thus a study of state unemployment compensation operations found that 90 percent of claims were paid within three weeks (Goodsell 1985).

Two studies—one conducted in the mid-1980s and the other in 2000–2001—approached the question of state administrative performance by asking middle- and upper-level managers in ten states—Arizona, Delaware, California, Indiana,

**Table 9-1** State Government Employment, March 2000

| State | Population rank | State employees, all functions (FTE, thousands)[a] | | | State employees, all functions, per 10,000 residents | | |
|---|---|---|---|---|---|---|---|
| | | FTE all functions | Rank | Percentage of workforce in higher education | Number | Rank | Percentage change in employment, all functions, 1990–2000 |
| Alabama | 23 | 80 | 20 | 40.8 | 179 | 20 | 0.7 |
| Alaska | 48 | 23 | 40 | 19.1 | 365 | 2 | 3.8 |
| Arizona | 20 | 65 | 26 | 38.3 | 126 | 43 | 29.0 |
| Arkansas | 33 | 49 | 34 | 36.0 | 183 | 18.5 | 24.3 |
| California | 1 | 355 | 1 | 34.8 | 105 | 49 | 9.5 |
| Colorado | 24 | 66 | 24 | 56.6 | 153 | 32.5 | 20.8 |
| Connecticut | 29 | 66 | 25 | 22.9 | 193 | 13 | 12.6 |
| Delaware | 45 | 24 | 39 | 30.1 | 303 | 3 | 13.6 |
| Florida | 4 | 185 | 4 | 27.0 | 116 | 47 | 16.0 |
| Georgia | 10 | 120 | 11 | 33.6 | 147 | 37 | 7.1 |
| Hawaii | 42 | 55 | 31 | 15.6 | 453 | 1 | 11.1 |
| Idaho | 39 | 23 | 41 | 36.7 | 175 | 23 | 21.1 |
| Illinois | 5 | 128 | 9 | 33.3 | 103 | 50 | −12.0 |
| Indiana | 14 | 83 | 18 | 56.5 | 136 | 40 | −7.2 |
| Iowa | 30 | 55 | 30 | 43.6 | 189 | 15 | −3.8 |
| Kansas | 32 | 43 | 36 | 42.4 | 158 | 18.5 | −14.1 |
| Kentucky | 25 | 74 | 22 | 33.9 | 183 | 29.5 | −1.3 |
| Louisiana | 22 | 95 | 15 | 30.1 | 212 | 9 | 12.1 |
| Maine | 40 | 21 | 43 | 29.8 | 161 | 28 | −6.6 |
| Maryland | 19 | 91 | 16 | 30.0 | 173 | 25 | 3.1 |
| Massachusetts | 13 | 96 | 14 | 26.9 | 151 | 35 | 2.6 |
| Michigan | 8 | 142 | 6 | 47.7 | 143 | 38.5 | −1.2 |
| Minnesota | 21 | 73 | 23 | 47.8 | 149 | 36 | 4.9 |
| Mississippi | 31 | 56 | 29 | 31.7 | 195 | 12 | 17.9 |
| Missouri | 17 | 91 | 17 | 30.1 | 163 | 27 | 23.0 |
| Montana | 44 | 18 | 46 | 35.1 | 199 | 10 | 6.3 |
| Nebraska | 38 | 30 | 38 | 33.6 | 174 | 24 | 1.3 |
| Nevada | 35 | 22 | 42 | 33.0 | 112 | 48 | 17 |
| New Hampshire | 41 | 19 | 45 | 35.5 | 152 | 34 | 16.5 |
| New Jersey | 9 | 133 | 8 | 21.1 | 158 | 29.5 | 18.5 |
| New Mexico | 36 | 48 | 35 | 41.5 | 263 | 4 | 20.3 |
| New York | 3 | 251 | 3 | 18.5 | 132 | 41 | −11.8 |
| North Carolina | 11 | 123 | 10 | 34.9 | 153 | 32.5 | 15.3 |
| North Dakota | 47 | 16 | 47 | 41.7 | 246 | 5 | 5.5 |
| Ohio | 7 | 136 | 6 | 47.2 | 120 | 45 | −2.1 |
| Oklahoma | 27 | 64 | 32 | 39.6 | 187 | 16.5 | −1.6 |
| Oregon | 28 | 53 | 30 | 25.9 | 156 | 31 | 2.2 |
| Pennsylvania | 6 | 150 | 5 | 33.8 | 122 | 44 | 17.6 |
| Rhode Island | 43 | 20 | 44 | 27.1 | 187 | 16.5 | −4.8 |
| South Carolina | 26 | 79 | 21 | 31.9 | 196 | 11 | −0.5 |
| South Dakota | 46 | 13 | 49 | 35.6 | 177 | 21.5 | 0.1 |
| Tennessee | 16 | 81 | 19 | 42.5 | 143 | 38.5 | 2.2 |
| Texas | 2 | 269 | 2 | 33.4 | 129 | 42 | 20.7 |
| Utah | 34 | 49 | 33 | 50.8 | 221 | 8 | 32.7 |
| Vermont | 49 | 14 | 48 | 36.1 | 224 | 7 | 3.7 |
| Virginia | 12 | 119 | 12 | 40.5 | 168 | 26 | 1.8 |
| Washington | 15 | 112 | 13 | 40.9 | 191 | 14 | 23.3 |
| West Virginia | 37 | 32 | 37 | 36.2 | 177 | 21.5 | −4.8 |
| Wisconsin | 18 | 64 | 28 | 43.3 | 119 | 46 | −4.3 |
| Wyoming | 50 | 11 | 50 | 27.6 | 226 | 6 | 3.1 |
| Total | — | 4,083 | — | 34.7 | 145 | — | 6.3 |

SOURCE: U.S. Bureau of the Census 2002.

[a] Full- and part-time employees expressed as full-time equivalents (FTE).

Michigan, New York, South Dakota, Tennessee, Texas and Vermont—about the performance of the units that they headed (Elling 1992; Elling, Thompson, and Monet 2003). To be sure, some administrators may dissemble or misperceive reality. But it is useful to assess administrative performance from the perspective of those who are actually "in the trenches."

In the most recent survey, when asked how effective their unit had been in accomplishing its goals and objectives in the past year, roughly three-quarters of the managers gave their unit a rating score of seven or higher on a scale where ten equaled "totally effective." Managers were also queried about the extent to which particular conditions or practices impeded the "efficient and effective administration of the programmatic responsibilities" of their units. In 2000–2001, of 65 potential impediments to effective management, only 14 were seen to be "serious" or "very serious" by a quarter or more of the responding managers. More than half of these problems concerned the availability or use of personnel—low salaries that hamper recruitment of good employees (58 percent of responding managers reported this to be a "serious" or "very serious" impediment), a problem adequately rewarding outstanding employees (54 percent), difficulty filling key staff vacancies (46 percent), complexity of personnel procedures for recruiting (37 percent) or hiring staff (28 percent), an inability to retain experienced employees (35 percent), and difficulty disciplining or dismissing low performing staff (34 percent). Several others involved the adequacy of financial resources such as insufficient legislative appropriations (40 percent of managers reported that this was a serious impediment) and legislative program expansion without sufficient additional funding (33 percent). It is also interesting that of the eight most serious impediments to effective management reported by managers in the 1982–1983 study, all but two ranked among the top eight in the more recent survey.

Judgments about bureaucratic performance often conflict because we apply differing, sometimes contradictory, standards. Three important standards of public bureaucratic performance are efficiency, effectiveness, and political/public accountability. The first two standards can be applied to public, private, and nonprofit organizations alike. An efficient organization gets the most out of a given amount of resources. If more highway litter is collected at a comparable or a lower cost, efficiency has increased. Effectiveness is goal-oriented. An effective organization gets the job done. However efficiently administered, does a program solve or ameliorate a problem? For instance, does vocational training improve the odds that incarcerated felons will secure jobs upon their release from prison and be less likely to engage in future criminal activity?

A major problem with the "public bureaucracy is inefficient" argument is that efficiency is not the only quality that we want public bureaucracies to display. Another important value is accountability. Accountability has two dimensions. A "process" dimension is concerned with the constitutionality or legality of administrative actions—with honesty, observance of due process, impartiality, and decency in dealing with the public. More demanding expectations concerning this standard distinguish public from private administration. Ensuring process accountability may require administrative practices that are neither cost effective nor efficient. Achieving process accountability is an important source of the so-called administrative "red tape" about which citizens complain.

Responsiveness is a second dimension of accountability. Whose goals should state bureaucracies strive to achieve? Specifying to whom administrators should be responsive is difficult since they live in a world of multiple legitimate but competing "authority figures." Is primary responsibility owed to the governor or to the legislature? What about responsiveness to those served by an agency's programs? What if what a governor or the legislature wants done conflicts with constitutional standards or professional norms?

We know little about the public's priorities in these matters, although some insight is provided by a survey of the citizens of Iowa (Bundt and Lutz 1999). Among nineteen qualities that could be reflected in the operations of state administrative agencies, the five that Iowans ranked highest were that they be trustworthy, financially responsible, ethical, accountable, and "fair and impartial." Agency efficiency ranked sixth while effectiveness ranked ninth. That Iowa state agencies should be "resulted-oriented" ranked sixteenth. In the eyes of Iowans (and we suspect many other Americans), administrative efficiency and effectiveness are not to be singlemindedly pursued to the exclusion of other important goals.

## IMPROVING STATE BUREAUCRATIC PERFORMANCE: RESHAPING OR REPLACING STATE ADMINISTRATIVE AGENCIES?

Although state bureaucracies typically perform better than their critics admit, their performance is not ideal. This section examines some efforts to improve state administration.

### Improving State Administration with Organizational Redesign

Going back to the founding of public administration as a field of study in the late nineteenth century, there is a tradition of seeing the sources of management problems as resulting from faulty administrative structures. Governments at all levels have frequently engaged in efforts to redesign those structures in the hope of enhancing administrative performance.

*The Bureaucratic Form of Organization.* We have been using the term bureaucracy loosely, but it has a technical meaning as a particular type of formal organization, one that is common to all sectors of society. "Bureaucratic" characteristics include:

• Systematic division of organizational tasks. Bureaucracies emphasize division of labor and specialization of function.

• Arrangement of organizational units in a hierarchy. Authority flows downward from a single head at the top, while responsibility flows upward to this individual. Bureaucracy embodies the principle of monocratic authority.

• Employment of persons based on their possession of technical competence relevant to an organization's tasks. Bureaucracy embraces the norm of neutral competence.

• An elaborate set of rules governing organizational operations.

Public administration doctrine prior to around 1970 stressed designing organizations along bureaucratic lines to ensure administrative success. Organizations based on these principles supposedly are capable of delivering services reliably and consistently while treating citizens fairly. The hierarchy of authority in them is seen as facilitating accountability to elected officials.

As state administrative systems evolved they often deviated from this bureaucratic ideal. One of the reasons why is that organizational arrangements may reflect the efforts of various and competing political actors, such as governors, legislators, and interest groups, to structure agencies in ways that will enhance the odds that particular programs will be implemented in ways that they prefer. Moreover, as states took on new tasks, they often assigned them to new, single-function agencies, further complicating the structure of state administration. By the middle of the twentieth century state bureaucracies often contained one hundred to two hundred units.

*The Dynamics of Reorganization.* Traditional public administration doctrine also stressed the desirability of fitting individual bureaucracies together as a system. Wasteful duplication of effort and uncoordinated service delivery would be reduced as numerous separate agencies were combined into a smaller number of broadly functional units such as transportation, natural resources, or human services. Combined with the familiar pyramidal structure of higher-level administrators closely supervising lower-level units and employees, such consolidation clarifies lines of responsibility and enhances the accountability of the bureaucracy as a whole. Not only is control by individual agency heads enhanced, but when such heads are appointed by the governor so is gubernatorial control. Reorganizers also urged abandonment of the practice of electing officials who had administrative responsibilities (such as auditors, treasurers, or secretaries of state), and the heading of agencies with boards or commissions, because such arrangements hamper gubernatorial control.

Traditional reorganization doctrine was so persuasive that twenty-six states accomplished major administrative restructuring in the quarter century after 1965 (Conant 2000). States reduced the number of agencies by as much as 80 percent with existing agencies often being combined into a smaller number of large, multifunctional "cabinet" departments. While proponents of reorganization typically promise monetary savings, reducing the number of agencies may save little money either because the eliminated agencies had minuscule budgets or because their functions continue to be performed by other agencies. Still, administrators believe that reorganization improves agency performance (Elling 1992). The clearest consequence of reorganization has been to increase administrative accountability, especially to the governor.

*New Strategies to Enhance Administrative Performance: TQM and REGO*

Numerous contemporary observers dismiss reorganization of the bureaucracy as being largely irrelevant to the challenges that confront state governments and their administrative agencies. Critics believe that bureaucratic-style organizations are too inflexible and resistant to change. They are insufficiently nimble for the new age. Bureaucracy's emphasis on hierarchy and top-down management is viewed as a problem because the lower-level employees most involved in delivering services have too little say in how this is to be done. Excessive emphasis on hierarchy and close supervision supposedly results in too many layers of organization between those at the top of the agency and those at the bottom, hampering communication and reducing an organization's ability to respond to feedback from its environment. These maladies are magnified because public bureaucracies are monopoly providers of services not subject to the desirable discipline of market competition.

Total Quality Management (TQM) and reinventing government (REGO) are two newer approaches to enhancing administrative performance. Proponents of TQM argue that organizational ineffectiveness stems not from lazy or uncaring employees but from management processes that have been badly designed by higher-level managers. They believe that agencies must view those they serve as customers whose needs come first. To achieve this, TQM strives to

- eliminate much of middle management.
- devolve authority to empower lower-level employees.
- encourage group problem solving and team management.
- emphasize the measurement of results, both in terms of customer satisfaction and other standards, to ensure continual improvement in quality.

This logic was sufficiently persuasive that thirty-two states had initiated TQM efforts by the mid-1990s (Chi et al. 1997).

Although TQM is one important source of inspiration for REGO, the latter is more skeptical than TQM about the utility of public bureaucracies in providing services. One key to reinvention is catalytic government, defined as a government that "steers but does not row" (Osborne and Gaebler 1993, ch. 1). While governments must determine what is to be done, what services will be provided, and how they will be paid for, actual service delivery need not be the responsibility of government bureaucracies. Closely related is REGO's call for "injecting competition into service delivery" (1993, ch. 3). Greater reliance on private or nonprofit organizations to deliver services is an obvious implication of these two principles taken together.

Both TQM and REGO favor flatter bureaucracies with fewer layers of organization between upper- and lower-level employees. This saves money, as supposedly superfluous middle-level managers are eliminated while lower-level employees, now subject to less close supervision, are empowered. In many states significant progress toward this goal has occurred (Brudney, Hebert, and Wright 1999; Brudney and Wright 2002). Going too far in this direction may, however, reduce the accountability of public managers to elected officials (Morgan et al. 1996).

The debate over flattening bureaucracies flows over into the debate over empowering lower-level employees. Service quality may be improved if the lower-level employees who are directly involved in implementing programs are given more authority. But, given continuing concerns about administrative fairness and due process in dealing with citizens, how much autonomy for employees is desirable? How much freedom over clients and customers do we want to grant to child protection staff, state police officers, psychiatric hospital staff, tax auditors, or prison guards?

Brudney, Hebert, and Wright (1999) and Brudney and Wright (2002) provide the best picture of what the states have done by way of reinvention. These studies assess reinvention in terms of the implementation of eleven specific reforms. In 1994 the most commonly implemented changes were training in customer service, strategic planning, and efforts to empower lower-level agency personnel. Using an additive scale that measures the extent to which each of the eleven reforms had actually been implemented in a given state, Brudney, Hebert, and Wright find wide variation in reinvention in the states (see Table 9-2). Moreover, while certain states had accomplished more reinvention than others, no state had a reinvention score of 30, a score indicative of at least partial implementation of each of the eleven reforms. Similar state data for 1998 indicate, on the one hand, that full implementation had increased for all eleven of the forms of reinvention. On the other hand, save for the use of strategic planning, no other reform was reported to have been fully implemented by more than 30 percent of the responding administrators. Clearly, REGO remains at the "talking" rather than the "doing" stage in many states.

*REGO and Contracting for Services*

Debate over reinvention is most heated concerning various forms of privatization. Contracting with private or nonprofit organizations for the delivery of services is the most widespread form of privatization in state government. Nearly three-fourths of state officials surveyed in 1998 said their units contracted out the provision of various services (Brudney and Wright 2001). Nearly one-third of the units expended 20 percent or more of budgeted funds in payments to contractors. Contracting has expanded from "hard" services, such as road construction or building maintenance, to "soft" services, such as adoption and foster care, mental health treatment, child support enforcement, substance abuse treatment, processing of Medicaid claims, regulation of child care facilities, and employee training and placement. Some states have experimented with privately run correctional institutions.

The most prevalent justification for contracting out is that private or nonprofit organizations can provide services of equal or better quality more cheaply. Roughly half of the state administrators surveyed by Brudney and Wright (2001) felt contracting of services had improved service quality while 19 percent felt quality had

**Table 9-2** Extent of Implementation of Various Elements of "Reinvention," by State Administrative Agencies

| State | Reinvention score (rank) | State | Reinvention score (rank) | State | Reinvention score (rank) |
|---|---|---|---|---|---|
| Alabama | 17.81 (50) | Louisiana | 23.40 (18) | Ohio | 23.46 (17) |
| Alaska | 19.71 (46) | Maine | 21.78 (31) | Oklahoma | 27.00 (4) |
| Arizona | 25.71 (10) | Maryland | 20.22 (40) | Oregon | 28.04 (2) |
| Arkansas | 21.13 (34) | Massachusetts | 25.80 (9) | Pennsylvania | 21.12 (35) |
| California | 20.25 (39) | Michigan | 22.23 (28) | Rhode Island | 18.26 (49) |
| Colorado | 24.32 (13) | Minnesota | 26.93 (5) | South Carolina | 26.11 (7) |
| Connecticut | 26.31 (6) | Mississippi | 21.85 (30) | South Dakota | 23.16 (21) |
| Delaware | 20.36 (38) | Missouri | 22.10 (29) | Tennessee | 20.00 (43.5) |
| Florida | 28.32 (1) | Montana | 23.39 (19) | Texas | 27.60 (3) |
| Georgia | 22.25 (27) | Nebraska | 21.48 (33) | Utah | 25.03 (12) |
| Hawaii | 20.46 (37) | Nevada | 20.00 (43.5) | Vermont | 19.87 (45) |
| Idaho | 23.05 (23) | New Hampshire | 18.70 (47) | Virginia | 24.07 (14) |
| Illinois | 22.88 (25) | New Jersey | 20.73 (36) | Washington | 26.06 (8) |
| Indiana | 23.36 (20) | New Mexico | 18.60 (48) | West Virginia | 23.03 (24) |
| Iowa | 24.06 (15) | New York | 25.63 (11) | Wisconsin | 23.59 (16) |
| Kansas | 20.11 (42) | North Carolina | 20.17 (41) | Wyoming | 23.10 (22) |
| Kentucky | 21.50 (32) | North Dakota | 22.70 (26) | | |

SOURCE: Brudney, Hebert, and Wright 1999.

declined. They were more divided on cost savings, however, with 35 percent saying contracting had saved money, 30 percent saying it had made no difference, and 29 percent saying costs had risen. Hiring contractors also makes sense when an agency has only a limited or short-term need for certain services. Purchased services may more readily be terminated or reduced should a state confront fiscal difficulties. Roughly one-fifth of the managers in ten states surveyed in 2000–2001 by Elling, Thompson, and Monet (2003) felt that relying on contractors to provide services guaranteed flexibility when reductions in service levels or staffing became necessary.

Other considerations also drive the contracting process. State government employees in many states are more heavily unionized than are private sector workers. Hence contracting may be a way to lower labor costs, if not also "bust the unions." While public sector unions may believe that this is the primary reason that jurisdictions shift from in-house to contracted service delivery, in the 2000–2001 state survey only 2 percent of managers acknowledged this to be a factor prompting the use of contracting.

Contracting rarely works as well as its proponents assert. While costs have often declined, sometimes this is because the quantity or quality of service being provided has also declined. Although competition may cause contractors to deliver better services, the need to make a profit may tempt them to skimp on quality. Another problem is that competition among qualified providers is often absent, especially in less populated areas and for specialized services. Smith and Smyth (1996) found that little competition existed for the contracts to provide substance abuse treatment services in North Carolina and that "once created a contract tends to be renewed routinely" (286).

Corruption may also subvert the contracting process. Bid rigging, bribery, and kickback scandals are common in the history of contracting. Freedman (1994) argues that some governors, whose traditional patronage appointment powers have been limited by the courts, now practice "new patronage" based on steering government contracts to political supporters. Effective contracting requires that specific performance standards be written into contracts and that contractor performance be closely monitored. Writing precise performance criteria is difficult, however, especially when the services involved are complex. Monitoring of contractor performance and auditing contractor records is typically limited and/or haphazard (Auger 1999). Moreover, good monitoring is not cheap, and when effective monitoring systems are in place the costs of such systems, combined with other costs of contract administration, may largely negate other savings.

Contracting raises accountability concerns because it lengthens the chain of command. Lines of authority and responsibility now run not just from a governor or the legislature to an agency head and then down to the level at which services are delivered in an agency, but on to private or nonprofit service providers as well. Finally, contracting raises liability issues. Depriving an individual of his or her life, liberty, or property is the ultimate in governmental power. Placing such authority in the hands of private actors is controversial and explains why few states have contracted for the operation of maximum-security correctional institutions, and why they remain doubtful about its suitability for other regulatory functions (Gormley 1996b, Thompson and Elling 2000). Demands for accountability in contract administration may ultimately come to exceed those that currently exist for direct delivery of public services because of "the fear that contractors are not motivated by a public service commitment and are not subject to the range of accountability mechanisms applicable to public employees" (Cooper 1994, 107).

While contracting out should be one of the tools that state governments use in delivering services, the growing literature on contracting and other privatization options suggests that states should exercise caution in selecting candidates for privatization and make sure that all relevant costs are realistically calculated. Significant resources must be devoted to contract administration, especially the drafting of specific contract language, and to monitoring of contract compliance. State agencies should also maintain some service capacity of their own, both as a standard against which to judge the performance of private providers and to guard against interruptions in service delivery associated with contractors' withdrawal.

## MANAGING THE PERSONNEL OF STATE BUREAUCRACIES

Although contracting out may reduce the number of employees directly employed in service delivery, others will have to be hired to perform the tasks that ensure that a system of catalytic government works well. Moreover, many functions will continue to be performed by those who are directly employed by state governments. Hence the ability of state governments to hire, motivate, and retain a productive corps of administrative employees will remain an important determinant of administrative performance.

Until well into the twentieth century, getting and retaining a state government job was largely a matter of a person having the "right" partisan affiliation or personal connections. Beginning in the late nineteenth century, civil service reformers challenged such patronage practices, arguing that effective government required the hiring and retention of public employees on the basis of merit—that is, on the basis of their education, relevant employment experience, or actual job performance. Independent civil service commissions would ensure adherence to such merit principles. The result would be a competent corps of politically neutral civil servants. Such a system is consistent with bureaucratic values. Today three-fourths of the states have comprehensive civil service systems.

*State Personnel Processes: Competence, Organizational Effectiveness, and Accountability*

While defenders of civil service arrangements argue that they ensure that "only the best shall serve the state," contemporary critics charge that such systems often fail to achieve this goal. Civil service arrangements have clearly improved the quality of state administration. No state can effectively meet the demands placed on it today using pure patronage arrangements. Anne Freedman's (1994) discussion of the corrosive effects of patronage-based practices in Illinois state government is instructive on this point. Although the state has numerous dedicated, hardworking, and competent employees, many of them have been demoralized by the state's patronage practices. Nor is it just "good government" civil service reformers who have criticized the Illinois system. Since the mid-1970s, three U. S. Supreme Court decisions have struck at the state's patronage-based practices. In its 1990 *Rutan* decision the Court rejected the state's argument that those it hires must be supporters of the governor's party or else they will not be motivated to work effectively, or will subvert the governor's program. Instead, the Court maintained that the

> Inefficiency resulting from the wholesale replacement of large numbers of public employees every time political office changes hands belies this justification. And the prospect of dismissal after an election in which the incumbent party has lost is only a disincentive to good work. Further, it is not clear that dismissal in order to make room for a patronage appointee will result in replacement by a person more qualified to do the job since appointment often occurs in exchange for the delivery of votes, or other party service, not job capability (quoted in Freedman 1994, 4).

To be sure, traditional civil service arrangements have not invariably contributed to effective state administration. Among the more serious impediments to effective management identified by managers surveyed in both 1982–1983 and 2000–2001 (Elling, Thompson, and Monet 2003) are several that related to state personnel practices. The next few sections discuss some contemporary challenges to state personnel systems.

**Table 9-3** Average Monthly Earnings, Full-time State Government Employees, March 2000

| State | Rank | Average monthly earnings | Percentage change from 1990 | State | Rank | Average monthly earnings | Percentage change from 1990 |
|---|---|---|---|---|---|---|---|
| California | 1 | $4,451 | 29.4 | Arizona | 27 | $3,055 | 41.5 |
| New Jersey | 2 | $4,075 | 8.4 | Kentucky | 28 | $3,051 | 21.2 |
| Michigan | 3 | $3,934 | 30.9 | Idaho | 29 | $3,022 | 37.6 |
| Connecticut | 4 | $3,909 | 47.9 | North Carolina | 30 | $3,012 | 30.9 |
| Minnesota | 5 | $3,892 | 38.7 | Indiana | 31 | $2,990 | 42.5 |
| New York | 6 | $3,859 | 36.7 | Maine | 32 | $2,983 | 33.9 |
| Alaska | 7 | $3,842 | 29.5 | Montana | 33 | $2,931 | 28.8 |
| Colorado | 8 | $3,779 | 43.5 | Hawaii | 34 | $2,926 | 27.0 |
| Rhode Island | 9 | $3,772 | 50.3 | Utah | 35 | $2,880 | 37.4 |
| Wisconsin | 10 | $3,710 | 42.3 | Georgia | 36 | $2,849 | 34.2 |
| Massachusetts | 11 | $3,683 | 26.3 | Arkansas | 37 | $2,842 | 42.8 |
| Iowa | 12 | $3,656 | 43.9 | Alabama | 38 | $2,841 | 42.0 |
| Washington | 13 | $3,551 | 36.5 | North Dakota | 39 | $2,826 | 41.0 |
| Nevada | 14 | $3,444 | 19.8 | Oklahoma | 40 | $2,821 | 45.9 |
| Illinois | 15 | $3,441 | 24.5 | New Mexico | 41 | $2,811 | 40.1 |
| Pennsylvania | 16 | $3,436 | 47.9 | Louisiana | 42 | $2,807 | 40.3 |
| Ohio | 17 | $3,369 | 42.5 | Tennessee | 43 | $2,786 | 35.6 |
| Maryland | 18 | $3,323 | 37.1 | South Dakota | 44 | $2,777 | 41.2 |
| Oregon | 19 | $3,269 | 26.8 | Mississippi | 45 | $2,752 | 44.0 |
| Virginia | 20 | $3,229 | 27.4 | South Carolina | 46 | $2,741 | 37.0 |
| Delaware | 21 | $3,222 | 44.9 | West Virginia | 47 | $2,694 | 42.4 |
| Vermont | 22 | $3,153 | 37.6 | Missouri | 48 | $2,678 | 44.4 |
| Florida | 23 | $3,149 | 32.6 | Wyoming | 49 | $2,589 | 40.4 |
| Texas | 24 | $3,095 | 50.9 | Nebraska | 50 | $2,514 | 48.2 |
| New Hampshire | 25 | $3,079 | 36.3 | | | | |
| Kansas | 26 | $3,071 | 29.4 | 50-state average | — | $3,374 | 26.6 |

SOURCES: U.S. Bureau of the Census 2002; U.S. Bureau of the Census 1991.

*Compensating State Government Administrative Employees.* Because state governments—like all governments—are labor-intensive, employee pay and benefits constitute a significant part of their budgets. In 2000 the monthly pay of a full-time state employee averaged $3,374—or over $40,000 annually (U.S. Bureau of the Census 2002).[2] The pay of state employees varies greatly, however, as Table 9-3 indicates.

Differences in cost of living explain some of the interstate variation in the pay of state government employees (Gold and Ritchie 1993). But while adjusting for cost of living narrows interstate pay differences, it does not eliminate them. For example, cost of living alone cannot explain why the average pay for Minnesota state government employees in 2000 was 55 percent higher than that of Nebraska state government employees.

2. Earlier I noted that many state government employees work in higher education. Many of these employees are themselves well educated. Hence their salaries tend to be higher as well, on average about 14 percent higher in 2000. Thus across the fifty states the average monthly earnings of non–higher education full-time state government employees was $3,221, while for all state government employees it was $3,374.

Since state governments must often compete with private sector employees for workers, how well states pay compared to the private sector is of importance.[3] Looking at pay for all state employees in seven states, and controlling for the characteristics of individual workers (education, experience, gender, race, etc.), Belman and Heywood (1995) found that California and Wisconsin state employees earned about 2 or 3 percent more than their counterparts in the private sector in those states, while in Mississippi and Illinois they earned about 2 percent less, and in Indiana and Michigan there was virtually no difference. Research also indicates that while lower-level state employees with less education may earn more than private sector workers with comparable education, better-educated state employees in higher-level administrative or professional jobs typically earn considerably less than similarly educated and employed private sector workers (Gold and Ritchie 1993; Belman and Heywood 1995; Miller 1996).

A state that fails to pay competitive salaries will typically have trouble recruiting and retaining employees. In fact, almost 60 percent of the managers surveyed in the 2000–2001 comparative state management study felt that low salaries hampered their ability to recruit good employees (Elling, Thompson, and Monet 2003). Voluntary employee turnover is undesirably high in many states; this is especially true in states that pay least well (Elling 1997; Selden and Moynihan 2000). Just keeping up with inflation is a problem for many state compensation systems. While the salaries of full-time state employees increased by about 27 percent during the 1990s, the inflation rate during the decade was almost 34 percent.

*Are State Employees Too Hard to Fire?* Many citizens could care less if state employees are poorly paid. In their eyes the problem is that they are too hard to fire. For the period from 1993 to 1995, the average annual dismissal rates in eighteen states averaged about one dismissal for every 100 employees (Elling 1999). Whether or not dismissal rates of this magnitude are too low can be debated (Elling 1999; Rainey 2003). State personnel directors think that their own state's personnel system has succeeded in protecting employees from adverse personnel actions unrelated to their actual ability to perform and in ensuring the political neutrality of the state workforce (Hays and Kearney 1992). But this accomplishment may come at the price of rules and procedures that make it difficult to discipline or discharge poorly performing state employees. Indeed, this is what one-third of the managers surveyed in the 2000–2001 comparative state management study reported to be the case (Elling, Thompson, and Monet 2003).

*"Deregulating" State Personnel Management.* Making it easier to get rid of low-performing employees is only one of a number of changes advocated to reform

---

3. Comparing pay in the two sectors is complicated. One reason is that certain jobs exist primarily, if not exclusively, in the public sector so that determining what constitutes an appropriate nongovernmental benchmark job is difficult if not impossible. Average state employee pay across all jobs may exceed that for the private sector in a state because state government employs relatively more employees with either more education or with skills that are in greater demand.

state personnel processes. A central concept is that personnel functions should be "deregulated" or "decentralized," with more authority for recruiting, hiring, appraising, training, rewarding, and disciplining employees being given to individual administrative agencies and operating managers. Jerrell Coggburn (2000) measured the extent to which states have deregulated their personnel systems based on whether they have put in place one or another of nineteen different reforms. Alabama, North Dakota, Oregon, South Carolina, Utah, and Virginia had deregulated their state personnel processes the most—their scores ranged from 13 to 15—while Florida, Hawaii, Nevada, and Rhode Island had done the least—their scores were three or less. The average number of reforms adopted was roughly eight. The most widely adopted changes were allowing operating agencies to determine promotion criteria (98 percent of states), allowing them to develop selection criteria for positions (71 percent), eliminating veterans' and minority preferences for promotions (71 percent), allowing operating agencies to control hiring process (69 percent), and relaxing restrictive selection rules (67 percent).

The fact that various personnel reforms have been only partially embraced in many states reflects some doubts about their desirability. Supporters of the civil service value of a politically neutral workforce are opposed to certain reforms, while public sector unions doubt that agency managers will treat employees fairly if given expanded personnel authority. Coggburn (2000) finds that more extensive state employee unionization is associated with less reform.

### The Challenge of Equal Opportunity and Diversity

Civil service's stress on "objective merit" has reduced discrimination based on race, ethnicity, age, gender, and disability. Moreover, state governments have addressed discriminatory practices or effects in their personnel systems in response to federal and state laws and court rulings. The share of state government jobs held by women and minorities has increased substantially in the past thirty-five years. By 1995 the proportion of female state government employees was only 6 percent less than would be expected based on their presence in the national population, with African American females' share of state jobs exceeding their population presence by 24 percent. African American and Hispanic men were much less well represented, however, with the former holding 17 percent fewer jobs than would be expected based on their presence in the population and the latter holding 38 percent fewer jobs (Riccucci and Saidel, 1997).

The concentration of women and minorities in lower-level jobs is the major employment equity issue today. To be sure, female and minority employees hold a larger share of higher-level state jobs that pay better and entail more responsibility than in the past. Between 1964 and 1999 the proportion of female state agency heads grew from 2 percent to 25 percent while the proportion of African American agency heads increased from 1 percent to 7 percent and the proportion of all minorities combined increased from 8 percent to 13 percent (Bullard and Wright 1993; "Women in State Government" 2000).

Greene, Selden, and Brewer (2000) have developed the most sophisticated measure of the extent to which various groups of state government employees are equitably distributed across the entire range of state government jobs, a measure that they call *rho*.[4] Hispanic American women (rho=0.27) and Native American women (rho=0.54) were most concentrated in lower-level/lower-paying state jobs. All groups of male employees other than Hispanic American males are overrepresented in higher-level jobs with white non-Hispanic males having a rho of 1.48 and Asian American men having a score of 1.82.

Table 9-4 provides detail on patterns for particular states. Males hold a disproportionate share of higher-level jobs in all but one state (see columns 1 and 2). Such overrepresentation exhibits considerable interstate variation, however, with male employment statistics ranging from just under 1.00 in Louisiana to 1.58 in North Dakota. The rho statistics for particular racial-ethnic groups (regardless of gender) are also highly variable across the states. Thus African American state employees (column 3) hold a disproportionate share of higher-level state jobs in nineteen states and do especially well in Massachusetts, California, Ohio, Washington, Illinois, Maine, and Michigan.

The less favorable circumstances of women and minorities in state employment are by no means entirely due to overt discrimination. But racism and sexism persist. Stereotypes about the abilities of women and minorities are a key part of "sticky floors" (jobs with limited promotion potential), "glass ceilings" that limit advancement, and "glass walls" that restrict employment of women or minorities in units with certain functions. Efforts to improve the employment status of women and minorities have been controversial, especially when they have taken the form of affirmative action. Opponents charge that affirmative action unfairly discriminates against better-qualified white males. While this may occasionally be so, there is little evidence that female or minority candidates for promotion are being systematically "leapfrogged" over better-educated or more experienced white or male state employees, or are otherwise less well qualified (Bullard and Wright 1993; Olshfski and Caprio 1996). The slow increase in the proportion of minorities or women in higher-level public jobs suggests that affirmative action has produced incremental change at most.

---

4. Rho measures both the proportion of all jobs held by employees of a particular gender or racial-ethnic background and the organizational (and salary) level of the jobs held by such employees in state government. The measure gives heavier weight to the representation of members of a particular group at higher than at lower levels. If a particular group of employees, white males for instance, holds the same proportion of jobs at all levels of the state job hierarchy, then *rho* has a value of 1.00. Values of rho below 1.00 indicate the concentration of members of that group in lower-level/less well-paying jobs while a value of rho greater than 1.00 indicates that members of a given group hold a disproportionate share of higher-level/better-paying state administrative jobs. For more detail on the calculation of rho, see Greene, Selden, and Brewer (2000), especially 390–392.

**Table 9-4** Representation by Gender and Race/Ethnicity (RHO) at Various Levels of the Administrative/ Salary Hierarchy, 1995

| State[a] | Gender | | Race/Ethnicity | | | | |
|---|---|---|---|---|---|---|---|
| | Female rho | Male rho | African American rho | Hispanic American rho | Asian American rho | Native American rho | Non-Hispanic white rho |
| Alabama | .78 | 1.28 | .56 | .32 | 1.18 | .47 | 1.15 |
| Alaska | .77 | 1.11 | .89 | .53 | 1.05 | .61 | 1.12 |
| Arizona | .58 | 1.44 | 1.05 | .54 | .77 | .28 | 1.12 |
| Arkansas | .83 | 1.18 | .97 | .25 | .57 | .78 | 1.01 |
| California | .68 | 1.21 | 1.68 | .53 | .94 | 1.08 | 1.57 |
| Colorado | .58 | 1.40 | .93 | .68 | .57 | .88 | 1.04 |
| Connecticut | .60 | 1.33 | 1.27 | .60 | .77 | 1.09 | 1.02 |
| Delaware | .63 | 1.44 | .67 | .43 | 3.78 | .54 | 1.02 |
| Florida | .65 | 1.40 | .97 | .66 | 1.30 | 1.35 | 1.04 |
| Georgia | .81 | 1.24 | .79 | .37 | 1.00 | .93 | 1.08 |
| Idaho | .57 | 1.45 | .51 | .20 | .66 | .33 | 1.04 |
| Illinois | .64 | 1.33 | 1.48 | .49 | 1.21 | 2.33 | .94 |
| Indiana | .74 | 1.30 | 1.06 | .52 | 2.49 | .76 | .99 |
| Iowa | .79 | 1.21 | .98 | .70 | .67 | 1.22 | 1.00 |
| Kansas | .57 | 1.48 | .90 | .47 | 1.19 | .83 | 1.02 |
| Kentucky | .73 | 1.29 | .88 | .42 | .80 | .21 | 1.01 |
| Louisiana | 1.00 | .99 | .82 | .25 | .56 | .80 | 1.12 |
| Maine | .57 | 1.46 | 1.43 | .77 | .22 | .11 | 1.01 |
| Maryland | .66 | 1.36 | .87 | .33 | .74 | .64 | 1.09 |
| Massachusetts | .70 | 1.30 | 1.89 | .48 | .53 | .82 | 1.00 |
| Michigan | .61 | 1.35 | 1.36 | .63 | 1.60 | 1.04 | .92 |
| Minnesota | .65 | 1.30 | 1.01 | .53 | .43 | .79 | 1.02 |
| Mississippi | .90 | 1.14 | .38 | .38 | 1.52 | .18 | 1.36 |
| Missouri | .59 | 1.49 | .76 | .54 | 2.30 | .96 | 1.01 |
| Montana | .64 | 1.33 | .33 | .33 | .62 | .24 | 1.05 |
| Nebraska | .52 | 1.53 | .98 | .40 | .66 | .45 | 1.02 |
| Nevada | .66 | 1.26 | .99 | .35 | .58 | .84 | 1.08 |
| New Hampshire | .64 | 1.38 | .42 | .11 | .22 | 1.37 | 1.01 |
| New Jersey | .60 | 1.37 | 1.32 | .37 | .43 | .92 | 1.07 |
| New Mexico | .63 | 1.41 | 1.17 | 1.11 | 1.02 | .23 | 1.00 |
| New York | .60 | 1.39 | 1.29 | .47 | .94 | .64 | 1.11 |
| North Carolina | .88 | 1.13 | .81 | .25 | .61 | .61 | 1.06 |
| North Dakota | .46 | 1.58 | .11 | .81 | 3.11 | .12 | 1.03 |
| Ohio | .63 | 1.38 | 1.65 | .83 | 1.40 | .76 | .91 |
| Oklahoma | .64 | 1.42 | .89 | .30 | 1.82 | .52 | 1.07 |
| Oregon | .59 | 1.37 | 1.33 | .39 | .80 | .71 | 1.02 |
| Pennsylvania | .58 | 1.44 | 1.32 | .44 | .76 | 1.54 | .99 |
| Rhode Island | .58 | 1.43 | .91 | .17 | .75 | .35 | 1.08 |
| South Carolina | .78 | 1.27 | .55 | .31 | 1.54 | .83 | 1.19 |
| South Dakota | .48 | 1.57 | .18 | .11 | 4.46 | .08 | 1.05 |
| Tennessee | .73 | 1.31 | 1.04 | .18 | .45 | 1.63 | .99 |
| Texas | .69 | 1.35 | .97 | .48 | .82 | 1.51 | 1.24 |
| Utah | .47 | 1.55 | .89 | .42 | .72 | .32 | 1.01 |
| Virginia | .67 | 1.35 | .98 | .28 | .48 | .91 | 1.05 |
| Washington | .63 | 1.30 | 1.49 | .46 | .98 | .85 | 1.00 |
| West Virginia | .57 | 1.53 | .70 | .44 | 6.15 | 1.42 | .99 |
| Wisconsin | .54 | 1.44 | 1.21 | .71 | .77 | .99 | .99 |
| Wyoming | .64 | 1.40 | 1.24 | .32 | 2.18 | .06 | 1.05 |

NOTE: I am grateful to Professor Sally Selden for providing me with this state-by-state breakdown. See also Greene, Selden and Brewer 2000. See footnote 4 for an explanation of RHO.

[a] Data were not available for the states of Hawaii and Vermont.

*The Challenge of Collective Bargaining*

As of 2001, state employees in thirty states possessed collective bargaining rights based on legislation (26 states) or gubernatorial executive order (4 states).[5] In twenty-one states, union density (the percentage of state employees with bargaining rights covered by a collective bargaining contract) exceeds 50 percent.[6] State government unionization is most extensive in those states with a history of strong private sector unionization, such as those in the Northeast, the Midwest, and the "Pacific Rim" states of California, Oregon, Washington, Alaska, and Hawaii. With the exception of Florida, state employee unions are weak or nonexistent in states in the South, Southwest, or Mountain West.

The consequences of collective bargaining for state administration are far from clear. The diversity of state laws on the matters subject to negotiation, and the differing political and economic environments in which collective bargaining occurs, virtually ensures highly variable effects. Still, collective bargaining has affected the operation of civil service systems, the costs of state government, and administrative performance.

Collective bargaining and civil service practices often coexist. Unions join civil service advocates in opposition to patronage practices and support protections against dismissal for non-work-related reasons. But merit principles may be compromised by unions' emphasis on seniority as the primary criterion for promotion, salary increases, or layoffs. This preference also hampers efforts to increase the gender or racial/ethnic diversity of the state workforce.

Some critics contend that union-negotiated wage and fringe benefit settlements inflate budgets and force tax hikes. With respect to wage increases, research suggests a modest impact with public sector unions generally having less impact than their private sector counterparts (Kearney 2001). According to one study, the average unionized state government employee earned about 7 percent more than one who worked in a non-unionized setting (Belman, Heywood, and Lund 1997). Moreover, state fiscal stringency has prompted union flexibility on compensation, often in return for guarantees that layoffs will not occur. Flexibility has also been encouraged by threats to contract out the provision of services to for-profit or not-for-profit providers.

Public sector unions—particularly those with many female members—have been in the vanguard of "comparable worth" efforts. Advocates of comparable worth argue that job classes that disproportionately employ women have lower rates of pay

5. Although New Mexico adopted a collective bargaining law in the 1990s, it was "sunsetted" out of existence a few years later. In 2000 the governors of Missouri and Kentucky signed executive orders giving state employees bargaining rights. In 1999 the 1996 Maryland executive order authorizing state employee collective bargaining was codified into law. I am grateful to Professor Richard Kearney and Professor Greg Saltzman for helping me to update the data in Kearney (2001).

6. These states are Alaska (61 percent), California (58 percent), Connecticut (75 percent), Florida (73 percent), Hawaii (71 percent), Maine (61 percent), Massachusetts (58 percent), Michigan (53 percent), Minnesota (61 percent), New Hampshire (56 percent), New Jersey (64 percent), New York (74 percent), Oregon (60 percent), Pennsylvania (63.4 percent), and Rhode Island (68 percent) (Kearney 2001).

because "women's work" is systematically undervalued. There is considerable debate on this point, and the courts have refused to embrace the comparable worth argument. Still, by the late 1990s, twenty-one states had adjusted pay ranges in ways that resulted in significant salary increases to women (and men) employed in traditionally female-dominated job classes (Gardner and Daniel 1998).

Although some observers contend that administrative performance is impaired as unionized employees gain a greater say in decisions traditionally reserved for managers, there is little systematic evidence that collective bargaining hampers productivity or reduces the quality of government services. Even in highly unionized states such as California or Michigan less than 5 percent of managers considered "limits on managerial authority due to collective bargaining" to be a serious impediment to effective management (Elling, Thompson, and Monet 2003). As previously noted, states that pay their employees better have more success in holding on to them (Elling 1997; Selden and Moynihan 2000), and better-paying states are often those with workforces that collectively bargain. Since employee turnover likely impacts administrative performance adversely, the existence of state employee unions makes a positive contribution to administrative performance.

Although unions are often suspicious of TQM or REGO initiatives—especially when such initiatives occur in conjunction with budget cuts and contracting out—they are not opposed to all such efforts. Management experts recommend more emphasis on employee training and career development, and unions support efforts to enhance the skill levels of their members (Kearney 2001). They also tend to support efforts to empower lower-level employees and often favor the "flattening of bureaucracies" by eliminating layers of middle management. The process of collective bargaining in general could be considered a vehicle for achieving the participative management and employee empowerment touted by TQM and REGO enthusiasts, albeit not solely on management's terms.

## ADMINISTRATORS AND OTHERS: STATE ADMINISTRATIVE PERFORMANCE IN A POLITICAL CONTEXT

The politics-administration dichotomy posited by Woodrow Wilson in the 1880s held that efficient and effective administration would result if trained professionals with considerable job security handled administrative tasks. For their part, elected officials were to establish agencies, authorize their programs, and specify the amount of money and number of personnel to be made available to those agencies. As a description of contemporary reality such a dichotomy is flawed. The difficulty of crafting complex policy, combined with the fact that political officials control resources crucial to administrative success, causes administrators to believe that policy making cannot remain the sole preserve of elected officials. Hence it is hardly surprising that state administrators devote as much as one-fourth of their time to policy development activities (Elling 1992). At the same time, elected officials seek to influence how state policies are implemented. State agencies make too much difference in the lives of constituents for elected officials to allow them to function in splendid isolation.

*State Bureaucrats as Policy Shapers*

Bureaucratic influence in the policy-making process stems from several sources. First, career bureaucrats often know best how to deal with problems. Public health officials, for example, can be expected to know more than anyone else about a state's health problems and its public health programs. Second, state agencies possess discretionary authority. No law can be written so precisely as to eliminate completely the need for choice in implementing its provisions. Moreover, it is unwise for elected officials to limit administrative discretion unduly since policy implementation is often improved if administrators can respond to feedback and make adjustments according to the circumstances in individual cases. In deference to bureaucratic expertise, elected officials often grant agencies broad authority to develop the procedures and regulations necessary to implement programs. Finally, agencies may develop "constituencies" that contribute to administrative influence as the beneficiaries of the programs that an agency administers become supporters of those programs and the agency itself.

A study of state agencies that administer air pollution programs (Potoski and Woods 2000) illustrates the policy-shaping and administrative roles played by state agencies. Top state officials with responsibilities in this policy area in thirty-eight states were surveyed as to the impact of various actors on developing emissions standards, developing ambient air standards, monitoring of ambient air quality, pollution source monitoring, enforcement, and granting of permits.[7] Across these six areas of activity the relevant state agency was significantly more influential (influence score of 26) than were industry or environmental interest groups (scores of 16 and 13, respectively), the state legislature (influence score of 11), or the governor (score of 10.5). Even in the case of the two arenas that involve the most policy making—developing source emissions standards and setting ambient air standards—state clean air agencies ranked as the most influential actor with respect to the former while they ranked right behind the U.S. Environmental Protection Agency with respect to the latter.[8]

Does the active role that state bureaucracies play in the policy-making process mean that we are confronted with runaway state bureaucracies? Such a conclusion is as wrong as believing that state bureaucracies and bureaucrats invariably leave policy making in the hands of elected officials while passively awaiting their marching orders. Administrative influence is relational. As more nonadministrative players get into the game, the relative power of an agency itself declines. Administrative expertise is less persuasive in an era when modest alterations in existing programs may seem insufficient (Rourke 1991). Moreover, bureaucrats are appointed officials

7. For a given area of activity, the influence of a particular actor could range from 1 (not influential) to 5 (very influential). The maximum possible influence score for a given actor across all six areas of activity was 30.

8. I am grateful to Dr. Neal Woods of the University of South Carolina for providing me with specific data on this point.

in a political system where popular election is a powerful source of legitimacy. Those who act unilaterally are likely to be castigated for exceeding their authority. Most administrative power is "derivative power," exercised at the sufferance of others. The abolition of an agency or the transferring of its programs is rare. But both occur. More common is the narrowing of administrative discretion as a consequence of elected officials' displeasure with how that discretion has been used.

One important element of the influence net of state agencies includes federal government actors such as the Congress, other federal agencies, and the federal courts. Potoski and Woods (2000) found that the average influence wielded by the U. S. Environmental Protection Agency was only slightly less than that of the state air pollution control agency itself. The federal courts have forced states to increase funding for, or modify the operations of, correctional institutions and facilities for the mentally ill, developmentally disabled, and children (O'Leary 1994). Federal (and state) court decisions concerning patronage practices, collective bargaining, sexual harassment, comparable worth, and affirmative action have had important consequences for state personnel systems. Having sketched the broad outlines of interaction between state agencies and other actors, I will now focus on bureaucratic relations with the governor, the state legislature, and the public in various guises—organized interest groups, clients of agencies, and ordinary citizens.

### The Governor as Chief Bureaucrat

To be successful, governors often need a state's bureaucracy. Although gubernatorial relations with administrative agencies are sometimes conflictual, usually they are not (Elling 1992). During his three terms as Michigan's governor, Republican John Engler was no fan of big government. Nevertheless, one of his aides had this to say about Michigan's bureaucracy: "The biggest surprise we faced when moving to the governor's office . . . was in working with the bureaucracy. We now had to recommend programs that could be effectively implemented and we needed state agency assistance on that. We were surprised at how many really good people were over there" (Elling and Kobrak 1995).

Until quite recently governors were often chief executives in name only. This is much less true today. In 1964 only one-third of agency heads surveyed in all fifty states reported that the governor exercised more control and oversight over their units than did the legislature while 44 percent said the legislature exerted more control (and 23 percent said the two had equal influence). By 1999 almost half of surveyed agency heads (49 percent) said the governor exercised more control while only 27 percent said this about the state legislature (Wright 2002).

Administrative reorganization has enhanced gubernatorial influence. Governors in more than half of the states can initiate organizational changes that take effect unless the legislature objects within a specified time period (Rosenthal 1990). Personnel system reform has also enhanced gubernatorial leverage over the bureaucracy. Nearly every state has shifted personnel management responsibilities from a semiautonomous civil service commission to a central personnel agency. In more than three-fourths of the states the head of this unit is either appointed by the governor and reports directly to him or her, or is appointed by a department head who is a gubernatorial appointee (National Association of State Personnel Executives 2000). Many states have also increased the number of higher-level administrators subject to gubernatorial appointment on the grounds that they are significantly involved in shaping policies as well as administering them. Some, however, worry that this trend threatens excessive politicization of the management of public programs and is but a thinly veiled attempt to reintroduce patronage practices into state administration (Freedman 1994).

Michigan's Republican governor John M. Engler (1991–2003) was one governor who understood that reshaping the bureaucracy was a key to advancing his policy agenda. He transferred environmental protection responsibilities from the state's Department of Natural Resources—an agency headed by a commission over which the governor had less direct control—to a new Department of Environmental Quality headed by a direct gubernatorial appointee, one presumably more responsive to his more business-oriented environmental policies. He eliminated the board that oversaw the Department of Corrections. Engler also combined the Departments of Mental Health and Public Health into a new Department of Community Health and increased the proportion of department services that were contracted out. As an early champion of welfare reform, he replaced the state's Department of Social Services with a Family Independence Agency. Finally, he used his appointments to the state's Civil Service Commission to reshape state personnel policies in ways that state employee unions, at least, thought were damaging to their interests.

While governors are more powerful than ever in formal terms, aggressive performance of the role of chief bureaucrat remains the exception. One reason is that they have many other things to do. These other obligations, such as providing policy leadership for the legislature, may be both more pressing and more interesting. The complexity of a state's administrative structure may discourage involvement. Moreover, some governors believe that an excessively intrusive management style is ineffective (Cox 1991).

Most of the time involvement with state bureaucracies is very much a matter of governors picking their spots. What prompts gubernatorial interaction with a state agency? Governors may focus on agencies with the biggest budgets or on those administering programs central to the goals of their administrations. They may not intervene unless a crisis arises in the administration of a particular program that has the potential for serious political fallout (Elling 1992; Weinberg 1977). Although waiting for crises to occur may seem a risky management strategy, even governors with strong formal powers must often embrace such a strategy to function effectively as chief bureaucrat.

### The Legislature as Bureaucratic Overseer

State legislatures can tap an impressive array of resources in seeking to influence bureaucracies. These include approving agency budget requests, modifying agency programs or organization, investigating agency operations, and confirming the governor's appointments to top administrative posts. These resources, and others, are why legislatures continue to matter in state administration even as the influence of governors has grown. In 1994 agency heads in all fifty states were asked to estimate how much influence the legislature had across four domains: determining the total agency budget, establishing the budgets for specific agency programs, instituting major policy changes, and changing the content of rules and regulations (Hebert 2000). The total influence score for the legislature (where 0 = no influence and 12 = high influence) was 9.40 while gubernatorial influence was only slightly greater, at 9.47. Recall as well from the ten-state management survey cited earlier in the chapter that how the state legislature deals with an agency's budget often creates problems for agencies in achieving their goals.

Legislatures are not all equally well prepared for the task of overseeing the bureaucracy, however. Effective oversight requires a combination of persistence and knowledge. Legislatures with longer sessions, with lower rates of member turnover, and with more extensive staff support find it easier to provide direction to their state's bureaucracy. Potoski and Woods (2000) found that when a state's legislature was more highly professionalized, the influence of the agency itself on state clean air policy and programs decreased significantly. As Chapter 6 indicates, however, state legislatures with these characteristics are not numerous.

### State Bureaucracies and Organized Interests

Citizens, whether organized or unorganized, have a stake in what state bureaucracies do. Interest groups—well organized but not broadly representative—may exert undue influence on state administration. Especially in the case of agencies created to regulate segments of the economy, the result may be a "captured" agency—one that is solicitous of the interests of the targets of regulation but neglectful of the interests of the broader public that is supposed to benefit from regulation.

Agencies and interest groups interact because each has resources useful to the other. Agencies contact groups to acquire information on the effects of their programs, to secure feedback on proposed regulations, and to gain technical information needed for agency operations. For their part, organized groups contact agencies both to seek information about agency programs and to try and shape the content of rules and regulations (Elling 1992). Such contacts may improve agency performance and help citizens to access services to which they are entitled.

Interest groups may also compromise administrative performance. They may encourage bias in rule application or distort agency priorities in ways that hurt the general public. This is less frequent when a larger number of groups contend for influence over agency affairs since the agency is less likely to be beholden to any single one and may be able to play one group off against another. Since, as discussed in Chapter 4, the state interest group universe has grown more diverse, such a situation is more likely today than in the past. In a fifty-state study across a wide range of state agencies both "professional associations" and "clientele groups" were seen by agency heads as having less influence on agency budget decisions, major policy changes, or the content of rules and regulations than either legislators or governors, with the overall influence of associations and clientele groups averaging in the "slight" range (Hebert 2000).

Interest groups are also less powerful because many states have expanded public representation in administrative decision-making processes. Requiring hearings on environmental issues and mandating the appointment of public members to state occupational licensing boards has facilitated public access. More than two-thirds of the states have "proxy advocacy" units that represent citizens in the deliberation of state agencies that determine the rates that electric and gas utilities may charge (Gormley 1996a). Facilitating public comment on proposed state air pollution agency policies has been found to increase the influence of environmental groups while not simultaneously increasing the influence of industry-affiliated groups (Potoski and Woods 2000).

### State Bureaucracies and the Public Encounter: Clients, Customers, or What?

One yardstick for judging an agency's performance is how well it meets the needs of those individuals or groups for whom it exists. One of the purported virtues of the bureaucratic model is that similar cases are treated similarly. Various studies of citizens' contacts with bureaucracies, some of which were cited earlier in this chapter, suggest that most citizens are treated well and that the bureaucrats with whom they deal are helpful. Only 7 percent of the state managers surveyed as part of the 2000–2001 comparative state management study felt that "agency employees not dealing fairly or helpfully with clients" was a serious problem (Elling, Thompson, and Monet 2003).

Citizens who believe they have been treated badly by state agencies can pursue various avenues of redress. They can contact various state elected officials for help in dealing with an administrative agency. Citizen contact with state legislators can help solve particular problems and may even lead to more substantial changes in agency procedures or the laws that they implement. Administrative actions are also regularly challenged in the courts, although the costs of and possibilities for delay inherent in the legal process limit the judiciary's value as an avenue of appeal for the average citizen. All states have open records or freedom-of-information laws designed to facilitate citizen access to materials upon which state agencies base their actions. Some states have adopted variants of the Scandinavian institution of the ombudsman—an official who investigates citizens' complaints about problems with government agencies.

Both TQM and REGO argue that improvements in governmental performance require that agencies adopt a customer orientation. Adopting such an orientation is complicated by the ambiguous meaning of "customer" in the public sector. Hyde (1995) distinguishes among those served or impacted by public agencies in terms of how much choice or influence they have. "Customers" are service recipients who have the most choice and influence over the service process. An example might be students at a state university, or residents who select between different state parks for camping. Those citizens who have legal or contractual ties with agencies are "clients"—recipients of welfare benefits might be an example. Those with the least amount of choice or recourse are "captives." This latter category is similar to Barzelay and Armajani's (1992) conception of "compliers." Governments frequently require individuals or organizations to behave in certain ways. If they do not, then penalties may be imposed on them. When asked to pay state taxes citizens are "compliers." So are inmates in state correctional facilities as well as those business firms subject to consumer protection, worker health and safety, environmental protection, and anti-discrimination laws.

Agencies may have both customers and compliers, and how the former fare is related to how the latter are treated. Such agencies cannot make compliers completely happy without compromising the reason that they exist in the first place: to collect taxes, to isolate lawbreakers from the general population, to protect the health and safety of workers, to enhance the quality of a state's natural environment, or to protect various citizens from unlawful discrimination. Environmental groups complain that environmental protection agencies worry too much about the needs of compliers—the individuals or firms who may be polluting—and too little about the needs of the broader public that benefits from a cleaner environment. My point is not to take sides in this debate. The point is that ambiguity regarding the concept of customer in these settings is one reason why controversy exists.

Despite complications such as these, state agencies are seeking to serve citizens and taxpayers better. Brudney and Wright (2002) found that both "systems for measuring customer satisfaction" and training in customer service for agency employees had been widely adopted by the late 1990s. Computers and information technology can also help state agencies better serve citizens. Darrell West (2001) found that 25 percent of state government websites offered at least one service that was fully executable online. The most commonly available services online include filing tax forms, securing publications or databases, registering a complaint, registering a vehicle, and buying a hunting or fishing license. Using an "e-government index," West finds that Indiana, Michigan, Texas, Tennessee, Washington, California, New York, Pennsylvania, Florida, and Ohio were the ten leading states. Still, the growth of state "e-government" efforts is hampered by inevitable telecommunication and computer bugs, by the fact that many citizens—and especially senior citizens and the poor—are not yet connected to the Internet, and by concerns about privacy and the security of confidential information that citizens may have to provide to access services.

### STATE BUREAUCRACIES AND ADMINISTRATION IN A CHALLENGING ERA: SOME REFLECTIONS

Concerns about state government performance quickly become concerns about state bureaucracies and administration. This is why efforts to "reinvent" government, or to install systems of "total quality management," are so attractive. Unfortunately, some proponents of TQM and REGO seem oblivious to the limits of their prescriptions in governmental settings. The inappropriateness of a simplistic customer-focus approach noted earlier is one example of this problem. Another is the hostility of REGO to traditional bureaucracies with their emphasis on hierarchy. It has been argued that in its treatment of authority in public organizations REGO has "misapprehended the political, legal, and constitutional context of public sector management reform. Reinventing government must recall that *public sector hierarchies are as much accountability devices as management tools*" (Zajac and Al-Kazemi 1997, 379, emphasis added). It is through hierarchy that democracies help to ensure the responsiveness of bureaucrats to popularly elected officials. Since success has many parents but failure is an orphan, it is also likely that the successes of TQM or REGO have been exaggerated to some extent. State administrative employees regularly seek ways to do their jobs better so as to benefit both those who receive services and those who pay for those services through their taxes. If "quality improvement" and "reinvention" stimulate such efforts then they will have made a difference for the better. But, as has been true of other past efforts to enhance state administrative performance, both TQM and REGO are likely to leave a legacy that is more modest than advocates expect.

Concerns about the accountability of state bureaucracies may well increase in the twenty-first century. State administrators are important policy shapers who have breached the walls that once limited their involvement in the policy-making process. Policy making is improved by the involvement of bureaucrats and bureaucracies. While we rightfully prefer that the governor and the legislature exclusively make major policy decisions, elected officials are fallible. They often find it hard to look beyond the next election. With greater security of tenure, and the benefit of professional expertise, administrators can broaden the horizons of elected officials and point out deficiencies in proposed policies that those officials may wish to ignore.

The efforts of governors, legislatures, the courts, and the public to exert more influence over the affairs of state bureaucracies suggest that "runaway" agencies are rare. The intervention of non-administrative actors in administrative affairs raises questions, however, with regard to how much efficiency and effectiveness must be sacrificed in order to enhance accountability or responsiveness. What is the proper balance to be struck between leaving an administrative agency alone to do its thing, on the one hand, and looking over its shoulder or putting handcuffs on its wrists, on the other?

State programs are typically administered in a reasonably efficient and effective manner. Unfortunately, the greater scope of state administrative responsibilities means that even if bureaucracies perform better than in the past, the aggregate costs of inefficiency or ineffectiveness remain great. The incompatibility of the standards to which we hold state bureaucracies means their performance can never be good enough. Instead, changes will occur in the tradeoffs that elected officials and citizens will accept. Sometimes improving efficiency and effectiveness will be emphasized. But just as often we may value accountability or responsiveness more highly.

**REFERENCES**

Auger, Deborah, A. 1999. "Privatization, Contracting, and the States: Lessons from State Government Experience." *Public Productivity and Management Review* 22: 435–454.

Barzelay, Michael, and Babak Armajani. 1992. *Breaking through Bureaucracy: A Vision for Managing Government.* Berkeley: University of California Press.

Belman, Dale, and John Heywood. 1995. "State and Local Wage Differentials: An Intrastate Analysis." *Journal of Labor Research* 16: 187–201.

Belman, Dale, John Heywood, and John Lund. 1997. "Public Sector Earnings and the Extent of Unionization." *Industrial and Labor Relations Review* 50: 610–628.

Brudney, Jeffrey, and Deil S. Wright. 2001. "Privatization Across the American States: Assessing and Explaining the Scope of Contracting by State Administrative Agencies." Paper presented at the annual meeting of the American Political Science Association, San Francisco, Calif., August 30–September 2.

———. 2002. "Revisiting Administrative Reform in the American States: The Status of Reinventing Government During the 1990s." *Public Administration Review* 62: 353–361.

Brudney, Jeffrey, F. Ted Hebert, and Deil S. Wright. 1999. "Reinventing Government in the American States: Measuring and Explaining Administrative Reform." *Public Administration Review* 59: 19–30.

Bullard, Angela, and Deil Wright. 1993. "Circumventing the Glass Ceiling: Women Executives in American State Governments." *Public Administration Review* 53: 189–202.

Bundt, Julie, and Gene Lutz. 1999. "Connecting State Government Reform with Public Priorities: The Iowa Test Case." *State and Local Government Review* 31(2): 78–90.

Chi, Keon, Drew Leathersby, Cindy Jasper, and Robert Eger. 1997. *Managing for Success: A Profile of State Government for the 21st Century.* Lexington, Ky.: Council of State Governments.

Coggburn, Jerrell. 2000. "Personnel Deregulation: Exploring Differences in the American States." *Journal of Public Administration Research and Theory* 11: 223–244.

Conant, James. 2000. "Management Consequences of the 1960–1990 'Modernization' of State Government." In *Handbook of State Government Administration,* edited by J. Gargan. New York: Marcel Dekker.

Cooper, Phillip. 1994. "Reinvention and Employee Rights: The Role of the Courts." In *New Paradigms for Government: Issues for the Changing Public Service,* edited by Patricia Ingraham, Barbara Romzek, and Associates. San Francisco: Jossey-Bass.

Cox, Raymond. 1991. "The Management Role of the Governor." In *Gubernatorial Leadership and State Policy,* edited by Eric Herzik and Brent Brown. Westport, Conn.: Greenwood.

Elling, Richard C. 1992. *Public Management in the States: A Comparative Study of Administrative Performance and Politics.* Westport, Conn.: Praeger.

———. 1997. "Slip-Slidin' Away? Patterns of Employee Turnover in American State Bureaucracies." Paper presented at the annual meeting of the American Political Science Association, Washington, D.C., August 28–31.

———. 1999. "Dissin' the Deadwood? Patterns in the Dismissal of Civil Servants in American State Bureaucracies." Paper presented at the annual meeting of the Southwestern Political Science Association, San Antonio, Texas, April 1–3.

Elling, Richard C., and Peter Kobrak. 1995. "The Bureaucracy: An Ambiguous Political Legacy." In *Michigan Politics and Government: Facing Change in a Complex State,* edited by William Browne and Kenneth Verburg. Lincoln: University of Nebraska Press.

Elling, Richard C., Lyke Thompson, and Valerie Monet. 2003. "The Problematic World of State Management: The More Things Change the More They Remain the Same." Paper presented at the annual meeting of the Midwest Political Science Association, Chicago, April.

Freedman, Anne. 1994. *Patronage: An American Tradition.* Chicago: Nelson-Hall.

Gardner, Susan, and Christopher Daniel. 1998. "Implementing Comparable Worth/Pay Equity: Experiences of Cutting Edge States." *Public Personnel Management* 27: 475–489.

Gold, Steven, and Sarah Ritchie. 1993. "Compensation of State and Local Employees: Sorting Out the Issues." In *Revitalizing State and Local Public Service,* edited by Frank Thompson. San Francisco: Jossey-Bass.

Goodsell, Charles. 1985. *The Case for Bureaucracy: A Public Administration Polemic.* 2d ed. Chatham, N.J.: Chatham House.

———. 1994. *The Case for Bureaucracy: A Public Administration Polemic.* 3d ed. Chatham, N.J.: Chatham House.

Gormley, William. 1996a. "Counterbureaucracies in Theory and Practice." *Administration and Society* 28: 275–297.

———. 1996b. "Regulatory Privatization: A Case Study." *Journal of Public Administration Research and Theory* 5: 243–260.

Greene, Vernon, Sally Coleman Selden, and Gene Brewer. 2000. "Measuring Power and Presence: Bureaucratic Representation in the American States." *Journal of Public Administration Research and Theory* 11: 379–402.

Hays, Steven, and Richard Kearney. 1992. "State Personnel Directors and the Dilemmas of Workforce 2000: A Survey." *Public Administration Review* 52: 30–38.

Hebert, F. Ted. 2000. "Governors as Chief Administrators and Managers." In *Handbook of State Government Administration,* edited by John Gargan. New York: Marcel Dekker.

Hyde, Albert. 1995. "Improving Customer Service Quality: Changing Concepts, Goals and Methods, An Afterword." *Public Manager* Fall: 25–27.

Jenks, Stephen, and Deil Wright. 1993. "An Agency-Level Approach to Change in the Administrative Functions of American State Governments." *State and Local Government Review* 25: 78–86.

Kearney, Richard C, with David G. Carnevale. 2001. *Labor Relations in the Public Sector.* 3d ed. New York: Marcel Dekker.

Michigan Department of Civil Service. 1987. *Public Perceptions of State Employment in Michigan.* Lansing: Michigan Department of Civil Service.

Miller, M. L. 1996. "The Public/Private Pay Debate: What Do the Data Show?" *Monthly Labor Review* May: 18–29.

Morgan, Douglas, Kelly Bacon, Ron Bunch, Charles Cameron, and Robert Deis. 1996. "What Middle Managers Do in Local Government: Stewardship of the Public Trust and the Limits of Reinventing Government." *Public Administration Review* 56: 359–366.

National Association of State Personnel Executives. 2000. *State Personnel Office: Roles and Functions,* 4th ed. Lexington, Ky.: Council of Governments.

O'Leary, Rosemary. 1994. "The Expanding Partnership Between Personnel Management and the Courts. In *New Paradigms for Government: Issues for the Changing Public Service,* edited by Patricia Ingraham, Barbara Romzek, and Associates. San Francisco: Jossey-Bass.

Olshfski, Dorothy, and Raphael Caprio. 1996. "Comparing Personal and Professional Characteristics of Men and Women State Executives: 1990 and 1993 Results." *Review of Public Personnel Administration* 16: 31–39.

Osborne, David, and Ted Gaebler. 1993. *Reinventing Government: How the Entrepreneurial Spirit Is Transforming the Public Sector.* New York: Penguin Books.

Potoski, Matthew, and Neal Woods. 2000. "Designing State Clean Air Agencies: Administrative Procedures and Bureaucratic Autonomy." *Journal of Public Administration Research and Theory* 11: 203–221.

Rainey, Hal. 2003. "Facing Fundamental Challenges in Reforming Public Personnel Administration." In *Public Personnel Administration: Problems and Prospects,* 4th ed., edited by Steven Hays and Richard C. Kearney. Upper Saddle River, N.J.: Prentice Hall.

Rosenthal, Alan. 1990. *Governors and Legislatures: Contending Powers.* Washington, D.C.: CQ Press.

Rourke, Francis. 1991. "American Bureaucracy in a Changing Political Setting." *Journal of Public Administration Research and Theory* 1: 111–129.

Riccucci, Norma, and Judith Saidel. 1997. "The Representativeness of State-Level Bureaucratic Leaders: A Missing Piece of the Representative Bureaucracy Puzzle." *Public Administration Review* 57: 423–430.

Selden, Sally, and Donald P. Moynihan. 2000. "A Model of Voluntary Turnover in State Government." *Review of Public Personnel Administration* 20: 63–74.

Smith, Steven, and Judith Smyth. 1996. "Contracting for Services in a Decentralized System." *Journal of Public Administration Research and Theory* 6: 277–296.

Thompson, Lyke, and Richard C. Elling. 2000. "Mapping Patterns of Support for Privatization in the Mass Public: The Case of Michigan." *Public Administration Review* 60: 338–348.

U.S. Bureau of the Census. 1991. *Public Employment: 1990.* Washington, D.C.: Government Printing Office.

———. 2002. *State Government Employment and Payroll Data.* Available at www.census.gov/govs/www/apesst.html. Accessed March 2002.

Weinberg, Martha. 1977. *Managing the State.* Cambridge, Mass.: MIT Press.

West, Darrell. 2001. *State and Federal E-Government in the United States, 2001.* Available at http://www.insidepolitics.org/egovt01us.html.

"Women in State Government." 2000. *Spectrum: The Journal of State Government* Spring: 12–15.

Wright, Deil. 2002. "Public Administration Revolutions in the American States: A Half-Century of Evolving Roles and Responsibilities Among State Agencies and Administrators in the Federal System." Third Annual Lent D. Upson Lecture, Graduate Program in Public Administration, Wayne State University, Detroit, Mich., March 20.

Zajac, Gary, and Ali Al-Kazemi. 1997. "Reinventing Government and Redefining Leadership." *Public Productivity and Management Review* 20: 372–383.

## SUGGESTED READINGS

Chi, Keon, Drew Leathersby, Cindy Jasper, and Robert Eger. 1997. *Managing for Success: A Profile of State Government for the 21st Century.* Lexington, Ky.: Council of State Governments. A wide-ranging review of efforts to enhance state government performance and service delivery via Total Quality Management and other initiatives.

Elling, Richard. *Public Management in the States.* Westport, Conn: Praeger, 1992. Drawing on a 1980s survey of administrators in ten states, this study explores the problems confronting state bureaucracies, how managers have sought to address those problems, and how a wide range of actors affect the state administrative process.

Gargan, John J., ed. 2000. *Handbook of State Government Administration.* New York: Marcel Dekker. An extensive collection of chapters examining the context of state government administration, discussing basic state government management practices, and exploring the administration of particular state functions.

West, Darrell. 2001. *State and Federal E-Government in the United States, 2001.* Available at http://www.insidepolitics.org/egovt01us.html. This study examines the extent to which governmental services are available online and explores other features of governmental Web sites. It includes a summary "e government index" ranking the states.

CHAPTER 10

# *Fiscal Policy in the American States*

JAMES C. GARAND AND KYLE BAUDOIN

When political scientists talk or write about politics, they often focus on "who gets what, when, and how" (Lasswell 1936) or "the authoritative allocation of values for a society" (Easton 1953). At the heart of these definitions is the idea that when it comes to politics, there are winners and losers. Some individuals and groups benefit from decisions made in the political process, others find themselves worse off as a result of political decision making. Politics, in the view of Lasswell and Easton, is about determining who the winners and losers are—in other words, which segments of society receive things of value (e.g., direct payments, pork-barrel projects, tax breaks) and which segments absorb the costs of those benefits (e.g., increased taxes, direct costs).

At the core of these debates over who wins and who loses in American state politics is money. State governments decide how much of the resources of the private economy are devoted to the public sector, and this decision involves winners who receive the benefits of government programs and losers who pay the costs of those programs. Once political decision makers have determined the size of government, state governments allocate (or do not allocate) dollars to various individuals or groups, and they tax (or do not tax) other individuals or groups to pay for the resources that they allocate. State governments decide the public priorities of their political systems—that is, whether public schools or the urban poor or local sheriffs or tobacco farmers or other groups receive resources allocated to the public sector, as well as how much of these resources will be (or will not be) received. State governments also decide who will finance these priorities. Who bears the costs of government programs can be made for one point in time (e.g., do the rich pay higher taxes today or do the poor pay higher taxes today?) or dynamically (e.g., should the costs of government be borne by current taxpayers or by future taxpayers?). Finally, state governments decide, within certain constraints, whether they will balance their budgets—i.e., whether they will spend more than they bring in, or vice versa.

The spending and taxing decisions that state governments make have important ramifications for the lives of citizens residing in those states. Over the past decade state governments have spent resources that constitute a bit more than 13 percent of the state personal income of their citizens, so government spending and taxing decisions in the American states involve a nontrivial share of the private economy. Moreover, state governments have a major share of responsibility in a number of policy areas, including education, transportation, social welfare, health, and public safety. A substantial share of the policy instruments used by state governments to solve policy problems involves the expenditure of monetary resources and the development of revenue sources to pay for those instruments. Moreover, many of the major problems facing American society are within the purview of state governments. How state governments allocate resources can have a substantial impact on the degree to which those problems persist or are otherwise solved or alleviated.

In this chapter we explore expenditure and tax patterns in the American states during much of the post–World War II period. We first discuss the size of state government, focusing on how it is measured and how patterns of government size have fluctuated over time. We also consider various explanations for variation in government size, both across states and over time. Second, we consider the spending priorities of the states—i.e., the distribution of expenditures among various spending areas. What are the shares of state spending allocated to education, welfare, highways, and health and hospitals? What explains these relative spending priorities? Third, we discuss the source of state government revenues, particularly in terms of state tax policies and priorities. Where do states obtain revenues to support government spending? What are the different sources of tax revenues? What explains patterns of tax and revenue levels, both across states and over time? Finally, we consider the issue of budget deficits and surpluses in the American states. Most state governments are required to balance their budgets, but the degree to which states run deficits or surpluses varies considerably.

## THE SIZE OF STATE GOVERNMENT

One of the major allocation decisions made by state governments involves the determination of the overall size of the public sector relative to that of the private sector. While one can describe politics in terms of governments' decisions to allocate resources to some competing claimants but not others, such decisions are dependent upon the existence of the governmental sector in the first place. Arguably, the preferred size of the public sector relative to the private sector is one of the great dividing issues in contemporary American politics, separating liberals and conservatives, Democrats and Republicans, and those with high incomes, moderate incomes, and low incomes.

The American states vary considerably in terms of the size of their governments, but what explains these patterns is less clear, as there has been less attention directed at explaining the size of the public sector at the subnational level. Garand (1988a) tests five models of state government size using data on the fifty American states from 1945 to 1978, and then extends this analysis to encompass data through 1984 (Garand 1993). Kapeluck (2001) extends the data set even further to include data through 1998. Many of the explanatory models used in research on state government growth are borrowed explicitly from research conducted at the national or cross-national levels (see, for example, Lowery and Berry 1983; Lewis-Beck and Rice 1985; Cameron 1978; Lybeck 1986), though some of the explanatory models are unique to subnational governments in federal systems.

### Measuring the Size of State Government

There has been some debate in the literature about how to measure the size of state government. At the core of the concept of government size is the notion that state governments reach into and influence both the workings of society and the lives of their citizens. Presumably, any measure of government size would account for the extent of that involvement by state governments. Unfortunately, there are not sufficient measures of all of the dimensions of state government activity; for instance, the magnitude of state regulation of individual activity is very difficult to measure.

Most scholars rely on measures of government size that account for the degree to which state governments draw resources from the private sector and/or produce outputs that are introduced into and have an effect on the state policy system. The most common measures of government size use state expenditures, usually in per capita terms or as a share of some indicator of the size of the state economy. The use of per capita state expenditures, measured by dividing state expenditures by state population, or of state expenditures as a share of economic output, is designed to "standardize" measures of government size. Obviously, states with large populations or large economies will spend more in raw dollars on the public sector than states with small populations or small economies, so it is important to divide state expenditures by population or economic output to account for these differences explicitly.

In this chapter we measure the size of state government in terms of total state expenditures as a share of total state personal income. Total personal income serves as a rough surrogate for the size of the private economy. Other available measures, such as Gross State Product (GSP), are more comprehensive measures of state economic activity, but unfortunately are not available for the entire postwar period.

### Patterns of Government Growth

In Figure 10-1 we present trends over time in the mean size of government in the American states from 1945 to 2000. The growth in the size of the public sector in the American states in the postwar era is undeniable. The mean size of the states' public

**Figure 10-1** Trends in Mean Size of State Government, 1945–2000

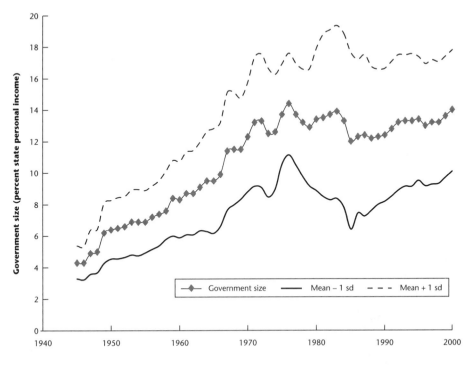

SOURCE: U.S. Bureau of the Census, *Statistical Abstract,* various years.

NOTE: Reports trends in mean government size over time along with standard deviation bands representing one standard deviation above and one standard deviation below the mean.

sectors was just over 4 percent of state personal income at the end of World War II, and it had grown to about 14 percent by 2000. State governments are clearly drawing substantially more resources from their state economies than they did in 1945.

Growth in the size of the public sector in the American states was fairly steady in the first few decades after World War II. The twenty-three years from 1945 to 1967 were marked by what are essentially incremental increases in government size over time, with few deviations from the trend. The pattern of steady increases was broken during the mid-1960s, at which time there was a bit more variability over time but an overall trend toward greater state government growth. The boom in state government size during the 1960s and 1970s coincides with the Great Society programs, which resulted in a period of government growth at the federal level and increased grants from the federal government, particularly in terms of revenue-sharing programs and increases in federal support for entitlement programs. Dramatic surges are evident in 1967, from 1969 through 1971, and from 1974 through 1976, but clearly the period from 1945 to the late 1970s is characterized by a pattern of steady growth in the size of the public sector over time.

On the other hand, after 1977 the size of the public sector stopped growing in comparison to the private sector. During this time the trend in mean government size leveled off between 12 percent and 14 percent of total state personal income. Following the peak of a bit more than 14 percent in 1976, the mean size of state government fell to 12 percent in less than a decade, with significant declines occurring from 1976 to 1979 and 1983 to 1985. State government size leveled off (and declined) at a time when federal support was in decline, due in part to larger budget deficits at the federal level. Mean state government size reached its low point in 1985, after which the years from 1986 to 2000 witnessed a steady, yet incremental rise in the size of government, much like the period from 1950 to the late 1960s.

It is also noteworthy that there is considerable variation in government size across states. In Table 10-1 we present data on the size of government in the fifty American states for 2000. The average state allocates 14 percent of total personal income to the public sector, with a standard deviation of 4.4 percent. Most states allocate between 12 and 18 percent of personal income to state government, but there are several states that fall outside of that range. At the top end is Alaska (37.3 percent), which has an extraordinarily large public sector due to the large amount of revenue derived from oil and gas production and revenues. Other states with relatively large public sectors include New Mexico (22.8 percent), Vermont (20.9 percent), Hawaii (20.2 percent), Wyoming (20.1 percent), and West Virginia (19.9 percent). On the other hand, some states allocate less of their resources to the public sector; these states include Florida (10.8 percent), Nevada (10.8 percent), Colorado (10.9 percent), Illinois (10.9 percent), Texas (11.2 percent), Maryland (11.5 percent), Georgia (11.6 percent), and New Hampshire (11.6 percent).

*Explaining Government Size in the American States*

Several theories have been tendered in the scholarly literature to explain patterns of government size, both across states and over time. These explanations fit into two broad categories (Lowery and Berry 1983). The first, the *responsive government* explanation, suggests that government grows and contracts as a function of demands by citizens for more or less government. The second, the *excessive government* explanation, suggests that the impetus for government growth rests with government itself, and that government grows because government, and not necessarily the citizenry, supports and takes action to create an expanded public sector. Clearly, responsive government explanations are compatible with classic notions of democratic theory and representative government, insofar as government size is depicted as a reflection of the preferences of citizens. On the other hand, excessive government explanations are more cynical about the determinants of government size, suggesting that the size of the public sector reflects more the views of government actors than of citizens.

Among responsive government explanations, *Wagner's Law* has been perhaps the most widely cited and tested. Wagner (1877) suggests that government grows as a function of economic and social changes that accompany industrialization and

**Table 10-1** Share of State Total Personal Income Allocated to Government Spending, in Total and in Four Spending Areas, 2000 (in percentages)

|  | Government size | Spending areas | | | |
|---|---|---|---|---|---|
|  |  | Education | Highways | Welfare | Health |
| Alabama | 15.8 | 6.2 | 1.1 | 3.3 | 1.6 |
| Alaska | 37.3 | 7.5 | 3.6 | 5.2 | 0.9 |
| Arizona | 13.8 | 4.6 | 1.3 | 2.6 | 0.9 |
| Arkansas | 16.9 | 7.0 | 1.3 | 3.5 | 1.2 |
| California | 15.1 | 5.0 | 0.6 | 3.7 | 1.1 |
| Colorado | 10.9 | 3.9 | 1.0 | 2.3 | 0.4 |
| Connecticut | 12.9 | 3.0 | 0.6 | 2.5 | 1.3 |
| Delaware | 18.2 | 6.1 | 1.4 | 2.4 | 1.2 |
| Florida | 10.8 | 3.4 | 0.9 | 2.2 | 0.8 |
| Georgia | 11.6 | 4.9 | 0.7 | 2.6 | 0.7 |
| Hawaii | 20.2 | 5.7 | 0.7 | 3.2 | 1.8 |
| Idaho | 15.7 | 5.8 | 1.6 | 2.7 | 0.5 |
| Illinois | 10.9 | 3.2 | 0.6 | 2.6 | 0.8 |
| Indiana | 13.0 | 5.0 | 1.3 | 2.6 | 0.5 |
| Iowa | 15.6 | 5.7 | 1.9 | 3.0 | 1.2 |
| Kansas | 12.8 | 5.2 | 1.9 | 1.8 | 0.6 |
| Kentucky | 17.0 | 5.6 | 1.7 | 4.4 | 0.9 |
| Louisiana | 16.6 | 5.4 | 1.1 | 3.1 | 1.9 |
| Maine | 17.7 | 4.1 | 1.3 | 5.1 | 1.0 |
| Maryland | 11.5 | 3.3 | 0.8 | 2.3 | 0.8 |
| Massachusetts | 13.4 | 2.6 | 1.3 | 3.0 | 0.9 |
| Michigan | 15.4 | 6.3 | 0.9 | 2.9 | 1.4 |
| Minnesota | 15.8 | 5.3 | 1.0 | 3.6 | 0.5 |
| Mississippi | 19.1 | 6.0 | 1.7 | 4.4 | 1.6 |
| Missouri | 11.9 | 4.1 | 1.0 | 2.8 | 0.8 |
| Montana | 19.1 | 5.9 | 2.2 | 2.8 | 1.3 |
| Nebraska | 12.8 | 4.4 | 1.3 | 3.1 | 0.9 |
| Nevada | 10.8 | 3.8 | 1.0 | 1.4 | 0.4 |
| New Hampshire | 11.6 | 3.6 | 0.9 | 2.9 | 0.5 |
| New Jersey | 12.0 | 3.3 | 0.5 | 2.0 | 0.7 |
| New Mexico | 22.8 | 8.3 | 2.3 | 3.8 | 1.7 |
| New York | 15.7 | 3.4 | 0.5 | 5.0 | 1.1 |
| North Carolina | 14.9 | 5.7 | 1.2 | 2.9 | 1.1 |
| North Dakota | 19.3 | 5.9 | 2.4 | 3.7 | 0.6 |
| Ohio | 14.6 | 4.3 | 1.0 | 3.0 | 0.9 |
| Oklahoma | 13.8 | 5.9 | 1.6 | 1.2 | 0.7 |
| Oregon | 17.6 | 5.1 | 1.1 | 3.4 | 1.6 |
| Pennsylvania | 13.9 | 3.7 | 1.0 | 3.9 | 0.9 |
| Rhode Island | 15.9 | 4.0 | 0.8 | 4.0 | 0.9 |
| South Carolina | 17.7 | 5.5 | 1.3 | 3.8 | 1.6 |
| South Dakota | 13.1 | 3.8 | 2.0 | 2.6 | 0.6 |
| Tennessee | 12.0 | 3.9 | 1.1 | 3.7 | 0.7 |
| Texas | 11.2 | 4.3 | 0.9 | 2.2 | 0.8 |
| Utah | 17.3 | 7.2 | 1.8 | 2.9 | 1.3 |
| Vermont | 20.9 | 8.7 | 1.5 | 4.6 | 0.5 |
| Virginia | 11.8 | 4.3 | 0.1 | 2.0 | 1.0 |
| Washington | 14.8 | 5.1 | 0.9 | 2.9 | 1.1 |
| West Virginia | 19.9 | 6.1 | 2.2 | 4.6 | 0.6 |
| Wisconsin | 16.1 | 5.3 | 1.1 | 2.5 | 0.8 |
| Wyoming | 20.1 | 6.2 | 2.9 | 2.3 | 0.9 |
| Mean, all states | 14.0 | 5.1 | 1.3 | 3.1 | 1.0 |

S O U R C E S : U.S. Bureau of the Census, *State Government Finances,* various years; U.S. Bureau of the Census, *Statistical Abstract,* various years.

urbanization. As a society moves from an agrarian base to an industrial base, per capita income increases, and this provides citizens with more discretionary income and makes them more accepting of public solutions to various policy problems. Moreover, industrial societies have more concentrated populations, and this creates externalities (e.g., increased traffic congestion, pollution) that can best be addressed through the public sector. For instance, traffic lights, environmental regulation, crime control, and extensive sewage treatment facilities are generally not necessary in the lightly populated rural areas that characterize agrarian societies, but in urbanized industrial societies these are necessities that require the expenditure of government funds. Given this theory, one would expect states with high levels of industrialization and urbanization to have larger public sectors than states with lower levels of industrialization and urbanization. Thus far the evidence in favor of Wagner's Law is decidedly mixed (Lowery and Berry 1983; Garand 1988a, 1993; Boix 2001). Most recently, Kapeluck (2001) finds little support for the argument that state per capita income is related positively to government size, though he does find support for the hypothesis that highly urbanized states have larger public sectors.

A second responsive government explanation, the *party control* explanation, suggests that government grows or contracts in response to the ideological leanings of the party that controls government. When the liberal party controls state government, so the argument goes, government size should increase, but when the conservative party controls state government the size of government should decrease, remain the same, or increase at a smaller rate. In the American context, this theory would lead one to expect that state governments would grow more during Democratic regimes than during Republican regimes. Here again, the empirical evidence for this theory is somewhat mixed, with some scholars finding this expected relationship (Garand 1985; Lewis-Beck and Rice 1985; Blais, Blake, and Dion 1993) while others fail to uncover this relationship (Garand 1988a; Lowery and Berry 1983; Kapeluck 2001).

Third, the *interparty competition* model is based on the idea that state governments are more responsive to the policy preferences of constituents when there is a high level of competition between the parties—i.e., when the Democrats and Republicans are of roughly equal strength. During such periods, proximity to the next election should spur increased spending as the two parties compete with one another for the affections of the electorate (Kiewiet and McCubbins 1985; Lowery and Berry 1983). On the other hand, when one party controls state government completely, one would expect upcoming elections to have very little effect on the size of government, since the party in power is not sufficiently threatened by the out-party to respond with increases in government spending. To date, the level of support for this model in empirical tests in the American states has been weak (Kapeluck 2001).

Fourth, the *political culture* explanation posits that government grows as a function of the prevailing political culture in a given political system. Some state political systems are known for their liberal political cultures; in these states, citizens see a legitimate role for government in solving policy problems, and so one would expect to see an expanded public sector. On the other hand, other state political systems are known for their conservative political cultures. These states are characterized as having citizenries that are less trusting of government solutions to policy problems, and so one would expect a smaller public sector (Garand 1993; Kapeluck 2001).

Fifth, the *fiscal constraints* explanation gives special emphasis to the role of institutional design constraints placed in the way of increases in government size. For instance, some states have tax and expenditure limitations written into their constitutions, and this places an impediment in the way of elected officials interested in expanding the size of government, though the empirical evidence in support of this hypothesis is spotty (Bails 1990; Cox and Lowery 1990; Howard 1989; Joyce and Mullins 1991). Moreover, other states have initiative and referenda structures that permit citizens to have a direct say in state fiscal matters, and these structures have been found to be related to lower levels of state spending (Matsusaka 1995).

Finally, some scholars have speculated that government size varies as a function of the *political needs* of state electorates. Some states have populations that are dominated by citizens who place high demands on government for goods and services. For instance, citizens both over the age of 65 and under the age of 18 are high demanders (or at least high users) of government services, so states with populations dominated by individuals in these age groups are likely to have larger public sectors that result from the increased pressure for expanded government placed on elected officials. Moreover, states with large minority populations also face pressure for increased spending, as do states experiencing poor economic performance (i.e., high unemployment, low economic growth). Both Garand (1993) and Kapeluck (2001) find support for the political needs explanation, with the size of various high-demand groups in the population having a positive effect on government size.

The excessive government explanations, on the other hand, portray governmental actors as important players in promoting increases in the size of the public sector, even above and beyond that demanded by citizens. Perhaps the most prominent of these theories is the *fiscal illusion* theory, which suggests that governmental actors support an increased public sector and hide from voters the true costs of government; the result is that citizens underestimate the cost of government and hence demand more government spending than they otherwise would if they were cognizant of the true cost of government. This theory is based on the premise that government adopts revenue collection mechanisms that make it difficult for citizens to estimate how much they are paying in taxes. For instance, income taxes are usually paid using a withholding mechanism; taxpayers receive a pay check in which taxes have already been collected, so they are unlikely to consciously recall their tax bill. Likewise, deficit spending (financed through borrowing) is a way of hiding the true costs of government; when this happens, government spending is higher than the amount of revenue collected, but the cost of government spending is deferred until it is paid as loan repayments by future taxpayers (Lowery and Berry 1983; Garand 1988a; Kapeluck 2001).

Second, the *bureau-voting* model posits that public employees are self-interested actors who prefer larger government to smaller government. Because government employees have a self-interest in seeing larger government, they are more likely to turn out on election day, and are more likely to vote for candidates who support an enhanced public sector. The result is that candidates for office who support a larger governmental sector are advantaged by the electoral support that they receive from a high-turnout segment of the electorate that supports increases in government size (Corey and Garand 2002; Garand, Parkhurst, and Seoud 1991; Garand 1988a; Kapeluck 2001).

Third, the *bureau information monopoly* explanation also posits a strong role of government bureaucrats in facilitating increases in the size of government (Niskanen 1971). The core concept underlying this theory is *information asymmetry*—that is, the idea that government bureaucrats, who are charged with administering laws passed by legislatures, have more information about the day-to-day workings of the policies that they administer than the legislators charged with making policy. When bureaucrats interact with legislators, primarily in institutional settings such as the budget process and through testimony before legislative committees, they use their informational advantages over legislators to manipulate legislators into supporting larger budgets for their agencies and departments. The result is that government grows at a faster pace than it would otherwise.

Fourth, the *intergovernmental grant* explanation suggests that state government grows as a function of the influx of intergovernmental grants from the federal government. As funds flow from the federal government to state governments, the size of the public sector increases in recipient states. This might seem like an obvious expectation, though it is not necessarily the case that states would increase overall spending as a result of receiving additional funds from the federal government. In fact, it is possible that intergovernmental grants perform a replacement function— that is, when states receive intergovernmental grants they use these funds to lower the tax burden of their own citizens. There is a fair amount of evidence that intergovernmental grants do result in higher state spending than would have occurred otherwise, suggesting what economists refer to as the "flypaper effect" as federal funds "stick" with the recipient government rather than leading to lower taxes. However, there is some evidence that federal funds get translated into increased state spending at less than a one-to-one ratio (Borcherding 1977; Garand 1988a, 1993), though Kapeluck (2001) finds that a dollar of federal grant funds generates more than a dollar increase in state expenditures.

Fifth, the *constituency size* explanation suggests that the number of constituents represented by legislators is positively related to growth in the size of the public sector. Legislators are seen as being subject to less constituency monitoring as the number of constituents they represent increases. This results in diminished accountability, which permits legislators to translate their own preferences for increased spending into policy-making behavior. Moreover, small constituency size usually means a legislature with a larger number of members, and this increases the costs that interest groups must pay to "buy" the votes necessary to put together a coalition in favor of increased spending. In tests conducted using state-level data, empirical support for this theory has been fairly strong (Gilligan and Matsusaka 1995; Thornton and Ulrich 1999; Kapeluck 2001).

Finally, the *concentration-displacement* explanation, also referred to as the "ratchet effect" explanation, suggests that government grows as a function of crises or catastrophes that require an immediate infusion of public-sector spending (Peacock and Wiseman 1961). An example of this would be World War II, during which time the U.S. government increased the size of the public sector dramatically in order to fund the war effort. The idea here is that the mass public is likely to support the initial increase in government size, given the crisis atmosphere that is created. However, when the crisis or catastrophe is over, the responsive government theories would predict that government size would revert to its pre-crisis levels. In fact, so the argument goes, the size of the public sector decreases somewhat after the crisis but does not return to pre-crisis levels. The mass public gets used to and becomes tolerant of the higher level of spending associated with the crisis, so when the crisis is over there is little demand to return to the tax levels that existed before the crisis. This theory would seem to be very appropriate for considering growth in the size of the public sector in areas pertaining to homeland security, particularly in the wake of the terrorist attacks of September 11.

### EXPENDITURE POLICY AND PRIORITIES

Once state governments have decided how much they are going to draw out of the private economy to support government programs, they must then decide the relative allocations among the competing claimants for government funds. In other words, what share of the budget is allocated to education or welfare, or health, or highways? These allocations can be thought of as representing policy priorities, insofar as they reflect the relative weights that state policy makers give to competing policy areas. Decisions about the allocation of funds to various policy areas are often heated and difficult to make. Given a limited, yet growing amount of resources, state governments must reach strategic compromises regarding the allocation of revenue to specific policy areas. The tradeoffs made by policy makers that are at the heart of state politics will be considered later in the chapter.

*Spending in Specific Policy areas*

In Figure 10-2 we present the trends in mean share of state personal income allocated to the education, highways, welfare, and health and hospital spending areas from 1945 to 2000. As one can readily observe, in 1945 states spent little in all areas relative to the size of the private economy; in no policy area did states allocate even as much as 1 percent of total state personal income, and no policy area was particularly favored by state governments. The immediate postwar environment brought new policy and programmatic spending ideas to the American states. Education, highways, and welfare saw an increase in spending before 1950, and education

**Figure 10-2** Trends in Mean Share of State Personal Income Allocated to Various Spending Areas, 1945–2000

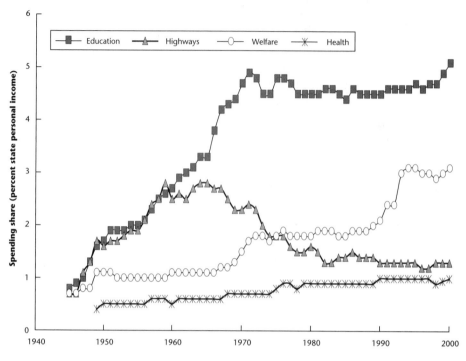

SOURCES: U.S. Bureau of the Census, *State Government Finances*, various years; U.S. Bureau of the Census, *Statistical Abstract*, various years.

and highways exhibited substantial increases throughout the 1950s. During the early 1960s education spending continued to increase dramatically, while highways spending leveled off and began to decline as a share of total personal income. Starting in the early 1970s the trend in education spending flattened, while just a few years earlier the trend in welfare spending turned upward. By the late 1990s, education spending remained in a dominant position relative to other spending areas, with welfare spending on the upswing and in the second position. Highways spending was on a long-term downward trend but still in the third position, but health spending was beginning to move upward.

*Education.* Controlling and funding education has always been within the domain of local and state governments, and over time the American states have taken on an increasing role in funding education. In recent years state government spending on education has surpassed that of local governments, with federal spending on education lagging well behind; in 2000 state revenues constituted 50.7 percent of revenues targeted toward education, compared with 42.4 percent from local governments and 6.9 percent from the federal government (U.S. Census Bureau 2001, 154). The data in Figure 10-2 suggest that education has been the single largest beneficiary of state spending in the last forty years. The quarter century from 1945 to 1970 witnessed a rise in education spending priorities from less than 1 percent to nearly 5 percent of total state personal income. In the last thirty years, the funding allocated to education has leveled off, with only minor changes occurring in the 1970s. Nonetheless, education is, and has been for some time, the highest priority and the most important area of state policy.

The patterns revealed in Table 10-1 suggest some variation in state education spending priorities across the states in 2000. The average state allocates 5.1 percent of its total personal income to public education, with a standard deviation of 1.4 percent. At the high end, Vermont, New Mexico, Alaska, Utah, and Arkansas all allocate more than 7 percent of total personal income to public education, while Massachusetts, Connecticut, Illinois, Maryland, New Jersey, Florida, and New York all spend less than 3.5 percent of total personal income on education. This variation might reflect, among other things, birth rates and the number of school-age children in the population, the reliance on private schools for the provision of education services, and the priority given to education by the state electorate.

*Highways.* Perhaps the most dramatic change in spending priorities during the postwar era involves the highways area. Highways spending underwent a meteoric rise during the highway construction boom of the 1950s, only to be followed by a steady but gradual decline over the next two decades. As Figure 10-2 indicates, state spending on highways peaked during the 1960s. At least in part this growth in spending represented the infrastructure build-up associated with the construction of an interstate highway system. Highways spending increased dramatically as the federal and state governments cooperated to construct a highway system that could presumably transport the military resources of the United States to any location in the most efficient manner possible. With the 1960s came the beginning of a gradual decline in highways spending, and by the early 1980s highways spending as a share of total personal income had returned to its pre-1950s levels.

As shown in Table 10-1, the average state spent just 1.3 percent of total personal income on highways in 2000, with relatively little variation around that mean. Several states—Alaska, Wyoming, North Dakota, New Mexico, West Virginia, Montana, and South Dakota—allocated more than 2 percent of the private economy to highways; note that most of these states are lightly populated states with large geographic areas. As many as fifteen states spend less than 1 percent of personal income on highways; at the bottom of the list are Virginia, New Jersey, New York, Connecticut, Illinois, and California. These bottom six states obviously spend a large amount of public money on their highways, but as a share of total personal income their level of spending pales in comparison to other states.

*Welfare.* As chapter 11 shows, the term *welfare* is generally used in reference to a wide range of programs that are intended to alleviate the burdens of poverty. As seen in Figure 10-2, investments in welfare programs were relatively modest through the 1950s and early 1960s, representing just over 1 percent of state total personal income. Starting with the late 1960s, there was a substantial upward trend in welfare spending; by 1976 rising welfare spending had surpassed declining high-ways spending. During most of the late 1970s and 1980s welfare spending hovered just below 2 percent of total state personal income, but during the 1990s wel-fare spending surpassed the 2 percent threshold and moved rapidly to 3 percent of total personal income. By the mid-1990s welfare spending had leveled off at about 3 percent.

The initial rapid surge in spending during the late 1960s is due in part to Lyndon B. Johnson's Great Society programs, including Medicaid. These programs were an offensive attack in the "War on Poverty," and they included a substantial intergov-ernmental grant component that helped to spur increased spending by the states. The second major upward adjustment of the early 1990s was met with increasing disdain for welfare among the mass public and helped to spur the welfare reform of 1996 that ushered in the TANF (Temporary Assistance to Needy Families) pro-gram, which replaced AFDC (Aid to Families with Dependent Children). The wel-fare restructuring of the mid-1990s was designed to return autonomy to the states, allowing more control of the specifics of their welfare programs. The leveling-off of welfare spending also reflects strong economic performance during the 1990s that helped to reduce welfare rolls and keep growth in welfare spending to a minimum.

As can be seen from Table 10-1, most states spend between 2 and 4 percent of total personal income on welfare programs. The most "generous" states are Alaska (5.2 percent), Maine (5.1 percent), New York (5.0 percent), West Virginia (4.6 per-cent), and Vermont (4.6 percent). This high level of priority directed toward wel-fare programs is most likely a function of a combination of welfare need (e.g., high poverty rates), ability to pay, and political liberalism of the population. On the other extreme, five states—Oklahoma, Nevada, Kansas, Virginia, and New Jersey—allocate 2 percent or less of total personal income to welfare programs.

*Health and Hospitals.* Relative to some of the other spending areas, the trend in health and hospitals spending in the American states shows no significant move-ment since World War II. In a total of forty-eight years, the mean spending on hos-pitals doubled from 0.5 to 1 percent of total personal income, but overall these fig-ures indicate that public health care was a relatively low priority in the American states during the postwar era. To be sure, this low priority for public health care spending is at least partly due to the dominant role played by private medicine and private insurance. In 2000 health and hospitals remains a relatively small item on the budgets of most states. The average state allocates 1 percent of total personal income to spending on health and hospitals. Even the highest-spending states, in-cluding Louisiana (which has a large charity hospital system), Hawaii, New Mexico, Mississippi, South Carolina, Oregon, and Alabama, spend just over 1.5 percent of total personal income on health and hospitals. The lowest-spending states, includ-ing Nevada, Colorado, Indiana, Idaho, New Hampshire, Minnesota, and Vermont, spend 0.5 percent or less of personal income on health and hospitals.

Overall, the general sense that one garners from examining the growth and change in spending in these four areas in the postwar era is that dynamic change is evident in some areas, while stability is the case for others. In the years immediately following World War II, all spending areas were nestled at roughly the same level. Since then, fifty years have passed and variation abounds. While state governments have grown, they have not chosen to allocate the extracted revenue equally across the spending areas. Some areas have benefited from the revenue stream, while others have seen little or no overall growth.

*Explanations for Changing Expenditure Priorities*

What explains changing spending priorities over time? As suggested by Ringquist and Garand (1999), changes in expenditure priorities can occur for a number of reasons. First, the policy-relevant values of voters and state policy makers may change. For instance, increases in education spending might be a function of changes in the education values of a given state's electorate; a state electorate that placed little emphasis on education spending during, say, the 1950s might take a very pro-education stance during a later period. This shift in values may result in the election of governors and state legislators who are more pro-education than previous policy makers, and the result could be a shift in priorities to favor education spending.

Second, states have demographic, social, and economic characteristics that influence state policy priorities, so it would not be a surprise that changes in those characteristics will result in shifts in policy priorities over time. The most obvious examples relate to the age distribution in a given state's population. A baby boom and resulting increase in the school-age population will likely result in much greater demand for education spending, and one would expect the relative share of the private economy devoted to education spending to increase. Alternatively, an aging population might be associated with lower demand for education spending but greater demand for, say, public health spending.

Third, changes in the source of funds for specific state programs might result in a shift in priorities. Some revenue sources are dedicated to specific policy areas—for instance, gasoline taxes are often dedicated to highway construction and road maintenance—and an increase or decrease in funds coming from a targeted revenue source may force state policy makers to adjust the priority given to the targeted spending area. Alternatively, changes in intergovernmental grants from the federal government are likely to have an effect on spending priorities. If, for instance, there are substantial reductions in federal grants for highway construction, state policy makers might be forced to adjust the amount of resources devoted to highways.

Fourth, another source of change in state expenditure priorities is tradeoffs among competing policy areas. A tradeoff occurs when spending in one or more policy areas is affected negatively by spending in another area. The notion of an expenditure tradeoff was first used to describe the "guns vs. butter" tradeoffs at the national level during the 1960s. Scholars speculated that increases in defense spending (i.e., "guns") during the 1960s came at the expense of spending on social programs (i.e., "butter"), and there was a substantial literature built around the debate over whether guns vs. butter tradeoffs actually occurred (Russett 1982; Domke, Eichenberg, and Kelleher 1983; Mintz 1989; Mintz and Huang 1990). The concept of a tradeoff is not necessarily limited to defense and social spending, so there is no reason why such tradeoffs cannot occur in the American states. For instance, Garand and Hendrick (1991) explore the interrelationships among spending changes for education, highways, welfare, and health and hospitals. The evidence for tradeoffs is not overwhelmingly strong, but there is some evidence that tradeoffs do occur.

Finally, state expenditure priorities can be affected by shocks or events that prompt higher or lower levels of funding. The events surrounding the attack on the World Trade Center on September 11, 2001, are cases in point. State governments will most certainly need to adjust their spending priorities to account for the increased likelihood of terrorist activity in the future. It is also likely that there will be federal grant funds for homeland security, and state governments will be able to tap into these funds to support higher spending priorities for anti-terrorism efforts.

### TAX POLICY AND PRIORITIES

In order to fund government programs, states generate revenue through various means. Revenue can come from a number of sources, including taxes, intergovernmental grants, and charges for government goods and services. In Table 10-2 we report the percentage of total and general revenue, respectively, derived from intergovernmental grants, taxes, charges, miscellaneous revenue, insurance trust revenue, and utility and liquor store revenue; these data are reported for all states combined in 2000. As may be seen, intergovernmental grants-in-aid, mostly from the federal government, contribute a large portion (approximately 28 percent of general revenues in 2000) to states' coffers. However, taxation (55 percent) is by far the largest revenue source and is the one over which states have the most control. Among the various taxes, individual income taxes represent the biggest source of revenue for the states, with almost 20 percent of general revenues coming from this source. General sales taxes are a close second with approximately 18 percent of general state revenues, though when combined with selective sales taxes (8 percent) sales taxes represent almost 26 percent of general state revenues. In combination, license taxes, corporate income taxes, and other taxes represent only about 10 percent of general state revenues. Finally, current charges and fees comprise about 11 percent of general revenue, and miscellaneous general revenue makes up roughly an additional 9 percent.

The focus of this section is on taxation. Obviously, states rely on other sources of revenue as well, but as Table 10-2 shows, taxes represent a large share of general revenues. Moreover, the other major source of state revenue, intergovernmental grants, is discussed in detail in Chapter 2 of this volume.

### Tax Regressivity

Methods of taxation and the political and economic consequences of each method vary greatly. One of the most important characteristics of a state tax system is how it treats low- and high-income individuals. Some tax systems are largely redistributive in nature, insofar as they place less of a tax burden on lower-income individuals relative to that of higher-income individuals, while other tax systems place a lower tax burden on higher-income citizens.

Based on the burden the tax imposes on different income groups, taxes are typically lumped into three categories. First, a *progressive* tax is a tax in which the rate of taxation increases as individuals' incomes increase. For instance, in most states the individual income tax is progressive, insofar as individuals pay a higher tax rate as their income rises. The argument behind such taxes is that lower-income individuals have

**Table 10-2** State Revenue Sources as a Share of Total and General Revenue, 2000 (in percentages)

| | Revenue sources as a share of | |
|---|---|---|
| Revenue source[a] | Total revenue | General revenue |
| Intergovernmental | 21.77 | 27.88 |
| Taxes | 42.80 | 54.81 |
|   General sales | 13.85 | 17.74 |
|   Selective sales | 6.17 | 7.90 |
|   License | 2.59 | 3.32 |
|   Individual income | 15.40 | 19.72 |
|   Corporate income | 2.58 | 3.30 |
|   Other | 2.21 | 2.83 |
| Current charges | 6.86 | 11.35 |
| Miscellaneous general | 6.65 | 8.52 |
| Insurance trust | 21.24 | b |
| Utility | 0.36 | b |
| Liquor store | 0.31 | b |

SOURCE: U.S. Bureau of the Census, *State Government Finances*, 2002.

[a] Definitions of these items can be found in U.S. Bureau of the Census (2000).
[b] Not included in general revenue.

less discretionary income than higher-income individuals, and hence that it is "fair" to tax those with lower incomes at a lower rate. On the other hand, a *regressive* tax is one in which the share of individuals' income devoted to taxes increases as income declines. In other words, with a regressive tax low-income individuals pay a higher share of their income to taxes than higher-income individuals. Sales taxes are often considered to be regressive, since individuals with low incomes spend more of their income than those with high incomes on consumption that is subject to sales taxes. Finally, *proportional* taxes do not differentiate individuals in terms of the share of income devoted to taxes. In this case high- and low-income individuals pay the same effective tax rate.

*Patterns of Tax Policy and Priorities Over Time*

Taxes constituted about 7 percent of state personal income in 2000; recall that state public sector spending constitutes about 14 percent of state personal income, so the other 7 percent of state personal income goes for intergovernmental grants, current charges, and miscellaneous revenues. As is the case with government expenditures, there was a general increase in tax shares of personal income from 1960 until the early 1980s, at which point the trend flattened and remained just below or around 7 percent until 2000.

What is the distribution of different taxes over time? In Figure 10-3 we present trends in the mean share of total personal income devoted to sales, individual income, corporate income, gasoline, and license taxes in the American states from

**Figure 10-3** Trends in Taxes as a Share of State Personal Income, Various Taxes, 1960–2000

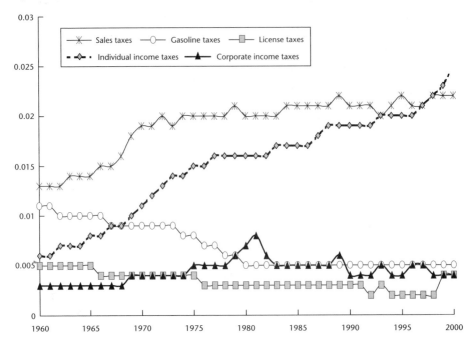

SOURCES: U.S. Bureau of the Census, *Statistical Abstract,* various years; U.S. Bureau of the Census, *State Government Finances,* various years.

1960 to 2000. Several general conclusions are suggested by these trends. First, it would appear that two taxes—sales taxes and individual income taxes—are on the increase, while the other tax types—gasoline taxes, license taxes, and corporate income taxes—exhibit a decline over time. States appear to place much greater reliance on sales and individual income taxes over time. Second, the diversity of state tax systems has declined considerably. Diverse tax systems are characterized by having many tax types and by having tax revenue distributed relatively evenly among different tax types. For instance, a diverse tax system would be one in which sales, personal income, corporate income, gasoline, and license taxes all contributed roughly equal amounts to tax revenues. Diversity more aptly described the tax system during the early 1960s, with all of these tax types making a reasonably large contribution to total tax revenue. However, over time the role of sales and personal income taxes has grown dramatically while gasoline, license, and corporate income taxes declined. The result is that sales and personal income taxes are the major components of state tax policy, by 2000 representing approximately two-thirds of state tax revenue. Clearly, the typical state tax system has come to rely on much less diverse sources of tax revenue over time.

*Sales Taxes.* For most of the post–World War II era, the sales tax has been the dominant method of taxation employed by the states. Not only was this the primary form of state taxation until the early 1990s, but the states have moved to this form of taxation incrementally, and only in a few cases have they decreased the sales tax. The period between 1960 and 1972 saw the largest increase in sales tax collections; during this period the sales tax moved from about 1.3 percent of total personal income to over 2 percent. From 1973 to 2000, the sales taxation share has been relatively static, or perhaps trending slightly upward, with only minor variation.

The sales tax has come under criticism from a number of quarters. First, sales taxes are seen by many observers as a form of fiscal illusion; sales taxes are added to the purchase price in a manner that de-emphasizes the tax in the minds of consumers. Dramatic sales tax increases might spark public outcries, but consumers are unlikely to differentiate small tax increases from inflationary price increases, so small sales tax increases are likely to be interpreted and absorbed as small price adjustments.

Second, sales taxes are generally viewed as being highly regressive—i.e., low-income individuals pay a higher share of their income to sales taxes than high-income individuals. To be sure, low- and high-income individuals pay the same sales tax rate. However, low-income individuals typically spend a higher share of their income on consumption, and hence they are more likely than high-income individuals to pay sales taxes on what they do with their income. The regressivity of sales taxes varies across the states. Some states apply the sales tax to food, utilities, and/or medicine, which in combination accounts for a higher share of income for those with low incomes than for those with high incomes.

Third, the elasticity of the sales tax hinges heavily on the items covered by state law, as well as on the economic conditions affecting consumers in the state. If some transferable or substitutable items are not covered by the sales tax, consumers will avoid the purchase of those items in favor of those not covered by the sales tax. This is particularly the case in recent years, when the availability of products that can be purchased over the Internet means that consumers can avoid sales taxes in their home states by purchasing products from Internet vendors residing in states with low sales tax rates or no sales tax altogether. This trend has prompted many state governments to ask Congress to pass legislation mandating that citizens of one state purchasing products over the Internet in another state be required to pay the sales tax for their home state.

Finally, economic conditions in a given state affect consumption, and consumption-dependent sales tax collections are often affected by declining economic conditions. Simply, when the economy is performing poorly individuals collectively make fewer purchases and sales tax revenues will decline or grow more slowly. This is also true for other types of tax collections, but sales tax revenues are especially susceptible to economic cycles. The result is that state policy makers cannot always depend on sales taxes as a stable source of revenue during periods of economic slowdown.

*Individual Income Taxes.* While the revenue extracted via the sales tax has remained relatively unchanged since the early 1970s, the individual income tax has shown a substantial upward trend since 1960. Beginning in 1960, individual income taxes represented just above a mere .05 percent of total state personal income. Over the course of the next four decades individual income taxes grew steadily as a share of total personal income, and by 2000 income taxes had approached the 2.5 percent threshold and surpassed sales taxes as a share of personal income. The increased share of the private economy going to individual income taxes likely has two sources. First, the increase in income tax revenue could reflect increasing income tax rates. Holding the income tax base constant, an increase in tax rates would generate additional revenue. Second, income taxes typically are progressive, meaning that individuals pay a higher share of their income to individual income taxes as their incomes increase. As per capita income has increased steadily in the United States over the past four decades, more individuals are moved into higher tax brackets. The result of this "bracket creep" is that more individuals are paying a higher share of their income to individual income taxes.

The income tax is easily applied in most states, as it is tied heavily into the federal personal income tax and is usually removed from employees' pay through a standard withholding mechanism. The resources extracted from the income tax are contingent on two factors: the tax code and the economic vitality of the state. States vary considerably in their income tax rates, the progressivity of their tax structure, as well as the use of exemptions and deductions. For instance, some states allow many exemptions and deductions, which are written into the tax law and can reduce the amount of revenue the state draws from the income tax. In addition, the state of the economy clearly has an effect on individual income tax collections. If the economy of a particular state is faltering, the income attained by its inhabitants will likely grow at a slower rate or be diminished, and this will reduce the amount that can be obtained through the income tax.

*Motor Fuel Taxes.* The motor fuel tax directly affects motorists as they purchase gasoline. Added to each gallon of fuel consumed at the time of the purchase, the gas tax influences the price consumers pay during each refueling. This attribute, while a hidden cost to most consumers, adversely affects the sale of gasoline, a vital source of energy in our modern economy.

As one can see from Figure 10-3, gasoline taxes were at a peak in 1960, at which time these taxes were the second highest source of state tax revenue, only behind sales taxes. The amount of revenue the motor fuel tax provides to the states has declined since 1960. The bulk of the reduction occurred between 1960 and 1980, and since 1980 the tax garnered from the sale of gasoline has remained stagnant around 0.5 percent of states' personal income. By the late 1960s motor fuel taxes were surpassed by individual income taxes as a source of state tax revenue, and since 1980 even the value of corporate income taxes has occasionally surpassed that of motor fuel taxes.

*Corporate Income Taxes.* The corporate income tax is a levy that extracts resources from businesses as a percentage of their net incomes. In Figure 10-3 we also depict the trends in corporate income taxes over time. As the figure illustrates, corporations, which represent some of the largest income generators in the states, are not a source tapped for state government revenue. Corporate income taxes represent a relatively low share of the private economy, not reaching 1 percent of total personal income even at its height. Corporate income taxes started in the early 1960s at below 0.5 percent of total personal income, but increased modestly throughout the 1970s, reaching their high point in 1981. After that year the trend in corporate income taxes was reversed, with a downward trend continuing through 1990, at which point the trend in corporate income taxes flattened and remained relatively stable throughout the 1990s.

The corporate income tax is typically categorized as progressive in that it usually taxes the more successful corporations at a higher rate, though the progressivity of the tax varies across the states. The corporate income tax is fraught with complexity and ambiguity. The confusion stems from the global nature of the modern corporation. If a product is manufactured in Massachusetts, but the raw materials originate in Malaysia, and the corporate headquarters are in Delaware, who claims the tax on the profit? The phenomenon of globalization is in part responsible for the low and decreasing tax revenue acquired from business, but political factors are also part of the story. In an attempt to lure and attract business to their states, policy makers will often include corporate tax breaks as incentives. The resulting competition produces a "race to the bottom," insofar as states compete with one another to provide the most favorable corporate tax climate. The granting of corporate tax breaks, usually under the rubric of job creation and economic development, is often controversial and plays to political divisions in the states. There is a considerable scholarly debate about whether corporate tax breaks actually have the desired effect on economic development.

*License Taxes.* States also obtain revenue from the licensing of certain objects and activities. These include the registration of motor vehicles and operators licenses. The trend indicated in Figure 10-3 is one of relatively little change, with minor reductions in the revenue extracted via license taxes. In 1960 license taxes comprised 0.5 percent of state total personal income and fell to less than half that by 1998. In the 1970s the trends for license taxes and corporate income taxes met and diverged, with corporate tax collections exceeding license taxes collections ever since.

Overall, the conclusions drawn from Figure 10-3 suggest a strong rise of the personal income tax as a formidable source of revenue for states. The sales tax has been and remains one of the two largest sources of tax revenue extracted by the states, but sales and personal income taxes are not the only sources of income the states employ. States rely on a myriad of funding flows to supply their programmatic needs. The diversity affords states some insulation from specific economic or external conditions that could otherwise result in serious budgetary shortfalls. The multiplicity of sources also allows states to spread the burden of taxation across many different groups. Finally, Figure 10-3 suggests a pattern in which states, while maintaining diverse methods of taxation, are beginning to rely more heavily on two specific forms, the personal income tax and the sales tax. If tax system diversity is a good thing, the two-tax system upon which many states rely raises questions about the ability of state governments to insulate themselves from economic slowdowns or negative external conditions.

### Determinants of Tax Revenues

For most types of taxes, the amount of revenue generated is a function of two characteristics of the tax system. First, we can use the term *tax base* to refer to the amount of resources in a given state that is subject to taxation for a given tax. For personal income taxes, for instance, states define what is taxable income, and the total taxable income in a given state is the base and subject to taxation. Second, the *tax rate* is the share of the tax base that is taken by state government in the form of taxes. For instance, if an individual earns $100,000 per year in taxable income (i.e., the individual's tax base) and the income tax rate is 5 percent (assuming a flat tax rate), the total tax taken from that individual is $5,000. When one adds together the taxable income for all individuals in a given state and applies the appropriate tax rate, this yields the total of tax revenue generated by that specific tax. So, if taxable income in a given state were $10 billion, a flat rate of 5 percent would generate $500 million in personal income tax revenue.

The tax rates adopted by state governments are largely a function of decisions made through the political process. For each tax type, there is considerable variation across the states in terms of general tax rates, and this variation reflects both the need for revenue and the predisposition of state electorates and policy makers to support government programs. In terms of need, some states have strong demands for public-sector goods and services that place pressure on state government to find revenue sources (including taxes) to support that spending. For instance, states with large school-age populations exhibit considerable demand for education spending; the result is that state electorates and policy makers face considerable pressure for increases in tax rates, particularly if intergovernmental grants and other funding sources are not available to pick up the slack. In addition, the ideological predisposition of state electorates and policy makers might be related to tax rates. Relatively conservative states will resist increases in tax rates, often even in the face of demand for greater expenditures; on the other hand, relatively liberal states will tend to view taxes as a necessary evil and be more likely to support tax rate increases as an appropriate means of paying for increased spending in important policy areas.

It is also noteworthy that the mix of taxes adopted by state governments is a function of decisions made in the political process. Different tax types have different implications for the citizens of the states, and state policy makers most certainly take these implications into account when determining the mix of taxes imposed on their citizens. Perhaps the most obvious example relates to the relative use of sales and personal income taxes in a given state. As noted above, sales taxes are generally viewed as regressive, since lower income individuals pay a higher share of their income to sales taxes than higher income individuals. On the other hand, income taxes are generally more progressive, insofar as income tax rates usually increase as taxpayers' incomes increase. The potential for manipulating the mix of sales and income taxes in order to achieve partisan or ideological political ends is certainly in evidence. States with a predisposition toward income redistribution and anti-poverty programs might be expected to downplay the sales tax and emphasize the personal income tax, particularly an income tax with a steep rise in tax rates as income increases. On the other hand, states for which income redistribution and anti-poverty programs have a lower priority would be expected to give a higher priority to sales taxes.

The tax base in a given state is determined by a wider range of factors, some of which are under the direct control of state policy makers, some of which are not. State governments are generally free to define what the theoretical tax base is for any given tax, and this will affect the level of revenues generated and has potential political implications. For instance, in determining the tax base for sales taxes, states can define taxable sales to include all sales, or they can exempt certain items such as food, medicine, clothing, or utilities. Including all sales in the tax base for the sales tax is likely to have the effect of making the sales tax more regressive; individuals with lower incomes will spend a higher share of their income on taxable consumption goods than individuals with higher incomes. Exempting food, medicine, clothing, or utilities takes out of the equation a major component of purchases by lower-income individuals, and so exempting these goods makes the sales tax less regressive. State governments can also make the personal income tax more or less progressive, or else can exempt other kinds of income from the income tax, and this has an effect on the tax base for this tax.

The tax base for a given tax is also affected by circumstances that are not directly under the control of state governments. In particular, the state economy has a major effect on the tax base (and ultimately, tax revenues) for most taxes, since the tax base expands when economic times are good and contracts when economic times are bad. Consider income taxes as an example. When economic times are bad (i.e., when economic growth is slow or nonexistent, when unemployment is high) personal incomes upon which the personal income tax is based will decline; some individuals who were working will be unemployed (and hence not earning income), while others who are employed will be forced to work fewer hours (and hence will earn less income), and still others who are unemployed will have less of a chance of entering the work force than when economic growth is strong. On the other hand, when the economy is vibrant and growing, previously unemployed individuals become employed individuals (and hence earn income that is subject to taxation), those who were employed work more hours and get raises (and hence earn additional income that is subject to the income tax), and in states with progressive income tax structures, some individuals earn more income, move into higher tax brackets, and hence pay a higher share of their income to income taxes. The end result is that under conditions of economic growth the tax base for the income tax increases, and, even holding the tax rate constant, this in turn results in a high level of income tax revenues. The same is true for sales taxes, which are highly dependent on the state of the economy. Ultimately, state economic performance has a strong effect on the tax base and the level of tax revenues available for allocation in the policy process.

It is for this reason that the predictability of state tax collections is typically lower than that for expenditures. When policy makers adopt a budget, the expenditures that they envision being spent are subject to relatively little uncertainty. It is true that some entitlement programs require states to provide funds to all eligible individuals, regardless of what was initially budgeted, and there is some uncertainty about the number of individuals who will be eligible to receive entitlement payments during the upcoming year. There also may be minor deviations from expected expenditures arising from administrative action. However, for the most part there is a fairly close connection between the amount of money appropriated and the amount spent. In the case of tax collections, there is much more uncertainty. Estimates of tax revenue are often based on forecasts of the economic behavior of citizens and the performance of the economy. While economic forecasts are reasonably accurate, they are not perfect, and the result of even a small deviation from expected economic performance can be a lower level of state revenues than anticipated. If the economy performs worse than expected, the size of the tax base for economy-dependent taxes will be smaller than expected, and the result is that tax revenues will be lower than expected. This can have the effect of forcing unanticipated reductions in spending, sometimes during the middle of the fiscal year or biennium.

### DEFICITS AND SURPLUSES

Thus far we have discussed state expenditures and revenues almost as if they are independent of one another. While the decision processes for expenditures and revenues are often conducted separately in the American states, ultimately most state governments are required to bring expenditures and revenues in their budgets into balance, or at least to produce a budget in which expenditures do not exceed revenues. Budget deficits are prohibited constitutionally by most state governments, and the result is that the legacy of deficit spending at the U.S. federal level has stood in sharp contrast to the experience in the American states, where deficits are uncommon.

Over the long run, budget deficits in the American states are relatively rare occurrences. From 1961 to 2000, 83.1 percent of all state-year cases were balanced or in surplus, meaning that only 16.9 percent of cases were in deficit. Most important, the trend toward budget surpluses was on the rise until very recently. During the 1960s, in only about two-thirds of state-year cases did revenues exceed expenditures, but the share of states with surpluses increased to over three-fourths during

**Table 10-3** Years with Budget Surpluses, by State, 1961–2000

| State | Number of years with budget surpluses | | State | Number of years with budget surpluses | |
|---|---|---|---|---|---|
| | n | Percentage | | n | Percentage |
| Alabama | 30 | 75.0 | Nebraska | 36 | 90.0 |
| Alaska | 27 | 67.5 | Nevada | 37 | 92.5 |
| Arizona | 39 | 97.5 | New Hampshire | 25 | 62.5 |
| Arkansas | 38 | 95.0 | New Jersey | 34 | 85.0 |
| California | 34 | 85.0 | New Mexico | 40 | 100.0 |
| Colorado | 38 | 95.0 | New York | 32 | 80.0 |
| Connecticut | 27 | 67.5 | North Carolina | 39 | 97.5 |
| Delaware | 27 | 67.5 | North Dakota | 34 | 85.0 |
| Florida | 38 | 95.0 | Ohio | 39 | 97.5 |
| Georgia | 36 | 90.0 | Oklahoma | 33 | 82.5 |
| Hawaii | 22 | 55.5 | Oregon | 34 | 85.0 |
| Idaho | 36 | 90.0 | Pennsylvania | 32 | 80.0 |
| Illinois | 34 | 85.0 | Rhode Island | 24 | 60.0 |
| Indiana | 31 | 77.5 | South Carolina | 36 | 90.0 |
| Iowa | 30 | 75.0 | South Dakota | 33 | 82.5 |
| Kansas | 37 | 92.5 | Tennessee | 35 | 87.5 |
| Kentucky | 28 | 70.0 | Texas | 40 | 100.0 |
| Louisiana | 30 | 75.0 | Utah | 34 | 85.0 |
| Maine | 32 | 80.0 | Vermont | 28 | 70.0 |
| Maryland | 29 | 72.5 | Virginia | 38 | 95.0 |
| Massachusetts | 21 | 52.5 | Washington | 35 | 87.5 |
| Michigan | 35 | 87.5 | West Virginia | 31 | 77.5 |
| Minnesota | 39 | 97.5 | Wisconsin | 35 | 87.5 |
| Mississippi | 35 | 87.5 | Wyoming | 37 | 92.5 |
| Missouri | 34 | 85.0 | | | |
| Montana | 36 | 90.0 | All states | 1,661 (2000) | 83.05 |

SOURCE: Calculated by the authors.

the 1970s (76.8 percent) and to over 90 percent during the 1980s (94.6 percent) and 1990s (95.2 percent). Clearly, in the past two decades budget deficits have become increasingly rare, occurring less than 10 percent of the time.

The trend in the mean size of state budget surpluses is also on the rise. The only years for which states had a mean budget deficit are in the early 1960s and 1971; in all other years, the mean for the states is positive, indicating a tendency toward surpluses. During the 1960s, the mean budget surplus across states and years was 2.1 percent of state expenditures. The mean budget surplus increased to 5.3 percent of state expenditures during the 1970s and to 10.8 percent of state expenditures during the 1980s, before leveling off at 9.7 percent of state expenditures during the 1990s. Clearly, states have been better positioned in recent years to avoid budget deficits and set aside resources for future programs or "rainy-day" funds. This trend is now at an end, however, with the large budget deficits that many state governments have experienced in 2002 and that are looming in the next few years.

In Table 10-3 we present data on the number and percentage of years with budget surpluses or balanced budgets, broken down by state. Based on these results, it is clear that some states are much more prone to budget deficits than others. On one hand, several states have budget surpluses all or almost all of the time. Two states—New Mexico and Texas—had a budget surplus in all 40 years from 1961 to 2000, while several others (Arizona, Minnesota, North Carolina, and Ohio) had a surplus in 39 of 40 years. On the other hand, several states regularly fail to balance their state budgets. Massachusetts was in surplus only 52.7 percent of the time, while three other states—Hawaii (55.5 percent), Rhode Island (60.0 percent), and New Hampshire (62.5 percent)—had a surplus in only a small majority of years.

However, the number of states with unbalanced budgets promises to increase in the next few years. During the 1990s, the booming economy resulted in huge revenue increases, and states responded with a combination of increased spending and tax cuts. With the economy stagnating in the past few years and likely to continue to do so over the next year or two, state revenue levels are unlikely to keep up with the current level of demand for public goods and service. States are facing budget deficits, in some cases very large budget deficits, and as a result many state governments are confronting the rather painful choice of reducing spending, increasing taxes, or some combination of the two.

## CONCLUSION

In this chapter we have discussed patterns and explanations of expenditures, taxes, and deficits in the American states. If one is to draw any conclusions from the foregoing discussion, one must begin with general trends in spending, taxes, and deficits over the past forty or fifty years. Clearly, the American states are very different today than they were at the end of World War II. During the 1950s, the size of the public sector was very modest, on average hovering around 4 percent of total state personal income. However, over the next four decades the public sector began to take a substantially increasing share of economic output. By the time of the late 1990s, American state governments absorbed a bit more than 13 percent of state economic output. The increase in spending was accompanied by commensurate increases in revenues, particularly taxes and intergovernmental grants, and the result over time has been an increasing tendency for state governments to balance their budgets and run budget surpluses. It is indisputable that the American states are major players in the policy process in the United States, and their role has been increasing at a steady pace since the end of World War II.

What explains these changes in the states over the past four decades? It is clear from our discussion that patterns of expenditures and taxes are determined by both policy instruments within the control of state governments as well as social, demographic, and economic conditions that are outside the direct control of state governments. The role of these social, demographic, and economic conditions cannot be overstated. Increases in state spending as a function of demands from state citizenries that are largely (but by no means exclusively) determined by its social and demographic characteristics. States' economic contexts also influence the demand for government services by determining the level of self-sufficiency or dependency in the population. Social, demographic, and economic conditions also influence the amount of tax revenues available for policy makers to allocate; for instance, states with impoverished populations facing weak economic conditions are less likely to generate sufficient revenue to support state programs. The end result is that state policy makers are substantially dependent on the context represented in their states' economic, social, and demographic circumstances. Even well-meaning state policy makers might find themselves in a situation that makes it difficult for them to make progress in solving the problems faced by the populations.

Of course, social, demographic, and economic conditions have had a major impact on state governments struggling with budget deficits in the past two years and for the immediate future. The economic slowdown in 2001 and 2002 has had a dramatic negative impact on state revenues, as derived from both state taxes and intergovernmental grants from the federal government. The reduction in revenues has come at a time when social and demographic conditions have placed considerable pressure on state governments for increased or, at the very least, constant levels of spending. The effects of social and demographic attributes on the demand for state government services are too numerous to detail here. But when combined with declining or stagnant revenues brought on by economic slowdown, the result is that many state governments are facing a considerable disconnect between the demand for government goods and services and the ability to support such services. The political battles that will result from high demands for government spending and the low supply of revenues promise to make state politics very interesting over the next few years.

But what state governments do—either at the direction of their state electorates, or else on their own—also has a discernible effect on expenditures, taxes, and deficits and surpluses. State governments make explicit decisions about the level of expenditures and the allocation of expenditures to various claimants for government goods and services. State governments cannot always control the state economic, social, and/or demographic conditions that influence revenue levels, but they can define the state tax base and the taxation rates for various taxes under their control. Within some constitutional and legal constraints, state governments can also determine the relative balance between expenditures and revenues, and this determines both whether states balance their budgets and the magnitude of their surpluses or deficits. Any effort to ascertain the determinants of state expenditures, taxes, and deficits and surpluses must account for the decisions made by state policy makers and the influence that citizens have on the actions of those policy makers.

**REFERENCES**

Bails, Dale. 1990. "The Effectiveness of Tax-Expenditure Limitations: A Reevaluation." *American Journal of Economics and Sociology* 49(2): 223–238.

Blais, Andre, Donald Blake, and Stephane Dion. 1993. "Do Parties Make a Difference? Parties and the Size of Government in Liberal Democracies." *American Journal of Political Science* 37(1): 40–62.

Boix, Charles. 2001. "Democracy, Development, and the Public Sector." *American Journal of Political Science* 45(1): 1–17.

Borcherding, Thomas. 1977. "The Sources of Growth in Public Expenditures in the United States, 1902–1970." In *Budgets and Bureaucrats: The Sources of Government Growth,* edited by Thomas Borcherding. Durham, N.C.: Duke University Press.

Cameron, David. 1978. "The Expansion of the Public Economy: A Comparative Analysis." *American Political Science Review* 72(4): 1243–1261.

Corey, Elizabeth C., and James C. Garand. 2002. "Are Government Employees More Likely to Vote? An Analysis of Turnout in the 1996 U.S. National Election." *Public Choice* 111 (April): 259–283.

Cox, James, and David Lowery. 1990. "The Impact of the Tax Revolt Era State Fiscal Caps." *Social Science Quarterly* 71(3): 492–509.

Domke, William, Richard Eichenberg, and Catherine Kelleher. 1983. "The Illusion of Choice: Defense and Welfare in Advanced Industrial Democracies, 1948–1978." *American Political Science Review* 77(1): 19–35.

Easton, David. 1953. *The Political System: An Inquiry into the State of Political Science.* New York: Knopf.

Garand, James C. 1993. "New Perspectives on the Size of Government in the American States: A Pooled Analysis." Paper presented at the conference on The Politics of State Economic Development: Prospects and Problems in State Economic Intervention. Chicago.

———. 1988a. "Explaining Government Growth in the U.S. States." *American Political Science Review* 82(3): 837–849.

———. 1988b. "Measuring Government Growth in the American States: Decomposing Real Growth and Deflator Effects." *American Politics Quarterly* 17(3): 405–424.

———. 1985. "Partisan Change and Shifting Expenditure Priorities in the American States, 1945–1978." *American Politics Quarterly* 14(3): 355–391.

Garand, James, and Rebecca Hendrick. 1991. "Expenditure Tradeoffs in the American States: A Longitudinal Test, 1948–1984." *Western Political Quarterly* 44(4): 915–940.

Garand, James C., Catherine Parkhurst, and Rusanne Seoud. 1991. "Bureaucrats, Policy Attitudes, and Political Behavior: An Extension of the Bureau Voting Model of Government Growth." *Journal of Public Administration Research and Theory* (April): 177–212.

Gilligan, Thomas, and John G. Matsusaka. 1995. "Systematic Deviations from Constituent Interests: The Role of Legislative Structure and Political Parties in the States." *Economic Inquiry* 33 (July): 383–401.

Howard, Marcia. 1989. "State Tax and Expenditure Limitations: There is No Story." *Public Budgeting and Finance* 9(2): 93–90.

Joyce, Philip G., and Daniel R. Mullins. 1991. "The Changing Fiscal Structure of the State and Local Public Sector: The Impact of Tax and Expenditure Limitations." *Public Administration Review* 51(3): 240–253.

Kapeluck, Branwell Dubose. 2001. "Government Growth in the American States, 1946–1997: A Test of Twelve Models." Paper presented at the annual meeting of the Southern Political Science Association, Atlanta, November 7–10.

Kiewiet, D. Roderick, and Matthew McCubbins. 1985. "Congressional Appropriations and the Electoral Connection." *Journal of Politics* 47(1): 59–82.

Lasswell, Harold. 1936. *Politics: Who Gets What, Where, When, and How?* New York: McGraw-Hill.

Lewis-Beck, Michael, and Tom Rice. 1985. "Government Growth in the United States." *Journal of Politics* 47(1): 2–30.

Lowery, David, and William Berry. 1983. "The Growth of Government in the United States: An Empirical Assessment of Competing Explanations." *American Journal of Political Science* 27(4): 665–694.

Lybeck, Johan. 1986. *The Growth of Government in Developed Economies.* Brookfield, Vt.: Gower.

Matsusaka, J. G. 1995. "Fiscal Effects of the Voter Initiative: Evidence from the Last 30 Years." *Journal of Political Economy* 103(June): 587–623.

Mintz, Alex. 1989. "Guns vs. Butter: A Disaggregated Analysis." *American Political Science Review* 83(4): 1285–1293.

Mintz, Alex, and Chi Huang. 1990. "Defense Expenditures, Economic Growth, and the Peace Dividend." *American Political Science Review* 84(4): 1283–1293.

Niskanen, William. 1971. *Bureaucracy and Representative Government.* Chicago: Aldine.

Peacock, Alan, and Jack Wiseman. 1961. *The Growth of Public Expenditure in the United Kingdom.* Princeton, N.J.: Princeton University Press.

Ringquist, Evan, and James C. Garand. 1999. "Policy Change in the American States." In *American State and Local Politics: Directions for the 21st Century,* edited by Ronald E. Weber and Paul Brace. New York: Chatham House.

Russett, Bruce. 1982. "Defense Expenditures and National Well Being." *American Political Science Review* 76(4): 767–777.

Thornton, Mark, and Marc Ulrich. 1999. "Constituency Size and Government Spending." *Public Finance Review* 27(6): 588–598.

U.S. Census Bureau. 2000. "Chapter 7: Revenue." *Federal, State, and Local Governments: Government Finance and Employment Classification Manual.* Washington, D.C.: U.S. Government Printing Office.

———. Various years. *State Government Finances.* Washington, D.C.: U.S. Government Printing Office.

———. Various years. *Statistical Abstract of the United States.* Washington, D.C.: U.S. Government Printing Office.

Wagner, Adolf. 1877. *Finanzwissenschaft.* Leipzig: C.F. Winter.

## SUGGESTED READINGS

Bahl, Roy W. *Financing State and Local Government in the 1980s.* New York: Oxford University Press, 1984. A classic summary of the economics and politics of state and local government financing.

Berry, William, and David Lowery. *Understanding United States Government Growth: An Empirical Analysis of the Postwar Era.* New York: Praeger, 1987. This is a strong summary of various models of government growth at the federal, state, and local levels. Many of the models of government growth described in this book are directly applicable to state government growth.

Council on State Governments. *Book of the States.* Lexington, Ky.: Council on State Governments, various years. An invaluable source of data on state expenditures and taxation over time.

Dye, Thomas. *Politics, Economics, and the Public: Policy Outcomes in the American States.* Chicago: Rand McNally, 1966. A classic book on expenditure and tax policy in the American states.

Garand, James C. "Measuring Government Growth in the American States: Decomposing Real Growth and Deflator Effects." *American Politics Quarterly* (October 1988): 405–424. A basic discussion of the effect of different inflation rates in the public and private sectors on state government growth; includes state-by-state estimates of the amount of government growth explained by differences in inflation rates.

Hansen, Susan B. *The Politics of Taxation: Revenue Without Representation.* New York: Praeger, 1983. This is one of the best books written on taxation and fiscal politics in the American states.

Sears, David O., and Jack Citrin. *Tax Revolt: Something for Nothing in California.* Cambridge, Mass.: Harvard University Press, 1985. One of the best books written on the tax revolt in California in the late 1970s, and more broadly a classic book on the politics of state fiscal policy.

# CHAPTER 11

# Transforming State Health and Welfare Programs

MARK CARL ROM

State governments face the most difficult budgetary conditions in a generation (NGA 2003). Tax revenues are down, and spending—especially for medical programs—is escalating rapidly. As the federal government seems little inclined to help states in these fiscally bleak times, states face tough choices, in health and welfare programs. Fiscal pressures will accelerate ongoing changes in program goals, clientele, and service delivery. The changes create new opportunities and challenges for those who administer the programs, those who are affected by them, and those who hope to study their causes and consequences.

This chapter focuses on the most important state programs that deliver medical services and economic support to the needy. I attempt to answer several questions: What are the major health and welfare programs in our nation, and what roles do the states play in designing, funding, and implementing them? What patterns characterize state programs over time and across the states with respect to recipients, benefits, and expenditures? What are the states now doing to reform their health and welfare programs? What are the politics of these programs? What are the states doing to promote personal health and economic independence so that these medical and income support programs will be less necessary in the future?

## THE PROGRAMS

America's health and welfare are tightly connected. Our health and welfare programs have not been closely coordinated, however, and they may be becoming less so.

Both health and welfare programs have delivered income support and medical care to well-defined, and often fairly narrow, groups—in particular, the elderly and those in poverty. These programs have helped millions by staving off deprivation and disease, yet they have failed to ensure a nation of independent, prosperous, healthy individuals. And they have always sought to remedy problems rather than to prevent them.

Social welfare programs either transfer income or provide services to individuals to improve the quality of their lives. The vast majority of social welfare spending is not aimed specifically at those in poverty, however, nor is all of it visible. For example, Social Security, the largest national social welfare program, paid more than $400 billion dollars to the elderly, their dependents, survivors, and the disabled in 2000 (U.S. Bureau of the Census 2002, 347). Medicare, a purely national program that provides medical benefits to the elderly, cost the federal government nearly $220 billion in 2000 (U.S. Bureau of the Census 2002, 97). Public K-12 education, the largest social welfare program funded by state and local governments, cost these governments almost $360 billion in 2000 (U.S. Bureau of the Census 2002, 133). Many additional billions of dollars are invisibly transferred through tax breaks for housing, education, medical care, and pensions (Howard 1997).

Yet these social expenditures are not commonly regarded as welfare. *Welfare* usually refers to those programs that provide public assistance only to the poor. (These programs are also called "means tested.") Overall, American governments spent nearly $400 billion in 1998, or about one-fourth of their total social expenditures, on these welfare programs. State and local governments, for their part, paid nearly 30 percent of these welfare expenditures (U.S. Bureau of the Census 2002, 343).

Medical programs are the largest welfare programs, consuming almost half of the nation's welfare spending, with state and local governments paying nearly 30 percent of this amount. Nearly three-fourths of state and local spending on welfare is devoted to medical care, primarily through the Medicaid program. States spend more on health care for the poor than they do on all other medical programs.

Cash assistance programs make up the second largest block of welfare spending, accounting for about one quarter of all welfare spending. The states pay 20 percent of this amount, and less than one quarter of state welfare expenditures goes to cash assistance programs, with the largest such programs being Temporary Assistance for Needy Families (TANF), Supplemental Security Income (SSI), and general assistance (GA). The states play a minor role in all other welfare programs (e.g., nutritional assistance, job training, or educational aid to the poor), as almost all state spending provides either medical or cash assistance.

State welfare spending is outlined in Table 11-1. Two features are striking. Medical programs are large and growing; cash assistance and job training programs are smaller and shrinking (though the states are spending somewhat more on such items as foster care, housing benefits, low-income education, and energy assistance). Real spending on welfare did not increase between 1992 and 1998. Medic-

**Table 11-1** Cash and Noncash Benefits for Persons with Limited Income, 1992–1998

| Program | Federal[a] | State and local[a] | Percentage of state and local welfare spending | Percentage change 1992–1998 state and local spending |
|---|---|---|---|---|
| Medical benefits[b] | 113,779 | 82,610 | 72 | 6 |
| Medicaid | 100,177 | 77,187 | 67 | 8 |
| Veterans | 9,603 | — | 0 | 0 |
| General assistance | — | 4,956 | 4 | –21 |
| Indian health service | 2,099 | — | 0 | 0 |
| Maternal and child health | 678 | 424 | 0 | –15 |
| Cash aid[b] | 73,872 | 20,690 | 18 | –20 |
| TANF/AFDC | 11,286 | 10,227 | 9 | –25 |
| SSI | 29,656 | 3,945 | 3 | –10 |
| EITC | 25,300 | — | 0 | 0 |
| Foster care | 3,730 | 3,303 | 3 | 18 |
| Pensions for needy veterans | 3,071 | — | 0 | 0 |
| General assistance | — | 2,625 | 2 | –30 |
| Food benefits[b] | 33,451 | 2,060 | 2 | –5 |
| Housing benefits[b] | 26,897 | 2,614 | 2 | 474 |
| Education[b] | 16,989 | 1,137 | 1 | 8 |
| Social services[b,c] | 7,300 | 5,153 | 5 | –15 |
| Jobs and training[b] | 3,785 | 71 | 0 | –91 |
| Energy assistance[b] | 1,257 | 64 | 0 | 62 |
| Total | 277,332 | 114,401 | 100 | 0 |

SOURCES: U.S. Bureau of the Census 2002, 344, Social Insurance and Human Services No. 524; U.S. Bureau of the Census 2002, 343, Social Insurance and Human Services No. 523.

TANF/AFDC = Temporary Assistance for Needy Families/Aid to Families with Dependent Children; SSI = Supplemental Security Income; EITC = Earned Income Tax Credit.

[a] In millions of 1998 dollars.
[b] Includes other programs not shown separately.
[c] Nonfederal expenditure is a rough estimate.

aid, TANF, SSI, and GA soak up almost 90 percent of state welfare spending, with Medicaid and TANF accounting for the vast majority. To understand state welfare programs, we must focus on these four programs—especially the biggest two.

## Medicaid

Medicaid provides medical care to low-income persons who are aged, blind, disabled; to poor families with children; and increasingly to certain other pregnant women and children (for a discussion of Medicaid eligibility, services, and financing, see U.S. House, *The Green Book* 2000, 889–930). Created during the Great Society efforts of the mid-1960s, Medicaid is an entitlement program. In an *entitlement program,* any person eligible for benefits can obtain them; the government is obligated to provide the benefits necessary to fill all claims. The federal government and state governments share responsibility for Medicaid. The federal government establishes program guidelines (concerning eligibility, services, and financing), and the state governments design and administer the program. The state and federal governments split the cost of the program based on the federally established matching rate that requires the more affluent states to pay a higher share of the cost.

The federal government requires that states provide a broad list of medical services within Medicaid, including inpatient and outpatient hospital services as well as physicians' services, to the categorically needy. States are allowed to offer additional services (such as the provision of drugs, eyeglasses, or psychiatric care), and they are also permitted to establish limits on recipients' use of the services (for example, on the number of hospital days reimbursed).

All but one state must provide Medicaid to individuals in *categorically needy* groups—for example, those eligible for SSI or TANF. (Arizona is the exception; since 1982 it has run a medical program for low-income residents as a demonstration project.) States can also, at their option, provide coverage to the *medically needy,* individuals who do not meet the income or resource standards of the categorically needy but otherwise meet Medicaid standards. As of the year 2000, thirty-nine states offered at least some services to the medically needy. States are required to provide more extensive services to the categorically needy than the medically needy.

Medicaid does not have its own team of doctors. Instead, states reimburse private health care providers for delivering services to Medicaid recipients. The states decide, within federal guidelines, the reimbursement rates. Because some states set these rates so low that few doctors wanted to take Medicaid patients, states are now required to set reimbursement rates high enough so that Medicaid services will actually be available to recipients, at least to the extent that they are available to other residents in the state. Health care providers cannot charge Medicaid patients additional fees above these amounts.

Medicaid eligibility historically has been linked to participation in other welfare programs, in particular Aid to Families with Dependent Children (AFDC), which was replaced by TANF in 1996, or SSI. The federal government began gradually expanding coverage for other low-income pregnant women and children beginning in the mid-1980s. More recently, the State Children's Health Insurance Program (SCHIP), created by Congress in 1997, further expanded eligibility for medical services to uninsured children in families with incomes above the federal poverty level. Eligibility for Medicaid is broadest for children in poverty: seven out of ten poor children under five years of age received benefits, compared with only three of ten poor adults between the ages of forty-five and sixty-four (U.S. House, *The Green Book* 1996, 886).

All individuals who are eligible for Medicaid are entitled to receive benefits, although many, in fact, do not claim them. Federal and state governments are obligated to pay for the medical services obtained by eligible recipients. These governments thus can neither budget precisely how much they will spend on Medicaid each year nor limit expenses to a fixed amount. As a result, this open-ended entitlement program has become the biggest challenge for state budgets.

*Temporary Assistance to Needy Families*

The welfare map was rewritten in 1996 when the federal government terminated AFDC and established the TANF program in its place. To understand what TANF is, it is useful to understand first what AFDC came to be.

AFDC was created as a minor and uncontroversial element of the Social Security Act of 1935, with the intention that it would be a temporary program to provide income support to widows and their families. It did not turn out that way, however. Fifty years after its creation, AFDC provided assistance to more than 14 million Americans. Most AFDC parents were not widows but mothers who were divorced, separated, or never married. Few AFDC recipients had paid employment, even though most mothers today do earn income by working. Nearly two-thirds of adults receiving AFDC had been "on the dole" for eight or more years. Finally, almost two-thirds of the recipients were nonwhite minorities (see U.S. House, *The Green Book* 1996, 473, 474, 505). A large proportion of adult AFDC recipients were unmarried, minority mothers with little earned income who remained on the rolls for years. AFDC came to be seen as a program that discouraged marriage and work, encouraged out-of-wedlock childbearing and dependency, and primarily served people of color (Gilens 1999).

Presidents since Richard Nixon, and more recently congressional Republicans, vowed to get rid of this politically unpopular program. President Bill Clinton famously campaigned on the promise to "end welfare as we know it," and when the Republicans took control of the Congress in 1994 they pressured Clinton to do just that. In 1996 the Congress approved, and Clinton signed, the bill to end AFDC and create TANF in its place (Weaver 2000).

TANF differs from AFDC in several important ways. First, the states have much more power over TANF than they did over AFDC. The states can determine who is eligible for TANF, what obligations they face and what benefits they receive, and how the programs will be designed, implemented, and evaluated. (The states must still submit reports to the U.S. Department of Health and Human Services detailing how they are spending federal funds.) States can deny benefits to any family or category of poor family—and some are doing so with gusto. States can require certain behaviors in return for benefits; Wisconsin, for instance, effectively requires employment or community service as a condition for receiving TANF benefits. Some states even decided not to run uniform TANF programs, delegating responsibility for program operation to the counties.

Second, AFDC was an entitlement to individuals and TANF is not. The federal government gives each state a block of funds to pay for the program each year, with a state's grant based on the average amount it received from the federal government for AFDC. The states are required to spend at least 80 percent as much as they had for AFDC in 1994; if they meet certain work requirement goals, they need spend only 75 percent as much. The states can use a substantial portion of their TANF funds for purposes other than providing cash benefits.

A third important difference between TANF and AFDC is that the main goal of TANF is to promote work, not provide income support to poor families. The states are required to enroll increasing shares of their caseloads in job-related activities; by the year 2002, 50 percent of the single parents and 90 percent of the two-parent families in the TANF caseload were to have been working or the state faced financial penalties. States with declining caseloads have lower work participation requirements. This suggests that the states can meet these requirements either by placing recipients in work activities or removing them from the welfare rolls. Which technique states choose is a matter of great interest.

TANF is much more concerned with changing recipient behavior than was AFDC. To discourage dependency, the federal government will not allow its funds to provide benefits to families for more than five years, although a small portion of the recipients can be exempted from these time limits. The states are allowed to cut benefits off earlier if they wish. To discourage childbearing, states may deny benefits to unmarried teenagers and their children or to children born while their mothers were receiving benefits. States may require school attendance by the parents if they have not completed high school. States may also require "personal responsibility" contracts as a condition of enrolling in TANF, and thirty-five do so (State Policy Documentation Project 1999). While the states are not exactly Big Brother, they can increasingly be Stern Parent.

*General Assistance*

Poor people who do not qualify for TANF are almost—but not quite—out of luck. Many states have their own general assistance programs to provide cash, medical assistance, and other services to low-income individuals who are not eligible for other welfare programs (Uccello and Gallagher 1998). The term *general assistance* is a generic term for the entire group of purely state programs, which vary widely. Some GA programs cover broad categories of people who are ineligible for federal assistance, such as able-bodied adults without children, certain two-parent families with children, and the not quite elderly or disabled. Other states provide benefits only to narrow groups (such as those who have applied for SSI but are not yet receiving benefits) or in special circumstances (as when a home is destroyed by a natural disaster). In 1996 forty-one states had some form of general assistance, with thirty-two offering statewide programs, and at least some counties in nine other states had GA programs. Eight states—Alabama, Arkansas, Louisiana, Michigan, Mississippi, Oklahoma, Tennessee, and Wyoming—have no GA programs at all (Thompson 1995). Only twelve states provide financial assistance to all financially needy persons who do not qualify for federal welfare programs. GA programs provide more medical assistance than income support. In 1998 medical care made up nearly two-thirds of state GA spending, and states are gradually spending more for medical services and less for cash assistance (U.S. Bureau of the Census 2002, 344).

*Supplemental Security Income*

Established by the federal government in 1972 to replace several other federal programs that provided grants to the states, the SSI program provides cash payments to elderly, blind, or disabled persons who are also poor. Maximum SSI benefits are available to these individuals who are without other resources; benefits are reduced as a recipient's earned income rises or if the recipient is living with another person. SSI recipients may also be eligible for Social Security, Medicaid, and food stamps.

The fourth largest state-supported welfare program, SSI is gradually becoming more federal. The federal government establishes eligibility requirements, sets national benefit levels, and administers the program; states have the option of supplementing the federal benefit standard. All but seven states—Arkansas, Georgia, Kansas, Mississippi, Tennessee, Texas, and West Virginia—provide some form of supplemental benefits, though these benefits are typically quite small. The federal government pays for federal benefits and administration; the state governments fund the supplemental benefits and their administrative costs (for details, see U.S. House, *The Green Book* 2000, 232–235). Federal SSI benefits are indexed to inflation, so recipients receive the same cost-of-living adjustments as do Social Security beneficiaries; state benefits are not indexed.

## THE POLITICS

The Medicaid, TANF, SSI, and GA programs together spend more than $240 billion each year to assist about 44 million recipients. Except for GA, the programs are a complex mix of federal and state designs, funds, and administration. What factors influence the design and operation of these programs? Although these elements include economic and demographic attributes, political factors ultimately dominate. The reasons for this are clear. Economic and demographic conditions provide policy makers with opportunities and constraints, but these conditions do not by themselves make policies: politicians do. The politicians make program decisions based on their electoral concerns, their ideological beliefs, and their pragmatic judgments about what is best for their constituents, state, and country.

*Federalism*

Authority over health and welfare policy is shared—not always cordially—among state and national governments. This has three main implications for state policies. First, states do not have sole jurisdiction over health and welfare policy: they are constrained by national laws. On the one hand, states must provide certain services and follow specific rules; on the other, they cannot adopt proposals they prefer if these conflict with federal law.

Second, state and federal governments often attempt to gain control over health and welfare programs while at the same time attempting to shift burdens to the other party. Efforts toward control can be seen in federal mandates on the states, by which the federal government requires the states to perform certain functions, and state requests for waivers from these mandates, whereby the states seek to escape from these requirements and establish their own standards. States, moreover, are often tempted to play these programs in such a way that they obtain the maximum federal financial support at minimum cost to themselves. The states have greater incentives to manipulate welfare financing than does the federal government. Unlike the federal government, the states' constitutions prohibit them from running budget deficits, so the states literally cannot afford to be as generous as the federal government.

Third, state governments compete and, at times, cooperate with each other. Some of the competition is political, as ambitious politicians strive to build their national reputations by developing innovative programs to address social problems. The competition can also be economic, as politicians seek to make their states more attractive for businesses and workers. Political and economic competition can lead in different directions; politicians have reasons for making their states distinctive, but not so distinctive that they scare away economic resources.

*Internal Politics*

State policy choices are also influenced by political, economic, and demographic factors that vary across states and over time. The political cultures, ideologies, institutions, and public opinions of the states all can affect their health and welfare policies. The economic conditions of the states, their wealth and the sources of it, can influence state politicians as they choose among policies. The states also differ in the age of their populations, the composition of their families, and the ethnicity of their citizens, each with potential significance for the states' policies.

Political culture is "the particular pattern of orientation to political action in which each political system is embedded" (Elazar 1972, 84–85). This orientation may be found among politicians and the general public, and it may affect their understanding of what politics is and what can be expected from government, influence the types of people who become active in politics, and influence the ways in which they practice politics and formulate public policy (Sharkansky 1969, 67).

In moralistic political cultures, "both the general public and the politicians conceive of politics as a public activity centered on some notion of the public good and properly devoted to the advancement of the public interest" (Elazar 1970, 174). Traditionalistic or individualistic political cultures, in contrast, view politics as a way of preserving the status quo or gaining personal enrichment, respectively, as explained in Chapter 1. Moralistic political cultures thus tend to be more activist and generous in their health and welfare programs than traditionalistic or individualistic states. A state's political culture changes only slowly, moreover, so it is the most stable of the political variables.

Political ideology involves the durable views of politicians about what the government should do and how it should do it. Most basically, Americans have either conservative or liberal ideologies regarding health and welfare programs; liberals are in favor of expanded benefits and more inclusive eligibility standards, and conservatives prefer more restrictive benefits and eligibility. Political culture is related, but by no means identical to, political ideology. Moralistic states are not necessarily liberal, nor are individualistic states invariably conservative, although traditionalistic states almost always are conservative (Erikson, Wright, and McIver 1993, 150–176.) Political conservatives in moralistic states might believe that government best helps the poor by making welfare difficult to obtain; liberals in individualistic states might seek to increase welfare spending merely to enhance their own political fortunes.

The political institutions of American governments—their legislatures, bureaucracies, political parties, interest groups, electoral systems—can also influence health and welfare policies. In general, governments with professional legislatures and competent bureaucracies are more active in developing programs and open-handed in supporting them. Interest groups are more involved, and more influential, in some states than in others and in some issues than others (Thomas and Hrebenar, Chapter 4 in this volume). States with more highly mobilized publics and more competitive elections are also more likely to support social welfare programs (Holbrook and Van Dunk 1993).

Policy makers pay attention to public opinion, and these opinions vary across the states, over time, and among health and welfare issues (Berry et al. 1998). It should come as no surprise that citizens of Minnesota and Mississippi, for example, have different opinions about the appropriate role of their governments in social policy and that state policies in part reflect these opinions. Still, the sentiments of the nation as a whole also change over the years, with the public looking more favorably on the recipients of welfare in the 1960s than in the early 1980s and mid-1990s. The American public also appears to be more sympathetic to programs that provide goods and services (such as food and health care) to the poor rather than give them cash (Cook and Barrett 1992). Certain types of recipients are more politically popular. The "deserving poor" (for example, the disabled, children, and the elderly) are viewed sympathetically and provided greater governmental support, whereas the "undeserving poor" (for example, young men or women bearing children out of wedlock) are scorned by the public (Katz 1986). Public approval for programs that promote work is much stronger than for programs that don't (Mead forthcoming). The public opposes the idea of "welfare" but supports programs that help the poor help themselves.

Interest groups are also active in welfare and, especially, health politics. Medical providers—doctors, nurses, hospitals, insurers—all have an interest in how health programs are designed, administered, and financed. Certain types of patients—particularly the elderly and disabled—also have organizations that routinely promote their claims (welfare mothers, in contrast, usually do not). Interest groups are less pronounced in income-assistance programs, where the main actors are typically welfare officials, charities, and religious organizations.

*Economic and Demographic Factors*

The principal economic factors influencing health and welfare policies are both cyclical and structural. Whenever the economy goes into recession, for example, the number of individuals eligible for these programs increases (as more people become poor) and program costs rise; when the economy is growing faster, fewer individuals receive benefits and costs are reduced. This cyclical effect, however, is overshadowed by broader structural changes in the American economy and demography during the last couple of decades that increased the prevalence of poverty within certain groups, especially women and children, even during times of prosperity (Blank 1997).

The causes for these economic and demographic changes are complex and hotly debated. They involve such issues as the decline in well-paying blue-collar jobs, the increase in temporary or part-time jobs lacking benefits, the increase in single-parent families through divorce and, particularly, childbearing out of wedlock, and the perceived rise in a more permanent underclass apparently locked in poverty. Still, the absolute wealth of the country—and so the potential resources available for health and welfare programs—has increased substantially every decade since the 1940s, though these gains have not been shared equally by all groups or all states.

The economic and demographic characteristics of the states provide the context in which the politicians operate. States that are richer have more resources to devote to health and welfare programs, if they wish to do so. States with more favorable demographics have fewer welfare needs. But neither resources nor needs determine what policies will be chosen. Policy makers do.

*Interstate Competition*

Although the states are politically independent of each other, they are all part of a nationwide economic and political system. State politicians seeking to develop a national reputation accordingly have incentives to conduct bold policy experiments. When running for president, Bill Clinton and George W. Bush pointed to the educational reforms they pioneered as governors of Arkansas and Texas, respectively. Former Wisconsin governor Tommy Thompson used his welfare experiments as a springboard to appointment as Bush's Secretary of Health and Human Services. If the innovations prove successful or politically attractive, other states often imitate them. This pattern of state innovation and diffusion is well-recognized in American politics (Walker 1969).

States are also engaged in economic competition with each other regarding finance, commerce, and labor. Politicians find it far easier to run for reelection if they can boast that under their direction the state has a booming economy, rising incomes, high employment rates, and low taxes. This interstate economic competition has led some scholars to conclude that states are ill-suited to have responsibility for redistributive programs (see especially Peterson 1995). The logic behind this claim is simple. If a state offers generous health and welfare benefits, it will become a "welfare magnet" attracting the poor who need these benefits and repelling the affluent who pay the taxes to support them. Politicians are more sensitive to the concerns of the affluent because they are more important politically. As a result, politicians have strong incentives to keep their states from becoming welfare magnets; in fact, states have incentives to provide welfare programs that are less generous than their neighbors. If each state acts the same way, welfare benefits would become increasingly stingy and welfare eligibility increasingly stringent as the states "race to the bottom."

Whether states have been "welfare magnets" or will "race to the bottom" is an unsettled question. If generous states exert magnetic attraction to the poor, the pull is fairly weak. Some scholars find evidence of welfare magnets; others do not (for evidence of welfare magnets see Peterson and Rom 1990 and De Jong and Graefe 2002; for counter evidence, see Schram, Nitz, and Krueger 1998). But whether welfare magnets exist in fact, it is clear that many politicians find the phrase a useful rhetorical device to attack welfare generosity. And although state-provided welfare benefits have tended to decline in recent decades, it is not at all clear that states are racing to the bottom (Berry, Fording, and Hanson 2003; Rom 1998). Still, there is growing evidence that interstate competition puts pressure on states to restrict the generosity of their welfare systems (Bailey and Rom 2002).

*Policy Implications*

These political, economic, and demographic factors affect health and welfare policies in subtle and complex ways. All American governments are subject to their influence, but the impact of each factor differs for each state, varies between state and national governments, and changes over time. There is no single pattern of evolution for health and welfare policies, though a few observations might be offered.

States tend to be more parsimonious than the federal government in their efforts to restrain eligibility and benefits. The federal government, in contrast, is typically more generous in expanding health and welfare eligibility criteria and benefit levels. The programs under more state control (such as TANF and GA) tend to have smaller rolls that are more prone to shrink, whereas programs for which the federal government has primary responsibility for establishing eligibility criteria (such as Medicaid and SSI) tend to have larger rolls likely to expand. Such tendencies are not absolute; many states award benefits, especially medical care, to more residents than the federal government requires, and the federal government at times acts to tighten welfare eligibility or benefits.

It is worth remembering, however, that state health and welfare policy choices are far more complicated than a simple tallying of economic, demographic, and political forces would suggest. Policies vary among the states for unique historical reasons. An unusually forceful leader, a public scandal, a temporary surge in public opinion, all can have lasting effects on policy choice.

**THE PATTERNS**

Let us now turn to the patterns—and the anomalies—in health and welfare policies. Let us first examine the broad trends since 1970 in recipients, benefits, and ex-

**Figure 11-1** Annual Welfare Expenditures per Recipient

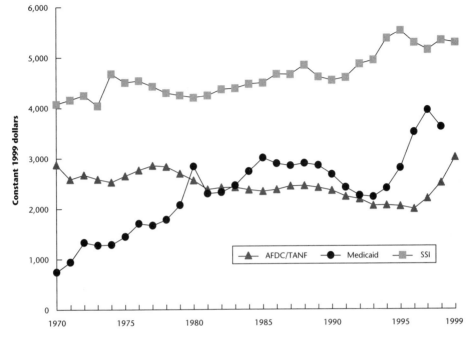

S O U R C E S : U.S. House, *The Green Book* 1998, 2000; CMS 2002b.

penditures for AFDC/TANF, Medicaid, and SSI; comparable data do not exist for GA programs.

*Trends in Benefit Levels*

Benefit trends for TANF/AFDC, Medicaid, and SSI are shown in Figure 11-1. The most important trend is that real Medicaid benefits increased by more than 280 percent between 1970 and 1998 (medical benefits are annual expenditures per recipient, adjusted for changes in medical prices). AFDC benefits, in contrast, decreased by more than 30 percent from their peak in 1977 to 1995. Between 1994 and 2000, real maximum TANF benefits in the median state declined by another 10.5 percent. Only six states raised benefits enough to offset inflation (U.S. House, *The Green Book* 2000, 382, 384). Though cash TANF benefits continued to decline in recent years, average spending per recipient increased substantially. The first reason for this is that federal spending for TANF has been roughly constant since 1996, and the states are required to spend 75 to 80 percent of their 1996 amounts. As TANF caseloads have declined substantially, more is spent per person still in that program. Second, TANF funds can be spent for a wide variety of purposes other than cash benefits. Still, it is difficult to compare AFDC expenditures—which consisted primarily of cash benefits—to TANF expenditures, which can go towards cash benefits, work activities, child care, administration, and various other activities.

**Figure 11-2** Welfare Recipients, 1970–2001

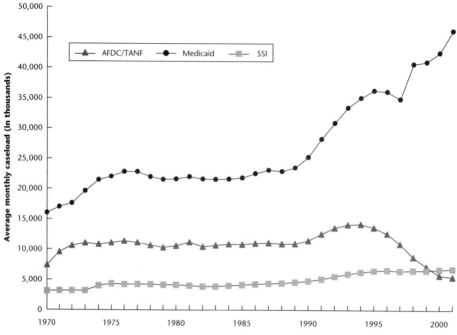

SOURCES: U.S. House, *The Green Book* 2000; CMS 2002b.

Better to be poor and elderly than poor and a single parent, at least as far as welfare benefits go: SSI benefits were much larger than TANF/AFDC benefits for the entire period. The differences in benefits between state and federal governments are even more striking. Average SSI benefits per person are much more generous than TANF benefits, in large part because the federal government sets and fully funds a minimum benefit level for SSI. These federal benefits have also been indexed to inflation since the mid-1970s (and indeed slightly over-indexed). As a result, real federal SSI benefits grew at least slowly during these decades, whereas state supplements declined sharply. Twenty-one states supplemented federal SSI benefits continuously between 1975 and 1999, yet real state-funded benefits for aged couples declined an astonishing 78 percent in the median state during that period, and benefits for aged individuals fell by 68 percent (U.S. House, *The Green Book* 2000, 236–239).

*Trends in the Number of Recipients*

AFDC/TANF, Medicaid, and SSI annual caseloads between 1970 and 2001 are shown in Figure 11-2. Medicaid and AFDC caseloads grew substantially in the early 1970s, then stabilized through most of the 1980s. Both programs began growing strongly again in the late 1980s. Since the mid-1990s, however, Medicaid and TANF

**Figure 11-3** Welfare Spending, 1970–2000

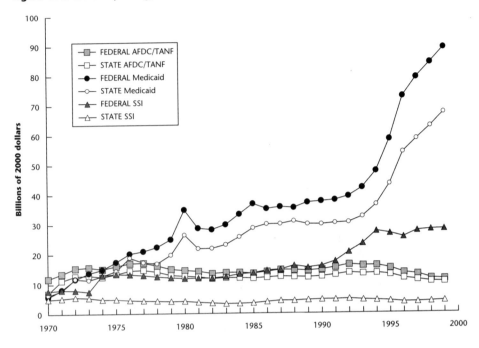

SOURCE: U.S. House, *The Green Book* 1998, 2000.

caseloads diverged dramatically, with Medicaid rising rapidly and TANF falling sharply. SSI caseloads, in contrast, have grown slowly during the entire period.

The recent trend—strong growth in Medicaid rolls, sharp decline in TANF, and stability in SSI—is especially important for state politics and policy. This trend was not caused purely by economic or demographic changes. It reflects the clear preference of state and national politicians for providing medical care to the elderly, disabled, or children who are poor and for withholding income support from impoverished, working-age adults.

### Trends in Expenditures

Total real federal and state spending on AFDC/TANF, SSI, and Medicaid between 1970 and 2000 is shown in Figure 11-3. State and federal spending on Medicaid dwarf expenditures on SSI and AFDC/TANF. Real state and federal expenditures on Medicaid rose more than twice as rapidly as spending on SSI, and TANF expenditures actually fell somewhat. State and federal governments both shared in the growth of Medicaid's spending, with the state governments carrying about 40 percent of the burden. Medicaid's extraordinary growth, fueled both by rising caseloads and benefits, has thus been a burden to state and federal governments alike. If welfare spending is a threat to state budgets, the peril comes from health care, not income support.

Future trends in expenditures are hard to predict, at least for the health programs. Medical prices are poised to rise rapidly again; in 2001 and 2002 medical care costs grew by more than 10 percent annually, far greater than the rate of inflation or growth in the economy. If caseloads continue to grow, total medical spending will rise yet more rapidly. Sharp increases in spending are unlikely for TANF. As the states are no longer required to provide benefits to any category of recipients, nor required to provide any particular benefits, the states could restrain spending even if needs grew.

### State Welfare Benefits and Recipients

The national trends this decade have thus featured diverging recipient populations, program expenditures, and benefit levels, with Medicaid and SSI growing and AFDC/TANF and GA shrinking. These trends have not affected all states equally, nor have all states responded in the same way to changing times.

*Benefits.* Welfare benefits vary dramatically across programs and among the states (Table 11-2). The average annual Medicaid expenditure per recipient in the states in 1998 was $3,856. (This represents the average across the states, not the average across recipients. California, with over 7 million Medicaid recipients, is given the same weight as Alaska, which has one-tenth that amount.) Average annual TANF benefits per family were almost the same ($3882) while TANF expenditures per person were $2637. Per person Medicaid expenditures were higher than TANF expenditures in every state except California, Idaho, Kansas, Oregon, Vermont, Wisconsin, and Washington. These states generally had either quite low Medicaid spending (California, Oregon, Vermont, and Washington) or high TANF spending (Idaho and Wisconsin). In 1998 the most generous state (Alaska) paid TANF families seven times as much as did the least generous (Mississippi); New York's average Medicaid expenditures per recipient were more than five times as large as in Washington, the state that spent the smallest amount. These differences are much greater than the cost-of-living variations in the states, and so indicate real differences in how the states treat their low-income residents.

Cash benefits are an accurate indicator of a state's generosity to its needy; the higher the benefit, the more generous the state. This is not necessarily true for total expenditures, however. It is possible for one state to deliver the same level of medical care as another state at a lower cost, for example. States with higher Medicaid expenditures thus do not necessarily offer better medical care. TANF spending does not necessarily represent generosity in benefits, either. For instance, California spends over two-thirds of its TANF funds on cash benefits; Idaho spends just 16 percent.

There is now little relationship between state generosity in Medicaid and TANF. Of the ten states with the highest TANF benefits per family, five also had Medicaid expenditures in the highest ten, but three states were among those with the lowest ten Medicaid expenditures. Massachusetts, Minnesota, New York, Rhode Island, and Connecticut had spending in the highest ten in both categories; California,

**Table 11-2** Mean Annual Welfare Benefit per Family or Expenditure per Recipient, Fiscal Year 1998

| State | Medicaid expenditure per recipient (rank) | TANF cash benefit per family (rank) | TANF expenditure per recipient (rank) |
|---|---|---|---|
| Alabama | 3,609 (25) | 1,675 (49) | 1,471 (45) |
| Alaska | 4,429 (12) | 8,028 (1) | 2,790 (16) |
| Arizona | 3,238 (37) | 3,345 (31) | 2,117 (30) |
| Arkansas | 3,240 (36) | 2,000 (45) | 1,951 (37) |
| California | 2,010 (48) | 6,315 (3) | 2,915 (14) |
| Colorado | 4,172 (16) | 3,606 (26) | 2,882 (15) |
| Connecticut | 6,351 (3) | 5,548 (10) | 2,779 (17) |
| Delaware | 4,141 (18) | 3,246 (32) | 3,210 (10) |
| Florida | 2,986 (40) | 2,741 (39) | 1,508 (43) |
| Georgia | 2,465 (47) | 2,842 (37) | 1,863 (39) |
| Hawaii | 2,746 (44) | 6,237 (4) | 2,215 (26) |
| Idaho | 3,450 (30) | 3,081 (33) | 6,005 (2) |
| Illinois | 4,526 (10) | 3,369 (30) | 1,594 (41) |
| Indiana | 4,222 (15) | 2,752 (38) | 1,963 (36) |
| Iowa | 4,093 (19) | 3,955 (22) | 2,521 (24) |
| Kansas | 3,786 (22) | 3,563 (27) | 4,571 (5) |
| Kentucky | 3,763 (23) | 2,636 (40) | 1,574 (42) |
| Louisiana | 3,308 (34) | 1,910 (47) | 1,084 (49) |
| Maine | 4,382 (13) | 4,415 (15) | 2,632 (21) |
| Maryland | 4,436 (11) | 3,727 (24) | 2,522 (23) |
| Massachusetts | 5,075 (8) | 6,059 (5) | 3,475 (9) |
| Michigan | 3,188 (38) | 4,288 (18) | 2,743 (18) |
| Minnesota | 5,431 (6) | 5,734 (7) | 2,675 (20) |
| Mississippi | 2,969 (41) | 1,214 (50) | 671 (50) |
| Missouri | 3,501 (29) | 2,924 (35) | 1,942 (38) |
| Montana | 3,583 (27) | 4,414 (16) | 2,016 (34) |
| Nebraska | 3,566 (28) | 3,878 (23) | 3,051 (12) |
| Nevada | 3,605 (26) | 3,457 (29) | 2,211 (27) |
| New Hampshire | 6,449 (2) | 5,005 (12) | 3,769 (7) |
| New Jersey | 5,188 (7) | 4,113 (20) | 2,069 (31) |
| New Mexico | 2,617 (46) | 4,596 (13) | 2,004 (35) |
| New York | 7,907 (1) | 5,758 (6) | 3,878 (6) |
| North Carolina | 3,437 (32) | 2,635 (41) | 2,051 (33) |
| North Dakota | 5,475 (5) | 4,059 (21) | 3,715 (8) |
| Ohio | 4,742 (9) | 3,675 (25) | 1,699 (40) |
| Oklahoma | 3,440 (31) | 2,607 (43) | 2,164 (29) |
| Oregon | 2,696 (45) | 4,572 (14) | 5,896 (3) |
| Pennsylvania | 3,992 (20) | 4,378 (17) | 2,627 (22) |
| Rhode Island | 6,001 (4) | 5,726 (8) | 3,013 (13) |
| South Carolina | 3,393 (33) | 1,891 (48) | 1,461 (46) |
| South Dakota | 3,976 (21) | 3,531 (28) | 2,054 (32) |
| Tennessee | 1,718 (49) | 2,039 (44) | 1,502 (44) |
| Texas | 3,071 (39) | 1,974 (46) | 1,343 (47) |
| Utah | 2,868 (42) | 4,253 (19) | 2,675 (19) |
| Vermont | 2,831 (43) | 5,527 (11) | 3,093 (11) |
| Virginia | 3,242 (35) | 2,949 (34) | 2,408 (25) |
| Washington | 1,446 (50) | 5,569 (9) | 2,204 (28) |
| West Virginia | 3,627 (24) | 2,878 (36) | 1,133 (48) |
| Wisconsin | 4,254 (14) | 6,788 (2) | 7,219 (1) |
| Wyoming | 4,163 (17) | 2,622 (42) | 4,926 (4) |

S O U R C E S : U.S. House, *The Green Book* 2000; U.S. Department of Health and Human Services, Administration for Children and Families 2003; Department of Health and Human Services, Health Care Financing Administration 2003.

Hawaii, and Washington were among the most generous in TANF benefits and low-est spenders in Medicaid. Two of the ten states (Mississippi and Tennessee) with the lowest TANF benefits also had Medicaid expenditures in the lowest ten. The states with the greatest contrast between their programs include California, Washington, Hawaii, Mexico, Vermont, and Oregon, all of which differed by thirty or more positions in the rankings (all had low Medicaid spending and high TANF benefits). Another way of showing the relationship between these variables is the correlation coefficient. When the coefficient equals 1 a perfect relationship exists; when it equals 0 the variables are not related at all. The correlation between TANF benefits and Medicaid expenditures across the states is only 0.29 (as compared to 0.59 in 1995).

The trend toward lower real benefits in AFDC has continued in TANF, and has affected all states: once inflation is taken into account, no state had a higher maximum in 2000 than in 1970. The decline has also been large, and felt everywhere. In the median state, maximum TANF benefits for a family of three fell by almost 50 percent during this period (U.S. House, *The Green Book* 2000, 390). The states with the smallest decline were Maine and Wisconsin, where maximum benefits fell by 21 percent; in Texas, maximum benefits shrank by 69 percent. The declines were not concentrated in the most generous states, either. Benefits in the most and least generous states fell by similar proportions.

The more affluent states support more generous social welfare programs than do their poorer peers. In general, a state with per capita personal income $1,000 higher than that of another state pays annual TANF benefits that are $160 higher. This relation is not ironclad, however. Some states with higher incomes nonetheless have lower benefits, and vice versa. In Utah, for example, average TANF family benefits are $4,253 per year and per capita income is $22,200; in Louisiana, per capita income is the same but TANF benefits are only $1,910.

The gap between TANF benefits and typical household incomes grows larger as the benefits fall lower. In the ten most generous states, average TANF benefits per family ($6,175) averaged about 20 percent of per capita income ($29,820). In the stingiest ten states, average family TANF benefits ($2,060) were less than 10 percent of household income ($22,900). States with the highest (and lowest) incomes reveal a different picture, however. In the ten states with the highest per capita incomes (averaging $32,300), mean TANF family benefits were $4,317, and TANF benefits averaged 13 percent of per capita income. In the ten states with the lowest incomes (averaging $24,100), mean TANF family benefits were $2,700, and the average benefit was 13 percent of per capita income. The low benefit states tend to be poor and the high benefit states tend to be more affluent, but poor states do not necessarily offer lower benefits and richer states higher benefits.

*Recipients.* The differences in the size of the welfare populations across programs, over time, and among the states are remarkable (Table 11-3). The states had 2.5 percent of their residents enrolled in TANF on average in 1998. Yet California has seventeen times more TANF beneficiaries, relative to its population, than does

**Table 11-3** Welfare Recipients as a Percentage of the Population, 1998

| State | AFDC/TANF percentage (rank) | Change 1995–1998 | Medicaid percentage (rank) | Change 1995–1998 |
|---|---|---|---|---|
| Alabama | 1.2 (4) | –53.4 | 12.1 (23) | –4.3 |
| Alaska | 4.9 (46) | 144.3 | 12.1 (24) | 6.9 |
| Arizona | 2.1 (24) | –50.1 | 10.9 (14) | –8.1 |
| Arkansas | 1.3 (5) | –48.2 | 16.7 (42) | 17.5 |
| California | 6.1 (50) | –27.9 | 21.7 (48) | 36.3 |
| Colorado | 1.3 (8) | –52.8 | 8.7 (3) | 10.7 |
| Connecticut | 3.5 (42) | –31.7 | 11.6 (21) | 0.1 |
| Delaware | 1.4 (13) | –57.9 | 13.6 (30) | 24.2 |
| Florida | 1.7 (17) | –60.4 | 12.8 (28) | 4.4 |
| Georgia | 2.4 (29) | –54.5 | 16.0 (39) | 0.3 |
| Hawaii | 5.0 (48) | 170.2 | 15.5 (37) | 52.4 |
| Idaho | 0.3 (1) | –84.0 | 10.0 (9) | 1.4 |
| Illinois | 3.9 (44) | –32.2 | 11.3 (17) | –14.1 |
| Indiana | 1.8 (18) | –39.6 | 10.3 (13) | 6.4 |
| Iowa | 2.3 (27) | –32.5 | 11.0 (16) | 2.8 |
| Kansas | 1.3 (7) | –56.1 | 9.2 (4) | –7.9 |
| Kentucky | 3.0 (37) | –36.7 | 16.4 (40) | –1.4 |
| Louisiana | 3.1 (38) | –46.9 | 16.5 (41) | –9.0 |
| Maine | 3.2 (39) | –33.4 | 13.7 (31) | 10.1 |
| Maryland | 2.3 (25) | –48.5 | 10.9 (15) | 32.7 |
| Massachusetts | 2.7 (32) | –37.2 | 14.8 (33) | 23.1 |
| Michigan | 3.4 (41) | –43.2 | 13.9 (32) | 14.7 |
| Minnesota | 3.0 (34) | –23.5 | 11.4 (18) | 10.9 |
| Mississippi | 1.9 (20) | –63.3 | 17.7 (44) | –8.6 |
| Missouri | 2.7 (31) | –42.2 | 13.5 (29) | 3.4 |
| Montana | 2.0 (21) | –47.5 | 11.5 (19) | 0.8 |
| Nebraska | 2.1 (23) | –13.3 | 12.7 (27) | 23.6 |
| Nevada | 1.5 (14) | –45.2 | 7.3 (1) | 6.8 |
| New Hampshire | 1.4 (9) | –42.2 | 7.9 (2) | –6.3 |
| New Jersey | 2.3 (28) | –39.9 | 10.0 (10) | 1.2 |
| New Mexico | 4.3 (45) | –29.0 | 19.0 (46) | 11.7 |
| New York | 5.0 (47) | –26.8 | 16.9 (43) | 1.2 |
| North Carolina | 2.3 (26) | –46.1 | 15.5 (34) | 2.6 |
| North Dakota | 1.4 (10) | –38.3 | 9.8 (7) | 2.0 |
| Ohio | 3.0 (36) | –43.0 | 11.5 (20) | –16.6 |
| Oklahoma | 2.1 (22) | –43.4 | 10.3 (11) | –14.8 |
| Oregon | 1.4 (12) | –55.9 | 15.6 (38) | 8.3 |
| Pennsylvania | 3.0 (35) | –38.3 | 12.7 (26) | 24.3 |
| Rhode Island | 5.4 (49) | –11.4 | 15.5 (36) | 13.5 |
| South Carolina | 1.6 (16) | –54.4 | 15.5 (35) | 15.2 |
| South Dakota | 1.3 (6) | –42.5 | 12.3 (25) | 21.6 |
| Tennessee | 2.8 (33) | –46.8 | 33.9 (50) | 21.2 |
| Texas | 1.9 (19) | –51.7 | 11.8 (22) | –13.7 |
| Utah | 1.4 (11) | –38.3 | 10.3 (12) | 26.5 |
| Vermont | 3.3 (40) | –27.7 | 21.0 (47) | 22.7 |
| Virginia | 1.5 (15) | –45.4 | 9.6 (6) | –6.8 |
| Washington | 3.6 (43) | –31.5 | 24.8 (49) | 111.3 |
| West Virginia | 2.4 (30) | –56.6 | 18.9 (45) | –11.3 |
| Wisconsin | 0.8 (3) | –79.9 | 9.9 (8) | 10.4 |
| Wyoming | 0.5 (2) | –81.7 | 9.6 (5) | –10.5 |

S O U R C E S: Department of Health and Human Services, Health Care Financing Administration 2003; Department of Health and Human Services, Administration for Children and Families 2003; U.S. Bureau of the Census 2002.

Idaho: California has 6.1 percent of its residents enrolled in that program while Idaho has 0.3 percent. (Differences in the absolute size of the rolls are much larger, with Idaho having about 4,000 recipients and California nearly 2 million.) TANF rolls were shrinking almost everywhere in the late 1990s (though they have grown very slightly again in the early 2000s), with the average decline 36 percent between 1995 and 1998; only in Alaska and Hawaii did the rolls continue to grow.

The Medicaid picture is more complex. The states have much larger Medicaid caseloads than TANF caseloads, of course, but the interstate variation is also larger. More than one-third of Tennessee's residents are enrolled in the TennCare program, for instance, and only 7 percent of Nevada residents receive medical care from Medicaid. More puzzling are the trends. Between 1995 and 1998 Medicaid enrollment in the states, as a percentage of the population, grew by just one percentage point. This modest increase masks the dramatic changes experienced in the states. At the extremes, Washington's caseload more than doubled relative to its population, whereas caseloads in Oklahoma and Ohio fell by about 15 percent. Medicaid expansions tended to swell the caseloads, while TANF reductions tended to depress them (as many families that left the TANF also left Medicaid, even though they were still eligible for benefits).

The relationship between program generosity and caseload might seem obvious: states with higher benefits would have relatively larger caseloads. Yet this has not been true for every program and for all times. For TANF, the correlation between caseloads and average benefits is 0.55; if a state paid $1,000 more in TANF benefits than another state, we would expect that the state would have a 0.4 percent larger share of its population in the program. Again, there are exceptions, with some states offering relatively high benefits and having relatively low caseloads, and vice versa. Wisconsin's TANF benefits are the second highest in the country, but it has only 0.8 percent of its population on the rolls; Louisiana paid the fourth smallest benefits, but over 3 percent of its residents received payments. For Medicaid, there is no relationship between per recipient expenditures and caseload size. Paradoxically, the highest proportion of welfare recipients are found in the more affluent states with higher benefits (such as California and New York) as well as in the poorer states with lower benefits (such as West Virginia and Mississippi).

## The Transformations

During the 1960s and 1970s the federal government was the leading innovator in social welfare policy. It is no more. The states, once again, are where the main policy experiments are being conducted. The federal government is responsible for this by omission and commission: It failed to enact comprehensive health care reform in 1994, and it delegated substantial control over welfare to the states in 1996. The states, for their part, have been eager to gain control over these policy areas (as long as this control does not cost them too much) and willing—at least some have been willing—to innovate to solve their problems.

## HEALTH CARE REFORM

The states continue to be the leaders in health care reform—and they continue to have good reasons to be. State health expenditures, especially those for Medicaid, along with education remain the largest items in many states' budgets. At the extreme, Tennessee expected to spend about 30 percent of its 2002 budget on Medicaid (NASBO 2002). Medical costs also continue to rise. Because virtually all state constitutions require balanced budgets, the states, unlike the federal government, are unable to finance health programs by running deficits. The number of Medicaid recipients has also been growing, as a result of factors such as federal mandates and also other measures beyond state control (such as the growing number of people without private health insurance). Meanwhile, public demand for health services continues to increase. The pressures of rising costs, rising demand, and rising numbers of the uninsured create powerful incentives for states to change the way they deliver health care. Fully forty-seven states took action in 2002, or have proposed actions for 2003, to control Medicaid expenditures (NASBO 2002).

State health care reform proposals are usually built around three main goals. The first is to control costs, both for the state's citizens and for the state itself. The second is to provide access, so that the health care needs of the citizens—at least those citizens that state political systems determine are worthy of support—are met. The third goal, high-quality care, is also important but is more controversial and difficult to define.

To accomplish these goals, state policy makers have focused their efforts on four major types of reforms. They have sought to enroll Medicaid recipients in managed care programs, expand insurance coverage for children and other vulnerable populations, control short- and long-term health care costs, and make insurance more affordable and available to the small-business community (Sparer 1998). This section examines managed care and insurance for children (for these and other topics, see Urban Institute 2002a).

### Medicaid Managed Care

Until the mid-1990s Medicaid, like most private health insurance, was a fee-for-service program. Medical providers who treated individuals covered by Medicaid were reimbursed for the services they provided. State governments established the reimbursement rates for the various services, the federal government required the states to set these rates high enough that the services would actually be available to Medicaid recipients, and medical providers were required to accept the reimbursements as payment in full for their services. Although this fee-for-service system neither pleased medical providers, who generally believed that the rates were too low, nor guaranteed access to care for Medicaid recipients, who often found that the services they needed were not easy to obtain, it did allow total costs to grow rapidly as providers sought higher payments and recipients sought more care.

Dissatisfaction with fee-for-service insurance led private companies to experiment with managed care programs. Although a wide array of such programs exist, one important element in many programs is that they are *capitated*—that is, the program receives a fixed amount of money per enrolled person to provide them a set of services. If the program spends less than this amount per patient it will run a surplus; if it spends more, it will incur a loss. This creates incentives for the program to reduce medical costs by delivering care efficiently, by minimizing unnecessary care, and, many fear, by withholding appropriate care. Managed care programs dominate the private health insurance market, with traditional fee-for-service plans covering less than a quarter of privately insured individuals.

Until 1997 federal Medicaid law did not allow the states to experiment with managed care programs unless they first obtained permission (through what were called Section 1115 or 1915 waivers) from the federal government. The Balanced Budget Act of 1997 eliminated the waiver requirement, however, so states no longer need federal permission to move their Medicaid populations into managed care programs (Sparer 1998). Most states moved swiftly to enroll their Medicaid recipients in managed care programs. As seen in Table 11-4, in 2001 fifteen states had at least three quarters of their recipients in such programs, and Washington and Tennessee had their entire caseload enrolled; only the two most rural states (Alaska and Wyoming) had no Medicaid recipients in managed care programs. Nationally, only one in ten Medicaid recipients was in a managed care plan in 1991; by 2001 nearly 60 percent were. Still, by the late 1990s the movement towards managed care had stalled, as the caseload outside of managed care was harder to move in, and existing managed care providers faced financial difficulties.

One prominent example of the state Medicaid managed care innovations is Tennessee's TennCare Program, implemented in 1994 (Conover and Davies 2000). TennCare was designed to cover Medicaid beneficiaries and also to expand coverage to those with preexisting health problems that left them uninsurable and those who did not have access to other employer- or government-sponsored insurance. TennCare's medical benefits are more generous than the federal government requires, but participants with incomes above the poverty line are required to pay premiums, deductibles, and co-payments based on their income. To encourage preventive care, however, all such services are free. TennCare was subsequently lauded as spending less per recipient than any other Medicaid program in the country (TennCare 2002a). At the same time, 85 percent of TennCare recipients reported that they were satisfied with the program (TennCare 2002b). On the other hand, TennCare "now clearly faces a crisis in which none of the alternatives—reducing coverage, cutting benefits, or increasing taxes—are attractive. . . . TennCare created financial incentives for private insurers to skim the healthiest patients and divert those with the highest costs into the public program" (Conover and Davies, 2000).

Medicaid managed care has sometimes improved health care delivery while reducing costs (Hurley and Zuckerman 2002). Caution remains in order, however. Cost savings are less than originally anticipated, as most Medicaid–managed care

**Table 11-4** Medicaid Managed Care, 2001

| State | Medicaid enrollment (in thousands) | Managed care enrollment (in thousands) | Percentage in managed care |
|---|---|---|---|
| Alabama | 652 | 350 | 54 |
| Alaska | 116 | 0 | 0 |
| Arizona | 549 | 528 | 96 |
| Arkansas | 444 | 258 | 58 |
| California | 5,487 | 2,871 | 52 |
| Colorado | 269 | 247 | 92 |
| Connecticut | 331 | 240 | 73 |
| Delaware | 102 | 83 | 81 |
| Florida | 1,923 | 1,185 | 62 |
| Georgia | 1,041 | 878 | 84 |
| Hawaii | 163 | 128 | 79 |
| Idaho | 134 | 38 | 28 |
| Illinois | 1,456 | 136 | 9 |
| Indiana | 617 | 433 | 70 |
| Iowa | 233 | 207 | 89 |
| Kansas | 205 | 118 | 58 |
| Kentucky | 608 | 490 | 81 |
| Louisiana | 826 | 57 | 7 |
| Maine | 222 | 96 | 43 |
| Maryland | 617 | 421 | 68 |
| Massachusetts | 955 | 616 | 65 |
| Michigan | 1,138 | 1,023 | 90 |
| Minnesota | 502 | 323 | 64 |
| Mississippi | 586 | 298 | 51 |
| Missouri | 840 | 379 | 45 |
| Montana | 73 | 47 | 64 |
| Nebraska | 202 | 151 | 75 |
| Nevada | 124 | 48 | 39 |
| New Hampshire | 79 | 6 | 8 |
| New Jersey | 759 | 459 | 60 |
| New Mexico | 332 | 212 | 64 |
| New York | 2,803 | 729 | 26 |
| North Carolina | 959 | 674 | 70 |
| North Dakota | 44 | 26 | 59 |
| Ohio | 1,293 | 278 | 22 |
| Oklahoma | 442 | 299 | 68 |
| Oregon | 413 | 361 | 87 |
| Pennsylvania | 1,369 | 1,037 | 76 |
| Rhode Island | 163 | 112 | 69 |
| South Carolina | 644 | 42 | 7 |
| South Dakota | 82 | 80 | 98 |
| Tennessee | 1,427 | 1,427 | 100 |
| Texas | 1,822 | 754 | 41 |
| Utah | 139 | 129 | 93 |
| Vermont | 129 | 78 | 60 |
| Virginia | 476 | 292 | 61 |
| Washington | 766 | 766 | 100 |
| West Virginia | 264 | 122 | 46 |
| Wisconsin | 515 | 267 | 52 |
| Wyoming | 40 | 0 | 0 |
| Total | 36,563 | 20,774 | 57 |

SOURCE: CMS 2001.

beneficiaries are mothers and children, and most Medicaid expenditures go to the elderly and disabled, a group for which it is difficult to contain costs (Holahan et al. 1998). Others have suggested that there is little care management in Medicaid managed care programs, as few beneficiaries are skilled at using these programs and few organizations adept at delivering them (Sparer 1998). The states are now under tremendous fiscal pressure to restrain Medicaid spending, but it is not easy to see how this can be done without limiting access or reducing service provision.

### State Child Health Insurance Program

The federal government created the State Child Health Insurance Program (SCHIP) in 1997 to help states create and expand programs providing medical care to low-income children (Dubay, Hill, and Kenney 2002). SCHIP is not a program dreamed up by the federal government and imposed on the states, however, as the states had already taken the lead in expanding medical care for poor children (in part through the Section 1115 waivers), and SCHIP was established in large part because of the political efforts of state governments. Prior to SCHIP's birth, thirty-four states were already offering care to more pregnant women and infants than the federal government required; twenty-four states were providing care to more children ages six and over; and eleven states had expanded care for younger children.

The federal government provides block grants to the states for SCHIP based on their proportion of the nation's poor (in families with incomes less than 200 percent of the poverty line) and uninsured children. The states, in turn, must provide matching funds (at a lower rate than for Medicaid). The states can use these funds to expand Medicaid, create a separate program, or both. Federal spending is capped at $40 billion for the program's first ten years, with the states expected to spend about half that amount.

The states are using their discretion to design an assortment of SCHIP programs (Dubay, Hill, and Kenney 2002). Sixteen states have incorporated SCHIP into their existing Medicaid programs, while the other 34 states have created separate programs. Twenty states have expanded eligibility for SCHIP above 200 percent of the poverty line; 11 states set eligibility below that line. To enroll children in the program, states have invested "unprecedented" resources in outreach. As a result, by 2000 rates of uninsurance among children had dropped from 23 percent to 18 percent, or by about one million individuals (Dubay, Hill, and Kenney 2002).

State innovations in health care are no panacea. Developing and implementing health care experiments require administrative expertise and integrated data systems—traits that have often been in short supply. The programs might be more expensive than expected, or they might not cover all those who need coverage. And, after all, experiments do fail. State experimentation is no guarantee of state success (Sparer and Brown 1996). States will continue to face substantial barriers in their efforts to improve access, enhance quality, and contain costs (Sparer 1998; Thompson and Dilulio 1998). Moreover, states are not always willing to innovate. One way to assess state innovation is through their willingness to expand health insurance coverage beyond federal requirements. By this standard, it appears that only about half the states have been highly or moderately innovative (Urban Institute 2002c). Still, the promise of medical coverage for our most vulnerable citizens is more nearly realized now than it was even a few years ago.

## WELFARE REFORM

TANF gives states much more authority and responsibility than did AFDC. Some states, such as Wisconsin, have totally redesigned their welfare programs (Mead, forthcoming). Other states have made much more modest changes. It is difficult to describe concisely how the states are using their new powers to design and implement TANF, in part because the states are doing so many different things (see Gallagher et al. 1998 for summaries; Urban Institute 2002b for reports).

*Work Requirements*

TANF's goal is work. The federal government requires all adult recipients to participate in work activities within two years of entering the rolls, although it exempts various parents from these requirements. The states have wide leeway to determine who must work, how soon work must begin, what counts as work, and what happens if a recipient does not comply with the rules.

*Exemptions.* States can decide how long they will allow a parent to stay at home with a young child before having to enter the workforce. About half the states exempt parents with children under age one from their work requirements. Two states set the exemption age at six months, twelve states set it at three months, and five states do not provide an exemption based on the age of the youngest child. Only five states allowed a single parent to remain with the child for more than a year before being required to work, and federal law gives the states incentives to set the exemption at one year or less. Eighteen states, moreover, set a cumulative time limit for how long a parent can be exempted from work (Gallagher et al. 1998, V-2).

*Work Starts.* Federal law requires that TANF recipients must begin work activities within twenty-four months, or sooner, at state discretion, unless they are exempted from these requirements. Only five states have adopted the twenty-four-month rule; most other states require recipients to begin work activities upon receipt of benefits, but because these activities differ so much—they can include such tasks as job search, job "readiness," or job skill training—it is hard to compare these rules (Urban Institute 2002d).

*Sanctions.* Federal law requires the states to penalize individuals who refuse to work, but the states can determine how big these penalties will be. Most states have sliding penalties that become more intense (lasting longer or reducing benefits further) as the recipient resists compliance. Fourteen states cut off benefits entirely at the first offense, and the other states have withheld benefits as their most extreme penalty. Twenty-one states remove the sanction immediately when the individual starts complying, and the rest of the states withhold benefits until sometime after the individual starts playing by the rules. In seven states a person judged to be continually out of compliance with the rules can never again obtain welfare benefits from the state (Urban Institute 2002d; Gallagher et al. 1998).

*Social Values*

Under AFDC, eligibility for two-parent families was sharply restricted, although each additional child brought an enrolled parent (usually a single mother) additional cash benefits. This feature made possible the claim that welfare was anti-marriage and pro-illegitimacy. Both provisions were eliminated by TANF. States now have the flexibility to reduce or eliminate additional benefits for children conceived while their mothers are on the TANF rolls. Twenty-one states have adopted some form of such "family caps," seventeen states offer no additional benefits, and five offer reduced benefits. In two states, Wisconsin and Idaho, benefits are not related to the size of the family (Urban Institute 2002d). Moreover, many states now award competitive grants or provide other kinds of program resources to community groups, counties, or local school districts that operate programs aimed at reducing out-of-wedlock pregnancy—especially teen pregnancy.

States can also determine which, if any, two-parent families are eligible for support. Thirty-five states now treat such families the same as one-parent families. Eight states have retained the restrictive criteria that existed for AFDC. The remaining states established eligibility rules less restrictive than under AFDC but more restrictive than the states treating two-parent families the same as single-parent families (Gallagher et al. 1998).

Congress must now reauthorize the TANF program (it needed to do so in 2002, but was unable to complete its deliberations). Sawhill et al. 2002 review the major issues: funding (some argue that the federal government should provide less money as the caseloads have declined so much; others respond that assisting the remaining caseload will be quite expensive), work requirements (President Bush wants to increase them; most governors seek flexibility), and benefit limits (as more recipients bump up against their lifetime benefit limits, controversy will increase as to whether those limits should be relaxed). In perhaps his most controversial welfare reform proposal, President Bush has called for Congress to award $300 million in TANF funding to states that institute programs promoting marriage through premarital counseling and to fund research on and bonuses for state initiatives that promote healthy marriages. Two states—Arizona and Oklahoma—are already using TANF funds specifically for marriage-strengthening activities (U.S. House 2001). But while public opinion supports marriage as an institution, it is quite skeptical about whether the government can or should promote marriage.

## PREVENTION

Our health and welfare programs provide care to the sick and assistance to the poor, especially poor women with children. They do relatively little to prevent individuals from becoming sick or from needing public assistance. American health and welfare programs emphasize treatment rather than prevention.

From a policy perspective this makes little sense, but there are good political reasons to emphasize treatment over prevention. Policy makers usually face the situation in which people need immediate assistance, and there is not enough money both to help them with their needs and to prevent others from requiring the same assistance later. As the demands for treatment are almost always louder than the requests for prevention, the former is politically favored over the latter. Yet the maxim is true: A dime of prevention is worth a dollar of cure. It is cheaper and easier to stay well than to become healed, to stay out of poverty than to get out. Most observers, conservative and liberal alike, agree that well-designed health and welfare prevention programs can be more effective and cost less than treatment programs.

State health and welfare policies have, to their credit, tilted somewhat more to prevention in recent years. Medicaid managed care has a better chance to emphasize wellness programs (that is, prenatal care, well baby care, and routine screenings, among others) than traditional Medicaid. Offering better medical care to children can lead to healthier, and we hope economically more independent, adults. States are experimenting with ways to help keep TANF recipients in school or in jobs, and to help deter unwanted pregnancies, as ways of helping the beneficiaries become economically self-sufficient. As a matter of policy, however, federal and state governments typically spend far more on treatment than prevention, at least on matters of public health. In the late 1980s the federal Centers for Disease Control and Prevention estimated that U.S. investment in prevention was less than 5 percent of U.S. spending on health care (CDC 1992). There is no reason to believe this imbalance has been corrected.

States that need most to emphasize prevention often have the worst current problems and are least able to look toward the future. Richer states, though, are better able to afford prevention. If a state is unified and committed enough politically—or if a political leader is able to persuade it that it should be—it might decide to spend on prevention despite its pressing treatment needs. Unity and commitment are necessary, as there are never enough resources, so spending on prevention dictates that some constituents in need of treatment will be ignored. Ignoring constituents is possible to the extent that policy makers concur that it must be done—and stick to this concurrence.

The combination of unity and commitment is scarce in partisan politics. But even when both political parties are committed to prevention they may have strong differences about what real prevention is. Liberals (and Democrats) in general view prevention as a set of positive incentives offered by the government. To keep individuals healthy, programs must provide them education or services so that they will be willing and able to become physically strong and economically self-sufficient. Conservatives (and Republicans) usually reject this view, placing responsibility for physical and economic health more squarely on individual citizens. Government, from the conservative perspective, mainly creates incentives for persons to become dependent and diseased by providing welfare and health benefits in the first place. Accordingly, government practices prevention best by ensuring that individuals bear the consequences of their own actions. (For an explanation of the differing perspectives of liberals and conservatives, see Lakoff 2002.)

Nonetheless, it is worth considering three questions. Why do people become ill, and so in need of medical care? Why do families become needy, and so in need of welfare? What can states do to prevent illness and neediness? Although the answers to the first two questions no doubt involve social and even metaphysical elements, I will focus on behavioral answers: People need medical treatment and welfare in part because of the way they behave. (The way people behave is, of course, affected by social forces and public policies.) State efforts at prevention therefore might need to address these behaviors.

Behavioral factors are largely responsible for about half of all premature deaths each year. The big three factors—tobacco use, poor diet and lack of exercise, and abuse of alcohol—cause in part 40 percent of all deaths and 75 percent of premature deaths. The other major factors—preventable microbial or toxic agents, firearms, sexual behavior, motor vehicles, and illicit drugs—account for the other 25 percent of premature deaths (McGinnis and Foege 1993).

The major behavioral factors that lead to welfare dependency are also clear. Families are most likely to spend long periods on welfare when children are born out of wedlock to young women who are poorly educated. At the end of the 1990s in the United States, the vast majority of the children living in female-headed families in which the mother was younger than twenty-one were poor; a large majority of these families received some form of public assistance.

The behavioral risks that damage public health or create the need for public assistance each have distinctive politics. None of these politics is simple or rational. All involve personal activities—smoking cigarettes, eating too much and exercising too little, drinking alcohol, shooting firearms, and having unsafe sex—that raise strong emotions in the political arena (Meier 1994). Because they involve highly personal behaviors of millions of individuals, they are difficult for governments to control or change. Still, state governments have made at least temporary public health progress on some of these issues. Smoking rates are falling, as is the frequency of drunk driving. Other behaviors have been less susceptible to change. The public's willingness to adopt healthier diets and sexual behaviors has not been firmly established. And America has not proved capable of greatly reducing its gun violence.

*Tobacco*

Tobacco use, especially cigarette smoking, is by far the largest threat to public health. Each year tobacco use is responsible for approximately 440,000 deaths from a wide variety of causes, such as cancer, cardiovascular disease, lung disease, and burns (CDC 2002b).

Our governments treated the tobacco industry gently for decades but now are taking an increasingly tough stance towards it, for several reasons. First, the scientific evidence is incontrovertible that smoking creates large health risks without producing any positive health benefits. Second, these health risks exist not just for the smokers themselves, but also for those who live or work with them, although the risks of "second hand smoke" have often been overstated (see Sullum 1994). Third, economic and social elites—who are also typically those with the most political resources—have become more hostile toward tobacco use because they themselves smoke less. In the mid-1990s about four out of ten high school drop-outs aged twenty-five and older smoked, for example, whereas only one in ten with college degrees did (National Center for Health Statistics 1998). Fourth, blame for tobacco use has been clearly placed on the tobacco industry itself. Often depicted as the merchant of death, the industry denied there was any link between smoking, addiction, and health problems, even as evidence of a connection mounted. The industry also targeted a particularly vulnerable and sympathetic group—children— in its advertising campaigns. Fifth, programs discouraging tobacco use need not cost much (through regulation) and indeed can raise substantial sums (through taxes). Sixth, various governments have decided that smoking-related health problems have imposed large costs on the public through the Medicaid and Medicare programs—and during the 1990s the states increasingly sued the tobacco industry for compensation.

The tobacco industry and users are not without their own political resources, of course, as Congress was reminded in 1998 when it considered legislation to tax and regulate cigarettes further (Derthick 2001). The industry's main resource is money. It spends far more to promote smoking than the government does to discourage it; for example, the tobacco industry spends millions every year on advertising, not including the advertising inherent in its sponsorship of sporting events (the Winston 500 automotive races, for example) and other activities. Tobacco interests also contribute extensively to political campaigns to ensure that their voice is heard. The tobacco users' main political strength is in their numbers. Because more than a quarter of the American public continues to smoke, politicians who threaten this activity (especially through taxation) face repercussions at the next election. (Indeed, Congress decided not to raise tobacco taxes in 1998 when the tobacco industry portrayed the measure as a voracious government's effort to raise billions of dollars in taxes from the public: Derthick 2001.) The tobacco industry's millions of smokers and millions of dollars notwithstanding, political strength is moving toward those who want to raise the cost and difficulty of smoking cigarettes.

State governments have acted with increasing vigor and creativity to discourage smoking. All fifty states obtained out-of-court settlements with the tobacco industry in which the industry will pay an expected $246 billion to the states over the next twenty-five years. Four states (Mississippi, Florida, Minnesota, and Texas) successfully pressed their own claims individually before the industry reached a global settlement with the other states in November 1998 (Action on Smoking and Health 1998). However, "most states have not kept their promise [to spend a significant portion of this money on anti-smoking policies]—only a handful of states have funded tobacco prevention programs at the minimum level recommended by the U.S. Centers for Disease Control and Prevention, and the majority of states have failed to fund prevention at even half the CDC minimum" (Campaign 2002a). With the states facing fiscal difficulties, most states have put substantial portions of their settlement to other uses.

States are also using various other means to reduce tobacco-related risks, although the intensity of the effort varies from state to state. Virtually every state requires smoke-free indoor air in some places to some extent. Only Alabama, Kentucky, North Carolina, and Tennessee—major tobacco producers—have no such laws. Forty-one states have laws restricting smoking in government work sites; thirty states regulate smoking in restaurants; twenty-one restrict smoking in private work sites; and some states regulate smoking in other locations, such as day care centers (for details, see CDC 1999). All states have cigarette excise taxes; thirteen states raised their tax rates between 1995 and 1998, and sixteen more states raised taxes in 2002 alone. Still, the taxes range from a low of 2.5 cents per pack in Virginia to $1.50 in New York, although the CDC estimates that the direct cost on society of each pack sold (from sickness and lost productivity) is $7.81.

The states seek to make it more difficult for youth to smoke. All states prohibit the sale and distribution of tobacco products to minors, and forty-two states have laws that bar minors from buying, possessing, or using tobacco products. No state allows vending machine sale of cigarettes to minors, and forty-one states provided additional restrictions to make youth access to vending machines more difficult. Only thirteen states have laws restricting tobacco advertising—up from nine in 1995—and most of these restrictions are quite modest (CDC 1999).

Laws do not necessarily mean results, of course, because state enforcement of tobacco laws is notoriously lax, particularly regarding sales to minors (see CDC 1999, for an analysis of the effect of state regulations on state smoking rates). Nevertheless, these laws do send a message concerning state priorities.

California has had perhaps the most ambitious smoking-control program. Beginning in 1988, when the state's voters approved Proposition 99, California raised cigarette taxes by twenty-five cents per pack and launched a high-profile television campaign (as well as education efforts by schools and doctors) financed by $80 million of the $780 million raised each year by the tax (Zamichow 1992). These policies, and changing social norms, caused California's smoking rate to fall farther and faster than the national average; the smoking rate in California dropped by 30 percent from the mid-1980s. And California continued to toughen restrictions. Beginning in 1998 California banned smoking in all public areas, including bars and restaurants.

American youth are not terribly impressed by all this. Smoking has become increasingly fashionable in middle and high schools, with smoking rates among ninth through twelfth graders rising substantially in the 1990s. In 2001 almost 30 percent of high school students had smoked cigarettes (Campaign 2002b).

*Diet and Activity*

Diet and activity contribute to more than 300,000 premature deaths each year, according to McGinnis and Foege (1993). The problem is not too little food and too much work, but just the opposite: Americans in general eat too much and exercise too little. Over one-half of American adults are overweight, and 20 percent are obese (Schoenborn, Adams, and Barnes 2002). Yet state and federal policy makers have done much less to reduce the threats to public health from obesity than from tobacco or alcohol.

The political dynamics of obesity make it exceptionally difficult for policy makers to take effective action to reduce its risks. As is true of smoking, the evidence for the harmful effects of excessive fatty foods and lack of exercise is strong, and political elites are generally sympathetic to the need for healthier diets and more exercise. College graduates are more than twice as likely to exercise regularly as those who did not graduate from high school (34 and 16 percent, respectively); those with incomes above $50,000 are much more likely to exercise than those with incomes below $10,000. Similarly, those with more education and higher income are less likely to be overweight than those with less education or income (U.S. Bureau of the Census 2002, 127).

Yet the other political liabilities associated with tobacco vanish as if in smoke. Obesity's risks do not directly influence the health of others, as smoking does, so no natural opposition to obesity exists from those who are more physically fit. The risks associated with obesity create few obvious villains. Unlike tobacco, virtually all foods can be part of a healthy diet, and no one food can be singled out as the culprit (there is no "smoking gun" in the food business). Nor is there an obvious (and cheap) way to regulate or tax foods or activity to induce better diets and more exercise. Even more than tobacco use, diet and exercise are regarded as purely personal activities that the government has no authority to regulate or tax. (In early 2003 a federal judge dismissed a lawsuit filed against the McDonald's fast-food chain blaming it for childhood obesity: Grimaldi 2003.) Of course, food is regulated in many ways (for example, for contaminants and truth in labeling), and sales taxes are often applied. But nowhere in the United States is food regulated or taxed on the basis of content. Moreover, purveyors of junk food spend opulently on advertisements, whereas advocates of healthier diets spend next to nothing. There is a large athletic products industry, of course, but it has a greater interest in selling fashion than in improving body-fat indicators.

As a result, there is no political momentum for legislatures to restrict diets or mandate exercise, and little political interest in more positive incentives. Any policy activity that occurs comes from public health officials (or, for example, nutritionists), who understand the importance of improved physical fitness and recognize the costs of providing health care to people suffering from obesity (Sturm 2002). Lacking regulatory authority, these officials have chosen to pursue an educational strategy to reduce the risks of obesity to public health. For example, CDC officials, working together with St. Louis University prevention researchers and Missouri Department of Health personnel, created a "Heart Health Project" in six poor, rural counties; the project substantially increased the use of walking trails among women with low educational levels (NCCDP 2001). The best place for state and local governments to intervene might be the schools, through the school lunch and physical education programs.

Still, the news is not promising. More Americans are overweight and fewer exercise vigorously than ever. During the 1990s, obesity rates increased by 60 percent among adults, doubled among children, and tripled among adolescents. More than 60 percent of adults do not get enough exercise to provide health benefits, and more than one-third of ninth through twelfth graders do not regularly engage in vigorous activity (NCCDP 2001).

*Alcohol*

Alcohol misuse accounts for 100,000 premature deaths annually. These deaths can occur through alcohol's effect on the body (for example, cirrhosis of the liver or fetal alcohol syndrome) and, more important, on behavior. When you go out this weekend, reflect on this: Half of all homicides, assaults, car and boat fatalities, drowning and fire fatalities, and the like can be attributed at least in part to alcohol consumption (McGinnis and Foege 1993). About 1,400 college-age students died of accidents involving alcohol in 1998, and an estimated two million (of eight million) college students drove while under the influence of alcohol. Over one-half million college students were unintentionally injured while under the influence, and another 600,000 were hit or assaulted by a student who had been drinking (Hingson et al. 2002).

There are old and new politics of alcohol. The (mainly religious) call for prohibition defines the old politics. The public health consequences or the costs and benefits of alcohol use did not enter into the debate; the debate was about whether drinking was a sin. These politics still prevail in many parts of the country. Although no states maintain prohibition, numerous dry counties dot the map (especially through the parts of the country known as the Bible Belt). It is no small irony that the Jack Daniels (a Tennessee bourbon) distillery is located in a dry county.

The new politics of alcohol are a hybrid of those for tobacco as well as diet and activity. One of the main differences is that there is no real elite opposition to alcohol, no doubt because those with more income and education drink as much as (if not more than) those with lower socioeconomic status. Alcohol use, moreover, is not seen (either medically or socially) as inherently harmful. Large portions of the public drink moderately, and medical research suggests that this might, in some circumstances, be healthful. The alcohol companies themselves urge their buyers to drink in moderation.

Although almost all tobacco use is politically vulnerable and almost no issues involving diet and activity are, the new politics of alcohol divides sharply between personal use and public misuse. In some central cities where personal alcohol consumption is itself seen as a major public health problem, there appears to be growing support for additional restrictions on the availability of alcohol (see, for example, Schneider 1997). In most places, however, additional policies to restrict purely personal use by adults have little political support. In contrast, public misuse—especially drunk driving—is being vigorously attacked around the country. Groups such as Mothers against Drunk Driving (MADD) and its offshoots (for example, Students against Drunk Driving, SADD) have mobilized much political and social support for their goal.

The states have led the way in these attacks, although not always willingly. The major impetus to state action was a 1984 federal law that required states to enact a minimum drinking age of twenty-one by 1986 or lose a portion of their federal highway funds (O'Malley and Wagenaar 1991). In 1982, for example, only fourteen states prohibited the purchase of alcohol by those under the age of twenty-one; all fifty states prohibited it by 1988. In 1998 Congress rejected a proposal requiring all states to adopt a uniform limit for the blood alcohol concentration (BAC) of 0.08 percent at which an automobile driver is considered intoxicated. Theories of federalism had less to do with this decision than lobbying by the beverage and restaurant industries. In 2001, though, Congress tied highway funding increases to the adoption of 0.08 BAC laws, and states are beginning to respond to this incentive. The combination of tougher drunk driving laws, increased penalties for violators, and expanded enforcement, together with changing social mores, has contributed to the substantial decrease in the rate of deaths, injuries, and accidents attributed to alcohol-influenced driving. Between 1990 and 1999, the proportion of traffic fatalities in which at least one person had a blood alcohol concentration of 0.10 or higher fell from 40 percent to 30 percent (U.S. Bureau of the Census 2002, 685).

### Firearms

Violent crime has again been in the news, but for two very different reasons. The frequency of violent crime—homicides, rapes, robberies, assault—has been dropping around the country since 1994. In 2001 the violent crime rate was at its lowest point since data have been collected (U.S. Department of Justice 2002). Still, there have been several highly publicized episodes of mass killings—most notably, the sniper attack that killed ten persons in the Washington, D.C., metro area and the slaughter at Columbine High School, in which two students killed twelve other students and a teacher before taking their own lives.

But whether we should be cheered by the trends or alarmed by the incidents, this much is clear: With firearms associated with almost 30,000 fatalities annually through homicides, suicides, and accidents, the toll taken on society by guns is unique among wealthy nations. Unique, also, is the widespread belief that gun ownership is a constitutionally protected citizen's right. (The Second Amendment states that "A well regulated Militia, being necessary to the security of a free state, the right of the people to keep and bear Arms, shall not be infringed." The legal debate is over whether this amendment guarantees an *individual's* right to bear arms.)

The politics of firearms are extraordinarily divisive (Spitzer 1995). No claim concerning the role of firearms in our society's violence goes unquestioned (for a summary of some of the controversies, see Witkin 1994; see also Lott 1997 and Ludwig and Cook 2002). Support for stricter gun control is broad among elites and the public as a whole, but opposition to controls is intense among gun owners and suppliers. Supporters of gun control recite with horror the toll taken by intentional and accidental gunfire each year. Gun advocates, for their part, correctly note that most gun owners pose no threat to public health; the others, the advocates contend, will pose a threat whether controls exist or not. As a result of the divisiveness of the politics of firearms, at least at the national level, the public is at times subjected to embarrassing debates about banning "assault weapons," as if such bans either would protect the public health or pose a threat to constitutional rights.

The extent of firearm violence varies widely from state to state and over time. In general, the southern and western states have much higher levels of violence than states in the Northeast or Midwest. Louisiana, for example, had more than 400 firearm-related violent crimes per 100,000 residents in 1995, whereas North Dakota had fewer than 10 per 100,000; the 50-state average was fewer than 200 per 100,000 residents (U.S. Department of Justice 1996, 319).

The states also have a wide variety of policies to regulate and control the purchase, carrying, or ownership of firearms, and many states have attempted to strengthen these laws in recent years. (For a state-by-state summary of laws and regulations concerning handguns, see U.S. Department of Justice 2000, 94–95.) The impact of these policies is difficult to measure (but see Ludwig and Cook 2002). Opponents of gun control argue that these results demonstrate that such control does not work to reduce violence. Supporters contend that in a society that so resembles an arsenal, the modest measures imposed by the states can hardly have much effect on reducing violence.

The largest current controversy concerns concealed-weapons laws. These laws generally allow any adult without a criminal record or history of mental illness to obtain a permit to carry (concealed) handguns virtually anywhere. In places that do not have these laws, a person must typically show a compelling reason to carry a concealed weapon. One scholar presents evidence that concealed-weapons laws reduce the frequency of violent crime by deterring criminals from attacking potential victims who may, after all, be armed and ready to retaliate (Lott 1997). This analysis has been widely, and convincingly, criticized (see, for example, Ludwig 1998a, 1998b; Webster et al. 1997).

The link between research and policy is always tenuous. But to the extent that the states are voting in this debate, it appears that they favor Lott's position. Approximately thirty-one states have concealed-weapons laws (depending on the source and definition; Council of State Governments 1998), with many of these laws enacted in the past decade. The most popular form of gun control appears now to be the laws that allow individuals to carry and, it is hoped, control their own guns.

*Sexual Behavior*

Alas, one of life's greatest pleasures is one of its greatest problems. Unprotected sexual intercourse can kill, injure, and deprive—and not just by transmitting the virus that causes AIDS. The good news is that AIDS is no longer the death sentence it once was; improved treatment regimes reduced the number of persons dying from AIDS from 33,000 in 1996 to 17,000 in 1999, though it remains one of the largest single causes of death for males aged twenty-five to sixty-four. (The sad news is that the number of Americans living with HIV continues to rise, from 275,000 in 1997 to 322,000 in 1999; CDC 2002a). But unprotected sexual intercourse also contributes to approximately 5,000 excess infant deaths (from unintended pregnancies), 4,000 extra deaths from cervical cancer (linked to certain sexually transmitted diseases), and 1,600 deaths from hepatitis B infection each year. In addition, some 12 million persons become infected with a sexually transmitted disease each year, and more than half of all pregnancies are unintended (McGinnis and Foege 1993). Whether or not one believes that the price of abortion is a human life, all should agree that the demand for abortion is far higher than we want.

The onset of AIDS has created special challenges for certain states' public health systems. Although every state has persons with AIDS (PWAs) as residents, AIDS is not spread uniformly across the country: California, Florida, and New York alone account for more about 40 percent of total AIDS cases up through 2001 (CDC 2002a). A large proportion—55 percent of all adults and nine out of ten children with AIDS—eventually receive Medicaid and thus become, at least medically, wards of the state (CMS 2002a). Typically, PWAs become eligible for Medicaid if they lose their own private insurance, their jobs, or their personal resources; through their eligibility in SSI or TANF; or through a state's "medically needy" category of Medicaid. The result is that much of the health care cost of AIDS is shifted to the public sector; in 2002 federal and state governments are expected to spend nearly $8 billion on AIDS through Medicaid. States with large numbers have thus been under tremendous pressure to contain the costs they have imposed on the public. A principal way states have tried to cope is to seek Medicaid waivers so that PWAs may receive home or community-based long-term care (rather than more expensive hospitalization); sixteen states are now doing this (CMS 2002a).

The politics of sex has been characterized by the struggle between those who view sexual behavior as a moral issue and those who consider it a policy issue only to the extent that sexual behavior threatens public health (Nice 1994; see also Lakoff 2002). The attitudes and policy preferences of those holding these views are fundamentally different. The former group believes that government policy should encourage or enforce only "moral" sex—that is, monogamous relations within a heterosexual marriage. The latter group argues that sexual relations between consenting adults are acceptable to the extent that they do not cause unintended pregnancies or spread disease; as a result, this group favors education concerning "safe sex" as the appropriate policy. State policies toward sexual behavior have to a large extent mirrored these divisions within their populations; more conservative states use less sex education; more liberal states rely less on moral messages.

The politics of sex have been especially unhelpful in regard to welfare policy. Unprotected sexual intercourse, of course, is literally the beginning of the nonmarital births to teenagers that put the family at special risk of needing public assistance. But prevention policies that tell teenagers either to "just say no" or "just be safe" apparently have little impact on teenage pregnancy rates. It is intriguing—a hopeful sign—that policies emphasizing both moral restraint and safer sex are more successful at reducing unwanted pregnancies and sexually transmitted diseases than either approach alone (Manlove et al. 2002). Still, the United States has the highest rates of teen pregnancy in the industrialized western world (National Campaign 2002).

It is also apparent that youth who become pregnant, or who impregnate, often have academic, economic, and emotional difficulties before the conception occurs. Dropping out of school, living in poverty, and having little hope for the future help create the conditions that lead teenagers to become parents (Dryfoos 1990; Lawson and Rhode 1993). Research suggests that it is important to address teenagers' social conditions as a way to prevent teen pregnancies. Rather than focusing on pregnancy prevention by itself, public policy needs to improve the educational, economic, and emotional circumstances of adolescents most at risk (Sawhill 2001; Kirby 2001). The best form of birth control is the realistic hope for a better future if childbearing is delayed. Providing such realistic hope for teenagers is not always an easy task even for parents. The states face even greater challenges in providing this hope.

## CONCLUSION

Each year federal and state governments spend over $400 billion providing health care and welfare to assist needy individuals in the United States. We should not underestimate the help this assistance provides. Without it, millions of Americans would suffer worse health and meaner poverty—and many would not survive.

Most government spending on public assistance is channeled through just four programs: Medicaid, TANF, SSI, and GA. The greatest part of this welfare does not consist of giving cash to the poor; programs that provide cash assistance cost only about one-third as much as those that provide medical services, and the proportion spent on health care is steadily growing. Although Medicaid and TANF are federal programs, the states carry a heavy burden in financing and operating them. During recent decades, Medicaid benefit levels have grown, recipient rolls have expanded, and total expenditures have soared. TANF rolls, in contrast, have fallen dramatically since 1996, with expenditures also falling at a slower rate.

These trends have not affected all states equally. Tremendous variation exists among the states in welfare benefits, caseloads, and expenditures. State policy responses to their health and welfare problems have also varied as a result of the specific political, economic, and demographic conditions existing within each state. Still, all states face similar pressures: Their constitutions forbid them from running deficits, and economic competition with their peers restrains their abilities to raise taxes as well as their interest in redistributing income.

The states are now struggling with ways to design their health and poverty programs so that services are provided to those most in need without encouraging others to become dependent on governmental largesse. State governments are also striving to develop ways to deliver these services while controlling costs. In doing so, the states are engaged in a period of extraordinary policy innovation—especially now that the federal government has given them substantial flexibility to conduct their experiments.

We can hope that these policy experiments will go beyond assisting the sick and the poor to preventing sickness and poverty. The barriers to doing so are high, of course. It is difficult for states to focus on prevention when there are so many demands for treatment. It is difficult to change individuals' behavior so that they will become healthy and independent. Yet such prevention is essential. Healthy citizens are less likely to become dependent on government support. Prosperous citizens are likely to need fewer medical services from the government. The best way for states to control their health and welfare spending is for them to help create healthy and independent citizens.

## REFERENCES

Action on Smoking and Health. 1998. Website at http:\\ash.org.

Bailey, Michael A., and Mark Carl Rom. 2002. "A Wider Race? Interstate Competition Over Health and Welfare Programs." Paper presented at the annual conference of the Midwest Political Science Association, Chicago, April 25–27.

Berry, William D., Richard C. Fording, and Russell L. Hanson. 2003. "Reassessing the 'Race to the Bottom' in State Welfare Policy: Resolving the Conflict Between Individual-Level and Aggregate Research." *Journal of Politics* 65(2): 327–349.

Berry, William D., Evan J. Ringquist, Richard C. Fording, and Russell L. Hanson. 1998. "Measuring Citizen and Government Ideology in the American States." *American Journal of Political Science* 42(1): 327–348.

Blank, Rebecca. 1997. *It Takes a Nation: A New Agenda for Fighting Poverty.* Princeton, N.J.: Princeton University Press.

Campaign for Tobacco Free Kids. 2002a. *State Tobacco Settlement.* Website at http://tobaccofreekids.org/reports/settlements/.

———. 2002b. "State High School Smoking Rates and Rankings." Website at http://www.tobaccofreekids.org/research/factsheets/pdf/0173.pdf.

CDC (Centers for Disease Control and Prevention). 2002a. *HIV/AIDS Update.* Website at http://www.cdc.gov/nchstp/od/news/At-a-Glance.pdf.

———. 2002b. *Tobacco Control: State Highlights 2002.* Website at http://www.cdc.gov/tobacco/statehi/statehi_2002.htm.

———. 1999. "State Laws on Tobacco Control—United States, 1998." *Morbidity and Mortality Weekly Report* 48: No.SS-3.

———. 1992. "Estimated National Spending on Prevention—United States." *Morbidity and Mortality Weekly Report* 41(July 24): 529–531.

CMS (Center for Medicare and Medicaid Services). 2002a. *Medicaid and AIDS and HIV Infection: Fact Sheet.* Website at http://cms.hhs.gov/hiv/hivfs.asp.

———. 2002b. "Medicaid Person Years and Recipients." Accessed at http://cms.hhs.gov/researchers/pubs/datacompendium/2002/02pg34.pdf.

———. 2001. "2001 Medicaid Managed Care Enrollment Report." Accessed at http://www.cms.gov/medicaid/managedcare/mcsten01.pdf.

Conover, Christopher J., and Hester H. Davies. 2000. "The Role of TennCare in Health Policy for Low-Income People in Tennessee." Washington, D.C.: Urban Institute. Website at http://www.urban.org/UploadedPDF/occa33.pdf.

Cook, Fay Lomax, and Edith J. Barrett. 1992. *Support for the American Welfare State: The Views of Congress and the Public.* New York: Columbia University Press.

Council of State Governments. 1998. "State Concealed Weapons Laws: Note." Website at http://ssl.csg.org/index/1998/98ssl85.pdf.

De Jong, Gordon F., and Deborah Roemke Graefe. 2002. "Welfare Reform and Migration: Moving to Benefits; Moving From Restrictions." Paper prepared for Northwestern University–University of Chicago Joint Center for Poverty Research.

Derthick, Martha A. 2001. *Up in Smoke: From Legislation to Litigation in Tobacco Politics.* Washington, D.C.: CQ Press.

Dryfoos, Joy G. 1990. *Adolescents at Risk: Prevalence and Prevention.* New York: Oxford University Press.

Dubay, Lisa, Ian Hill, and Genevieve Kenney. 2002. *Five Things Everyone Should Know About SCHIP.* Washington, D.C.: Urban Institute. Website at http://www.urban.org/UploadedPDF/310570_A55.pdf.

Elazar, Daniel J. 1972. *American Federalism: A View from the States.* 2d ed. New York: Thomas Y. Crowell.

———. 1970. "The States and the Political Setting." In *Policy Analysis in Political Science,* edited by Ira Sharkansky. Chicago: Markham.

Erikson, Robert S., Gerald C. Wright, and John R. McIver. 1993. *Statehouse Democracy: Public Opinion and Policy in the American States.* Cambridge: Cambridge University Press.

Gallagher, L. Jerome, Megan Gallagher, Keven Perese, Susan Schreiber, and Keith Watson. 1998. *One Year after Federal Welfare Reform: A Description of State Temporary Assistance to Needy Families (TANF) Decisions as of October 1997.* Washington, D.C.: Urban Institute.

Gilens, Martin. 1999. *Why Americans Hate Welfare: Race, Media, and the Politics of Antipoverty Policy.* Chicago: Chicago University Press.

Grimaldi, James V. 2003. "Legal Kibitzers See Little Merit in Lawsuit Over Fatty Food at McDonald's." *Washington Post.* January 27, E10.

Hingson, R., T. Heeren, R.C. Zakoes, A. Kopstein, H. Wechsler. 2002. "Magnitude of Alcohol-Related Mortality and Morbidity Among U.S. College Students Ages 18–24." *Journal of Studies on Alcohol* 63(2): 136–144.

Holahan, John, Stephen Zuckerman, Alison Evans, and Suresh Rangarajan. 1998. "Medicaid Managed Care in Thirteen States." *Health Affairs* 17: 43–63.

Holbrook, Thomas M., and Emily Van Dunk. 1993. "Electoral Competition in the American States." *American Political Science Review* 87: 955–962.

Howard, Christopher. 1997. *The Invisible Welfare State: Tax Expenditures and Social Policy in the United States.* Princeton, N.J.: Princeton University Press.

Hurley, Robert, and Stephen Zuckerman. 2002. *Medicaid Managed Care: State Flexibility in Action.* Washington, D.C.: Urban Institute. Website at http://www.urban.org/UploadedPDF/310449.pdf.

Katz, Michael B. 1986. *In the Shadow of the Poorhouse: A Social History of Welfare in America.* New York: Basic Books.

Kirby, Douglas. 2001. *Emerging Answers: Research Findings on Programs to Reduce Teen Pregnancy.* Washington, D.C.: National Campaign to Prevent Teen Pregnancy.

Lakoff, George. 2002. *Moral Politics: How Liberals and Conservatives Think.* Chicago: University of Chicago Press.

Lawson, Annette, and Deborah L. Rhode, eds. 1993. *The Politics of Pregnancy: Adolescent Sexuality and Public Policy.* New Haven, Conn.: Yale University Press.

Lott, John. 1997. *More Guns, Less Crime.* Chicago: University of Chicago Press.

Ludwig, Jens. 1998a. "Concealed-Gun-Carrying Laws and Violent Crime: Evidence from State Panel Data." *International Review of Law and Economics* 18: 239–254.

———. 1998b. "Guns and Numbers." *Washington Monthly* (June): 50–51.

Ludwig, Jens, and Philip Cook, eds. 2002. *Evaluating Gun Policy: Effect on Crime and Violence.* Washington, D.C.: Brookings Institution.

Manlove, Jennifer, Elizabeth Terry-Humen, Angela Romano Papillo, Kerry Franzetta, Stephanie Williams, and Suzanne Ryan. 2002. *Preventing Teenage Pregnancy, Childbearing, and Sexually Transmitted Diseases: What the Research Shows.* Washington, D.C.: Child Trends. Website at http://www.childtrends.org/PDF/K1Brief.pdf.

McGinnis, J. Michael, and William H. Foege. 1993. "Actual Causes of Death in the United States." *Journal of the American Medical Association,* November 10, 2207–2212.

Mead, Lawrence. Forthcoming. *Statecraft: Welfare Reform in Wisconsin.* Princeton, N.J.: Princeton University Press.

Meier, Kenneth J. 1994. *The Politics of Sin: Drugs, Alcohol, and Public Policy.* New York: M. E. Sharpe.

NASBO (National Association of State Budget Officers). 2002. *State Expenditure Report 2001.* Website at http://www.nasbo.org/Publications/PDFs/nasbo2001exrep.pdf.

NCCDP (National Center for Chronic Disease Prevention and Health Promotion). 2001. *Preventing Chronic Diseases: Investing Wisely in Health.* U.S. Department of Health and Human Services, Centers for Disease Control. Website at http://www.cdc.gov/nccdphp/pe_factsheets/pefs_pa.pdf.

NGA (National Governors Association). 2003. "State Budget Outlook Remains Bleak." Website at http://www.nga.org/.

National Campaign to Prevent Teen Pregnancy. 2002. Website at http://www.teenpregnancy.org/resources/data/genlfact.asp.

National Center for Health Statistics. 1998. Website at http:\\www.cdc.gov\nchswww\fastats.

Nice, David C. 1994. *Policy Innovation in State Government.* Ames: Iowa State University Press.

O'Malley, Patrick M., and Alexander Wagenaar. 1991. "Effects of Minimum Drinking Age Laws on Alcohol Use, Related Behaviors, and Traffic Crash Involvement by American Youth: 1976–1987." *Journal of Studies on Alcohol* 52(5): 478–491.

Peterson, Paul E. 1995. *The Price of Federalism.* Washington, D.C.: Brookings Institution.

Peterson, Paul E., and Mark C. Rom. 1990. *Welfare Magnets: A New Case for a National Welfare Standard.* Washington, D.C.: Brookings Institution.

Rom, Mark Carl. 1998. "What Race! To Where? A Critique of the 'Race to the Bottom' Slogan." Paper presented at the Wilson International Center for Scholars, Washington, D.C., April.

Sawhill, Isabel. 2001. *What Can Be Done to Reduce Teen Pregnancy and Out-of-Wedlock Births?* Washington, D.C.: Brookings Institution.

Sawhill, Isabel, R. Kent Weaver, Ron Haskins, and Andrea Kane, eds. 2002. *Welfare Reform and Beyond: The Future of the Safety Net.* Washington, D.C.: Brookings Institution.

Schneider, Saundra K. 1997. "Medicaid Section 1115 Waivers: Shifting Health Care Reform to the States." *Publius* 27(2): 89–109.

Schoenborn, Charlotte A., Patricia F. Adams, and Patricia Barnes. 2002. "Body Weight Status of Adults: United States, 1997–1998." *Advance Data from Vital and Health Statistics.* Department of Health and Human Services, Centers for Disease Control and Prevention, National Center for Health Statistics.

Schram, Sanford, Lawrence Nitz, and Gary Krueger. 1998. "Without Cause or Effect: Reconsidering Welfare Migration as a Policy Problem." *American Journal of Political Science* 42(January): 210–230.

Sharkansky, Ira. 1969. "The Utility of Elazar's Political Culture: A Research Note." *Polity* 2: 67.

Sparer, Michael S. 1998. "Devolution of Power: An Interim Report Card." *Health Affairs* 17: 7–16.

Sparer, Michael S., and Lawrence D. Brown. 1996. "States and the Health Care Crisis: Limits and Lessons of Laboratory Federalism." In *Health Policy, Federalism, and the American States,* edited by Robert F. Rich and William D. White. Washington, D.C.: Urban Institute.

Spitzer, Robert J. 1995. *The Politics of Gun Control.* Chatham, N.J.: Chatham House.

State Policy Documentation Project. 1999. *Personal Responsibility Contracts: Exemptions and Sanctions.* Website at http://www.spdp.org/tanf/prcexsanc/.

Sturm, Roland. 2002. "The Effects of Obesity, Smoking and Drinking on Medical Problems and Costs." *Health Affairs* 21(2): 245–253.

Sullum, Jacob. 1994. "Just How Bad Is Secondhand Smoke?" *National Review,* May 16, 51.

TennCare. 2002a. "Federal Study: TennCare is Lowest-Cost Health Program in the Nation." Website at http://www.state.tn.us/tenncare/TennCarelowest.html.

———. 2002b. "TennCare Members More Satisfied with the Program." Website at http://www.state.tn.us/tenncare/2002survey.html.

Thompson, Frank, and John Dilulio, eds. 1998. *Medicaid and Devolution: The View from the States.* Washington, D.C.: Brookings Institution.

Thompson, Lyke. 1995. "The Death of General Assistance in Michigan." In *The Politics of Welfare Reform,* edited by Donald F. Norris and Lyke Thompson. Thousand Oaks, Calif.: Sage.

Uccello, Cori E., and L. Jerome Gallagher. 1998. *General Assistance Programs: The State-Based Part of the Safety Net.* Washington, D.C.: Urban Institute.

Urban Institute. 2002a. "Health Policy Online." Website at http://www.urban.org/content/Issues InFocus/HealthPolicyOnline/HPOnline.htm.

————. 2002b. *Publications on TANF.* Website at http://www.urban.org/.

————. 2002c. *States as Innovators in Low-Income Health Coverage.* Website at http://www.urban.org/UploadedPDF/900546.pdf.

————. 2002d. *Welfare Rules Database.* Website at http://newfederalism.urban.org/WRD.

U.S. Bureau of the Census. 2002. *Statistical Abstract of the United States, 2001.* Washington, D.C.: U.S. Government Printing Office. Website at http://www.census.gov/statab/www/.

U.S. Department of Health and Human Services, Administration for Children and Families. 2003. "Statistics." Accessed at http://www.acf.dhhs.gov/news/stats/caseload.htm.

U.S. Department of Health and Human Services, Health Care Financing Administration. 2003. Form HCFA 2082.

U.S. Department of Justice. 2002. "Violent Crime Rates have Declined since 1994." Website at http://www.ojp.usdoj.gov/bjs/glance/viort.htm.

————. 2000. *Sourcebook of Criminal Justice Statistics.* Washington, D.C.: U.S. Government Printing Office.

————. 1996. *Sourcebook of Criminal Justice Statistics.* Washington, D.C.: U.S. Government Printing Office.

U.S. House of Representatives, Committee on Ways and Means. Various years. *The Green Book.* Washington, D.C.: U.S. Government Printing Office.

U.S. House of Representatives, Committee on Ways and Means, Subcommittee on Human Resources. 2001. *Hearings on Welfare and Marriage Issues.* Washington, D.C.: U.S. Government Printing Office.

Walker, Jack L., Jr. 1969. "The Diffusion of Innovation in the American States." *American Political Science Review* 63: 830–899.

Weaver, R. Kent. 2000. *Ending Welfare as We Know It.* Washington, D.C.: Brookings Institution.

Webster, Daniel W., Jon S. Vernick, Jens Ludwig, and Kathleen J. Webster. 1997. "Flawed Gun Policy Research Could Endanger Public Safety." *American Journal of Public Health* 87: 918–921.

Witkin, Gordon. 1994. "Should You Own a Gun?" *U.S. News and World Report,* August 15.

Zamichow, Nora. 1992. "Anti-Smoking Effort Works, Study Finds." *Los Angeles Times,* January 15, Section 5.

## SUGGESTED READINGS

Sawhill, Isabel, R. Kent Weaver, Ron Haskins, and Andrea Kane, eds. 2002. *Welfare Reform and Beyond: The Future of the Safety Net.* Washington, D.C.: Brookings Institution. This book contains twenty essays that focus on the record of welfare reform, specific issues likely to be debated as Congress prepares to reauthorize TANF, and a broader set of policy options for low-income families. It is a well-written, thoughtful, and accessible volume that provides a wide-ranging guide to the various complex issues that Congress must address as it considers the future of the nation's antipoverty policies.

Thompson, Frank, and John Dilulio, eds. 1998. *Medicaid and Devolution: The View from the States.* Washington, D.C.: Brookings Institution. Scholars and state health officials assess the policy and management implications of various options for transferring more authority over Medicaid to the states. They investigate Medicaid financing, benefits, and beneficiaries; long-term care; managed care; safety net providers; and the appropriate division of labor between the federal government and the states. The authors question the capacity of individual states to improve health care for the poor.

Urban Institute. 2002. *Publications on TANF.* Website at http://www.urban.org/. This website contains an annotated list of 145 research publications by the Urban Institute on the Temporary Assistance to Needy Families program as well as many other research reports on related issues.

U.S. House of Representatives, Committee on Ways and Means. 2000. *The Green Book, 2000.* Washington, D.C.: U.S. Government Printing Office. This is the single best publication on United States social welfare programs. The *Green Book* provides legislative histories, program descriptions, and many helpful data tables. The publication is usually updated annually.

# CHAPTER 12

# The Politics of Education

KENNETH K. WONG

Public education is shaped by the U.S. political system. First, federalism creates a de-centralized structure of educational governance. It facilitates a division of power and control among the three levels of government—federal, state, and local. Although the federal government has expanded its involvement in educational policy since the 1960s, public education remains the primary responsibility of state and local government. Second, pluralist democracy maintains a process of checks and balances in educational policy. Not only can competing interests gain access to decision making, institutional rules and procedures also mediate governmental functions at each level of our federal system. In other words, governing structure and political process are key factors in understanding the politics of education in the United States.

This chapter aims to specify how political institutions address competing demands in the educational policy arena. It starts with an overview of the division of power among the three levels of government in education. These roles include the somewhat restrained federal involvement in education, the states' constitutional authority, and the strong tradition of local control. The chapter then focuses on the politics and policy at the state level. First, it considers stability and change in school governance, including a discussion of the role of formal and informal actors. Second, the chapter examines in detail the states' efforts in promoting funding equity. Third, it considers the research on state efforts to promote accountability and choice in public schools. Finally, the chapter concludes with a discussion of emerging issues in state politics of education.

## FEDERALISM AND PUBLIC SCHOOLS

Decision making in educational issues has undergone major changes during the evolution of American federalism. While the federal government has assumed new responsibilities, state and local governments continue to dominate the creation and implementation of educational policy.

Historically, the federal government has adopted a permissive attitude in education that is consistent with the design of dual federalism. Article I, Section 8 of the U.S. Constitution specifies the "enumerated powers" that Congress enjoys, but the Tenth Amendment granted state autonomy in virtually all domestic affairs, including education. Sovereignty for the states was not dependent on the federal government but instead came from the states' citizenry. Consistent with this view, James Madison, in *The Federalist Papers,* which were first published during 1787 and 1788, suggested a line of demarcation between the federal government and the states. He wrote, "The federal and state governments are in fact but different agents and trustees for the people, constituted with different powers, and designed for different purposes" (Hamilton, Madison, and Jay 1961: No. 46, 296).

The dual structure was further maintained by local customs, practice, and belief. It came as no surprise that in his description of the American democracy in the mid-nineteenth century, Alexis de Tocqueville opened his seminal treatise by referring to the local government's "rights of individuality." Observing the state-local relations in the New England townships, de Tocqueville wrote, "Thus it is true that the tax is voted by the legislature, but it is the township that apportions and collects it; the existence of a school is imposed, but the township builds it, pays for it, and directs it" (de Tocqueville 2000, 63). Public education was primarily an obligation internal to the state. The division of power within the federal system was so strong that it continued to preserve state control over its internal affairs, including the *de jure* segregation of schools, many decades following the Civil War.

Federal involvement in education sharply increased during the Great Society era of the 1960s and the 1970s. Several events converged to shift the federal role from permissiveness to engagement. During the immediate post–World War II period, Congress enacted the G.I. Bill to enable veterans to receive a college education of their choice. The Cold War competition saw the passage of the National Defense Education Act in 1958 shortly after the Soviet Union's satellite *Sputnik* successfully orbited the earth. At the same time, the 1954 landmark Supreme Court ruling *Brown v. Board of Education* and congressional enactment of the 1964 Civil Rights Act sharpened federal attention to the needs of disadvantaged students. Consequently, the federal government adopted a major antipoverty education program in 1965, Title I of the 1965 Elementary and Secondary Education Act (ESEA).

The ESEA, arguably the most important federal program in public schools in the last four decades, signaled the end of dual federalism and strengthened the notion of "marble cake" federalism where the national and subnational governments share responsibilities in the domestic arena. Prior to the 1965 law, there was political deadlock on the role of federal government in Congress. The states outside of the South were opposed to allocating federal funds to segregated school systems. Whereas some lawmakers refused to aid parochial schools, others wanted to preserve local autonomy from federal regulations. Political stalemates were reinforced by behind-closed-doors bargaining among the few powerful committee chairs (Sundquist 1968).

The eventual passage of ESEA and other social programs marked the creation of a complex intergovernmental policy system that is unique in American history. To avoid centralization of administrative power at the national level, Congress increased its intergovernmental transfers to finance state and local activities. During the presidency of Lyndon Johnson, categorical (or single purpose) programs, including Title I, increased in number from 160 to 380. By the end of the Carter administration, there were approximately 500 federally funded categorical programs. Particularly important was the redistributive focus of many of these categorical programs that were designed to promote racial desegregation, protect the educational rights of the handicapped, assist English language learners, and provide supplemental resources to children from at-risk backgrounds. Despite several revisions and extension, ESEA Title I continues to adhere to its original intent "to provide financial assistance . . . to local educational agencies serving areas with concentrations of children from low-income families to expand and improve their educational programs . . . which contribute particularly to meeting the special educational needs of educationally deprived children." [1]

Federal engagement in redistributive policy is recorded in spending priorities. According to an analysis of federal spending in public schools between 1970 and 1994, Wong (1999) found that federal aid to redistributive programs showed persistent growth in real dollar terms. During the twenty-four-year period, these programs increased from 36 to 62 percent of the total federal spending in elementary and secondary schools. However, federal redistributive support declined during the Reagan presidency. In constant dollars, federal funding for these programs dropped by almost 11 percent between 1980 and 1985. Beginning in the last two years of the George H. Bush administration and throughout the Clinton presidency, there was strong federal support for education. Between 1992 and 1994, for example, Head Start saw a jump from $1.6 billion to $2.2 billion in constant dollars.

With congressional enactment of the No Child Left Behind Act of 2001, President George W. Bush is further expanding federal involvement in educational accountability for all children. The federal law requires annual testing of students at the elementary grades in core subject areas, mandates the hiring of "highly qualified teachers" in classrooms by 2005–2006, and grants state and local agencies substantial authority in taking "corrective actions" to turn around failing schools. Further, the law allows parents to take their children out of failing schools. Equally significant in terms of federal intervention is the legislative intent in closing the

---

1. Elementary and Secondary Education Act of 1965, Pub L., No. 89-10, Sec 201, 79 Stat. 27 (1965). Codified as amended at 20 U.S.C. Sec 6301 (2002).

achievement gaps among racial/ethnic subgroups as well as income subgroups. To support these efforts, the federal government increased its allocation to the Title I program by $1.7 billion to a total of almost $11 billion, in addition to over $900 million for early reading initiatives.

Historically, the redistributive goals of the federal government did not always receive state and local support. Based on a comparative analysis of federal roles in education, health care, and housing and community development, Peterson, Rabe, and Wong (1986) documented various patterns of state and local response to federal expectations. Two major patterns were found. While intergovernmental cooperation was strong in activities pertaining to economic growth, conflict often occurred in redistributive programs. The lack of full federal funding can be a source of intergovernmental contention. The federal government promised to provide 40 percent of the funds for special education, but in reality its funding level seldom went over 25 percent of program costs. Local and state agencies were also reluctant to change their practices in light of the federal focus. Perhaps most interesting of all, though, was the observation that intergovernmental tension became increasingly manageable with the passage of time. Professional exchange and identification across intergovernmental levels were instrumental in resolving program conflict and facilitating communication (Wong 1990). It remains to be seen if this pattern is repeated as the federal government begins implementing the No Child Left Behind Act, its latest redistributive program.

### GOVERNANCE AND MANAGEMENT: STABILITY AND CHANGE

While the federal role addresses redistributive issues, states assume constitutional and policy authority over much of the jurisdictional territory of public education. Clearly, our constitutional framework enables each of the fifty states to maintain its own educational system. From a constitutional-legal view, localities are political subordinates of the state, and local powers can be granted only with the consent of the state legislature (see Chapter 2 in this volume on this point). Despite interstate variation in governing tradition and culture (Elazar 1972; Wirt 1977), local districts are seen as agencies of the state educational system. The states enjoy substantial control over compulsory attendance, accreditation, curriculum, graduation standards, and such housekeeping matters as calendar, records, and accounting procedures.

In practice, once their legal status has been established, local governments enjoy substantial control over critical resources that can be used to sustain their existence. Localities can select their own political representatives, decide on fiscal policies, and choose the scope of their services. Localities generally maintain more discretion over district organization, guidance and counseling, pupil-teacher ratios, staff recruitment, and extracurricular activities. Nonetheless, on school funding and accountability issues, the balance of power has shifted toward greater state control in recent years.

*Local Control within State Constitutional Framework*

In the 1940s, there were almost 109,000 school districts. The smallest districts often had difficulty recruiting qualified teachers, upgrading physical facilities, and maintaining an enriched curriculum. To provide more uniform educational services in an economical manner, states began to consolidate districts. As of 2003, there were 13,522 independent school districts governing over 90,000 schools across the nation. School district consolidation occurred at a much faster pace than the consolidation of local governments overall. While school boards constituted 70 percent of all local governmental bodies in 1942, they accounted for about 15 percent in 2002. Although four out of five school districts are responsible for fewer than 3,000 students, the average size of districts has grown over the years. Today, about a third of the districts are located in five states: California, Texas, Illinois, Nebraska, and New York.

While the number of school districts has changed significantly over the years, district governance and administration have remained remarkably stable. The dominant mode for the selection of school board members is a nonpartisan election held in an off-year from the local general election. Board members can be elected from subdistricts or district-wide (at-large). Term limits are not usually placed on board membership. These elections are rarely contested and usually involve very low voter turnout. Even fewer voters are likely to attend board meetings, which are often held on a monthly basis. Given the low political interest in school board politics, many researchers note the dominance of civic elites and interest groups in these elections. However, a few exceptions are found in major cities. Although an overwhelming majority of school boards are popularly elected, those in Baltimore, Boston, Chicago, Cleveland, New York, Oakland, Philadelphia, Trenton, and several other cities are appointed either by the mayor or jointly by the mayor and the governor.

*Selection of State Officers*

At the state level, the selection of the state school board, though far from uniform across the fifty states, is largely an appointive process. Governors in thirty-one states (or 62 percent) appoint the state school boards, as Table 12-1 shows. This group of states includes Florida, where in 2002 the state board was composed of the governor's cabinet. Beginning in January 2003, however, Governor Jeb Bush began appointing a state board to oversee both public schools and colleges. In Georgia the state board lost the substantial power it once wielded due in part to 1996 legislation that shifted power from the board to the superintendent and in part to gubernatorial decisions to replace 9 of its 11 members (see Jacobson 1997). In Illinois in 1997 the governor gained new power to appoint a chair when the state board membership was cut from 17 to 9. Gubernatorial appointment may be based on different formal criteria. For example, New Jersey stipulates that 3 of its 13 board members be women. Illinois provides partisan and regional balance in its state board.

**Table 12-1** School Board and Chief State School Officer Selection Methods, by State

| State board selection | | Chief state school officer selection | | | |
|---|---|---|---|---|---|
| | | By election | | By appointment | |
| | | Nonpartisan (6) | Partisan (8) | State board (26) | Governor (9) |
| By election (10) | Nonpartisan | | | Hawaii, Nebraska, Nevada, Utah | |
| | Partisan | | | Alabama, Colorado, Kansas, Michigan | Texas |
| | By local school board members | | Washington | | |
| Mixed (3) | Both elected and appointed | | Indiana | New Mexico, Ohio | |
| By appointment (36) | Governor | California, Georgia, Idaho, North Dakota, Oregon | Arizona, Montana, North Carolina, Oklahoma, Wyoming | Missouri, New Hampshire, Vermont, West Virginia, Alaska, Arkansas, Connecticut, Florida, Illinois, Kentucky, Louisiana, Maryland, Massachusetts | Delaware, Iowa, Maine, New Jersey, Pennsylvania, South Dakota, Tennessee, Virginia |
| | Legislature | | | New York | |
| | Jointly by governor and legislature | | South Carolina | Mississippi, Rhode Island | |
| None | | Wisconsin | | | Minnesota |

SOURCE: Based on author's analysis of information in "State Education Governance" 2002.

Besides the governor, other political institutions may be involved in the selection of school boards. The legislature and the governor in three states jointly appoint their boards. In South Carolina, while the governor appoints 1 member, the state legislature appoints the remaining 17 members. In Mississippi the governor selects 5 members and the legislature the remaining 4 members. In Rhode Island 9 members are appointed by the governor and 2 by the legislature. Further, the state board in New York is solely appointed by the legislature. Three states (Indiana, New Mexico, and Ohio) use a combination of gubernatorial appointment and the elective process. For example, while 10 of the 11 board members in Indiana are appointed by the governor, the chief of the board is elected. Indiana also takes into consideration partisan balance on the board and requires that it include four educators. Only

20 percent of the states have an elected board. Of these ten states, four use a non-partisan ballot and five rely on partisan election. In Alabama, which has a partisan-elected board, the governor serves as the board president. In Washington the members of the state board are elected by local school board members. Wisconsin and Minnesota no longer have a state school board.

The scope of the state board has gradually broadened. Six states grant the state board an authority that includes postsecondary education. These include Florida, Idaho, Missouri, Oregon, New York and Pennsylvania. In Florida, Governor Bush's mandate to appoint a K-20 board is designed to improve policy coherence at all levels of education. In New York the board oversees public schools, higher education, cultural institutions, and licensed professions.

While most governors appoint their state school board, most chief state school officers are selected by the state board. As of January 2002, the board appoints its school chief in twenty-six states while the governor appoints the top executive in only ten states. Fourteen states elect their school chiefs. While eight states hold partisan election, six use a nonpartisan ballot to select their top school officer. As suggested in Table 12-1, the thirteen states in the western region are more likely to have a popularly elected chief school officer. Of the fourteen states that elect the school chief, seven are located in the West.

In considering the selection methods for both the board and the school chief, several systems of governance seem to emerge. As shown in Table 12-1, there is no state that maintains a popularly elected school governance system, namely an elected board and an elected chief officer. The closest approximation is Washington, where the school chief is popularly elected and the board is elected by local school board members. In contrast, the most common method of selection, practiced in twenty-four states, is an appointive system for both the board and the school chief. The remaining states tend to use a combination of selection methods. Twelve states have an appointed board but a popularly elected school chief. Nine states have an elected board but an appointed state school officer.

*Fragmented Power in the Legislative Process*

Legislative politics plays an important role in shaping educational policy because it is central to taxation, expenditure, and constituent concerns. School legislation often constitutes a part of a larger revenue package. Given the fact that over 80 percent of state monies are distributed through formulae written by lawmakers, the legislative process can be highly competitive.

Difficulties in forming the needed political coalition are likely to be magnified in two circumstances in the legislative process. The first occurs when the legislative authority structure in education is fragmented. In their comparative state study, Rosenthal and Fuhrman (1981) found interstate variation in legislative priority on education. Very often, education committee chairs do not overlap with the membership on the ways and means and the appropriations committees. In each budgetary cycle, education has to compete with other major domains, such as welfare assistance, transportation, and higher education. Given this fragmentation, newly adopted education programs may not be fully implemented due to insufficient funding. Likewise, partisan splits between the legislature and the governor's office, as well as between the two houses within the legislature, are likely to present political obstacles in enacting spending and taxing bills.

The second circumstance that leads to difficulty in formation of the necessary political coalition involves the conflict embedded in the big city–suburban split within the legislature. An example is Illinois, where the legislative feud between Chicago and the rest of the state has been a crucial factor in explaining state revenue and spending policy that affects Chicago schools. Suburban and rural legislators rarely vote for tax increases to provide additional aid to the fiscally stressed Chicago schools. A state's ability to offer aid to strapped schools is thus limited by urban-suburban-rural contentions. Racial factors may further contribute to these cleavages. In other words, in states with major cities (e.g., Chicago in Illinois, Philadelphia in Pennsylvania), state aid allocation is determined by intense political bargaining.

Recently, legislative politics has focused on raising academic standards and public school choice (i.e., charter schools). During the early 1990s, Republican-dominated legislatures allied with Republican governors in several states successfully adopted major reform legislation, including charter schools. In the last few years, however, leaders from the two major political parties seem ready to support a wide range of state-led initiatives to improve school performance and accountability (see discussion later in the chapter).

*Influence of Non-Governmental Actors*

Leadership at the state and district levels has to resolve competing demands from diverse sources. While business interests have pushed for better student performance, parents and community organizations voice concerns over teacher quality, school safety, and the physical conditions of schools. Further, equal educational opportunities have been promoted by national and statewide coalitions that focus on "group rights" for low-income and minority children (Orfield and Eaton 1996).

Among the most important organized interests that exercise direct influence on educational policy is the teachers' union (McDonnell and Pascal 1979; Moe 2001; Loveless 2001). While affiliates of the American Federation of Teachers (AFT) are active in urban districts in the Northeast and Midwest, National Education Association local chapters organize teachers in most other districts. The former, when compared to the latter, is seen by the school board as more adversarial in the bargaining process. In his study of Chicago's teachers' union (an AFT affiliate), Grimshaw (1979) suggested that the union has gone through two phases in its relationship with the school administration. During the organizing phase, the union largely cooperated with the district and state administration in return for a legitimate role in the policy-making process. Cole (1969) also found that union recognition was a key objective in the 1960 teachers' strike in New York City. In the second phase, which

Grimshaw (1979) characterized as "union rule," the union became independent of local and state political leadership. Instead, it looked to the national union leadership for technical support and political guidance, thereby engaging in tough bargaining with the school management over better compensation and working conditions. Consequently, Grimshaw argued that local policymakers "no longer are able to set policy unless the policy is consistent with the union's objectives" (1979, 150).

Another contending interest is the increasingly well-organized taxpaying public, a substantial portion of which no longer has children in the public schools (Kirst 1980). The aging population has placed public education in competition with transportation, public safety, community development, and health care over budgetary allocation. Discontent with property taxes became widespread during the time of the much-publicized campaign for Proposition 13 in California. Between 1978 and 1983, of the 67 tax or spending limitation measures on state ballots across the nation, 39 were approved (Citrin 1984). In communities with a substantial representation of retirees (such as those in Florida), referenda for school taxes have met with greater skepticism. More recently, business-organized lobbying groups have been successful in pushing for higher academic standards and strong accountability measures. In districts where public schools fail repeatedly, political leaders seek alternative ways of delivering schooling services, including privatization or creating charter schools.

### POLITICS OF SCHOOL FUNDING

In public school funding, the federal government has always been a junior partner. With federal funds accounting for somewhere between 5 and 10 percent of public elementary and secondary education revenue in the last several decades, funding responsibility for K-12 education is shared between state and local governments. Since the 1980s, state governments have generally assumed primary fiscal responsibility, with local governments providing the rest of the necessary revenue. In his longitudinal analysis of educational funding across the fifty states, Wong (1999) found that the state share was only 38.3 percent in 1959. A reversal of responsibility between local and state governments occurred during the late 1970s and early 1980s. Due to local fiscal retrenchment, responsibility for funding education shifted from local to state sources. Since the mid-1980s, the state share of total school revenues has either exceeded or stayed close to the 50-percent level. The prominence of state fiscal support signals the rising influence of the state in determining how the K-12 education pie will be divided in response to competing demands in the policy-making process.

During the 1990s, states maintained relatively stable levels of funding responsibility. The average percentage of elementary and secondary revenue provided by states was approximately 49 percent, but there is much variation to be noted. In Table 12-2, the fifty states are divided into five groups, according to level of funding responsibility. These groups are labeled "High," "Mid-to-High," "Mid," "Low-to-Mid," and " Low" responsibility states. At the extremes are Hawaii, in which almost

**Table 12-2** State Funding Responsibility Measured by Percentage of All Public Elementary and Secondary School Revenues, 1992–2000

| State | 1991–1992 | 1993–1994 | 1995–1996 | 1997–1998 | 1999–2000 | Average |
|---|---|---|---|---|---|---|
| High responsibility states (states 1–10) | | | | | | |
| Hawaii[a] | 90.3% | 90.0% | 89.8% | 89.0% | 88.8% | 89.6% |
| New Mexico | 73.8 | 73.6 | 73.9 | 72.2 | 71.5 | 73.0 |
| Washington | 71.6 | 69.7 | 68.0 | 66.0 | 63.5 | 67.8 |
| North Carolina | 63.6 | 64.0 | 64.5 | 67.3 | 67.6 | 65.4 |
| Delaware | 65.9 | 64.4 | 66.6 | 64.4 | 65.6 | 65.4 |
| Alaska | 68.0 | 67.1 | 66.1 | 62.2 | 58.9 | 64.5 |
| Kentucky | 67.0 | 65.9 | 65.3 | 61.7 | 60.7 | 64.1 |
| West Virginia | 67.1 | 64.6 | 63.0 | 62.7 | 61.7 | 63.8 |
| Idaho | 61.8 | 60.4 | 64.3 | 62.7 | 61.1 | 62.1 |
| Alabama | 58.8 | 59.3 | 61.3 | 62.5 | 62.2 | 60.8 |
| Mid-to-high responsibility states (states 11–20) | | | | | | |
| Oklahoma | 62.2 | 58.8 | 59.3 | 61.6 | 58.4 | 60.1 |
| California | 65.9 | 56.2 | 55.8 | 60.2 | 60.3 | 59.7 |
| Arkansas | 59.9 | 57.8 | 60.0 | 57.7 | 60.2 | 59.1 |
| Utah | 57.2 | 54.9 | 58.6 | 61.0 | 59.2 | 58.2 |
| Kansas | 42.4 | 57.8 | 57.3 | 57.9 | 62.4 | 55.6 |
| Mississippi | 53.5 | 54.5 | 57.8 | 55.4 | 56.2 | 55.5 |
| Minnesota | 51.6 | 55.1 | 58.2 | 52.3 | 60.0 | 55.4 |
| Indiana | 52.9 | 52.3 | 54.3 | 51.4 | 52.3 | 52.6 |
| Louisiana | 54.8 | 53.0 | 50.3 | 50.4 | 49.5 | 51.6 |
| Michigan | 26.6 | 28.7 | 66.8 | 66.0 | 64.6 | 50.5 |
| Mid responsibility states (states 21–30) | | | | | | |
| Wyoming | 50.0 | 52.2 | 51.3 | 47.0 | 51.9 | 50.5 |
| South Carolina | 48.3 | 46.2 | 52.9 | 51.5 | 52.8 | 50.3 |
| Georgia | 47.7 | 50.7 | 51.9 | 51.2 | 47.9 | 49.9 |
| Iowa | 47.3 | 48.2 | 49.0 | 51.3 | 50.6 | 49.3 |
| Florida | 48.4 | 49.8 | 48.6 | 48.8 | 49.5 | 49.0 |
| Oregon | 30.6 | 39.5 | 54.1 | 56.8 | 57.1 | 47.6 |
| Maine | 49.8 | 48.3 | 47.0 | 45.5 | 44.6 | 47.0 |
| Montana | 41.8 | 51.4 | 48.6 | 46.9 | 44.7 | 46.7 |
| Tennessee | 42.2 | 46.8 | 47.9 | 47.7 | 45.8 | 46.1 |
| Wisconsin | 39.4 | 38.7 | 42.9 | 53.7 | 54.0 | 45.7 |
| Low-to-mid responsibility states (states 31–40) | | | | | | |
| Arizona | 42.4 | 41.5 | 44.1 | 44.3 | 43.6 | 43.2 |
| Texas | 43.4 | 40.2 | 42.9 | 44.2 | 44.2 | 43.0 |
| Colorado | 42.8 | 43.5 | 43.8 | 43.4 | 41.3 | 43.0 |
| North Dakota | 44.8 | 42.8 | 42.1 | 41.1 | 40.2 | 42.2 |
| Ohio | 40.8 | 40.8 | 40.7 | 41.2 | 42.5 | 41.2 |
| New York | 40.3 | 38.2 | 39.7 | 39.7 | 44.8 | 40.5 |
| New Jersey | 42.2 | 40.4 | 38.6 | 39.8 | 41.2 | 40.4 |
| Rhode Island | 38.5 | 39.0 | 41.5 | 40.1 | 41.3 | 40.1 |
| Pennsylvania | 41.4 | 40.3 | 39.8 | 38.7 | 37.8 | 39.6 |
| Connecticut | 40.7 | 40.3 | 38.0 | 37.3 | 40.2 | 39.3 |

**Table 12-2** *(Continued)*

| Low responsibility states (states 41–50) | | | | | |
|---|---|---|---|---|---|
| Missouri | 38.0% | 38.3% | 40.2% | 39.7% | 37.6% | 38.8% |
| Vermont | 31.6 | 31.3 | 27.8 | 29.4 | 73.6 | 38.7 |
| Maryland | 38.2 | 38.9 | 38.2 | 39.0 | 39.0 | 38.7 |
| Massachusetts | 30.7 | 34.1 | 38.3 | 40.7 | 43.7 | 37.5 |
| Nebraska | 34.3 | 32.7 | 31.6 | 33.1 | 36.6 | 33.7 |
| Virginia | 31.1 | 30.8 | 31.1 | 31.4 | 42.6 | 33.4 |
| Nevada | 38.7 | 32.8 | 32.0 | 31.8 | 29.1 | 32.9 |
| South Dakota | 27.0 | 26.1 | 29.7 | 35.6 | 34.5 | 30.6 |
| Illinois | 28.9 | 28.2 | 27.3 | 28.4 | 30.8 | 28.7 |
| New Hampshire | 8.5 | 8.2 | 7.0 | 9.3 | 55.8 | 17.8 |
| All States | 47.7 | 47.8 | 49.4 | 49.5 | 51.7 | 49.2 |

SOURCE: Calculated by the author using data from the U.S. Department of Education, National Center for Education Statistics, Common Core of Data.

a Hawaii is a special case because it has only one school district. Hawaii is not included in analysis of intra-state equity (for example, between districts) due to this feature of its public education system.

90 percent of elementary and secondary school revenue is provided by the state, and New Hampshire, where less than 10 percent of revenue comes from the state. The ten states with the highest funding responsibility account for nearly two-thirds of annual education revenue, while states with low funding responsibility supply one-third of the state's education budget.

What accounts for the variation in state fiscal role across the fifty states? What are the political and institutional factors that contributed to a greater state share of the school funding? And what are the political constraints?

### School Funding System Overturned by Judicial Actions

Efforts to reduce funding disparities across districts have led many states to absorb a higher share of educational costs. School finance litigation and court rulings have heightened the public attention to interdistrict inequalities (Wise 1972; Guthrie, Garms, and Pierce 1988; McDermott 1999). The structure of the plaintiffs' argument is seemingly straightforward—disparity in local taxable wealth is closely linked to spending differences, which contribute to inequities in schooling opportunities and quality. In virtually all judicial challenges, taxpayers in districts with low property values are found to carry heavy tax burdens. Students in these high tax–low wealth districts do not seem to benefit from the fiscal well-being of the state as a whole.

Beginning in the 1970s up to the present, about half of the states have either faced rulings or remain in the process of dealing with major lawsuits that challenge the constitutionality of the state finance system in public education. As Table 12-3 shows, state high court rulings have shifted in favor of the plaintiffs in the last three decades. The number of decisions in favor of the defendant states declined from seven in the 1970s to six in both the 1980s and the 1990s. At the same time, the

**Table 12-3** State High Court Decisions on Constitutionality of State Finance System, 1970s–1990s

| Ruling | 1970s | | | 1980s | | | 1990s | | | Totals |
| | Number of rulings | Percentage of total rulings | States | Number of rulings | Percentage of total rulings | States | Number of rulings | Percentage of total rulings | States | |
|---|---|---|---|---|---|---|---|---|---|---|
| Finance system ruled constitutional | 7 | 58 | Arizona Idaho Michigan Ohio Oregon Pennsylvania Washington | 6 | 55 | Colorado Georgia Maryland Oklahoma Wisconsin | 6 | 35 | Arkansas Minnesota North Dakota Oregon Rhode Island Virginia | 18 |
| Finance system ruled unconstitutional | 5 | 42 | California Connecticut New Jersey Washington West Virginia | 5 | 45 | Arkansas Kentucky Montana Texas Wyoming | 11 | 65 | Alabama Arizona Arkansas Massachusetts Missouri New Hampshire New Jersey Ohio Tennessee Vermont Wyoming | 21 |
| Total | 12 | 100 | | 11 | 100 | | 17 | 100 | | 39 |

SOURCE: Author's analysis of information on the Web site of the Education Commission of the States, February 2000.

number of rulings that declared state funding systems unconstitutional increased from five in both the 1970s and the 1980s to eleven in the 1990s. In other words, while 58 percent of the decisions in the 1970s were in favor of the status quo, 65 percent of the rulings overturned the status quo during the 1990s. In 1997 alone, courts found the funding systems in Ohio, Vermont, and New Hampshire unconstitutional. Consequently, the eighteen states that violated their constitutions had to restructure their funding systems to reduce interdistrict inequity.

Judicial involvement in reforming the statewide school finance system started in 1967 in California when John Serrano and other parents, concerned about poor school services for their children in the Los Angeles area, brought a class action suit against the state of California. In the landmark ruling *Serrano v. Priest* (1971), often referred to as *Serrano I*, the California Supreme Court handed down a six-to-one decision in favor of the parents. According to this ruling, significant interdistrict disparities in school spending due to uneven distribution of taxable wealth violated the equal protection provisions of the state constitution. In this case, sharp disparity in school spending existed between the wealthy Beverly Hills district and the nearby Baldwin Park district. While the former had a tax rate that was less than half as much as the latter, it was able to come up with twice as many school dollars on a per student basis during 1968–1969. As the court opinion stated, "affluent districts can have their cake and eat it too; they can provide a high quality education for their children while paying lower taxes. Poor districts, by contrast, have no cake at all" (96 Cal. Rptr. 601 at 611–12). Shortly after the court decision, the California legislature adopted what became the first of several school finance reform plans during the 1970s (Levin et al. 1972; Kirst and Somers 1981). At the same time, parent plaintiffs in several other states filed similar charges.

However, within two years, *Serrano I* was brought into question by a U.S. Supreme Court ruling on a case in Texas. In *San Antonio Independent School District v. Rodriguez* (1973), a 5-to-4 decision reversed a federal district court ruling. It concluded that since education does not constitute a fundamental interest under the U.S. Constitution, the state can choose to preserve local control by not interfering in interdistrict fiscal inequities. In line with *San Antonio,* the supreme courts of Arizona (1973), Washington (1974), Oregon (1976), Colorado (1976), Idaho (1975), and several other states ruled that the statewide system did not violate the state constitution despite interdistrict funding inequity.

Despite *San Antonio,* the pressure for a more equitable allocation of state funds continued. Among the most significant state rulings that rejected the local control notion in *San Antonio* was *Serrano II* (1976) in California. In the post–*Serrano II* period, the state supreme courts in Washington, Wyoming, and several other states also ruled unconstitutional their state school financing systems. Costly services for special needs students were brought to the states' attention by big-city districts in several legal suits, including *Seattle v. Washington.* (1978). Further, the court overturned the school funding systems in Texas (1989), Kentucky (1989), New Jersey (1990), Vermont (1997), Ohio (1997), and New Hampshire (1997).

The New Jersey ruling, in contrast to rulings in most other states, paid particular attention to the concentration of social needs in inner-city schools. The court, in *Abbott v. Burke II* (1990), recognized additional costs to address the needs of disadvantaged pupils in urban areas, estimating that programs to "reverse the educational disadvantage the children start out with" in urban districts would cost about $440 million for the first year. Immediately following the court decision, the Democratic governor proposed $2.8 billion in new and increased taxes to fund new services for the poorest schools. However, the reform and tax-increase plan was substantially compromised following key Republican wins in the gubernatorial and legislative election. After years of fiscal conservatism under Governor Christine Todd Whitman, the new Democratic administration of James McGreevey is attempting to address the intent of the *Abbott* decision despite the current economic downturn.

Judicial impact has not been confined to the eighteen states where the state funding was successfully challenged. In many states, judicial pressure and, in some cases, anticipation of judicial challenges have brought about reform in the state aid allocation. Utah and Washington, for example, have "foundation programs" establishing base-line revenue for students in poor districts. Districts are required to levy local property taxes up to a state-designated maximum. State dollars are channeled to make up the difference between local tax revenue and the minimum level of school spending. To supplement the foundation programs, many states have adopted various complicated multi-tiered schemes. Under "power equalizers," state aid guarantees an equal amount of local tax returns at different levels of tax levy. Further, several states primarily use "resource equalizers" that either specify the state share in local spending (known as "percentage equalizers") or equalize the taxing returns of districts to finance schools (known as "district power equalizing"). Unlike foundation programs, equalizing systems do not place a fixed dollar limit on state support.

Increase in state aid is often a result of political bargaining. In order to gain a legislative coalition for a reform package, policy makers often adopt the "leveling up" strategy where no districts would suffer a reduction in their state support. Taxpayer dollars may be more widely distributed in two-party competitive states where political elites want to see their constituencies benefiting from state allocation. In other words, an increase in state transfers to poor districts is seldom achieved at the expense of the more affluent communities.

Electoral concerns substantially shaped legislation to address interdistrict inequity in Kansas, California, New Jersey, New York, and Washington (Berke, Goertz, and Coley 1984). Texas offers a good example of the politics of sectoral rivalry. In 1989 Texas's educational finance system was ruled unconstitutional. In a 9-0 reversal of the appellate court's ruling, the state's supreme court pointed out, "Districts must have substantially equal access to similar revenues per pupil at similar levels of tax effort. Children who live in poor districts and children who live in rich districts must be afforded a substantially equal opportunity to have access to educational funds" (*Edgewood Independent School District v. Kirby* [1989]).

The ruling set off fierce partisan conflict and interest group contention that lasted three years. Having gone through various reform plans, the Republican governor and the Democratic-controlled legislature produced a compromise bill in 1990. Senate Bill 1 would have provided $500 million more to the state's 1,056 districts; in other words, no district would come out as a loser. However, the seemingly modest increase in state support and the scattering of these funds prompted a district judge to reject the plan (Harp 1990). The prospect of school finance reform was substantially enhanced with the election of a Democratic governor, Ann Richards, whose campaign included state educational funding as a key issue. After numerous delays and last-minute give-and-take, the governor and the legislature produced yet another legislative proposal in June 1993.

The proposed reform called for the state to reallocate "excess" local tax revenues from the richest 10 percent of the districts to support the statewide teacher retirement system, thereby freeing more state funds for the poorest districts. The plan would use property taxes collected from the affluent communities to support schools in the fiscally depressed communities. While the plan was shaped by the Robin Hood principle, it did not commit additional state tax dollars. In other words, the state's political leaders remained constrained by middle-class concerns and made no serious attempt to call for an increase in state taxes to fund schools.

*State Response to Federal Programs for the Disadvantaged*

The prominent state role in school spending has been further encouraged by the adoption of legislation that promotes equal educational opportunity. In this regard, federal school policy during the Great Society era of the mid-1960s and the 1970s has played a crucial role. While federal funds constitute less than 10 percent of all school revenues, federal programmatic guidance has clearly stimulated state activity in addressing special needs. Currently, all states are providing their own funds for special education. Twenty-eight states fund their own compensatory education, and twenty-one states support bilingual instructional services.

During the 1980s, however, an increasing number of states shifted from the federal categorical model to an allocative system that weights special-needs students more heavily than others in the general-aid formula. This alternative arrangement was used by only five states during the mid-1970s (Leppert et al. 1976). The shift from categorical to pupil weightings occurred at a time when states assumed greater autonomy in the climate of Reagan's New Federalism. By the 1980s, it had become popular in distributing funds for the handicapped. Of the states that provide compensatory programs, thirteen adhere to pupil weighting and fifteen retain categoricals. In bilingual education, six use pupil weights and fifteen allot funds through categorical grants.

States' policy framework on equity issues can have distributive consequences. For example, politics in California is substantially shaped by urban interests. Urban lawmakers dominate various influential legislative offices and committee chairs— the speaker of the house, the president pro tempore of the senate, the chair of the assembly's ways and means committee, the chair of the senate appropriations committee, and the chairs of the education committees in the two houses (Timar 1992). To respond to their urban constituencies, the legislative leaders have funded a wide range of categorical programs. Indeed, on the average, 26 percent of the urban district's total school funds are state categorical sources as compared to only 13 percent in the suburban districts. For example, Los Angeles receives 31 percent of its school revenues from state categoricals, while its wealthy southern suburb, Palos Verdes, obtains only 8 percent of its funds from categorical programs. In the case of California, state allocation has been beneficial to the urban districts.

*Property Taxpayer Revolts*

The pressure toward a greater state role, according to studies on constituent politics, has been enhanced by citizen-based campaigns against local increases in property tax levy. Within five years following California's Proposition 13, well over half of all states enacted some form of legislation curbing governmental spending and restricting property tax levy increases. Between 1976 and 1990, thirty-six states experienced a property tax revolt (Mullins and Joyce 1995).

Indeed, signs of taxpayer opposition to school levies had begun to emerge prior to the passage of Proposition 13 in California in 1978. As early as 1970, a majority of school bond requests had failed to meet with the approval of voters across the nation (Piele and Hall 1973). In California, for example, local taxpayers were so dissatisfied with a sharp increase in local school contributions during the Reagan governorship that, between 1966 and 1971, they rejected 50 percent of all local tax increases for school operation and 60 percent of the school bond levies for capital improvements (Levin et al. 1972). Discontent among property tax payers became more widespread during the time of the much-publicized campaign of Proposition 13. According to a national Gallup Poll at the time, when asked to identify their dissatisfaction with various taxing sources for public schools, 52 percent of the respondents mentioned property tax, as compared to only 20 percent citing state sources (Phi Delta Kappa 1984). In 1978 alone, voters in California, Colorado, Idaho, Montana, Nevada, Oregon, Utah, and several other states pushed for limitation of property tax increases. Consequently, major property tax limitation measures were adopted in California, Idaho, and Massachusetts.

Where the local taxpayer movement is well organized, there is evidence that the state begins to assume greater financial responsibility for local school cost (Williams 1982; ACIR 1980; Gold 1985; Urban Institute 1983). After the passage of Proposition 13, California's state share in nonfederal school revenues jumped from less than 50 percent to more than 70 percent. The state share also went up in Massachusetts and Idaho to make up for the lost local revenues after the adoption of tax-limiting measures. The role of the state becomes more complicated where spending limits on both the state and local sources were adopted, such as in Colorado, New Jersey, and Tennessee. In these states, it is more likely that both state and local spending on education exhibit a slow growth pattern. However, a faster rate of decline at the local level may result in an increase in the percentage of the state share.

Taxpayers' concerns can illuminate territorial divisiveness. Illinois is a good example of how school finance reform can be frustrated by fragmentary politics. In 1992 voters opposed a constitutional referendum that would have directed the state to be the primary funder in public education. The initiative was supported by 57 percent of the voters, yet was 3 percent short of what was needed to enact a constitutional referendum. As expected, support was the strongest from Chicago, and opposition came mainly from the surrounding middle-class suburbs. Indeed, the city-suburban rivalry is exacerbated by racial and income differences. While whites constitute only 12 percent of the enrollment in the Chicago public schools, students in the suburban schools predominantly come from white, middle-class families.

With a fiscally conservative Republican governor and the senate under the leadership of a Republican from a middle-class suburb west of Chicago, it seemed unlikely that the state legislature would launch any major reform in school finance. Then politics took a dramatic turn in 1997 when the governor reversed his earlier position on school finance reform. When the legislature rejected his proposal to increase state income tax to lower the local tax burden in funding schools, the governor returned with a new reform package that relied on users fees and sales taxes. The 1997 "compromise" reform legislation guaranteed a foundation level of $4,225 to every student in the state for three years beginning in the fall of 1998. At least for a brief period of time, fragmentary politics gave way to coalitional politics in Illinois.

Michigan offers another example of what happens when state aid to schools does not receive statewide political support. Prior to 1993, Michigan state government's share of school costs declined steeply, partly because of the recession and decline of the auto industry (Wong 1999). The state's limited role is seen in two different examples, one relating to Detroit and the other to a small rural district. Detroit, the state's major city, is clearly isolated from the governing institutions at the state level. The state-city relations deteriorated during the long tenure of Mayor Coleman Young. In addition, the demographics have worked against the city. While Detroit maintained 22 percent of the house seats in the 1960s, it controlled fewer than 14 percent of the seats in the 1980s.

The suburban communities, on the contrary, now hold 30 percent of the house seats. Just at the time when Detroit's influence was in decline, the state legislature became increasingly reluctant to provide additional aid to the city schools. In 1973, for example, the state legislature raised the minimum level of required local levy, which was substantially higher than what Detroit was taxing at the time (Mirel 1993). To avoid risking a significant loss in state aid, Detroit had to impose a higher millage on its already shrinking property tax base. Although Detroit presently receives more than half of its revenues from the state, there is very limited political support for a more activist state in general.

The latter point is illuminated by the failure of the state to intervene in the Kalkaska district in the rural northwestern lower peninsula area (Wilkerson 1993). The district's levy proposal had been rejected three times by the community, whose residents were mainly retirees with no school-age children. In response to the district's appeal for $1.5 million in state aid to keep the school open for ten more weeks, the state legislature cited that the state codes could not compel the district to stay open (unlike California laws). In the absence of a state subsidy, the district was forced to close the schools ten weeks early. In short, even in a fiscal crisis like the one in Kalkaska, the state leadership, restrained by a broader taxpaying constituency, decided not to step in and assume greater responsibility in educational funding.

In late 1993 Michigan politics took a dramatic turn when the Republican governor and the legislature produced a compromise that would replace two-thirds of the local property tax revenues with state taxes. Among the facilitating factors for the bipartisan reform was the fact that Michigan's property tax burden was 30 percent higher than the national average (ACIR 1992). Michigan voters subsequently approved a measure that raised the state sales tax from 4 to 6 percent, increased the tax on cigarettes by three times, and created other users fees (Federal Reserve Bank of Chicago 1994). The adopted measure also slightly reduced the state's personal income tax from 4.6 to 4.4 percent. Clearly, the plan served to reduce the property tax burden for homeowners and, to a limited extent, business property owners as well. It remains to be seen whether the shift to a greater state role will actually reduce the disparity between the have-nots (such as Detroit and rural districts) and the haves (such as suburban communities outside of Detroit).

### Effects of the Leveling-Up Strategy

A key policy question is whether the states' leveling-up strategy has the effect of narrowing the gap in fiscal capacity among districts. Using the latest available state-by-state information, Wong (1999) analyzed the extent to which disparity persisted between the 5th and 95th percentiles of the districts in each state. To standardize the measure of interdistrict inequity, the author developed the spending gap index, derived by dividing the excess per pupil spending in the wealthier districts by the statewide per pupil spending. As Table 12-4 shows, the spending gap index for all fifty states in 1999 averaged 0.29 (or 29 percent of the statewide per pupil spending). In other words, the gap seems modest.

There are, to be sure, interstate variations. Seven states had a fairly wide disparity gap that exceeded 0.40 (or 40 percent of per pupil spending). These included Alaska, Illinois, New Hampshire, Montana, Vermont, Kansas, and Arizona. In contrast, nine states had a modest disparity gap of less than 20 percent between the haves and the have-nots. These were California, Washington, Alabama, Delaware, Iowa, North Carolina, West Virginia, Florida, and Nevada. Hawaii and Washington D.C., both of which are basically unitary systems without subdivisions, are the exceptions, exhibiting no disparity gap.

### THE NEW LANDSCAPE IN STATE-LED REFORM

Political scientists are keenly interested in the balance of power between the state and local communities. A great deal of systematic research has focused on the notion of centralization of state authority. While the notion of centralization remains relevant, recent legislation on educational accountability, choice, and takeover of districts and schools provides a new empirical basis to rethink the state role. A hybrid of state authority appears to have emerged in that we now see both centralizing and decentralizing tendencies occurring at the same time, often within the same state.

Over the past decade states have taken a more active role in educational reform. As an initial step toward rethinking the changing role of the state relative to district authority, we will consider three state-led reform initiatives. These are state policies on testing and performance standards, adoption of choice-based programs, and enactment of takeover legislation over low-performing districts and schools.

### Pressuring Schools to Meet Higher Standards

Many states have established accountability standards, and a few of them are ready to take more direct intervention, such as taking over failing districts or a cluster of low-performing schools. This tendency toward state-led accountability is likely to grow, as the federal No Child Left Behind Act of 2001 requires a stronger state role in raising student performance. The law specifically requires states to

**Table 12-4** Classification of States by Spending Gap Index Between Fifth and Ninety-Fifth Percentiles of District in Spending per Pupil, 1999

| State | Spending per pupil (A) | Disparity between fifth and ninety-fifth percentiles (B) | Spending gap index (B/A) | Actual B/A[a] |
|---|---|---|---|---|
| U.S. average | $6,835 | $1,958 | 0.44 | 0.29 |
| Alaska | $8,743 | $6,625 | 1.20 | 0.76 |
| Illinois | $7,185 | $4,057 | 1.04 | 0.56 |
| New Hampshire | $6,742 | $3,459 | 0.87 | 0.51 |
| Montana | $6,214 | $2,984 | 0.81 | 0.48 |
| Vermont | $7,938 | $3,495 | 0.79 | 0.44 |
| Kansas | $6,211 | $2,744 | 0.70 | 0.44 |
| Arizona | $5,033 | $2,122 | 0.64 | 0.42 |
| Missouri | $6,143 | $2,252 | 0.59 | 0.37 |
| North Dakota | $5,830 | $2,060 | 0.57 | 0.35 |
| Massachusetts | $8,444 | $2,850 | 0.54 | 0.34 |
| Idaho | $5,218 | $1,889 | 0.53 | 0.36 |
| South Dakota | $5,521 | $1,891 | 0.52 | 0.34 |
| Ohio | $6,999 | $2,246 | 0.52 | 0.32 |
| Minnesota | $7,051 | $2,318 | 0.51 | 0.33 |
| New Jersey | $10,283 | $3,708 | 0.51 | 0.36 |
| New York | $10,029 | $3,387 | 0.50 | 0.34 |
| New Mexico | $5,748 | $1,863 | 0.49 | 0.32 |
| Texas | $6,145 | $1,918 | 0.49 | 0.31 |
| Arkansas | $5,470 | $1,816 | 0.49 | 0.33 |
| Maine | $7,595 | $2,248 | 0.48 | 0.30 |
| Oklahoma | $5,394 | $1,730 | 0.48 | 0.32 |
| Pennsylvania | $7,824 | $2,292 | 0.47 | 0.29 |
| Wyoming | $7,421 | $2,330 | 0.46 | 0.31 |
| Michigan | $7,662 | $2,374 | 0.45 | 0.31 |
| Nebraska | $6,422 | $1,861 | 0.45 | 0.29 |
| Connecticut | $8,800 | $2,812 | 0.44 | 0.32 |
| Tennessee | $5,343 | $1,496 | 0.41 | 0.28 |
| Oregon | $7,027 | $1,847 | 0.39 | 0.26 |
| Indiana | $6,871 | $1,726 | 0.38 | 0.25 |
| Rhode Island | $8,242 | $2,000 | 0.38 | 0.24 |
| Mississippi | $5,014 | $1,143 | 0.35 | 0.23 |
| Georgia | $6,417 | $1,583 | 0.35 | 0.25 |
| Kentucky | $5,922 | $1,337 | 0.33 | 0.23 |
| Wisconsin | $7,716 | $1,723 | 0.32 | 0.22 |
| Maryland | $7,496 | $1,716 | 0.32 | 0.23 |
| Colorado | $6,165 | $1,394 | 0.32 | 0.23 |
| Virginia | $6,839 | $1,426 | 0.32 | 0.21 |
| Louisiana | $5,652 | $1,253 | 0.32 | 0.22 |
| California | $6,298 | $1,227 | 0.30 | 0.19 |
| South Carolina | $6,114 | $1,255 | 0.30 | 0.21 |
| Utah | $4,331 | $934 | 0.28 | 0.22 |
| Washington | $6,394 | $1,260 | 0.28 | 0.20 |
| Alabama | $5,601 | $1,090 | 0.28 | 0.19 |
| Delaware | $8,030 | $1,466 | 0.27 | 0.18 |
| Iowa | $6,547 | $1,150 | 0.26 | 0.18 |
| North Carolina | $5,990 | $1,090 | 0.26 | 0.18 |
| West Virginia | $7,093 | $922 | 0.20 | 0.13 |
| Florida | $5,691 | $781 | 0.19 | 0.14 |
| Nevada | $5,736 | $714 | 0.16 | 0.12 |
| District of Columbia | $9,933 | $0 | 0.00 | 0.00 |
| Hawaii | $6,487 | $3 | 0.00 | 0.00 |

SOURCES: Based on author's analysis of data reported in *Education Week* 2002 and U.S. Bureau of the Census, 1999.

a "Spending per pupil" based on U.S. Bureau of the Census figures from 1999, "Spending gap" from *Education Week,* resulting in the need to distinguish "Actual."

administer annual assessments in reading and mathematics and to measure "adequate yearly progress" of all students, including those who enroll in special education programs and those who are English language learners. The federal law also sharpens its focus on narrowing the achievement gap among racial groups.

To examine the scope of a state's standards and accountability framework, we consider multiple measures regarding state mandates on testing and standards. As Table 12-5 shows, these measures include the number of tests given in grades 1 to 8 in English and mathematics, number of tests given in grades 9 to 12 in English and mathematics, statewide practice in assigning ratings to all schools, state efforts to identify low-performing schools, and state listing of low-performing schools. These measures, based largely on data as of 2000, are then summed in terms of a score on state accountability standards on testing and academic policies. The table shows that strong accountability states include Alabama, California, Florida, West Virginia, North Carolina, Louisiana, New Mexico, Maryland, Tennessee, Virginia, and Kentucky. Among the states that play a limited accountability role are Nebraska, Wyoming, New Jersey, New Hampshire, Montana, Minnesota, Maine, and Iowa.

State efforts toward accountability notwithstanding, the implementation of the federal No Child Left Behind Act is not likely to occur rapidly. With dozens of states suffering from budgetary shortfalls in 2003, states are likely to delay their response to costly federal mandates. According to a fifty-state report card on the anniversary of the federal legislation, only five states received federal approval on their accountability plan (Education Commission of the States 2003). Further, only half of the states were prepared to monitor performance of various subgroups and to undertake corrective actions in failing schools. Over 80 percent of the states were not ready to meet the federal expectation on placing highly qualified teachers in the classroom.

*Launching Choice-Based Programs*

Dissatisfied with low performance in public schools, an increasing number of policy makers and reformers are focusing on market-like competition as the driving force to raise student performance (Hirschman 1971). In reviewing the range of choice-based initiatives, Greene (2002) has developed an "Education Freedom Index" for each of the fifty states. This index uses four components (weighted equally) to determine the school choice climate: charter schools, subsidized private schools, home-schooling, and public school choice. As Table 12-6 suggests, Arizona provides the highest degree of school choice to families, while Hawaii maintains the least choice. During 2000 and 2001, Florida showed the greatest gain toward school choice, while Utah regressed on choice climate.

There are state variations across the four components. While public school choice (such as citywide magnet programs) was widely implemented, subsidized private school choice from either governmental or nongovernmental sources was absent in eleven states. Thirteen states did not have legislation on charter schools, while only two states did not allow for home-schooling in 2001.

**Table 12-5** State Testing and Standards Policies, 2000–2001

| State | English and mathematics tests given grades 1–8 | Elementary and middle school testing score[a] | English and mathematics tests given grades 9–12 | High school testing score[b] | State assigns ratings to all schools[c] | State identifies low-performing schools[d] | Number of schools determined to be low performing in 1999–2000 | State score for testing and standards policies |
|---|---|---|---|---|---|---|---|---|
| Alabama | 12 | 0.75 | 8 | 1.00 | Yes | | 150 | 2.75 |
| California | 14 | 0.88 | 6 | 0.75 | | Yes | 3,144 | 2.63 |
| Florida | 12 | 0.75 | 6 | 0.75 | Yes | | 401 | 2.50 |
| West Virginia | 12 | 0.75 | 6 | 0.75 | Yes | | 7 | 2.50 |
| North Carolina | 12 | 0.75 | 5 | 0.63 | Yes | | 44 | 2.38 |
| Louisiana | 12 | 0.75 | 4 | 0.50 | Yes | | 57 | 2.25 |
| New Mexico | 12 | 0.75 | 4 | 0.50 | Yes | | 25 | 2.25 |
| Maryland | 14 | 0.88 | 2 | 0.25 | | Yes | 93 | 2.13 |
| Tennessee | 12 | 0.75 | 3 | 0.38 | | Yes | 48 | 2.13 |
| Virginia | 10 | 0.63 | 4 | 0.50 | Yes | | 736 | 2.13 |
| Kentucky | 7 | 0.44 | 5 | 0.63 | Yes | | 149 | 2.06 |
| Nevada | 8 | 0.50 | 4 | 0.50 | Yes | | 10 | 2.00 |
| South Carolina | 12 | 0.75 | 2 | 0.25 | Yes | | | 2.00 |
| Texas | 12 | 0.75 | 2 | 0.25 | Yes | | 146 | 2.00 |
| Colorado | 8 | 0.50 | 3 | 0.38 | Yes | | | 1.88 |
| Indiana | 6 | 0.38 | 4 | 0.50 | Yes | | 39 | 1.88 |
| Arizona | 12 | 0.75 | 8 | 1.00 | | | | 1.75 |
| Utah | 16 | 1.00 | 6 | 0.75 | | 2004 | | 1.75 |
| Massachusetts | 7 | 0.44 | 2 | 0.25 | | Yes | 2 | 1.69 |
| Connecticut | 6 | 0.38 | 2 | 0.25 | | Yes | 28 | 1.63 |
| Delaware | 6 | 0.38 | 2 | 0.25 | Yes | | | 1.63 |
| New York | 4 | 0.25 | 3 | 0.38 | | Yes | 105 | 1.63 |
| Oregon | 6 | 0.38 | 2 | 0.25 | Yes | | 47 | 1.63 |
| Vermont | 6 | 0.38 | 2 | 0.25 | | Yes | 39 | 1.63 |
| Michigan | 5 | 0.31 | 2 | 0.25 | Yes | | 92 | 1.56 |
| Wisconsin | 5 | 0.31 | 2 | 0.25 | | Yes | 223 | 1.56 |
| Idaho | 12 | 0.75 | 6 | 0.75 | | | | 1.50 |
| Kansas | 4 | 0.25 | 2 | 0.25 | Yes | | 3 | 1.50 |
| Missouri | 4 | 0.25 | 2 | 0.25 | | Yes | | 1.50 |
| Oklahoma | 6 | 0.38 | 1 | 0.13 | | Yes | 25 | 1.50 |
| Mississippi | 14 | 0.88 | 4 | 0.50 | 2002 | | | 1.38 |
| Arkansas | 11 | 0.69 | 3 | 0.38 | 2004 | | | 1.06 |
| Washington | 8 | 0.50 | 4 | 0.50 | future | | | 1.00 |
| Alaska | 10 | 0.63 | 2 | 0.25 | 2000 | | | 0.88 |
| Georgia | 10 | 0.63 | 2 | 0.25 | 2002 | | | 0.88 |
| South Dakota | 7 | 0.44 | 3 | 0.38 | | | | 0.81 |
| Ohio | 4 | 0.25 | 4 | 0.50 | | | | 0.75 |
| Rhode Island | 6 | 0.38 | 3 | 0.38 | | future | | 0.75 |
| Pennsylvania | 5 | 0.31 | 3 | 0.38 | | | | 0.69 |
| Hawaii | 6 | 0.38 | 2 | 0.25 | | | | 0.63 |
| Illinois | 6 | 0.38 | 2 | 0.25 | 2002 | | | 0.63 |
| North Dakota | 6 | 0.38 | 2 | 0.25 | | | | 0.63 |
| Iowa | 4 | 0.25 | 2 | 0.25 | | | | 0.50 |
| Maine | 4 | 0.25 | 2 | 0.25 | | | | 0.50 |
| Minnesota | 6 | 0.38 | 1 | 0.13 | | | | 0.50 |
| Montana | 4 | 0.25 | 2 | 0.25 | | | | 0.50 |
| New Hampshire | 4 | 0.25 | 2 | 0.25 | | | | 0.50 |
| New Jersey | 4 | 0.25 | 2 | 0.25 | | | | 0.50 |
| Wyoming | 4 | 0.25 | 2 | 0.25 | | | | 0.50 |
| Nebraska | 2 | 0.13 | 1 | 0.13 | | | | 0.25 |

SOURCE: Adapted by the author from *Education Week* 2001b.

[a] Sixteen total elementary and middle school English and mathematics tests were the highest number given; states giving sixteen tests were given a score of 1, all other states were given a fraction of 1 based on number of tests.

[b] Eight total high school English and mathematics tests were the highest number given; states giving eight tests were given a score of 1, all other states were given a fraction of 1 based on number of tests.

[c] A score of 1 is given to states that assign ratings to all the schools as of 2000–2001. A few more states are expected to do so starting in 2002.

[d] A score of 1 is given to states that identify low-performing schools as of 2000–2001. A few more states are expected to do so in the future.

**Table 12-6** Education Freedom in the States

| State | EFI 2001 score | EFI 2001 rank | EFI 2000 rank | Change in rank | Charter score | Private score | Home-school score | Public choice score |
|---|---|---|---|---|---|---|---|---|
| Arizona | 2.94 | 1 | 1 | 0 | 4.69 | 0.31 | 1.86 | 4.91 |
| New Jersey | 2.43 | 2 | 4 | 2 | 1.38 | 0.85 | 2.93 | 4.57 |
| Delaware | 2.4 | 3 | 7 | 4 | 2.28 | 0.57 | 1.85 | 4.90 |
| Florida | 2.39 | 4 | 35 | 31 | 1.91 | 2.51 | 1.13 | 4.01 |
| Minnesota | 2.37 | 5 | 2 | −3 | 1.75 | 1.70 | 1.12 | 4.93 |
| Wisconsin | 2.36 | 6 | 3 | −3 | 1.47 | 0.93 | 2.11 | 4.94 |
| Texas | 2.32 | 7 | 6 | −1 | 1.59 | 0.28 | 2.93 | 4.50 |
| Missouri | 2.26 | 8 | 19 | 11 | 1.27 | 0.28 | 2.93 | 4.55 |
| Michigan | 2.26 | 9 | 11 | 2 | 1.94 | 0.57 | 1.57 | 4.95 |
| Oklahoma | 2.23 | 10 | 31 | 21 | 1.05 | 0.00 | 2.93 | 4.95 |
| Idaho | 2.20 | 11 | 12 | 1 | 1.02 | 0.00 | 2.93 | 4.84 |
| Colorado | 2.16 | 12 | 8 | −4 | 1.84 | 0.28 | 1.67 | 4.84 |
| Indiana | 2.15 | 13 | 25 | 12 | 1.25 | 0.57 | 2.27 | 4.53 |
| California | 2.11 | 14 | 21 | 7 | 1.71 | 0.57 | 1.69 | 4.49 |
| Maine | 2.09 | 15 | 9 | −6 | 0.00 | 2.36 | 1.45 | 4.57 |
| Oregon | 2.06 | 16 | 5 | −11 | 1.26 | 0.57 | 2.32 | 4.08 |
| New Hampshire | 2.04 | 17 | 16 | −1 | 0.85 | 0.85 | 1.87 | 4.57 |
| Nebraska | 2.02 | 18 | 13 | −5 | 0.00 | 0.85 | 2.26 | 4.96 |
| New Mexico | 2.02 | 19 | 23 | 4 | 1.03 | 0.28 | 2.43 | 4.31 |
| Kansas | 1.96 | 20 | 30 | 10 | 0.60 | 0.57 | 2.54 | 4.13 |
| Illinois | 1.94 | 21 | 24 | 3 | 0.96 | 1.16 | 1.46 | 4.16 |
| Pennsylvania | 1.86 | 22 | 33 | 11 | 1.40 | 1.16 | 0.75 | 4.14 |
| Louisiana | 1.84 | 23 | 26 | 3 | 1.00 | 0.85 | 1.18 | 4.36 |
| Connecticut | 1.84 | 24 | 10 | −14 | 0.87 | 0.85 | 0.72 | 4.94 |
| Vermont | 1.83 | 25 | 28 | 3 | 0.00 | 1.82 | 1.30 | 4.19 |
| Ohio | 1.82 | 26 | 18 | −8 | 1.26 | 0.91 | 0.57 | 4.55 |
| North Carolina | 1.80 | 27 | 38 | 11 | 1.69 | 0.00 | 1.51 | 4.00 |
| Washington | 1.79 | 28 | 20 | −8 | 0.00 | 0.57 | 1.70 | 4.91 |
| Montana | 1.79 | 29 | 37 | 8 | 0.00 | 0.28 | 2.73 | 4.14 |
| Wyoming | 1.79 | 30 | 40 | 10 | 0.54 | 0.00 | 2.39 | 4.22 |
| South Dakota | 1.78 | 31 | 15 | −16 | 0.00 | 0.00 | 2.23 | 4.90 |
| Arkansas | 1.76 | 32 | 17 | −15 | 0.48 | 0.00 | 1.62 | 4.94 |
| Iowa | 1.76 | 33 | 14 | −19 | 0.00 | 1.00 | 1.09 | 4.95 |
| New York | 1.75 | 34 | 27 | −7 | 1.29 | 0.85 | 0.32 | 4.53 |
| Georgia | 1.68 | 35 | 41 | 6 | 1.18 | 0.00 | 1.51 | 4.04 |
| Massachusetts | 1.66 | 36 | 22 | −14 | 1.53 | 0.57 | 0.00 | 4.56 |
| Mississippi | 1.64 | 37 | 34 | −3 | 0.08 | 0.28 | 2.11 | 4.11 |
| Alaska | 1.62 | 38 | 42 | 4 | 1.03 | 0.28 | 2.86 | 2.30 |
| South Carolina | 1.59 | 39 | 43 | 4 | 1.25 | 0.00 | 1.05 | 4.05 |
| Tennessee | 1.53 | 40 | 36 | −4 | 0.00 | 0.28 | 0.98 | 4.86 |
| Alabama | 1.50 | 41 | 39 | −2 | 0.00 | 0.00 | 1.95 | 4.06 |
| Virginia | 1.47 | 42 | 44 | 2 | 0.45 | 0.00 | 1.37 | 4.04 |
| Kentucky | 1.44 | 43 | 47 | 4 | 0.00 | 0.00 | 1.64 | 4.12 |
| North Dakota | 1.43 | 44 | 32 | −12 | 0.00 | 0.28 | 0.49 | 4.93 |
| Nevada | 1.40 | 45 | 48 | 3 | 1.03 | 0.28 | 1.46 | 2.84 |
| Maryland | 1.37 | 46 | 46 | 0 | 0.00 | 0.28 | 1.53 | 3.68 |
| West Virginia | 1.36 | 47 | 49 | 2 | 0.00 | 0.85 | 0.16 | 4.45 |
| Rhode Island | 1.35 | 48 | 45 | −3 | 0.68 | 0.57 | 0.00 | 4.14 |
| Utah | 1.34 | 49 | 29 | −20 | 0.87 | 0.00 | 0.00 | 4.48 |
| Hawaii | 0.88 | 50 | 50 | 0 | 1.56 | 0.00 | 1.21 | 0.75 |
| Average: | 1.8676 | | | | 0.9608 | 0.5604 | 1.6136 | 4.3374 |

SOURCE: Compiled from the *2001 Education Freedom Index,* as developed by Jay P. Greene, The Manhattan Institute for Policy Research, 2002.

Perhaps the most important market-like initiative is the charter school reform. With thirty-seven states and the District of Columbia operating a total of over 2,000 charter schools, charter school reform takes on a national character as an alternative to failing public schools. As new charter schools are established to meet rising parental demands, a key issue is the quality of the schooling opportunities provided to students in various settings. Charter schools of the 1990s were designed to circumscribe institutional constraints such as union power. By relaxing school admissions policy on student selection, public charter schools aim to keep parents satisfied with the public schools instead of opting for nonpublic schools (Raywid 1985; Wong 1992).

Although charter schools are labeled as public schools, they are distinctive in several major aspects. The school's charter or contract explicitly states the conditions and expectations for outcome-based performance (Bierlein 1997; Hill 1997). The authorizing agency can be the local school board or other legal entities such as universities. Once established, charter schools enjoy substantial autonomy in setting teachers' salaries and work conditions, although they are bound by state regulations regarding safety, health, dismissal, and civil rights. School funding follows students to the charter schools, which are operated on a multiyear renewable contract.

Thirty-six states and the District of Columbia have passed laws providing for the creation of charter schools. In the 1999–2000 academic year, 1,689 charter schools were in operation, and an additional 305 were approved to open in 2000–2001. At least one district in California has converted to a system of charter (or contract) schools. Enrollment in charter schools increased to about 2.5 percent of the nation's public school student population in 1999–2000. In Arizona, California, and Michigan, charter enrollment figures are much higher.

Do charter schools create a competitive environment that causes regular public schools to make greater efforts to raise their performance? The rationale of competition has been widely cited, but the evidence in support of this claim is mixed (see Wong and Shen 2001).

Competitive effects of charter schools are constrained by legislative compromise. Based on interviews and policy/legal analysis in four states, Hassel (1999) found that legislative compromise has played a significant role in reducing the competitive impact of charter schools. Laws that cap the number of charter schools, cushion the financial blow to traditional district schools, or reduce the autonomy of charter schools all contribute to reducing the impact a charter school can make.

In a study of five urban districts, Teske and his associates (2001) attributed the modest effects of competition to several factors. The effects of charter school competition are lessened by financial cushioning and by a lack of school-level penalties for losing students to charter schools. Growing student populations may also reduce the competitive effects; even though traditional public schools are losing relative market share, the absolute number of their students remains constant. In districts where charter schools did have an impact, piecemeal rather than system-wide changes were made, mostly concerned with expanding the school day by offering new add-on programs.

Charter schools also vary in their effects on racial segregation or stratification, a concern widely shared by skeptics of school choice initiatives. Wong and Shen (2001), for example, found that California and Michigan have quite different charter school landscapes. Although each state has relatively strong charter legislation and a larger number of charter schools, the two states differ in terms of innovation and stratification effects. In California, for example, there is a clustering of high-achieving students by race. In Michigan, there seems to be less stratification. Other differences between the two states include the extensive involvement of higher education institutions in Michigan and the large number of home-school–focused charter schools in California. These and other differences may account for the varying degree of stratification in the two states.

Another prominent market-like reform is the state-funded voucher experiments in Milwaukee and Cleveland. These experiments signal that an unusual kind of political alliance has emerged to address the growing concerns with failing public schools in the inner city. This new alliance consists of two core segments of the Republican and Democratic parties. Frustrated with the low quality of schooling opportunities for their constituencies, lawmakers and religious and community leaders in African American neighborhoods (a traditional core of the Democratic party) have parted company with the teachers' union (another Democratic core) and supported a more radical solution to the crisis in urban education. In Milwaukee, Polly Williams, a black state lawmaker, and Howard Fuller, a black activist and former superintendent, became the most outspoken supporters of the state-funded voucher program, which began in 1990. In Cleveland, Fannie Lewis, a Democratic member of the city council, spearheaded the 1994 passage of the choice program in the Ohio legislature.

Joining the Democratic core were Republican governors and their business allies who saw choice as a mechanism not only to improve school performance and market efficiency but also to weaken the influence of the teachers' union. In both Milwaukee and Cleveland, this unique alliance was gradually broadened to include the Catholic Church and a wide range of business interest groups. Seeing a broadening of support, key proponents of choice have attempted to increase the demand and supply of choice programs. For example, Milwaukee's mayor, John Norquist, favored raising the income ceiling on eligibility. Pro–school choice advocacy groups, such as the Heartland Institute in Chicago, continue to play an active role in organizing lobbying efforts in state capitals.

The Cleveland voucher program has gained national prominence. The program started in the fall of 1996 and was immediately challenged in court for violating the "establishment clause," as students were allowed to choose religious schools. The program was restricted to lower elementary grades during the initial phase. In its first year, about two-thirds of the nearly 2,000 participants enrolled in kindergarten or first grade, and about 25 percent had attended private schools in previous years.

The Cleveland program was challenged on the ground that over 90 percent of its students enroll in sectarian schools. In December 2000 a federal appeals court ruled that the enrollment pattern had the "impermissible effect of promoting sectarian schools." But in June 2002 the U.S. Supreme Court ruled 5-4 that the Cleveland voucher program did not violate the First Amendment's Establishment Clause, which separates the affairs of religious institutions and the government.

The Supreme Court's *Zelman v. Simmons-Harris* (2002) decision generates two long-lasting consequences that are likely to redefine public educational institution. First, the decision is likely to spread the voucher experiment to a growing number of states, just like the charter school movement over the last decade. Second, with state funding support, parental demand for school choice will grow. In response, diverse suppliers of schooling service will emerge. These include faith-based organizations, discontented parents and teachers, as well as non-profit and community-based organizations. If the voucher movement grows as fast as the charter school reform, the supply of public schooling in the next ten years will be significantly different than the existing service delivery system. However, the voucher movement, like the charter school reform, may be tied to state policies promoting greater accountability (Fiske and Ladd 2000). As parents exercise school selection, the information needed for accountability and school performance will not subside.

### Takeover As a Reform Strategy

In response to the public call for accountability, states have begun to allow for takeover of the school district, either by a state authority or by the mayor. Most states have had provisions for state takeover of local school districts, but states rarely invoked them, except in cases of clear financial mismanagement or illegal activity (Cibulka 1999). Some of the more recent state takeover laws focus more on breaches of academic accountability. Twenty-four states allow state takeover of local school districts, permitting state officials to exert authority over a district in the case of "academic bankruptcy" or woefully low-performing schools, but only eleven states have exercised the law.

School district takeover is currently becoming an important political and policy issue in many states. In Missouri, for instance, school districts in both the City of St. Louis and Kansas City are facing possible takeovers by the State Board of Education (*St. Louis Post-Dispatch* 2001; *Kansas City Star* 2001). In New York there is discussion of a takeover by state education officials of the Roosevelt school district on Long Island (*Education Week* 2001). In these and other instances, state or mayoral takeover seems to be an attractive option to turn around failing school districts.

In analyzing the facilitating factors and barriers for turning around failed schools, the most important distinction is between "city/mayoral" vs. "state" takeovers. In one sense, this is an artificial distinction. In all cases the state authorizes mayoral takeover. However, mayoral takeovers are unique because instead of granting power to a state-selected oversight board, the state allows a mayor and mayor-appointed officials to run the district.

Several differences are seen between districts under mayoral control and those that were subject to state takeover (Wong and Shen 2002). Although the racial makeup of the student body is similar across the two types of districts, city takeover districts have more than four times the number of schools than the state takeover districts, and about five times the number of students to handle. Thus when mayors decide to take over the educational system, they take on an enormous challenge.

Mayoral takeover cities also differ from state takeovers because, unlike state-appointed superintendents, mayors are politically accountable to their constituents. If parents and residents are unhappy with the progress of educational reform, they can choose to vote the mayor out of office. When state-appointed officials are put in charge, however, it is sometimes difficult to see who is accountable if the district does not improve.

Another important difference between city and state takeovers is the balance of revenue coming from city vs. state sources. Mayoral takeover districts receive a significantly larger percentage of their education revenue from local sources. With more revenue from local sources, mayors in these districts have more leverage to ask for and gain increased local control of the schools. In the state districts, state revenue makes up about 70 percent of total revenue, and this number increased from 1992 to 1997. In contrast, the mayoral takeover districts receive approximately 50 percent of their total revenue from the state. We can also interpret this difference in terms of increased accountability. State takeover districts are more accountable to the state than city takeover districts because in the state takeover districts, states are funding a greater portion of total district revenue. In city takeovers, there is greater accountability to local taxpayers because local taxpayers fund a majority of the district's revenue.

To be sure, there are variations in the implementation of takeover reform. Chicago, Boston, and Cleveland are examples of an integrated governance structure, where the mayor exercises fairly complete control over all aspects of the district functions (Wong and Shen 2002). Integrated governance in these cities has been facilitated by the following factors: (1) Mayoral vision on outcome-based accountability; (2) broad public dissatisfaction with "a crisis" in school performance over several years preceding integrated governance; (3) state leadership that is dominated by Republicans who are willing to "empower" the mayoral office to address school problems; (4) strong business support that has translated into adoption of corporate management practices to address complex bureaucratic problems in school districts; and (5) weakened legitimacy of traditionally powerful service provider groups (unions) and service demand groups (racial and neighborhood-based groups).

Mayors who maintain integrated governance have indicated a strong commitment to enhance management efficiency in their city services. These mayors are keenly aware of the ongoing challenge of retaining productive resources within the city (Tiebout 1956). Unless city services provide optimal cost-benefit ratios to the middle class, cities are likely to face a declining revenue base as taxpayers move to more desirable areas nearby. To stem the flight, these mayors have decided to bring public schools into the overall city strategy to improve service quality and management. An insulated school system would mean business as usual, where the mayor lacks direct control over the use of about one-third of the local property tax revenues. To the extent that schools can become an economic development strategy for the city as a whole, these mayors may be able to restore public confidence in public schools, thereby changing the market-like dynamics of middle class migration to the suburbs.

In three other cities, Oakland, Calif., Washington, D.C., and Baltimore, the takeovers look a little different. Washington, D.C., and Baltimore can be characterized as maintaining a quasi-integrated governance system. The mayor, or in the case of Washington, D.C., a citywide reform board, exercises some formal control over the school system as a whole. Yet the degree of control, when compared to the three cases of integrated governance, is less than complete. These three "quasi-integrated" systems are still dominated by traditional politics in education and are not moving toward an accountability-based policy framework. Several political barriers to integrated governance exist in Washington, D.C., and Baltimore. For example, in Baltimore the legislature is not willing to give power directly to the mayor because of partisan and territorial politics. The mayor actually lost some of his authority, sharing it now with the governor and the Maryland state department of education. In D.C., the higher-level legislative body, the Congress, stripped the city of major functional authority and would not relinquish it until D.C. improved its management. In Oakland, Mayor Jerry Brown is still trying to establish control over the school district. He has made progress, but has not been able to avoid the political quarrels that prevent systemic change in the district.

State takeovers in Compton, Calif., and Lawrence, Mass., have led to bitter fights between the state and local authorities. Assessing the state takeovers in New Jersey and elsewhere before 1996, *Education Week* (1996) observed that, "in case after case, when state administrators have tried to elbow out local officials and run a failing district themselves, improvements have come at the heavy cost of lawsuits, bitter media battles, and confused and angry teachers and parents." An analysis of standardized testing calendars highlights a difference in accountability between mayoral and state takeovers, and that may be a source of discontent in the state takeover cases (Wong and Shen 2002). In the state takeover city of Hartford, Conn., for instance, the public has little to say about the future of superintendent Tony Amato. The state-appointed board of trustees makes the hiring decision, and many residents believe that Amato will leave for a larger district. This rumor started when, in Spring 2000, Amato was "caught applying for the superintendent's post in San Francisco even though his current contract had not expired—and in spite of his pledges to stay in Hartford for a while" (*Hartford Courant* 2000a). Also at issue is the perception that the state is infringing on local control. Again in Hartford, Amato angered parents and local residents when he "made sweeping generalizations about the inadequacy of music programs" (*Hartford Courant* 2000b).

Whether mayoral control can be widely adopted beyond these few cities depends on various conditions. First, the political capital of the mayor is a key element. Second, the appointment of competent administrators and board members by the mayor is a political process. Third, governance improvement needs to permeate through a complex multi-layered school policy system. For example, mayoral control in Baltimore has recently been constrained by gubernatorial involvement in school board appointments. Finally, governance reform needs to facilitate effective educational practices in order to improve student performance.

## HIGHER EDUCATION AS A DISTINCT POLICY ARENA

When compared to elementary and secondary education, higher education has several structural features that tend to shape how politics is played out at the state level. First, higher education is often seen by state political leaders as central to their effort to promote economic growth. With increasing frequency, governors ally with their state higher education institutions to compete for business investment in high tech and manufacturing industries. Research grants and patents on invention are touted as major sources for job creation. Consequently, state universities are run more like a business corporation than a public agency (Lucas 1994).

Further, universities and colleges are not restricted by compulsory attendance laws. State government has continued to support student choice of institutions and programs of study. In fact, students' freedom to select has been strengthened by a number of federal and state grants and loans that are provided directly to eligible individual students, who in turn can take the grants and loans to another institution. In light of the market-like dynamics in student enrollment, which is further complicated by a fluid faculty labor market, universities have maintained substantial autonomy over their academic mission, program, and student admissions. While an increasing number of states have created statewide coordinating boards for oversight purposes (Hearn and Griswold 1994; Hines 1988), these boards seldom take over the management of under-performing institutions (as in the case of state and city takeover of low-performing districts and schools).

Finally, higher education has increasingly become a contested terrain over social and moral issues. According to a content analysis of 163 ballot measures between 1993 and 2000, McLendon and Eddings (2002) found 12 highly politicized ballot measures on issues that ranged from race-based admissions policy, homosexual rights, English as the official language, and state lotteries. The authors observed that "the higher education community became very deeply involved in the politics of ballot passage and defeat for many of these issues" (McLendon and Eddings 2002, 211). In short, morality-based, high salience politics is likely to shape public debate on the role of higher education across the states.

## CONCLUSION

The twentieth century brought about many changes in public school governance. Among the most significant changes are the rapid consolidation of districts, increase in state fiscal role, growth of federally funded programs for the disadvantaged, and the expansion of school choice programs. Politically, there has been a greater involvement of governors, legislatures, and mayors in public schools in recent years. This latest surge of political leadership in education is ironic. In the beginning decades of the twentieth century, partisan leadership and politics were on retreat due to the reform efforts of the Progressive movement. It was only during the racial and urban crisis of the 1950s and 1960s that political leaders felt the political pressure to mediate conflicts in public schools. However, by the late 1980s and throughout the 1990s, an increasing number of governors and big-city mayors have made the decision to lead the public school system. Clearly, the relationship between the political leaders and the schools has been reconfigured over the last century.

Regardless of who is in charge, there are significant challenges to improving public education in America. Thirty percent of children in urban areas are poor compared to 18 percent for the nation as a whole. Urban schools are twice as likely to enroll minority children than the national average. While only 23 percent of fourth-graders in high poverty schools performed at the basic level or higher in the National Assessment of Educational Progress reading tests, almost 70 percent of their peers did so in schools with less poverty outside the urban setting (Wong 1999). In the context of a global, networked economy, schools are increasingly divided by technological know-how. Even more fundamental is the uneven distribution of teaching quality among schools and districts.

In response to public demands for better school performance, states have initiated a wide range of reform initiatives. This chapter has discussed several of these reforms, including efforts to narrow funding disparity, strengthen accountability, expand schooling choice, and takeover of failing districts and schools. Like previous reforms, the current reforms face political resistance and organizational barriers. At the same time, they promise to improve the life chances of some of the program participants. Nevertheless, for students who are keen on understanding and improving the quality of public schools, the current reforms will provide a rich empirical base for charting the next steps. Indeed, this is an exciting time to choose educational politics and governance as a field of study.

## REFERENCES

Advisory Commission on Intergovernmental Relations (ACIR). 1992. *Significant Features of Fiscal Federalism.* Vol. 2. Washington, D.C.: ACIR. Table R-2.
———. 1980. *Significant Features of Fiscal Federalism.* Washington, D.C.: ACIR.
Berke, Joel, Margaret Goertz, and Richard Coley. 1984. *Politicians, Judges, and City Schools: Reforming School Finance in New York.* New York: Russell Sage Foundation.
Bierlein, Louann. 1997. "The Charter School Movement." In *New Schools for a New Century,* edited by D. Ravitch and J. Viteritti. New Haven, Conn.: Yale University Press.

Cibulka, James. 1999. "Moving Toward An Accountable System of K-12 Education: Alternative Approaches and Challenges." In *Handbook of Educational Policy*, edited by G. Cizek. San Diego, Calif.: Academic Press.

Citrin, Jack. 1984. "Introduction: The Legacy of Proposition 13." In *California and the American Tax Revolt*, edited by T. Schwadron. Berkeley and Los Angeles: University of California Press.

Cole, Stephen. 1969. *The Unionization of Teachers: A Case Study of the United Federation of Teachers*. New York: Praeger.

de Tocqueville, Alexis. 2000. *Democracy in America*. Edited and translated by H. Mansfield and D. Winthrop. Chicago: University of Chicago Press.

Education Commission of the States. 2003. *A Report on State Progress in No Child Left Behind*. Education Commission of the States website at www.ecs.org. Accessed January 2003.

*Education Week*. 2002. "Quality Counts 2002: Building Blocks for Success." January 10, 68–70.

———. 2001a. "N.Y. State Eyes District Takeover." March 28.

———. 2001b. "Quality Counts 2001: A Better Balance." http//educationweek.org/sreports/qc01/articles/qc01story.cfm?slug=17exec_sum.h20

———. 1996. "Ill Will Comes With Territory In Takeovers." June 12.

Elazar, Daniel. 1972. *American Federalism: A View from the States*. 2d ed. New York: Thomas Y. Crowell.

Elementary and Secondary Education Act of 1965. Pub L. No. 89-10, Sec 201, 79 Stat. 27 (1965). Codified as amended at 20 U.S.C. Sec 6301 (2002).

Federal Reserve Bank of Chicago. 1994. *Chicago Fed Letter*. Chicago: Federal Reserve Bank of Chicago. May, No. 81.

Fiske, Edward, and Helen Ladd. 2000. *When Schools Compete: A Cautionary Tale*. Washington D.C.: Brookings Institution.

Gold, Stephen. 1985. "State Aid for Local Schools: Trends and Prospects." In *Public Schools: Issues in Budgeting and Financial Management*, edited by John Augenblick. New Brunswick, N.J.: Transaction.

Greene, Jay. 2002. *2001 Education Freedom Index*. New York: The Manhattan Institute.

Greenhouse, Linda. 2002. "Ruling in Ohio Case: Majority Says Cleveland Program Offers 'True Private Choice.'" *New York Times*, June 28, A1.

Grimshaw, William. 1979. *Union Rule in the Schools*. Lexington, Mass.: D.C. Heath.

Guthrie, James, Walter Garms, and Lawrence Pierce. 1988. *School Finance and Education Policy*. Englewood Cliffs, N.J.: Prentice Hall.

Hamilton, Alexander, James Madison, and John Jay. 1961. *The Federalist Papers*. New York: Mentor.

Harp, Lonnie. 1990. "Finance Reform Is Struck Down by Texas Judge." *Education Week*. October 3, 1.

*Hartford Courant*. 2000a. "Investing In Mr. Amato." June 5.

———. 2000b. "Amato's Shooting From Hip Continues To Backfire." July 23.

Hassel, Bryan. 1999. *The Charter School Challenge: Avoiding the Pitfalls, Fulfilling the Promise*. Washington D.C.: Brookings Institution.

Hearn, James, and Carolyn Griswold. 1994. "State-Level Centralization and Policy Innovation in U.S. Postsecondary Education." *Educational Evaluation and Policy Analysis* 16: 161–190.

Hill, Paul. 1997. "Contracting in Public Education." In *New Schools for a New Century*, edited by Diana Ravitch and Joseph Viteritti. New Haven, Conn.: Yale University Press.

Hines, Edward. 1988. *Higher Education and State Governments*. ASHEERIC Higher Education Report No.5. Washington D.C.: Association for the Study of Higher Education.

Hirschman, Albert. 1971. *Exit, Voice, and Loyalty*. Cambridge, Mass.: Harvard University Press.

Jacobson, Linda. 1997. "Ga. Governor Purges Board to End Bickering with Schrenko." *Education Week*. January 15, 21.

*Kansas City Star*. 2001. "Missouri Lawmakers Again Weigh State Takeover of KC School District." April 23.

Kirst, Michael W. 1980. "Review of Dilemmas in School Finance." *American Journal of Education* 88(4): 502–505.

Kirst, Michael W., and S. Somers. 1981. "California Educational Interest Groups: Collective Action as a Logical Response to Proposition 13." *Education and Urban Society* 13(2): 235–256.

Leppert, Jack, Larry Huxel, Walter Garms, and Heber Fuller. 1976. "Pupils Weighting Programs in School Finance Reform." In *School Finance Reform: A Legislator's Handbook,* edited by Joseph Callahan and William Wilken. Washington D.C.: National Conference of State Legislators.

Levin, Betsy, et al. 1972. *Paying for Public Schools: Issues of School Finance in California.* Washington D.C.: Urban Institute.

Loveless, Tom, ed. 2001. *Conflicting Missions? Teachers Unions and Education Reform.* Washington, D.C.: Brookings Institution.

Lucas, Christopher. 1994. *American Higher Education: A History.* New York: St. Martin's Press.

McDermott, Kathleen. 1999. *Controlling Public Education: Localism versus Equity.* Lawrence: University Press of Kansas.

McDonnell, Lorraine, and Anthony Pascal. 1979. *Organized Teachers in American Schools.* Santa Monica, Calif.: Rand Corporation.

McLendon, Michael, and Stuart Eddings. 2002. "Direct Democracy and Higher Education: The State Ballot as an Instrument of Higher Education Policy Making." *Educational Policy* 16(1): 193–218.

Mirel, Jeffrey. 1993. *The Rise and Fall of an Urban School System: Detroit, 1907–81.* Ann Arbor: University of Michigan Press.

Moe, Terry. 2001. *Schools, Vouchers, and the American Public.* Washington, D.C.: Brookings Institution.

Mullins, Daniel, and Phillip Joyce. 1995. *Tax and Expenditure Limitations and State and Local Fiscal Structures.* Center for Urban Policy and Environment, School of Public and Environmental Affairs, Indiana University. December.

Orfield, Gary, and Susan Eaton. 1996. *Dismantling Desegregation.* New York: New Press.

Peterson, Paul E., Barry G. Rabe, and Kenneth K. Wong. 1986. *When Federalism Works.* Washington, D.C.: Brookings Institution.

Phi Delta Kappa. 1984. *Gallup Polls of Attitudes toward Education 1969–1984: A Topical Summary.* Bloomington, Ind.: Phi Delta Kappa.

Piele, Philip, and John Hall. 1973. *Budget, Bonds, and Ballots.* Lexington, Mass.: Lexington.

Raywid, Mary Ann. 1985. "Family Choice Arrangements in Public Schools: A Review of Literature." *Review in Educational Research* 55(4): 435–467.

Rosenthal, Alan, and Susan Fuhrman. 1981. *Legislative Education Leadership in the States.* Washington, D.C.: Institute for Educational Leadership.

*St. Louis Post-Dispatch.* 2001. "Most Candidates Say They Would Take Over Schools If They Fail." February 28.

"State Education Governance at a Glance." 2002. *The State Education Standard* Spring: 38–42.

Sundquist, James L. 1968. *Politics and Policy: The Eisenhower, Kennedy, and Johnson Years.* Washington, D.C.: Brookings Institution.

Teske, Paul, Mark Schneider, Jack Buckley, and Sara Clark. 2001. "Can Charter Schools Change Traditional Public Schools?" In *Charters, Vouchers and Public Education,* edited by Paul Peterson and David Campbell. Washington D.C.: Brookings Institution, 188–214.

Tiebout, Charles. 1956. "A Pure Theory of Local Expenditures." *Journal of Political Economy* 64: 416–424.

Timar, Tom. 1992. "Urban Politics and State School Finance in the 1980s." In *The Politics of Urban Education in the United States,* edited by John Cibulka, Rodney Reed, and Kenneth Wong. London: Falmer Press.

Urban Institute. 1983. *State and Local Fiscal Relations in the Early 1980s.* Washington, D.C.: Urban Institute.

U.S. Bureau of the Census. 1999. *Education Finance Survey.* Washington, D.C.: Government Printing Office.

Wilkerson, Isabel. 1993. "Tiring of Cuts, School District Plans to Close Schools." *New York Times,* March 21, 20.

Williams, M. 1982. "Earthquakes or Tremors? Tax and Expenditure Limitations and School Finance." In *The Changing Politics of School Finance,* edited by Nelda Cambron-McCabe and Allan Odden. Cambridge, Mass.: Ballinger.

Wirt, Frederick. 1977. "School Policy Culture and State Decentralization." In *The Politics of Education,* edited by Jay Scribner. Chicago: University of Chicago Press.

Wise, Arthur. 1972. *Rich Schools, Poor Schools: The Promise of Equal Educational Opportunity.* Chicago: University of Chicago Press.

Wong, Kenneth. 1999. *Funding Public Schools: Politics and Policy.* Lawrence: University Press of Kansas.

———. 1992. "The Politics of Urban Education as a Field of Study: An Interpretive Analysis." In *The Politics of Urban Education,* edited by Cibulka, Reed, and Wong, 3–26.

———. 1990. *City Choices: Education and Housing.* Albany: State University of New York Press.

Wong, Kenneth, and Francis Shen. 2002. "Do School District Takeovers Work? Assessing the Effectiveness of City and State Takeover as a School Reform Strategy." *State Education Standard* Spring: 19–23.

———. 2001. "Institutional Effects of Charter Schools: Innovation and Segregation." Paper presented at the annual meeting of the American Educational Research Association, Seattle, April 10–14.

## SUGGESTED READINGS

Cremin, Lawrence. *American Education: The Metropolitan Experience 1876–1980.* New York: Harper and Row, 1988. This historical study examines the transformation of schools and colleges and of the media of popular communication within the broader societal context.

Guthrie, James, Walter Garms, and Lawrence Pierce. *School Finance and Education Policy.* Englewood Cliffs, N.J.: Prentice Hall, 1988. This book offers a comprehensive treatment of school finance politics and policy.

Gutmann, Amy. *Democratic Education.* Princeton: Princeton University Press, 1987. This study proposes a democratic theory of education. The author addresses fundamental issues of values, aims, control, and participation.

Mintrom, Michael. *Policy Entrepreneurs and School Choice.* Washington D.C.: Georgetown University Press, 2000. This study examines the leadership role in promoting educational innovation and reform.

Peterson, Paul, Barry Rabe, and Kenneth Wong. *When Federalism Works.* Washington D.C.: Brookings Institution, 1986. This book proposes a differentiated understanding of the politics in implementing federal programs in education, housing, and health care. While redistributive programs involve more conflicts, developmental policy is characterized by state and local cooperation.

Wong, Kenneth, and Francis Shen. "Do School District Takeovers Work? Assessing the Effectiveness of City and State Takeovers as a School Reform Strategy." *State Education Standard* Spring 2002:19–23. Based on an analysis of management and student performance data in several districts, the authors assess the impact of takeover strategy on issues of accountability and performance.

CHAPTER 13

 # Economic and Social Regulation

MATTHEW ESHBAUGH-SOHA AND
KENNETH J. MEIER

Regulatory policy, those efforts by the government to alter the behavior of individuals and corporations, has many objectives. Ostensibly, most state governments cite the need to protect the "health, welfare, and morals" of the population, a state-level version of the federal concept of "public interest." From such broad, overreaching goals, several other, narrower regulatory objectives come to the forefront. First, much of regulation is designed to protect individuals from the ill effects of marketplaces. Markets, of course, work perfectly as long as there is perfect competition among the firms; everyone has full information about prices, products, and their effects, and there are no externalities (your consumption of a good does not negatively affect another individual). Correcting market failures is one goal of regulation. Second, at times these economic reasons for regulation get perverted by the political process, and regulation is used to protect firms or individuals from competition. Competition creates winners and losers; if some product is crucial (an adequate supply of fresh food, for example), then a logical argument can be made that regulation would benefit consumers by protecting producers from ruinous competition. Sometimes such arguments, however, simply reflect industry efforts to exploit consumers by avoiding competition. Third, states sometimes regulate for equity reasons. The current distribution of income or policy benefits may not coincide with the preferences of those in power. Most states, for example, require telephone companies and utility companies to provide a base level of services to poor individuals (or elderly) at a price below cost. These services are then subsidized by higher prices charged to other consumers. Fourth, states regulate to protect public goods, those goods that if provided to one person must be provided to all.

The classic case of public goods regulation used to be broadcasting when the indus-try relied exclusively on the over-the-air spectrum (rather than cable or other forms of delivery). The protection of clean air and water fall under this justifica-tion. Fifth, states regulate to reduce uncertainty. Insurance regulation, in part, is de-signed to reduce a policyholder's uncertainty that the insurance company will actu-ally be able to pay off a claim.

Given these many reasons for regulation, that states would regulate a wide vari-ety of industries and behaviors should come as no surprise. The following section provides a brief overview of the scope of state regulatory policy. To provide some order to the chaos, the second section introduces a policy framework that will focus on a few key concepts—salience, complexity, capacity, and ideology. Four case stud-ies of state regulation then use these concepts to show how regulatory policy is made.

## THE SCOPE OF REGULATION

Regulation in recent years is often divided into economic regulation and social regulation. Economic regulation concerns traditional economic questions such as who can provide a good, what price should be charged, and what situations should hold in the marketplace. Social regulation covers a much larger set of activities, everything from forcing businesses to avoid pollution to restricting access to abor-tion services. In practice, the distinction between social regulation and economic regulation is less clear since policies often have multiple goals and correcting an economic problem often has social consequences and vice versa.

### Economic Regulation

Traditional economic regulation focused on the three threats to perfect compe-tition—monopoly, information asymmetry, and externalities. Where and when state governments could apply economic regulation, however, is the subject of a long political struggle between states and the federal government (see Eisner 1993). In some cases the federal government preempted state regulation; in some cases regulation is shared; in other cases the states enjoy a virtual monopoly on regulatory authority.

When the federal government asserted control over interstate commerce, the regulation of intrastate commerce remained at the state level. States, as a result, can and do regulate prices and entry for intrastate railroads, trucking firms, and bus companies. One visible manifestation of the regulation of intrastate commerce shows up in the variation in state limits on trucks hauling double or triple trailers, a practice permitted by some states and banned by others.

The interstate versus intrastate distinction has led to a variety of cases of shared economic regulation (and social regulation). Intrastate telephone rates and local service rates are set by state governments while interstate rates are subject to federal jurisdiction (although the federal government prefers to let the market handle much of this regulation). Banks, savings and loans, credit unions, and other financial intermediaries can seek either a federal or a state charter, which determines if the state or the federal government will be the primary regulator (the federal government retains some jurisdiction through deposit insurance).

In some cases this joint jurisdiction has led to a competition between states and the federal government. In the 1980s and 1990s, as the federal government backed away from aggressive consumer protection regulation, state governments, often led by attorneys general, moved in. Similarly, state aggressiveness in antitrust policy or tobacco regulation policy has at times provided a spur to the recalcitrant hide of federal regulators.

The regulation of other major industries occurred on a case-by-case basis with little concern for a comprehensive approach to regulation at either the state level or the federal level. Electrical utility companies consciously sought state regulation to avoid the possibility of state and local governments simply taking over their monopolies and running them as government enterprises (Anderson 1980). Insurance regulation was delegated to state governments by a federal law exempting the industry from federal antitrust proceedings if state regulation applied (Meier 1988). Regulation of the alcohol industry, both retail and wholesale, was delegated to state governments via legislation implementing the repeal of prohibition (Meier 1994). Health care regulation grew out of joint federal-state programs to provide health insurance (Medicare, Medicaid) and the escalating costs of health care. The regulation of occupations—doctors, lawyers, cosmetologists, funeral home operators—as well as the general regulation of business was left to the states by default.

### Social Regulation

Although social regulation is often associated with the federal programs of the 1960s and 1970s (environmental protection, worker safety, etc.), states have an extensive history in social regulation as part of their effort to protect the health, welfare, and morals of the population. Some of these state duties grew out of public health concerns such as public sanitation and the spread of communicable diseases while others grew out of welfare policy such as delinquency laws or laws protecting children.

A set of highly visible joint federal-state programs exists in environmental protection and workplace safety. In both cases, states can gain primary authority over these state-federal programs by meeting certain federal standards, and approximately half of the states do so. Environmental protection includes not just programs to protect clean air and clean water but also pesticide regulation and the regulation of surface mining reclamation. Workplace safety is generally perceived to be about the Occupational Safety and Health Administration (OSHA) programs, but each state also runs an extensive workers' compensation program to insure against workplace injuries. Workers' compensation programs impose far more restrictions on local businesses via insurance requirements than does OSHA.

In recent years, a different form of social regulation has reasserted itself and attracted a great deal of attention by political scientists who designate the area as "morality policy" (Mooney 2001). Morality policy concerns the regulation of activities that relate to first principles, those deeply held beliefs of citizens that define what is right and wrong. States have been drawn into morality policy in the areas of gambling, drug and alcohol policy, sexual behavior, and abortion, among others. Some scholars argue that morality policy is fundamentally different from other regulatory polices in structure, design, and objectives (Meier 1994; Mooney 2001). Others see it as an extension of long-term efforts to regulate public welfare and morals, issues that ebb and flow with history (Tatalovich and Daynes 1998).

### A POLICY FRAMEWORK

Policy makes an enormous difference in politics because different policies offer different incentives for political and bureaucratic actors. Upon classifying public policy into four distinct categories, Lowi (1972, 299) argued that "policies determine politics." Regulatory policy, for example, encourages conflict between citizens, interest groups, bureaucrats, and politicians. After all, when government regulates, it attempts to control behavior or limit choices available to individuals and groups in society (Meier 1985, 1).

The broader policy literature also supports policy as essential to the explanation of government processes. Executives, for example, have leadership incentives to support civil rights policy (Ripley and Franklin 1991), whereas the legislative branch dominates the adoption and implementation of agriculture policy (Meier 1985). Other research in American politics, such as that concerning representation and voting behavior, concur that different policies produce different incentives for politicians and encourage different political and policy outcomes (see, among others, Hill and Hurley 1999).

### The Salience and Complexity of State Regulatory Policy

Given that different policies produce different political responses, policy type should illuminate our understanding of state regulatory policies. We think that political activity varies according to the salience and technical complexity of a regulatory policy (Gormley 1986), and that this will help explain how regulatory policy affects and is affected by state government (see Gerber and Teske 2000). Figure 13-1 depicts four policy areas according to Gormley's (1986) salience-complexity typology.

A salient issue leads to public attention to and debate about the costs and benefits of policy problems and solutions. It affects a sizeable portion of the general population (Gormley 1986, 598) and is important to the public. Salience can also vary within a policy area and change over time as a problem worsens, demographics change, or the issue is redefined (Gormley 1986, 599). Hence education policy is salient when state administrators reveal standardized test scores while tax policy is salient as tax day nears.

Complexity refers to technical issues that cannot be addressed or answered by the average person. Technically complex policy requires "specialized knowledge and training" (Gormley 1986, 598). Hence the adoption and implementation of complex policy usually occurs behind closed doors. An example of a technically com-

**Figure 13-1** The Complexity and Salience of Public Policies

|  | Complex | Not complex |
|---|---|---|
| Salient | Clean air regulation | Gay civil rights |
| Not salient | Insurance | Procedures |

SOURCE: Adapted from Gormley (1986).

plex policy is the regulation of electric utilities. We all know that we must pay our electric bills in order to stay warm during cold winter months. But only the technically informed know what needs to be regulated to ensure fair prices for heat during cold winter months.

*Four Actors in State Regulation*

The politics of regulatory policy differ by policy type because, depending on the policy's complexity or salience, political actors have different reasons to advocate or oppose regulatory policies. We examine four actors in our assessment of state regulatory policy: politicians, citizens, bureaucrats, and interest groups.[1]

Politicians adopt and shape regulatory policy. They debate bills in the legislature or sign them into law. Politicians prefer salient policies but avoid complex ones given their incentives to respond to public opinion. Because politicians are held accountable to voters every two to six years, policies of public concern are most likely to be on a politician's agenda. Salient policies demand that politicians respond to public opinion or face electoral consequences (Erikson, Wright, and McIver 1993). When a policy is technically complex, however, politicians are unlikely to look to the public for guidance. Because the public rarely understands such issues, the public is unlikely to hold politicians accountable on complex issues when they run for reelection. Hence politicians will defer to experts who understand how to implement complicated policies. Politicians may still shape complex policies, but without taking cues from the public.

Citizens are generally disinterested in politics. Like politicians, they voice support of or opposition to salient policies but eschew complex ones. As V.O. Key (1966) once aptly noted, citizens are but an echo chamber; they respond to issues that are important to politicians. Complexity also limits the range of citizen activ-

---

1. We recognize that courts play a prominent role in regulatory policy, especially in clean air and gay civil rights policies. However, we see the courts as an arena in which citizens or business groups seek to influence policy, rather than an institution that independently affects state regulatory policy.

ity. Most citizens simply do not have the expertise or understanding to know what maximum level of $NO_2$ is required for breathable air. Nevertheless, because state politicians respond to citizens' policy concerns (Erikson, Wright, and McIver 1993), citizens have an incentive to be vocal on issues that are easy and uncomplicated.

Both complexity and salience drive bureaucratic activity. If a policy is salient, bureaucrats must be responsive to citizens and politicians. They must "look over their shoulders" at politicians who have incentives to make sure policy is implemented according to public opinion (Gormley 1986, 610). If a policy is complex, bureaucrats will use their expertise alone to direct regulation. They have little reason to follow politicians or citizens when policies are complex because citizens and most politicians rarely understand them. As state bureaucracies have recently grown in size and become more professional (Rosenthal 1998), and bureaucrats have become more responsible for ensuring that policies are implemented efficiently and effectively, state bureaucrats have progressively become more important in the implementation of regulatory policy.

Interest or business groups have no regard for either a policy's complexity or its salience. Interest groups concern themselves with regulations that directly affect their business and operations and seek to manipulate regulations in their favor regardless of an issue's complexity or salience (Gormley 1986, 604). Their effectiveness in limiting or extending state regulations, nevertheless, depends on an issue's salience and complexity. Because business groups often oppose regulation that might benefit the collective good, they shun the public spotlight. As such, they flourish when issues are low in public salience. When an issue is also high in technical complexity, business groups also benefit because politicians and citizens will defer to their policy expertise.

### Capacity and Ideology

Although salience and complexity may indicate who within a state regulatory policy area might be involved in its adoption and implementation, they do not necessarily explain differences in regulation across states. Two other factors—ideology and capacity—are related to state performance and are useful concepts in comparing states' approaches to regulatory policy. Those states with greater capacity and an ideology favoring a particular type of regulation will be more apt to adopt that regulatory policy.[2] The reader might think of capacity as a necessary condition for policy influence. Without capacity government actors may be forced to respond to the pressures of interest groups. Possessing capacity, government can significantly influence the regulatory process; the direction of that influence depends, however, on its predominant ideology.

Ideology measures a state's fundamental predisposition toward regulation. Basically, a state whose citizens support policy regulation is more likely to adopt and

---

2. These dimensions also vary by complexity and salience—ideology is more important when an issue is salient; capacity is more important when an issue is complex.

implement regulatory policies. A liberal state is more likely to support the regulation of air pollution, for example, than a conservative state (Lester 1990). A state's "liberalism" will not always determine whether or not a state will regulate different policies, but it gives a good indication of the propensity for a state to regulate.

A state's capacity is its ability to regulate when politicians, citizens, bureaucrats, and business groups demand regulation. Capacity relates to "the ability to anticipate and influence change; make informed and intelligent decisions about policy; attract and absorb resources ... and evaluate current activities to guide future actions" (Honsdale 1981, 578). Clearly, sufficient capacity is needed for effective policy implementation. An agency constrained by inadequate funding will not be effective in implementing policy (Mazmanian and Sabatier 1989). Moreover, a less professional legislature will devote less time and energy to legislate adequate standards of control.

## FOUR STATE REGULATORY POLICIES

We have selected four policy areas based on Gormley's (1986) typology for more in-depth discussion.[3] The first category comprises those policies that are salient and complex, thus producing simultaneous pressures for expertise and accountability. Clean air policy in particular is complex yet usually salient to the general public.[4] Policies that are not salient but are complex comprise the second category. Insurance regulation, as an illustration, is complicated but usually unknown to the public at large. Insurance regulation demands expertise at the expense of bureaucratic accountability. Third, gay civil rights policy is salient to most of the public; but similar to civil rights policy generally, it is usually not complex. Accountability is the operative mechanism with gay civil rights. Procedural policy, finally, refers to day-to-day ordinary functions of state regulatory administration such as inspections, licensing, procurement, and so forth. Despite its importance to government, it is neither complicated nor highly salient. In procedural policy, there is little pressure for either bureaucratic accountability or expertise.

We also examine these four policies across states to incorporate ideology and capacity. State ideology and capacity will condition the propensity for a policy area to be regulated by individual states. Even if a policy area is salient, effective regulation is impossible without sufficient capacity. Regulation is also unlikely to be prominent in a state without ideological support for it.

This range of policies gives us variance on our dependent variables and produces different expectations for state regulation by policy area. Policy dimensions allow us to assess how different regulatory policies affect and are affected by state governments. In particular, we note which actors dominate which policies and what kind of politics pervades each policy area. Ideology and capacity are also im-

---

3. An extensive assessment of Gormley's typology can be found in Gerber and Teske (2000).
4. We characterize clean air and gay civil rights policies as salient, even though they are not always of interest to the public. They are relatively more salient than other state regulatory policies.

portant to explain state regulatory policy in a comparative context. Both factors suggest which states will regulate policy areas and which ones will not. Our approach seeks to demonstrate in broad terms how regulatory policy operates and who benefits. Within these broad strokes, myriad nuances can move policy in one direction or another. No short essay can do justice to the wide range of regulatory policies in fifty states, but a general pattern can be established that permits other areas to be examined in a comparative perspective.

Before we begin our discussion, a word about American federalism. State regulatory politics are not exclusively state-driven. Most regulation is also influenced by the federal government. Just as different policies affect different state regulatory outcomes, different policies also motivate federal actors to be involved in state regulatory policy. These reasons, we believe, vary by policy type. Scholars use several analogies to highlight American federalism and its consequences for state regulatory policy (see Chapter 2). In general, federal involvement in regulation (the vertical dimension) should limit politicians' influence (see Wood 1992), yet horizontal competition between states should increase political leadership (Lowry 1992).

We also discuss federal influences on state regulatory policies in three of the policy case studies below. First, clean air policy mandates federal involvement in the regulation of air pollution even though states have substantial influence over air pollution control. As a result of prevailing wind patterns, the federal government must regulate air pollution to ensure that all states have similar air qualities and are, therefore, not polluting to the detriment of other states. Second, although state governments have a clear and direct incentive to regulate the insurance industry, the federal government also plays a modest role. Through federal tax laws, and as a direct regulator of insurers who provide coverage for federal employees, the federal government influences what is essentially a state-driven policy area. Finally, the federal government has become more involved in gay civil rights, especially since the 1992 presidential election (Haeberle 1999). Both presidents and legislators have contributed to the gay rights debate by modifying the military's position on employing gay men and women (as Clinton did by executive order in 1993) or limiting gay civil rights protections through the Defense of Marriage Act (DOMA).

## CLEAN AIR POLICY

Clean air policies are intended to reduce air pollution, such as exhaust from trucks and cars (mobile sources) or discharge from coal-fired utilities or factories (stationary sources), to improve human health and limit damage to property and the environment. Because clean air policy is highly complex yet salient, bureaucrats and interest groups are more involved in the regulation of air pollution than politicians and citizens. Moreover, clean air policy encourages a mixture of state and federal involvement, with states having the primary responsibility for maintaining the quality of their air. Finally, those states with the capacity to enforce air pollution controls and that are ideologically predisposed to support clean air policy will be more effective regulating air pollution than other states handcuffed by limited re-sources and countervailing ideologies.

### The Complexity and Salience of Clean Air Policy

The complexity of clean air regulations is self-evident. With each extensive amendment to the Clean Air Act, legislators and experts have balanced economic and environmental costs, calculated national ambient air quality standards, and set deadlines for compliance. The adopters and implementers of clean air policy have had substantial expertise to determine what emissions level will have the most bal-anced impact on the economy and the environment. Indeed, standard calculations for pollution controls now rely on benefit-cost analysis, which measures whether the benefits of environmental regulations (what we gain from them) are greater than their costs (what we lose from them) (Freeman 2000, 192).

Clean air is also salient. It concerns a sizeable portion of the population, and a policy is also salient, according to Gormley (1986, 601), when a "necessity [in this case the air we breathe] is imperiled." The public is also generally concerned with environmental degradation (Dunlap 1989). When given a choice between eco-nomic growth and environmental protections, the public sides with the environ-ment, or at least agrees that one does not necessarily succeed at the expense of the other (see Page and Shapiro 1992).

Highly complex and salient policies create simultaneous pressures for account-ability and expertise. In this policy area high complexity repels politicians, but salience encourages them to take a public position (Gormley 1986). Amid conflict-ing pressures, politicians will favor style over substance. They will advocate clean air legislation to appease their constituents but are unlikely to affect substantively the implementation of clean air policy because they lack technical understanding of how air pollution should be regulated. Politicians leave these technical decisions to upper-level bureaucrats and professionals. Although they are compelled to listen to politicians when an issue is salient, expertise gives bureaucrats significant discretion over the complexity of clean air policy (Ringquist 1995, 167). Interest groups, par-ticularly industry activists resistant to regulations, should also affect the level of state air pollution controls. Their expertise can help shape legislation and administrative rules. Finally, citizens might influence clean air policy because it is salient, but their message will only be generally one in favor of clean air regulations, without know-ing whether to support specific controls or reject alternative policies. Citizen influ-ence in such areas is likely to be more effective when coupled with some policy ex-pertise. Environmental interest groups have recognized this fact and sought to develop an independent source of policy expertise (Sabatier and McLaughlin 1990).

### Clean Air Policy: A Case Study in Regulation

Initially, air pollution was considered a local problem. Only industrial cities ex-perienced it and sought to regulate it (Jones 1975). As air pollution emerged as a crisis in many more cities, the federal government reacted with a piece-meal approach to legislating regulations. In the 1950s and early 1960s, national legislation provided technical aid and funding to state and local government, but federal authorities could only cajole, not coerce states into controlling air pollutants. The responsibility to control air pollution rested with state and local governments to set voluntary air pollution standards and plans for their implementation.

The environmental movement of the late 1960s and early 1970s changed the regulation of air pollution forever. Consistent with Downs's (1972) issue-attention cycle, citizens and environmental groups became actively interested in air pollution regulation. They focused the nation's attention on environmental problems with Earth Day rallies on April 22, 1970, and argued that a federal presence was needed to effectively limit pollution. Citizen involvement is one reason why the locus of clean air policy shifted in 1970 from state to federal control (see Cohen 1995, chapter 2).

Activists argued that federal legislation was required to limit the adverse effects of interstate pollution. The pollution emitted from smelters and automobiles does not rise into the air and simply fall to the ground, polluting only the area around it. Prevailing wind patterns carry air borne pollutants to areas far from its source. Pollution from coal-burning power plants in the Midwest is responsible for much acid precipitation and related problems in upstate New York and New England. Because air pollution controls in the state of Ohio are likely to benefit other states in the northeast to a much greater extent (Rabe 2000, 44), some states are reluctant to regulate their industries and automobiles. The federal government, environmentalists argue, must be involved.[5]

As the public demanded more stringent pollution controls in the late 1960s, the federal government seized an opportunity to control air pollution across the nation. Two ideologically distinct politicians were the impetus behind the adoption of the 1970 Clean Air Act. Senator Edmund Muskie (D-Maine) authored several federal clean air statutes throughout the 1960s. Although he had advocated an incremental federal approach to handling air pollution, the environmental movement compelled the senator from Maine to espouse even stricter standards and greater federal involvement. President Richard Nixon, driven by his belief that the environmental vote was crucial to his 1972 reelection campaign, also advocated a stronger federal role. Together, Muskie and Nixon generated the most comprehensive air pollution legislation to date, setting stringent federal guidelines to control air pollution across the nation.

The 1970 act provides three broad guidelines for air pollution control, each implemented by the Environmental Protection Agency (EPA), the federal agency re-

---

5. This argument is surfacing once again. The Bush administration has sought to limit clean air regulations under the 1990 amendments. State support and opposition to these changes follow the prevailing winds argument well. State attorneys general in northeastern states oppose rules that would relax requirements for the nation's older coal-fired power plants; state attorneys general from midwestern states that burn coal for energy support relaxing strict clean air regulations (Pianin 2002).

sponsible for monitoring and enforcing clean air regulations under the Clean Air Act. First, the EPA established national ambient air quality standards (NAAQS). NAAQS are acceptable levels for six pollutants—carbon monoxide, particulate matter, nitrogen dioxide, sulfur dioxide, ozone, and lead—in the "ambient" or outside air. NAAQS are designed with a primary goal to protect human health and secondary goals to protect property and the environment (see Ringquist 1993, 47). Second, the Clean Air Act required emissions standards for stationary sources of air pollution, such as smelters, coal-burning plants, and factories. Third, it mandated specific goals for automobile emission reductions and timetables for compliance. Amended again in 1977 and 1990, the Clean Air Act of 1970 provides the statutory foundation for clean air regulation at the state and federal levels. The 1990 amendments, in particular, limited the impact of acid rain by requiring the use of low-sulfur coal (Bryner 1995, 82).

Despite significant federal control over clean air policy in the early 1970s, states' roles in air pollution control increased significantly (Ringquist 1993, 63). The Clean Air Act mandated that states have the "primary responsibility" for controlling air pollution. State authorities draft State Implementation Plans (SIPs) to guide air pollution regulations. Moreover, states generally spend more on pollution control than does the federal government (Bryner 1995, 12; Rabe 2000). States can also exceed federal air regulations if they choose so policy entrepreneurs have incentives to pursue environmental controls at the state level. Encouraging state politicians in this role is the rising influence of direct democracy—in the form of either initiatives or referenda—through which citizens directly support clean air regulations (Rabe 2000). Citizens generally support pollution controls unless there are significant private costs (Melnick 1983, 37), so states are likely to enact and implement air pollution controls.

Industry may have more influence than citizens over state clean air laws because industry directly affects the state economy. Industry may bring jobs and economic prosperity to a state and could threaten to leave if states regulate too stringently. Indeed, if one state regulates, but other neighboring states do not, industry could leave the regulated state for another state with less regulation (see, among others, Rabe 2000, 44). Industry also has the resources and incentives to understand a complex policy that affects its bottom line. If industry can influence bureaucrats' development and maintenance of air pollution regulations, they might deter states' propensity to limit industrial pollution. Ringquist (1993, 119) found, however, that more industry influence in a state's economy increases the strength of a state's air pollution controls. Contrary to the conventional wisdom, therefore, states and their bureaucrats responsible for regulating air pollution appear to be powerful enough to resist coercion from industry lobbyists.

Despite these separate influences on federal and state development of air pollution controls, state and federal authorities do not operate independently when combating air pollution. Air pollution regulations require balance between state and federal authorities so that much of what has become clean air policy was hammered out with EPA and state coordination. Called cooperative or conjoint federalism, the EPA works with state and local governments to achieve air pollution reduction goals. In effect, the EPA establishes standards, but implementation of these standards rests with the states (see also Bryner 1995, 23–24). States submit implementation plans for meeting and maintaining national ambient air quality standards fixed by federal clean air statutes. These plans usually set pollution emissions limits for existing stationary sources (Ringquist 1995, 152). Once approved by state governments, if acceptable to federal standards, the state plans become federally supervised, but monitored and enforced by state authorities. Although citizens and politicians "got the clean air ball rolling," so to speak, bureaucratic discretion and expertise are needed to develop standards and enforce controls. The federal-state interaction on clean air policy is one of state bureaucrats agreeing with federal bureaucrats on acceptable SIPs.

State and federal cooperation, moreover, is present across both stationary- and mobile-source emissions. Along with existing stationary sources of pollution regulated by the 1970 Clean Air Act, any new stationary-emissions source must also meet state and federal standards. States have considerable discretion in granting permits for newer facilities. They issue permits for only those new facilities that meet new source standards. Moreover, new sources of pollution cannot cause the air quality in the region to exceed its collective standards for stationary emissions. If a new source of pollution will surpass a region's limits, then older plants must offset the regional increase in air pollution with a decrease in existing pollution levels. Consistent with the concept of conjoint federalism, state permits for new industrial facilities must comport with the EPA's "New Source Performance Standards" (Bryner 1995, 144), and new facilities must install the best control technology available (Ringquist 1995, 167).

Cooperation between state and federal authorities is also evident in the regulation of mobile-source emissions, such as cars and trucks. The federal government sets some standards for emissions on the national level. Moreover, federal involvement is needed to encourage automakers to produce and sell cleaner-burning automobiles (Lowry 1992). States are responsible for developing maintenance and inspection programs for automobile emissions. These programs might include tail-pipe emissions limitations, or traffic and parking regulations such as carpooling, park and ride programs, or carpool lanes.[6] In addition, states act as a laboratory for federal regulation guidelines. California, for example, introduced mobile-source emissions controls in the late 1960s, standards that were later incorporated into the Air Quality Act of 1967 (Davies 1970, 54) and Clean Air Act of 1970. After 1970 California continued to enforce standards more stringent than federal standards and remains a forceful advocate of stronger environmental regulation. Whether stationary or mobile sources of pollution, states and federal authorities, particularly expert bureaucrats, cooperate to enforce federal clean air statutes.

6. Technically these are referred to as HOV, or High Occupancy Vehicle, lanes.

*Capacity and Ideology*

Although complexity and salience suggest who will regulate clean air in any state, capacity and ideology indicate which types of states will be actively involved in clean air policy regulations and help explain interstate differences in air pollution regulations. Lester (1990) initially argued that successful state implementation of environmental policy rests on a state's commitment to the environment (its ideology) and its capacity to implement federal environmental statutes. A pro-environment state with the capacity to implement air pollution laws will regulate more than a state that neither supports environmental regulations nor has the resources to implement clean air laws. Policies are not simply created by the federal government and implemented uniformly across the states. Instead, state policy officials adjust their efforts to comport with state goals and resources.

We support this argument in Table 13-1. States with more capacity to regulate air pollution have stronger air pollution regulations. The bivariate correlation between clean air strength and state budgets for fighting air pollution is 0.49. Moreover, those states with a higher liberalism score tend to have stringent air pollution regulations according to a significant Pearson's r of 0.29. The anecdotal evidence supports this finding as well: the state of California has one of the highest liberalism scores and the strongest ranking for the regulation of air pollution.

*Summary*

As salience and complexity suggest, clean air policy involves a mixture of different actors. Citizens pushed politicians to develop controls, but substantive regulations have been hammered out in cooperation between federal and state bureaucrats. Because they do not usually offer technically complex advice, politicians rarely influence clean air policy beyond its adoption. Indeed, federal politicians can affect clean air enforcement, but only with blunt, procedural tools such as budget cuts and appointments to the EPA (Wood 1988). We also notice that states vary in their regulation of air pollution. Those states with capacity and citizen support have stronger air pollution regulations than those states lacking in capacity and a supportive citizenry.

## INSURANCE REGULATION POLICY

Everyone knows what insurance is.[7] It is a means of protecting one's income, health, and property. Automobile owners in most states know, for example, that they must buy automobile insurance to drive legally. Those who have had speeding tickets or accidents also know that their premiums—what they pay to be insured—increase because they are higher insurance risks than more cautious drivers. We

---

7. Most definitions of insurance are not that insightful. Mayerson (1962, 2) defines insurance as "the business in which insurance companies engage." Ned Flanders thinks insurance is a form of legalized gambling. Mehr and Cammack (1972, 17–23) define insurance according to its component parts: loss, risk, peril, and hazard.

**Table 13-1** Indicators of State Preferences to Regulate Air Pollution

| State | Clean air strength[a] | State liberalism[b] | Budget for clean air[c] |
|---|---|---|---|
| Alabama | 3 | 0.78 | 509 |
| Alaska | 7 | 0.74 | 109 |
| Arizona | 7 | 0.85 | 2,122 |
| Arkansas | 1 | 0.85 | 220 |
| California | 10 | 0.97 | 11,022 |
| Colorado | 4 | 0.96 | 984 |
| Connecticut | 9 | 0.91 | 804 |
| Delaware | 1 | 0.98 | 257 |
| Florida | 7 | 0.91 | 733 |
| Georgia | 4 | 0.80 | 817 |
| Hawaii | 4 | 0.79 | 164 |
| Idaho | 2 | 0.77 | 223 |
| Illinois | 7 | 0.93 | 1,743 |
| Indiana | 6 | 0.84 | 904 |
| Iowa | 5 | 0.84 | 421 |
| Kansas | 2 | 0.77 | 216 |
| Kentucky | 7 | 0.93 | 945 |
| Louisiana | 5 | 0.76 | 396 |
| Maine | 3 | 0.94 | 169 |
| Maryland | 3 | 0.91 | 751 |
| Massachusetts | 6 | 1.10 | 1,336 |
| Michigan | 8 | 0.88 | 1,294 |
| Minnesota | 5 | 0.94 | 519 |
| Mississippi | 1 | 0.76 | 339 |
| Missouri | 5 | 0.82 | 309 |
| Montana | 2 | 0.87 | 362 |
| Nebraska | 4 | 0.83 | 165 |
| Nevada | 2 | 0.85 | 171 |
| New Hampshire | 6 | 0.97 | 170 |
| New Jersey | 9 | 0.98 | 2,602 |
| New Mexico | 1 | 0.84 | 383 |
| New York | 5 | 1.05 | 3,271 |
| North Carolina | 8 | 0.77 | 787 |
| North Dakota | 1 | 0.72 | 132 |
| Ohio | 8 | 0.89 | 1,161 |
| Oklahoma | 5 | 0.77 | 264 |
| Oregon | 6 | 1.01 | 1,494 |
| Pennsylvania | 8 | 0.89 | 2,421 |
| Rhode Island | 6 | 1.00 | 199 |
| South Carolina | 6 | 0.75 | 506 |
| South Dakota | 1 | 0.57 | 56 |
| Tennessee | 3 | 0.76 | 728 |
| Texas | 7 | 0.80 | 3,353 |
| Utah | 3 | 0.78 | 349 |
| Vermont | 3 | 1.17 | 166 |
| Virginia | 8 | 0.85 | 1,022 |
| Washington | 8 | 0.98 | 616 |
| West Virginia | 2 | 0.83 | 442 |
| Wisconsin | 9 | 0.86 | 832 |
| Wyoming | 1 | 0.90 | 180 |

SOURCES: Clean air strength rankings are for 1987 (Ringquist 1993, 106); ideology scores are for 1999 and are adapted from Erikson, Wright, and McIver (1993; see php.indiana.edu/~wright1/); budgets are for 1970s and 1980s (Ringquist 1993).

[a] Rankings run from 0 to 10, with a higher number indicating more overall state support for air pollution regulatory policies.
[b] Scores are positive mean scores, ranging from 0 to over 1. The further away from 0 a state is, the more liberal that state is. These numbers represent Erikson, Wright, and McIver's (1999) scores added to 1.
[c] Numbers are average expenditures on air pollution regulations in thousands of 1982 dollars.

might know what insurance is, but most of us know little about how government regulates those companies who sell insurance to automobile owners, primarily because few studies have explored the political consequences of insurance regulation (but see Meier 1988; Orren 1974). This lack of scholarly attention is remarkable given that insurance is the largest regulated industry in the United States and almost exclusively regulated by state governments. In this section we highlight the dimensions of state insurance regulation, define insurance, and detail how it is regulated.

*The Complexity and Salience of Insurance Regulatory Policy*

Insurance regulation is a policy area typically characterized by high complexity and low public salience. Most people realize that they must pay insurance premiums to drive their cars or trucks, but few understand how rates are set, what insurance companies do with their premiums, and why premiums increase from time to time. Moreover, as long as insurance customers are able to shop around for the best deal and avoid large, inexplicable increases in their premiums, most Americans simply accept insurance premiums as a part of life, much like paying taxes, without concerning themselves with its regulation by government.

In policy areas that are complex yet unsalient, policy experts thrive and direct regulation, while citizens and politicians remain on the sidelines. Expert bureaucrats and industry groups affected by regulation dictate the extent of insurance regulations. Key decisions are likely to be made by these few individuals with a direct interest in insurance. The public is usually excluded from the decision making because the issues are too obscure and complicated. Of elected representatives, only those who have a particular interest in insurance regulation are likely to involve themselves in overseeing regulation of insurance. Executives, likewise, are unlikely to pay attention or attempt to persuade others on issues that are complex, yet unsalient (see Eshbaugh-Soha 2002).

*Insurance Policy: What It Is and How It Is Regulated*

The insurance industry is a large component of national and state economies, whether in terms of the amount of money spent on insurance per year, or the number of people employed by the industry. Americans paid $727 billion in premiums in 1999 to life insurance companies and $287 billion to property and casualty companies in 1999 (U.S. Bureau of the Census 2001, 748–749). The insurance industry employed over 2.2 million persons in 1997 (*Life Insurance Fact Book* 1998, 58).

The insurance industry is categorically divided into two component parts: life and health, and property and casualty insurance. Life and health insurance policies protect families and individuals in the case of death or illness. Insurers sell three basic products: life insurance, annuities, and health insurance. By buying life insurance—either as whole life, term, group, or universal life coverage—one can protect one's family by providing some financial security in the case of untimely death. Annuities protect against the financial difficulties of old age. Similar to social security, annuities pay the policyholder income from a pre-specified start date until his or her death. Health insurance, finally, pays health care costs for those afflicted with sickness or disease.

Life insurance companies play a prominent role in the economy because premiums are usually paid for many years before a claim is made. Insurance companies invest premiums paid for life and health insurance policies in the economy (the scope of such investments is regulated by state law). Life insurance companies held nearly $3.1 trillion in assets through 1999, two-thirds invested in corporate stocks and bonds (U.S. Bureau of the Census 2001, 749). The regulation of life and health insurance companies primarily concerns licensing of companies to sell insurance in the fifty states. Even though companies must be licensed in a state to sell insurance in that state, the barriers to enter and exit the insurance industry in many states are low and regulations fairly unrestrictive. (New York is an exception; see Meier 1988, 6). Some states also aggressively regulate these companies under a variety of anti-discrimination statutes (for example, prohibitions against discrimination against blind persons). For health insurance companies, cost containment has been a perennial issue.

Property and casualty (PC) insurance makes up the second category. Simply put, PC insurance protects an individual's property in case it is damaged or destroyed. The largest component of PC insurance is automobile insurance. Other areas include workers compensation, homeowners, and general liability insurance. Because PC insurers must pay claims at a faster rate than life insurance companies, the PC insurance sector is less important to the economy than health and life insurance companies (Meier 1988, 11). Nevertheless, the PC insurance sector invests a considerable amount of its assets in stock.

If barriers to enter and exit the insurance industry are few (Meier 1988), then how do states regulate insurance industries? First, some states regulate insurance rates. This happens more so in PC insurance than in life or health insurance. States regulate life insurance rates only indirectly by requiring specific mortality tables, which calculate the probability of death at several ages (Mayerson 1962, 335). Insurers must use these tables to determine premiums for different age groups. Although all states monitor rates, states regulate PC insurance rates differently. Some states are free market states; they let the market decide how much insurers will charge customers for automobile and homeowners insurance. Other states are non-competitive regulators of the insurance prices. About two-thirds of the states allow a rate-setting board to set rates and rate increases (Meier 1988, 44).

Second, states regulate access to insurance (Meier 1988, 45). Under state law, insurance companies are not required to insure high-risk applicants, but states provide access to drivers who cannot purchase standard insurance. States may increase access through a shared-risk system, where states require insurers to share the costs of high-risk drivers, or marketing assistance plans (MAPs). MAPs are voluntary organizations that locate insurance companies who will underwrite high-risk drivers. The state of California, for example, offers the California Automobile Assigned Risk Plan (CAARP) to provide insurance to high-risk drivers unable to purchase insurance elsewhere. CAARP processes insurance requests of high-risk drivers in need of insurance and puts them in touch with participating insurance companies. Applicants to the plan are divided among the insurance companies in the state relative to the percentage of the insurance market each company holds in the state. States also provide access to SR-22 insurance, required of drivers who have had their license revoked for driving or alcohol-related offenses.

State and federal governments have regulated the insurance industry—whether life and health or PC—since the early twentieth century (Meier 1988, chapter 4) for many reasons (Meier 1988, 46–47; see Mayerson 1962, 66). First, states regulate insurance companies to make sure that the insurer-insured contract is upheld. States make sure that insurance companies remain solvent, that is, that they exist to pay claims when the insured make claims. Second, because consumers have little knowledge of the individuals who sell insurance or about the complexities of policies, states mandate that insurance policies are clear to understand and are fair in price. Third, whether through subsidies, shared-risk pools, or discrimination laws, states regulate the insurance industry to guarantee access to insurance for those who need it.

States regulate insurance. But which actors—bureaucrats, industry groups, politicians, or consumer groups—are involved in and explain the regulation of insurance? In a comprehensive analysis of state insurance regulation, Meier (1988) finds that bureaucrats are prominent actors in determining state insurance policy, with industry less influential. Although this contradicts not only Gormley's expectations but also Stigler's (1971) theory of regulation, it makes sense. The insurance industry is not a unified industry: life and health differ from property and casualty insurance companies in their goals. Moreover, individual agents have different goals than insurance companies and, therefore, different reasons for wanting or not wanting state regulations in their workplace. Each state, however, regulates insurance differently, and the politics of insurance regulation varies a great deal from state to state.

*Capacity and Ideology*

State capacity to regulate is key to which states are free market systems and which are noncompetitive regulators of insurance. Greater capacity—whether in greater fiscal resources to regulate insurance or more professionalized legislatures—should have a significant impact on a state's regulation of insurance. More funds mean that states can pay more bureaucrats to monitor insurance rates and access plans. Some states such as Wisconsin, New York, California, and Florida have highly professional bureaucracies that play an important role in regulating the industry. In other states, insurance regulatory capacity is weak, and the industry has the advantage. Capacity also matters in the legislature. A professionalized legislature is more likely to have expert staff and members whose primary concern is insurance and its fairness to consumers. The state of California, for example, has a highly professionalized legislature and several policies, such as CAARP, that encourage access to insurance. Because insurance is not usually salient and consumer groups and citizens are rarely involved in insurance regulation, ideology likely has little influence over the regulation of insurance across the fifty states.

*Summary*

Insurance regulation is a fairly complicated policy area, but one that is usually not salient.[8] Research shows, however, that our policy dimension does not fit insurance regulation perfectly (Meier 1988). The insurance industry influences insurance rates and access to insurance but does not dominate the policy process. Instead, state bureaucrats have influence over rates and access to insurance, especially in states with greater capacity. Political elites and consumer groups might also affect the regulation of insurance in the unlikely event that the policy area becomes salient.

## GAY CIVIL RIGHTS POLICY

State intervention in the rights of gays and lesbians has become more prevalent in recent years, as both sides of the debate have become increasingly vocal. On the one hand, opponents of gay civil rights argue that state protections based on sexual orientation amount to states' sanctioning lifestyles that are morally questionable. On the other hand, supporters argue that individuals, regardless of their sexual orientations, should be protected from discrimination; civil rights, jobs, and housing should be irrelevant to what homosexual men and women do in their private lives. Indeed, the debate about gay civil rights, whether one supports or opposes them, may be categorized according to two broad dimensions: privacy and discrimination. The regulation of gay and lesbian rights is, therefore, about whether states restrict private activities, or whether they restrict others (employers, landlords, etc.) from limiting the public rights of homosexuals.[9]

Unlike air pollution and insurance regulations, which assess the economic costs and benefits of policies or activities, gay and lesbian civil rights are intended to do more than just improve the economic well-being of gay men and women. Gay civil rights policies also involve social regulation in that they regulate the behavior of individuals in society (see Anderson 2000, 11). In other words, gay civil rights not only concern policies that involve economic resources, such as domestic partner benefits, but also the allocation of non-monetary social resources, such as state protection from discrimination or the freedom to act privately as one chooses. The crux of the gay civil rights movement is often framed as identity politics, whereby gays and lesbians have sought affirmation of their identities through non-economic means (Bailey 1999). Within this context, we highlight the complexity and salience of gay and lesbian rights policies, underscore the importance of capacity and ideology in protecting or restricting freedoms for gay men and women, and note the recent rise of the issue to the level of federal intervention.

---

8. In relatively rare situations a crisis can make insurance regulation salient. The liability insurance crisis of the mid-1980s was such an example and even led to a state referendum in California that altered how insurance was regulated. In 2002 Texas experienced an insurance crisis when mold claims resulted in several homeowners insurance companies leaving the state.

9. By "public" rights we mean the rights of gay men and lesbian women to work, live, or socialize where they wish.

*The Complexity and Salience of Gay Civil Rights Policy*

Gay civil rights policy is highly salient, yet not complex. Often framed as morality politics (Haider-Markel and Meier 1996), gay civil rights policy encourages public debate, whether from those who support or oppose it. The importance of gay politics to both sides encourages a black and white debate, where one is either for gay civil rights and lifestyles or one is not. Extreme tactics and rhetoric typically characterize the public discourse of gay civil rights policy (Bull and Gallagher 1996). From one perspective, furthermore, gay civil rights are salient because to some people they amount to "an affront to community values" (Gormley 1986, 601).

Like civil rights policy based on race or gender, gay civil rights are not complex (Haider-Markel and Meier 1996). Gay civil rights affect many deeply, and they are sufficiently uncomplicated that most citizens have an opinion either in favor of or against the regulation of gay and lesbian rights. Being a subset of morality politics, gay civil rights are easy to understand and mobilize against. Gay civil rights policy is an easy issue, in which one only needs a gut feeling to form an opinion on it.

The combination of high salience yet low complexity shapes the politics of gay civil rights and hints at which political actors are involved in their adoption or implementation. Gay and lesbian civil rights policy encourages active politicians and citizens, yet eschews the influence of bureaucrats and business groups. Low complexity means that most citizens or citizen groups[10] have an opinion about the policy, and high salience means that they will indicate publicly their support or opposition to gay and lesbian civil rights. Politicians have electoral concerns, so they respond to citizens on salient issues. Conversely, bureaucrats do not have an informational advantage on uncomplicated issues and must respond to citizens' and politicians' concerns on salient issues. The propensity of a state to enforce or implement gay and lesbian rights policies is thus a function of citizens' and politicians' policy preferences. Finally, businesses or business groups[11] may oppose gay civil rights because they fear a loss of business but may value gay customers as a potential new market (Green 2000). Either way, businesses may not have a substantial impact on the regulation of gay and lesbian rights due to its high salience and low complexity.

*Gay Civil Rights Policy: A Case Study in Regulation*

Gay civil rights policy is an area of growing interest in the American political system. Questions about gays in the military, hate crimes against gays, and the private rights of gay and lesbian partners have recently permeated the national news. Although issues about homosexuality have existed throughout American history, whether in art, literature, or politics, debates about political and social rights for

10. To maintain consistency across policy types, we use "citizens" or "citizens groups" to refer to those who either support gay and lesbians civil rights, such as the National Gay and Lesbian Task Force (NGLTF) or the Human Rights Campaign, or oppose gay civil rights, e.g., the Christian Coalition.

11. "Business groups" in this subsection refers to business owners who may or may not be affected by the expansion or restriction of gay civil rights at the state and local levels. The real group battle is between those citizen groups who either support or oppose gay civil rights.

gay men and women did not reach national prominence until the Stonewall riots in June 1969 (Duberman 1993).

Despite the fervor surrounding the 1960s civil rights movement, gays and lesbians were virtually silent and did not initially demand equality. They lacked a charismatic leader, such as Martin Luther King Jr. or Malcolm X, and did not have a national platform to demand protection from discrimination. When police raided the Stonewall nightclub in a prominently gay part of New York City, angry members of the gay community rioted against discrimination, marking a new beginning for the gay civil rights movement.

This anger and frustration with a system of discrimination and harassment quickly turned to constructive political involvement. Several gay civil rights groups organized around the country. The National Gay and Lesbian Task Force, for example, filled "the void where no national work was being done on behalf of gays" (quoted from Rimmerman, Wald, and Wilcox 2000, 62). The NGLTF, founded in 1973, raises awareness and provides information about gay and lesbian issues. Similarly, the Lambda Legal Defense and Education Fund, also founded in 1973, helps gays and lesbians fight for equality through the courts.

Many local communities also responded in support of gay civil rights. Beginning with East Lansing, Michigan, in March 1972 (Button, Rienzo, and Wald 1997, 65), cities have passed ordinances protecting the rights of gay and lesbian citizens. The East Lansing ordinance, and many that followed, prohibited discrimination based on sexual orientation not only for city jobs, but also for housing, public accommodations, and private sector employment. Since 1972 hundreds of cities and some states have passed discrimination protections specifically for sexual orientation.

Despite the initial fervor surrounding Stonewall, the gay civil rights movement has evolved slowly. Protections from discrimination in places of employment, housing, and public accommodation have progressed in a piece-meal fashion (Cohan 1982). Even today, homosexual men and women are neither protected from discrimination the way other minorities are nor allotted the same freedoms to do what they choose in the privacy of their own homes. Gay men and women are not legally protected from being fired or being "redlined" when purchasing a house because sexual orientation is not held to the same "strict scrutiny" as are race and gender. Both consensual sex and marriage, two institutions protected by government for heterosexual couples, are not protected to the same extent for gays and lesbians. Most successful efforts to achieve state discrimination protections or gain reasonable access to privacy simply motivate gay civil rights opponents into action. Nevertheless, as politically active gays and lesbians began to assert their right from political and social persecution, politicians, citizens, and interest groups have played a more active role in the politics of gay civil rights. Actors in the gay civil rights debate divide into either advocates or opponents of gay civil rights, and the gay civil rights debate concerns two areas of contention.

The first area of debate relates to the public activities of gay men and women. Here, advocates of gay and lesbian rights argue that homosexuals should be guaranteed the same rights as heterosexuals. Employers should be prevented from firing an employee simply because of his or her sexual orientation. Just as it is illegal to reject a real estate application because an individual is African American or Hispanic, moreover, homosexuals should be protected from similar acts of discrimination. Laws or ordinances, supporters argue, are necessary to ensure that sexual orientation does not preclude U.S. citizens from living ordinary lives and being allotted fundamental protections granted to others. Opponents of anti-discrimination statutes claim that sexual orientation does not deserve protection. They claim that discrimination is already illegal, and laws that protect gays and lesbians amount to granting "special rights."

Both sides concur that the right to not be discriminated against is fundamental. The gay civil rights debate concerns more specifically whether or not sexual orientation is adequately protected under existing laws, or if legislation is needed to specify it as a category worthy of state protection. Button, Rienzo, and Wald (1997, 126) illustrate the potential need for anti-discrimination protections in a telling example. In 1991 Cracker Barrel restaurants fired eleven employees in accordance with their new policy refusing to employ those "whose sexual preferences fail to demonstrate normal heterosexual values which have been the foundation of families in our society" (quoted from Button, Rienzo, and Wald 1997, 126). Despite significant media attention and some protests, Cracker Barrel did not rehire the eleven employees. Without local, state, or federal civil rights protections, these employees lacked any legal recourse and were without a job. Gay civil rights advocates maintain that protections are needed in similar situations to prevent firings unrelated to job performance. Besides, business' argument that employing gays and lesbians is harmful to business is debatable, in light of the evidence: Gay civil rights protections have little or no impact on business growth in states and cities with these laws (Button, Rienzo, and Wald 1997, 125).

Despite the difficulty in requiring private businesses to not discriminate on the basis of sexual orientation, discrimination statutes have been passed at the local and state level. Because success may expand the scope of conflict and produce even more opposition (Haider-Markel and Meier 1996), gay civil rights ordinances have progressed slowly, from protecting city employees, for example, to branching out to public accommodations, housing, and private employment. Of course, the salience and low information complexities of gay civil rights mean that public opinion shapes policy outputs. Local and state protections against discrimination based on sexual orientation follow public opinion quite well (see capacity and ideology section below). Those states and localities that are liberal and tolerant promote regulation of discrimination; those areas that are conservative and religious do not.

Public salience can be a double-edged sword for supporters of gay civil rights. Just as advocates can tap broad public opinion against discrimination, opponents can frame ordinances as promoting "special rights" and the gay agenda. Indeed, as protections for sexual orientation mounted in the early 1990s (Button, Rienzo, and Wald 1997), opponents of "special rights" have sought to restrict them. Through statewide referenda and initiatives, citizens groups have moved to restrict city councils and state legislatures from protecting gay civil rights (Donovan, Wenzel, and Bowler 2000). Initiatives of the late 1980s and early 1990s attempted to repeal local gay civil rights ordinances.[12] Since *Romer v. Evans* (517 U.S. 620, 1996), however, in which the Supreme Court struck down a series of initiatives limiting discrimination protections based on sexual orientation, direct democracy has been used less frequently as a tool to limit gay civil rights (Donovan, Wenzel, and Bowler 2000, 180). When initiatives have passed, they tend not to demand extreme change but instead incrementally reduce gay civil rights protections. The success of a majority of state and local antigay initiatives (Gamble 1997; Haider-Markel 1999; but see Donovan and Bowler 1998) also provides incentives for politicians to further their own political careers as crusaders for moral values (Donovan, Wenzel, and Bowler 2000).

The right to privacy of homosexual men and women, or the private lives of homosexuals, is also important to gay civil rights policy. Simply put, policy makers must ask, should gays and lesbian couples be granted the same privacy rights as heterosexual couples? Should state law allow consensual sex, which is often taken for granted between heterosexual couples? Moreover, should gays and lesbians be allowed to marry just as heterosexual couples are? Advocates argue that government should not regulate the private lives of American citizens, whether gay or straight. Opponents claim, conversely, that not restricting gay and lesbian privacy encourages and promotes homosexuality as a legitimate and healthy lifestyle, which opponents argue it is not.

The right to privacy generally extends to issues of consensual sex or equal rights and equal recognition under the law as couples. Each of these is generally sanctioned by state governments for heterosexual couples, yet circumscribed or banned for homosexuals. Although fourteen states have antisodomy laws that apply to both heterosexual and homosexual sex (Welch, Thomas, and Ambrosius 1999, 529),[13] the laws have been enforced disproportionately against homosexuals (Button, Rienzo, and Wald 1997, 40). The Supreme Court case, *Bowers v. Hardwick* (478 U.S. 186 1986), was a case about the right of homosexual men to engage in consensual sex in the privacy of their own home. Writing for the majority, Justice Byron White argued that the right to privacy does not cover homosexual sodomy. The Court held this even though the right to privacy protects aspects of heterosexual sex. But in June of 2003 the Supreme Court reversed its stance on sodomy in the case of *Lawrence v. Texas* (#02-0102). It struck down a Texas ban on gay sex as an unconstitutional violation of privacy and overturned the *Bowers* decision, and appears to cover sodomy statutes in other states as well.

Same-sex marriages are also related to gay civil rights policy. Proponents argue that legal marriage between gay partners would legitimize homosexuality as a so-

12, An example relates to the Colorado for Family Values initiative, later rejected by the Supreme Court in *Romer v. Evans,* which would have overturned Boulder and Aspen's gay civil rights ordinances.

13. Sodomy is illegal only for homosexuals in five states (Welch, Thomas, and Ambrosius 1999, 529).

cially acceptable lifestyle and grant partners legal advantages given to heterosexual spouses, such as insurance, inheritance, and hospital visitation rights. Opponents maintain that legalizing gay marriages would only strengthen the gay civil rights agenda, which is immoral and dangerous (Lewis and Edelson 2000, 200). The opposition has successfully framed gay marriages as an affront to the sanctity of marriage between a man and a woman. Indeed, only the state of Hawaii had extended the right to marriage to gays and lesbians through the courts, but even it has since used a referendum to reverse the state supreme court's decision (Donovan, Wenzel, and Bowler 2000, 164).[14] Through the beginning of 1998, twenty-six states passed legislation banning same-sex marriages, and eleven more had bills under consideration (Lewis and Edelson 2000, 200).

Political opposition to gay marriages is not surprising in light of the public opinion data. Whereas 83 percent of the American public supports protection from discrimination based on sexual orientation (Lewis and Edelson 2000, 194; see Lewis and Rogers 1999, 121), the public is not supportive of privacy issues for homosexuals. Public opposition to same-gender sex has remained strong over time, with at least 67 percent of the public against it since 1977 (Lewis and Edelson 2000, 195). In a policy area driven by salience and a lack of complexity, the public (including various citizens groups) has a strong influence over governmental decisions. When the public does not support gay marriages, politicians eschew supporting them. Whereas state and local government may have been ready to protect sexual orientation from discrimination because public opinion also supports these protections, state and federal laws have moved to limit, or at least not protect, the privacy rights of gays and lesbians due to public opposition to homosexual marriages and consensual sex.

The executive and legislative branches have been decidedly mixed in their support of gay civil rights. Bill Clinton made gay civil rights an issue during his 1992 presidential campaign. He promised to address the growing controversy surrounding gay men and women in the military; once in the White House, however, he encountered substantial opposition from members of Congress, the public, and members of the military establishment, including the Joint Chiefs of Staff. Clinton settled for a "don't ask, don't tell" policy, which prevented the military from asking its rank-and-file their sexual orientation, yet precluded soldiers and sailors from "coming out of the closest" while active members of the U.S. military.

After Hawaii permitted gay marriages, the U.S. Congress moved to regulate and restrict the legality of gay marriages under the Defense of Marriage Act (DOMA). Social conservatives demanded that Congress restrict the scope of gay civil rights. Otherwise, all states might be forced to recognize gay marriages under the full faith

---

14. Vermont legally recognizes "civil unions," similar to marriage, but these are recognized only in Vermont. Civil unions give gay couples insurance, adoption, health care, and property rights similar to those allotted to heterosexual married couples (see http://www.vermontgayandlesbianweddings.com).

and credit clause of the Constitution, which mandates that states recognize the public acts, records, and proceedings of all other states. Many conservative lawmakers argued that allowing homosexual couples to marry trivializes the institution of marriage and encourages children to become homosexual (see LeLoup and Shull 1999, 164). Opponents maintained that the law violated full faith and credit and was just an election year political gambit (Lewis and Edelson 2000). President Clinton eventually signed the Act into law before his reelection victory in 1996, despite his earlier support for gays in the military. The DOMA barred the federal government from recognizing gay marriages and mandated that states need not recognize gay marriages from other states. Ironically, the U.S. Supreme Court—packed with social conservatives who also staunchly support state authority in the Constitution—might eventually declare DOMA unconstitutional given its possible infringement on the full faith and credit clause.

### Capacity and Ideology

Capacity and ideology are two dimensions of politics that help us determine those states that will favor gay civil rights and those opposed. States must be sufficiently in favor of gay civil rights to protect them. Ideology is especially important because public opinion (or the state's liberalism) is likely to have a substantial impact on the adoption of gay civil rights protections because gay civil rights policy is salient to the public. Because states rarely enforce the laws discussed in this chapter other than via highly visible court cases, capacity becomes much less important.

Table 13-2 shows that ideology, but not capacity, helps explain the propensity of states to adopt legislation protective of gay civil rights. State liberalism (ideology) is important. With a Pearson's r of nearly 0.7, more liberal states are simply more likely to be pro–gay civil rights. By way of example, Connecticut, a state that is highly liberal at 67.10, is also ranked highly in support of gay civil rights. Mississippi, a conservative state, is least supportive of gay civil rights legislation. Legislative professionalism, which measures the capacity of state legislatures to adopt gay rights policies and oversee their implementation, has little relationship to gay civil rights laws. Vermont, for example, is not very professional but strongly supports gay civil rights.

### Summary

Gay and lesbian civil rights policy follows our expectations of high salience and low complexity. Citizens, groups, and their opinions have an enormous impact on gay civil rights policy at the state level. Because the public tends to support laws that prevent discrimination against homosexuals, politicians adopt them. The gay civil rights movement has not been as successful preventing government interference over privacy issues for the same reason: the public opposes homosexual sex and marriage, and politicians therefore do not adopt privacy rights protections for gays and lesbians.

**Table 13-2** Indicators of Potential State Support for Gay Civil Rights Policies

| State | Gay civil rights rankings[a] | Legislative professionalism[b] | State liberalism[c] |
|---|---|---|---|
| Alabama | −82 | 0.06 | 0.78 |
| Alaska | −40 | 0.32 | 0.74 |
| Arizona | −25 | 0.09 | 0.85 |
| Arkansas | −65 | 0.04 | 0.85 |
| California | 54 | 1.00 | 0.97 |
| Colorado | −35 | 0.07 | 0.96 |
| Connecticut | 81 | 0.12 | 0.91 |
| Delaware | −10 | 0.03 | 0.98 |
| Florida | −67 | 0.22 | 0.91 |
| Georgia | −39 | 0.04 | 0.80 |
| Hawaii | 42 | 0.14 | 0.79 |
| Idaho | −80 | 0.01 | 0.77 |
| Illinois | −5 | 0.02 | 0.93 |
| Indiana | −20 | 0.06 | 0.84 |
| Iowa | −11 | 0.05 | 0.84 |
| Kansas | −82 | 0.04 | 0.77 |
| Kentucky | −22 | 0.08 | 0.93 |
| Louisiana | −61 | N/A | 0.76 |
| Maine | 2 | 0.04 | 0.94 |
| Maryland | 4 | 0.06 | 0.91 |
| Massachusetts | 64 | 0.17 | 1.10 |
| Michigan | −19 | 0.32 | 0.88 |
| Minnesota | 24 | 0.11 | 0.94 |
| Mississippi | −90 | 0.04 | 0.76 |
| Missouri | −40 | 0.07 | 0.82 |
| Montana | −37 | 0.03 | 0.87 |
| Nebraska | −27 | N/A | 0.83 |
| Nevada | 8 | 0.06 | 0.85 |
| New Hampshire | 66 | 0.09 | 0.97 |
| New Jersey | 70 | 0.26 | 0.98 |
| New Mexico | 11 | 0.04 | 0.84 |
| New York | 6 | 0.49 | 1.05 |
| North Carolina | −80 | 0.04 | 0.77 |
| North Dakota | −35 | 0.01 | 0.72 |
| Ohio | −4 | 0.12 | 0.89 |
| Oklahoma | −92 | 0.06 | 0.77 |
| Oregon | 34 | 0.11 | 1.01 |
| Pennsylvania | −33 | 0.27 | 0.89 |
| Rhode Island | 68 | 0.04 | 1.00 |
| South Carolina | −70 | 0.08 | 0.75 |
| South Dakota | −37 | 0.01 | 0.57 |
| Tennessee | −30 | 0.06 | 0.76 |
| Texas | −18 | 0.16 | 0.80 |
| Utah | −77 | 0.04 | 0.78 |
| Vermont | 97 | 0.01 | 1.17 |
| Virginia | −87 | 0.09 | 0.85 |
| Washington | 9 | 0.16 | 0.98 |
| West Virginia | −35 | 0.05 | 0.83 |
| Wisconsin | 60 | 0.13 | 0.86 |
| Wyoming | 5 | 0.01 | 0.90 |

S O U R C E S : Gay rights rankings are for 2000 (Keen 2002); legislative professionalism rankings are for 1999 (Berry, Berkman, and Schneiderman 2000); ideology scores are for 1999 and adapted from Erikson, Wright, and McIver (1993; see php. indiana.edu/~wright1/).

[a] Rankings run from −100 to +100, with a higher number indicating more state support for gay civil rights policies.
[b] Scores run from 0 to 1, with 1 indicative of a highly professional state legislature.
[c] Scores are positive mean scores, ranging from 0 to over 1. The further away from 0 a state is, the more liberal that state is. These numbers represent Erikson, Wright, and McIver's (1999) scores added to 1.

## PROCEDURAL POLICY

"Street level" politics are the least dynamic of policy dimensions. Being low in complexity and salience, few actors have an interest in these policies. For policies in this area, standard operating procedures are the norm. Generally, bureaucrats follow a set of routines that evolve slowly over time, yet remain stable and highly predictable (Jones 1985). Nevertheless, street level regulatory policies affect industry or state politics. They only do so at such an immeasurable level that interest groups, industries, bureaucrats, or politicians rarely get excited enough to be bothered by them.

Just as these policies rarely attract the interest of the public and politicians, they also rarely attract the interest of political scientists and thus are not well studied. Of the ten policy areas that Gormley (1986) classifies as low in salience and complexity, six have not generated any systematic studies (housing inspections, nursing home inspections, blue laws, billboard regulation, restaurant inspections, motor vehicle inspections) and two have generated only a single study (building inspections, Jones 1985; liquor licensing, Meier 1994). Of the other two, one is not an area of state regulation (broadcast regulation) and the other has recently become very salient and thus transformed its politics greatly (election regulation).

Despite the logical reasons for thinking that the politics in procedural areas will differ from that in other areas of regulation, we have little systematic demonstration of that difference. A set of recent studies by Allen (1999, 2002) on what he calls mundane policies includes some of the low salient, low complexity regulatory policies. His work finds that the traditional political economy models such as those discussed in the previous sections perform poorly in mundane policy areas. This work suggests that different approaches and new models are needed if we desire a better understanding of regulatory policies that often escape below the political radar screen. There is quite likely to be a politics involved in procedural policy, but it is not the same type of politics that occurs in other regulatory policy areas.

## CONCLUSION

Regulatory policy at the state level covers a wide range of substantive policy areas, each with a somewhat unique form of politics. The broad outlines of regulatory policy, however, can be understood (at the state level or any other level) using a few concepts and the relationships between these concepts. We have argued and illustrated with case studies that a combination of salience and complexity determines who gets involved in regulatory policy. Salience attracts the interest of politicians and citizens and thus generates demands for accountability. Complexity advantages expertise and repels both citizens and politicians who rarely have the ability to meaningfully participate in policy debates. Bureaucrats (and industry actors where an industry is involved) are always present. As policies become more complex, they gain advantages in the process. Complexity also makes accountability more difficult as issues of effectiveness and competence tend to dominate.

After determining who is likely to participate or participate effectively, the next question is the content of public policy. For government actors, either bureaucrats or politicians, to play a key role, they must have the capacity to act, that is, the resources and expertise to deal with a problem. Without that capacity, policy decisions revert to industry actors with governments merely ratifying the results. With capacity, however, governments become an independent force. The types of policies that government actors then pursue are a function of ideology. Liberal states are more predisposed to regulate economically. Social regulation follows a similar pattern, although both nonlibertarian conservatives and liberals are likely to support regulation that is consistent with their values.

## REFERENCES

Allen, David W. 2002. "Mundane Cash Management Policies in the American States." *Social Science Journal* 39(1): 1–18.

———. 1999. "Political Economy and Adoption of Policies Affecting Everyday Life in the American States." *Social Science Journal* 36(3): 393–411.

Anderson, Douglas D. 1980. "State Regulation of Electrical Utilities." In *Regulation,* edited by James Q. Wilson. New York: Basic Books.

Anderson, James E. 2000. *Public Policymaking: An Introduction,* 4th ed. New York: Houghton Mifflin.

Bailey, Robert W. 1999. *Gay Politics, Urban Politics: Identity and Economics in the Urban Setting.* New York: Columbia University Press.

Berry, William D., Michael B. Berkman, and Stuart Schneiderman. 2000. "Legislative Professionalism and Incumbent Reelection: The Development of Institutional Boundaries." *American Political Science Review* 94: 859–874.

Bryner, Gary C. 1995. *Blue Skies, Green Politics: The Clean Air Act of 1990 and Its Implementation,* 2d ed. Washington D.C.: CQ Press.

Bull, Chris, and John Gallagher. 1996. *Perfect Enemies: The Religious Right, the Gay Movements, and the Politics of the 1990s.* New York: Crown Publishers.

Button, James W., Barbara A. Rienzo, and Kenneth D. Wald. 1997. *Private Lives, Public Conflicts: Battles Over Gay Rights in American Communities.* Washington, D.C.: CQ Press.

Cohan, A. S. 1982. "Obstacles to Equality: Government Responses to the Gay Rights Movement in the United States." *Political Studies* 30: 59–76.

Cohen, Richard E. 1995. *Washington at Work: Back Rooms and Clean Air.* Boston: Allyn and Bacon.

Davies, J. Clarence III. 1970. *The Politics of Pollution.* New York: Pegasus.

Donovan, Todd, and Shaun Bowler. 1998. "Responsive or Responsible Government?" In *Citizens as Legislators,* edited by Shaun Bowler, Todd Donovan, and Caroline J. Tolbert. Columbus: Ohio State University Press.

Donovan, Todd, Jim Wenzel, and Shaun Bowler. 2000. "Direct Democracy and Gay Rights Initiatives after *Romer.*" In *The Politics of Gay Rights,* edited by Craig A. Rimmerman, Kenneth D. Wald, and Clyde Wilcox. Chicago: University of Chicago Press.

Downs, Anthony. 1972. "Up and Down with Ecology: The Issue-Attention Cycle." *Public Interest* 28: 38–50.

Duberman, Martin. 1993. *Stonewall.* New York: Dutton.

Dunlap, Riley E. 1989. "Public Opinion and Environmental Policy." In *Environmental Politics and Policy,* edited by James P. Lester. Durham: Duke University Press.

Eisner, Marc Allen. 1993. *Regulatory Politics in Transition.* Baltimore: Johns Hopkins University Press.

Erikson, Robert S., Gerald C. Wright, and John P. McIver. 1993. *Statehouse Democracy: Public Opinion and Policy in the American States.* New York: Cambridge University Press.

Eshbaugh-Soha, Matthew. 2002. *Signaling Influence: Presidential Statements and their Power over Policy.* Ph.D. dissertation, Texas A&M University.

Freeman, A. Myrick III. 2000. "Economics, Incentives, and Environmental Regulation." In *Environmental Policy,* 4th ed., edited by Michael E. Kraft and Norman J. Vig. Washington, D.C.: CQ Press.

Gamble, Barbara. 1997. "Putting Civil Rights to a Popular Vote." *American Journal of Political Science* 41: 245–269.

Gerber, Brian J., and Paul Teske. 2000. "Regulatory Policymaking in the American States: A Review of Theories and Evidence." *Political Research Quarterly* 5(December): 849–996.

Gormley, William T. 1986. "Regulatory Issue Networks in a Federal System." *Polity* 18: 595–620.

Green, John C. 2000. "Antigay: Varieties of Opposition to Gay Rights." In *The Politics of Gay Rights,* edited by Rimmerman, Wald, and Wilcox.

Haeberle, Steven H. 1999. "Gay and Lesbian Rights: Emerging Trends in Public Opinion and Voting Behavior." In *Gays and Lesbians in the Democratic Process,* edited by Ellen D. B. Riggle and Barry L. Tadlock. New York: Columbia University Press.

Haider-Markel, Donald P. 1999. "Redistributing Values in Congress: Interest Group Influence Under Sub-Optimal Conditions." *Political Research Quarterly* 52: 113–144.

Haider-Markel, Donald P., and Kenneth J. Meier. 1996. "The Politics of Gay and Lesbian Rights: Expanding the Scope of the Conflict." *Journal of Politics* 58: 332–349.

Hill, Kim Quaile, and Patricia A. Hurley. 1999. "Dyadic Representation Reappraised." *American Journal of Political Science* 45: 109–137.

Honsdale, Beth. 1981. "A Capacity Building Framework: A Search for Concept and Purpose." *Public Administration Review* 41: 577–589.

Jones, Bryan D. 1985. *Governing Buildings and Building Government.* University: University of Alabama Press.

Jones, Charles O. 1975. *Clean Air: The Policies and Politics of Pollution Control.* Pittsburgh: University of Pittsburgh Press.

Keen, Lisa. 2002. "News Analysis." *Washington Blade,* November 9, A9.

Key, V. O. Jr. 1966. *The Responsible Electorate.* Cambridge, Mass.: Belknap Press.

LeLoup, Lance T., and Steven A. Shull. 1999. *The President and Congress: Collaboration and Combat in National Policymaking.* Boston: Allyn and Bacon.

Lester, James P. 1990. "A New Federalism? Environmental Policy in the States." In *Environmental Policy in the 1990s,* edited by Norman J. Vig and Michael E. Kraft. Washington, DC: CQ Press.

Lewis, Gregory B., and Jonathan L. Edelson. 2000. "DOMA and ENDA: Congress Votes on Gay Rights." In *The Politics of Gay Rights,* edited by Rimmerman, Wald, and Wilcox.

Lewis, Gregory B., and Marc A. Rogers. 1999. "Does the Public Support Equal Employment Rights for Gays and Lesbians?" In *Lesbians and Gays in the Democratic Process,* edited by Riggle and Tadlock.

*Life Insurance Fact Book, 1998.* 1998. New York: American Council of Life Insurance.

Lowry, William R. 1992. *The Dimensions of Federalism: State Governments and Pollution Control Policies.* Durham: Duke University Press.

Lowi, Theodore J. 1972. "Four Systems of Policy, Politics and Choice." *Public Administration Review* 32: 298–310.

Mayerson, Allen L. 1962. *Introduction to Insurance.* New York: Macmillan.

Mazmanian, Daniel A., and Paul A. Sabatier. 1989. *Implementation and Public Policy.* Lanham, Md.: University Press of America.

Mehr, Robert I., and Emerson Cammack. 1972. *Principles of Insurance,* 5th ed. Homewood, Ill.: Richard D. Irwin.

Meier, Kenneth J. 1994. *The Politics of Sin.* Armonk, N.Y.: M.E. Sharpe.

———. 1988. *The Political Economy of Regulation: The Case of Insurance.* Albany: State University of New York Press.

———. 1985. *Regulation: Politics, Bureaucracy, and Economics.* New York: St. Martin's Press.

Melnick, R. Shep. 1983. *Regulation and the Courts: The Case of the Clean Air Act.* Washington, D.C.: Brookings Institution.

Mooney, Christopher Z. 2001. *The Public Clash of Private Values.* New York: Chatham House.

Orren, Karen. 1974. *Corporate Power and Social Change: The Politics of the Life Insurance Industry.* Baltimore: Johns Hopkins University Press.

Page, Benjamin, and Robert Shapiro. 1992. *The Rational Public: Fifty Years of Trends in Americans' Policy Preferences.* Chicago: University of Chicago Press.

Pianin, Eric. 2002. "White House Warned on Easing Clean Air Rules." *Washington Post,* January 9, A2.

Rabe, Barry G. 2000. "Power to the States: The Promise and Pitfalls of Decentralization." In *Environmental Policy,* 4th ed., edited by Kraft and Vig.

Rimmerman, Craig A., Kenneth D. Wald, and Clyde Wilcox, eds. 2000. *The Politics of Gay Rights.* Chicago: University of Chicago Press.

Ringquist, Evan J. 1995. "Environmental Protection Regulation." In *Regulation and Consumer Protection,* edited by Kenneth J. Meier and E. Thomas Garman. Houston: Dame Publications.

———. 1993. *Environmental Protection at the State Level: Politics and Progress in Controlling Pollution.* Armonk, N.Y.: M.E. Sharpe.

Ripley, Randall B., and Grace A. Franklin. 1991. *Congress, the Bureaucracy, and Public Policy.* Chicago: Dorsey Press.

Rosenthal, Alan. 1998. *The Decline of Representative Democracy: Process, Participation, and Power in State Legislatures.* Washington, D.C.: CQ Press.

Sabatier, Paul A., and Susan M. McLaughlin. 1990. "Belief Congruence between Interest Group Leaders and Members." *Journal of Politics* 52(August): 914–938.

Stigler, George J. 1971. "The Economic Theory of Regulation." *Bell Journal of Economics and Management Science* 2: 3–21.

Tatalovich, Raymond, and Byron W. Daynes. 1998. *Moral Controversies in American Politics: Cases in Social Regulation.* Armonk, N.Y.: M.E. Sharpe.

U.S. Bureau of the Census. 2001. *Statistical Abstract of the United States.* Washington, D.C.: U.S. Government Printing Office.

Welch, Susan, Sue Thomas, and Margery M. Ambrosius. 1999. "The Politics of Family Policy." In *Politics in the American States,* 7th ed., edited by Virginia Gray, Russell C. Hanson, and Herbert Jacob. Washington, D.C.: CQ Press.

Wood, B. Dan. 1992. "Modeling Federal Implementation as a System: The Clean Air Case." *American Journal of Political Science* 36: 40–67.

———. 1988. "Principals, Bureaucrats, and Responsiveness in Clean Air Enforcements." *American Political Science Review* 82: 213–234.

## SUGGESTED READINGS

Anderson, James E. 2000. *Public Policymaking: An Introduction,* 4th ed. New York: Houghton Mifflin. In *the* textbook for public policy in the United States, Anderson describes key theories and frameworks that political scientists use to explain public policy and applies them to recent examples in politics.

Button, James W., Barbara A. Rienzo, and Kenneth D. Wald. 1997. *Private Lives, Public Conflicts: Battles Over Gay Rights in American Communities.* Washington, D.C.: CQ Press. This quintessential book on gay civil rights details the movement from its symbolic beginnings at Stonewall through recent struggles over referenda and initiatives.

Lowry, William R. 1992. *The Dimensions of Federalism: State Governments and Pollution Control Policies.* Durham: Duke University Press. The author uses a horizontal-vertical typology of environmental policy to underscore the importance of federalism to the American republic.

Meier, Kenneth J. 1988. *The Political Economy of Regulation: The Case of Insurance.* Albany: State University of New York Press. This book explores the nuances of insurance regulations in a political science context and offers a political science explanation of insurance regulation.

Ringquist, Evan J. 1993. *Environmental Protection at the State Level: Politics and Progress in Controlling Pollution.* Armonk, N.Y.: M.E. Sharpe. A well-written and comprehensive account of state environmental protections; the author develops both air and water pollution regulations at the state level and balances qualitative explanation with quantitative evidence.

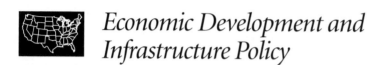

# CHAPTER 14

# Economic Development and Infrastructure Policy

MARTIN SAIZ AND SUSAN CLARKE

Already engaged in global competition for investment, American states were drawn into another aspect of globalization with the terrorist attacks of September 11, 2001. In addition to the terrible human losses, the economic impacts were enormous. The effects of these attacks continue to ripple through the U.S. economy, although New York City and Washington D.C. suffered the most immediate and devastating impacts. The attacks disrupted some 10,000 businesses in New York City and spurred the relocation of an estimated 30,000 employees to Connecticut and New Jersey (Lyne 2002). Faced with these economic losses, the state of New York and New York City created a pool of $500 million in economic incentives—loans, loan guarantees, tax breaks—to persuade large businesses not to leave Manhattan. Even though the funds were intended to go only to firms likely to relocate, Daniel Doctoroff, the city's deputy mayor for economic development and rebuilding, conceded that some of the $500 million in incentives would likely go to companies "that never had any intent to leave. . . . Everyone lies about it" (Lyne 2002).

The scale and magnitude of the terrorist attacks are unprecedented in American history, but these concerns with economic well-being and the effectiveness of public policy incentives are familiar issues for state governments. Indeed, they are increasingly salient matters as state governments cope with globalization and economic transformation. Not long ago, national borders protected state and local economies from the challenges of global capitalism. Today, with the help of free trade agreements, and advanced by a revolution in worldwide communications, global competition is transforming the economy of the United States. Industries that were thought of as state or national assets commonly migrate across borders and oceans. Parts suppliers and production subcontractors to domestic industries are often located in far-away lands. At home, state policy makers face an emergent "new economy," a knowledge-based economy in which wealth is created through skills, information, technology, and innovative capacity rather than through the physical assets, such as natural resources or transportation links, important in the past. Each year, state and local governments spend billions of dollars on economic development programs designed to grow, attract, and retain businesses and jobs that will integrate their states with a global economy and locate their economic futures in the vibrant sectors of the new economy.

As we demonstrate here, the tools used to promote state economic development vary among states and over time; historically, they often involved public policies that cut the costs of doing business—such as lowering taxes or targeted tax incentives, providing land or subsidies to firms, and building needed infrastructure. More recently, many states are targeting growth processes, regions, and economic sectors, rather than individual firms; they do so by participating in public-private partnerships, establishing venture capital funds and foreign trade offices, offering seed money for new ventures, encouraging collaboration and networking among clusters of firms, creating high-tech research centers at public universities, and other innovative strategies.

All these initiatives fall under the label of state economic development programs. There is little agreement among scholars, however, that economic development programs actually work—meaning that they change the quality and quantity of economic activity in the state. Thus there is some controversy as to whether state economic development programs are good public policy. And more than economic calculations are at stake: these policy issues create a political dilemma for public officials. While it is not clear that economic development policies work as planned, it is also unclear that such expenditures are a complete waste. So, even if public officials suspect that economic development policies are not effective, it can be difficult to ignore the pleas of a distressed community for public subsidies when a local company is threatening to relocate. Considering the potential political benefits gained from claiming to protect jobs and businesses against the unlikely event that the incentives later will be shown to be inconsequential, public officials tend to support these programs even in the absence of solid evidence that they accomplish the intended goals.

The many faces of globalization, along with the continuing political and economic uncertainties surrounding economic development decisions, contribute to a distinctive climate for state economic development policy makers. In turn, the dynamics of the new economy, the sheer diversity and complexity of recent state economic development programs, and the emergent global marketplace in which states must compete prompt us to rethink our assumptions about this policy arena. Four dimensions merit special attention in this chapter: (1) the significance of federalism and globalization in shaping state economic development options; (2) the changing definitions of the problems that emphasize investment in the infrastructure, locational incentives, and entrepreneurial "solutions" to state economic development issues; (3) periodic shifts in orientation of state policy among conventional cost-reduction, smokestack-chasing strategies and more entrepreneurial policy approaches; and (4) the enduring debate on the effectiveness of state economic development policies in influencing state growth and development. These issues signal realignments in the politics of making state economic development policy in the coming years.

### FEDERALISM, GLOBALIZATION, AND STATE ECONOMIC DEVELOPMENT POLICY

The objective of state economic development policy is to bring about more economic activity in a particular location. However, unlike national governments, states cannot control the movement of raw materials, capital, or workers across their borders. They cannot affect the supply of money or the rate of interest on borrowed funds. Most important, state governments cannot command business to invest; they can only hope to induce investment by offering or creating incentives to promote the desired economic activity. Hopefully, these incentives will stimulate new investment that would otherwise not be made in that location.

That said, the states offer low interest loans, loan guarantees, special tax breaks, and outright grants of cash and land to attract and retain private businesses in the state. If a company's site needs improvement, some state governments will prepare the ground for development, bring utility lines to the site, or link it to the transportation system by building roads and tracks. If labor is a problem, they will train workers for individual firms or reimburse them for the costs of customized job training. Among other services, the states use their power of eminent domain on behalf of industries to consolidate multiple land parcels into single developable units. States link businesses to university research, underwrite vocational education to upgrade the skills of the local labor force, and develop industrial parks to compensate for perceived shortages of industrial land. Almost every state offers programs that help businesses export their products to foreign markets, and the governors commonly embark on overseas trade missions to promote their state's firms. More indirectly, states induce investment by granting tax incentives to businesses in general or by reducing personal taxes to entice corporate managers and entrepreneurs to come to the state. The states do these and many other things to overcome the constraints imposed on states by the American federalist system.

### Federalism and State Policy Choices

The decentralized American federal system places many responsibilities on state and local governments but provides few resources to help meet these burdens. As a result, the states compete with each other for investment that brings jobs and tax revenues to the state. Paul Peterson (1981) argues that business and residents are attracted to places with the most favorable ratio of taxes paid to services received. In Peterson's view, states have a common interest in policies that promote economic activity to employ residents and to generate tax revenues. States need these revenues to provide good services and thus enact development policies under the implicit threat that residents and firms will leave if they perceive that the benefit-tax ratio is no longer favorable.

Yet when states offer incentives to retain and attract companies, they are in the position of having to act without sufficient information. They are uncertain of the deals being offered by other states as well as the needs of the firms they are trying to attract or keep from leaving. Because most state governments pursue this strategy and few dare disengage from the competition, they often promise more than is wise or necessary to secure the deal, often with no guarantee that the benefits will outweigh the costs. State incentive packages ratchet upward because only the firm knows what it really needs, and states do not want to make a bid that is too low to attract the firm (Jones and Bachelor 1986). As a result, businesses can play states off each other to get the best deal. Governments take part in this process because there are political advantages to winning the investment competition with other states (Wolman 1988; Wolman and Spitzley 1996).

This competitive environment of bidding up incentives across states sometimes resembles the spiral of decisions in an arms race (Hanson 1993; Peretz 1986). More than thirty-five states, for example, competed in 1993 to be the site for Mercedes-Benz's new sports-utility vehicle plant. With Mercedes-Benz in the "auctioneer's" seat, states presented custom-tailored incentive packages to entice them to locate in their state. Alabama's $300 million winning package included tax breaks, promises to buy the vehicles for the state fleet, payments to workers while in training, commitments to develop the new site, and construction of a welcome center for visitors to the plant, as well as more traditional infrastructure development (Mahtesian 1994). Alabama continued on this path in 2002 by granting $118 million in incentives to Hyundai to locate a new assembly plant in the state.

Periodically, public officials grow weary of the competition and attempt to establish truces in these bidding wars. In 1993 the National Governors Association adopted voluntary guidelines on tax breaks and subsidies aimed at winding down the bidding for private investment (Wyatt 1994). More recently, the Maryland legislature attached a "cease-fire" provision to a job-creation tax credit bill directing the governor to negotiate an agreement with his counterparts in Delaware, North Carolina, Pennsylvania, Virginia and West Virginia (Mahtesian 1996). Several attempts have been made to get the U.S. Congress to intervene. The Federal Reserve Bank of Minneapolis published a report urging Congress to exercise its regulatory authority over interstate commerce to end competitive business-recruitment. To date, eleven states have passed resolutions urging Congress to do something about states luring businesses from other states. Rep. David Minge (D-Minn.) introduced the "Distorting Subsidies Limitation Act" in 1997, but the bill failed to attract the minimum number of sponsors. It seems that economic truces between states are likely to be unstable, and calls for congressional action short-lived. With few incentives for cooperation, governors continuously sacrifice collaborative strategies to respond to pressures to compete in a globalized economy.

*Globalization and State Policy Choices*

It is clear that state economic growth and development processes now must be considered in the context of larger trends. Growth no longer can be captured within politically bounded and relatively closed economies. Investment flows and decision makers are international rather than local or national. The most salient features of globalization include the greater mobility of capital, a new international division of labor with many production jobs moving outside the United States, the elimination of national trade barriers, new information and transportation technologies, and global competition increasingly driven by innovation rather than the costs of land, labor, and capital (Reich 1991). These features alter the investment priorities of firms and the policy options of states.

State policy makers are faced with the need to make their communities competitive in a global arena, where increasingly mobile capital and new telecommunications technologies make locations appear interchangeable to firms. The traditional interjurisdictional competition for investment takes on a new dimension when the costs of production are lower outside the United States and all states are potential losers. In the absence of a national industrial policy, states have been compelled to craft their own responses to the diverse effects of globalization trends.

## CHANGING PROBLEM DEFINITIONS: ECONOMIC DEVELOPMENT AS A POLICY PROBLEM

One of the complications inherent in the study of state economic development is that it is often politically advantageous for the proponents of almost any policy initiative to cast their proposal in terms of its potential to enhance the economy. But if economic development is defined as any and all policies that directly or indirectly enhance the economy, the policy arena becomes undistinguishable from other arenas. A more precise definition is called for. To this end, we define economic development policy as those policies intended to encourage new business investment in specific locations in the hopes of developing the economy by producing jobs and enhancing and diversifying the local tax base (Eisinger 1988, 4). This definition allows us to consider the full range of problem definitions states use to diagnose their development needs and identify appropriate solutions, from infrastructure programs to efforts to affect firms' locational decisions to more process-oriented strategies to encourage indigenous growth.

*States As Economic Policy Activists*

The American states are not newcomers to the practice of economic development. They have been involved in promoting economic growth since the first days of the Republic. The current array of economic development policies is only the latest stage in a continuing, albeit wavering, process of state intervention in economic activities. Prior to 1800 most of the U.S. population lived and worked on small, self-sufficient farms. Commercial farming was insignificant because the cost of transporting crops was overwhelming. The cost of transporting a ton of goods thirty miles overland was roughly equivalent to transporting them three thousand miles overseas from Boston to London (Takaki 1990, 75). States built infrastructures (ports, roads, bridges, and so forth) to facilitate the movement of goods to the coast and then to other eastern cities or overseas. As competition developed between eastern seaports, the states rushed to build canals. Cumberland (1971) estimates that the public investment in canal building was $432 million, of which $300 million was paid by the states and $125 million by local governments. The federal government contributed only $7 million (North, Anderson, and Hill 1983).

By 1860 the Northeast, West (Illinois, Indiana, and Ohio), and South were economically integrated. Both the Northeast and the South depended on the West for the production of foodstuffs. The Southeast specialized in cotton production and supplied the textile factories in the Northeast. The South and the West purchased manufactured goods from the East (North 1966). This transition was spurred in large part by technological improvements that enabled, then led to demands for, an integrated transportation system, setting in motion the forces leading to what Taylor (1977) called the transportation revolution. The economic role of the states did not end with financing harbors and canals. The states contributed 48 million of the 179 million acres allocated to railroads for development of rail systems (North, Anderson, and Hill 1983). After the railroads came highways with automobiles, then air transportation, all of which involved state government financing and improved the movement of goods and information and further stimulated economic growth.

State economic development policies, outside of helping build transportation networks, however, have a sporadic history. State economic development policy as an activity separate from transportation policy became a formal function of state government in Alabama, Florida, Maine, and North Carolina in the 1920s. In other states economic development planning was adopted as an aspect of participation in the New Deal economic recovery programs in the 1930s and 1940s or as a way to coordinate industrial production in World War II. But except for a few in the South, all states had phased out their economic development agencies by the 1950s (Eisinger 1988).

Only within the last three decades has economic development policy resurfaced as a major concern among the states' governors. Prior to the 1980s, Herzik (1983) described economic development as a "cyclical" policy—one that grows in concern, peaks, and then steadily declines. But since the mid-1970s the issue of economic development has been a perennial state issue. Throughout the 1980s, and continuing through the 1990s and into the twenty-first century, governors have ranked economic development with education, highways, corrections, welfare, and health care as enduring state policy issues. Today every state recognizes economic development as an integral part of state government.

*Variations in State Problem Definitions*

Citizens and public officials in each state, however, understand their economic development problems differently, and thus their policy solutions differ as well. Policy making for state economic development is especially intriguing because of competing problem definitions. Policy makers draw on various theories of economic growth in defining and diagnosing state development problems—they help policy makers pinpoint what causes these problems and what the appropriate solutions might be (Rochefort and Cobb 1994). Traditional locational or "smokestack-chasing" strategies, for example, reflect a theory of economic growth that emphasizes the importance of low costs for basic production factors—land, labor, raw materials, and capital—in attracting investment to a particular location.

In the wake of global competition, however, a different economic model is emerging. According to this theory, state development problems stem not from high production costs but from environments not receptive to new and innovative technologies and business activities. From the perspective of this theory, the problems of economic development are not loss of investment but potential relegation to a global backwater as innovation centers grow elsewhere. State officials persuaded by this new perspective are experimenting with policies that emphasize flexibility, risk taking, and market structuring on the part of state government to encourage innovation and to minimize barriers to innovation (Clarke and Gaile 1998).

The sheer diversity of state policy responses to these problem diagnoses is impressive. According to the latest comprehensive data source, the states offered 974 separate economic development programs (NASDA 1998).[1] Some programs, such as industrial revenue bonds and tax incentives for the purchase of industrial machinery, are offered by all states. All states also offer direct financial assistance to firms through direct loans, grants, loan guarantees or other interest subsidies. Other programs are more distinctive, such as New Hampshire's Economic Development Ventures Fund, which provides grants and loans through non-profit community development corporations and worker cooperatives for projects that will create economic opportunities for low- and moderate-income citizens.

To make sense of this array of state economic development policies (for a comprehensive list of policy instruments, see Sternberg 1987), we classify strategies in terms of their infrastructure investment objectives and their business promotional objectives; we further distinguish the latter as incentives aimed at influencing locational decisions or at facilitating entrepreneurial growth processes.[2]

---

1. This does not include programs funded primarily by the federal government, basic state taxes such as income, sales, and property taxes, and subsidies offered to induce compliance with environmental regulations.

2. Our state program data are drawn from the *Directory of Incentives for Business Investment and Development in the United States* for 1983, 1986, 1991, 1994, and 1998 (*Directory of Incentives*, various years). The directory presents the state programs in a narrative format that includes a description of the incentive, its terms, conditions, and eligibility criteria. The program information is self-reported by the states in a standardized format. Another frequently used data source, the *Industrial Development and Site Selection Handbook* ("the Conway data"), is also based on self-reporting but is more oriented towards industrial recruitment strategies. It slights entrepreneurial programs and reports merely the presence/absence of programs rather than the narrative detail included in the *Directory of Incentives*. State economic development policy efforts continue to expand. As reported by the *Directory of Incentives* (various years), the number of economic development programs rose from 465 in 1983 to 974 in 1998, more than doubling the number of incentive programs in fifteen years.

## ALTERNATIVE STRATEGIES FOR ECONOMIC DEVELOPMENT

Three major policy strategies dominate the state economic development agenda: infrastructure strategies, locational incentives, and entrepreneurial strategies. Briefly, strategies for infrastructure emphasize the construction and maintenance of physical infrastructure such as roads and highways to encourage and support development. Locational incentives seek to reduce the costs of doing business in relation to other locations; they may be aimed at attracting businesses that wish to relocate, retaining those tempted by other states to relocate, or encouraging existing businesses to expand in place. In contrast, entrepreneurial strategies emphasize facilitating growth processes rather than influencing particular firms in their choice of location.

Each of these policy paths implies distinctive strategies that reflect different understandings of the logic underlying economic development processes. That said, policy makers must also be pragmatists and seek orientations that accord with the political dispositions of state voters. While these investment and promotional strategies do not entail mutually exclusive choices, each state nevertheless exhibits a distinctive economic development policy profile. We compare these state policy profiles by developing a standardized index of policy attributes for each of the three policy orientations: the infrastructure investment approach, the locational incentive approach, and the entrepreneurial approach.[3]

### The Infrastructure Development Approach

Although traditional infrastructure strategies center on the provision of seemingly prosaic fixed assets such as highways, sewers, and waste treatment plants, there is a sense of crisis surrounding infrastructure policy, and the very term itself is subject to debate. Perry (1994) traces the evolving taxonomy from a focus on internal improvements in the early nineteenth century to the concern with public works projects in the Great Depression era to the more inclusive and systemic view of infrastructure systems. In contrast to a specific focus on bridges or roads, the term infrastructure now signifies a concern with both the technological systems of physical facilities and the roles, particularly the economic role, these assets play in future growth and development. This link between infrastructure and development became prominent in the 1970s, when economic development needs displaced historical concerns with health, safety, and environmental needs as the primary justification for infrastructure investment (Felbinger 1994). In the absence of national infrastructure policy initiatives, however, there is a concern that there will be continued underinvestment in public infrastructure, with potentially negative effects on national and subnational policies.

3. To construct our indexes, we coded the 3,730 program descriptions from the 1983, 1986, 1991, 1994, and 1998 editions of the *Directory of Incentives for Business Investment and Development in the United States (Directory of Incentives,* various years). Our standardized index scores are the ratio of attributes to programs for each state for the infrastructure, locational, and entrepreneurial incentive approaches. For full details of index construction and tests of validity, see Saiz 2001b.

*Federalism and Infrastructure Investment.* In the early 1980s, Choate and Walter's report (1981) on public capital infrastructure, *America in Ruins,* galvanized public attention. Choate and Walter argued that local economic development was hampered by obsolete and deteriorating public facilities. Their diagnosis of an infrastructure crisis demanded a national policy response. Federal participation in infrastructure provision, however, has been erratic and reluctant. The national government has perceived most public works projects as having primarily local impacts and has thus been averse to taxing or borrowing for such purposes (GAO 1993; Rivlin, 1995).

Federal capital spending for the nation's infrastructure peaked in the 1960s. Since 1970 there has been a precipitous decline in federal support for state and local infrastructure—a loss in constant dollars of more than 60 percent in federal grants-in-aid between 1970 and 1990. State and local governments now account for 90 percent of all public works spending, with a growing share (43 percent) of those expenditures by special purpose governments such as public authorities and special districts (Leigland 1994). By the mid-1980s, federal efforts were characterized as an ad hoc federal infrastructure strategy that emphasized aid for transportation programs; trust fund financing rather than grants-in-aid; and support for research, management, training, technical assistance, and demonstration projects (Man and Bell 1993, 19).

In the past, this aversion to federal action was overcome by framing local infrastructure issues as national problems: politicians justified the 1956 National Highway Act for defense purposes and claimed the Water Pollution Control Act of 1972 would ensure national standards for water quality. After 9/11 state governments and national policy makers began to assess state and local infrastructures in terms of their interdependencies and vulnerability to attack. Framing infrastructure issues in terms of security problems redirects attention to "critical infrastructures" rather than infrastrucure systems as a whole or only public facilities.[4] The concern for improving the condition of the nation's infrastructure is now overshadowed by a concern for its protection. Governors are playing a critical role coordinating state and local resources to enhance security at major airports and protect communications and power networks, bridges, public buildings, and supplies of drinking water. But one of the dilemmas is that in many regions, such as the Pacific Northwest, elements of these critical infrastructures are primarily privately operated and not subject to government control. And it is not clear who is in charge if state infrastructures are threatened: emergency-management systems are traditionally funded and directed by the federal government while state governments provide disaster assistance.

Even with these recent threats, therefore, the federal government's responsibilities in financing and regulating development of infrastructure continue to be in

---

4. Critical infrastructures include information, telecommunications, transportation, energy, water, health care, and financial services and the information systems that support them, with a special emphasis on emergency preparedness communications.

question. Despite numerous proposals for new funding to invigorate state infrastructure investment, there are few breaks in this national policy gridlock. One important exception to this stalemate was the passage of the Intermodal Surface Transportation Efficiency Act of 1991 (ISTEA), authorizing expenditures for intermodal transit—highways, mass transit, and safety and research programs—as well as nonroadway enhancements such as greenways, bike paths, and historic preservation (U.S. Department of Transportation 1993). It gave the states a prominent and flexible policy role, in exchange for providing 20 percent of funding, and brings new interests into the transportation policy arena by requiring states to share planning for new transportation projects with metropolitan planning organizations (MPOs) (Kincaid 1992). The successor legislation to ISTEA, the Transportation Equity Act of 1998 (TEA-21), retained many of the innovative aspects of ISTEA; it also cast transportation policy as an international issue by funding transborder transportation corridor planning by state and local governments.[5]

*State Infrastructure Policy Agendas.* Infrastructure investment is the most traditional state investment and development tool and a good gauge of state involvement in economic development. The traditional agenda centers on financing infrastructure; more recently, public construction of sports stadiums and public investment in information highways are salient issues in addition to the concern for critical infrastructure.

State and local governments rarely debate whether infrastructure investment and maintenance are necessary; rather, the central issues are how to provide and pay for them. Even where the national government pays significant infrastructure construction costs, as in the highway programs, states and localities are responsible for the continued maintenance of these facilities. This stewardship is expensive, and it is tempting to defer maintenance; indeed, until recently the incentives of federal capital grants for replacement and renewal activities perversely encouraged delays on maintenance until deteriorating structures became eligible for federal funds (Perry 1994).

Historically, taxes and bond financing supported most state public works activities, but the financing has become increasingly complex. In passing the National Highway System Designation Act of 1995, Congress encouraged states to come up with new financing approaches such as organizing infrastructure banks and experimenting with toll roads (Ota 1998). California offers several prototypes of public-private partnerships, technological innovations, and private financing to construct transportation infrastructure. The state Department of Transportation, for example, entered into franchise agreements with private investors in order to construct transportation facilities that otherwise faced political stalemates. One project involved construction of four express toll lanes on the median strip of state route 91,

5. The CORBOR programs—the Coordinated Border Infrastructure (CBI) and the National Corridor Planning and Development (NCPD) discretionary grant programs—are signature features of the TEA-21 program (see U.S. Department of Transportation 1998).

which links Orange County and Riverside County; the private partners provided most of the financing, which is to be repaid by tolls collected electronically as cars enter the express lane with debit card transmitters on the car's dashboard.

In today's competitive context, many state and local officials see sports stadiums as infrastructure assets with important revenue-generating potential. While some sports stadiums are privately financed (for example, the San Francisco Giants' Pacific Bell Park, or the Boston Celtics' Fleet Center), most rely on substantial public subsidies. Teams often threaten to leave town if they don't get new stadiums and public subsidies to support them. Today the St. Louis Cardinals, Minnesota Twins, Arizona Cardinals, San Diego Padres, Kansas City Royals and Chiefs, and the New York Yankees and Mets are all seeking new stadiums while Chicago, Boston, Detroit, and New Orleans are planning major renovations (Mihoces 2002). Although relocation is rare, cities are hostage to these cyclical threats since sports leagues enjoy a monopoly: national leagues create an "artificial scarcity" of teams by limiting the number of teams and controlling where they will be placed. Indeed, the owners of major league baseball periodically threaten to eliminate teams to boost revenues.

By continually threatening to leave if cities do not meet their demands, sports teams create their own version of the arms race described above. St. Louis and the state of Missouri, for example, paid the full costs (estimated at $300 million) of building the TransWorld Dome football stadium in St. Louis to attract the Rams from Los Angeles, throwing in a new practice facility and a $29 million relocation fee to sweeten the deal. When St. Louis later unsuccessfully sued the National Football League for conspiring against the city over the franchise price, the city attorney described it as "the worst sports deal in history" (Mahtesian 1998).

As in other economic development deals, the costs and benefits seem skewed toward private interests. Team owners and players clearly gain from the subsidized stadiums, but the state and local benefits are less obvious. The usual taxpayer share in stadium construction is 80 to 100 percent, mostly for construction, but governments often pay for land and street improvements (Barringer 1997). For example, to build the Seahawks Stadium in Seattle, the public put up $300 million in taxpayer funds while the Seahawks' owner, a founder of Microsoft, invested $130 million. To raise these public funds, supporters draw on state and local sources that might be used for other projects; stadium deals also place financial burdens on many who have neither the interest nor the ability to attend sporting events.

While most citizens enjoy sports, polls, referenda, and elections consistently show few are willing to pay for sports stadiums with public funds. They see little reason to do so since most economic assessments fail to show increases in per capita income, wages, or even net employment associated with stadium development (Rosentraub et al. 1994). Furthermore, fairness issues take on a clarity in sports financing that is often missing from other economic development debates. Despite the post–Super Bowl euphoria in Denver, the Denver Broncos' demands for a new stadium prompted one official to ask, "What about Mrs. Martinez?" The imaginary Mrs. Martinez may be unable to pay the ticket prices at the new stadium and will never see a game but will have to pay increased taxes to raise public funds for the stadium. In a sense, such arrangements transfer dollars from people who pay sales taxes—especially middle- and lower-class citizens—to owners and players who spend it elsewhere. When tax-free bonds are issued, all federal taxpayers end up subsidizing sports stadiums. Perhaps this explains the current ambivalence among voters in financing sports stadiums. Charlotte's voters rejected financing a new basketball arena, as have voters in Minneapolis and Houston. Stadium projects in Los Angeles, Phoenix, San Diego, Chicago, and St. Louis all faced organized opposition (Mihoces 2002).

Recent information technology changes are likely to reshape state infrastructure agendas by the end of the century. Technological changes provide new ways of communicating and producing, but they also transform social and political dynamics in unanticipated ways. Into the next century state infrastructure politics are likely to reflect the changing nature of global competition, persistent tensions in intergovernmental relations, the continual question of public finance, as well as the particular social and economic conditions in each state.

Many states are taking the lead in developing innovative information infrastructures. In the early 1990s, for example, Iowa financed and built its own fiber-optic network to ensure universal service and maintain public control. North Carolina, in contrast, formed a public-private partnership with twenty-eight state telephone firms to build the North Carolina Information Highway (NCIH) in 1995, the first statewide broadband network. Rewiring the state is part of North Carolina's economic development strategy: officials anticipated that the existence of a statewide information highway will attract businesses to North Carolina because they will not have to build their own private networks (Richter 1994, 68). While it is difficult to track these business impacts, high schools, community colleges, and state agencies using the NCIH for distance learning and training purposes are key users and beneficiaries of the network.

Similarly, Illinois's Century Network connects more than 5,600 government agencies, schools, museums, and other public institutions. Illinois went one step further, launching Illinois VentureTech in 2000, a technology-based economic development program investing $2 billion in state resources into a multi-pronged agenda including education, research and development, health sciences, biotechnology, and information technology programs. By taking the investment lead, the state hopes to create a new image encouraging further business investment. This massive investment program moved Illinois to a tie for first place in the 2001 Digital State surveys (ranking states' use of technology to improve government services) and prompted an increase in business incubators and more commercialization of university research (Towns 2002).

To gain a more precise sense of state infrastructure policy agendas, we examined state programs that offered incentives either to communities or private companies to develop infrastructure. In 1983 no state offered an infrastructure assistance program, but by 1998 twenty-five states did; Alabama and Pennsylvania each have six infrastructure programs, while Illinois, Mississippi, New Mexico, and Washington have four programs. The Gund Foundation worked with the state of Ohio to draw up a comprehensive infrastructure development plan for Cleveland, carried out by the Build Up Greater Cleveland public-private partnership (Licate 1994).

Our index of state infrastructure programs (Table 14-1) measures the commitment of states to infrastructure policies in relation to their overall economic development policy effort. The higher the score, the greater the state's commitment to infrastructure. An examination of infrastructure index scores shows that the magnitude of the index scores has remained about the same over time. This is because the number of programs highlighting transportation or infrastructure incentives adopted by the states is low in relation to the total number of incentives the state offers. In 1998 there was an increase in infrastructure programs as a share of overall economic development effort; in some states, like Texas and Pennsylvania, this reflects a resumption of previous efforts; but in states such as Alabama, New Mexico, Illinois, and Washington, the index shows a marked increase in infrastructure initiatives.

### The Locational Incentive Approach

Locational economic development policies aim at improving a community's ability to compete with other locations for industry, jobs, and economic growth. This policy orientation is grounded in economic location theory, which suggests that, other things being equal, firms will seek those locations where the combined costs of land, labor, capital, energy, and transportation are minimal (Weber 1984). Thus the state seeking a competitive advantage over other states must create an advantageous price structure for these "production factors," thereby creating a comparative locational advantage.

Common tools used in making locations more attractive to investors include low-interest financing (frequently offered in the form of industrial revenue bonds), tax credits, abatements, deferments and exemptions, subsidized employee training, and assistance with site selection and preparation (Fosler 1988). The rubric of locational economic development policy also includes the notion of creating a "positive business climate" or a pro-business atmosphere. These are vague concepts, but the associated policies often include low taxes and regulatory policies designed to keep production costs low, such as right-to-work laws and relaxed environmental legislation (Plaut and Pluta 1983).

Recently, Boeing CEO Philip Condit announced that his company was looking to relocate its headquarters from Seattle to Chicago, Dallas, or Denver, challenging state and local boosters to pony up an incentive package to lure its 500 employees. These bids exemplify locational incentive strategies. Chicago and Illinois won the competition with a $63 million offer including $41 million in state tax credits, ten years of income tax grants for Boeing's employees, $20 million in job training, technology, and capital improvements, and $2 million in property tax abatements and improvements to Midway Airport's hangars. The deal illustrates a classic zero sum

**Table 14-1** Infrastructure Economic Development Policy Indexes

| State | 1983 | 1986 | 1991 | 1994 | 1998 |
|---|---|---|---|---|---|
| Alabama | 0.00 | 0.00 | 0.08 | 0.12 | 0.30 |
| Alaska | 0.00 | 0.00 | 0.00 | 0.00 | 0.11 |
| Arizona | 0.00 | 0.00 | 0.00 | 0.00 | 0.00 |
| Arkansas | 0.00 | 0.00 | 0.00 | 0.04 | 0.05 |
| California | 0.22 | 0.20 | 0.25 | 0.25 | 0.18 |
| Colorado | 0.11 | 0.14 | 0.08 | 0.08 | 0.10 |
| Connecticut | 0.00 | 0.00 | 0.00 | 0.00 | 0.00 |
| Delaware | 0.00 | 0.00 | 0.00 | 0.00 | 0.00 |
| Florida | 0.00 | 0.00 | 0.11 | 0.05 | 0.13 |
| Georgia | 0.00 | 0.00 | 0.00 | 0.04 | 0.00 |
| Hawaii | 0.08 | 0.07 | 0.07 | 0.14 | 0.10 |
| Idaho | 0.00 | 0.00 | 0.00 | 0.00 | 0.00 |
| Illinois | 0.00 | 0.00 | 0.08 | 0.04 | 0.14 |
| Indiana | 0.19 | 0.15 | 0.16 | 0.16 | 0.08 |
| Iowa | 0.00 | 0.00 | 0.00 | 0.00 | 0.05 |
| Kansas | 0.00 | 0.00 | 0.08 | 0.12 | 0.08 |
| Kentucky | 0.20 | 0.33 | 0.27 | 0.27 | 0.16 |
| Louisiana | 0.00 | 0.00 | 0.00 | 0.00 | 0.04 |
| Maine | 0.00 | 0.00 | 0.00 | 0.13 | 0.09 |
| Maryland | 0.00 | 0.00 | 0.00 | 0.00 | 0.00 |
| Massachusetts | 0.00 | 0.00 | 0.00 | 0.00 | 0.00 |
| Michigan | 0.07 | 0.06 | 0.13 | 0.20 | 0.27 |
| Minnesota | 0.15 | 0.06 | 0.10 | 0.10 | 0.22 |
| Mississippi | 0.00 | 0.00 | 0.08 | 0.12 | 0.12 |
| Missouri | 0.00 | 0.17 | 0.13 | 0.07 | 0.06 |
| Montana | 0.13 | 0.05 | 0.05 | 0.00 | 0.14 |
| Nebraska | 0.00 | 0.00 | 0.00 | 0.00 | 0.00 |
| Nevada | 0.00 | 0.00 | 0.00 | 0.00 | 0.00 |
| New Hampshire | 0.29 | 0.14 | 0.40 | 0.11 | 0.18 |
| New Jersey | 0.27 | 0.13 | 0.14 | 0.09 | 0.11 |
| New Mexico | 0.00 | 0.00 | 0.11 | 0.08 | 0.17 |
| New York | 0.06 | 0.06 | 0.08 | 0.12 | 0.06 |
| North Carolina | 0.00 | 0.00 | 0.00 | 0.00 | 0.00 |
| North Dakota | 0.00 | 0.00 | 0.00 | 0.00 | 0.00 |
| Ohio | 0.00 | 0.00 | 0.00 | 0.14 | 0.14 |
| Oklahoma | 0.00 | 0.00 | 0.00 | 0.00 | 0.00 |
| Oregon | 0.43 | 0.33 | 0.27 | 0.00 | 0.17 |
| Pennsylvania | 0.17 | 0.23 | 0.27 | 0.32 | 0.33 |
| Rhode Island | 0.10 | 0.07 | 0.08 | 0.08 | 0.04 |
| South Carolina | 0.13 | 0.09 | 0.06 | 0.30 | 0.33 |
| South Dakota | 0.00 | 0.00 | 0.00 | 0.00 | 0.00 |
| Tennessee | 0.30 | 0.33 | 0.40 | 0.36 | 0.29 |
| Texas | 0.40 | 0.40 | 0.08 | 0.14 | 0.19 |
| Utah | 0.33 | 0.25 | 0.11 | 0.00 | 0.00 |
| Vermont | 0.33 | 0.00 | 0.00 | 0.00 | 0.00 |
| Virginia | 0.00 | 0.00 | 0.05 | 0.00 | 0.00 |
| Washington | 0.20 | 0.20 | 0.20 | 0.11 | 0.24 |
| West Virginia | 0.00 | 0.00 | 0.00 | 0.00 | 0.13 |
| Wisconsin | 0.14 | 0.11 | 0.07 | 0.08 | 0.09 |
| Wyoming | 0.00 | 0.00 | 0.00 | 0.00 | 0.00 |
| U.S. mean | 0.09 | 0.07 | 0.08 | 0.08 | 0.10 |

SOURCES: Computed from program descriptions in *Directory of Incentives*, various years.

game: 80 percent of the jobs are transfers, few new jobs were created, and Chicago gained at Seattle's expense (Lyne 2001).

*Attributes of Locational Policy Orientations.* We assess the degree to which states pursue a locational economic development approach by measuring the extent to which their policies reflect key attributes of the locational orientation. First, we distinguish programs whose primary purpose is to reduce costs by offering direct financial subsidies to businesses. Second, we include policies that indirectly reduce costs to business such as when states offer tax relief or accelerated depreciation on capital expenditures. Third, from these programs we eliminate those that target specific areas or economic sectors (other than manufacturing), leaving only nontargeted, administratively passive programs that require little initiative on the part of a governmental agency to implement. Thus the attributes of locational economic development policies show an acceptance of prevailing economic forces; other than attempting to lower costs within the state, the economic role of state governments remains subordinate to private sector decisions (Eisinger 1988; Fosler 1988).

*Changes in Locational Orientations.* The locational policy index measures the degree to which state governments have adopted policies with locational attributes in relation to the state's overall economic development policy effort. Thus states with higher index scores (as shown in Table 14-2) demonstrate greater commitment to a locational policy orientation than do states with lower scores. Over time, Colorado, Idaho, and South Dakota consistently emphasize locational policy orientations; South Carolina and Nevada recently emerged as states giving priority to locational strategies. Table 14-2 suggests no obvious regional pattern to these locational policy orientations, although less densely populated, less urbanized states and southern states with historical usage of locational policies appear to be the most prominent adopters of this strategy.

Most states do not seem to be pursuing locational approaches as single-mindedly as in the past. Between 1994 and 1998 twelve states increased their locational index scores while the scores in thirty-six states declined. The average value of the locational indexes dropped substantially every year since 1983, despite increases in the total number of state economic development programs in each of these periods. New state programs are more likely to include more entrepreneurial attributes.

### Entrepreneurial Economic Development Policy Approaches

Entrepreneurial policies are grounded in a theoretical model of economic development processes that emphasize the wealth-generating capacities of innovative activities as the engine of economic growth. Rather than attempting to influence business locational decisions, state policy makers use public resources and authority to encourage new markets and economic ventures. This sometimes requires public officials to act like business entrepreneurs by taking risks and creating opportunities in hopes of generating a more vibrant state economy (Eisinger 1988; Clarke and Gaile 1998).

**Table 14-2** Locational Economic Development Policy Indexes

| State | 1983 | 1986 | 1991 | 1994 | 1998 |
|---|---|---|---|---|---|
| Alabama | 2.40 | 2.40 | 2.15 | 1.82 | 1.40 |
| Alaska | 2.25 | 2.75 | 1.36 | 1.11 | 0.84 |
| Arizona | 2.50 | 2.67 | 2.67 | 2.00 | 1.64 |
| Arkansas | 2.50 | 2.33 | 1.56 | 1.19 | 1.58 |
| California | 1.67 | 1.70 | 1.58 | 1.58 | 1.00 |
| Colorado | 2.56 | 2.43 | 1.92 | 1.83 | 1.90 |
| Connecticut | 2.00 | 1.88 | 1.65 | 1.37 | 1.66 |
| Delaware | 2.00 | 2.13 | 1.46 | 2.09 | 1.56 |
| Florida | 2.27 | 2.10 | 1.47 | 1.05 | 1.08 |
| Georgia | 2.33 | 1.29 | 1.29 | 1.50 | 1.82 |
| Hawaii | 2.17 | 2.14 | 1.93 | 1.79 | 1.60 |
| Idaho | 2.50 | 2.43 | 2.43 | 2.22 | 2.00 |
| Illinois | 2.30 | 1.89 | 1.31 | 1.38 | 0.81 |
| Indiana | 1.88 | 1.80 | 1.79 | 1.74 | 1.04 |
| Iowa | 2.10 | 2.00 | 1.56 | 1.45 | 1.10 |
| Kansas | 2.50 | 1.91 | 1.25 | 1.64 | 1.31 |
| Kentucky | 1.60 | 2.00 | 1.91 | 2.00 | 1.53 |
| Louisiana | 1.83 | 1.93 | 1.53 | 1.67 | 1.58 |
| Maine | 1.85 | 1.71 | 1.92 | 1.63 | 1.68 |
| Maryland | 1.57 | 1.63 | 1.42 | 1.20 | 1.26 |
| Massachusetts | 1.77 | 1.79 | 1.38 | 1.45 | 1.29 |
| Michigan | 2.21 | 1.56 | 1.33 | 1.65 | 1.33 |
| Minnesota | 1.46 | 1.76 | 0.90 | 0.85 | 0.56 |
| Mississippi | 1.83 | 1.83 | 1.92 | 1.77 | 1.38 |
| Missouri | 2.00 | 1.54 | 1.40 | 1.46 | 1.23 |
| Montana | 2.25 | 1.53 | 1.60 | 1.39 | 1.36 |
| Nebraska | 2.00 | 1.63 | 1.73 | 1.73 | 1.85 |
| Nevada | 2.50 | 1.17 | 1.17 | 1.22 | 1.89 |
| New Hampshire | 2.43 | 2.43 | 2.60 | 1.21 | 0.55 |
| New Jersey | 1.91 | 1.63 | 1.36 | 1.30 | 0.89 |
| New Mexico | 1.80 | 2.20 | 2.00 | 1.38 | 1.71 |
| New York | 2.13 | 1.72 | 1.19 | 1.12 | 1.19 |
| North Carolina | 2.20 | 1.22 | 1.50 | 1.36 | 1.56 |
| North Dakota | 1.91 | 2.00 | 1.69 | 1.56 | 0.90 |
| Ohio | 1.69 | 1.50 | 1.46 | 1.71 | 1.33 |
| Oklahoma | 2.29 | 2.22 | 2.10 | 1.92 | 1.71 |
| Oregon | 1.86 | 1.44 | 1.36 | 1.35 | 1.28 |
| Pennsylvania | 1.67 | 1.27 | 1.05 | 1.32 | 1.21 |
| Rhode Island | 2.10 | 1.79 | 2.00 | 2.00 | 1.61 |
| South Carolina | 2.13 | 2.09 | 2.39 | 2.09 | 2.60 |
| South Dakota | 2.75 | 2.20 | 2.13 | 1.89 | 2.00 |
| Tennessee | 2.10 | 2.33 | 2.30 | 2.36 | 1.53 |
| Texas | 1.60 | 1.60 | 1.83 | 1.24 | 0.94 |
| Utah | 2.67 | 2.75 | 1.67 | 1.78 | 1.42 |
| Vermont | 2.00 | 1.75 | 1.71 | 1.71 | 1.58 |
| Virginia | 2.13 | 1.79 | 1.60 | 1.57 | 1.28 |
| Washington | 2.40 | 2.40 | 1.80 | 1.68 | 1.10 |
| West Virginia | 2.00 | 2.00 | 2.06 | 1.54 | 1.60 |
| Wisconsin | 1.86 | 1.44 | 1.27 | 1.08 | 0.78 |
| Wyoming | 2.75 | 1.83 | 2.00 | 1.67 | 1.33 |
| U.S. mean | 2.10 | 1.91 | 1.69 | 1.57 | 1.39 |

SOURCES: Computed from program descriptions in *Directory of Incentives*, various years.

These entrepreneurial policies are recent additions to the states' economic development policy arsenal, most having been adopted during and after the recession of the early 1980s (Sherman, Wallace, and Pitney 1995). This entrepreneurial approach generates new roles for state governments, particularly a more central role in efforts to create jobs and facilitate growth processes (Osborne 1988, 249). Leadership, information, strategic planning, public-private partnerships, and policy brokering become the new tools of state economic development (Bradshaw and Blakely, 1999). In New York's Industrial Effectiveness Program/Manufacturing Extension Partnership, for example, the state helps firms identify and develop strategies to improve their management and improve efficiency and to expand the market for state businesses. Similarly, the Massachusetts Technology Collaborative sponsored the development of the Massachusetts Medical Device Industry Council, a trade association and network of medical device manufacturers.

Although economic development processes are still driven primarily by private sector decisions, state government initiatives provide critical support for these processes. Creating an entrepreneurial "climate" in the state can promote new economic activity (Goetz and Freshwater 2001); this can occur through strategic clustering and targeting of existing programs and organizations or by establishing new public-private institutions. These new organizations, generally outside the governmental arena and staffed by development professionals, provide a means of coordinating investment decisions. They often also furnish means for overcoming the historic restrictions on state debt capacity still in place in many states. They often have independent financing authority and can leverage private-sector investments with public funds in ways not available to state agencies. For example, quasi-public state organizations may supply "seed" money to stimulate new business formation or to fund the research needed to bring technological innovations to the market. These state organizational innovations allow state governments to be more flexible and versatile than bureaucratic structures normally permit; advocates claim they permit the state to anticipate, specialize, experiment, evaluate, and adjust to changing economic forces (Fosler 1988, 4).

*Attributes of Entrepreneurial Economic Development Orientations.* Several core attributes of entrepreneurial economic development programs distinguish them from more conventional locational economic development approaches. First are programmatic features that target entrepreneurs by limiting incentives to high-technology and small businesses or to firms at high-risk (start-up, new product, technology transfer, and basic research) stages of development. Venture capital programs, for example, normally have this attribute. Second are programs that target growth-producing economic sectors, identified by Sternberg (1987, 159) as banking, education, and communications. Third, following observations by Bowman (1987), we include attributes of programs that attempt to improve the capacity of a firm or individual to take advantage of, or adjust to, new production processes. Customized job training, technical or entrepreneurial assistance for individual firms, business incubators, and programs aimed at the rehabilitation of plants (or the provision of new infrastructure) to take advantage of new technologies, for example, typically show this attribute. Lastly, we isolate features of programs that work through public-private partnerships, such as local or state development (and credit) corporations that expand financial opportunity by leveraging private capital with public dollars, thereby increasing the pool of local investment funds (Saiz 2001b).

*Changes in Entrepreneurial Orientations.* The index score reflects the degree to which state governments adopted policies with entrepreneurial attributes in relation to their overall economic development policy effort. Again, the higher the value, the greater the state reliance on this approach. A clear trend can be seen in Table 14-3 toward adoption of policies with more entrepreneurial attributes. Between 1983 and 1998 the average index increased by more than 150 percent as all fifty states showed greater use of entrepreneurial approaches. By the end of the 1990s, New York, New Hampshire, and North Dakota were placing the greatest emphasis on entrepreneurial approaches. These states ranked high in the early indicators and maintained their positions by consistently adding programs with entrepreneurial attributes. Arkansas, Minnesota, Massachusetts, and North Carolina—entrepreneurial policy leaders in the late 1980s and 1990s—seemed to be moderating their approaches.

In line with Eisinger's contention (1988) that states will maintain a mix of traditional and entrepreneurial economic development policies, our indexes show that states continue to combine approaches. As Bradshaw and Blakely (1999) see it, these new orientations are more likely to focus than to replace earlier strategies. Some states take a leadership role in adoption of entrepreneurial economic development strategies while other states, such as Illinois, Indiana, Louisiana, Michigan, Texas, and West Virginia, consistently fall in the middle range on both measures. This apparent balancing act is not surprising when we consider the political context of policy adoption. Although states increasingly are adopting new approaches with entrepreneurial attributes, these new policies are an overlay on previously adopted development programs characterized by locational attributes. Given the difficulty of terminating programs with influential beneficiaries, the shift toward entrepreneurial orientations is likely to be slow, partial, and uneven. Some analysts would argue that it could even be reversed. Tennessee's Saturn deal, Alabama's Mercedes-Benz package, and other such mega deals could signal the return of smokestack-chasing (Guskind 1993; Mahtesian 1994).

### Why Do States Adopt Different Strategies?

While rising levels of state economic development activism can be interpreted in terms of the incentives embedded in decentralized federalism structures, the reasons why states favor one orientation rather than another are less clear. The logic of competitive federalism may be sufficient for explaining conventional cost-reduction strategies; the use of state authority to shape market structures, to create public-private partnerships, or to pursue strategies involving higher-risk and longer-term investments is less explicable. In a recent study, Saiz (2001a) used the

**Table 14-3** Entrepreneurial Economic Development Policy Indexes

| State | 1983 | 1986 | 1991 | 1994 | 1998 |
|---|---|---|---|---|---|
| Alabama | 0.30 | 0.30 | 0.62 | 0.65 | 1.15 |
| Alaska | 1.00 | 1.25 | 1.57 | 1.56 | 1.37 |
| Arizona | 0.00 | 0.00 | 0.00 | 0.45 | 1.00 |
| Arkansas | 0.30 | 0.33 | 1.88 | 2.65 | 1.53 |
| California | 0.56 | 0.50 | 0.58 | 0.58 | 1.29 |
| Colorado | 0.11 | 0.14 | 0.50 | 0.42 | 0.60 |
| Connecticut | 0.93 | 0.76 | 0.90 | 1.05 | 1.50 |
| Delaware | 0.40 | 0.50 | 1.08 | 0.45 | 1.17 |
| Florida | 0.64 | 0.80 | 1.42 | 2.14 | 1.92 |
| Georgia | 0.50 | 1.86 | 1.59 | 1.31 | 1.12 |
| Hawaii | 0.25 | 0.21 | 0.50 | 0.71 | 1.10 |
| Idaho | 0.38 | 0.14 | 0.14 | 0.22 | 1.00 |
| Illinois | 0.50 | 0.61 | 1.08 | 1.08 | 1.75 |
| Indiana | 0.56 | 0.70 | 0.89 | 0.84 | 1.92 |
| Iowa | 0.30 | 0.50 | 0.78 | 0.75 | 1.48 |
| Kansas | 0.38 | 0.45 | 1.33 | 1.24 | 1.31 |
| Kentucky | 1.10 | 1.33 | 1.18 | 1.27 | 1.32 |
| Louisiana | 0.50 | 0.53 | 0.68 | 1.00 | 1.46 |
| Maine | 0.77 | 0.86 | 0.77 | 0.81 | 1.23 |
| Maryland | 1.14 | 1.00 | 0.96 | 1.24 | 1.33 |
| Massachusetts | 1.31 | 1.36 | 1.76 | 2.00 | 1.71 |
| Michigan | 0.71 | 1.00 | 1.17 | 1.25 | 1.13 |
| Minnesota | 1.00 | 0.65 | 1.95 | 2.05 | 1.56 |
| Mississippi | 0.08 | 0.50 | 0.58 | 0.62 | 1.15 |
| Missouri | 0.58 | 1.33 | 1.60 | 1.54 | 1.81 |
| Montana | 0.38 | 1.05 | 1.20 | 1.43 | 1.86 |
| Nebraska | 0.38 | 0.63 | 1.00 | 1.00 | 1.00 |
| Nevada | 0.00 | 0.92 | 0.92 | 0.78 | 1.33 |
| New Hampshire | 0.57 | 0.57 | 0.40 | 2.05 | 2.18 |
| New Jersey | 0.73 | 0.81 | 1.73 | 1.76 | 2.00 |
| New Mexico | 0.60 | 0.40 | 0.22 | 0.85 | 1.00 |
| New York | 0.69 | 1.17 | 1.89 | 1.79 | 2.19 |
| North Carolina | 0.40 | 2.44 | 2.20 | 2.09 | 1.44 |
| North Dakota | 0.82 | 0.83 | 1.13 | 1.06 | 2.15 |
| Ohio | 1.19 | 1.50 | 1.54 | 1.21 | 1.57 |
| Oklahoma | 0.29 | 0.33 | 0.30 | 0.92 | 1.33 |
| Oregon | 1.00 | 1.44 | 1.55 | 1.59 | 1.78 |
| Pennsylvania | 0.92 | 1.91 | 1.91 | 1.36 | 1.63 |
| Rhode Island | 0.30 | 0.93 | 0.69 | 0.69 | 1.25 |
| South Carolina | 0.38 | 0.64 | 0.56 | 0.57 | 0.73 |
| South Dakota | 0.25 | 0.40 | 0.38 | 0.56 | 0.78 |
| Tennessee | 0.80 | 0.44 | 0.40 | 0.36 | 1.71 |
| Texas | 0.60 | 0.60 | 0.58 | 0.95 | 1.69 |
| Utah | 0.67 | 0.25 | 1.11 | 1.11 | 1.67 |
| Vermont | 1.00 | 1.08 | 1.29 | 1.36 | 1.58 |
| Virginia | 0.63 | 0.79 | 0.75 | 1.17 | 0.89 |
| Washington | 0.20 | 0.40 | 0.70 | 1.53 | 1.76 |
| West Virginia | 0.63 | 0.73 | 0.82 | 1.46 | 1.60 |
| Wisconsin | 1.00 | 1.22 | 1.20 | 1.44 | 1.61 |
| Wyoming | 0.00 | 0.83 | 0.50 | 1.00 | 2.00 |
| U.S. mean | 0.57 | 0.80 | 1.01 | 1.16 | 1.45 |

SOURCES: Computed from program descriptions in *Directory of Incentives*, various years.

above indexes as indicators in a pooled times series analysis to predict the adoption of state economic development strategies between 1983 and 1994. His analysis supports the hypothesis that the approach to economic development a state government chooses to pursue is largely determined by the degree to which its neighbors pursue locational approaches, other factors held constant.[6] Perhaps more notable is the negative relationship between a state's neighbor's locational scores and its efforts to pursue an entrepreneurial strategy.[7] Here the data suggest that the adoption of locational strategies not only increases the likelihood that one's neighbors will also pursue a locational approach but decreases the likelihood that bordering states will seek entrepreneurial strategies.

These findings suggest that states that adopted entrepreneurial economic development strategies did so in a context that was relatively free of economic competition, while states in more competitive contexts curtailed similar efforts because they feared neighboring states would raid their industries. This analysis confirms the apprehensions of policy analysts and economists who worry that locational strategies lead to a zero-sum game. From a local political standpoint, it makes little difference to the governor of Indiana that the jobs he or she claims to have created were actually lured from Michigan. Yet from a national perspective, no new economic benefits were produced; indeed, some workers may have moved needlessly. Because of these concerns, the rise of entrepreneurial strategies (because they emphasize new business development) made policy analysts hopeful that governments could engage in economic development in a way that would lead to the creation of new wealth. Analysts were also hopeful that entrepreneurial policies (especially those that fostered the development of human capital) would help state and local governments to cope with the consequences of economic globalization (Clarke and Gaile 1998). If these new policy orientations appeared to improve a community's well-being, then other jurisdictions might follow suit. Unfortunately, the evidence shows that this scenario is unlikely to occur.

## THE POLICY EFFECTIVENESS DEBATE

But do state economic development policies make a difference? This simple question is a hard one to answer because experts disagree on what "success" would look like, how to measure it, and how to sort out the effects of public policies from other changes also affecting state economic development. This lack of consensus among the experts leaves state policy makers without much guidance or strategic information in making their decisions. Economic development officials admit they see only a weak relationship between their efforts and economic improvement

---

6. The effect of a state's neighbor's policy is large and robust: a one-unit increase in the average locational score of a state's neighbors increases a state's locational strategy score by .91—a considerable result given that the average locational score for all states over the ten-year period is only 1.75.

7. In this case, a one-unit increase in a state's neighbor's average locational scores decreases the state's entrepreneurial policy efforts by .82.

(Rubin 1988). Given the political context and uncertainty about the effectiveness of their tools, policy makers are tempted, in Rubin's words, to "shoot anything that flies; claim anything that falls."

In the face of the trends and changing conditions reshaping state economic development policy making, state policy makers are reassessing what they know about policy effectiveness and what they need to know to make better decisions.

*Do Taxes Matter?* Probably. If we look at the effects of basic tax structures—not specific tax incentives or economic development strategies—on economic growth, early studies generally showed that state taxes have little to do with higher rates of economic growth (Wasylenko 1981, 1984). Other elements, such as proximity to markets, labor supplies, transportation, and utility costs, tended to be more important than taxes. But over the past two decades, there is evidence that lower taxes may be associated with more business activity (Bartik 1991). At the metropolitan level, taxes may have more influence on location decisions because the cost differences that exist between major economic regions are less relevant—so taxes become more important (Peretz 1986).

How taxes matter is not always clear. Until recently, survey work showed that surprisingly few employers mentioned taxes or other inducements as a primary reason for choosing to invest (Bridges 1965). After interviewing officials from companies that accepted state incentives, Harrison and Kantor (1978) found that in every case "the company took actions according to its own plans, then learned about the existence of the tax credits and applied for them, often at the explicit urging of the state officials in charge of the program." But now it appears that the importance of tax incentives may vary by industrial sector: executives in relatively technology-intensive industries appear to view taxes as an increasingly important cost factor. For these companies, traditional location factors matter less when high-value, low-weight products make it possible to serve distant markets (Blair and Premus 1987). Rather than just accepting or rejecting the notion that taxes or tax incentives can influence business decision making, it is important to consider the effects on a sector-by-sector basis.

Answering this basic question is complicated because only corporate managers can tell us whether lower taxes or more tax incentives are justified; obviously, they have every reason to overstate the importance of economic development incentives in order to encourage officials to sweeten the deal (Donahue 1997). To avoid this, we can assess whether economic development programs make a difference by using statistical techniques to analyze the relationship between state incentive programs and various economic outcomes. Unfortunately, as Clarke and Gaile (1992, 193) conclude, attempts to assess the effects of economic development are "a quagmire of good intentions and bad measures."

*Can We Measure the Effects of Policy Strategies?* Here is where it becomes clear that there is little consensus on what economic development policy success means. Are we looking for changes in general aggregate indicators such as employment, income, and capital investment, or should we seek particular measures such as the movement, expansion, or creation of firms and jobs? If the latter, what about questions of the quality or type of economic growth? Many environmentalists, for example, question the use of job growth as a measure of economic well-being since it brings along more congestion and pollution; better to focus on increased per capita income as an indicator, they would argue.

Even if we could agree on what a successful economic development policy should do, it is very difficult to determine whether the effects are actually caused by the policy adopted or some other factors affecting the state economy independent of the policy strategy. And, as we have demonstrated above, states combine several economic development approaches in making policy. Some approaches may be more effective than others, but the combined effect obscures the contribution of any particular policy.

To further complicate the issue, some of the most vital factors shaping state economic development are not easily captured by traditional policy measures. Many states are relying on tourism and travel for economic development; even though jobs and wages in the tourism industry tend to be low skill and low wage, tapping into the dynamic tourism sector is an attractive option. Not surprisingly, taxing visitors' lodging and car rentals is more politically popular than increasing taxes for residents. Unfortunately, there is currently no adequate state-level measure of the development impact of tourism. States are also turning to gambling and lotteries to raise state revenues and generate economic development. By late 2002, 39 states had lotteries, 11 states authorized casinos, and 24 states had state-tribal gaming compacts for casino gaming on tribal lands (NCSL 2002). While this does not seem to be sustainable economic development, it does generate jobs and revenue for the state; in Arizona, Kansas, and Oregon, some of the lottery revenues are earmarked for economic development while Indiana's Build Indiana Fund is financed in part by gaming revenue.

*Are Some Types of Policies More Effective Than Others?* Maybe. Here again, early studies of state locational incentives showed they were ineffective (Bridges 1965), but recent studies are more ambivalent (Peirce 1994). Many studies arrive at different answers because they are looking at different success measures or find different effects for different policies at different time periods. Hansen (1984), for example, finds that incentives reduce employment growth but increase the rate of business start-ups. Kale (1984) reports industrial development incentives actually decreased employment growth in the 1960s and early 1970s but increased growth in the later 1970s.

Sometimes it seems that sheer levels of economic development policy activity or expenditures make a difference. Higher general investment in economic development programs, for example, seems to boost manufacturing employment growth (de Bartolome and Speigel 1995; Koropeckyj 1997). On the other hand, Brace's (1993) study of economic development policy activism in four states reveals a negative relationship between high policy usage and income growth. These disputes are useful reminders that what we decide to measure influences our assessments; it is also the case that overnight benefits are unlikely and that the potential beneficiaries of these policies must be taken into account in any assessment. Bartik's (1991) review, for example, concludes that incentives can have positive effects on long-term business growth and labor market conditions, including prospects for African Americans and less-educated workers.

There is some evidence that specific types of policies matter. Saiz's (2001b) analysis shows a statistically significant relationship between the adoption of entrepreneurial economic development strategies and increased manufacturing employment. But in comparing the effects of entrepreneurial and locational strategies, Saiz finds no evidence that locational strategies have positive impacts on state economic growth. Indeed, his analysis suggests that locational approaches are associated with decreases in employment in the finance, insurance, and real estate sectors. A further boost for entrepreneurial approaches comes from Langer's (2001) finding that states adopting more entrepreneurial policies have more equitable distributions of income than states pursuing more traditional subsidy strategies.

*Does Evidence Matter?* Given the prospect that previous evaluations of economic development strategies are less relevant for new economic conditions in the states, a reconsideration of the effectiveness of these state strategies is called for (Accordino 1994; Buss 2001). But even in the absence of compelling evidence of policy effectiveness, state policy makers continue to support economic development agencies and programs. Reports by state officials on spending for economic development operations are collected by the National Association of State Development Agencies (NASDA) and shown (in constant dollars) in Figure 14-1.[8] The data reflect trends in the more active economic development programs in the 1980s and 1990s and provide some indication of the level of policy effort in different states.

Agency budgets climbed rapidly in the 1980s showing a near fivefold increase in constant dollars by 1990. During this time, real expenditure growth averaged more than 50 percent per year. The rate of growth slowed in the early 1990s but returned to robust growth by the end of the decade, reflecting the robust economic growth of the middle and late 1990s. Steady increases since 1992 suggest the durability of economic development appropriations even in the face of widespread state budget reductions. These historical trends suggest that, overall, state economic development spending may increase (albeit only nominally) despite recessions.

For individual states, however, economic downturns and budget shortfalls can force cuts in economic development budgets. Indiana's governor cut $50 million from the state's 21st Century Research and Technology Fund in 2002 until budget shortfalls are resolved. In 2002 economic uncertainty led California's governor to propose over $35 million in economic development program cuts at the same time

8. While the data capture the value of some financial incentives such as the capitalization of revolving loan funds, venture capital, or other financing programs, it is primarily reflective of operating costs for program operations including job training, advertising, and technical assistance programs. Notably missing are the costs of tax subsidies given to businesses and financing granted from loan pools created in past years or from off-budget sources such as pension funds.

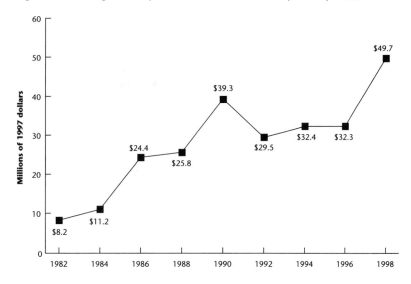

**Figure 14-1** Average State Expenditures for Economic Development Operations

SOURCE: National Association of State Development Agencies, "State Development Expenditure Survey," 1992, 1994, 1996, 1999.

as reactivating the California Economic Strategy Panel, a group responsible for devising a state economic development strategic plan. In Tennessee state legislators considered eliminating the state tourism and economic development departments as a contingency budget measure while New York state legislators, dealing with the same grim realities, increased the governor's $750 million budget for economic development initiatives to $1.2 billion. Economic uncertainty makes states more sensitive to the costs of their economic development programs but also more aware of the need to enhance their state's development prospects.

## THE NEW POLITICS OF STATE ECONOMIC DEVELOPMENT POLICIES

In a paradoxical turn of events, states and regions may become the new arenas for global competition. As firms scan the globe for the locations best fitting their needs, their menu of possible locations is less likely to be defined by national boundaries and more likely to reflect specific configurations of features and amenities sought by the firm. California's strongest competitors for investment, for example, may be provinces or regions in Europe or Latin America rather than other states in the United States. This means that the decision context for state officials is now broader than state or national boundaries. These changing politics of scale are exemplified by the formalization of regional markets transcending national boundaries, such as those created by the North American Free Trade Agreement. While our decentralized federal structure historically encouraged arms-race-type bidding wars among the states, globalization forces appear to encourage a different type of competition. The issue is whether states can adjust to this turbulent environment and capture these new sources and forms of growth and wealth.

This new context forces us to reconsider our assumptions about state economic development policies. While federalism still fosters interjurisdictional competition, globalization trends are altering locational calculations. State officials are caught up in interpreting what these trends and conditions mean for economic development in their states. As our data show, their policy responses vary widely. This indicates that these trends impact states in different ways but also suggests that states with similar features are choosing different solutions to their development dilemmas. Many states continue to emphasize the need to be competitive with other states in attracting firms and investment with locational incentives. Given our decentralized federal system, it is hard to imagine this interstate competition disappearing completely. But it is also true that the changing nature of global competition and the demands of the new economy are prompting more attention to state incentives that support innovation and growth processes rather than subsidies for specific firms. Thus we continue to find evidence of a shift over time toward more entrepreneurial approaches even as states balance this new orientation with more traditional approaches.

In an era in which technological changes radically alter the costs of production as well as the costs of overcoming distance, states also are increasingly responsible for infrastructure investments. In contrast to the segmented infrastructure programs of the past, these new state policies emphasize integration of infrastructure systems, competition rather than regulation, and complex financing arrangements. Since 9/11 these issues are framed in terms of the security of critical infrastructures; states are struggling to balance these security needs with their economic development agendas.

Overall, these strategy shifts and different mixes of policy orientations over time may be in response to changing state political conditions or the waxing and waning of state commitments to activist, expensive economic development initiatives (Eisinger 1995). It is also possible they reflect an intentional, evolutionary effort to adjust and adapt state economic development strategies to a fluid and uncertain context. In particular, the escalating costs of industrial recruitment—the megadeals—are fueling an increasingly critical view of the use of business incentives. One estimate is that state and local governments lose nearly $15 billion annually from tax breaks and subsidies for businesses (Peirce 2000). Critics claim they create windfalls for business, fail to create net job increases, promote inequities among firms and industries within a state, and reduce the opportunities for state action on other programs—such as education and transportation—important for economic growth (Snell 1998; Kearns 2001).

Although it seems an uphill battle, groups opposed to the use of incentives to lure businesses sometimes pursue legal action to prevent their use. Others have called on the U.S. Congress to use the federal interstate commerce clause to limit interstate competition for industry. More than ever, states are being asked to justify program dollars. Performance standards and accountability measures provide more transparency in budget processes; this is a first step in determining who benefits from tax incentives and subsidies and how productive these investments are in reality. Only Maine, Minnesota, and North Carolina have comprehensive incentive reporting requirements disclosing all firm-specific incentives. In 1989 only two states had standards to ensure that benefits produced by economic development policies outweigh their costs; today more than twenty-nine states have such laws (CFED 1996). Several states now are using performance-based incentives whereby companies assisted must reach agreed-upon employment and revenue goals if they are to enjoy the full value of incentives. Louisiana, Ohio, and Texas pioneered the use of "clawbacks" for reclaiming some of the value of incentives when job goals are not achieved or a company leaves the state prematurely.

The political changes associated with globalization remind us that economic equity—for workers, areas, businesses—is an integral, if implicit, aspect of economic development strategies. For many American communities, globalization brings increasing inequalities and social polarization between those benefiting from these economic changes and the many with less certain futures (Kanter 1995). Perhaps these deteriorating social conditions will serve as grounds for political action. But the state political conditions—such as coherent party structures and interparty competition—that Hwang and Gray (1991) reason might encourage the mobilization of broad constituencies and the articulation of alternative economic and social agendas are less predictable in the face of globalization and devolution. The logic of interstate competition and the pressures of globalization imply that directing policy attention to those seen as less productive and less competitive in a global era will not be considered in a state's long-term interest.

Short of political mobilization, states could address these equity concerns as well as bolster their roles in the new economy by incorporating workforce development issues into their economic development agendas. Federal programs such as the Workforce Investment Act and TANF (Temporary Assistance for Needy Families) direct resources to state and local governments for workforce development. But even with resources available, state and local governments find these human capital agendas more difficult to develop than traditional economic development agendas. Workforce development is vulnerable to different time horizons, uneven resources, underinvestment, and the lack of "ownership" of an organizational infrastructure capable of supporting and sustaining long-term initiatives. States with enviable track records in economic development innovations rarely demonstrate the same acumen when it comes to workers.

Workforce systems present particularly difficult problems. As Mossberger (2000) points out, incentives to cooperate are "absent, uncertain, or unevenly distributed across industries and firms" in the case of workforce programs. As a result, business participation is often weak and episodic, as is the mobilization of strategic public officials and agencies—a stark contrast to the "feeding frenzy" typifying locational policies. Partnerships around workforce issues are typically fragile, short-term, and opportunistic rather than strategic; businesses are wary of working with less familiar state labor and employment agencies, and these agencies often have adversarial views of business (Giloth 2003). This suggests that the politics of the new economy will be shaped by these significant differences between workforce development and the more conventional politics of economic development.

In short, the state context is more politicized in regard to economic development issues than previously assumed. State political institutions are evolving as well and often feature new organizational approaches to carrying out development policies (Clarke and Gaile 1998). Increasingly, state development politics are characterized by nonelected public and private actors as well as organizations and partnership arrangements that cannot easily be labeled as either public or private; often this includes foundations and nonprofit organizations. In the last decade, states veered between two organizational paths, sometimes privatizing specific state economic development functions and other times taking the lead in new policy strategies. Although Kentucky privatizes some economic development activities, it recently also established the Kentucky Innovation Commission with a Commissioner of the New Economy charged with creating and promoting a knowledge-based economic strategy for the state. In each instance, states are designing new institutional and organizational arrangements with sufficient scope, responsiveness, and flexibility to provide the foundation for economic development. These new arrangements allow state officials to think "outside the box" and to circumvent established interests and outdated ideas in considering policy options. Whether these new arrangements also will represent the voices of those often adversely affected by globalization trends or encourage state officials to address their needs remains to be seen.

**REFERENCES**

Accordino, John J. 1994. "Evaluating Economic Development Strategies." *Economic Development Quarterly* 8: 218-229.

Barringer, D. 1997. "The New Urban Gamble." *American Prospect,* September–October, 28–34.

Bartik, Timothy J. 1991. *Who Benefits from State and Local Economic Development Policies?* Kalamazoo, Mich.: W. E. Upjohn Institute for Employment Research.

Blair, John P., and Robert Premus. 1987. "Major Factors in Industrial Location: A Review." *Economic Development Quarterly* 1: 78–85.

Bowman, Ann O'M. 1987. "Tools and Targets: The Mechanics of City Economic Development." A research report of the National League of Cities. Washington, D.C.: National League of Cities.

Brace, Paul. 1993. *State Government and Economic Performance.* Baltimore: Johns Hopkins University Press.

Bradshaw, T. K., and E. J. Blakely. 1999. "What Are 'Third-Wave' State Economic Development Efforts? From Incentives to Industrial Policy." *Economic Development Quarterly* 13: 229–244.

Bridges, Benjamin. 1965. "State and Local Inducements for Industry, Part II." *National Tax Journal* 18(1): 1–14.

Buss, Terry F. 2001. "The Effect of State Tax Incentives on Economic Growth and Firm Location Decisions: An Overview of the Literature." *Economic Development Quarterly* 15: 90–101.

CFED (Corporation for Enterprise Development). 1996. "Is Growth Tied to State Incentive Programs?" *Innovations Newsletter* #3. July.

Choate, Patrick, and Susan Walter. 1981. *America in Ruins: Beyond the Public Works Pork Barrel.* Washington, D.C.: Council of State Planning Agencies.

Clarke, Susan E., and Gary L. Gaile. 1998. *The Work of Cities*. Minneapolis: University of Minnesota Press.

———. 1992. "The Next Wave: Local Economic Development Strategies in the Post-Federal Era." *Economic Development Quarterly* 6: 187–198.

Cumberland, John H. 1971. *Regional Development Experiences and Prospects in the United States of America*. The Hague: Mouton.

de Bartolome, Charles A. M., and Mark M. Speigel. 1995. "Regional Competition for Domestic and Foreign Investment: Evidence from State Development Expenditures." *Journal of Urban Economics* 37: 239–259.

*Directory of Incentives for Business Investment and Development in the United States*. Various years. Washington, D.C.: Urban Institute.

Donahue, John D. 1997. *Disunited States*. New York: Basic Books.

Eisinger, Peter. 1995. "State Economic Development in the 1990s." *Economic Development Quarterly* 9: 146–158.

———. 1988. *The Rise of the Entrepreneurial State: State and Local Economic Development Policy in the United States*. Madison: University of Wisconsin Press.

Felbinger, Claire F. 1994. "Conditions of Confusion and Conflict: Rethinking the Infrastructure-Economic Development Linkage." In *Building the Public City*, edited by David C. Perry. Newbury Park, Calif.: Sage Publications.

Fosler, R. Scott, ed. 1988. *The New Economic Role of American States*. New York: Oxford University Press.

GAO (U.S. General Accounting Office). 1993. *Federal Budget: Choosing Public Investment Programs*. Washington, D.C.: U.S. Government Printing Office.

Giloth, Robert, ed. 2003. *Workforce Development Politics: Civic Capacity and Performance*. Philadelphia: Temple University Press.

Goetz, S. J., and D. Freshwater. 2001. "State-level Determinants of Entrepreneurship and a Preliminary Measure of Entrepreneurial Climate." *Economic Development Quarterly* 15: 58–70.

Guskind, Robert. 1993. "The New Civil War." *National Journal*, April 3, 817–821.

Hansen, Susan B. 1984. "The Effects of State Industrial Policies on Economic Growth." Paper presented at the annual meeting of the American Political Science Association, Washington, D.C., September 2.

Hanson, Russell L. 1993. "Bidding for Business: A Second War between the States?" *Economic Development Quarterly* 7: 183–198.

Harrison, Bennett, and Sandra Kantor. 1978. "The Political Economy of State Job-Creation Business Incentives." In *Revitalizing the Northeast*, edited by Richard Sternlieb and Roger Hughes. New Brunswick: Rutgers University Center for Urban Policy.

Herzik, Eric. 1983. "The Governors and Issues: A Typology of Concerns." *State Government* 51: 58–62.

Hwang, Sung-Don, and Virginia Gray. 1991. "External Limits and Internal Determinants of State Public Policy." *Western Political Quarterly* 44(June): 277–298.

Jones, Bryan, and Lynn Bachelor. 1986. *The Sustaining Hand*. Lawrence: University Press of Kansas.

Kale, Steven. 1984. "U.S. Industrial Development Incentives and Manufacturing Growth during the 1970s." *Growth and Change* 15(1): 26–34.

Kanter, Rosabeth Moss. 1995. *World Class: Thriving Locally in the Global Economy*. New York: Simon and Schuster.

Kearns, Monica. 2001. "Retooling State Economic Development Policy for the New Economy." Denver: National Conference of State Legislatures.

Kincaid, John. 1992. "Developments in Federal-State Relations, 1990–91." *The Book of the States, 1992–93*. Lexington, Ky.: Council of State Governments.

Koropeckyj, Sophie. 1997. *Do Economic Development Incentives Matter?* Regional Financial Associates. Accessed at www.rfa.com/samp/ecodev.stm.

Langer, L. 2001. "The Consequences of State Economic Development Strategies on Income Distribution in the American States." *American Politics Research* 29: 392–415.

Leigland, James. 1994. "Public Infrastructure and Special Purpose Governments: Who Pays and How?" In *Building the Public City*, edited by Perry.

Licate, Jack. 1994. "Cities Can Take Back Their Infrastructure." *Governing* (July): 68–71.

Lyne, Jack. 2002. "New York's $500M Incentive Package Aims to Retain Lower Manhattan Firms." *Site Selection.* Accessed May 12, 2002, from www.conway.com/ssinsider.

———. 2001. "$63 Million in Incentives, Last-second Space Deal Help Chicago Land Boeing. *Site Selection.* Accessed May 12, 2002, from http://www.conway.com/ssinsider.

Mahtesian, Charles. 1998. "The Stadium Trap." *Governing* (May): 22–26.

———. 1996. "Saving the States From Each Other: Can Congress Dictate an End to the Great Smokestack Chase?" *Governing* (November): 15.

———. 1994. "Romancing the Smokestack." *Governing* (November): 36–40.

Man, Joyce Y., and Michael E. Bell. 1993. "Federal Infrastructure Grants-in-Aid: An Ad Hoc Infrastructure Strategy." *Public Budgeting and Finance* 13: 9–22.

Mihoces, Gary. 2002. "Senate Looks at Antitrust." *USA Today,* February 14, 2C.

Mossberger, Karen. 2000. "School-To-Work Programs and the Challenges of Business-Education Partnerships in Urban Economic Development." Paper presented at the annual meeting of the American Political Science Association, Washington, D.C., August.

NASDA (National Association of State Development Agencies). 1992, 1994, 1996, 1998. *Economic Development Expenditures Survey.* Washington, D.C.: NASDA.

NCSL (National Conference of State Legislatures). 2002. "Economic and Tourism Development." Accessed at www.ncsl.org/programs/econ/.

North, Douglass C. 1966. *The Economic Growth of the United States, 1790 to 1860.* Englewood Cliffs, N.J.: Prentice-Hall.

North, Douglass C., Terry Anderson, and Peter Hill. 1983. *Growth and Welfare in the American Past.* Englewood Cliffs, N.J.: Prentice-Hall.

Osborne, David. 1988. *Laboratories of Democracy.* Boston: Harvard Business School Press.

Ota, Alan K. 1998. "Governors' Pleas Nudge Senate Into Action on Highway Bill." *Congressional Quarterly Weekly Report,* February 28, 481–482.

Peirce, Neal R. 2000. "Tax Subsidies for Footloose Firms: Two New Reasons to Stop." National Academy of Public Administration, Alliance for Redesigning Government. May 7. Accessed at www.alliance.napawash.org/ALLIANCE/.

———. 1994. "The When, How, and Why of Wooing." *National Journal,* February 26, 488.

Peretz, Paul. 1986. "The Market for Incentives: Where Angels Fear to Tread." *Policy Studies Journal* 5: 624–633.

Perry, David C. 1994. "Introduction: Building the Public City." In *Building the Public City,* edited by Perry.

Peterson, Paul E. 1981. *City Limits.* Chicago: University of Chicago Press.

Plaut, Thomas, and Joseph Pluta. 1983. "Business Climate Taxes and Expenditures, and State Industrial Growth in the United States." *Southern Economic Journal* 50(September): 99–119.

Reich, Robert. 1991. *The Work of Nations.* New York: Alfred A. Knopf.

Richter, M. J. 1994. "Let the States Help Pave the Information Superhighway." *Governing* (November): 72.

Rivlin, Alice. 1995. *Reviving the American Dream.* Washington, D.C.: Brookings Institution.

Rochefort, David A., and Roger W. Cobb. 1994. "Problem Definition: An Emerging Perspective." In *The Politics of Problem Definition,* edited by David A. Rochefort and Roger W. Cobb. Lawrence: University Press of Kansas.

Rosentraub, M., D. Swindell, M. Przybylski, and D. Mullins. 1994. "Sport and Downtown Development Strategy: If You Build It, Will Jobs Come?" *Journal of Urban Affairs* 16: 221–239.

Rubin, Herbert J. 1988. "Shoot Anything That Flies; Claim Anything That Falls: Conversations with Economic Development Practitioners." *Economic Development Quarterly* 2: 236–251.

Saiz, Martin 2001a. "Politics and Economic Development: Why Governments Adopt Different Strategies to Achieve Similar Goals." *Policy Studies Journal* 29: 203–214.

———. 2001b. "Using Program Attributes to Measure and Evaluate State Economic Development Activism." *Economic Development Quarterly* 15: 45–57.

Sherman, Don Grant II, Michael Wallace, and William D. Pitney. 1995. "Measuring State-Level Economic Development Programs, 1970–1992." *Economic Development Quarterly* 9: 134–145.

Snell, Ron. 1998. *A Review of State Economic Development Policy.* Denver: National Conference of State Legislatures.

Sternberg, Ernest. 1987. "A Practitioner's Classification of Economic Development Policy Instruments, with Some Inspiration from Political Economy." *Economic Development Quarterly* 1: 149–161.

Takaki, Ronald. 1990. *Iron Cages.* New York: Oxford University Press.

Taylor, George R. 1977. *The Transportation Revolution, 1815–1860.* New York: M. E. Sharpe.

Towns, Steve. 2002. "Successful Venture." *Government Technology,* September 5. Accessed at www.govtech.net/.

U.S. Department of Transportation. Federal Highway Administration. 1998. *TEA-21-Transportation Equity Act for the 21st Century: Fact Sheets.* Accessed at www.fhwa.dot.gov/tea21/factsheets/index.htm.

———. 1993. *Intermodal Surface Transportation Efficiency Act of 1991: Selected Fact Sheets.* Washington, D.C.: U.S. Government Printing Office.

Wasylenko, M. 1984. "Disamenities, Local Taxation, and the Intra-Metropolitan Location of Households and Firms." In *Research in Urban Economics,* edited by Robert Ebel. Greenwich, Conn.: JAI Press.

———. 1981. "The Location of Firms: The Role of Taxes and Fiscal Incentives." In *Urban Government Finance: Emerging Trends,* edited by Roy Bahl. Beverly Hills, Calif.: Sage Publications.

Weber, Melvin. 1984. *Industrial Location.* Beverly Hills, Calif.: Sage Publications.

Wolman, Harold. 1988. "Local Economic Development Policy: What Explains the Divergence between Policy Analysis and Political Behavior?" *Journal of Urban Affairs* 6: 19–28.

Wolman, Harold, and D. Spitzley. 1996. "The Politics of Local Economic Development." *Economic Development Quarterly* 10(May): 115–150.

Wyatt, Cathleen Magennis. 1994. "Zero-Sum Games." *State Government News,* April, 28–32.

## SUGGESTED READINGS

Blakely, Edward J., and Ted K. Bradshaw. 2002. *Planning Local Economic Development: Theory and Practice.* Beverly Hills, Calif.: Sage Publications. This revised edition of a classic volume addresses the nuts-and-bolts of economic development policy making, including the planning process, high-technology economic development strategies, and implementation of local economic development initiatives.

Buss, Terry F. 2001. "The Effect of State Tax Incentives on Economic Growth and Firm Location Decisions: An Overview of the Literature." *Economic Development Quarterly* 15: 90–101. Buss reviews the conflicting results in the tax study literature on the relationship of taxes and economic growth as well as on the effectiveness of tax incentives in influencing business location decisions.

Eisinger, Peter. 1988. *The Rise of the Entrepreneurial State: State and Local Economic Development Policy in the United States.* Madison: University of Wisconsin Press. Eisinger develops an analytical framework for comparing "supply-side" state policies designed to reduce the costs of land, labor, capital, and taxes with "demand-side" entrepreneurial strategies aimed at facilitating growth processes through the active intervention of state governments. He traces the evolution of these approaches and surveys evidence for the effectiveness of specific strategies in contributing to growth.

Fisher, Peter S., and Alan H. Peters. *Industrial Incentives: Competition among American States and Cities.* Kalamazoo, Mich.: W. E. Upjohn Institute, 1998. The authors examine a range of incentives in the 24 most industrialized states and in a sample of 112 cities in those states to assess the extent to which incentive policies target distressed areas and particular types of firms, subsidize competition between cities, and provide discretionary implementation opportunities.

Saiz, Martin. 2001. "Politics and Economic Development: Why Governments Adopt Different Strategies to Achieve Similar Goals." *Policy Studies Journal* 29(2): 203–214. Saiz assesses the forces that drive governments to engage in economic development activity and the reasons states and communities adopt different strategies with a pooled times series analysis using indicators of interstate competition, fiscal stress, and state ideology collected between 1983 and 1994. His findings indicate that economic development strategy choices are largely a function of inter-jurisdictional competition.

# Name Index

# Subject Index

Note: page numbers in italics indicate illustrations.